PRIME TIMES,
BAD TIMES

PRIME TIMES, BAD TIMES

ED JOYCE

Doubleday
NEW YORK
1988

DESIGNED BY PETER R. KRUZAN

Library of Congress Cataloging-in-Publication Data
Joyce, Ed. 1932–
    Prime times, bad times / by Ed Joyce. — 1st ed.
        p.   cm.
    Includes index.
1. Television broadcasting of news—United States—History.
2. Joyce, Ed. 1932– .   3. Television producers and directors—
—United States—Biography.   4. CBS Television Network—History.
I. Title.
PN4888.T4J69   1988
070.1′9—dc19   87-36587
                                                                      CIP
ISBN: 0-385-23923-8

BG

FOR MAUREEN

I should have
kissed her more
and argued less

ACKNOWLEDGMENTS

When the King in Lewis Carroll's *Through the Looking Glass* told the Queen, "The horror of that moment I shall never, never forget," she responded with a splendid bit of advice: "You will, if you don't make a memorandum of it." Certainly, the writing of this book was facilitated by the written record of various events preserved in my files. Conversations and events which have been re-created were reconstructed from such written materials as well as from memory, my own and those of others.

I am thankful to James L. Brooks, who not only encouraged me to write this book but sought out Lynn Nesbit of ICM, who, to my good fortune, agreed to serve as my agent.

Lynn led me to Herman Gollob, who became the editor of this book; I am grateful for both his patience and his impatience. Cynthia Barrett and Judy Sandman, who at different times were his editorial assistants, challenged statements, questioned facts, and helped hack through the thicket of my prose.

To friends at CBS a special thank-you. I hope their future is as bright as their distant past. They deserve better than the chaos so many of us helped create over the past few years.

And finally to my wife, Maureen, my daughter, Brenda, and my son, Randall, my deepest gratitude. They were wonderful when the times were good, superb when the times were not. Careers are interesting. Families are forever.

PROLOGUE

An invitation to lunch from Gene Jankowski, the President of the CBS Broadcast Group, had come as a small surprise. As I walked to the restaurant on a bright warm day in the spring of 1986, I could see the first green leaves appearing on the trees of New York's Central Park. It had been over four months since Gene had removed me as President of CBS News and more than two months since I'd resigned completely from CBS. Crossing West Sixty-fifth Street, I tried to recall how many years Gene and I had known one another. Nearly twenty, I figured, and I could recall only one other occasion when we'd had lunch alone together.

I approached his table at Shun Lee West with a certain curiosity. I had a hunch about the purpose of our lunch. It was after the spring rolls but before the spicy chicken when the subject was raised.

"Ed, I hear you're writing a book," he said.

"I am," I told him, and I waited.

Gene toyed awkwardly with his chopsticks for a moment, then he asked, "What kind of book will it be?"

"Gene, I think television has undergone a permutation. It'll never again be what it was under Paley. The old man's famous whim of steel could be an awesome force. He could be dead wrong but he called the shots. The era of the great entrepreneur is over. Now, television's just another business. Instead of the world's biggest candy store, CBS is one more American corporation."

Gene didn't disagree with me. We talked about this for a few minutes and then he came to the point.

"I hope this won't be one of those gossipy books."

I laughed. "Gene, prepare yourself. I'm going to tell things the way they happened."

"Ed, you're a young man. You're going to want to work in this business again."

I didn't have to open a fortune cookie to get that message. I smiled. By then Gene's wrist was buried in a blue Tiffany's shopping bag. He produced a sterling silver paperweight with my initials on it.

"This is to hold down the pages of your manuscript and to remind you of your friends."

We shook hands and went different ways. Gene returned to his office at CBS, to the challenges of declining network audiences and a diminished advertising marketplace. I returned to my typewriter and the book I hoped would be an accurate, if painful, account of what it was like to run one of the world's most distinguished news organizations during an unprecedented period of upheaval, of libel suits and takeover attempts.

To understand that upheaval and its impact on CBS News, it helps if you know that alone of the three networks CBS News consistently measures itself by its past.

In the late 1930s Edward R. Murrow and a handful of very young men at CBS created something which had never existed before: America's first broadcast news service. Until then news was something one read, often days after the event itself had taken place. Murrow and his colleagues changed all that. Their radio reports from Europe on the eve of the Second World War and later during the war itself were the beginnings of CBS News as it exists today.

Living as we do in an age when television is the primary source of news for most Americans, it's hard to think of it as the infant of American journalism. CBS began broadcasting its first nightly news program on television in 1948; Douglas Edwards was the anchorman, a title which had not yet been coined. The broadcast was seen only in New York, Boston, Philadelphia, and Washington, D.C. Not until 1951, when the coaxial cable reached the West Coast, could Edwards open his broadcast by saying, "Good evening, everyone, from coast to coast."

The value system which shaped those broadcasts had been in place for not much more than a decade. Whatever professional standards existed at

CBS News in 1948, 1951, and, for that matter, today, have their roots in those early Murrow years. They are a reflection not only of Murrow but of the man who founded CBS, William S. Paley.

It was Paley who early on recognized the value and prestige of CBS News. As a result, the businessmen who ran the other networks allowed and even encouraged their own news departments to compete on the same sensible ground. Three similar traditions of broadcast journalism evolved, but it was CBS which set the standard.

For almost forty years the country has had the benefit of network television news—not just its regularly scheduled news broadcasts, but its special coverage of elections, conventions, summit meetings, and those grim and terrible times when one of our leaders has been the victim of an assassin's bullet. The benefits which have come from an open reliable flow of information during a time of crisis are almost incalculable. For a large and diverse nation based on a concept of consensus, it's been a remarkable service, all the more remakable when you realize that this service has had to coexist on that small plate of glass in your home with car chases and sitcoms, with football games and soap operas. It moves from remarkable to amazing when you realize that the ultimate responsibility for the network news divisions has rested in the hands of the same businessmen who have shaped the rest of American television as it exists today.

Because of a sense of tradition, a certainty about the importance of the role of the network in providing news, those businessmen and their successors fought off invasions from advertisers, from their own affiliates, and from the government itself. To their everlasting credit they did this at times of substantial risk.

Now an era of junk bonds and debt/equity ratios is endangering that legacy.

In February 1986, I wrote a letter of resignation to Gene Jankowski. In it I referred fondly to CBS and described it as a "valued institution." I wonder if he grasped my meaning. It is a valued institution. Valued highly by Drexel Burnham and First Boston and Goldman Sachs. And that may be its undoing.

During my last four years at CBS News, first as Executive Vice President and then as President, I was at the center of the most turbulent era in the history of one of America's important institutions.

What's it like when the phone rings and it's the head of the CIA asking you to hold back on a story?

What judgments were made and what standards used in covering a terrorist hijacking?

What were the challenges in San Francisco and Dallas during the 1984 political conventions when, as President of CBS News, you found yourself in simultaneous disputes with the political parties, the CBS affiliates, and your own network over the CBS News coverage?

These events, as it turned out, are part of this book, but only part. They are events on the grand stage of the history of CBS News. Offstage the performances were not always so grand. They took place amidst a series of onslaughts against "the house that Murrow built."

What was it like during one twelve-month span when CBS found itself besieged on numerous fronts: the Westmoreland libel trial, an attempt by the Fairness in Media group allied with Senator Jesse Helms to "become Dan Rather's boss," the move by the flamboyant Southern entrepreneur Ted Turner to take over CBS, the acquisition by Ivan Boesky, the now infamous Wall Street arbitrageur, of millions of dollars' worth of CBS stock, leaving no doubt that CBS, in the language of Wall Street, was "a company in play"?

To answer such questions I've relied on an extensive personal file for this period. My two secretaries, Josephine Franc and Shirley Marrano, were not only meticulous; they were compulsive savers as well. My debt to them became apparent as I unpacked carton after carton of memos, telephone logs, appointment calendars, speeches, transcripts of testimony before Congress, depositions, and other material.

As I look back in the aftermath of these events and reflect on what took place, I think the logical beginning for the story is a phone call I received one morning in the fall of 1981.

PRIME TIMES,
BAD TIMES

My secretary sounded flustered. She knew I was in conference with the Black Citizens for a Fair Media and I'd told her to hold all calls.

"I didn't know whether to interrupt or not," she said. "But I thought you'd want to know that Dan Rather has called twice."

"You did the right thing," I said. "Did he say what he wanted?"

"Yes . . . he wants to know if he can come by at ten-thirty this morning to have a cup of coffee with you."

"That's only twenty minutes from now," I said. "Call him back and tell him the coffee will be waiting."

At this time I was the general manager of WCBS-TV, the CBS-owned television station in New York. Frequently it seemed my life was just one long meeting. We were planning a new hour of news at 5 P.M., starting a new magazine program at 7:30 P.M., choosing a new advertising agency, hiring a new retail sales manager. Somehow I couldn't recall having this many meetings when I was running the CBS television stations in Chicago and Los Angeles. New York is headquarters for CBS, and the frequency and size of the meetings seemed to expand in direct proportion to the bureaucracy which needed to be serviced. This morning, at least, was a little different. I was meeting with the leader of a community organization. Black Citizens for a Fair Media is a watchdog group which monitors both the hiring practices and the on-air performance of New York television stations.

Emma Bowen, its leader, is a smart tough lady who knows her way

1

around the New York media. For the last hour she'd really grilled me on the station's employment record.

"Emma, I know we're scheduled to meet until eleven," I said, "but my secretary has just told me Dan Rather has called twice asking to see me. I don't know what's so important, but I'd really like to meet with him. Can I owe you one?"

"We're just about done. Don't worry. I know where to find you."

After I walked Emma to the elevator, I returned to my office and waited for Rather, using the time to go through the morning mail. I'd last heard from Rather in 1979. I was in charge of WBBM-TV then, the CBS station in Chicago. Rather had gotten an offer from Roone Arledge of ABC. His agent, Richard Leibner, frequently called me, warning that Rather would go if CBS didn't "get serious." My name in those days often appeared in newspaper stories listing the candidates who might replace Bill Leonard when he retired as President of CBS News. It was obvious Leibner saw me as a channel for delivering his message to the brass at CBS. He was right. One afternoon the call came not from Leibner but from Rather, who was having dinner that night with Gene Jankowski and John Backe, then the President of CBS. After that phone call, my message to New York was blunt:

"Either put some cards on the table with Rather or be prepared to lose him."

The campaign that Rather and his agent waged was successful. The cards that CBS placed on the table were extraordinary. Walter Cronkite, who'd often talked about but never specified a retirement date, was given a million-dollar-a-year, long-term contract in exchange for leaving the *Evening News* and being generally available for three months out of each year. He was also named to the CBS Board of Directors. On January 28, 1980, Dan Rather signed a new contract with CBS naming him as Cronkite's replacement. Even though the succession wouldn't take place until 1981, the terms were spelled out, codifying for Rather the kinds of prerogatives accumulated over the years by Cronkite on a de facto basis. The contract even assured his participation in management decisions involving the *Evening News*. Much was written at the time about "yet another million-dollar contract for a television news star." The reporters writing those stories didn't have a clue as to the actual magnitude of a deal which involved high up-front payments and interest-bearing deferred-income funds.

While all of this was happening at CBS News, I was being shuttled around the CBS television stations. From Chicago I was sent to Los

Angeles to run KNXT Television. Then in February 1981, I was brought to New York to manage the flagship station, WCBS Television. The station was located in the same building, the Broadcast Center, which headquartered CBS News. Once the home of the Sheffield Dairy Farms, the building is so complex and so sprawling that I had come into it each day for eight months without once encountering Rather. I was looking forward to our coffee together.

Even though he'd enlisted my aid in building a fire under CBS in 1979, I barely knew Rather. I'd worked with him in the late sixties and early seventies when I was an executive producer in radio for CBS News. Most of our work together had been overseas, on assignment in Paris or Naples. I remembered him as eager to please and enormously hardworking. Paradoxically, those were the qualities which seemed to divide people at CBS News into two camps. To one he was the good soldier, a thoughtful, considerate co-worker. To the other he was "Driven Dan," manipulative and ambitious. I leaned toward the first group. Over the years I'd watched Rather pay his dues with assignments in Dallas and Washington, in London and Vietnam. Maybe I was influenced because I knew he'd grown up poor in the Texas of the Depression. My own roots are planted in that dry soil of the Southwest. "None of his critics matter now," I thought. Dan Rather was the anchorman of *The CBS Evening News,* the most prestigious air role in American television.

The Dan Rather who came into my office that morning didn't look like someone who was enjoying being "king of the hill." He looked tired. Passengers coming off an eighteen-hour flight from Hong Kong move with the same kind of weariness he was showing as he reached out for the coffee I handed to him.

He looked around my office. "So this is where all those high-powered decisions about New York television get made."

I smiled at that. "Now you know where to send the bombs."

"No bombs . . . I promise. How does it feel to be back on your old stomping grounds?"

"I was news director here for seven years," I said. "But there have been so many changes it's taken months to get a handle on things. In some ways it was easier going cold to Chicago and Los Angeles."

"This outfit has really moved the Joyces around, hasn't it?"

"You're a veteran of that, too," I said. "The impulse to throw rocks at moving vans is probably not unknown to the Rathers."

Rather seemed to be relaxing. As I poured him a second cup of coffee, I asked, "How are you finding your new life?"

"This ratings business is a whole new world to me," he said. "I wish I understood it better. It's worrisome to know that fewer people are watching the *Evening News* now than they did when Walter was here."

Rather had reason to be concerned about ratings. In the first three months after taking over from Cronkite, the audience for the broadcast dropped by slightly more than a rating point, which amounted to 815,000 homes using television. By July, ABC News had actually moved into first place for one week. The pressure this was placing on CBS News was obvious from the fatigue in Rather's face.

"That brings me to the reason I asked to see you," he said. "Ed, I just assumed that because they've only recently brought you back to run the flagship station, you were off any list of candidates to replace Bill Leonard when he retires. But lately Gene Jankowski has been mentioning your name whenever the subject comes up. I wanted you to know I've told Gene that if that should happen, I'd be comfortable with it."

If my name was surfacing again in conversations about the President's job, it was news to me and that was what I told Rather.

"If you assumed I was out of the running, Dan, so did I. Why would CBS move me here from California only to move me again a few months later? But I appreciate what you told Gene and it's good of you to share it with me."

"It's important I add something," he said. "Yours is not the only name Gene has mentioned. There are others I told him I could support, but you are one of those names."

That struck me as a curious postscript. "Look," I said, "if CBS decides in its wisdom to turn to me, I'll accept and be honored. If they choose someone else, I'll wish him well and get back to planting this big patch of ground I've just dug up. Besides," I added, "Leonard isn't scheduled to retire for another six months."

Rather put down his coffee cup. "It can't wait that long," he said very quietly, and he left.

As it turned out, this was only the first of many meetings I would have in the years to come with Dan Rather which would leave me sitting alone in my office asking myself, "What was that all about?" I was stunned at the way he was writing Leonard off. From what I knew, Leonard had played a major role in orchestrating the departure of Cronkite and the signing of Rather as his replacement. It was Leonard who flew to Washington the day of the Rather announcement to break the news to Roger Mudd. For years Cronkite had taken summers off and Mudd was his designated replacement when he was gone. Mudd had assumed that when Cronkite retired he would be his successor. Mudd had been outspoken in his dismissal of Rather as a Texas-style Sammy Glick and he was furious about learning of his selection as Cronkite's replacement just an hour and twenty minutes before its public announcement. He left the CBS News bureau and never returned. Later that afternoon he issued a public statement which minced no words. "The Management of CBS and CBS News has made its decision on Walter Cronkite's successor according to its current values and standards. From the beginning I've regarded myself as a news reporter and not as a newsmaker or celebrity." Eight months later he joined the staff of NBC News. Leonard had to know the likely price for selecting Rather would be the loss of Mudd but he was unequivocal in his choice. Now, almost two years later, Rather seemed eager for Bill to be replaced and soon.

And what was the point of coming to my office to tell me he would be comfortable with me but then pointing out that several others were also acceptable? I ended up concluding that he had probably covered all the candidates in this fashion. Whoever got the job would know that Jankowski had first tested the water with Dan Rather.

For several years, newspaper stories had included me in their lists of those who might one day run CBS News. In a 1978 New York *Times* story, I was described as "a young dark horse." By 1980 the *Times* news service had upgraded my status. They ran a story taken from the Chicago *Tribune* describing me as "the favorite for the CBS News presidency," adding that I had the support of Gene Jankowski, "whose budget cutting practices are similar to Joyce's." Under my management WBBM Television in Chicago not only had moved into first place with all of its news broadcasts but had done so with a very lean budget.

If that had earned me the support of Gene Jankowski and had made me a favorite for the News presidency, he never said a word to me. Not once did I ever have a conversation about it with anyone running CBS.

After Rather's visit, I found myself thinking more often about CBS News. Why were they having such problems? Could these be solved? The biggest obstacle facing Leonard's successor, particularly if he came from outside, would be a Luddite reaction to change. The News Division was filled with prideful people who dated back to the Murrow and, of course, to the Cronkite era. They weren't likely to take kindly to the idea that CBS News needed improving. These were the same people who talked about Roone Arledge at ABC as though he was a television parvenu who, through some fluke, had gained membership in their club. Arledge was, in fact, much better than that. As President of ABC News, he had revitalized a moribund news organization. He had introduced a new pace and the use of computer graphics to the ABC News product. His critics at CBS seemed to fixate on this as though a concern for presentation was somehow antithetical to good journalism. They seemed particularly blind to the fact that ABC News was outclassing them in the special-events coverage of the big breaking stories. During the Iranian hostage crisis, for example, it was ABC, not CBS, which in a bold innovative step carved out the 11:30 P.M. time period for special coverage of this story each night. Out of this grew the *Nightline* broadcast. Using the interviewing skills of Ted Koppel, one of their correspondents, they took advantage of the new satellite technology to interconnect the nation and the world for a nightly analysis of the major news stories. Because *Nightline* dealt so quickly and so lucidly with the big breaking stories, it helped develop an impression that an era had passed and ABC News would be the leading television news organization in the 1980s.

Arledge had also managed to raid CBS News for some of their best people. Half a dozen correspondents, including Hughes Rudd, Sylvia Chase, John Lawrence, and Richard Threlkeld, departed CBS. Arledge had also lured away three talented producers, two directors, and four associate producers.

NBC had made forays of its own into the CBS camp. A half dozen producers and an equal number of correspondents, including Roger Mudd and Marvin Kalb, joined NBC's ranks. Some of this discord was captured in a 1981 *TV Guide* article, "The House of Murrow under Siege," which made a compelling case that "after years of dominance, CBS News has lost key people—and some of its competitive edge—to rival networks." The joke which circulated in the CBS News Washington Bureau at that time asked, "Will the last person to leave the bureau for ABC News please turn out the light."

Each night at 7 P.M., after our New York broadcast had concluded, I studied *The CBS Evening News*, trying to put myself in the place of the viewer who, after nineteen years of the calm, reassuring presence of Walter Cronkite, now found Dan Rather in the anchor chair. No two men could be more different. If you were looking for counterparts in the animal kingdom, Walter would be a Great Dane, or perhaps an Old English mastiff—calm, secure in himself. Dan would have to be placed in the hound or terrier class—quivering with nervous energy, bred for the chase.

No attempt had been made to reflect or accommodate those different qualities in the way the broadcast was presented or produced. Rather

6

looked like a gangly nephew wearing one of his uncle's oversized suits. Even the way the director placed Rather alongside the graphic displays used to illustrate stories was wrong. He was reducing the anchorman to a Lilliputian scale. "CBS News," I thought, "is going to need a crash course in basic television production."

The editorial makeup of *The CBS Evening News* seemed just as anti-quated. At least half of the broadcast on most nights was made up of the incrementa of government produced each day by its Washington Bureau. It was as though the producers didn't realize there was actually a real country west of the Alleghenies. That would be a tough nut to crack. After all, this was the way CBS News had always done it during those years when Cronkite anchored the most watched news broadcast on network televi-sion. If there was a problem, wasn't it because viewers weren't taking to Rather? Cronkite's enormous personal popularity had spanned so many years the broadcast itself was almost secondary. It was basically the same broadcast a viewer might have seen when Cronkite replaced Douglas Edwards in April 1962. By 1981 there had been a proliferation of broad-cast news. Local television had expanded. All-news radio stations had sprung up across the country. There'd been a growth of news on indepen-dent television stations, and there was now a twenty-four-hours-a-day Cable News Network.

Cronkite had for years described his broadcast as a headline service. This "journal of record" approach left little time for original reporting, for the enterprise story or background report. Somehow that half-hour broadcast would have to accommodate more than just the headlines.

In the days that followed, I began to receive frequent phone calls from Richard Leibner, Rather's agent. Leibner's firm, N. S. Bienstock, dealt almost exclusively with clients in television news. It represented a cross section of on-air and behind-the-scenes people (producers and directors) not only at the networks but at local television stations around the coun-try. Leibner ran the business with his wife, Carole Cooper, and I'd known them for years, dating back to my days as a New York news director. In a negotiation for a weatherman, he'd once induced me to put more money on the table by pleading with me to "give the kid a little dignity." He was a shrewd man who, it seemed to me, had always had a fix on what the market would bear. He represented a number of our anchor people and reporters at WCBS-TV, so the reasons to call me were numerous. The calls would always start with a greeting of "Hi, babe," followed by a joke so tasteless I would pray my phone wasn't bugged. He would allot a few minutes to his clients at my station, spend an equal amount of time disparaging our anchor people and reporters who were represented by other agents, and then move to the raison d'être for his call.

"Dan should have gone to ABC." Leibner's pitches were often preceded by an abrupt shift into high whine.

"That's crazy," I said. "You got a deal for him which made him a rich man."

"Hey . . . Arledge would have paid more. Dan wanted to stay at CBS. Now they're killing him."

"Richard . . . who is they?"

"Fouhy and Lane. They wanted Mudd."

Ed Fouhy was the CBS News Vice President in charge of all hard-news activities. John Lane was his deputy. Fouhy was a CBS News veteran. After years in a variety of producer roles he resigned to join NBC News. He returned to CBS News in the late seventies as Washington Bureau chief. Bill Leonard had recently moved him to New York and made no secret that the move was intended to promote his chances for becoming President.

"Mudd's gone," I said. "Dan's got the job."

"Yeah . . . tell that to those two guys."

Leibner ticked off a string of requests Rather had made, from extra producer help to an investigative unit. All, he claimed, had been listened to and then ignored. At the time of this call near the end of October, the alarm bells at CBS were clanging. Not only did ABC's *World News Tonight* move into first place for two weeks but in the second week CBS actually ended up third behind both ABC and NBC.

The quiet tapping of tombstone chisels could be heard throughout CBS. This was now a serious situation. Without a leadership position, the price of thirty-second commercials was dropped by as much as $10,000 to an average of $30,000 a spot. This decline in viewership also had an impact on the audience for the local news broadcasts of the CBS affiliates, a group not known for its patience with failure. A general mind-set was developing both inside and outside CBS that Rather didn't have the qualities audiences looked for in an anchorman. Inside CBS News itself there was a sense of failure, which was increasingly being laid at Rather's door. Mudd may have been lost but, as *TV Guide* pointed out, CBS News had "a stellar relief pitcher in Charles Kuralt, who, when he replaced Cronkite for three weeks [in the summer of 1980], inspired an extraordinary cascade of fan mail." The article quoted Shad Northshield, executive producer of *Sunday Morning*, which Kuralt anchored each week. "Everyone has always said he was good," Northshield said, "but few realized he was that good." That word of support for a colleague seemed to convince the Rather camp that a coup was being planned.

"Dan and I know what Northshield is up to," Leibner said. "He takes those shots in the press because he'd like to see Dan fall on his ass and Kuralt step in." Leibner didn't stop there. "You tell me why Fouhy and Lane will give Northshield anything he needs, whatever correspondent he wants for *Sunday Morning,* but when the *Evening News* wants somebody, they are always on some other assignment."

I would ultimately learn that this was untrue.

"Where is Leonard in all of this?" I asked.

"He's letting Fouhy and Lane handle everything while he gets *Up to the Minute* on the air." This was a new afternoon broadcast produced by CBS News, which would, as it turned out, have a short life span.

Scarcely a week would go by without a phone call or a visit from Leibner with another litany of complaints about CBS News, always ending with a mournful "Dan should have gone to ABC." I was undoubtedly just one stop on a delivery route he'd established. The Rather camp was waging an offensive, trying to make sure whatever change resulted from the decline in the fortunes of the *Evening News* did not involve its anchor chair.

Rather was not able to hide his tension at broadcast time. He appeared on the air looking ill at ease, often stumbling in his reports. If he had to read a story with a touch of humor in it, he would force a strained smile, but during the story which followed the smile would still be there, regardless of the subject.

As I watched these broadcasts, I began to wonder myself if he was crossing some threshold over which he would be unable to return. How long could he perform like this before an irretrievable portion of the television audience voted no with their dials? How much of the problem, I wondered, was Rather, and how much was the organization which supported him?

The day Egyptian President Anwar el-Sadat was assassinated the answer seemed apparent.

ABC News walked away with the story. It seemed as though they were everywhere, interviewing key people in Egypt and the world capitals. What's more, they presented their coverage in a clear, coherent flow of information. CBS News, by contrast, seemed disorganized, particularly in the crucial early hours of this breaking story. They redeemed themselves a bit when their Cairo Bureau chief was the first to learn that Sadat had died.

Despite the inadequacy of the CBS News coverage, Rather looked better than he'd appeared in the past seven months. He seemed alive and sure of himself, qualities which were lacking in his regular nightly appearances.

The questions raised by these contradictions were ones which would have to be answered by whoever would be given the task of reversing the decline of *The CBS Evening News*.

T he fact that I was asking myself such questions was a reflection of the many turns my career had taken over the years at CBS.

When I was a young reporter-producer-broadcaster at WCBS Radio in New York in the early sixties, becoming President of CBS News seemed as remote as being elected to the papacy. I'd even been reluctant to accept my first management job in 1966 at WCBS as radio news director, but it turned out to be a good decision because I was given the opportunity to help design CBS's first all-news radio station. In 1969 I moved to CBS News as executive producer for their radio coverage of special events. I probably would have stayed there forever if the former sales director from the radio station hadn't moved up the ladder and become the general manager of WCBS Television in New York. He was desperate to find a news director and offered the job to me.

I set some sort of tenure record for the volatile world of New York television. Seven years may not seem a long time, but in television, news directors are changed about as often as managers of professional baseball teams.

Then in 1977 my world expanded when I became the Vice President for all news for all five CBS-owned television stations in New York, Philadelphia, Chicago, St. Louis, and Los Angeles. News Departments were growing in size and importance. They had become the locomotive which pulled each station's economic train.

A kind of caste system prevailed at CBS. There were those who actually put broadcasts on the air. News people were in this group.

Then there were people who ran things, the CBS executives. The general managers of the television stations belonged to that group. They were almost without exception former salesmen. They'd been placed in those jobs by senior managers who were themselves former salesmen and who felt a comforting bond with others who perceived television primarily as a lucrative carrier of advertising. To those of us in the newsrooms it seemed as if they not only thought alike, they looked alike, as though they had all been cloned in some back room of Paul Stuart, the expensive men's clothing store on Madison Avenue. To us they were the "42 Longs," the only suit size we told one another you would ever see in an executive dining room at Black Rock, the headquarters building on Sixth Avenue.

By the late seventies, operating a television station had become a more complex business than ever before. A station could not be successful unless its news broadcasts attracted an audience large enough to produce the high ratings which a Sales Department could translate into dollars. In many cities that involved the kind of competition reminiscent of the newspaper circulation wars at the turn of the century or during the 1920s. Wearing a 42 Long didn't necessarily prepare you for this.

The general manager of WBBM-TV in Chicago was a lively former salesman whose social life had earned him the sobriquet "Disco Dave" in the local press. This was not especially reassuring to his superiors in New York. They were watching what they believed was a downward curve in a station they thought of as a key profit center.

The station's news broadcasts were anchored by Bill Kurtis and Walter Jacobsen, both of whom had reputations in the Midwest as serious journalists. Yet they were consistently number two and sometimes number three in the ratings. The ABC station WLS-TV was the favorite of Chicago viewers, particularly in the working-class neighborhoods. All of this was a growing problem for my boss, Tom Leahy.

Leahy was the President of the CBS Television Stations Division. Before that he'd been the general manager I'd worked for at WCBS-TV. He was tough and direct, a product of the Irish Bronx. I knew he could be surprisingly indulgent toward the eccentricities of people who worked for him—as long as they produced. If they didn't produce, it was only a matter of time before I'd hear him muttering, "I don't bandage lepers." With WBBM-TV failing to move ahead, Disco Dave would have been wise to curtail his nightlife. He didn't and Leahy began to boil. On a fall day in 1978 he brought Disco Dave into New York for a meeting. Later that day I was on a plane for Chicago, the new general manager of WBBM-TV.

If improving the news hadn't been seen as the key to the success of WBBM, if I hadn't worked closely with Leahy for years, if he hadn't been willing to take a chance, I never would have been admitted to the world of the 42 Longs. I knew that and I was determined to move WBBM-TV into first place. After years of running a News Department, it was exhilarating finally to have an entire station to work with. News, programming, sales, advertising, finance, community affairs, a large technical staff. I knew it would take an entire station effort, not just a push by the News Department if we were going to succeed.

I prayed for some good stories we could sink our teeth into. We got two beauties. The great blizzard of '79 paralyzed Chicago for weeks. First with snow, then with days of record cold. We set out to make ourselves the city's central source of information. Many of the city's neighborhoods were immobilized and they remained that way with streets unplowed. The mayor at that time, Michael Bilandic, would go on our air and tell viewers their streets were "as clean as the Indianapolis Speedway." In the pre-television era he could have gotten away with that. A viewer would simply have assumed his was an unlucky block in a city of plowed streets. But our coverage included pictures from helicopters showing miles of unplowed streets. The mayor paid the price in the next Democratic primary. Voters remembered the blizzard. Bilandic was rejected in favor of his scrappy opponent, Jane Byrne.

The station began to pull together. I turned to the Sales Department with a challenge to "help pay for all of this coverage." They sold sponsorship of all our special reports to Standard Oil of Indiana. Working with our Advertising and Promotion Department, we developed new campaigns for our news broadcasts.

Then came the second big story. The visit of the first Polish Pope to a city with the largest Polish population outside of Warsaw. The other Chicago stations didn't blanket the story with coverage. I made a decision to preempt our network for hours of special coverage. Our coverage gained us viewers who stayed with the station for years. WBBM moved into the number one position.

It was a golden period. Number one in news, costs under control, sales booming, profits up. To make it even sweeter, we were succeeding with news broadcasts which were the antithesis of the "happy talk" school of local television news which had proliferated across the country. I found myself in the pleasant position of having met the expectations of my bosses in New York with our success in news as well as surprising them with my prowess at the bottom line.

That became obvious during a visit to Black Rock. I had flown into New York to present a business review of WBBM. This was a report on the current status and future projection of ratings, sales, costs, and profit for the station. It was a glowing analysis. The station was delivering close to a 50 percent return on sales. CBS had a money machine in the Midwest. I did the presentation for Tom Leahy and his staff. Gene Jankowski dropped in for a quick "attaboy." Afterward, as I was getting ready to leave for the airport, I sat alone with Leahy in his office.

"Ed, this is a business of cycles. You run hot, and then you run cold, and if you're lucky you run hot again. Right now, you're a very hot ticket."

It was as though I had suddenly mastered nuclear physics. This probably said more about the attitude of the CBS brass toward news people in general than it did about me. It seemed to me that sales and finance were mostly matters of common sense and a lot less complex than running a News Department.

The mandate to a general manager was unvarying: "Be number one but protect the profit." Balancing these twin imperatives resulted in CBS asking me to make two more cross-country relocations in an astonishingly short period of time. In the summer of 1981 I was sent to Los Angeles to manage KNXT Television. Less than a year after that move, I was back at WCBS-TV, my old station in New York, this time as its general manager.

Now, after only eight months, there might be another change in store. It seemed to me that Bill Leonard would almost have to be replaced by someone from outside CBS News. In a period of decline, in-house candidates become identified with the problems. That might be unfair, but in my mind the competition for the job was quickly being reduced to two people, Van Sauter, the President of CBS Sports, and me.

I came close to being unique at CBS in 1981. I was someone who'd come up through their newsrooms but had been given layers of business experience in the ranks of general management.

One other person had a similar background, Van Sauter. Our careers over the years I've just described paralleled one another's to an extraordinary degree. In the 1960s when I was the news director for the CBS all-news radio station in New York, he held the same job in Chicago. We'd both been on-air reporters.

The first time I met Sauter was in 1968. The radio division had assembled the news directors of its seven radio stations for a conference. I've always disliked group meetings. I've attended them and I've run them and I've never liked them. The physical confinement in one room, sometimes for days, is something I find agonizing. I noticed someone else whose loathing for this kind of meeting matched or even exceeded my own. At the far end of a long horseshoe table a large, almost portly man looked as if he might be in pain. He sat silently for hours as the meetings droned on. Swirls of acrid pipe smoke rose from his bushy black beard. In those days Van Sauter hadn't developed a sense of personal style. In blue jeans with an old sweater draped over a bulky frame, he looked like the actor Sebastian Cabot with a wardrobe provided by Goodwill.

That evening after the first day's meeting had concluded, some of the news directors adjourned to a nearby bar where we could begin some real shop talk. After the first round of drinks, Jim Zalian, the news director from KNXT in Los Angeles, got up and headed toward the bar.

"Can I get you anything?" he asked.

Van looked up from his beer. "Zalian," he said, "you can get me the fuck out of here and back to Chicago."

"If you're going for passes," I said, "get me one, too."

Zalian began to laugh. "You guys don't know how to have a good time. Joyce, what would you rather be doing?"

I thought about it for a moment. "A root canal therapy?"

In the years to come, in a variety of jobs, Van and I would find ourselves sitting at similar tables for similar meetings. We would immediately pick up the thread of our "I hate this more than you do" competition.

The year I became a television news director, 1970, my replacement at CBS News was Van Sauter. Not much more than a year later, he'd gone back to Chicago as the news director for WBBM-TV.

In 1974 Van tried his hand as a local anchorman in Chicago, but he failed quickly at this, he said, because "I wasn't able to make love to the camera." Soon afterward, CBS News offered him the job of Paris Bureau chief. I lost track of him during this period. Paris Bureau chief would have to be near the top of anyone's list of great jobs. So the news in 1976 that Van Sauter was returning to New York to become Vice President for Program Practices baffled me. That was the fancy title for the CBS censor. It was hard to imagine Sauter as the guy who would now review all of the Heckel and Jeckel children's cartoons for violence, approve the feminine hygiene commercials, and give his "yea" or "nay" to the Sonny and Cher divorce jokes before their reunion show could go on the air. I just assumed it was the pressure of alimony payments and two sons approaching college age. Reasons like this had sent a lot of good news people into more lucrative fields such as public relations.

"Too bad," I thought, and that was about the extent of my requiem.

I certainly had no premonition that two years later Van and I would be sharing a bottle of wine on the deck of a fifty-four-foot boat which was his new home in Marina Del Rey, California. I was, by then, Vice President for News for the CBS Television Stations Division and he was the new Vice President and general manager of KNXT, our station in Los Angeles. He was explaining how Southern California real estate prices had turned him into a sailor.

"I couldn't afford a house here," he said. "Not one I'd want to live in. I figured living on a boat would at least have a little style."

"On this boat," I said, "with that beard you look like an outtake from *The Sea Hawk* but in L.A. you're just another pretty face."

Actually, Los Angeles was taking note of the new general manager of CBS's troubled television station. The man sent from New York to breathe some life into a last-place station wasn't another three-piece-suiter from New York. He was a bearded eccentric who lived aboard a boat in Marina Del Rey and went to work wearing an open shirt, chinos, and Top-Siders. Not that unusual in the movie colony perhaps, but hardly the expected demeanor of a CBS executive. By then I'd watched Van gradually assemble "the act," an artfully constructed persona of beard and pipe and portly shuffle, all cloaked in a variety of wrinkled chinos, safari jackets, and shoes from L. L. Bean.

It was fun to watch. The act was done that skillfully. It worked wonders with the press. Profiles and interviews of this colorful new GM appeared with enough regularity to help create a perception of KNXT as a reenergized station. This was an important opinion shift and he brought it about with great skill. I'd never gotten this kind of close-hand look at Van at work before.

I spent several months of 1978 in Los Angeles helping to design and implement an expanded news broadcast. The station's early news would run from 4:30 P.M. to 7:00 every weekday. This particular afternoon we were toasting its progress.

"You've now got the longest news broadcast in the history of television," I said. "What could go wrong?"

"Sure," he said. "You can fly back to New York and tell Leahy it was fine when you left."

We were interrupted by the arrival of two yards of blond hair. It was draped over the shoulders and down the back of a young woman who was Van's date for the evening. She'd just completed filming a small part in a science-fiction film. Van was discovering that the state of California had repealed middle age for men who worked in television and who had virtually unlimited expense accounts.

"You know I'm about to get on a plane and fly to New York," I said. "You don't have to look so damned happy."

"Don't worry," he said. "It's a keen disguise."

Many months later I spent another weekend in Los Angeles and turned on the television set in my hotel room to watch the news. After the sports I was about to turn the set off and leave for dinner when I saw a face I recognized from somewhere. Then it clicked. The blond vision which had suddenly materialized that afternoon on the fantail of a boat in Marina Del Rey now did the weekend weather on KNXT.

By then I was deeply involved in a television station of my own, WBBM-TV in Chicago. In May 1979 the Arbitron rating service had just come in, giving a first place to our news broadcast. We were all on a great high. It didn't even matter that we'd been hit with a spring snowstorm which was tying up the city. My secretary buzzed me to say it was Van Sauter on the phone.

"He's probably calling to congratulate me," I thought. A classy thing to do. KNXT had, by then, come a long way up out of its own ratings cellar but was still struggling to break through into a second place position.

"How's it going?" I said.

"Joyce, you may have the ratings but I'm sitting here on my boat, it's seventy-eight degrees, there's not a cloud in the sky, and I'm about to open some wine."

"You bastard," I said. "After I quote you the Arbitron book, let me read you the Nielsen overnights. They're glorious."

"Fuck your ratings. I've got the sunshine," and he hung up.

Over the years, we could joke about the presidential sweepstakes in which we'd both been entered.

"If I get it I'll send you back to be the Paris Bureau chief," I told him.

"And I'll open a Dublin Bureau for you if I get the job," he's answer. "Don't forget we have a deal."

If you've ever worked in a large organization, you may be familiar with, you may even have experienced this sort of relationship. For a number of reasons it stopped short of an actual friendship. Except for the few months in Los Angeles we never actually worked together. Most of the time we were in different cities. Even when we were in the same town Van led a bachelor's life and I was hard-core married, so we were unlikely to "hang out" together.

But on the occasions when our jobs at CBS brought us together we enjoyed one another's company, and at gatherings of CBS executives we would seek one another out. When CBS brought its Presidents and Vice Presidents together for company seminars, it invariably chose the location and the hotel on the basis of the caliber of the golf course. The meetings would be held in the morning and the afternoons would be left as free time. A large corps of CBS executives, all wearing shirts with alligators on their chests, would dash for the links. Van and I, who grew up in newsrooms believing in H. L. Mencken's maxim, "Never trust a journalist who plays golf," would dash instead for the Hertz counter at the hotel and rent a car for an afternoon of sightseeing. We were grateful for one another's company but were content to allow CBS to schedule future occasions for camaraderie.

In July 1980 the professional leapfrog the two of us had been playing for years resumed. Van was shipped back to New York as the President of CBS Sports. I was sent to Los Angeles to replace him as the Vice President and general manager of KNXT. I was thrilled. I already knew a lot of the people there; I liked them and I liked the station. After Chicago winters the thought of living in Southern California was a major attraction. More importantly, the station had some problems and I wanted to solve them. If KNXT had been the dominant station in Los Angeles, if it had been trouble-free and running smoothly, I would have made a mistake by going there. It would have been a maintenance job, which, in television, is the equivalent of quicksand. No thank-yous for continued success but multiple fingers pointed in your direction if a glitch develops.

The news expansion of 1978 had lifted the station out of the cellar. But for over a year the station had been sitting on a plateau, unable even to stay consistently in second place, much less aim its sights at number one. I believed two serious errors had been made. On the late news at 11 P.M. Connie Chung had been paired with Marcia Brandywine as Southern California's first all-female anchor team. Both of them were fine anchorpersons, but after the applause for a symbolic gesture toward social innovation died down, the harsh reality was that the two of them didn't work very well together. The station ran a poor third in that time period. The bigger error, in my judgment, involved the 6 P.M. news. Van had hired Brent Musburger, the CBS sportscaster, as an anchorman. Brent flew to New York each weekend for his network sports assignment and flew back to Los Angeles in time for the Monday evening broadcast. Brent is one of the best sports announcers in the business. He's intelligent and energetic. His ability to ad-lib a lucid flow of information involving games, players, and scores makes it obvious that he knows his field. But he is not a journalist. He hasn't spent his life staking out police stations, covering politics, and handling all of the assignments that produce not only the expertise but the credibility which an anchorman ought to bring to his job. He would have to be removed. I'd known him and admired him for a number of years and I dreaded having to tell him he didn't belong in an anchor chair.

A few days after my arrival I shared some of this with Van. He'd flown back to Los Angeles because he was about to be married to Kathleen Brown, daughter of the former California governor Edmund "Pat"

Brown and sister of the then current governor, Jerry Brown. We were seated in the office I'd just inherited from Van and he'd been briefing me on KNXT.

"Hey, big guy," he said. "It's your station now. Obviously the late broadcast hasn't worked. You'll have to make changes. If I'd stayed here I would have had to change it, too."

"You obviously don't agree with me about Brent," I said.

"Look, I know where you're coming from," he replied. "I've always felt Brent made it work, but I understand how you feel."

A few days later Van offered Brent an expanded and more lucrative role as the on-air managing editor of *The NFL Today.* Brent resigned and moved back to New York. I hired Jess Marlow, a respected veteran of NBC in Los Angeles, to replace him.

Now I was left to deal with a new nightly half-hour magazine show, *Two on the Town.* The new broadcast was now in production and was scheduled to premiere in less than two months. Van had told me he'd "planned on putting everything else aside about four weeks before it was to go on the air and get really involved."

This surprised me. A nightly magazine show is a major undertaking for a local television station. When I worked with Van on his news expansion in 1978, I'd been impressed by the long hours and the enormous energy he poured into everything he was doing. Now his station was embarking on another expansion and he was admitting he had yet to get "really involved."

I came away from that discussion believing Van had been bored for the past year. It seemed as though his attention span hadn't extended beyond his first eighteen months at KNXT.

The magazine represented not just an opportunity to present stories which reflected the life of Southern California; it was a chance to break the choke hold syndicators had on the 7:30 P.M. time period. Years earlier, the Federal Communications Commission decreed that the 7:30 P.M. time period on television could no longer be programmed by the networks. The time period was given back to the local stations in the mistaken belief that they would provide a service to their communities. What the local stations did almost without exception was to purchase reruns of sitcoms and game shows. Over the years the television syndicators even produced first-run game shows for sale to local stations for this time period. So much for the FCC's noble experiment in legislating community programming. If KNXT could make its magazine work, not only would we have a locally produced program on the air each night in that time period, we could produce it at a smaller cost than we'd have to pay for five nights of smirking game show hosts. It was absolutely the right direction for the station and I spent my first two months at KNXT driving the program director and the show's producer to the edge of exhaustion. I asked for a remake of the show's opening, a change in the music, reedits of some stories, complete deletion of others. For two guys who'd been working for months on their own, it must have been traumatic, but I wanted that show to succeed.

At my first meeting with the stations' Advertising Department I was told that the station's entire advertising budget for the year had been spent and there was no money left with which to advertise our new magazine. I made two phone calls. The first to Tom Leahy, my boss in New York, to tell him that the station was having a great sales year and that the first two magazine broadcasts were in the can and looked terrific. Then I told him it was a shame we couldn't advertise them since there wasn't a nickel left in the advertising budget even though we had five months of the year still left facing us.

"I'll get back to you," he said.

The second call I made was to Van Sauter, telling him about my first call. There was silence on the other end of my line, then laughter.

"I'd do the same thing if I were in your shoes," he said. "I'd better find a reason to call Jankowski so I can tell him about this before Leahy gets to him."

"My guess," I said, "is that you are now five minutes too late."

Van called me a week later.

"Boy, have I taken a lot of shit on your advertising budget."

"What are you telling them?" I asked.

"I'm reminding them that KNXT is giving them an extra million dollars in unanticipated sales this year. I told Jankowski to give Joyce his advertising money and let me pay attention to the NFL schedule."

We were both dealing with a classic dilemma faced by the managers of CBS-owned television stations. Sometimes a station pulled in several million dollars of unexpected commercial revenues. This could be because news ratings took off or the advertising marketplace in the area happened to surge. This was always welcome news at Black Rock, where the extra money would quickly be used elsewhere or designated as profit. The Broadcast Group might use it to deal with its own problems. If not, it would be passed through to the Corporation, which might use the money for some new venture. CBS at that time was busy expanding in a variety of nonbroadcast areas, including toys, magazines, musical instruments, and motion pictures. A general manager quickly learned that a cost problem was his problem and not something he could solve with the additional revenues generated by his Sales Department. There was a Catch-22 quality to all of this. He might make an all-out push in news coverage of a big story. The Pope visiting Chicago or canyon fires in Los Angeles are prime examples. Good coverage would result in a lasting increase in ratings for the news broadcasts which the Sales Department could translate into additional revenues. But after the applause died down and the general manager finished taking his bows, he could find himself forced to make reductions at his station in order to deal with the costs incurred by his success. The reality was that we were managing cash cows for CBS. A healthy streak of cynicism was sometimes the best solution for dealing with this. Van knew he'd blown the advertising budget. He also understood that I was playing the old game of "look at the mess I've inherited." We were midway through the third quarter of the year and finding somewhere between half a million and three-quarters of a million dollars at KNXT would have meant making cuts which I didn't want to make. I wanted a pass and I got one.

Two on the Town got the promotion it deserved and it began to attract an audience.

While I was settling into life in Southern California, Van was refocusing his energy in the world of television sports. Even on the other side of the country I could see Sauter touches in the newspaper and magazine stories about CBS Sports. Van's public assertion that "I don't know anything about sports but I do know something about television" was picked up with delight by the nation's television writers.

I was in my eighth month at KNXT, probably the happiest I've ever been in a job. After the blizzards of Chicago my wife and I were luxuriating in our first full winter in Southern California. Maureen had just finished redecorating yet another new house.

I wasn't the only one who thought running KNXT was a great job. One evening after dinner I was waiting outside Chasen's for the valet to bring me my car. Bob Wood was standing there, too. He was once President of CBS Television and in the 1960s had been the general manager for KNXT. He'd been gone from CBS for a number of years but remained an almost legendary figure in broadcasting. We talked for a minute.

"I want to give you some advice," he said. "You won't take it but I'll give it anyway. It's inevitable that you will get a call from somebody running CBS. They'll want you to come back and take some job there. Don't do it.

The day I left here, it was never as good again. You've got the best job in television."

Four days later, in January 1981, Tom Leahy flew to Los Angeles and asked me to come back to New York and run WCBS-TV, the flagship station.

That night I walked into the house with a bottle of champagne. Maureen began to cry. Every new job at CBS had been an occasion for great jubilation in our life. This time it was different.

We realized how happy we'd been. I talked about calling Leahy in the morning and telling him we'd moved so often in such a short time that I'd like to sit this round out. By the end of the evening the champagne was gone and so was any hope of staying in California. The possibility of someday running CBS News was just too important. We knew, both of us, that the chances of that happening would be less likely if I said no.

We talked about moving back to the apartment on Central Park West we'd rented to a tenant. We thought of friends we both missed.

"May this be," I said, holding up an empty glass in a toast, "the move that leads us both to interesting times."

I wouldn't be wrong.

It was almost four o'clock on a rainy afternoon in the first week of November 1981.

I'd been standing outside the CBS Broadcast Center for at least twenty minutes trying without success to hail a cab. I'd gotten a call from Tom Leahy asking me to come to his office in Black Rock at four. It was almost four-fifteen when I got there.

"Sorry I'm late, but catching a cab at this time of day is a pain in the ass, especially when it's raining."

"I wouldn't know," Leahy said. "I never use public transportation."

He had a company car and a driver, and this was an old joke between us. Many people at CBS would look at you with disbelief if you told them Leahy had a sense of humor. When they saw him at meetings he was all business and he had a reputation for asking tough, pointed questions. Even though I'd worked closely with him for eight years, I'd come prepared to field a barrage of questions about WCBS-TV. I began to reach into my briefcase when Gene Jankowski came in the office and closed the door. The contrast between these two couldn't have been greater. Leahy had a streetwise quality like the kid who swiped your pencil box at recess but also got straight A's in math. Jankowski was the Boy Scout leader you never had. A burly man who looked as though he might have been a college wrestler, he may have been the most consistently optimistic person I'd ever met.

Jankowski wasted no time getting to the point.

"In a few days I'm going to make an announcement that Van Sauter is going to be the next President of CBS News. I wanted you to know that."

"I appreciate your telling me in advance," I said. "It means a great deal. Van will do a fine job."

If I'd been alone with Leahy I might have added, "This will give me a few days to practice a phony smile." I didn't think Jankowski would appreciate the black humor. It's not that I didn't believe Van would do well. I thought he was pretty good. It was just that I knew I'd run better newsrooms and better stations than he had and, damnit, I'd wanted to go to CBS News. I was waiting for Jankowski to provide an exit line so I could take a walk and sort some of my feelings out, but he didn't move. He had another announcement.

"I'm also creating a new job. One that's never existed before at CBS News . . . Executive Vice President . . . a clear-cut number two job, and I'd like you to take it."

At that point my brain was on overload. For years I'd been running newsrooms, then television stations. What would it be like not being the guy in charge? But if I didn't take this, would I always regret not having gone to CBS News at a time when the challenges were so clear?

"Gene, can I ask you a question?"

"I'd expect you to."

"Do you really need a number two guy?"

"Absolutely," he said. "There are too many people there who will oppose any kind of change. If I send just one of you, they'll isolate you and you'll fail."

"We've never really discussed the News Division," I said. "It's a great organization but it's being overtaken and people there don't seem to know it. If if doesn't change it runs the risk of being fossilized."

I was beginning to warm to my subject.

"I want to be part of that change but I have to set one condition."

Gene looked puzzled. "What condition is that?"

"I have to hear directly from Van that this job is not something he's just accepting because you want it. I want to hear from him that it's something he wants."

Leahy, who had sat through this without saying a word, looked at Gene and said, "That's smart."

"Van told me he thinks it's an inspired idea," Jankowski said. "He's out of town . . . I'll have him call you at home tonight."

The rain had let up and instead of going back to my office I decided to walk to my apartment. I strolled slowly up Sixth Avenue toward the park, feeling simultaneously worried and exhilarated. There was no doubt that I wanted to go to CBS News. No job could be more challenging and exciting, but I had to remind myself that I wouldn't be going to the job I'd been hoping for. What would it be like working for Van? It would be hard for me to see him as a boss. We'd spent so many years as peers that it would require an adjustment on my part. If we disagreed on some matter I would no longer be in a job where mine was the final decision. How did he feel about the creation of a number two job? Was he just agreeing to the idea to please Jankowski? All of these thoughts were jumbled in my mind as I walked home. I also wanted to share this with my wife. Maureen had paid some prices for my moves up the ladders of CBS. Would she think it had all been worthwhile? We'd been married since our teens—so long now that she qualifies as my oldest friend. When our two children had gone away to college she'd started a second career, first an an editor for a microfilm publishing house, then as a reporter for a suburban newspaper. All of that had gone out the window when CBS started moving us around the country . . . and she'd been so damned happy in California.

As it usually turns out, she saw things with clear eyes.

"Where would you rather be . . . WCBS or CBS News?" she asked.

We were standing on our terrace overlooking Central Park West. The rain had cleared the air and we could watch the joggers returning from the park and the limousines pulling up to Tavern on the Green.

"That's a good question," I said. "CBS News."

"Then we should be happy about this. A couple of years ago you would have been thrilled to be offered this job."

"Then why am I not smiling?"

"Because your pride's hurt. You've spent years being amused by Van and now he'll be your boss."

"Ouch!" I said. "How have we ever stayed married so long?"

"Because I'm a smart woman and I'm smart enough to see that you and Van will work very well together."

We were interrupted by Operator 51. That's a special CBS operator who channels phone calls to CBS executives and knows where to find them anywhere in the world at any hour. It was Van trying to reach us.

"Congratulations, big guy," he said.

"Hell, congratulations to you. You're exactly what they need right now, Van."

"Let's see if they feel that way in a month," he said, laughing.

"Van, I don't know if Gene repeated what I said this afternoon, but I told him everyone should have the right to pick their own people and that

I would only take this if it was something you wanted. I want you to know I really mean that."

"Ed, as far as I'm concerned, we go there as a team. There is a huge amount of work ahead of us."

That was important for me to hear. Nothing Van could have said would have been more welcome. I would have to adjust to a number two role, but if we established right from the start that we were functioning as a team, then I could make this a meaningful job.

"Well, you've got yourself a deal, then," I said. "I guess this means I don't get to collect on Dublin."

A few days later Van and I were sitting in Gene Jankowski's office waiting for him to return from CBS News. The announcement of our appointments was scheduled to be made the next day and, as a courtesy, he was meeting with Bill Leonard's key executives to inform them of the changes in advance. The group would include Ed Fouhy, the Vice President for News Coverage, and his deputy, John Lane. It would also include Roger Colloff, the Vice President for Public Affairs (an area of CBS News which included *60 Minutes* and the *CBS Reports* documentaries); Bob Chandler, the Vice President for Administration; and Ernie Leiser, the Vice President with responsibility for special-events coverage.

All of them except for Colloff were veterans of CBS News. Each, without exception, had believed himself at various times in his career to be a candidate for the presidency of the News Division.

"Does Gene really think he can tell these guys and then hold off a public announcement until tomorrow?" I asked.

"I know," said Van. "Every reporter in the country will have this story by the end of the day . . . but you know Gene."

I did know Gene. He would leave that meeting having told a group of Vice Presidents to hold what he'd shared with them in confidence until tomorrow. He'd be surprised and then disappointed when he learned that the story of our appointments had swept CBS News before he'd even gotten back to his office.

There was a naïve quality about Gene Jankowski. For that reason he'd often been underestimated. The son of a Polish-American blue-collar worker from Buffalo, he'd gone to Canisius College in upstate New York. His goal was to become another Martin Manulis, one of the producers in the Golden Age of television. Instead, Gene had gone into sales, eventually moving through a number of executive sales jobs. I'd first known him at WCBS-TV when he was the station's director of sales. In 1974 he became director of finance and planning, the head bean counter of the

CBS Television Stations Division. At CBS, to move from the fast-track sales world to a dull financial job was unprecedented. The sales people were shocked; it was as though he'd become a Mormon missionary. It was one of those times when Jankowski was underestimated. By 1976 he was controller for the Corporation and now he was President of the Broadcast Group, the financial heart of the company.

If any of his optimism had been chipped away, he didn't show it when he came back to his office. But then he closed the door.

"How'd it go?" Van asked.

"Don't expect a welcoming committee."

"That bad?" I said.

"There was total silence after I made my announcement, so I asked if there were any questions. I got one: Why'd I have to send two of you? Fellas, this too shall pass . . . they'll get over it."

"Any words of wisdom before we begin?" I asked.

"Just go to work on the *Evening News*. It's too important to be allowed to fall apart."

Then, almost as an afterthought, he added, "You know, you're going to have to do something about the *Morning News*. We have affiliate stations who are talking about canceling it." Gene grinned. "You'll make it work. That's why I picked you."

The announcement was released to the press the next day, November 10, 1981. Predictably, word leaked out and our appointments were reported in that morning's New York *Times*. Van and I would both join CBS News in two weeks. Van would serve as second-in-command to Leonard until Bill retired in March 1982.

There wouldn't be much time for Van and me to talk before we started our new jobs. As outgoing President of CBS Sports, Van would be out of town for most of that period. He was about to leave for Hawaii, where he would join Bill Leonard and the other CBS division chiefs for the annual meeting of the CBS Affiliates Board. Both of us were spending our days trying to wind down our current jobs. That evening on the telephone we had a brief conversation and it dealt mostly with Dan Rather.

"I don't like this two-week waiting period before we start," I said. "It's going to impose a level of anxiety on that place that's not healthy."

"And Leonard won't be there as a sounding board," Van said. "The nervousness will make its way to Rather."

"He needs less tension, not more," I said. "Some nights he looks like his face is going to crack."

"Why don't you have dinner with Rather while I'm gone," Van suggested, "and take his temperature."

Two nights later I was seated at one of the banquette tables at Alfredo's, which was close enough to CBS for Dan to be able to join me after his broadcast. I'd asked John, the owner, to make sure we weren't disturbed. Dan arrived shortly before eight. He stopped briefly at another table to say hello to Tom and Patti Leahy and then joined me.

"Welcome . . . and I do mean welcome," he said.

"That's good of you to say," I answered. "I really want to pick your brain tonight, but before we get started, would you like a drink before dinner?"

"No, thank you. It's been a long day. I have a lot to tell you and I know you have questions for me. If I have a drink, I'll be no good to you."

We ordered dinner and I looked directly at Dan.

"How bad is it?"

"It's . . . bad. We're in trouble. Make no mistake, CBS News is still a strong organization, but we've lost our edge and Van Sauter and Ed Joyce have not arrived one minute too soon."

For the next hour I listened to a stunning denunciation of the management of CBS News. Each volley of criticism would be preceded by an expression of admiration or a comment on Dan's long relationship with the accused.

"Bill Leonard is a good friend and I owe him a great deal, but Bill is winding down at the very time CBS News needs to be wound up. Bill and Ed Fouhy have both kept homes in Washington, and they're on their way to the airport by noon on Friday and not back in their offices till late morning on Monday."

I asked him about Sandy Socolow. Socolow was the executive producer of the *Evening News,* the same job he'd held when Cronkite had anchored the broadcast. Rather's answer began with a tribute to Sandy's years of dedicated service . . . then he made a transition to the word "but."

"Sandy Socolow has no greater admirer than Dan Rather, but these are grueling killer jobs, and if there is such a thing as executive producer burnout, Sandy may have it."

No disclaimer preceded his denunciation of the three Vice Presidents he seemed to hold personally responsible for his declining fortunes—Ed Fouhy, John Lane, and Washington Bureau chief Jack Smith.

"They've made a pact to take care of one another," he said. "Leonard brought Ed to New York for one purpose, to position him as his replacement. John and Jack have dedicated themselves to making that happen, but instead of taking hold and making that happen, they've all played a pat hand."

"Dan, how are they going to react to our arrival?"

His answer was delayed by the waiter bringing coffee, then by Tom Leahy dropping by our table to say good night.

"Let me get back to your question," Rather said. "Fouhy will leave if he can find another job. Lane has CBS News tattooed on his backside. He'll stay if you want him, and so will Jack Smith."

"What about Colloff and Chandler?"

"Bob is very good at what he does and he'll be hoping you two are smart enough to recognize that. Roger knew Bill when they were in Washington. He's the kind of eager young guy you find on congressional staffs. Bill brought him up here with no journalism experience, made him his aide, and then rewarded him with the job he's got. Roger is ambitious and smart enough to know he's lucky to be here. He'll be looking for ways to get on board."

Over my coffee I studied Rather. He looked tired. His face was lined. He'd worked awfully hard to get where he was. The old curse that warned: "Beware of what you want because you may get it" seemed to have descended on him and to be taking a terrible toll.

"Ed, let me ask you a question now," he said. "You and Van have both been involved with turnaround situations before. Where will you start in trying to turn this situation around?"

I paused before I answered. Van and I hadn't had time together to really discuss this. But after everything Rather had been saying this evening, I couldn't very well be unresponsive to his question.

"We'll all be in a better position to answer that a few weeks from now," I said. "But let me rattle off some quick reactions. First of all, your broadcast doesn't fit you. It still fits Walter. It's his headline service. Even the look is wrong. They don't know how to shoot you. But, Dan, the problem goes beyond the way your broadcast is put together."

I described for Rather my reaction to their coverage on the day of the Sadat assassination.

"If CBS loses viewers to ABC during coverage of a big story like that, they may like what they see and never come back. I'm sorry it that's overly critical at our first meeting, but you asked me the question."

Dan looked like a *Price Is Right* contestant who'd just won the big trip to Hawaii.

"Ed . . . first of all . . . you're not overly critical. Second, thank God someone is saying this. I can't tell you how many times some of us would look at one another and say, 'Are they watching? Do they know how bad this is?' "

It was now close to ten o'clock and we were the last table still occupied. I called for the check, and said to Rather, "Be of good cheer . . . it's all doable."

Later that night Van called from Hawaii. It was almost midnight here. In Hawaii it was early evening and he was on his way to the Affiliate Board dinner. The conference was taking place at the Mauna Kea resort hotel on the large island.

The network meets with its affiliates in much the same way Ford or General Motors gets together with its dealers. You can have the greatest product line in the world but it's worthless unless you have the outlets to market and sell what you produce. CBS at the time owned five television stations. Its network programming, however, was carried by approximately two hundred other stations throughout the fifty states. Although independently owned and operated, these stations are affiliated with the CBS Television Network in a complex relationship involving payments to the stations for carrying the network programs. They are also given windows of local commercial time in the network programming which they may sell to their own advertisers. The compensation from the network varies according to the size of the stations, which range from those in big cities such as Washington, D.C., and San Francisco to those in small towns such as Chico and Eureka.

Each November, CBS meets with the members of the Affiliate Board. This is an important, often contentious, meeting. These are the affiliates who have been elected by the other stations in their region of the country to represent their interests and who frequently are asked to voice their complaints in meetings with the network.

At this morning's meeting CBS News had unveiled a plan for a one-hour news program. The Affiliate Board members had practically hooted them out of the room.

Van described all of this, saying he couldn't believe how poorly prepared CBS had been in their presentation of an obviously controversial proposal to the Affiliate Board.

"Were there any affiliates on their side?" I asked.

"If there were, I didn't see them," he said.

"Did you know they were going to unveil this?"

"About an hour before the meeting started, Leonard mentioned it to me."

"How did you handle it during the presentation?"

"When the shit started to fly, I just stared out the window and smoked my pipe."

"What a shame," I said. "That was like going to a political convention with no delegate support in your pocket. It'll be years before we can push that issue again."

"If then," Van said. "Right now, those affiliates want to see some evidence that *The CBS Evening News* is not going to be allowed to go in the tank."

A one-hour news broadcast would be a great breakthrough and would provide the opportunity for CBS News to pioneer new forms of news coverage. It would also require the affiliate stations to give back to the network a half hour of their valuable local time, something they would have been loath to do in the best of times. To have proposed this at a time when CBS News was in such a state of disarray was sheer idiocy.

A rational discussion with the affiliates at a later and more propitious time might have developed some sensible accommodation for a one-hour news broadcast. Instead, the proposal drew battle lines which I am afraid have become permanent impediments to a national service of great potential value.

A number of affiliates were so alarmed they subsequently entered into relationships with outside suppliers of news material, such as Ted Turner's Cable News Network. C. P. Persons, whose WKRG-TV in Mobile, Alabama, was a CBS bulwark in the South, later told me he acquired the rights to purchase and broadcast CNN specifically to replace *The CBS Evening News* if it was expanded to an hour.

After describing the fiasco of the one-hour-news proposal, Van asked, "How did your dinner with Rather go?"

"The man is terrified," I said. "His dream came true and it's all falling apart."

Van groaned. "I know what you mean. I've spent more time with him than you have. He's incredibly fragile, but he's the franchise. The only way we'll be able to make the changes we need to make is if Rather remains supportive and doesn't buy into the people who will be running into his office with their bitching. I figure I'll just have to spend a lot of time with him. I'm really going to have to marry the guy."

"You should hear him on the current management," I said. "Boy, is he pissed."

"I've heard him. He'd like us to go in and fire all of them."

"We can't do that," I said. "We carry enough baggage coming in from the outside. They've forgotten we both used to work there."

"I hear you," he said. "We'll just have to work around some of them."

"It's pretty clear to me that Socolow can't stay as executive producer."

"Any thoughts?"

"We probably ought to talk to Joan Richman and Howard Stringer."

Richman was executive producer of the *Weekend News* and Stringer was the executive producer of the CBS Sports documentary unit.

"I bounced both of those names off of Rather," I added. "He would work with either of them."

"Do you know them?" he asked.

"I've known Joan for years. She's very good. I gave Stringer his first news job in 1967. He's a very creative guy. I just don't know if he can do this line of work."

"Why don't you have lunch with each of them while I'm gone and we'll talk when I get back."

I had lunch with Joan Richman on Monday, November 16. Joan is an impressive woman. She is what novelists sometimes describe as Junoesque in stature, giving an immediate impression of her considerable strength and dignity. That impression is not misplaced. Joan started out as a researcher in the CBS News library, where I first met her in the 1960s. By 1969, when I joined CBS News, she was a producer in the special-events unit working on space shots, elections, and other major stories. Her ascent into the lofty realm of what had been, and in many ways was still, an old boys' club is a tribute to her talent and strength. Joan may have a knack for small talk. I've never managed to spark it, so I got right to the point.

"Why isn't the *Evening News* working?"

Joan laughed. "Are you going to have any easy questions?"

"Probably not," I said. "But I figure you might have given some thought to this one."

"Let me light another cigarette and I'll try to give you an answer," she said. "For a start, you guys are going to have to bring an end to the war between Rather and the assignment desks, particularly the domestic desk."

Joan described a divided newsroom with Rather on one side and the domestic and foreign editors on the other. The two editors controlled the bureaus with all of their correspondents and camera crews. Their two desks made the story assignments for breaking news. They also filtered the assignment requests from the various broadcasts, such as the *Evening News, Sunday Morning,* the *Weekend News.*

"I know it's been over ten years since I left CBS News," I said. "But isn't that the way it always worked? What's changed since Cronkite left?"

"Of course it's the way it's always worked. You want the assignment desks to react quickly. The difference is that Walter didn't make that many requests, and when he did, everyone clicked their heels and rushed to get it done. Dan is making a lot of requests and Fouhy and Lane have tried to protect the independence of the assignment process. I don't know what you two will have to do to solve this, but you've got to fix it."

"What sort of thing does Rather ask for?" I asked.

"It can vary from day to day," Joan said. "It might be an extra producer . . . I know he wants an investigative unit. Fouhy and Lane tell him, 'That's an interesting idea, we'll think about it,' and that response drives him up the wall."

"But that sort of request doesn't involve the assignment desks," I said.

"No, but it's part of the problem," Joan said. "The issue with the desks is very simple. They want to make assignments and then consider requests from the broadcasts, including the *Evening News*. Dan wants his requests to become automatic assignments."

"I've got another one for you," I said.

"As good as that one?"

"Maybe . . . You worked in special events. I always thought CBS News had just about invented that kind of coverage. Now I'm beginning to think they don't know how to do it anymore."

"Wait a minute," she said. "You can't just say special-events coverage. That unit also does the eleven-thirty P.M. special reports. They do that pretty well. It's on the big story where you've got to get on the air right now that there have been problems."

"Terrific," I said. "If the other networks have been on the air with better earlier coverage, then by eleven-thirty you're presenting history. I just don't understand how this happened."

"Edward, I'm going to say something important. CBS News has the best people in the world. They need leadership and direction. If Van and you supply that, everything will be fine."

Three days later I had lunch with Howard Stringer. In 1967 I'd hired Howard for an entry-level job at WCBS Radio. It was a kind of news clerk position, someone who would sit in the control room and make sure the technician had the tape inserts in order. Those were the short interviews with newsmakers and reports from correspondents in the field. Howard liked the entry part but wasn't convinced the level was acceptable.

"I did graduate from Oxford," he said.

I was then a grizzled news director of thirty-four and I thought this tall young man in his early twenties didn't fully appreciate the marvelous opportunity being offered. I opened my office door and pointed to a young fellow who was delivering coffee to the newswriters.

"When he's not delivering coffee," I said, "he's busy changing rolls of papers on the wire machines. When he goes home at night he can't get the ink out of his fingernails. Not the most challenging job for someone with a Ph.D. from Harvard, but he's terribly grateful for the opportunity to learn the news business."

Howard took the job.

He was an interesting young man, just back from Vietnam, where he'd served in the U.S. Army. In 1967, this was not that rare among young applicants but, in Howard's case, memorable because he was then, as he was in 1981, a citizen of Great Britain. The son of a Welsh mother and an English father who was a career airman in the RAF, Howard had received a scholarship to an English public school and had then gone on to Oxford, also on scholarship. After graduation from Merton College he decided to see what opportunities might exist in the United States for a bright young lad with an Oxford education. What he discovered was that holding a green card not only made a young man eligible for employment; it also made him eligible for the American draft.

Not long after I'd hired him, he left for a researcher's job in the CBS News election unit. In the years that followed he moved into *CBS Reports,* became a producer and then an executive producer. He'd distinguished himself with the five-part prime-time series "Defense of the United States" and other documentaries as well. He had worked with Bill Moyers to produce a disturbing look at arson in the South Bronx in the highly praised "The Fire Next Door."

Howard had enjoyed the patronage of a number of senior people at CBS News, men considerably older than himself. Executives and producers such as Bill Leonard, Bud Benjamin, John Sharnik, and Perry Wolff were all veterans whose credits and accomplishments, particularly in the documentary area, were legendary. They not only liked the talent and eagerness they saw in this young man; they found him a lively and witty colleague. The adroitness with which Howard can employ his Britishness to produce a smile or a laugh was terribly attractive to people in a tense business. It's an English quality which helps explain their abundant success as actors, diplomats, and ships' stewards.

At lunch Howard remembered our first meeting.

"I can see what progress in this company can do for you," he said. "When I first met you there was less gray in your hair."

"You, on the other hand, still have your sandy curls," I said. "Bit thinner on top, it seems to me."

Howard feigned a wince. "Hard but fair . . . the same qualities which convinced me to take that dreadful job in radio."

"Dreadful? If I hadn't hired you, who knows what you'd be doing now. Teaching at some dreary boys' school on the Isle of Wight?"

"It will be wonderful working for you again. I can see that now."

I brought up the same questions about the *Evening News* and special events I'd asked Joan Richman. Howard's knowledge of the special-events area was understandably vague, since he'd never worked in this area. He'd obviously given thought to the *Evening News.*

"It's really rather a boring broadcast, isn't it? I can't remember the last time I saw a correspondent actually use the visual elements of his story. Instead, it seems to be 'Here's my script and bugger all.' "

"You take months to prepare a documentary," I said. "Remember this is a nightly broadcast."

"I know people say that," he said. "I really think it's how you look at the structuring and the telling of a story. It's even how the correspondents work with the camera in the field. Do they all think they have to stare the camera down? Don't any of them ever watch *60 Minutes* and see Mike Wallace or Morley Safer doing a walking shot?"

"What reaction do you think you'd get if you said that to some of the correspondents?" I asked.

"The bright ones would understand. The others would tell me they're not actors."

We talked about trying to break away from a headline-service philosophy.

"I'd love to try that," he said, "to initiate stories just as we do in documentaries. I can assure you the new management will have its hands full trying to convince the bureaus, particularly the Washington Bureau, that it really means that."

After I left Howard that day, I reflected on how different from one another he and Joan were. If Joan was given a job to do, she'd move in a straight line. "Lord help anyone who didn't see her coming," I thought. Howard, on the other hand, would try to do it by charm. In the slower-paced, more reflective world of documentaries this had proven effective. It might be a quality which would ease some of the tensions which appeared to be plaguing Rather. But the pressure of meeting a daily deadline wouldn't always allow time for charm. Would Howard have some of Joan's steel when that happened? Interesting questions . . . interesting people. I'd try to summarize all this for Van when he got back.

Both Joan and Howard had talked about the organization which supported the *Evening News* and the other broadcasts as well. The size and diversity of the institution I was about to enter was remarkable. To the outside world CBS News seems to be a single entity, a kind of electronic newspaper. In actual fact, it's more analogous to a publishing enterprise responsible for a wide range of editorial products—the equivalent of a morning paper, an evening paper, and, today, even an overnight paper. Each is completely different, with different readerships. There are also the CBS News magazines, *60 Minutes* and others . . . a children's insert, *In the News,* delivered in the midst of the Saturday morning cartoons . . . a news syndication service to the nation which has no counterpart in the publishing world, a special-events capability which instantly provides the nation with a common bond of information during times of great urgency —the assassination of a President, the crash of a space shuttle, political conventions, election nights. CBS News requires an annual budget of more than $250 million dollars.

But undoubtedly when CBS News is mentioned most people think of the *Evening News.* It is this broadcast which more than anything else shapes the persona of the entire News Division. Its anchorman may become "the most trusted man in America," as Cronkite did, or in the case of Rather a few years later, be selected by a national news magazine as "one of the most influential Americans." In the fall of 1981, however, Dan Rather was something less than a face to be reckoned with in national television. Changing that was the challenge which lay ahead. The top three priorities facing Sauter and Joyce would be the *Evening News,* the *Evening News,* and the *Evening News.*

"Is that a new dress code for CBS News . . . rube chic?"

I was talking to Van, who was attired in a tweed jacket and a bow tie and on his head wore a billed cap with the emblem of Beechnut chewing tobacco emblazoned on the front. It was Monday morning, November 23, 1981 . . . our first day at CBS News. Even though my new secretary had spent the weekend getting the office ready, I was surrounded by unopened cartons of books, pictures, and all the other detritus of executive life I'd moved in and out of half a dozen offices.

Van grinned. "Maybe I'll wear this to Bill Leonard's staff meeting," he said.

"Not exactly Murrow's homburg or Collingwood's trilby," I said. "If you wear a cap like that, Bill will make you wipe your shoes before he lets you walk on his carpet."

My secretary laughed, and handed me some books, which I placed on a high shelf. It was a few minutes past eight. We'd all gotten in early to get our offices in order before everyone else arrived. Until Van moved into Leonard's office in the spring, we were sharing a three-room suite on the first floor of the Broadcast Center. Our two secretaries occupied the ten feet which separated us.

I walked into Van's office and closed the door.

"Speaking of Leonard's staff meeting . . . do you plan to make some remarks?"

"No, I'm just going to lay doggo at those meetings," he said. "I think both of us should just listen . . . listen and take notes. Not just at those meetings, either. Let's spend a few days just wandering around hearing what people say."

"I need to remind you," I said, "that I wasn't exactly subtle with Richman and Stringer about the fact that changes were in the wind."

"It's not a problem. I just don't think we should share specifics until we're prepared to announce them."

"Right now, there are lots of questions that need to be asked," I said. "It's like being a reporter again."

"One big difference." Van paused to pick up his phone and buzz his secretary. "Helen . . . bring in a couple of cold Tabs." He turned back to me. "When you're a reporter you can go home at night and forget your story. Whatever we come up with here will directly affect the quality of our lives for the next few years."

"Have you thought through the whole business of making changes while Bill is still sitting in the President's office?"

"I figure Bill will be a realist," he said. "We're expected to solve these problems now . . . not next spring when he retires."

I thought about that as I pulled up the metal ring on the can of soda.

"I think he will be," I said. "Remember, in 1978 they announced that Bill would replace Dick Salant in 1979. So there is some precedent here."

"God . . . remember how bitter Salant was about being forced to retire?" Van asked.

"My guess is Bill will go to extra lengths not to show any bruises in public," I said. "He has too much pride for that."

"Well," he said, "in about three hours when we go to his staff meeting, we'll find out."

Bill Leonard was already in his sixties when he was named President of CBS News. This prompted a spate of Pope John comparisons. He had later been asked to remain in the job for a year past the retirement age of sixty-five to provide managerial continuity during the Cronkite-Rather transition. But a lame-duck quality pervaded his administration from the start, a sense that he was holding the office until the senior management of CBS could decide on a permanent occupant.

For over a decade, from 1946 to 1957, Bill conducted a successful radio program called *This Is New York* on WCBS Radio in New York. Being a roving reporter in search of the unusual can be fun; it can also be damned hard work. In 1956, at the age of forty, Bill suffered a major heart attack. Not only did he fully recover; he went on to a new career at CBS News, as a correspondent for *CBS Reports*, producing and narrating such broadcasts as "Trujillo: Portrait of a Dictator" and "Thunder on the Right." In 1962 he headed the News Division's election unit. In 1964 he became Vice President for Public Affairs.

He was in this job when an underutilized executive producer named Don Hewitt pitched an idea for a weekly magazine program. Leonard not only responded enthusiastically; he championed the idea. *60 Minutes* may have been the inspiration of Hewitt, but it was Bill Leonard who not only got the show on the air but lobbied for its continuation during the early years when the broadcast was scheduled on Tuesday nights opposite *Marcus Welby, M.D.* In those years, no one dreamed that *60 Minutes* in a Sunday night time slot would attain and hold for years a position among television's top ten programs.

In the fall of 1975 Leonard was made a corporate Vice President based in Washington. This was a lobbyist job and it carried with it a number of attractive perks . . . a limousine, financial assistance in the purchase of a luxurious home, and a very large expense account. It was an opportunity for the good life, corporate style. Silver-haired and always overweight, Bill showed no indication of concern about the heart attack which had cut short his days as a radio reporter over twenty years earlier. Friends at CBS thought the lobbying job would be a low-pressure way to spend the remaining few years of a lifelong career at CBS.

Instead, three years later he was brought back to CBS News, this time as its President. It proved to be a difficult tour. The CBS News to which he returned was encountering competitive pressures it hadn't experienced for over a decade. The Cronkite-Rather transition didn't work out as Bill had hoped. Now, instead of a graceful retirement in the spring of 1982, his replacement had been brought on board seven months earlier and would begin his own reorganization while Bill still held the title of President.

At 11:30 A.M. on November 23, I was seated in Bill's office. It was time for his regular morning staff meeting, which opened somewhat stiffly. Van and I were received less like new bosses than like two candidates for admission to a club who were being vetted by the admissions committee. Bill welcomed both of us. Van sat quietly smoking his pipe, deferring to Bill, who asked John Lane to begin what I would later come to recognize as the morning ritual. Lane was Vice President and deputy director of news coverage. He'd been a senior producer and executive producer for the *Evening News.* At one time, he'd been the best Chicago Bureau chief people at CBS News could remember.

"John, fill us in on what's happening this morning," Leonard asked.

"Well . . . we have a lot of to-ing and fro-ing this morning," he said, and then began to read from a list of stories being covered around the world by CBS News. At any one time it seemed as if a third of CBS News was seated aboard an airplane. As he went down the list I noted there was no reference to stories the *Evening News* actually planned on using for the night's broadcast. I wondered if that was a reflection of the gulf between the broadcast and the assignment desks that Joan Richman had described.

And I studied the other executives in the room. Lane's boss was Ed Fouhy. For years, Fouhy had been the Washington producer for the *Evening News.* In 1974 he left to become a producer for NBC News but returned to become the Washington Bureau chief. Leonard had moved him to New York to position him as his eventual replacement.

Next to him was Bob Chandler. Chandler had come to CBS News as head of public relations from *Variety,* where he'd been a reporter. That was in the fifties, but in the years since he'd held a number of key jobs, among them supervising political coverage and public affairs. He was known for being both precise and blunt.

Ernie Leiser was there that morning, too. In the fifties Leiser had been a correspondent working for CBS News in Europe. Later he made a transition from reporting to production. To many at CBS News, Leiser was one of those people who'd always been "in charge." In fact, at one time he had the reputation of a newsroom tyrant.

The only one of the group I hadn't known for some years was Roger Colloff. Colloff was relatively new not only to CBS News but to broadcast journalism. In the seventies he'd held a variety of jobs in Washington, among them legislative assistant to Senator Walter Mondale. From 1972 to 1975 he worked in the lobbying office of CBS as director of government affairs. When Leonard returned to CBS News as its president, he brought Colloff with him as his assistant. Later he rewarded him by placing him in charge of public affairs, an area which included not only *60 Minutes* but all documentaries. The sudden rise of the thirty-five-year-old newcomer quickly earned him the nickname "Fast Track."

When Lane finished his report, Leonard turned to the rest of his executives, none of whom seemed to have anything to report that morning. The rest of the meeting was passed quickly and was devoted to pleasant small talk with Leonard acting like the gracious host of a small gathering of friends and acquaintances. Not a great deal of business took place.

Later in Van's office we compared notes.

"Do you think that was a typical staff meeting?" he asked.

4 1

"Hard to tell. After Lane's assignment report, it just shifted into a lot of old-boy badinage. All that was missing was a decanter of port and a box of fine Havanas. Maybe it was just a way of accommodating our arrival."

"I think Colloff is smart," Van said. "I don't think he's a problem. What did you think of Fouhy?"

"Being very formal . . . terribly correct . . . like a senior officer elected by the other POWs to deal with their captors."

"I don't know if Fouhy will ever buy in," he said. "Lane is another case. He'll try to make it work for us."

"I like John," I said. "You know, just before I went into Leonard's office, he stopped me. He said he'd done everything he could to help Fouhy get the President's job . . . said he felt he was the right man, but he would do everything he could to make it work for us."

Van nodded and brought up some of the other executives.

"God . . . Chandler is arrogant," he said. "I asked him to explain his job and he said at this stage I wouldn't understand it but I'd come to realize he was indispensable."

I began to laugh. "I like that. It's gutsy. He's telling you up front he's not somebody to be pushed around."

"What are we going to do with Leiser?"

"What do you mean?"

"I don't think you're wrong about special-events coverage. We'll have to find some face-saving job for Leiser."

I considered that for a moment before responding.

"This is going to confront us each time we make a change, you know . . . inevitably we will end up displacing people who are part of the history of this place."

"Well, we don't have any choice," he said, "but you know what we're going to end up with, don't you? A group of highly paid, not very busy 'formers'—former this and former that. And they are all going to see themselves as Keepers of the Flame."

"I hope that's not the case," I said. "I have a feeling there are people here who will welcome change as long as we don't start introducing acrobats and calliopes."

"Remember what I said. The first time we do something that's at all different, we'll hear the murmuring in the hallways: 'Boy, the flame really flickered that time.' "

"I guess it's the same thing a new administration faces in Washington," I said. "There's always some permanent shadow government."

I must have looked depressed. Van began to smile.

42

"Look at it this way," he said. "If it works, it won't matter. If it doesn't, it's someone else's problem . . . whoever replaces us."

My mood began to thaw. "You're right . . . let's hit it."

Van pushed back from his desk. "Rather tells me it's not the custom here for the new Presidents to spend much time around the *Evening News* areas. You want to pay them a visit?"

"Why not," I said. "Nobody expects the Spanish Inquisition."

As we walked toward the newsroom, heads turned at the sight of the two new executives wandering through. We did make an incongruous pair. Both in shirt sleeves, but there the similarity ended. I had on navy-blue trousers, a button-down shirt, a red tie, and suspenders. Van was in chinos, a bold check shirt, and a bow tie. To make the difference even more distinct, before leaving his office he'd put on another nylon billed cap. This one was red and on its front advertised "Red Man Chewing Tobacco." The cap was a remarkable distraction for the *Evening News* staff. Instead of being made nervous by our presence and by the questions we asked, they seemed to think they were being entertained.

The *Evening News* was located in a small area just behind the large CBS newsroom. Cameras were permanently placed around the anchor desk where Rather did his broadcast each evening. The editor and newswriters worked around its periphery. In the corner of the room was the small office Rather had inherited from Cronkite. Next to it was a small glass-enclosed room known throughout CBS News as the Fishbowl. In this area the executive producer and the senior producers of the broadcast coordinated and filtered the output of correspondents, producers, and camera crews in bureaus throughout the country and around the world.

Sandy Socolow stood up when we opened the Fishbowl door.

"Welcome," he said. "What brings you two gentlemen to our part of the building?"

"No particular agenda," Van said. "We were just wandering the halls, trying to find the men's room."

This produced a chuckle from the senior producers, Mark Harrington, David Buksbaum, and Linda Mason. Socolow took him seriously.

"I'm sure we can find a desk assistant to point the way," he said.

"Actually, we're here as a learning experience," I said, "trying to figure out how things work."

Socolow laughed. "That might be helpful for us all," he said, "but I'll be glad to answer questions about anything I understand."

"I'm curious about the assignment process," I said, "and how you work with the assignment desks to initiate stories."

4 3

Just then the door opened and Dan Rather entered.

"I see you've already met this troupe of accomplished dog robbers," he said, referring to the senior producers, "and, of course, you know our ace executive producer, Sandy Socolow."

That struck me as a bit odd since I'd obviously been talking with Socolow, who quickly responded, "I've known both of these gentlemen for years. We've just been answering some questions about the way things work."

"I was asking Sandy about the way the broadcast orders up stories through the assignment desks," I said. "But we can come back to that at a time when all of you aren't trying to get a broadcast on the air."

Sandy turned to Van and then to me. "Seriously, if either of you have any criticisms or suggestions I'd like to hear them."

Van responded immediately. "I'm concerned about the way the anchorman is being shot in relationship to the graphics," he said. "He's too small. You're subordinating a million-dollar anchorman to a four ninety-eight graphic."

I was pleased but surprised at hearing him say that. In going over my own observations of CBS News with Van, I had mentioned this repeatedly but he'd been unresponsive.

Socolow seemed agreeable. "I'll sit down with Richie Mutschler, the director, and see what we can do about that."

Rather appeared ecstatic. His face was glowing. The new head of CBS News had been asked about the *Evening News* and he didn't like the way they were making the anchorman look. At last someone was getting the priorities straight.

That evening Ed Fouhy and John Lane joined us in Van's office to watch the first feed of the *Evening News* at 6:30 P.M. John was studying the broadcast lineup sheet showing which stories the broadcast was using and in what order. He looked up over the top of his reading glasses and smiled at us.

"You two have been working your magic on the anchorman of *The CBS Evening News*. He seems happier and more relaxed than he's been in a long time."

Then he looked at Fouhy and added, "My brothers, right now Mr. Rather thinks the two of you are the answers to all of his problems. You haven't seen his dark side, and I pray to God you never do."

"What do you make of the way Lane and Fouhy react to Rather?"

It was early the next morning, about eight o'clock, our second day at CBS News. I was sitting in Van's office. He shook his head at my question.

"They obviously don't like him," he said.

"No . . . it's more than that," I said. "It's like a scene from *The Omen* where we're being warned to watch out for Damien."

"I can only assume," Van said, "that during what Dan perceived as his dark days, he thought those two guys were pulling against him. I don't know if they can ever fix that."

"A thought that's occurred to both of them, I'm sure. I get the feeling that the Rather enemies list has been carved in stone somewhere."

"It's not his enemies I'm concerned about," Van said. "It's his friends.

"Who do you mean?"

"Guys like Leibner . . . or David Buksbaum. He really relies on them . . . listens to what they say."

"Leibner you can understand," I said. "He helped make him a rich man. I can't figure out the Buksbaum relationship. For Rather it must be like having your own watchdog."

Van almost choked on the cold Tab he was drinking. "You are so right." He laughed. "One word from the master and he'll tear flesh out of your shoulder. We should find another good job for him and get him the fuck off that broadcast."

"Either that or get rabies shots," I said.

Buksbaum was a senior producer on the *Evening News*. A cigar-smoking veteran of what television news people refer to as the "crash and burn" school, Buksbaum was a contentious personality who tended to quarrel with his peers.

"Those people are always going to be a factor in Rather's life," Van said. "He seems to need them. I'd just like to isolate them from his day-to-day life."

"Enter the new bridegroom," I said. "Are you sure you like this job?"

"I do." Van's face broke into a broad smile. "It's better than being the censor." He looked at his watch. "Holy shit . . . it's after nine. Rather's probably in by now. I should go take his temperature. Where's my cap?"

Van's visits with Rather ranged from this sort of impromptu drop-in to more formal meetings which I would join. These were designed to share with the anchorman our early impressions. The main purpose was to make him feel he was at the center of whatever deliberations might lead to change. Most often the discussions took the form of questions from both Van and me about the impact various changes might have.

"Do you think if Socolow was made London Bureau chief it would soften the blow of being removed from the *Evening News?* Would Joan Richman be good at the special-events job? What could we do with Leiser? Does Stringer have the stretch to take over a hard-news broadcast?"

His answers to the questions were less important than the process of asking them.

As the days went on, a picture of CBS News seemed to be emerging, at least of the hard-news side. The hard fact was that the organization wasn't effectively servicing its most important broadcast and that issue transcended any other consideration. We had to continue to provide resources for *Sunday Morning,* the *Morning News,* and the weekend broadcasts. At the same time the assignment desks and the bureaus would soon learn that they would be measured by how well they responded to *The CBS Evening News.*

That weekend I came into my office. After a week of nonstop conversations about CBS News, it was pleasant to be alone. I felt by now as if I was on information overload. My brain was trying to process what I had collected wandering about the News Division listening to people talk about their jobs and their problems. With no phones ringing and no interruptions, I spread my notes across my desk and began to organize them into categories. Public affairs . . . hard news . . . the broadcasts . . . the assignment desks . . . the bureaus . . . special events . . . the budget . . . advertising and promotion.

Not everything needed or could get immediate attention. Public affairs could wait. There were documentaries in production and *60 Minutes* was a successfully operating world of its own. Time enough to get involved there. I checked it off.

The problem areas were the *Evening News* and the *Morning News* and, of the two, the *Evening News* was more crucial.

But despite what Jankowski might have thought, the *Evening News* was not a separate entity to be repaired like a ship in dry dock. There might be some quick cosmetic touches which would make the broadcast look better, but the real problems were larger than the broadcast alone.

To address that, we were going to need people in a number of key jobs who wanted to do more than maintain the grounds and paint the shutters of the "house that Murrow built."

By the end of that weekend, I had drafted a plan.

Phase One called for "A Large-Scale Staff Realignment" to improve:

A. The *Evening News*

B. The news-gathering process

C. The special-events capability

The plan called for an all-out effort to enhance the *Evening News,* including schemes for a new set, a new open, new graphics, a Rather's reporters team, and a revised format including such elements as live two-way interviews.

Phase Two would concentrate on efforts to "Rebuild the *Morning News.*" In this phase we would:

A. Evaluate all of the on-air talent

B. Realign the production staff if needed

C. Revise the format

D. Change the set

E. Change the music

F. Change the start time

Under each of those headings, I summarized my thoughts and I listed a number of key positions I felt we would have to refill with new people. I wanted to get all of this in some form I could place in front of Van so we could begin to discuss the actual steps we should take. It was fine to "wander around" or to "fall by" the Fishbowl. In fact, it was essential to do this. We were both ingesting so much information and so many impressions I had begun to worry about making changes on a piecemeal basis. But I also knew I would do well to remember the Latin phrase *summa sedes non capit duos,* which, translated literally, says "there's only room for one at the top."

Van was in charge and the more casually I presented the material, the less likely he might feel I was trying to rein him in or direct him.

On Monday morning, November 30, I walked into his office waving pieces of paper.

"You probably aren't aware," I said, "that CBS in its wisdom once sent me for a two-week crash course in bean counting at the Harvard Business School."

Van began lighting a pipe, giving me time to continue my monologue.

"By the time I left Harvard, not only had I mastered the principles of 'negative cash flow' and 'exponential smoothing' but I even learned how to draw up an action plan."

I dropped it on his desk and headed toward the door.

"Put it aside and read it later . . . See if you think if has any merit," I said, and left.

Half an hour later, Van came into my office holding the papers I'd given him.

"We have to get this done in the next thirty days," he said.

"That's not much time," I said. "Why not space it out?"

"First of all, Black Rock wants to see change," he said. "I think right now I could get some extra money out of Jankowski if I told him it was to enhance the *Evening News.*"

"You don't think the money will still be there in a couple of months?"

"I don't know . . . but there's another reason for moving quickly. People in the News Division are expecting changes. The longer we wait, the harder it will be to make them. We'll be like Leonard . . . the people here will be ours. Let's make these changes in a short space of time and then send a signal that it's over."

I started sweeping papers off my desk.

"Let's get at it," I said. "We don't have a lot of time."

First we decided to make Howard Stringer the new executive producer of *The CBS Evening News.* I'd taken Howard to a second lunch, and this time brought Van along. We both felt Howard would bring a fresh eye to the production and the editorial makeup of the broadcast. Equally important was his personality. The atmosphere of the Fishbowl was filled with what struck me as an unnecessary air of tension. Howard had enough British sophistication mixed with humor to change that atmosphere.

Joan Richman could also have handled the job, yet her weekend news broadcasts were not significantly different from the existing *Evening News* and there was at least a question as to how much of an ally for change she would be. But there was no doubt she could walk into special events and immediately start to take names and kick ass. As I'd done with Howard, I set up a lunch for Joan with the two of us. We both agreed that Joan would be ideal for the special-events job.

Changing just those two positions created a ripple effect. Before we were finished, a number of key jobs throughout CBS News would be filled with new faces. But we were working under two self-imposed conditions. We wanted to fill these key jobs from inside CBS News itself and we also wanted to find face-saving roles which we hoped would be acceptable to those who were being moved. In that way we hoped to minimize the trauma in an organization unaccustomed to change.

If we replaced Socolow with Stringer and then sent Socolow to London as bureau chief, we would be offering him the most prestigious and largest of the overseas bureaus. It had a symbolic importance dating back to the Murrow years. It was also the coordinating hub for other, smaller bureaus covering Europe, the Middle East, and Africa. All of that was fine, but what would we do then with Peter Kendall, the current London Bureau chief? Van wanted to bring Lane Venardos, the *Evening News* producer in Washington, to New York as a senior producer. He was well respected and he and Van were old friends and colleagues from their days together in Chicago television.

If we made the move with Venardos, Kendall could go to Washington as his replacement with the explanation that he'd been in London long enough and it was time for a rotation.

Joan Richman presented an interesting problem. She was willing to accept the job of Vice President for Special Events, but she also wanted to be the executive producer for the unit. Currently two people held these jobs. Ernest Leiser was the Vice President, Russ Bensley the executive producer. Joan made a compelling case that if she was going to accomplish what we expected of her, she'd have to wear both hats. Leiser and Bensley had both spent decades at CBS News. What would we do with them? We could slide Bensley into the *Weekend News* as its executive producer. Leiser presented more of a dilemma.

Van came up with the solution.

"Let's make him my assistant," he said. "We'll figure out what he does later. There's probably a lot of policy stuff I can dump on him."

The list went on. We needed a replacement for Stringer as executive producer of *CBS Reports*. We wanted to add one or two producers to the *Evening News*, find another job for David Buksbaum, name a new national editor who would work more compatibly with the *Evening News,* appoint some new domestic bureau chiefs. Each move triggered others. It was like three-dimensional chess.

Then there was the *Morning News.*

"In a funny way," I said, "the *Morning News* is a bigger challenge than the Rather broadcast."

Van nodded in agreement. "But the level of expectation is so much lower," he said. "If we could just come up with something that would demonstrate some growth, it would quiet those affiliates and Gene would be happy."

We had worked through most of the morning and then had broken for the Leonard staff meeting. Both of us had full afternoons. Bob Chandler was supposed to brief me on the system for preparing promotional spots for the *Evening News*. So it was sandwiches and cold Tabs in the office while we wrestled with the *Morning News*.

For thirty years CBS had been unable to find an audience for its morning programming. The list of those who'd tried was long and varied. Entertainers such as Jack Paar, Will Rogers, Jr., and Dick Van Dyke had come and gone. An assortment of CBS News correspondents had anchored the broadcast, among them Mike Wallace, Hughes Rudd, and Lesley Stahl. In fact, it seemed as if half the correspondents at CBS News had done a tour of duty in this hardship post and moved on. Over the years, CBS News had taken some odd roads. In the 1950s Walter Cronkite was teamed with Charlemane the Lion, a Bil Baird puppet. In 1973 CBS News hired Sally Quinn as the first female anchorwoman at CBS News. At the time, Quinn was a reporter for the "Style" section of the Washington *Post* who had earned a reputation for amusing but devastating stories on the parties given in the city's political and diplomatic circles. Her sole television experience before being abruptly dropped in the anchor chair

51

was a guest appearance on a Barbara Walters show. The results were so disastrous that the poor woman was practically hooted off the air. After such a public fiasco, CBS News seemed reluctant to compete for viewers in that time period.

Instead, it presented a straightforward hour of news each morning which it boasted was the best one-hour news broadcast on television. *The CBS Morning News* shared the two-hour block with *Captain Kangaroo* and the result was more a morning of public service than commercial television. The CBS senior management and even the affiliates seemed to accept as a fact of life the dominance of NBC's *Today Show*, which had pioneered the time period.

ABC changed the competitive dynamics in the mid-seventies when it premiered a new morning television show, *Good Morning America*, with David Hartman. This new show not only found an audience; it eventually overtook *The Today Show* in ratings. What's more, *GMA* was produced not by ABC News but by that network's Entertainment Division. As the audience for *GMA* increased, the CBS brass and the affiliates began to take a new and harder look at their own morning time period. In the face of this growing pressure, Leonard turned for his solution to the team that had produced the successful *Sunday Morning* broadcast, anchorman Charles Kuralt and executive producer Shad Northshield. *Sunday Morning* was a leisurely and literate broadcast which not only gave viewers the major stories but presented a variety of back-of-the-book features not usually covered on commercial television—classical music, jazz, media criticism, long thoughtful stories by CBS News correspondents which were allowed to run from five to ten minutes in length. This was a luxury for reporters not to be found in the other news broadcasts at CBS, where the average story ran under two minutes. Kuralt's easy, unruffled style provided the overlay for a broadcast which quickly became a weekly habit for millions of Americans. But it was Shad Northshield, the executive producer, who shaped and structured a program which spoke up rather than down to its viewers. Shad was a nature lover. As a result, viewers of *Sunday Morning* were treated each week to a closing story which incorporated glorious photography showing migratory birds in passage or insects skimming the surface of a flowing mountain stream. *Sunday Morning* not only showed there was an audience for this kind of television; it brought a shower of praise to CBS.

Because of their great success, Kuralt and Northshield were asked to solve Leonard's weekday problem. Kuralt was paired with Diane Sawyer, who was then the State Department correspondent for CBS News. *Sunday*

Morning was, in effect, expanded to a six-days-a-week schedule. During the week it was simply called *Morning* and it was every bit as classy a broadcast Monday through Friday as it was on Sunday. In October 1981 Jankowski had even expanded the weekday broadcast from one hour to ninety minutes in an effort to make it more competitive with its rivals.

Nothing seemed to help; the CBS jinx held firm. In 1981 *The CBS Morning News* achieved a Nielsen rating of 2.6, the same dismal rating the broadcast had received in 1980. *Good Morning America,* however, had a 5.2 rating, for the first time moving ahead of *The Today Show* with its 5.0.

Northshield's broadcast reflected the perfect sensibility for Sunday mornings when viewers could sit comfortably at home with cups of coffee and leisurely watch television. Unfortunately, few of them had that luxury on weekday mornings. Watching honeybees in flight or an eight-minute cover story by a correspondent on our endangered ecosystem demands concentration and commitment from a viewer. On weekday mornings viewers are gulping down their coffee, getting ready to go to work or school. They have only a short span of time to watch television. In fact, they tend to listen more than they watch and then they're out the door on their way to challenging and difficult days. Those who stay behind also have full days of their own ahead.

The problems with the *Morning News* went beyond its format. Kuralt seemed strangely uncomfortable and his partner Diane Sawyer even more so. She seemed cold, an austere blond beauty out of place next to the folksy Kuralt.

The plan I had given Van called for a revamp of *The CBS Morning News* but had stopped short of calling for a replacement for the anchors. Van seemed to have little doubt about the need to do this.

"Let's get Kuralt back doing those *On the Road* pieces for the *Evening News,"* he said, "and Rather would love to see Sawyer back covering the State Department. He can't stand Pierpoint."

Robert Pierpoint was the State Department correspondent and had been the number two correspondent at the White House during Rather's tour of duty there during the Nixon years.

"Shouldn't we talk to them first?" I asked.

"Why don't you set up some meetings for us. Set up one with Northshield, too. Let's find out where he's coming from. Can he do a broadcast that's not so fucking dull and listless?"

The next morning we met with Northshield in Van's office. At his suggestion I also invited Ed Fouhy and John Lane. At the Leonard staff meetings, their references to Shad invariably included mentions of his temperament, his hair-trigger reactions to criticism.

Much of Shad's career had been spent at NBC News. He had succeeded Reuven Frank as producer of *The NBC Nightly News.* Shad liked to boast about the number of times he'd been fired. For a lifelong veteran of NBC to have come, in his sixties, to an organization as xenophobic as CBS News and to have been generally accepted by the old guard was a tribute to his ability as a producer.

There were interesting similarities between Van and Shad. Both were large men with full beards. Both had strongly defined personas. If Van was the irreverent impresario, Shad was the crusty producer. The two acts were on a collision course.

Shad knew he was there to discuss the morning broadcast, and he waited for Van to take the lead. Van obviously had Shad's reputation for volatility in mind as he danced around his criticisms. Instead of "dull and listless," he talked instead about "a quicker pace and rhythm," about a "need to more accurately calibrate the perceptions of morning television viewers."

Shad wasn't buying it.

"Look," he said, "I know how to produce a television show. At least I think I can. No, I know I can. In fact, I'm good at it. But I guess I'm not smart enough to understand that stuff about calibrating perceptions and quicker pace and rhythm. I don't know what any of that means."

Fouhy and Lane shot one another an "oh boy, we warned them" look.

I jumped in. "Let's not kid one another. We all know what that means. It means trying to do a faster-paced broadcast with shorter pieces. You may not want to do that kind of show but that's another issue."

Shad looked at me like I just walked into the room.

"Yeah," he said. "I guess that is what I mean. I wouldn't want to do that kind of show."

The meeting went downhill from there.

If we wanted to make changes in the *Morning News,* it would obviously have to be done with a new executive producer. The question was: who? Until the morning of the meeting with Shad, George Merlis was just someone I'd once talked to about his ideas for local programming during the period when I'd been the general manager of WCBS-TV. Merlis had been the executive producer of ABC's *Good Morning America.* He was a former New York City newspaperman who had moved into television, where he'd worked on ABC's evening news broadcast and on *The Reasoner Report.* I remembered Merlis and suggested to Van that we talk with him.

The next evening, a Wednesday, Van and I met Merlis for drinks in the bar at the Metropolitan Club. A short man with dark curly hair, Merlis was not reluctant to reveal his bitterness at ABC for having fired him.

"What happened to you at ABC?" I asked him bluntly.

"I felt I should run the show, not Hartman and his agent. David was just too powerful and I was out. I'd like a chance to kick their ass."

Van was munching a handful of peanuts from the bowl on the table.

"Merlis, what can you tell us about the morning audience?"

"The first thing I can tell you is that it's plural . . . audiences. They wake up at different times, they leave the house at different times, and they stay with you for about twenty minutes."

For the next hour he discussed the peculiar nature of morning television and how it differed from the viewing experience at any other time of the day. He was critical of *The CBS Morning News,* calling it "slow and self-indulgent." He couldn't have been more prepared if he'd been working from a script. By the time the evening was over, I wouldn't have been surprised if he had turned to Van and said, "You need to more accurately calibrate the perceptions of morning television viewers."

We left the Metropolitan Club believing we'd found one answer to the morning dilemma. Merlis had actually produced a successful morning broadcast and his news background was strong enough to make him our candidate for the task of doing what no one at CBS News had been able to do in thirty years—build a competitive broadcast in the morning.

The next week, Van and I had lunch with Charles Kuralt at the Dorset Hotel to discuss the *Morning News.* Television viewers have associated Kuralt for years now with his *On the Road* stories about life in the small towns along the asphalt roads of America, but his career is more varied than most people realize. Charles Kuralt joined CBS News in 1956 as a radio newswriter. In 1959 he was named a correspondent. He was twenty-five years old and so impressive he was talked about as "the next Ed Murrow." As a correspondent, he worked out of New York and then Rio de Janeiro. In 1965 he proposed that he and a camera crew be allowed to wander the country in search of interesting stories. It took him two years to convince CBS News that this was a good idea. In the fall of 1967 he and a camera crew set off in a little camper bus for New England. The story which followed and was used on the *Evening News* lovingly panned across the New England hills and then moved in for a closer look at the brilliance of Vermont maples and New Hampshire oaks. A rich voice retaining just the faintest touch of a North Carolina boyhood described the scene by saying, "It is death that causes this blinding show of color, but it is a fierce and flaming death. To drive along a Vermont country road in this season is to be dazzled by the shower of lemon and scarlet and gold that washes across your windshield."

It's easy to think of Kuralt just as that jolly round fellow who has told us about wood carvers in Alabama and glass blowers in Maine. But that's a mistake. He takes pride in his explorations of homespun America, but they are stories he does with the same care he used when he covered a revolution in Cuba or a civil rights march in the South. Kuralt is a shy, reticent man with a tinge of sadness when he speaks. At our lunch he knew we were there to talk about the problems of the *Morning News* and he did everything he could to make it an easy conversation.

"If you fellows want to make a change in the morning," he said, "just tell me. I won't be terribly saddened at the thought of sleeping later in the morning. Six days a week of this is getting to be a strain."

We talked about what else he might like to do.

"I'd kind of like to get back to doing *On the Road* stories for the *Evening News*. That is, if you think there's a place for them on the kind of broadcast you want to see. I miss doing those stories and I do think they make a contribution."

Van quickly responded. "I think the *Evening News* lost something of importance when you stopped doing those stories for them," he said.

I asked Charles a few questions about what it would take to gear up the *On the Road* unit.

Almost as an afterthought Kuralt added, "Oh, one thing, I would like to keep on doing *Sunday Morning*. I'm kind of proud of what we've created there and I'd like to stay with it."

The lunch concluded with no definite resolution but with a clear knowledge that Kuralt would be cooperative if we wanted to make an anchor change on the *Morning News*. I left the Dorset that day telling Van we'd encountered "a rarity in television, a gentle, self-effacing man."

"God, yes," he said. "There aren't many of those. He's making it very easy."

Sharing adjoining offices, both Van and I had agreed that neither would pay attention to a closed door but would enter the other's office without announcement. Friday afternoon, December 4, I walked in while Van was on the phone. He put his hand over the mouthpiece and whispered. "Tony Schwartz, New York *Times*."

I listened in amazement as he told Schwartz that he planned to replace not only Shad Northshield on the *Morning News* but Kuralt and Sawyer as well. We hadn't told Shad or Charlie that such a move was definite and we hadn't even had our meeting with Diane.

When he hung up, I said, "Why are you telling him this?"

"It's important to have the *Times* on our side. Besides," he added, "I'm softening up resistance. I'm sending a signal that change is inevitable."

I'd watched the results of Van's handling of the press for years but always at something of a distance. This was my first real glimpse of how he went about it. I walked out of his office that afternoon shaking my head.

The next morning the New York *Times* ran a story with the headline "CBS News May Switch Personnel on Morning." In it Schwartz accurately quoted his "CBS source" as saying, "We do want a news program that better serves the needs of people who don't have time to watch television for long periods in the morning and need to get information quickly."

Sunday, December 6, was a particularly cold day in New York. The temperature had plunged into the low twenties. Van and I had arrived first at our table in the bar at the Dorset Hotel for our Diane Sawyer lunch. We had to assume she'd read the story in yesterday's *Times*. In fact, it was widely assumed at CBS that one of our first moves would be to find a replacement for her. Her performance had been so disappointing the black humorists of the News Division had dubbed her "the Ice Queen."

Diane Sawyer's path to television news had hardly been traditional. In 1963 she'd been chosen America's Junior Miss. After graduation from Wellesley College she became the weather girl for WHAS-TV in Louisville, Kentucky, her hometown. For four years she had been a press aide in the Nixon White House and was one of those loyal staffers who went to San Clemente with the deposed President to help him prepare his memoirs. In 1978 CBS News hired her for their Washington Bureau. This generated an outcry from many of their news veterans that she represented a compromise of journalistic objectivity. But Diane's excellent and tireless work earned her the State Department beat. The boos had turned to cheers and now Rather was even arguing for her return to that beat when—inevitably, he assumed—she was removed from the *Morning News*. Neither Van nor I had ever met Diane. Neither of us was prepared for the woman who joined us at our table. Coming in from the frost air of a New York December with flowing blond hair and sapphire eyes, she did look exactly like an ice queen, tall and lovely. But in minutes that impression thawed and revealed a witty, charming woman with a natural effervescence. It was hard to reconcile this Diane Sawyer with the one I watched on television each morning.

"You know, you're a totally different person than you appear on the air," I said.

This was obviously the moment she'd been waiting for.

"Is it true?" She looked at both of us searchingly. There was an awkward pause.

"Is what true?" Van asked.

"What the *Times* said . . . that you're removing me from the *Morning News?*"

Van didn't miss a beat.

"Diane, during a period like this gossip will inevitably make its way into the paper. You'll just have to learn to put it aside."

She was unrelenting.

"You still haven't answered my question. Is it true?"

"No decision has been made," Van said. "There has certainly been talk about it, even going so far as to consider returning you to the State Department beat. But these have only been discussions, and if people who take part in these discussions feel the need to pick up the phone and share this with some wretched person at a newspaper, it's regrettable, but I suppose in our peculiar business inevitable."

For a minute I forgot about being in Van's office when he had talked to the *Times*. His response was so convincing I found myself nodding in agreement.

"Let me ask you a question now," Van said. "I'm blown away by the difference that Ed mentioned. The way you are here at this table is so different from the lady I watch in the morning. Would you feel comfortable revealing some of those qualities on the air?"

For the next forty-five minutes we listened to Diane Sawyer's detailed analysis of why she hadn't been able to break out of the morning mold. Her complaints ranged from the kinds of interviews she was given to the formality of the relationship between Kuralt and herself and even to the set.

"Charles and I both work sitting on those high stools," she said. "That may be fine for a man, but try to imagine what it's like for a woman in a skirt sitting there with your feet off the ground. It's hard to look like you know what you're doing when you spend that much time worrying about what to do with your legs."

She was absolutely right. After lunch Van and I remained alone at our table for another few minutes.

"She is impressive," I said.

Van shook his head and laughed. "We're in trouble, Joyce. That woman is smarter than both of us."

As we got up to leave I asked him how he was going to pull Tony Schwartz back off that limb he'd left him on?

"What do you mean?"

"His story certainly left Diane poised for the high jump. I don't have another candidate. Do you?"

Van thought about that while we both wrestled into winter coats.

"Why don't you have lunch with Schwartz. Let him know that Diane may continue to play a role in the new *Morning News.*"

"And what do I say if he asks what the new *Morning News* will be?"

"Just tell him when we've got it set, we'll make sure he's covered."

As long as I could remember, Van had been treated well in the press. I'd just assumed it was merely a reflection of his natural skill in dealing with reporters. He was always good for colorful copy, having worked as a newspaper reporter in Detroit and Chicago before responding to the lure of broadcasting. What I hadn't seen at a distance but was now learning from the inside was the amount of time and effort he devoted to his press coverage. Dealing with the press was a significant part of his week—breakfast, lunch, constant telephone calls.

In early December, I joined Van for breakfast with Fred Rothenberg of the Associated Press and watched the skill with which he moved from "off the record" to "not for attribution" to "strictly for background." I began to understand better the origins of an article in the Los Angeles *Times* a few days earlier which had quoted Van as saying he "intended to honor the values and tradition of CBS News," but then went on to quote "sources closely acquainted with Sauter and his style of management who expect him to make wholesale changes at CBS News." At the end of the breakfast with the AP reporter he dangled the lure of access: a day behind the scenes at CBS News with a promise of open doors.

Our breakfast the next day with Sally Bedell of *TV Guide* was quite different. She was a tough, somewhat straitlaced reporter with abundant sources of her own. Van's performance that morning was more restrained. But even here he was franker in his criticisms of CBS News than I'd heard him be with anyone at the News Division itself with the exception of me. Each reporter was made to feel he was being allowed unique access to the thinking behind the changes which would take place at CBS News.

Reporters such as Bedell were very sparing with their agreement to an "off the record" conversation. Others were so delighted at what they perceived as the openness of the new chief of CBS News they became eager partners. In orchestrating the "CBS News Is on the Move" campaign, Van played Gepetto to some very aggressive reporters who never seemed to know when he was pulling their strings.

Not long after the sessions with Rothenberg and Bedell, I had lunch with Tony Schwartz of the *Times*. We were seated at a table at the Metropolitan Club and Schwartz was still gloating over the beat he'd scored on his changes at the *Morning News* story. He didn't seem bothered when I told him I thought Diane Sawyer would remain an important part of the broadcast. I avoided mentioning either Kuralt or Northshield.

"My story said 'may switch,'" he said, "and I know my source on the story is good."

I couldn't resist tweaking him by telling him I'd been sitting with Van in his office when they'd talked.

"I can't believe the things he tells me," he marveled. "What's his theory, just to trust the reporter not to burn him, and that's always worked?"

Without choking on my mashed potatoes, I muttered something about Van's "respecting your integrity as a reporter." What I didn't say was "You sap, he knows you won't burn a terrific source."

That week we met with Bill Leonard in his office and described the lunch with Diane Sawyer and our belief that there might be a lot more to Ms. Sawyer than anyone had yet seen on the air. Bill wasn't surprised. After all, he was the one who'd put her in that role in the first place. I think he felt frustrated himself that more of the qualities we all saw in her weren't coming through on the air. And he wasn't surprised at our talking about replacing Kuralt, but he warned us that he was hearing Kuralt was growing increasingly resentful at newspaper stories disparaging the *Morning News*.

"If you're going to replace him, you ought to get at it," Leonard said. "The longer this goes on, the more people are going to think you're being unkind to a very nice man."

Instead of responding directly to that, Van threw a curveball which genuinely stunned me.

"I think he should be pulled off *Sunday Morning*, too, so he can work full-time for the *Evening News*."

I looked at Bill, who seemed equally nonplussed.

"This is one of those times when Van and I disagree," I said.

Bill leaned forward in his chair. A flushed face is particularly noticeable under a thick head of white hair. There was no mistaking Bill's agitation.

"Look," he said. "You can take Kuralt off the *Morning News* and there will be a lot of people here who won't like it but they all understand the problems of that broadcast. But if you take him off *Sunday Morning* you're going to create a storm that neither of you two guys need."

"Bill, your counsel to Ed and me in this time of transition is just invaluable," he said. "We are very fortunate to be able to turn to you in areas like this."

Once back in our office area, Van was visibly annoyed.

"We can't be seen disagreeing with one another in front of these people," he said. "If they sense a split they'll move in on us and we'll never get anything done."

There was merit to that argument. Van had talked about coming to CBS as a team and we were functioning in that manner to a degree which was even exceeding my expectations. If we were working this closely together we could argue, we could disagree, but when the office door opened we should appear seamless in our decisions and actions.

"You're right," I said. "I believe that, too. But I shouldn't be hearing something like that Kuralt thing for the first time in front of Bill. At least give me a chance to tell you I think you're wrong."

Van nodded. "I hear you."

This was not the only occasion when Bill Leonard tried to provide wise counsel for the two of us. Van and I left the Broadcast Center one afternoon to visit Phil Donahue in the Central Park West apartment he shared with Marlo Thomas. After many years in Chicago, Donahue was anxious to move the production of his nationally syndicated talk show to New York and end his and Marlo's constant commuting. He was interested in contributing a segment for *The CBS Morning News* and even more interested in developing a larger role at CBS News. To have achieved his kind of success without being part of one of the three networks was, particularly at that time, a remarkable accomplishment. He was smart enough to know that he'd become a significant television star but that no single show could last forever. So his interest in finding a place with a network news division was understandable. The problem was that he was in partnership with a Midwestern television company which had every intention of remaining involved in all of Donahue's future plans. This would be a major concern for CBS News, which for many years had refused to work with outside producers in order to protect its claim that it alone was "solely responsible for the content of its news broadcasts." We laid all of this out for Leonard, who cut right to the bone in his response.

"Forget the second stage when he'd work full-time for CBS News. Let's assume he could shake loose his partners. What's the first stage?"

"He'd contribute one, maybe two segments each day for the *Morning News*," answered Van.

"Would he continue to do his syndicated talk show?"

"He'd have to. He's got contractual obligations."

"Then forget it. He can't be part of CBS News while he's still got a show on the air someplace else where he's pinching old ladies on the ass."

That wasn't a particularly accurate description of the Donahue audience, but is was Bill's way of reminding the two new kids on the block that they were back at CBS News and they'd do well to remember and respect its value system.

Bill continued to tell us that Kuralt was growing increasingly resentful. John Lane added the same warning about Shad Northshield. The *Times* story about their impending replacement was, according to Lane, a particular source of bitterness.

"Shad figured the *Times* heard that from somebody in authority," he said. "Otherwise they wouldn't have gone with the story."

The barrage of stories about impending changes was creating a pressure quite apart from any Black Rock mandate. If we didn't make a change in the *Morning News* soon, it wouldn't be surprising to find Kuralt and Northshield asking to be removed. We were, in effect, promoting change before we had alternatives in place. We could give Diane Sawyer another chance on a reformatted broadcast. George Merlis was standing in the wings eager to come to the *Morning News* as its new executive producer. But the linchpin of the current broadcast was Kuralt and if he left we had no one in line as a replacement. His was a terribly demanding role. It calls for someone with the traditional skills of an anchorman, the ability to read news copy, to handle changes and breaking stories. If we were going to become more competitive in the morning, we would need someone who could not only do that but also handle a variety of live interviews every day. Tom Brokaw of NBC News was an example of someone who'd been able to do it all and still project an engaging personality. As we looked through the ranks of CBS News correspondents, there were many fine journalists but no one available who struck either of us as an ideal morning anchor.

Each time we went down the list Van would mention Bill Kurtis. Kurtis was still an anchorman at WBBM-TV in Chicago. At different times in our careers Van and I had each worked with him there. In 1972 Van was the news director who convinced Kurtis to leave a job as West Coast correspondent for CBS News and come to WBBM-TV as their anchorman. By 1978 when I arrived as that station's general manager, Kurtis enjoyed considerable respect in that city as an anchorman who also covered stories as a reporter. His early coverage of the tragic effects of Agent Orange on the health of veterans who'd served in Vietnam placed the Agent Orange issue on the agenda of the national media.

The breakthrough for WBBM-TV and for Bill Kurtis in Chicago came in October 1979, when Pope John Paul II visited that city. This was at a time when I was the station's general manager. For months I had worked with the news and technical departments planning special coverage. When the Pope arrived our cameras were everywhere, from the ethnic neighborhoods he visited to the giant outdoor mass in Grant Park to the live concert where Luciano Pavarotti sang for the Pope. For days the station preempted network programming for this coverage. The result was something unique in the relationship between a television station and its audience. For two days after the Pope's departure it was virtually impossible to get a business call through the WBBM-TV switchboard. Viewers kept phoning hour after hour to say thank you for the coverage. WBBM-TV had covered the story on a scale not undertaken by the other Chicago stations. The results were lasting. The station attracted and held an audience for its evening news broadcasts which was larger than its competitors'. Bill Kurtis, who had anchored the special coverage, became an enormously popular figure in the Midwest. If Cronkite was "the most trusted man in America," Kurtis held the position of trust and respect in Chicago.

It was a role he savored. In one of the important cities of the world he was an esteemed citizen. I described all this for Van before telling him I thought Kurtis would have difficulty living without that adulation. He was a remarkably unsophisticated man. This had not hindered his growing role as Chicago's Mr. Journalism. As a result of his popularity, mishaps seemed to leave him unblemished.

Then, as now, some local television stations would send their anchormen on foreign assignments. It's a regrettable practice and largely an ego stroke for the anchorman, who arrives in some exotic location on a very tight schedule and indulges himself for a few days in the mistaken assumption he is "playing in the majors." Because the anchorman has little or no expertise in that area of the world, the result is seldom more than a series of shots showing Hometown Harry on Safari. It's picture-postcard journalism. Bill wanted to go to Teheran. During the Iranian hostage crisis Teheran was awash with Western news people, but part of the deal Kurtis had made with WBBM-TV prior to my arrival assured him foreign assignments. Judging from the size of the press corps which had descended on the Iranian capital, Teheran was safe. Bill had been pitching a story on disappearing wildlife which would have meant visiting the game parks of Africa. At least in Teheran there was ongoing news, and so he departed. During the few days he spent in Iran, Bill was struck by the fact that while the press reported each day on the demonstrations taking place around the American Embassy, life was relatively quiet in the rest of Teheran. Returning to Chicago with the accumulated wisdom of a week in Teheran, he began to publicly lecture the American press for its jingoistic coverage of the hostage crisis. After the first rhetorical flourish he had little to support such a charge. Knowing that there were two newspapers in Chicago that would be sensitive to this sort of indictment, I thought there would be hell to pay.

To my surprise Bill's public quotes were never challenged. No one was about to lay a glove on "Chicago's own." I told Van I thought Bill could have real problems adjusting to life in a less protected environment.

He listened without reacting. The amount of press coverage about imminent change in the *Morning News* had by now created its own imperative. Our list of candidates to replace Charles Kuralt in the morning consisted of one: Bill Kurtis. He was an experienced, successful anchorman with a background in both local and network television. If he had shortcomings, he also had the advantage of being available.

On Wednesday morning, December 9, Van and I quietly left our offices and flew to Chicago. From there we traveled to a hotel in suburban Lake Forest, Illinois. In a suite taken for the day, we sat down with Kurtis and described his promising future with *The CBS Morning News*. Not only the chance to anchor *The CBS Morning News* but the opportunity to do documentaries for the legendary *CBS Reports*. There was not a doubt in my mind that if we made the offer, Bill would take it.

Bill's most probing question that day in Lake Forest came when he asked who his co-anchor would be. When I answered with the name of Diane Sawyer, he smiled. I was sure I was reading his mind. He was thinking, "Good, no competition there."

Even as these changes for the *Morning News* were taking shape, we were implementing a series of appointments throughout CBS News. On December 2, we announced the Stringer, Socolow, Venardos, Kendall moves. This was followed shortly by the Richman, Leiser, Bensley changes. In the next few weeks close to thirty key jobs at CBS News would be filled with new people, the "best and the brightest" of CBS News. In a short space of time there would be a new national editor and new bureau chiefs in New York, London, Paris, Rome, Tel Aviv, Atlanta, Chicago, and

Los Angeles. Except for George Merlis, who would soon be hired for the *Morning News,* each of these jobs was filled from inside the News Division itself. More change than CBS News had seen in ten years was occurring in the span of a few weeks. There was even a new job for David Buksbaum. As the new Vice President for Operations, he would manage the camera crews, videotape editors, directors, and all of the News Division employees who kept the technical wheels turning. When Fouhy learned of our plan for Buksbaum he was less than enthusiastic.

"He's a loose cannon," he warned us. "We'll have nothing but problems."

It turned out to be a good move. Although his devotion to Rather remained complete, he was removed from the minute-by-minute mix of the broadcast, enabling Stringer to establish his own relationship with the anchorman without the hovering presence of a snarling gatekeeper. Happily, Buksbaum proved to have an affinity for technicians and their needs. For the first time in years, camera crews throughout the world would come to feel that there was someone in New York who understood and cared about their problems.

Before each set of announcements was made both Van and I would meet with Bill Leonard and walk him through the changes. Bill offered no quarrel when we unveiled our plans. I had the feeling that he might have made many of the same changes if imminent retirement hadn't made it too tempting to step away from the risk of bruising old friends and colleagues. Bill was enthusiastic about Stringer, but Sandy Socolow was an old friend. He asked us if he could break the news to Sandy.

"I'll tell him that no one can expect to stay in a job like that forever," he said, "and that the chance to be London Bureau chief is a fair, even generous offer. I think it will mean more if he hears it from me."

In the midst of these changes Rather's diminutive size on the screen had become a nightly joke between Van and me. Despite Socolow's assurance that he would discuss the issue with the director, nothing had changed. Each time Rather came on the screen appearing Lilliputian next to a giant map or a photograph of a newsmaker, we began to laugh.

One story using the emblem of one of the nation's automakers made Rather seem particularly tiny.

"What is this," Van asked, "the incredible shrinking anchorman?"

"You might be onto something," I said. "If Lily Tomlin would co-anchor . . ."

"Wait a minute," Van said. "Look at this next shot. He's a little larger."

"You're right," I said. "He's up to at least a dollar and a half."

Van's right hand began to rotate across his beard.

"Can you imagine this going on at one of your television stations?" he asked. "What would you have done?"

"I guess I would have gone into a control room and changed it."

The hand left the beard and picked up a phone.

"Helen, call the *Evening News* and tell them after the broadcast is over I want them to keep both the control booth room and the studio hot."

That night, Friday, December 4, at 8 P.M., both of us sat in chairs in the control room next to Richie Mutschler, the director. Rather was seated in his anchor chair. The instructions to Mutschler were brief.

Joyce: "Richie, ask the TD to put that graphic on the line monitor. . . . Now ask him to reduce its size. . . . No, more than that . . . smaller . . . smaller. . . . That's it."

Sauter: "Now let's see Dan next to the graphic. Ask the cameraman to move in tighter on Dan. No, make him larger than that . . . still bigger . . . O.K. Richie, that's the way we want to see the anchorman beginning Monday night."

That Monday night, December 7, Dan Rather, the principal communicator for *The CBS Evening News,* filled the television screen in the first perceptible revision in a series of changes which would begin the reversal of that broadcast's decline.

In 1981 when CBS News was undergoing these transformations, all of CBS was experiencing changes even more far-reaching.

William S. Paley was in the process of stepping aside. In the 1920s he'd built a small network of radio stations into an enormous communications empire.

Everyone who worked at CBS had felt the dominant presence of the man who cast the final vote on any issue he deemed significant. Paley's absolute power was simply a fact of life for all of us. "It's his candy store" was a frequently resorted to phrase which captured our acceptance of this "Chairman for Life."

We'd heard many times before that Paley was grooming a successor. But Paley's health and vigor kept him active into his eighties. His legendary lieutenant, Dr. Frank Stanton, actually made it as far as becoming Vice Chairman. But Stanton reached his own retirement age of sixty-five in 1973 with Paley still in the Chairman's office.

Before Stanton's retirement, Jack Schneider, the President of the Broadcast Group, got a tryout in 1969 as the Executive Vice President of CBS. But word began to circulate that Paley found him lacking in the necessary business skills. In 1971, he was replaced by Charles Chick Ireland, a former right-hand man to Harold Geneen of International Telephone and Telegraph.

Less than a year later Paley's grumblings had already begun when Ireland, in what some at CBS believed was a "wise career move," died of a heart attack at the age of fifty-one. This time Paley chose a man he called a "financial wizard." Arthur Taylor was thirty-seven years old, Executive Vice President and chief financial officer of International Paper. The wizard lasted four years. Paley acknowledged that Taylor was "indeed brilliant" and CBS earnings were at an all-time high. But Taylor, Paley said, "did not have all of the essential qualities to become my successor." Those apparently were what he spotted in John Backe, the forty-four-year-old head of the CBS Publishing Group.

"I had my eye on John Backe for some time," Paley said.

In 1976, Taylor was out, Backe was in. By April 1977, Paley was sufficiently confident of Backe's leadership to step down from the job of Chief Executive Officer. He remained as Chairman of CBS. Backe seemed to flourish in the CEO role. By 1981 earnings were even higher. The television network had pulled out of a prime-time slump and had wrestled the number one position back from ABC.

In May 1980, Backe spoke to the CBS affiliates at their annual meeting in Los Angeles. He talked glowingly about the accomplishments of CBS. That afternoon, flying back to New York with Bill Leonard, Backe was in an ebullient, expansive mood, optimistic about the future of CBS.

When the company plane reached New York he was asked to come to the Chairman's office. Once there, he learned that Paley didn't think he had the necessary qualities to become his successor. Backe was out and Tom Wyman was in.

Paley was now seventy-nine years old. His latest handpicked successor was fifty-one, and came to CBS from the Pillsbury Corporation in Minneapolis, where he'd been in charge of the Jolly Green Giant brand of packaged foods. It took a $1 million bonus to bring Wyman to CBS. That was in addition to an annual salary of $750,000. It also took the assurances of Paley and the Board of Directors that he would be allowed to run the company.

When Wyman came to CBS he assumed operational control of a corporation with businesses ranging from broadcasting, records, and publishing to children's toys and Steinway pianos. But it was broadcasting, not CBS Records or Holt, Rinehart & Winston, the book publisher, which shaped the identity of CBS. And this was more than public perception. The CBS Broadcast Group in 1981 contributed 41 percent of the total revenues of CBS, Inc. As Wyman would learn, the Broadcast Group was lucrative and complex. It was divided into separate divisions which included CBS News, the five owned and operated television stations, Radio, and the various components of the television network, Entertainment, Sports, along with Sales, Operations, and Affiliate Relations.

In the fall of 1981, Wyman had been in his job for a year and a half and he certainly gave the impression he was running things. That October he was profiled in the business section of the Sunday New York *Times*. He told the *Times*, "I don't think there's any question in anyone's mind that I'm running the company." Of Paley he said, "He is wonderfully tough-minded and asks spectacular questions. But the initiatives have been mine." To the average reader this was not a particularly startling statement. To Paley watchers it was stunning, a public relegation of Paley to the advisory sidelines.

For days we waited for an announcement from the Chairman's office that "Mr. Wyman has decided to return to his first love, the frozen food business in Minnesota." As the days went by with no such announcement, heads began to nod. Maybe this time Paley really was going to step down. The whispered refrain in the upper floors of Black Rock was: "Wyman's got the backing of the board, the old man can't touch him."

In that same month Wyman served notice on CBS News that a new day had dawned. He made a speech before the International Radio and Television Society at New York City's Waldorf-Astoria Hotel. In that speech he described the political conventions as being as much "out of hand" as the rest of the long political process leading to national elections. He told the group that CBS "does not plan gavel-to-gavel coverage of the 1984 conventions."

I'd gotten a preview of this the first time I met Wyman, more than a year earlier. It was the day after the 1980 Republican convention and Jankowski had flown to Chicago, where I was scheduled to present a business review of WBBM-TV. I remember meeting a tall man, at least six feet three, who seemed barely interested in my television station but obsessed by the convention he'd just attended. He couldn't believe the amount of money CBS had invested in its coverage or the amount it lost because it preempted regular prime-time programming. It was as though he had personally encountered the Bermuda Triangle of corporate profits.

Wyman was more worldly than his predecessors. He had been based for five years in Vevey, Switzerland, in the 1950s for the Nestlé Corporation. That day in my office in Chicago he placed a call to Paley, who was staying at the Plaza-Athénée in Paris and spoke enough French to be able to tell the operator, *"Je voudrais la chambre de Monsieur Paley, s'il vous plaît."* In a company filled with executives who had trouble ordering a bottle of French wine in a restaurant, that alone set him apart. He was a graduate of

Amherst who had written his master's paper on William Butler Yeats. I would eventually come to see this tall graceful man's droll sense of humor. I could believe that, of the senior executives at CBS, he alone might on occasion read a book for pleasure. Despite that, he talked about business in some abstract language shared only by other corporate CEOs. He was someone who could say, "Managing has to do with the animation and orchestration of people," and believe that he had spoken with precision and clarity. I'm afraid I didn't much like the man I met that day in Chicago.

As I listened to him instructing Jankowski on the writing off of gavel-to-gavel coverage and discussing the need to find a proper forum for the announcement, I was depressed that a decision of this significance was being mandated by someone who only a few months earlier was measuring the volume of frozen peas being moved off supermarket shelves. Now here he was. By the time he actually made that speech to the IRTS over a year later, I was beginning to identify the audience he was really trying to reach. It certainly wasn't the group of broadcast executives who buy the tickets and fill the tables at those lunches. Wyman was using that forum to speak past those broadcasters to a body called the "financial community." More specifically, he was addressing a handful of financial analysts who interpreted the value of broadcast stocks to that community. Men such as John Ready of Drexel Burnham, Joseph Fuchs of Kidder Peabody, or Anthony Hoffman of A. G. Becker. Executives at CBS would be hard pressed to recall hearing Wyman speak when he wasn't tuning his remarks to impress these analysts. It had been possible to hold an executive position at CBS for years without knowing those names, or for that matter, without spending a great deal of time thinking about "the shareholders." Wyman changed all of that. CBS was in a state of transition from the personal fiefdom of a great entrepreneur to an American corporation under the new leadership of a modern CEO. Wyman was using the podium of the IRTS to tell the analysts, the financial community, the shareholders, and his own executives that CBS stock would become more valuable because of a new management which understood the need to reduce costs. By announcing three years in advance that the traditional CBS News convention coverage would be curtailed he was seizing a symbolic opportunity to get the message across. It would not be the last time that CBS News would be used to drive home the point that the management of CBS was serious about cost control.

As 1981 drew to a close, however, the 1984 conventions seemed an eternity away. On the immediate agenda were the more pressing matters of staff reorganization, enhancement of the *Evening News,* and rehabilitation of the morning broadcast. During a Christmas season party at Jankowski's house in Weston, Connecticut, I learned that that list would also include a revamp of the entire graphic presentation of CBS News. I was sitting in his living room with a glass of white wine in my hand reminding Maureen that we'd first had dinner there in 1971, when Gene and I both worked for WCBS-TV in New York.

"They've done a lot with it since then," she said.

Gene came over and joined us.

"Gene, if I was an anthropologist, I could chart your history with this house," I said.

"What would it tell you?"

"That swimming pool out in back? That was added the year you became controller. And the tennis court? That went in the year you got the Broadcast Group. If you do any better, you're going to be the Squire of Kettle Creek Road."

There was a broad smile on his face.

"You're off a little," he said, "but not by much."

He started to get up to say hello to Jean and Dan Rather, who'd just come in. They stopped to talk with Brent Musburger, and Gene leaned over the edge of my chair.

"Paley would like to have dinner with you and Van on December 22. Are you free?"

I smiled. "I think I can clear my calendar. Anything I should be thinking about before that dinner?"

"Mostly it'll be a courtesy dinner, but without a doubt he'll bring up the CBS News graphics. He thinks they are a mess."

"He's not wrong about that," I said.

"Wyman can't believe Paley gets involved in that sort of thing," he said. "He thinks the Chairman manages too far down, but I tell him he's always been like that. Look, I won't tell Van or you how to deal with the problems of CBS News, but I am asking you to do something about the graphics. Every time I talk to the Chairman, he brings them up. You've got to get him off my back."

After we left the party I found myself thinking about the awe with which people at CBS regarded Paley.

In 1980, when I was running KNXT-TV in Los Angeles, Paley had come to the station for a business review. I was in a position to present a glowing picture and he was in a relaxed, expansive mood recalling his own days in that building in the 1940s when it originated network radio shows of Jack Benny, Bing Crosby, Edgar Bergen and Charlie McCarthy, and Burns and Allen.

"I used to keep an office up on the second floor," he said. "I'd take the Twentieth Century out here and stay for weeks at a time."

It was obvious the hallways and studios of this old building on Hollywood's Sunset Boulevard were filled with pleasant memories. His mood was so genial I was prompted to make a request.

"Mr. Paley," I said. "I'm going to ask you for a favor."

In an instant the glow of nostalgia left his eyes and I found myself looking at steel. Quickly, I held up a copy of his autobiography, *As It Happened.*

"I'd be most appreciative if you would sign my copy of your book," I said.

His expression returned to one of cordiality and he wrote a generous inscription on the flyleaf of the book.

Later that day I told my boss, Tom Leahy, I'd asked Paley to autograph his book for me.

"I'd love to have him do that," he said. "I just don't have the guts to ask."

Tom Leahy was one of the toughest executives I'd known. But the patriarchal figure of William S. Paley was so intimidating he was afraid to ask him to autograph a book.

Paley's power over those who worked for him at CBS was absolute. My initial glimpse of this came in 1967, when I was the news director for WCBS Radio in New York. It was my first job on the management side of broadcasting, a career change that came about because Marty Weldon, the station's splendid news director, died suddenly of a heart attack. A few days after Marty's funeral, Tom Swafford, the general manager, and I were standing side by side in the men's room. I heard him say, "Ed, I've been thinking. You ought to consider becoming the news director."

I stared at the wall.

"I like what I'm doing."

"I know . . . I know. But think about it for a few days and come see me."

For seven years I'd been on the air for that station. I'd never managed anything in my life. I'd been given a chance to be more than an announcer. I'd produced documentaries, I'd wandered the city as a roving reporter, and the station had once even allowed me to present a program of live jazz. For the past few years I'd had my own program in an afternoon lineup which included two alumni of NBC, Dave Garroway and Ken Banghart. Each day I got to meet and interview a parade of fascinating people intense with the issues of that age . . . people like Malcolm X, William F. Buckley—surely New York's most entertaining mayoral candidate since Jimmy Walker—Jackie Robinson, Allen Dulles. I thought I'd found a great way to earn a comfortable living. Now Swafford was asking me to think about a transition which not only would increase the number of hours I worked but would reduce my income from $40,000 a year to $25,000.

When Steve Flanders, the station's City Hall reporter, whom I revered, gave me unassailable arguments about why I had to take the job, I accepted.

A few months later the Newark riots erupted. In that summer of 1967 the urban riot was a plague visited upon the black neighborhoods of many American cities. That night in Newark, I joined Steve Flanders and Tony Brunton, another of our radio reporters, in the station's mobile unit. Frankly, I wanted to show that I hadn't become a deskbound paper shuffler. About ten o'clock, on a long, dark street near Newark Hospital, we pulled up behind a parked police car. Except for that car the street was deserted and we quickly realized the reason. The two cops were crouched on one side of their car exchanging gunfire with a sniper concealed on the roof of a nearby project. Within seconds the three of us were stretched on the ground under our mobile unit. At one point I whispered to Steve, who was lying next to me, "I want you to know I really like this job . . . I can't tell you how much I appreciate the advice you gave me."

Actually, I really did like the job. That was in part because I liked Swafford. Swaff was a trim man in his fifties with only one good arm and a year-round tan he maintained with a sunlamp. He was also a recovered alcoholic. Somehow he'd managed to work his way past that handicap, and the exuberance he brought to the radio station was contagious. He was almost obsessed with his vision for revising the format of WCBS. He wanted to build it into what was then called in the broadcasting business a "contemporary" music station, which played middle-of-the-road music and had a strong local news department. Swafford thought he'd already laid the cornerstone of his dream station with a morning program hosted by the same Pat Summerall who is today familiar to the viewers of NFL football games on CBS television. Pat was a former kicker for the New York Giants who'd broken into broadcasting at our station as a sports-caster. Swafford turned him into his morning-drive-time DJ and began an expensive advertising campaign promoting Pat as "Super Summerall." Ads appeared in all of the New York newspapers showing Pat Summerall in a Superman costume.

But even Swafford's suntan couldn't hide the worry lines on his face when he asked three of his department heads to come into his office on a Tuesday morning in mid-1967. Besides me, there was Maury Bencoyl, the program director, who would preside over the new music programs Swaf-ford intended to create, and Bob Hosking, who was the director of sales. He thought Swafford's intended format change was a potential money-maker and his sales force was poised, ready to go. Bob is today the President of CBS Radio.

Swafford closed the door of his office.

"This has to be a secret," he said.

That always gets your attention.

"I've just come from a meeting with Paley," he told us.

I'd worked at WCBS since 1959. I was twenty-six when I joined the station. Paley, for me, was a remote corporate deity whose name was invoked the way the ancient Greeks and Romans mentioned Zeus or Jove.

I'd not only never met him; I'd never even seen him. That would soon change.

"Paley thinks WCBS should become an all-news radio station," he continued.

"What did you say to him?" I asked.

"I told him Westinghouse did it first in New York with WINS, and I didn't think the market could support two all-news stations."

Hosking began to look as worried as Swafford.

"You're absolutely right," he said. "How did you leave it?"

"He asked me to give it further analysis. I'm going to see him again later this week. I'd like each of you guys to prepare your own analysis of the Paley proposal. Give it to me by the close of business tomorrow."

I prepared an analysis which said that such a station would be expensive to operate and slow to grow, but would capitalize on all the natural strengths of CBS. I thought the demand for staggering amounts of news material would mean either that CBS News would have to supply us with additional national and international material or that we'd have to find other resources. As for WINS, which was already an all-news station . . . when we were finished, I said, we'd be better than they were.

Swafford understandably was not pleased by my observations and recommendations. He was, however, characteristically generous.

"I wouldn't expect a news guy to tell me going all-news was a crappy idea."

Swafford, with Arthur Hall Hayes, President of CBS Radio, and Fred Ruegg, the Senior Vice President, met with Paley. They laid out for him a series of precise, cogent reasons against converting WCBS to an all-news radio station.

A few days later all three men were gone.

Hayes and Ruegg were out completely. Swafford, a favorite of Jack Schneider, President of the Broadcast Group, was spared total expulsion and was, instead, exiled to Venezuela to oversee a partial interest CBS held in a Caracas television station.

Years later when CBS had successful all-news radio stations in New York, Chicago, and Los Angeles, he would recall for people his dispute with Paley.

"Yeah, I'm the guy who told Paley his all-news idea would never work . . . and I really liked Venezuela."

Paley selected Joe Dembo as the new Vice President and general manager of WCBS Radio. At the time, Joe was in charge of all of the radio activity of CBS News. Two years earlier he'd been the news director for

WCBS Radio. I'd know him since 1959, when he left NBC, where he'd been a newswriter working on such programs as *The Today Show.* He'd first come to WCBS as the station's editorial director.

After the announcement of his appointment, Joe asked me to have lunch with him at Patsy's restaurant in the West Fifties. I was already seated at the table when he arrived. Joe Dembo is an intense man with a voice so deep he sounds like Darth Vader. When you first meet him it's somewhat startling because he's small enough to lend jackets to Michael J. Fox.

The lunch started on a great note.

"I want you to remain as news director," he said.

I was hoping he would say that. Not only had I begun to enjoy being a news director but the prospect of building an all-news station for CBS had me sitting up half the night. Swafford had called Joe and urged him to keep me in the job but it was his decision. Over the next hour, in between bites of Patsy's delicious hot sausages and peppers, I ran through my list of things that needed doing. After we first designed a format, we'd need to hire new writers, editors, reporters, technicians. As we were leaving I mentioned a timetable.

"I figure an easy six months to get all this done."

"The Chairman asked if we could be on the air with an all-news format in three months," Joe said.

He pushed open the door to the street and continued: "I told him yes."

In the time I worked for Joe Dembo he was a relentless, nitpicking, thankless, driving martinet . . . and I thought he was wonderful. He was, I believe, the best general manager in the history of CBS Radio.

When the Newark riots broke out, Dembo was already in his new job. The episode when Flanders, Brunton, and I were doing our best to keep a mobile unit between ourselves and a sniper ended shortly after 2 A.M., and I returned to the newsroom. It was too late to go home, so I slept on the couch in my office for a few hours. Daylight woke me. I sat at my desk for a few minutes and then headed toward the men's room to wash my face and shave. Walking through the small reception area on the sixteenth floor of Black Rock, where the station was located, I saw an elevator door open and Joe Dembo get off. I stopped and waited for him to reach me. I half expected to hear some thank-you for having put in a rough night.

"Did you hear what happened?" he asked.

"No," I said. "What?"

"The first editorial I've done as general manager. I recorded it yesterday and it ran this morning. The opening three words were missing. It was upcut by the technician. I'm in here to find whoever did it."

In a fury he wheeled off toward the control room. After a few steps he stopped abruptly, and over his shoulder he said, "If you don't hire some more writers soon we're never going to meet the date I promised Paley."

Without waiting for my response he resumed his march to the control room. If it had been someone else I think I would have been furious. Instead, I remember laughing and saying to myself, "That little prick won't be happy until this is a great radio station."

Needless to say, I redoubled my hiring efforts. I had one break going in. Five months earlier I had hired a morning newscaster who had turned out to be terrific. When I'd first heard about him he was working for ABC doing feature segments called *Flair Reports* for their radio network. I asked him to send me some tapes of his work and I liked what I heard. It wasn't just that he had a good voice and delivery; his writing style was distinctive, particularly the innovative way he incorporated audiotape segments.

His name was Charles Wood, but there was already a Charles Wood on the air somewhere else in the country. AFTRA, the performer's union, has a strict rule. If you are an active member using a full name such as Charles Wood, nobody else can call himself that even if it really is his name. So our Charles Wood used the name of Charles Osgood, and for years, until he joined CBS News, listening to morning radio in New York was infinitely more interesting because of Charles Osgood.

I still needed to hire a large number of reporters, writers, and editors. I knew it was also an opportunity to do some meaningful hiring. Joe Dembo agreed.

In 1967 there weren't many women in nonsecretarial jobs at WCBS and I don't recall any blacks at all. I'd like to believe it was more than being shot at in Newark that started me thinking, but seeing a neighborhood in flames can make you stop and reflect. The CBS Personnel Department was helpful when it came to locating women. We even raided wire services and newspapers for some of their bright women employees. But there was no such mechanism at CBS for finding blacks or, for that matter, other minorities. I called the Urban League and told them of my frustration.

"Blacks just don't think of CBS as a company which will accept them," I was informed. But they agreed to help circulate the word that I was open and eager for applications from qualified blacks. Gradually the applications began to trickle in. Jacob Wortham was, I believe, the first black newswriter to be hired at WCBS Radio. Then a phone call came from an applicant for a reporter's job. I made an appointment to see him. He was a

Philadelphia schoolteacher in his twenties who worked part-time as an announcer at a black radio station in that city. He turned out to be an impressive young man, but his experience was extremely limited. He didn't even have tapes of his work.

"Look," I said, "let me give you some wire copy and a typewriter. Take a couple of hours and write a few stories. Then I'll put you in a studio and we'll record you."

He looked at me as if I were asking him to step inside our revolving door . . . and maybe I was.

"You won't learn anything about me from that," he said. "Why don't you lend me a small tape recorder," he continued. "I'll go out and do a story and bring it back for you."

"Oh Christ," I thought, "what have I got here?" But I got a tape recorder and gave it to him.

A few hours later he was back. I told him I'd listen to the tape and get in touch with him in a few days. The next morning I closed the door to my office and played the tape. He'd gone up to Harlem and interviewed a black politician. I think it was Basil Patterson. Then he'd recorded a lead-in and a close. It wasn't great. But it wasn't terrible. I thought about it all morning and then I went in to see Dembo. I played the tape for him.

"I know his work is rough," I said, "but he's smart and he's aggressive. He didn't let me stuff him in a studio to read some rewritten wire copy. I'd like to take a chance."

Joe agreed but cautioned me to make it clear to him he'd have to show steady improvement once he got here.

I left Joe's office and placed a call to the Philadelphia number on the résumé I'd kept in my office. The person who answered gave me the number of an Atlanta hotel which was housing a convention for black DJs.

"Could you connect me with the room of Ed Bradley," I asked.

Ed answered and I laid it all out for him. His work was rough but he had enough promise to make us take a chance. He'd have to be able to handle lots of criticism.

"Ed," I said, "if you can accept that and you want the job, then it's yours."

There was a pause. "I want the job."

I hung up worrying that he didn't sound all that happy or enthusiastic about what, after all, was a pretty damn good job. Years later, when Ed Bradley was an established news star traveling the world for *60 Minutes*, we talked about that day.

"Remember when you called me in my hotel room in Atlanta?" he asked. "When you told me I had the job and we hung up . . . I sat there in my room and cried."

One by one our openings for reporters, writers, and editors were filled. Early July was our target date. As the time grew closer, Dembo and I both went through mood swings. One day we'd be totally confident that we were assembling the most professional radio news organization in broadcasting. Then we'd produce several hours of a simulated broadcast and convince ourselves that what we were building was the first news swamp. The broadcast seemed formless. But day by day it began to take shape. Our staff was now on board, our most recent rehearsals had gone well. We were as ready as we were likely to be.

On a rainy Sunday afternoon, I left my home in Connecticut and headed my car toward New York. I planned to stay in a hotel room close to the station so I would have no difficulty in being in the newsroom well in advance of our 5:30 A.M. debut. As I passed Stamford I turned on my car radio, tuned to CBS. Nothing.

"Hell," I thought, "what a time for my radio to go out." I turned the dial to the left and I could hear NBC. I turned it to the right and I heard WINS "All News All the Time." There was nothing wrong with my radio except when I turned it to 880, the frequency for WCBS. Every mile of the Merritt Parkway seemed to stretch out forever while I waited in vain to hear some sound come out of that spot on the dial, to hear an announcer apologize for technical difficulties which had taken the station briefly off the air. Near the Greenwich exit I saw a gas station. I wheeled off the Merritt and dashed for a phone booth. There I learned it was a technical problem, all right. A technical problem caused by pilot error, a first in my experience. A light plane had crashed into our AM transmitter, which was located on an island in Long Island Sound. The transmitter was in ruins and the station would be out of business for several days.

So the debut the next day of the first CBS all-news radio station was heard only by those with FM receivers. In 1967 comparatively few people listened to FM radio. FM had not become the medium of choice it is today for so many people. In those days, for example, an FM radio in a car was rare and expensive. For all of us who were involved that Monday morning, there was a sense of anticlimax.

"It's too bad no one is hearing this."

A few hours later we weren't quite so unhappy about that fact. We began to encounter the first of the opening-day glitches, tapes that didn't come up, live reports that weren't there, anchorpersons awkwardly coping with the challenge of being on the air for two hours at a time. I was by then sitting in Joe's office waiting for sandwiches we'd ordered. We were both making notes as we listened to his radio. The phone rang and I watched Joe impatiently pick it up. His executive slump disappeared as he sat up straight in his chair.

"Yes, sir," he said. "I'll be right up." He put his phone back on its cradle and began massaging the back of his neck. He looked stricken.

"Paley wants to see me," he said. "Do you think he knows about that tape that didn't come up?"

"Those things happen," I said. "We'll get better."

By the time those words were out of my mouth, Joe had his jacket on and was out the door.

I remained in his office taking notes. My lunch arrived from the Carnegie Deli, matzo ball soup, pastrami on rye, and a bottle of Dr. Brown's celery tonic. I left it sitting in the brown paper bag in which it came. The celebratory impulse which had prompted it had disappeared. Half an hour later Joe returned. He looked like he'd gone to the seashore. The color had returned to his face and he practically bounced into his chair.

"He likes it," he said. "He's up there listening and making notes. Just like us."

Out of his jacket Joe took several pages of his notes of Paley's notes. This was a practice which would be repeated frequently for the next two years. We were still groping for the form of the CBS brand of all-news radio and Paley unerringly would pick out something we were still grappling with and offer the solution.

Time and time again Joe would be summoned on short notice to the Chairman's office. Paley would read his notes to him. "Headlines on the half hour are important, but the listeners need a road map. Follow the headlines with a list of special features they can expect to hear in the next thirty minutes."

There was the matter of time checks.

"People like to set their watches. Why not give them a time tone to listen for at the start of each hour?"

It was hard to believe Paley could devote as much time as he did to listening to his radio station, but his notes were continuing evidence of his interest. Joe would listen and make his own notes. Back in his office, he, in turn, would read them to me and I would go back to the newsroom and try to make the ideas work. I used to needle Joe by telling him, "You've discovered the secret for handling Paley. You do whatever he tells you."

That really wasn't fair. We were all flattered by the amount of attention Paley was giving us, but there were times when we disagreed with him. For a while Paley wasn't happy with Charles Osgood as a radio anchorman. He liked his feature work but thought his reading as an anchorman was "too choppy." It was this offbeat delivery which we thought made Charlie so unique and so valuable. For months Paley never missed an opportunity to remind Joe that Charlie was "miscast."

The pleasure Paley was obviously taking in being right about his all-news venture may have suppressed any impulse he had to hand a plane ticket to Venezuela to another recalcitrant general manager, and as the months went on the soundness of his belief in all-news radio was increasingly supported by the growth of WCBS.

It was a period of major news, the assassinations of Robert Kennedy and Martin Luther King, the invasion of Czechoslovakia. In growing numbers, an audience sought the services of this all-news station. Advertisers began to come to the station for its upscale audience.

The CBS radio stations in Chicago and Los Angeles soon followed our example and changed to all-news formats. Paley was so proud of his creation he asked us to prepare a three-hour presentation on all-news radio which he would attend along with Dr. Frank Stanton, the President of CBS, and Jack Schneider, the President of the CBS Broadcast Group. Dembo and I were immersed in all-news radio. But we couldn't believe that the three senior executives of CBS were going to sit still for a three-hour presentation. Sit still they did. In fact, Paley seemed to delight in it all. He beamed at us as though we were his prize pupils reciting the *Iliad* in perfect Greek. I've often wondered if he wasn't enjoying the resonances of another era when he and other young men like himself were shaping and molding a brand-new medium.

Schneider tried to give the impression of listening, but you could actually see his mind wandering to what he undoubtedly considered the more important questions of prime time and up-front markets. CBS had recently announced the cancellation of *What's My Line* after a run of seventeen years.

Stanton stared down at his notepad for most of the three hours and seemed totally preoccupied. He'd probably taken a phone call from an irate LBJ fuming about some CBS News story from Vietnam. It didn't matter. Their inattention was no more important to us that day than the loss of our transmitter had been the first day of our all-news effort. At CBS it was enough to please an audience of one, if the happy listener was William S. Paley.

F ourteen years later I was once again preparing for a meeting with Paley. December 22, 1981, was the night Van and I had been asked to have dinner with him.

Frank Stanton was gone, Jack Schneider was gone. Paley was now seventy-nine years old. He still held the title of Chairman but no longer involved himself in the day-to-day operations of CBS. That he was still a force to acknowledge could be measured by Jankowski's eagerness to satisfy his complaints about CBS News graphics.

Paley was quite right in his dislike of the graphic presentation of CBS News. It was a mess. Not only was the typeface hard to read, but the style varied from broadcast to broadcast and wasn't even consistent within the *Evening News* itself. The maps were hard to decipher. The generic graphics for stories on the economy, blizzards, union strikes, and other recurring stories were a hodgepodge.

In advance of the dinner Van and I met with Thomas Geismar of the design consultant firm of Chermayeff and Geismar. We commissioned him to design a new graphic look for all of the hard-news broadcasts at CBS News. If Paley brought the subject up at dinner we'd be able to tell him change was underway.

The night of the dinner Van and I arrived together at 7:30 P.M. at Paley's Fifth Avenue apartment. Wyman and Jankowski got there at the same time and we all rode up in the elevator. The houseman took our coats in the foyer. The far wall of the foyer provided a thrilling flash of recognition. A huge painting of a young boy leading a horse. A Picasso. On the walls of

Paley's office at CBS there are paintings by Picasso, Kline, Rouault, and Giacometti, but nothing nearly as breathtaking as the extraordinary painting which hangs in the entrance of his apartment.

The houseman escorted us into the living room, where Paley was waiting. He was dressed in a dark blue suit and navy tie with tiny red dots. His silver hair looked as if it had received the meticulous attention of the world's most expert barber. He wore his seventy-nine years with grace and you could imagine what he must have been like at thirty-five.

It was fascinating to watch Wyman with Paley, particularly in contrast to Jankowski. Gene seemed to stand at attention, even when seated at the dinner table. Wyman, by contrast, was almost deliberately at ease, comfortably recessed in a deep chair, knees and elbows in a series of long graceful angles. He and Paley chatted amiably about a number of the most casual subjects. Rupert Murdoch. Paley didn't know him personally.

"Is he an attractive man?" he asked.

I don't remember Wyman's response. It didn't matter. It wasn't meant to matter. From time to time Paley would turn his head slightly to include the rest of us. It was a gracious gesture, much the way a Squire might include the Master of Hounds and his head lad before he got around to asking them about the new litter of pups. That moment came at the dinner table. As the soup bowls were being removed Paley turned to Van and said, "I hope you're going to give some thought to the look of the news broadcasts, to the graphics they're using."

Van was ready. "Gene has mentioned your concern, Mr. Paley. It's a concern both Ed and I share. As a matter of fact, we've retained the design consultant firm of Cheramayeff and Geismar to review all of the CBS News graphics and come back to us with recommendations for their improvement."

The Squire looked pleased. That litter might have promise.

"I'd like to see those when they're ready," he said.

I'd spoken to Geismar just before I left the office.

"We'll be able to show you something in a month," I said.

Paley smiled. "When Frank Stanton was here, he used to handle this sort of thing for me," he said. "Frank was very knowledgeable and very good at this. The way we look is terribly important, you know."

The subject of graphics was dropped and replaced by the dangers of editorializing in news broadcasts.

"Often it's your best people who want to do it," he warned. "But CBS News has to be as close to objective as possible."

He recalled for us his parting with Howard K. Smith. Smith was a

Rhodes scholar who worked for United Press in Berlin in 1940. Murrow hired him away to work for CBS. After the war Murrow hired Smith as his successor in London. He stayed in Europe until 1957, when he became chief Washington correspondent. During this period he became a frequent alternative to Murrow on *CBS Reports*. In 1961, when Murrow left CBS, Smith seemed clearly to be moving into the Murrow role. But executives at CBS were increasingly worried that Smith's commentaries on controversial issues were crossing the line between analysis and editorial. They went so far as to remove a closing line from Smith's script for a *CBS Reports* documentary on racial tension in Birmingham, Alabama. The line which they removed quoted Edmund Burke, who said, "The only thing necessary for the triumph of evil is for good men to do nothing."

"I told Smith, 'You're very good and very valuable. I'm sure the other networks know this. You'd be a loss to us. But if you want to do this you can't do it on CBS. You'll have to do it someplace else.' "

Smith left CBS as a result and soon joined ABC as the co-anchor of their evening news broadcast.

"It doesn't matter how much you like them," he said. "There'll come a day when they'll want to do this and you've got to stop them."

The evening concluded shortly before ten o'clock. As the houseman was handing me my coat, Paley walked over to say good night.

"Remember what I said about editorializing," he said. "Keeping that out of our news reports may be the hardest part of your job."

The days that followed the dinner with Paley were devoted to more change. Tom Geismar was hard at work redesigning the typographical look of CBS News. The Paley Project, we called it. But television had entered the age of electronic graphics as well. We had the technology to create an array of special effects for illustrating breaking news stories. Electronic wipes, simple animation, and other techniques were used regularly by ABC News but had generally been ignored at CBS.

Jeff Kreiner, a young associate director on the *Evening News,* came to me with a plea to be allowed to experiment with these new techniques. I'd thought until then that CBS lacked the equipment to do this. Kreiner claimed the barrier at CBS was psychological, not technical. I told him to make a tape showing what was possible for us to do on a real-time basis for a broadcast which would have to go on the air that evening. A few days later he was back. He and Steve Besner, a colleague from the *Evening News,* had a tape containing a variety of electronic illustrations.

It's easy to dismiss electronic graphics as glitz or Star Wars come to television. Many stories are inherently difficult for television to report coherently. Stories which require an understanding of spatial relationships, such as a mine disaster or the collision of two aircraft, are comprehensible if accompanied by the right graphics.

Television has often been accused of shying away from complex economic stories. There was truth to that charge. These stories were difficult to tell in terms a viewer could comprehend and retain. In 1981 the use of electronic illustrations coincided with an awareness that stories about business, government, and the growing unemployment rate had moved into the must-cover category.

The Kreiner-Besner tape which I screened for an enthusiastic Sauter became a kind of primer for Stringer's producers on the *Evening News*. Increasingly, they turned to directors for help in constructing their stories. These two young men, more than anyone else, created a new look for the stories reported on *The CBS Evening News*.

At the same time these visual changes were taking place, a change in editorial approach was also occurring. Change which remains controversial to this day. For years the Washington Bureau of CBS News had filled almost half the broadcast on an average night. The hearing room, the briefing room, the steps of the Capitol building were regular and familiar sights to news viewers. This began to change. In New York, Stringer started teaming correspondents such as Bernie Goldberg or Ray Brady with some of the sharp young producers from the *Evening News* staff. At the same time he was encouraging the bureaus to become more aggressive in submitting story ideas from their regions. Interesting suggestions began to trickle, then to pour in from correspondents in bureaus where the practice had been to wait for the assignment call from New York. An energetic correspondent such as Barry Petersen in San Francisco could quickly become an *Evening News* regular with stories whose locales ranged from Salt Lake City to Seattle.

Stories which would earlier have been covered solely in Washington were now sometimes given to other bureaus. Instead of a piece from a Washington correspondent at the Labor Department on the newest unemployment figures, those statistics might be used to introduce a story about the impact of unemployment in Detroit or Cleveland. This came as a shock to the Washington Bureau. For years they had been asked to cover the incrementa of official Washington.

"The bill is going in the hopper."

"The bill is in the hopper."

"The bill has come out of the hopper."

Washington was the largest of the CBS News bureaus. Unlike other bureaus, it works on a system of beats. The White House, the Hill, the various departments, such as State, Defense, Labor. And, of course, an assemblage of regulatory agencies. The bureau covers the most important capital in the world. It's the center of an enormous bureaucracy which affects almost every facet of life in the United States. So it's inevitable that national news broadcasts are heavily oriented toward their stories. But for years the Washington Bureau of CBS had provided an available quota of stories with which to fill the *Evening News.* When commercials are removed from that half-hour broadcast, approximately twenty-two minutes remain for actual news. Creating new competition for those precious minutes was bound to produce strains and we began to hear rumblings from our Washington Bureau.

Jack Smith, the Washington Bureau chief, had been in charge of the CBS News Chicago Bureau during the days when I ran WBBM-TV. We knew one another well enough for him to feel comfortable calling me to voice a warning.

"There's a lot of talk down here about you two guys being anti-Washington," he said.

"What's all that about?" I asked. "You know I'm not anti-Washington, but some of the stories are better if they're done by the other bureaus."

"It's getting harder to get a Washington story on the *Evening News,* and I have to tell you that's not going down very well with the folks here."

"Jack, you guys are getting some competition from the other bureaus," I said. "You can't count on automatically filling half of the broadcast with stand-uppers or what the Fishbowl calls 'thumbsucker' pieces. You know: 'Here's the way the Washington wind is blowing today.' "

"I know what you're saying," Jack said. "Remember, I ran the Chicago Bureau. But some of our good people aren't getting on the air."

"Jack, can you be more specific?"

"Well, there have been some good stories that Pierpoint has had over at State. They've either been boiled down for Rather 'Tell Stories' or incorporated in another story from Stahl or Plante at the White House."

"Jack, did Pierpoint get on the air more often before Van and I arrived?"

I knew the answer. Robert Pierpoint, the State Department correspondent, had occupied a secondary spot vis-à-vis Rather when they both reported from the White House for CBS News during the Nixon years. Rather was so open in his dislike of Pierpoint that the *Evening News* producers shied away from putting him on the broadcast.

Jack groaned at my question. "I know what you're getting at," he said.

86

"There's bad blood there. But Rita Flynn is number two at State and she can't get on the broadcast either. It's a hell of a situation when neither one of our State Department correspondents can get on the air."

"What's her problem?" I asked.

"That happened before you got here, too. She worked all day on a story which got dropped and she called Socolow to complain. She's a strong-willed woman and she didn't hide her unhappiness. Sandy must have told Rather."

I interrupted him. "Now in order to get on Rather's broadcast she'd have to be the only reporter there when Kim Philby redefected."

"I'm afraid you're right," he said. "Look, I know you think these are problems you inherited, but they're being played as part of an anti-Washington attitude in the front office."

"Well, that's not good for any of us," I said.

"And there are some quotes from Van which have gotten repeated to the folks down here."

I didn't ask him what the quotes were. I didn't have to.

"Jack, I've got another call coming through. In a few weeks I think both Van and I should come down and spend a couple of days in the bureau and see if we can't put some of this to rest. There may be changes taking place on the *Evening News,* but Washington is our most important bureau and it always will be."

"People in this bureau need to hear that," he said.

As I put the phone back in its cradle, I worried about the abruptness with which I'd cut Jack off. I didn't want to hear those quotes because I didn't want Jack to ask me if they were accurate.

Each evening after the broadcast Van and I would compare notes and then we'd head for the Fishbowl, where we'd share them with Stringer, Rather, and the senior producers. Our nightly arrival no longer created the shock it had produced the first week we were there. The sense of everyone being on a mogul alert was gone. Rather would invariably greet us with "Did anyone touch us up tonight?" or "On a scale of one to five, where would you put it?" Van would go through the notes.

"The lead story from the White House was hard to follow. Is employment up or down? It can't be both. . . . Dynamite piece from Tom Fenton in London. . . . NBC had great pictures of stranded cattle in that Nebraska blizzard. Where was our Chicago Bureau on that?"

If anything was left out of the list, I'd add it or amplify a point which might have been glossed over. The more detailed that list, the more Rather would relax. As Stringer watched, he quickly joined in what became a nightly exercise in self-criticism. These always stopped short when they touched on areas which might agitate the anchorman. One night I was concerned because NBC had managed to obtain an exclusive interview with Lech Walesa in Gdansk, Poland.

"We should have had that," I said. "He's not exactly J. D. Salinger. He does give interviews."

Stringer jumped in. "I should have stayed on top of that, but I spent all afternoon on the telephone with that flaming Washington Bureau."

"What's the problem there?" I asked.

"It's Pierpoint," he said. "Bob feels his credibility at State is being hurt because Marvin Kalb gets on the air at NBC on a regular basis and he doesn't."

Van and I both looked at Rather. The color left his face so quickly he looked like the underside of a very large mushroom. Stringer realized he'd transgressed one of the rules of the *Evening News* postmortems. Feel free to discuss anything as long as it doesn't upset the anchorman. There was an awkward moment of silence and then Van weighed in.

"He's like the rest of those fucks down there. All they want to do is interview pointy-heads and bureaucrats."

The room dissolved in a chorus of laughter and splotches of color began to return to Rather's face. He turned to his producers.

"I just wish," he said, "this new President of CBS News wasn't so reluctant to express his opinions."

Even with the limitations imposed by the anchorman's nervous system, these postmortems were still valuable. Preparing each night's broadcast was Stringer's responsibility. Once the broadcast was over, while it was fresh in everyone's mind, a critical discussion seemed a logical step toward improvement. During the Cronkite era, any self-examination immediately following the broadcast was confined to the *Evening News* staff. One of the prices to be paid for our new approach, however, was the risk of being quoted. As Jack Smith's phone call indicated, Van's comments on the Washington Bureau had been sufficiently colorful to warrant the widest distribution.

There was no doubt those nightly meetings were helping Rather to relax. It showed on the air and the results were beneficial. Rather is never able to keep the tension out of his face. He follows a familiar phrase such as "more news in a moment" with an odd grimace which never quite becomes a smile. His eyes glisten like wet grapes, his vocal pitch rises. We came to recognize these facial expressions as signs of anxiety.

As a reporter, this had never been a visible problem. Reporters are on camera for brief periods of time. They are the sprinters of television. For the anchor chair you have to train for the marathon. It's both a confining and a demanding role. For someone who savored writing and editing it could be a rewarding experience. If you were outgoing and at ease among people, as Cronkite was, the public opportunities were there to enjoy. Rather was ill at ease among strangers. His approach to his craft was more visceral than cerebral. He frequently said about himself that while he was a natural reporter he was not a natural anchorman. Now he was spending his days first preparing to read and then reading a few minutes of copy written by someone else. For each of us concerned with the success of *The CBS Evening News,* helping its anchorman maintain a steady emotional balance was an ever-present fact of life. We could also see that it was working. For the first time he began to look as though he might belong in that anchor chair. As he watched the activity around him, he seemed to relax. More an observer than a participant, he seemed reassured at the sight of a busy crew patching his leaky boat.

One patch which was applied in early January 1982 was a new opening for the *Evening News.* Rather had pressed Bill Leonard for a change shortly after he replaced Cronkite. Broadcast trivia collectors might recall that for a few months *The CBS Evening News* began with an artist's rendition of a satellite hovering over the planet Earth. Accompanied by electronic boops, beeps, and hums, it turned to reveal the United States lighting up with TV sets at twilight. Perhaps it was a reflection of a growing lack of confidence in the *Evening News* during this period, but Rather's new opening quickly acquired the name Death Star.

The Death Star had to go, but the question of its replacement troubled us. Changing it could make it a front-burner issue in much the way changing a masthead at a major newspaper or a corporate logo could suddenly demand the services of an executive committee.

Fortunately, Lou Dorfsman volunteered his services. Dorfsman was the creative director in charge of design for CBS. Lou had gotten wind that we had hired an outside consultant to revise the CBS News graphics and that we were a few weeks away from presenting them to Paley. The design czar was not about to sit quietly on the sidelines while the on-air look of a significant portion of CBS was being altered. Lou had, by now, gotten himself invited to the meeting at which we would present the proposals to Paley. It seemed a good idea to give him a preview of the recommendations. In my office Van and I laid out the rough draft of the changes, including eight-by-ten color photographs of the new typeface taken from control-room monitors showing exactly how it would look. For years Lou had exercised tight control over almost every aspect of design at CBS. The wonderful Tiffany image which CBS had maintained for so many years in this area was in many ways a result of Frank Stanton's trust in Lou's aesthetic judgments. For years he'd bullied many of us into higher standards of design by shamelessly invoking Stanton's name. Now Stanton was gone and with him a lot of Lou's clout, but if he took us on at the meeting with Paley, we'd be dead. Paley wouldn't ignore him on issues of visual taste. Lou pored over the material we'd given him without saying a word. There was no doubt Lou Dorfsman understood visual statements. He was one himself, with his thick head of hair and bushy mustache with just enough gray to befit a man in his sixties. That day he was wearing a tweed jacket with dark checks and, to make sure his artist side was covered, a purple tie. Five minutes must have gone by before he responded.

"I could say this was shit . . . or I could make some cockamamie changes . . . but it's not shit, it's good stuff."

"Will you tell that to the Chairman?" Van asked.

"I'm not going to break your balls. Sure I'll tell him. I don't know if he'll listen, but I'll tell him."

He paused to let this sink in.

"Now let me ask you guys something. What other changes are you planning where maybe I might be of some help?"

I had an inspiration. "Lou, we've got to do something about the way the *Evening News* opens."

"You mean that planet-of-the-carbuncles thing? You're right, it's crap. It's gotta go."

The deal was going down and it was a good one. Lou knew the Geismar designs were excellent and he'd support them, but in return he wanted some piece of the design action at CBS News. Stanton might be gone, but Lou was not going to allow himself to be frozen out of the design decisions. Many people, Lou foremost among them, believe he's a genius. In truth, he's terribly good and he proved it a few nights later.

Dorfsman joined Sauter, Stringer, and me in a control room. We were there to experiment not only with a new opening but with bumpers, those brief segments going into commercial breaks which tell viewers about other stories still ahead in the news broadcast. If they are effective they convince the viewer it would be premature to switch the dial. They also contribute a feeling of pace. ABC was using them, as was almost every television station in the country. CBS News had for years stubbornly shown a static wide shot of a not very interesting newsroom with a teletype clacking in the background. I had asked Elliott Schrager, who was a partner in a music production company and enjoyed a good reputation, to try his hand at some music to accompany the bumpers.

What he brought me was so melodic it seemed inappropriate for a news broadcast. I asked Stringer if he and Lane Venardos would spend a day with Schrager at the Sound Mixers studio at Forty-ninth Street and Broadway. Working with an electronic synthesizer, they created a mix of sounds and came back with a commanding bass phrase which became the familiar electronic sound signature of the *Evening News.*

The bumpers were quickly designed. An opening was a different matter. That night Rather was seated at his anchor desk while we experimented with a variety of openings. Montage effects with clips from upcoming news stories, wide shots of the newsroom followed by a camera zoom to Rather—they were all terrible. It was dispiriting. We'd taken a break and were sprawled against the desktops in the subdued light of the control room discussing some of the L.A. animators who were producing the current wave of high-tech material for commercials and motion pictures.

Suddenly Dorfsman spoke up.

"Guys, look at the monitor over on the right here."

It was the B monitor.

"Hey, Richie," I said, turning to the director. "Can we see that on the line monitor?"

It was a shot of Rather at the anchor desk.

"We keep doing this shtick about openings," Dorfsman said. "We futz around with this and futz around with that. It's all crapola. I know I'm supposed to be the big-time design maven here . . . and we ought to open with a whiz and a bang. But what's more important than the news?"

We looked at one another while he continued.

"Why don't you just let the guy say 'Good evening,' and then do the news. The news is your open."

Frank Stanton had been right to rely on Lou Dorfsman. While the three news executives were about to turn to a Hollywood animator, Dorfsman's idea was distinctive for its simplicity. No fanfare, no music, no animated gadgets whirling around the television screen. The anchorman simply said, "Good evening, this is *The CBS Evening News,* Dan Rather reporting." Then he immediately began to read the day's most important story.

We left the control room that evening with a new open for the broadcast and a package of new bumpers. If Paley approved the new graphics *The CBS Evening News* could quickly acquire a new look.

On the morning of January 28, 1982, Van and I arrived at Paley's office on the thirty-fifth floor of Black Rock. The headquarters building of CBS acquired that name because of the dark color of the Canadian black granite which sheathes its thirty-six stories. Architect Eero Saarinen designed a building so modern in appearance that Paley's office with its traditional furnishing seemed almost out of place. His desk was an old chemin de fer gaming table he found in Paris. Along one wall were an old architect's table and a long wooden antique lounge chair. And of course, there was his collection of art. A large black-and-white abstract by Franz Kline dominated one wall. Another wall held a cabinet containing a battery of television sets for viewing all the networks. But above that cabinet there was a grouping of exquisite paintings, including a Giacometti oil and a vivid Rouault. We were joined by Wyman and Jankowski and a few minutes later by Lou Dorfsman. Across the surface of a coffee table we laid out one by one approximately thirty eight-by-ten color photographs of the new graphics taken from control-room monitors. We had not only examples of a new white typeface with a thin black edging but a variety of other changes we hoped to make. A new dateline super, for example, with an elegant blue underlining.

The same eyes which had spotted and then purchased "La Voilette" off a wall in Matisse's apartment in Paris were taking a sustained critical look at what we hoped would soon be appearing on millions of television sets across the country. It was a bit intimidating.

As he moved from photograph to photograph, Paley asked a succession of questions. "Will these be as easy to read once the picture has been fed across the country and then transmitted to homes by the local stations? How will they look on black-and-white sets?"

Each time we answered, he looked to Lou Dorfsman for confirmation. True to his word, Lou was consistently supportive. Neither Wyman nor Jankowski took part in this. They sat on the sidelines as silent spectators. I remembered Wyman's line that "Paley managed too far down." Maybe he did, but his knowledge of what it actually took to put a program on the air was infinitely more comprehensive than Wyman's or, for that matter, Jankowski's.

Paley asked another question. "I like this very much, but won't it be confusing for viewers in New York if the local news looks different from the news on the network?"

Jankowski spoke for the first time and there was no doubt that in his dealings with Paley he had learned to distinguish the difference between a question and an order.

"Mr. Paley, Channel 2 will change to these new graphics at the same time CBS News does."

When we left Paley's office that morning, we had his endorsement for the changes. Wyman seemed faintly amused by the whole experience, anxious to return to a world of front-end investments, joint ventures, and first-quarter forecasts, the areas of real concern for a modern CEO. His only comment as he left us was "Well, I'm glad that's over."

Jankowski, on the other hand, seemed jubilant. We rode down in the elevator together. As he was getting off on the thirty-fourth floor to return to his office, he said, "Guys, thank you for this. My life will be a lot easier without his phone calls about our terrible graphics."

"Gene, somebody better tell Channel 2 they're about to acquire a new look," I said.

B y early 1982 almost everything at CBS News seemed to be falling into place. The changes on the *Evening News* were now apparent.

The combination of the new production elements, the cold open, the bumpers, the new graphics, and the tight shots of the anchorman created a quick impression of new vitality. Less apparent, but of greater significance, the conflict between the assignment desks and the broadcast had come to an end. Van and I had replaced the domestic assignment editor with Sam Roberts, a producer who'd spent many years working on the *Evening News.* The message to the organization was clear: the success of *The CBS Evening News* was a goal in which everyone had to share. The sweeping staff realignment emphasized the point that the new management was prepared to make whatever changes were required to bring about its success. I was pleased with the way Stringer was working with his producers and with the correspondents in the bureaus. But the discontent in the Washington Bureau troubled me. Van continued to be outspoken in his disdain for "all those bureaucratic news stories they want to cover."

I was anxious to sort this out. I wasn't sure myself if he really felt that way. More likely, I thought, he was just indulging his penchant for the rhetorical flourish. We'd talked about the reflex action of the *Evening News* and how it relied on the Washington Bureau to fill its broadcast. We both felt strongly that our news coverage would be improved if we could encourage and strengthen the other bureaus. But the nightly get-togethers in the Fishbowl often provided an irresistible opportunity for Van to entertain Rather and the others. Frequently he disparaged "those dipshits in Washington who think the world is made up of State Department briefings." The more outrageous he was, the more he delighted the group in the Fishbowl. I'd known Van for so many years I'd forgotten the impact he could have on a fresh audience. To me it was part of "the act," not to be taken seriously. For Rather and the others who were observing successful change occurring all around them, these sessions began to acquire the significance and intensity of group discussions one associates with the Esalin Institute in Big Sur, California. One afternoon I casually mentioned to Van that I had seen a new half-hour syndicated show which was just starting on Channel 7 in New York. The show was *Entertainment Tonight* and I said I thought they were very skillful in their use of television packaging and production techniques. Van expressed interest and said he'd make a point of watching it. That night in the Fishbowl as we were dissecting the broadcast, he glanced up at a bank of monitors and noticed that *Entertainment Tonight* was on the air. Van turned to the group and with his pipe directed their attention to the monitor.

"I wish you'd all make a point of watching that show," he said. "They have a lot to teach us about producing television."

"That's a bit much," I thought. I'd have to tell Van later I didn't mean to suggest they were that good, and besides, telling CBS News to study *Entertainment Tonight* was bound to raise some eyebrows. Instead, Rather nodded solemnly.

"I've heard about this show," he said. "I'll have a tape made so we can all watch it."

Rather was fascinated by the quick and favorable reaction to the new look of *The CBS Evening News*. Throughout the television industry there was a growing acknowledgment that his broadcast had turned a corner, was out of its slump, and that Rather himself seemed like a different person. Some of the same people who'd avoided eye contact with him were now telling him how great his show looked. As a result, he became intrigued by cosmetic touches in television.

One evening he appeared wearing a sleeveless wool sweater under his jacket. The amount of space in the nation's press devoted to that sweater was staggering. It would have taken Princess Di in a see-through blouse to crowd Dan's sweater out of the columns. He began to wear a sweater regularly. This happened at about the time the ratings for the *Evening News* began to climb. The sweater became Dan's lucky totem. In the coming years, if the ratings took a dip and Dan began to worry, a sweater would materialize regardless of the season. One July evening when the city of New York was in the grip of a muggy heat wave I looked at my monitor just as Dan was saying "Good evening," and there under his lightweight summer jacket was a heavy wool sweater. He's often told interviewers that he first wore the sweater by accident, that he'd had it on in the office and forgot to take it off for the broadcast. Those who believe that will also, to use one of his Texas expressions, believe that "thunder curdles milk."

I have to confess I enjoyed these post-broadcast rap sessions. The hours of the day passed with such velocity there was little opportunity for any kind of dialogue. Van and I worked so closely we had developed a kind of verbal shorthand in which we seemed to be finishing one another's sentences. Walking back to the Fishbowl each evening after the broadcast was something we both looked forward to. The *Evening News* producers had grown accustomed to our presence, and on the rare nights when we didn't show up, they actually expressed concern that something might be wrong.

One night as we entered, Stringer looked up and, to the amusement of the room, greeted us with "I see Butch and Sundance have arrived."

I turned to Van. "I think I'd prefer Stan and Ollie."

For years either of us could turn tension to laughter with the line "This is a fine mess you've gotten us into, Stanley."

The truth was, we made an effective team. The speed with which improvements had taken place was testimony to that. If Van liked to lean back in the post-broadcast atmosphere of the Fishbowl and indulge in flights of free association, they'd all have to adjust to it. In time they'd learn that not every discussion was a call for action.

For example, one morning during this period I arrived in my office to find a worried Howard Stringer waiting for me.

"Listen, mate," he said. "I think we're making a terrible mistake with this latest change."

"Howard, I know I'm going to sound dense, but what change are you talking about?"

"None of the producers thinks it will work either. It's bloody awful."

"Would it help if I walked out the door and came in again? Then you could begin by telling me what you're talking about."

Howard looked at me as if I were experiencing some bizarre lapse of memory.

"Doing away with our correspondents and replacing them with reporters-producers . . . having Dan voice-over all their stories. Do you think that's a good idea?"

"Oh, that's what this is about," I said. "First of all, you're not quoting

Van correctly. His idea was to have Dan and a small handful of star correspondents do all of the on-air work. Secondly, it's a terrible idea which I hope never happens, but it was nothing more than theoretical chat. Van was just having a good time."

Howard moved toward the door. "Well, I shall enjoy this day ever so much more now. We did say to one another afterward that you didn't join in, which is why I rushed in this morning to see you."

"Relax . . . tell your people they should feel flattered that Van feels comfortable enough with them to let his thoughts flow like that. But if you took it that seriously, what was Dan's reaction?"

"Be expecting a bit much from an anchorman, wouldn't it, to hear him say expanding his role was a bad idea."

Just before he opened the door he began to smile and shake his head.

"Van can be terribly persuasive when he carries on like that. Next time, can you tug your ear or scratch your nose? Send me some secret signal that it's not really going to happen?"

After Howard left I thought back to the previous night's discussion in the Fishbowl. It had seemed so clear to me that Van had merely been savoring his own swirl of impressions and intuitions. Yet Rather and his producers had come away believing they'd shared in a process which was about to further reshape CBS News. A few minutes later Van arrived following one of his regular breakfasts at the Dorset Hotel. I stuck my head in his office.

"Good morning," I said. "Before the day gets away from us you need to know the Munchkins on the *Evening News* went home last night believing they'd witnessed the dawn of a new era of group journalism."

Van gave me a blank look.

"They did?"

"Yeah, Stringer came to see me this morning. I told him you just felt comfortable sharing ideas with them."

"What a bunch of dipshits," Van said. "You know it's not the worst idea."

"Van, it would rip the place apart. It would eliminate what we now do with some degree of skill and replace it with something that has a strong probability of failure."

"There's no doubt," he said, "that it would generate a degree of grief neither of us needs in our lives, but the size of the talent payroll you and I looked at yesterday is a crusher. If you and I don't come to grips with it on our own, the Corporation will force us to deal with it."

He stopped for a moment to open a carrying case.

"But that's tomorrow's problem," he continued. "Today's priority is still the wretched *Evening News*. Wait till Rather sees this."

Out of the case he lifted a khaki farm cap with a camouflage pattern. He put it on his head. Across the front of its crown it proclaimed "Quaker Boy Turkey Calls—Choice of Champions."

"I think I'll stroll back and say hello to the animals."

While Van went on his morning Rather visit I stepped back in my office and looked at the stacks of talent contracts we'd both been studying for the past several days. We had read and been briefed by Art Sekarek, the Vice President for Business Affairs, on the hundreds of contracts CBS News had with its correspondents and producers.

It had been a sobering experience for both of us. The contracts showed an obvious pattern of escalation in both salary levels and special concessions which had developed during the previous three years. The News Division was carrying a mammoth talent payroll. First, there was the "millionaires club": Dan Rather, Walter Cronkite, Mike Wallace, Bill Moyers, and Don Hewitt, each of whose salaries exceeded $1 million a year. Below them a column of others ranging in salaries from $200,000 to just below the $1 million mark. Several veteran producers would soon be pushing $300,000. Correspondents whose contributions were at best marginal were earning more than $100,000 a year.

Van's musings of last night had really been a case of his groping out loud for a solution to a real problem. In addition, there was a welter of subparagraph language and side letters which made binding commitments for future assignments. Lesley Stahl, one of our White House correspondents, had language guaranteeing that in the event of an anchor opening on one of the two weekend news broadcasts she would become the replacement. Phil Jones, a Capitol Hill correspondent, had a side letter promising "a shot," whatever that meant, at filling in as a weekend anchorman. Art Sekarek was a very savvy executive. He'd spent a good part of his life negotiating contracts. As he ticked off one fat contract after another, he could see the astonishment on both our faces.

"I know," he said. "It's pretty rich."

"How did this happen?" Van asked.

"Simple," Art said. "There was a lot of press about the people we lost to ABC and NBC. The word came from Black Rock. Leonard was told not to lose any more people. We didn't. The agents loved it."

"This is madness," Van said, and he turned to me.

"Ed, I think all future contracts should be signed off by you."

"Sure, I'll do it," I said.

I had had no idea of the morass I was entering that day. In all of CBS no bog held more reptiles. It seemed obvious that something would have to be done to retard these escalating salaries. Almost 30 percent of our total budget was being used to pay a group of people who took increases of 25 or 50 or even 100 percent for granted. Another 20 percent of the budget paid the union, clerical, executive, and other support people. Half of the resources of CBS News were devoted to payroll. Not only were we a labor-intensive business, but a significant number of our laborers in electronic journalism were earning the kinds of salaries most people associated with motion-picture stars and heads of oil companies.

If Van wanted me to put the brakes on our contract offers, I was fully prepared to do so. Over the years I'd negotiated a lot of contracts and I had developed a reputation as a tough but realistic bargainer. I looked forward to the chance to restore control to an area which was soaking up the resources we would need to cover news. I enjoyed the frequency with which Van turned to me with instructions to "handle it." He concentrated a good deal of his time on dealing with Rather, Black Rock, and the press. That was fine with me, too. He juggled the three with remarkable dexterity. The transition period at CBS News was made infinitely easier because of this.

I never heard Paganini play the violin. I never saw Babe Ruth at Yankee Stadium. I did get to watch Van Sauter handle the press and he was a marvel. Roone Arledge, who had obsessed the TV writers and columnists for years, virtually disappeared from their pages overnight along with Sylvester "Pat" Weaver and Pinky Lee. Van was brilliant. He was able to do something I've never seen before or since. He used his press coverage to define and articulate himself to Rather and the troops at CBS News and at the same time to the upper management of CBS News. Two weeks after his arrival at CBS News, *Newsweek* devoted two pages to Van Sauter, the man "who has always gone against the flow of pinstripe decorum," at "a particularly uneasy time at CBS News." The article catalogued the woes of the News Division at length but stressed that "CBS clearly trusts in Sauter," and that Sauter believes "Dan Rather is the right man in the right job," and then quoted Rather as saying, "Van is the kind of officer who can drink with the enlisted men and still retain their respect."

The only dissenting voice, quoted the *Newsweek* article, was that of Joseph Benti, a onetime CBS News anchorman who had been a local anchorman at KNXT in Los Angeles during Van's tenure as general manager there. Benti described Van as "a consummate corporate games-man. Journalism isn't his highest goal. Making an impact is."

That criticism was quickly lost, however, in the echo of other newspaper and magazine articles which followed the *Newsweek* story. Variations of the *Newsweek* theme were repeated over and again. CBS News was on the march and look who's running the place . . . a onetime newspaperman with a beard, a pipe, and scruffy clothes. These stories predated any actual upturn in the fortunes of CBS News, but they created an aura of success which began to acquire its own momentum. Van's pursuit of press coverage in those early days showed a subtle grasp of the concept that perception can become reality.

The product of Van's labor was so voluminous it prompted a phone call from a troubled Stringer.

"I think the attention Van is getting is marvelous," he said. "I'm all for it. It's about time we had someone who knew how to handle that bunch. But Dan's feeling a bit left out. He's muttering about a growing 'cult of the personality.' "

"Keep your eye on this," I replied. "If he mentions it again, tell him you heard us talking about a press campaign for him. I'll call Geraldine Newton in the Press Department and make sure she's working on that."

The last thing in the world we needed was an anchorman with a threatened ego. I talked to the Press Department and they scheduled a number of press interviews for Rather. First with Fred Rothenberg, a young reporter from the Associated Press who was to spend a day with Dan in the CBS newsroom. But this kind of profile presented a problem. Rather is not just the anchorman of *The CBS Evening News,* he is also its managing editor. That title is window dressing. In no way does he perform the duties of managing editor as they have traditionally existed for decades in American journalism. Frequently Rather didn't arrive until late in the afternoon. Requests or demands from him were unlikely to produce any strong resistance. But there is a distinction between exercising power and providing regular managerial supervision. There is no doubt that he does the first even more than Cronkite, who was routinely referred to at CBS News as "the Eight-Hundred-Pound Gorilla." But it's a power that grows out of the barrel of a camera lens and exists uniquely in television. It is power without responsibility.

The day young Rothenberg arrived, the editorial and production staff watched in amazement as Dan Rather premiered in the new role of the "hard-charging managing editor." But by all accounts his performance was a critical success. It got a glowing review in the Associated Press. "It's 5 P.M., ninety minutes to airtime. Dan Rather is sitting at his horseshoe-shaped desk. Just another newsman, pounding a typewriter to beat another deadline." Then contradicting itself, the AP said that before the broadcast "Rather is Managing Editor."

In breathless fashion the article described Rather on the phone, talking to field producers and correspondents, asking questions, filling gaps in stories, suggesting angles to pursue, on the phone with resources in Washington, following a hunch that something was about to happen in Lebanon, trying to decide whether CBS had enough people in the Middle East if there was a crisis. Our own "Man for All Seasons," Dan performed every newsroom role that day. AP pointed out that "over the next hour and a half, Rather will write the copy that ties the 'Evening News' into a 22-minute summary of the day's events."

This came as somewhat of a surprise to John Mosedale, a member of the Writers Guild of America who was under the impression that that's what he did. Editor Lee Townsend seemed taken aback when Rather, under Rothenberg's watchful eye, handed him a piece of copy Lee had already gone over with the admonition: "Lee, trust your mother, but check it out."

The article concluded with the news that "the job does not seem to have changed Rather or his lifestyle, except that his hair is grayer. He still lives in the same apartment, tries to jog two miles every morning and is disarmingly polite to everyone he meets."

Rothenberg apparently believed that he saw a typical day in Dan Rather's professional life. Howard Stringer and Lane Venardos coined a phrase which is used to this day to describe Dan's behavior whenever a reporter shows up. Heads nod in immediate understanding when told that "Dan gave it the full Rothenberg."

The AP story appeared in newspapers across the country. This sort of article gave CBS affiliates a real morale boost. It also came at an ideal time. In early 1982 I was attending my first regional affiliates meeting in Palm Springs, California, at the La Quinta golf and tennis resort. Several times a year such conferences were held in different parts of the country. They were small enough so that at the lunches and dinners it was possible to come to know quite a cross section of these station operators. The CBS Affiliate Relations Department prepared advance briefing books telling not only what to expect but providing clues as to the identities of the smart operators and the dunces. The general manager of one station in Pennsylvania was described in one briefing book "as having completely rearranged everything since his installation as GM in July. So far," it said, "all the sound and fury hasn't accomplished anything. The station is still mired in last place." I would come to admire some of these affiliate operators for being good broadcasters with a keen sense of their own communities. I also came to dread being cooped up for days with the sort of fellow who ran a third-place station but felt compelled to tell me viewers in his area didn't "give a rat's ass about what happened in the Middle East." In 1982, however, they were all strangers to me.

The CBS Affiliate Relations Department had warned me I could expect to encounter protests about the role of Bill Moyers on the *Evening News*. That concerned me because I thought Bill Moyers's commentaries were profoundly important to the broadcast.

The dean of broadcast commentators was Eric Sevareid. For years this scholarly man had appeared each night on the *Evening News* placing in perspective the complex issues of our time. But Moyers was a different case. First, he went out in the field with camera crews to illustrate his points in stories dealing with such subjects as the abuse of PACs by some of the nation's legislators. The affiliates weren't sure they liked that. Many were certain they didn't. Second, he'd been LBJ's press secretary. How could he be fair to the Republicans? they asked. Moyers's reports about rising unemployment rates and his examinations of the impact of Reagan budget cuts on the lives of average Americans drew sharp protests from the White House which were echoed by many affiliates.

Stringer had worked with Moyers in the *CBS Reports* unit and their relationship was one of mutual trust. Of Stringer's contributions during this period, none was as significant as his ability to bring out the best in Moyers. Moyers had a clause in his contract which specified that if he and the executive producer of the *Evening News* reached an editorial impasse, the dispute would promptly be resolved personally by the President of CBS News. When Howard learned of this he came to see me.

"I've worked so long with Bill," he said, "that he'll listen to me if I tell him he's gone a bit off in one of his commentaries. But if there is some point where we're in disagreement, I'd like us to be able to come to you."

"That's fine with me," I said. "But it doesn't satisfy the terms of his contract."

"I won't be a problem. You and Bill will be able to discuss the issue. Van is so outspoken about being a right-winger in a sea of liberals I think Bill would stop listening and just get bloody-minded."

Because of Howard's instincts that Moyers would be comfortable with me in discussions of the line between commentary and editorializing, I came to know firsthand how scrupulous Bill tried to be.

Eventually I learned that these complaints about Moyers's alleged lack of objectivity most often came from a general manager or station owner who hadn't actually seen the broadcast in question. More likely he'd been accosted by one of his town's prominent citizens while trying to enjoy a game of golf or a Saturday night dinner-dance at the country club. A day or so later he'd get on one of those regional conference calls the affiliates regularly hold with one another. He'd mention the flak he was taking because of CBS News and learn that old Joe who ran a station in a neighboring state hadn't played tennis in three weeks because of this. Protests would then begin to make their way to CBS News.

Van knew I regularly reviewed the scripts for Moyers's commentaries before they went on the air. Any commentator worth listening to inevitably generated protests. I made that point to Van, adding that I thought we'd be getting similar outcries if a Democrat was sitting in the White House. Van was outspoken about his own right-wing beliefs, but he had never tried to impose his political views on the news organization. Because of this, he could accept that Moyers's LBJ association did not automatically prevent Bill from being evenhanded in his commentaries.

Besides, the ratings for the *Evening News* were beginning to increase. I was convinced that Bill gave the broadcast an intellectual edge. Moyers represented an attempt to extract accountability from an administration which had gotten used to a free ride from the media. His pieces may have been tough, but they were not unfair. It was ironic that some of the sharpest political coverage in television was coming from New York and not from Washington.

Van and I arrived in Palm Springs having agreed that we would, if challenged, be firm in our defense of Moyers. We didn't have long to wait for that opportunity. During these meetings each of the various sectors of the network gives a briefing to the assembled affiliates. In our case it was a progress report on CBS News from me. It was almost lunchtime when Van asked if there were any questions. From the slight rise of the speaker's platform I looked out at about sixty men, most of them in late middle age. Many of them wore sleeveless shirts or light sweaters. They were minutes away from a tennis court or a golf course and, for a moment, I thought we'd get a pass. Then after Van and I gave a progress report on CBS News, one general manager raised his hand.

"A lot of our viewers think Bill Moyers is trying to stop the President from reducing the budget."

Heads began to nod and a murmur of support ran through the room.

"I think a lot of us would like to know what can be done to make sure he's fairer in his reports."

Van turned to me and said, "Let me respond."

From the expressions on the attentive faces in front of me it was obvious this was the moment they'd been waiting for.

"In the time Ed and I have been at CBS News," Van began, "we have instituted a regular review process for the Moyers commentaries. That process is ongoing and will continue. Based on what we have seen to date we believe that Bill Moyers is a man of integrity and that we would be hearing the same criticism if there was a Democrat in the White House. Nevertheless, that review process will continue and I assure you that Ed and I are both determined that the news product of CBS will continue to be fair and balanced. Are there any other questions?"

The next hand that was raised belonged to an affiliate operator from Ohio who couldn't understand how Harry Reasoner could have flown into his city for a *60 Minutes* story and not have called or dropped by the station. The issue of Moyers's commentaries wasn't raised again and the meeting ended. The affiliates headed off for their afternoon of tennis or golf and Van and I walked out into the California sunshine.

"I'd hate to be facing this group if they're really on your case," he said.

"It must have been a lot of fun coming to these during the Vietnam War," I said.

"I suspect we haven't heard our last complaint about Moyers."

"You know what we ought to do," I said. "We ought to bring Bill to the big annual meeting in May. Let him talk to these guys so they can see for themselves that he doesn't have horns."

"Not the worst idea," Van said.

We were interrupted by Tony Malara, Vice President for Affiliate Relations.

"Nice presentation, guys. I'm glad the Moyers thing was put on the table. They've been on a tear about him. By the way, Wyman's here. His plane just landed. He's on his way to his cottage . . . I mean his room."

Malara was an excitable man whose silver beard and rotund figure were at odds with one another, as if the head of country singer Kenny Rogers had somehow been grafted onto the body of Nikita Khrushchev. He seemed particularly agitated that day, and as Van and I headed back to our room, I watched him spin across the La Quinta grounds with quick short steps before twirling into the offices of the hotel's general manager.

Later and under more relaxed circumstances Malara gave me an account of the events of that day which had caused his anxiety. His experience was a microcosmic example of the culture conflict which was sweeping CBS.

When Tom Wyman arrived as the new CEO for CBS he made no secret that one of his goals was to change the corporate culture. In attempting to accomplish this, Wyman strove to set a personal example by flying coach instead of first class, by taking cabs instead of limos, and by staying in hotel rooms rather than hotel suites. For years network executives had regarded these perks as a way of life, an unwritten part of their compensation package. When Wyman talked about the need to reduce costs he spoke to an understanding, even receptive executive corps. But when he targeted their special areas of executive privilege they reacted as if they had just been told to bring their lunch from home in brown paper bags. Then a consensus began to develop that this was merely a temporary phase. They knew how seductive it was to enter the world of corporate aircraft, waiting limousines, and hotel suites with well-stocked bars and complimentary baskets of fruit from the management. They assumed it was only a matter of time before Wyman dropped his stuffy Pillsbury ways and began to savor "the CBS style." It would be gradual, nothing sudden . . . the way he might realize it has been months since he'd worn a brown suit to the office.

When Malara learned that Wyman would attend the affiliates meeting in Palm Springs, he went to his boss, Jim Rosenfield, who was in charge of the television network.

"What sort of room should I set aside for Wyman?" he asked.

Rosenfield was emphatic.

"Not a room," he said. "Set him up in his own private cottage with a bedroom, living room, bar, kitchen, and terrace."

La Quinta had a number of these and they really were quite lavish. A few days later Wyman's secretary called Malara specifically to say that "Mr. Wyman wants to make sure he has nothing more than a single room."

Malara immediately called Rosenfield to report this. Rosenfield was again emphatic.

"Tom has to learn the way we do business when we are entertaining affiliates."

The day Wyman was scheduled to leave New York, his secretary called Malara in Palm Springs. She efficiently reminded Malara about the single room. Malara began to fret and went again to Rosenfield.

"No," Rosenfield said, "Tom's got to learn how we do it. Leave him in the cottage."

The corporate jet was scheduled to set down at the Palm Springs airport in just under six hours. As each hour went by, Rosenfield began to consider alternative methods of instructing Wyman in the special virtues of the CBS style. At the end of the fifth hour he grabbed Malara.

"You're right. We've got to get Tom a single room."

Malara spun into action, only to discover that in Palm Springs in midwinter, single rooms are not always available. La Quinta was fully booked. He and Rosenfield then made the kind of quick decision which should earn them a special niche in the network executive hall of fame. They obtained the master keys for the cottage and proceeded to lock the doors which led from the bedroom to the living room, the bar, and the terrace. The manager of La Quinta then instructed his staff to lead Mr. Wyman directly and only to the door of the cottage which opened into the bedroom. Wyman spent two nights in his La Quinta bedroom secure in his belief that a leader leads not just by saying but by doing.

According to the nineteenth-century German military theorist Karl von Clausewitz: "Usually a battle inclines in one direction from the very beginning, but in a manner hardly noticeable."

When I returned from Palm Springs, a struggle had begun which would cost CBS News millions of dollars and a significant portion of its reputation. In hindsight, the direction in which we were headed had been determined. At the time, it was "hardly noticeable."

During a staff meeting with Bill Leonard, I learned about an upcoming *CBS Reports* documentary which was scheduled to go on the air on January 23, just a few days away. It was one of a number of documentaries which were underway long before either Sauter or I arrived at CBS News. Leonard casually mentioned that he'd seen a final screening of the broadcast and that he thought it was "awfully good." The subject was Vietnam, the correspondent was Mike Wallace, and the producer was George Crile, whom neither of us knew. Leonard turned to Roger Colloff and asked him to set up a screening for Van and me.

A few mornings later we both arrived at a *60 Minutes* screening room to view "The Uncounted Enemy: A Viet Nam Deception." We said "hello" for the first time to George Crile and Ira Klein, the film editor on the broadcast. Howard Stringer had been the executive producer but for weeks we'd kept him too busy with the *Evening News* to be involved with the completion of the documentary, and he didn't join us. Andrew Lack, a producer from the *CBS Reports* unit, had been selected as the Stringer replacement, but he was so unfamiliar with the material that the burden of executive oversight fell on Colloff.

The *60 Minutes* screening room is set up like a tiny theater with several rows of comfortable movie-theater chairs and a large screen. The light went down and we began to watch a disturbing and seemingly thorough indictment of the American military high command during the war in Vietnam. Mike Wallace opened the broadcast by telling viewers the CBS News would "present evidence of what we have come to believe was a conscious effort—indeed a conspiracy at the highest levels of American military intelligence—to suppress and alter critical intelligence on the enemy leading up to the Tet offensive." For ninety minutes my eyes were riveted to the large screen as seven retired military officers and a former CIA official came forward to support the charge that these figures had been intentionally manipulated. Wallace grilled General William Westmoreland with these charges and the general seemed evasive, nervous, unable to offer facts with which to rebut these serious charges. The bottom line of the broadcast was that, as a result of this deception, Congress, the Joint Chiefs, the President, and, obviously, the American public were led to believe we were winning in Vietnam. Because of this falsehood, we were unprepared for the size and scope of the Tet offensive and, therefore, suffered losses on a scale which was unnecessary. The broadcast cut across ideological lines, confirming the worst suspicions of doves and enraging hawks. When it ended and the lights in the screening room went back on, we sat there for a moment readjusting to the brightness.

To no one in particular, I said, "God, that's powerful stuff."

Van turned to Crile. "That's a stunning broadcast." Then he asked, "What will Westmoreland think of this?"

Crile didn't know.

In what turned out to be a prophetic comment, I said to Crile, "The military will hate this. I hope you've saved your notes."

Crile seemed pleased by that challenge. "I have," he said.

A few days later Dan Stern and John Miller of the CBS Advertising Department showed an ad for the broadcast to Sauter, Chandler, and me. Van thought the ad didn't reflect the powerful broadcast he'd seen, and instructed them to "go back to the drawing board, and come back with something which shows the conspiracy which went on."

That request would haunt him for years to come. Stern and Miller came back with a mock-up of a full-page ad featuring a drawing of a group of men in uniform seated around a conference table with the word "Conspiracy" laid across it in large, bold letters.

On Friday, January 22, 1982, that ad ran in the Washington *Post* and the New York *Times*.

The broadcast aired on Saturday, January 23, 1982 at 9:30 P.M. and neither of us was surprised by the wide sweep of praise it produced. The New York *Times* commended it in an editorial, "War Intelligence and Truth." A few days later the conservative columnist William F. Buckley devoted a column to it in which he called it a "truly extraordinary documentary."

Our minds quickly turned to other pursuits. We'd both admired the broadcast, understood and shared Bill Leonard's enthusiasm. But it hadn't "happened on our watch." Bill had decided to leave in February, a few weeks ahead of his March 1 retirement date, and the broadcast seemed an ideal capstone to a distinguished career which had been rooted in the production of documentaries. Bill had come to the office infrequently during the past few weeks rather than show up for what had become a largely ceremonial job. Never once did he display any outward sign of anger at what had to have been a terribly uncomfortable situation for a proud and distinguished man.

After the trip to Palm Springs, not only did I learn for the first time about the Vietnam documentary, I also learned that Van and I had inherited a significant research study. CBS News had always publicly scorned such studies. Only newsworthiness, it was often repeated, should determine a broadcast's content, not knowledge gained from investigating the varying likes and dislikes of viewers. When Bob Chandler casually mentioned to me that the results of this study, which had been commissioned months earlier, would be available in a few days, I expressed my surprise.

Ostensibly, the purpose of the study was to design a better advertising campaign, but coming as it did at a time when the fortunes of the *Evening News* were declining, the questions it asked were especially pointed.

Van and I had both worked with such research when operating television stations, but we had not planned on doing so at CBS News. We had, in fact, worked with the same company which had just done the new study for CBS News, Eric Marder Associates. The Marder firm had interviewed in person more than 500 people in a cross section of cities around the nation. Those interviewed were asked a variety of questions which ranged from preference of single versus multiple anchors to the importance of scoops and the value of experience by newscasters.

The Marder people presented the results of their findings to Van and me. For two people accustomed to such studies, the results were clear. Overwhelmingly, the people interviewed told the researchers that "an experienced newscaster" was the most important factor in their choice of a television news broadcast. A few years later, "objectivity" would emerge as the most significant factor, but in 1981–82 the country seemed to be in the grip of the great Cronkite void. Walter had been off the air for months, but he continued, for most viewers, to be the perfect embodiment of the experienced newscaster. Now that we had this information, the question was: what do we do about it? Explaining a general principle of advertising, Arnold Becker of CBS Research told Bob Chandler that when marketing a product similar to competing products one tries to single out a desirable feature and claim that "it's yours alone." For example, one could announce that "Chandler's sugar is sweet," inferring that other sugars aren't, and thereby preempting that particular product benefit.

Van and I didn't even wait for the CBS Advertising Department to make recommendations. We quickly produced a series of in-house promotional spots proclaiming directly, not inferring, that Dan Rather was the country's "Most Experienced Anchorman." We simply ignored the experience of John Chancellor, Tom Brokaw, and Roger Mudd at NBC and Frank Reynolds and Peter Jennings at ABC. The promos showed clips of Rather covering the civil rights movement in the South; they showed him in Vietnam. They also mentioned *60 Minutes* and Rather's days in Dallas and London. These spots ran repeatedly for months.

The ratings for *The CBS Evening News* began to grow and future studies showed Rather leading all the current network anchors in the category of experience. It would take years for NBC and ABC to convince their viewers that their anchors were equally experienced.

No such advantage would develop for *The CBS Morning News* during the next two years. The new morning broadcast began under a shadow cast two months earlier by an uncharacteristically angry Charles Kuralt. In a tough speech he made in December 1981 in New Orleans, Charles said, "At the networks today there is an unseemly emphasis upon image and flash and the tricks of electronics as substitutes for the hard fact." He described Van Sauter as "charming, intelligent, and successful," but added, "The imperatives of journalism are not on his mind right now. He is not even thinking about the news, he is thinking about the stage set. Informing the viewer can wait."

Charles, whose pride had been severely and unnecessarily wounded, was mad as hell. He had reason to feel bruised and there was no doubt that Van had brought on this outburst by his orchestrations of press

1 1 0

coverage. My worry was that Van would now feel compelled to return the salvo and I urged him to exercise restraint.

"It'll be like fighting Santa Claus," I said as I came into his office carrying a copy of Kuralt's contract.

"That speech is going to acquire a life of its own if it's not shot down," he fumed.

"Look," I said, "we should be thinking about making Kuralt feel better about this new management," and I held up his contract.

"I can't believe this," I continued. "While Rather and Wallace and Moyers, even Hewitt, were getting million-dollar deals, the legendary Charles Kuralt doesn't seem to have a clue that a new gravy train has pulled into town."

"Really?" Van looked surprised. "That's what he gets for spending all those years with the shitkickers."

I spread Kuralt's contract on Van's desk.

"By taking him off the *Morning News*," I said, "he loses $215,000."

"Good," Van said. "Maybe he can make it up in speaker's fees."

"That, if I may say so, is my point," I said. "According to his contract, $180,000 is his base and he gets another $60,000 for *Sunday Morning*. That's $240,000, and while it's a nice salary, it's not the kind of money someone of Kuralt's stature should earn in this business. He might be less inclined to make speeches like that if he felt we had tried to be fair in our dealings with him."

"What do you suggest?" Van asked.

"I know we're worried about the cost of talent contracts, but this is different. Let's take him up over $400,000. It's less than he would earn if he stayed on the *Morning News*. Contractually, we don't have to do anything. He's got another three years left, but I think we need to do something and this strikes me as fair."

Van let out a sigh. "Eduardo, I'm sure you're right. Go ahead. Right now, I don't want to talk with him."

After leaving Van's office, I called Ed Fouhy and told him my plan to adjust the dollar terms of Kuralt's contract.

"I think that's the right thing to do," he said.

I looked at my desk calendar.

"I'm free tomorrow morning. See if you can get hold of Kuralt and bring him to see me then."

The next day Fouhy arrived with Kuralt, who seemed to be as ill at ease as I was. Since I knew full well his resentment was not without foundation, I was anxious that we stay focused on the future.

"Charlie," I said, "I'm told you handle your own contracts and that you don't have an agent."

"I've always been uncomfortable with the idea of an agent," he said, "and with previous management I never believed I needed one."

The room temperature dropped ten degrees. He wasn't going to make it easy. I let that previous management reference slide by but thought it ironic that under this new management he was about to get a hefty and voluntary pay increase.

"Well, I thought we might discuss an adjustment of your salary this morning."

Kuralt stiffened. There was another ten-degree drop.

"Before we start talking money, I think I'd better hear about my new assignment and decide if it's something I want to do."

"You pretty well spelled that out a few weeks ago at lunch with Van and me," I said. *"Sunday Morning* and *On the Road* stories for the *Evening News.* You tell me what you need to get the *On the Road* unit reactivated and I'll get it for you."

Charlie just nodded at that and the chill began to leave the room.

"I know the past few weeks have been awkward and unpleasant," I said. "I want you to know I'm truly sorry about that. If I had some way of erasing it I would. What I can do is to go beyond just telling you how important you are to CBS News and adjust your contract so at least you don't take a financial beating in addition to whatever other woes this new management has presented you with."

I'd never meant anything more in my life than what I'd just said and perhaps Charlie sensed that. Our conversation moved into the nuts and bolts of producing *On the Road* pieces—getting his old camera crew and editor, leasing a bus, and having a clear understanding that, while he welcomed suggestions from the *Evening News* staff, he would not be given assignments. By the time we discussed money, I'd agreed to a bit more than I had quoted Van, but I was happy to give it.

After Kuralt left I turned to Fouhy, who during our discussion had made helpful assurances to Kuralt that his old crew was there and waiting for him to return to the road.

"Well," I asked, "you know him better than I do. How did it go?"

"I think you were almost courtly in your approach. He's a proud man and I think you were right to do that."

I thanked Fouhy for his help and began to draft a deal memo for the Business Affairs Department outlining the new salary structure and assignments for Kuralt. As a result of that morning, I would be the executive in years to come who dealt with Charles Kuralt. Each time I would find him gentlemanly and responsive to whatever we were discussing, but always there was a sense of sadness which never quite disappeared.

In March 1982 the new morning broadcast premiered. Not everyone cheered on this latest effort. The removal of Kuralt had alienated a significant number of our own people and they were doubly incensed by his replacement, Bill Kurtis. It didn't matter that Kurtis had been a CBS News correspondent from 1970 to 1973. Just as it didn't matter that WBBM-TV in Chicago, where he'd been a successful anchorman, was generally considered to be the best local television news organization in the country at that time. To them, Kurtis was "a local anchorman."

Some of this feeling was reflected a few months later in a New York *Times* article about Kurtis with the headline "Can Minor League Anchorman Make It in Majors?" Given his network experience, some of that debate seemed misplaced. John Lane understood the resentment Kurtis engendered and spelled it out for me.

"If you're a CBS News correspondent who's spent the past ten years getting on and off airplanes for a living, you don't want to hear that Kurtis used to be a correspondent, too. All you know is that while you've been busting your ass, he's been a local anchorman going home to his own bed every night and earning half a million bucks a year."

So a sizable contingent was prepared to hate the new *Morning News,* and hate it they did. They hated the new open and matching graphics by John Leprevost and Jay Teitzel, two West Coast artists who had done a lot of the animation work for the Entertainment Division. They hated the bright new music by songwriter Joe Raposo and the faster pace of the broadcast. If they were in the Washington Bureau, they hated the fact that Kurtis and Sawyer now did the live interviews with Washington officials. They remained detractors even when the number of viewers grew enough to challenge *The Today Show* for the first time, and even two years later when the *Washington Journalism Review* annual poll showed that *The CBS Morning News* was the morning television broadcast its readers thought the best.

The negative attitude toward the broadcast was so pervasive I found myself spending more and more time with George Merlis, the executive producer, helping him break down walls. His requests to bureaus for crews and editors were frequently ignored. This was partly because of the new focus on the *Evening News* which was keeping the bureaus busy. But it also reflected their resistance to a broadcast which was now much closer in concept and execution to NBC's *Today Show* than to the old *CBS Morning News.*

At the end of each week I would preside over an editorial and production meeting with Merlis, his senior producers, and the two anchors. Each morning I watched the *Morning News* at home until about eight-thirty, then left for the office and watched the last few minutes there. At nine, I'd share whatever thoughts and impressions I had with Merlis and at nine-thirty give Van a fill-in on how the morning had gone. Van seldom watched more than a few minutes of the broadcast before he left for an 8 A.M. breakfast at the Dorset with someone from the press or from Black Rock. His inattention surprised me. He was zealous about watching the *Evening News,* even when he was out of New York and alone in a hotel room. The morning broadcast was so big and so sprawling he seemed unable to focus on it in the same way he could the half-hour *Evening News.*

One morning I gave Merlis a particularly hard time about Kurtis looking unprepared in several interviews. Afterward, when Van arrived in his office, I shared my exasperation with him and chided him, saying, "You really ought to try and watch more of the broadcast."

For a moment he seemed taken aback. Then he suddenly began to laugh. "I'm sorry," he said, "but I love it when you get so pissed off." He swallowed a gulp of cold Tab and wiped the corners of his eyes with the back of his hand.

"Believe me," he continued, "the *Morning News* is not a problem. Think of how many times it's been changed with new anchors and new producers. Salant must have changed it ten times. I figure we're good for at least three *Morning News*es on our watch."

I shook my head. "You're probably right. But it just seems we've got a shot with this one if we don't let down."

Van raised his red can of soda in a gesture of a toast. "You, sir, are doing exactly the right thing. When I leave the house in the morning I feel comfortable because I know you're on their case."

I felt myself shifting from high to low dudgeon.

"And I want you to know," I said, "how comforting it is each morning while I watch Merlis struggle with the dawn to know that you are midway through another order of creamed chipped beef on toast. You will probably be the first News president to die of the gout."

Just then his executive phone buzzed. This is the private system which connects the phones of a hundred CBS executives in New York. He picked it up and, following CBS protocol for users of this system, announced his identity.

"Van Sauter. . . . Good morning, Gene. . . . That's nice of you to say. I thought it was a good broadcast. . . . You're right about Diane Sawyer, that lady is dynamite. I thought Kurtis looked ill prepared on a couple of his interviews, but we're working on that."

I walked quietly toward the door and left Van to continue his conversation with Jankowski. He waved as I closed the door, his beard sculpted by a beatific smile.

If Van seemed content to let someone else shepherd the *Morning News,* it was obvious he didn't feel that way about the public-affairs area, the world of the documentary.

In the fifties and sixties, because of Edward R. Murrow, the center of gravity for CBS News was its Public Affairs Department, not the *Evening News* and its anchorman. Public affairs was *See It Now,* where Murrow conducted his epochal examination of Senator Joseph McCarthy, and later *CBS Reports,* where Murrow revealed the plight of the migrant worker in the controversial "Harvest of Shame." In those days *The CBS Evening News* with Douglas Edwards ran only fifteen minutes.

But the appointment of Walter Cronkite to the anchor chair marked a change. As Cronkite grew in popularity and influence, so did the resources available to the broadcast. Correspondents and crews were added. The length of the broadcast was increased from fifteen minutes to half an hour. During this period the identity of CBS News began to merge with its evening broadcast. By 1982 the public perception of CBS News was primarily shaped by its *Evening News* and by the anchorman whose familiar face was the television equivalent of a newspaper masthead.

Still, the documentary effort of CBS News in 1982 was distinguished, and by comparison with the documentary output of all three networks today, it was prodigious. The year seemed to have started well with "The Uncounted Enemy: A Viet Nam Deception." Thirteen other documentaries, most of which had been in production for the past year, would be scheduled throughout 1982. An hour on Pablo Picasso with Charles

Kuralt; the controversial "People Like Us" with Bill Moyers, which examined the human toll exacted by the Reagan budget cuts. There were other prime-time hours on subjects ranging from the parole system to a shopping mall in Kansas which the producer used as a metaphor for changing life in America. It was a good year for American television viewers and for CBS News. Van came up with an inspired idea—a collaboration of some of the disparate units of CBS News, Special Events, *CBS Reports,* and *60 Minutes* to produce a ninety-minute special report, "Central America in Revolt," a remarkable primer on the turmoil which was then beginning in Central America.

In March 1982, Van and I were both walking back to our offices from a screening in the Ford Building, which is opposite the CBS Broadcast Center on West Fifty-seventh Street. It was one of those rare March days in New York when even the dismal reaches of Fifty-seventh Street and Eleventh Avenue carry a suggestion of spring.

We'd just seen the hour on Picasso, which was scheduled for broadcast on March 27. It was narrated by Kuralt and written and produced by Perry Wolff, one of a handful of people who had shaped and defined the television documentary in the 1950s. An exhibition of Picasso's works had been held at the Museum of Modern Art in New York in the summer of 1980. Wolff had used the opportunity to trace on film the history of this great artist and to explore some of his recurring themes—death, pathos, and the duality of women. We were waiting for a stream of cars and trucks to pass before we crossed in mid-block. Van was shaking his head.

"You don't suppose Paley's having been both President and Chairman of the Museum of Modern Art was on their minds when they decided to do an hour on Picasso?" he asked.

"Then it's despotism in a good cause," I said cheerfully. "My God, that was glorious photography."

Van seemed surprised at my reaction.

"That glorious photography you admire so much will get a four rating if we're lucky."

"Nobody gives a shit about ratings for documentaries," I said. "That's the one area where we get a pass."

The traffic slowed and we crossed the street.

"Oh yeah?" Van replied. "Tell that to Bud Grant and Harvey Shepherd in the Entertainment Division. Every time we put on an hour like that, they're convinced again that we're total assholes."

The Entertainment Division of CBS begrudged relinquishing prime-time hours to CBS News for its documentaries. It was as though they were forced to make donations to a charity they didn't much believe in. As a result, documentaries at CBS were often scheduled on Christmas night or opposite the Academy Awards on NBC, time periods the network regarded as disaster areas.

"You worked with them when you were the censor," I said, "so I assume you're right, but who cares. They love *60 Minutes* because it's in the top ten. The day the ratings drop, Mike, Morley, Harry, and Ed . . . they're like *Hogan's Heroes* to those guys . . . yesterday's programming. We're just in different businesses."

By now we'd entered the Broadcast Center and were heading toward our offices.

"I'm not convinced," Van said, "that we can't come up with documentaries that will find an audience."

I left Van that morning feeling uneasy. Trying to produce documentaries which viewers would select over their favorite entertainment shows was a contradiction in goals. It would automatically rule out the kinds of subject matter which made the documentary an important contribution to television. There were a lot of reasons for producing documentaries, but ratings weren't among them. You produced them for the same reasons Mormons tithe, to give something back.

Van continued to feel differently. He argued that a demonstration of success in the Nielsen ratings would enable him to lobby Jankowski for the opportunity to embark on other projects, perhaps a regularly scheduled magazine. I offered several suggestions for documentary subjects. Illegal immigration was one issue I thought warranted at least an hour of prime time. My suggestion generated about the same enthusiasm Henry Ford II might have shown an executive who was recommending the return of the Model A.

Van regularly bombarded Roger Colloff with ideas for documentaries which would attract more viewers. The impact of this wasn't felt until 1983, when the documentary lineup included a re-creation of a nearly disastrous plane crash, an hour on intercollegiate basketball, and a report on the plight of the grizzly bear. The latter broadcast proved how difficult it is to compete with the patience and diligence of the National Geographic specials. Crew time ran out for the CBS News production unit and the hour on the grizzly contained not a single frame of original footage of the elusive bruin. The documentaries were weaker and there were fewer of them. In 1983 a budget squeeze reduced the total number of documentary hours in the CBS prime-time schedule to seven.

Van's desire to program the documentary hours with themes which

118

would attract additional viewers continued. It was as though he was determined to demonstrate to Jankowski that he was a realist who understood the requirements of prime time. I assumed that this was the result of conversations between the two of them. I knew the documentary had sometimes been the cause of dissension within CBS. Murrow's disagreements with Stanton and even with Paley were historic. But I'd always assumed these were disputes over specific broadcasts which were controversial. Van's reactions seemed to go beyond that. I was concerned, not just because of his feelings, but because he had a keener sense of the current attitudes at Black Rock than I did. In this new job I was seeing less of Jankowski than I had when I ran television stations. But he met frequently with Van and I had to believe that Van was reflecting their conversations. The two years Van had spent as the network censor had given him a working knowledge of the network which I simply didn't have. That process of acculturation had left him with an understanding of the key players and their concerns and priorities. In fact, just a few weeks earlier I had gotten a reminder of just how well he understood them.

It happened while I was seated aboard the CBS Gulfstream jet, taking part in the first of many "Ted Turner must be stopped" meetings. Along with other CBS executives, I was returning from a regional meeting of affiliates in Phoenix. Several of our affiliates had told us they'd been approached by the Turner people, who were trying to sell them news packages or even half-hour news segments of their Cable News Network. A number of these affiliates were seriously considering using this material to program their overnight time period. Most affiliates simply went off the air overnight or programmed old movies. Potential commercial revenues were too marginal to encourage many stations to invest in this time period. Turner, in his eagerness to crack the network affiliate structure and open up a new market, was offering his product at a bargain-basement price. The relationship of network and affiliate was largely monogamous and Turner's advance prompted the CBS network executives to behave like threatened spouses. They were on fire, particularly Jim Rosenfield, who was then in charge of the television network.

Rosenfield had joined CBS as a salesman in 1959 and had moved up through various executive sales jobs to become President of the television network in 1977. In 1981 he was named an Executive Vice President of the Broadcast Group but retained responsibility for the network. He was a man of considerable passion, with an enormous appetite for involvement and activity. He moved with an athletic lightness belying a 280-pound body which invariably entered rooms navel first. This day he was not about to let Ted Turner move in on his affiliates. Even then, long before any takeover attempts, Turner had become the bogeyman of CBS. The threat was not without foundation. Affiliates of all three networks had expanded their own local news efforts. A low-cost supplemental news service would and did have great attraction.

Our small aircraft began to take on the nature of a revival meeting in the sky.

"We can't let Turner into our tent. That would be terrible," Rosenfield exhorted. He stood in the aisle of the aircraft surrounded by his sales and affiliate relations executives, who were looking up from their seats.

"Terrible . . . really terrible," they responded in chorus.

"Guys . . . what are we going to do?"

They looked at one another in silence. Rosenfield turned toward Van, who had been quietly smoking his pipe and drinking a Tab.

"Van, could the News Division do anything in that time period?"

Van had been sitting there waiting for that question. He began a fascinating improvisation by telling them, "The clear and present danger is that this is the first unraveling of the relationship between CBS News and its affiliates."

So many network executives leaned forward I'm sure the pilot thought he was encountering wind shear.

After warning the flock that there was trouble right here in River City, he assured them that all was not lost, and Professor Harold Hill couldn't have done it better. Instead of a new band, a brand-new and exciting overnight news service. No trombones and oboes but two choices—a two-tier price structure. One price for something CBS could be proud of; another, lower price for something closer to Turner's secondary news service, CNN II.

"But," Van asked, "would the lesser service send the right signals to our affiliates?

"Perhaps," he answered his own question, "but I'm not convinced we'd hold them all, and if we lose this airtime to Turner this year, who else will take it from us next year?"

No one on that plane wanted CNN II. They wanted whatever Van thought would keep Turner at bay.

Once the plane had landed and we were alone together in a car on the way into Manhattan, I turned to Van.

"We're up to our ass in the *Evening News* and the *Morning News* right now. How the hell are we going to come up with an overnight broadcast?"

"Leiser doesn't have anything to do these days," he said. "We'll put him in charge."

It was hard to argue that Leiser, as assistant to the President, was not underemployed. The job of assistant to the President had been created just to make his previous job available for Joan Richman. The next day Van and I met with Leiser and asked him to take over the planning of this new overnight broadcast. He seemed pleased to have something to do and a few weeks later brought us his proposal. He presented it with much enthusiasm. Five hours a night of original programming, seven nights a week. Double-anchor teams, weather forecasters, sportscasters, additional crews, reporters, and producers in each domestic bureau as well as London, a total of over two hundred additional people. Van looked at his budget. We'd talked to him about something in the vicinity of $12 million. As we added up what he'd presented, it would require over $30 million to produce. Leiser looked sheepish, not an expression I'd seen before on the face of someone whose scowl had terrified several generations of producers and correspondents at CBS.

"I've never prepared a budget before," he said.

Van and I looked at one another and we both began to roar with laughter.

"Joyce, do you realize this thirty-year veteran we have entrusted with planning the first overnight news broadcast in the history of CBS News has just admitted he doesn't know what the fuck he's doing?" Without pausing for an answer, he continued: "Leiser, just for that you'll be the executive designated to stay up all night and watch this shit."

This was the first, but sadly not the last, *Nightwatch* budget cut. No one at the television network was apparently applying the same scrutiny to the question of the salability of *Nightwatch;* no one was asking if the 2 A.M. to 6 A.M. time period could generate enough sales revenues to at least pay for the cost of the new program. The answer, experience would teach us, was a resounding NO. By 1985 successive cuts would reduce the budget of $12 million to $4 million. What would start out as an overnight news broadcast with a team of rotating anchors would be reduced to an interview show with a single host which made no attempt to report the news. Television viewers seeking an overnight news broadcast would still have to watch CNN.

In early 1982, however, *Nightwatch* was just one more element traveling in a field of kinetic energy Van seemed to generate. If I disagreed with him on the matter of documentaries or found him shamelessly indiscreet in his dealings with the press, those were feelings I kept apart from our constant flow of activity. On balance, I thought we were working well together. Rather had dubbed us "Mr. Inside and Mr. Outside," and that was probably an apt description. Van relished the public part of his job, the speeches, dealing with the press, while I enjoyed the shirt-sleeves role. Both of us, by nature, preferred being involved with change rather than managing a status quo. But I think it's fair to say that my greatest satisfaction came more from planning and implementing change, whereas Van's came from the presentation and the representation of that change. Each of us possessed a portion of the other's skills but our real abilities were rooted in those differences.

There was one asset Van had which I certainly did not possess, his determination and endless patience in dealing with the anchorman. After one particularly good broadcast he greeted him with "Hello, champion," and the glow on Dan's face was so obvious that this salutation would become a permanent part of Van's repertoire of courtship.

"The anchorman obviously doesn't object to being called champion," I said to Van the next morning.

"I know," he admitted. "Isn't it remarkable?"

"Well, just keep him in that mind-set."

"There's got to be a way of spending more downtime with him," Van mused.

"What do you mean by downtime?"

"Away from here, where we could just hang out. It would give me a chance to get inside his mind and put out any fires that may be smoldering there."

"What does he like to do when he's not here?"

"That's the problem. He's not a man with a lot of interests. He's talked about fly fishing but I've never done it."

Some weeks later that changed. Van returned from a fishing trip to Jackson Hole, Wyoming, talking knowledgeably about trout flies, the Royal Coachman, the Bitch Creek Nymph, and the trouble he was having with his back cast. By spring the wall in his office held a photograph showing Van with the anchorman in the middle of a Connecticut river in their waders and fishing vests . . . the camera freezing the graceful patterns of leaders and lines swirling from their graphite rods.

For Van fishing became a real passion. Every opportunity to go fishing in the years to come would be seized and sometimes invented. As I would one day learn, it's easy to fall in love with the sport of fly fishing.

T he "inside" and "outside" roles Van and I had begun to develop were further defined on April 2, 1982, when Argentina invaded the islands it called the Malvinas and the British called the Falklands.

The warfare which resulted lasted for weeks and demanded an around-the-clock state of alert to handle frequent special reports. It was the most demanding news story since Van and I had arrived. I don't recall any discussion between us in which we agreed that I would be the "duty officer" for this story. It happened in the same seamless fashion which marked so much of what we did. I just assumed that I would be the one to spend nights and weekends in the newsroom and, quite honestly, that was where I wanted to be.

When network television covers a major news event the challenges are unique to electronic journalism. The process is an odd mixture of journalism and something which is best analogized in military terms, "the movement of men and matériel." For every correspondent the public sees, there are numerous camera crews, producers, and technicians who are essential for converting an unfolding news event into understandable, accurate news reports. This was an odd story to cover. Neither the Argentines nor later the British allowed American reporters to set foot on those barren islands in the South Atlantic. For days we reported news from the capitals of the two warring nations. While British warships steamed toward the area of conflict, the world waited to see if some negotiated settlement might take place which would preclude bloodshed.

CBS News sent a large contingent to Buenos Aires, about sixty people in all, including Bob Schieffer as senior correspondent. A former Fort Worth, Texas, newspaperman, Schieffer had joined CBS News in 1970 and had covered the Pentagon before being assigned to replace Rather at the White House. At the time of the Falklands conflict Schieffer was a national correspondent based in Washington and the anchor of the *Saturday Evening News*. London was the largest overseas bureau and it was home base for Tom Fenton, the chief European correspondent. Since the late sixties Fenton had been based in CBS News bureaus in Paris, Rome, Tel Aviv, and now London. During the Falklands crisis, viewers regularly saw Fenton with the latest report from the Ministry of Defence in London followed by a live switch to Buenos Aires, where Schieffer would offer the reaction from the Argentine generals. It was live, it was immediate, and, by the time the British fleet reached the South Atlantic, it was second-hand. The only reporters to witness the conflict were a handful of British war correspondents who provided pool coverage and their reports were obviously censored by the British military before being made public.

A big story such as this is a tonic for a news organization. I've seen it happen over and over again. Problems are put aside and animosities are submerged while everyone focuses on a single task. For weeks my days and nights were consumed by the logistical and editorial details of covering this war. As the British fleet began its engagement with the Argentine Navy and later during the invasion itself, CBS News developed techniques for telling the story. Animated graphics showing the air strikes by British Harrier jets were used in lieu of actual film or tape of the event. To make sure our interpretation of the military dispatches coming out of the Ministry of Defence was correct, we hired a retired U.S. Marine Corps general, Fred Haynes, who was able to study the terse reports from the British and translate them into understandable descriptions of military engagement.

But a major asset was our anchorman. This was a story Rather understood and one he approached with enormous energy. Of the scores of special reports which interrupted regular CBS programming during this period, all but a handful were done by Rather. If I was tiring from long seven-day workweeks, I could look at Rather, who was putting in the same schedule, and console myself that I didn't have to be ready on a few minutes' notice to appear in front of a camera looking and sounding alert. Because of the number of these interrupts, Rather's presence permeated all of CBS television. In the midst of Saturday morning cartoon shows,

Saturday and Sunday sports events, weekday soap operas, prime time, Rather was there with the latest from the Falklands. Rather even anchored the *Saturday Evening News,* which Schieffer normally handled. After that broadcast he came to see me and he talked about a number of other things before he unveiled the real reason for his visit.

"Ed, I don't know if you realize how much difference it makes having you in this newsroom throughout this story."

"You're good to say that," I told him, "but the truth is, I'd pay somebody for the chance to be doing this. It's why you get into this business in the first place."

"I know what you mean," he said. "It's a great job and there's no heavy lifting. But I want you to know that if our coverage is working, and I believe it is, it's because our people know you're in here right in the middle of it. That's not just a difference in this new administration; it's a principal difference."

Someone once said, "Flattery is all right as long as you don't inhale it." By the time I exhaled, I had had a lungful.

"It's exhilarating being the guy on site who has to make hard decisions," I said, perfectly willing to be told how good those decision had been.

"I'm afraid you're going to be facing one of those decisions tomorrow," he said.

Having just learned I was the world's most successful news executive, I was eager to learn of my new challenge.

"What's that?" I asked.

"My anchoring the Saturday news made a lot of sense," he said. "I'm here anyway doing all these interrupts. Tomorrow is more difficult. Mort Dean will be here to anchor the early evening broadcast and Charles Osgood the late Sunday broadcast. I know you're the one who'd have to tell them, but I urge you to let me anchor their broadcasts."

When an anchorman is sent out in the field to report on a major story, it is not uncommon for the correspondent who normally covers that area to feel slighted. The practice is known as "bigfooting." Removing another anchorman from his own broadcast so a bigger anchorman could sit there during a major story would be the ultimate bigfoot. I didn't hesitate. This story could give Rather the kind of reputation Cronkite had earned for anchoring unfolding events.

"Dan, you're right and you shouldn't be a part of telling them. I'll handle it. You plan on doing those two broadcasts tomorrow."

After Rather left my office I called Van at home and told him of my plan to have Rather do both Sunday broadcasts.

He had one question.

"Have you talked to Rather about this?"

"He really wants to do it," I said. "He's on a roll with this story and we should encourage that."

"I think it's an inspired idea," he said.

Rather anchored both broadcasts, a fact not appreciated by either Dean or Osgood. Neither of the other two networks news organizations immersed their anchormen in the coverage of this story in the same way. For weeks viewers of CBS network programs who were in the habit of watching NBC or ABC for their evening news broadcasts found themselves suddenly exposed to the new CBS anchorman of CBS. As our growing ratings would show, some of them liked what they saw and began to seek him out each evening. At a time when CBS was trying to establish Rather as the most experienced of the network anchors, his frequent appearance at all hours reporting the latest on a tense world crisis was a fortunate opportunity.

The war in the Falklands seemed to go on forever, with casualties mounting on each side. A side casualty was the CBS News budget. Maintaining an army of people in Argentina and beefing up London coupled with staggering satellite bills was adding up, and quickly. Late one Saturday evening I left the newsroom and returned home. Five minutes after my arrival the phone rang. It was Russ Bensley, the executive producer for the *Weekend News*.

"A photo agency has just offered us television rights for color photographs of the *Belgrano* sinking," he said.

The *Belgrano* was an Argentine troopship which had been sunk by the British Navy.

"How are they?" I asked.

"They show the ship going down surrounded by a scattering of life rafts."

"Is there much variety in the shots?"

"No, they're all basically the same."

"How much are they asking?"

"Twenty-five thousand dollars, and if we don't give them a quick answer, they're going to offer them to ABC."

I was rocked by the price tag. A normal price for exclusive stills offered by a photo agency would be five or six thousand dollars.

"That's a lot of dough, Russ. What do you think?"

"It's a lot of money but the sinking of that troopship has been a big story and this is the first look at what took place."

I swallowed hard and gave him his answer.

"Go ahead and buy them but let's try and keep that price tag to ourselves. If it circulates it could inflate the market for future stuff."

The still photos turned out to be a good investment. Bursts of orange color from life rafts on a gray sea provided an eerie contrast to the dark form of a giant troopship listing forward in the water on its way to the bottom of the South Atlantic. We used them for days. An announcement of the sinking of a ship by the Royal Navy acquires another dimension when you actually see the small life rafts filled with terrified survivors. Nevertheless, I did not circulate the cost of that glimpse. I didn't want Black Rock, which was beginning to sense the cost of our Falklands coverage, to know that I had laid out $25,000 for a handful of still photographs.

Because of the crisis in the Falklands, I almost didn't attend the annual Washington correspondents dinner. It's a black-tie affair put on by the radio and television reporters who regularly cover the capital, and is attended not only by the television and radio community but by the movers and shakers of Washington. Leaving the Falklands story, even for one night, made me uncomfortable. But John Lane, with whom I'd shared many long days and late-night telephone calls, reminded me that there were telephones in Washington, too.

"My brother," he said, "have no fear. If something comes up, you'll be found even if you're trying to hide. Besides," he added, "Van says he's not going and if neither one of you shows up it will be misinterpreted by people in our bureau."

It was Lane's usual sound advice, and by the end of the evening in Washington, I'd talked to enough people from the bureau to feel good about having gone. The next morning I made a note to tell John how right he'd been to urge me to go.

At National Airport I boarded the Eastern Shuttle and settled into a seat for the flight back to New York. The crowded plane took off and banked over Arlington. From the small cabin window I could see Arlington National Cemetery, where my mother and father are buried. I realized this was the first time I'd come to Washington without at least thinking about a visit to Arlington. They're buried side by side just down the hill from the JFK Memorial. Edward Joyce, Sr., would enjoy the proximity. Dad was a lifelong Democrat who fervently believed that FDR had saved the nation from a terrible revolution. If he'd lived he would have been a staunch supporter of Kennedy, who was not only a Democrat but had the added advantage of being Irish. What a shame that neither of my parents

127

was alive to know what had happened to their firstborn. If you'd followed the migrations of the Joyce family in the thirties and forties, it's not likely you would have been willing to bet the rent money on the chances of their oldest son becoming an American success story. It's an amazing country.

My parents were an unlikely couple. Robye Marzelle Baker, my mother, was a third-generation Texan, a conservative Protestant married to a Catholic liberal twenty years her senior. Her great-grandfather had been captured and paroled at Vicksburg and she had an ancestor who'd fought with Marion the Swamp Fox in the Revolutionary War. My father's father came from Galway, Ireland, and was to become a conductor on the Delaware, Lackawanna & Western. I have the wonderful gold pocket watch he used to keep the great train on schedule.

My father used to tell wonderful stories about growing up in Pike County, Pennsylvania, at the turn of the century. To my young ears they sounded like Tom Sawyer and Pudd'nhead Wilson combined. Mast Hope, where the Joyces lived, was a tiny quarry town on one bank of the Delaware River. The small house, which still exists, is set about one hundred yards back from the railroad track. For a young boy, or at least one young boy, it was like living in a seaport. Instead of tall ships, it was a long train with its sad whistle that made one feel mournful because you'd been left behind. My father was not one to be left behind.

After the third grade he never entered a classroom. He began to use the railroad the way later generations of hitchhikers would use the interstates. Decades later my grandmother would shake her head and describe my father at twelve years old rolling head over heels out of a boxcar as it slowed at the curve before the house.

"And always with a puppy under his arm or a kitten in his pocket," she'd add.

But the drive that was to turn her other children into teachers and nurses was about to change my father's life. Grandfather Joyce came off the train one night with the package that his wife had asked him to pick up in New York. It contained a telegraph key and a book on the study of Morse code. If her son wouldn't go to the school she was going to bring the school to him. In those days railroad telegraphers were in demand and that's what her son was going to become. My grandmother had no idea if the clicking sound from the small key was code or gibberish, but she knew for sure what it meant if she didn't hear it, and that would send her tearing after her eldest son with a stick in her hand and a mission in her heart. Years later my father could not describe this scene without an involuntary hunching of his shoulders, but he learned Morse code. And the Morse code was his ticket to the world beyond Mast Hope.

With the skill a mother's determination imposed on him, he became a railroad telegrapher and then, in his late teens and twenties, he became a "sparks," a ship's telegrapher. Aboard such merchant ships and passenger liners as the SS *Vestris* and SS *Momus* he sailed to South America and Europe. As a wireless operator he was considered an officer. Aboard the passenger ships, this meant dining with the passengers. It was at these tables, surrounded by women in long dresses and men in evening clothes, that my father acquired a grace and charm that remained throughout his life. In the solitude which was also part of the life of a ship's wireless operator, he discovered a passion for reading. Once as a youngster I read an article he'd written about Latin America and wondered out loud, "Where'd he learn all that?"

"University of the waves," he told me.

I didn't know he'd heard me and I didn't understand the answer.

But for so many young men of that time it was the American West which was still the last frontier. With money saved from a number of sailings, he gambled on the opportunities in Arizona. He fell in love with the West. And the West returned the feeling. In his early twenties he became the general manager of the huge Johnson ranch twenty-five miles outside of Willcox. In the first decade of this century the Old West was on its way out but it was not yet gone. For a young Easterner to run a large cattle spread was no small accomplishment. It couldn't be done without knowing how to handle a horse and how to handle yourself in a fight, and at least knowing one end of a gun from another. If this was a golden time in my father's life, it became more so when he and the ranch owner's daughter fell in love and were married. For a wedding present the newlyweds were given a smaller ranch of their own. Pulp novels of the time couldn't have written a rosier sunset ending. The couple was even blessed with two daughters, my half sisters Pat and Mickey. They were barely toddling when America entered the war with Germany and the first doughboys were being assembled for the encounter. In the true Western spirit, my father was one of the first to volunteer.

Leading men was second nature to a ranch manager and his experience as a telegrapher made him a natural to become an officer in the Signal Corps. First as a lieutenant, then as a captain, he took part in some of the worst fighting in that brutal, muddy war. He was repeatedly decorated for bravery and received the Purple Heart after being gassed and wounded in the Argonne-Meuse offensive. After convalescing in a French hospital, he was brought back to the United States. Like the young boy who had rolled out of Delaware, Lackawanna boxcars, he stepped off the troopship onto the docks of New York with two Alsatian shepherd puppies in the pockets of his olive greatcoat.

Back home in Arizona the folks around Willcox made their feelings clear. Throughout the war his letters to the hometown newspaper had been the subject of much discussion and admiration. They were glad Cap Joyce had made it home and they never failed to let him know it.

Years later Republic Pictures made movies with endings like that and the lights would go on and catch people brushing tears from their eyes. But this story was a long way from over. Cap Joyce was not the first war veteran to return home and find that the small world he'd left behind had changed. The war had changed him, too. Popular magazines of the day abounded with helpful hints on readjustment for the "boys from over there." But somehow he'd expected to make that readjustment to a life which had remained unchanged in the years he'd been gone, and that hadn't happened. The ranch was not in good shape, and he'd missed a part of his children's growing up. More worrisome was his wife Catherine's edginess. She was not as outgoing and full of laughter as he remembered her. As months went by he began to encounter odd reactions from neighbors on nearby ranches and from old friends when he mentioned Catherine. They changed the subject or looked the other way.

One November morning in Willcox a group of his ranch hands came looking for him.

"Cap," they told him, "there's something we gotta tell you."

What they had to tell him was that Jess, the ranch foreman, had been "steppin' out" with his wife.

"We woulda kept shut," they said, "but it didn't stop when you got home."

My father thanked the men, got in his Studebaker, and drove to the ranch, where he asked the foreman a straightforward question. The answer was affirmative, but no one but my father could describe how Jess phrased it, because a moment later he was dead with my father standing over him holding his Colt .45.

His next stop was the sheriff's office in Tombstone, where his first words were "Boys, I'm turning myself in. I've just killed a man."

The tabloids had a field day. Reporters from as far away as Chicago covered the trial of the young war hero who had "defended the sanctity of his home." The jury came back with a reduced charge of manslaughter. Judge Ernest McFarland, who years later would become Majority Leader of the United States Senate, sentenced him to two years in prison. Eighteen months later he was paroled to begin a new life. As part of that parole, it was determined that it would be best if he did not return to Willcox, where his former wife lived with their two children.

That prohibition caused him to move to Phoenix, where, in 1930, he met and married my mother. Her family had moved there from Texas. Her home was the Spur Cross Ranch, which my father had started up in nearby Cave Creek. The ranch wasn't suitable for livestock, but it was ideal for the herds of dudes who were arriving in large numbers to relax and play in "summer's winter home."

Tall and commanding in Stetson and boots, Cap Joyce could take the dudes safely and comfortably on overnight trail rides. They would sit around a campfire of fragrant mesquite and listen to this Westerner talk quietly and passionately about the Anasazi Indians, about different cow brands, about Amar, the Arabian mare he'd just gotten from the Kellogg farm in Battle Creek, Michigan.

Two months before I was born in 1932, the ranch was sold. By then the Depression had pretty much eliminated dudes as paying customers. There weren't a whole lot of jobs for unemployed ranchers right then. Ernest McFarland, the same man who'd sentenced Dad a few years earlier, helped him obtain an appointment as camp superintendent in the Department of the Interior's Division of Grazing on Emergency Conservation work. My parents and my brother Charles and I lived that winter in a CCC camp in a large tent supported by four wooden walls. The tent was heated by a big wood-burning stove, on which my mother cooked our meals. It was a life raft for the whole Joyce family.

By the end of the year an idea was developing in my father's mind which would carry us through most of the Depression. He created and published a small magazine of the Southwest called *The Last Frontier*. Part Southwest tourist hokum with a homespun column called "Under the Captain's Dome," it contained articles on Western lore and Indian rituals and a variety of ads for Navajo rugs and turquoise jewelry from trading posts in Arizona and New Mexico. One of my clearest memories as a child is sitting in the back seat of an old car speeding along one of those everlasting stretches of desert highway on the way to some isolated trading posts. Once there, I would play for hours with the Indian children while my father would horse-trade inside with the proprietor. If the owner of the trading post had no money to advertise, that was O.K., Dad would take a trade instead.

A six-inch ad with a photograph for a corn-dancer blanket and two bracelets. A second ad next month, another blanket and two turquoise rings. There were times when our small house in Phoenix and later Prescott would look like a trading post itself. *The Last Frontier* carried us through the Depression.

By 1940 the Depression was ending and California seemed the best place to find work. My folks gathered together for sale whatever we owned, including the Navajo rugs and jewelry they'd loved and wanted to keep for themselves. We were off on a journey which would repeat itself over and over again for the next ten years.

It turned out there were jobs, lots of them. Dad worked for the Office of Price Administration and the Bureau of Reclamation; he started up restaurants and ran nightclubs. I came to like the back seats of old cars and staring out the window at passing farmland, with rows of planted crops like daddy longlegs running alongside you. Always on our way to someplace else.

My reverie came to an abrupt end when the metallic sound of the stewardess's voice on the Eastern Shuttle reminded passengers to "please extinguish all cigarettes and return your seats to their upright position." Soon the bump of the landing gear on the runway at La Guardia Airport announced the end of another journey and I pulled my carry-on suitcase out of the overhead compartment and headed eagerly for the CBS Broadcast Center.

One of the items on my agenda that day was the annual May affiliates conference. In 1982 it was scheduled to be held in San Francisco and the date was drawing closer. Both Van and I were looking forward to this big meeting of all the affiliates. We'd been in our jobs for six months. Because of the reactions we encountered at the smaller regional meetings, we were confident that CBS News would get a warm reception at the May meeting. Late in the day of my return from Washington the two of us drew up a plan for our presentation.

Van would do the introductory remarks, which would include an overview of CBS News. Then I would describe the progress made by the *Morning News* and introduce Kurtis and Sawyer. After that, I'd present Kuralt and Moyers. Following a few words from each of them, Van would introduce Dan Rather, the anchorman of *The CBS Evening News.* Rather was scheduled to wind up the presentation with what we hoped would be an inspirational speech and we'd wait for the ovation.

As we got closer to the actual date of the convention, Van scheduled a fishing trip for himself in Wyoming. At the end of each day my phone would ring with a "checking in" call from Van. He called from pay phones outside local service stations or 7-Eleven stores. I'd hear the familiar "Hi. . . . What's goin' on?" and I'd give him a fill-in on what happened that day in the Falklands and any other developments at CBS. He'd been tired when he left and now he sounded rejuvenated. We were both ready and eager to go to San Francisco. Van would fly there from Wyoming on Friday, May 21. The affiliates would arrive on Sunday. Because of the war in the Falklands, I would stay in New York until midweek and arrive just in time for our CBS News presentation on Wednesday. During our last 7-Eleven/Broadcast Center phone conversation, I again ran down the list of CBS News participants and their arrival times in San Francisco. Besides the correspondents who would take part in the presentation, Ed Bradley, Andy Rooney, Morley Safer, and Harry Reasoner had been invited to attend the big dinner which would conclude the meetings.

"That's a dynamite lineup," Van said. "The affiliates will love it."

"What could go wrong?" I asked, a question which implied the existence of a law which demanded that a problem arise whenever a situation looked promising.

"No, we're in good shape," he said. "And I might add, you and I are richly deserving of a few days in San Francisco."

T he kind of week we experienced in San Francisco was not what we had anticipated.

For the past two months we'd been aware that Sally Bedell and Don Kowet of *TV Guide* were working on a story about how the Crile-Wallace "Uncounted Enemy" broadcast had been put together. Many of us knew Bedell. She was well sourced, hardworking, and meticulous. In short, a first-class reporter. Few of us knew Kowet. The issue of *TV Guide* carrying the piece hit the stands on Monday, May 24, 1982, the opening day of the CBS affiliates conference.

If Libyan terrorists had fired mortars into the Masonic Auditorium in San Francisco, where the convention was taking place, it couldn't have caused more of an uproar. The article, "Anatomy of a Smear," took a hard and unfavorable look at the journalistic ethics and procedures which went into producing the broadcast. The authors very cleverly avoided challenging the premise of the broadcast. Instead, they built a case that "CBS began the project already convinced that conspiracy had been perpetrated and turned a deaf ear toward evidence that suggested otherwise." With great specificity they leveled a series of charges claiming ethical and procedural abuses ranging from violations of CBS News's own written standards to outright distortion. The writers made it clear they had somehow obtained CBS's own unedited transcripts of interviews done for the broadcast.

Van called me that morning.

"Have you read it?"

"Unfortunately, I have. It's ugly. We've got to find out if it's true."

"I'm afraid of what that answer may be."

"What's it like there?" I asked.

"It's a shit storm. You can recognize a visiting affiliate by the *TV Guide* he's carrying."

"I just talked to Stringer."

"What does he say?"

"He's not very high on Crile. Says he's like one of those terribly bright guys from a good family who joins the CIA and spends the rest of his life believing the ends justify the means."

"Oh . . . wonderful. Just what I needed to hear. Guess what other broadcast Crile produced?"

"I can hardly wait," I said.

"Remember a couple of years ago . . . the hour CBS did on gays in San Francisco?"

"That was Crile?"

In 1980 "Gay Power," which was co-produced by Crile, so enraged the gay community in San Francisco that charges of unfairness were filed with the National News Council. The Council concluded that two of the allegations of unfairness were correct, citing a violation of CBS News's own written standards when applause from a later portion was inserted into a speech.

"Guess who the executive producer was?" Van asked.

"I don't think I want to know."

"Howard Stringer."

"Van, don't leave your hotel room. You can only get hurt."

He was headed for a meeting with Ralph Goldberg, then an associate general counsel for CBS, and Gene Mater, a Vice President on Jankowski's staff.

"I have no choice. If I don't do something fast, we'll lose control of this. Paley's talking about asking Archibald Cox to convene a blue-ribbon panel."

"Why don't you take Chandler? He's lived through a few of these. If there is a problem, CBS News has to clean its own house."

"I hear you. I'll call you after the meeting."

Van did take Chandler, along with Roger Colloff. He called me later that day to tell me he was going to ask Bud Benjamin to conduct an inquiry. I thought that was a wonderful idea and told him so. If CBS News had a "Mr. Documentary," it was Bud Benjamin. In the late forties and early fifties, he'd been a writer and producer of documentaries for RKO-

Pathé. In 1957 he was hired by CBS News to produce the historical series *The 20th Century* with Walter Cronkite.

Their weekly collaboration lasted until 1969. After that Benjamin produced a variety of documentaries for CBS News and in 1974 was named executive producer for *CBS Reports*. A year later he was reunited with Cronkite when he was selected as executive producer for *The CBS Evening News*. Now in his mid-sixties, he held the title of senior executive producer in the documentary area of CBS News. It would be hard to think of anyone at CBS News who was more respected and better-liked.

"After I call Bud," Van said, "why don't you touch base with him and see what he needs. And I'll go off and tell the wretched affiliates what we're doing."

That afternoon I met with Bud in my office. He is a tall, bespectacled white-haired man who is so polite and soft-spoken it would be easy to imagine him as the dean of a prestigious prep school for boys. As you come to know Bud, you realize that soft-spoken is not the same as soft. He seemed to feel the need to make one disclosure before accepting the assignment.

"You know I was a college classmate of Mike Wallace at the University of Michigan?"

"I didn't," I said, "but I know that won't influence what you're doing."

"You're right. It won't. I just wanted you to know it. This isn't a job I asked for. I wouldn't have. There's only one reason I'm taking it. I love CBS News. There's nothing more important than its reputation."

"Bud, the press will be all over you when this is announced."

"That's easy," he said. "I'm not going to talk with them. When I finish my report, I'll give a copy to Sauter and a copy to you. I can promise one thing. You won't be reading Bud Benjamin's opinions in the newspapers."

By midmorning on Wednesday, May 26, we were gathering in the auditorium for the CBS News presentation to several hundred affiliates, many of them joined by their wives. This is a kind of shareholders report the network provides each year, on the year past and the year ahead. The highlight for the affiliates is the chance to see and meet their network stars in the flesh. In the dressing-room area behind the large stage where our presentation would take place, the CBS News stars were beginning to assemble.

Van was talking with Bill Kurtis and Diane Sawyer. Charles Kuralt was chatting with one of the stagehands and Bill Moyers had just arrived. I walked over to Bill to say hello.

"What time did you get in?" I asked.

"Early evening," he said, "just in time for a quick dinner and bed."

"I did the same thing and, of course, I woke up on New York time. I've been awake for hours."

"That always happens to me when I fly west," he said.

"Have you seen Dan?" I asked.

"No, you're the first CBS News person I've run into."

"I think I'll call his room. You never know, the time change might have had the reverse effect on him."

There was no answer when I called Dan's room at the Fairmont. As minutes passed I began to worry.

I walked out to the lobby of the auditorium and began to pace back and forth, keeping a lookout so I could quickly escort him backstage when he arrived.

Suddenly, an obviously shaken Rather burst through the door. He saw me and rushed over.

"A man is about to come through that door. Get somebody to keep him away."

While I summoned security guards, Rather described what had happened.

"I've never seen him before. While I was crossing the street I saw him on the sidewalk and I could tell he recognized my face. That happens all the time but, out of the blue, he walked up and knocked me to the ground."

Dan said he'd quickly gotten to his feet and rushed into the auditorium.

The guards were waiting as the man who was following Rather came through the door. He was trim, in his thirties, with neatly cropped hair which showed a noticeable amount of gray. He wore chinos and a Lacoste short-sleeved shirt. The guards quickly hustled him into the arms of a nearby policeman.

"Dan, you're going to have to decide if you want to press charges," I said.

"I'm not likely to do that," he said. "It'll be the Chicago cabdriver all over again."

A few years earlier he'd gotten into an argument with a Chicago cabbie who claimed Rather refused to pay a $12.50 fare. The cabbie wouldn't let him out of the cab and kept driving. Rather finally opened the window of the speeding taxi and flagged down a police car. The cabbie eventually went to jail, but Rather was pilloried by Chicago columnist Mike Royko, who portrayed him as a big shot stepping all over a little guy.

This time he chose to let the matter drop. It was a glimpse of the dark side of celebrity. This was not the last such incident for Dan and eventually it became necessary for him to travel with one, sometimes two bodyguards. Former law enforcement officers guard him much the same way Secret Service agents protect elected officials. They sweep airports, they bypass lines, and when Rather walks into a ballroom or an auditorium and all eyes are on their man, their eyes are on the crowd. When he stays at a hotel, the switchboard will accept calls only for whatever code name he is using that day. In the following years this traveling entourage expanded to include producers and secretaries.

I took Dan backstage and got him a cup of coffee while he tried to regain his composure before our presentation. The affiliates were unaware of what had taken place and within a few minutes Dan said he was ready to go on.

By now the large auditorium was filled, and as we all walked to the wings, an announcer on a PA system made the first introduction.

"Please welcome Van Sauter, the President of CBS News."

Van stepped up to the podium on stage right. He wasted no time in getting to the subject which was on every affiliate's mind, the *TV Guide* article. He assured the affiliates that "CBS News will thoroughly examine the *TV Guide* charges with the same vigor and objectivity we bring to our own reporting."

In the offstage darkness I began to relax. This group was in a mood to help celebrate the resurgence of CBS News and felt they could do so once they'd been assured that no erosion of standards would be tolerated.

I came on next and introduced Bill Kurtis and Diane Sawyer. Each of them spoke about their enthusiasm for the new *Morning News*. Introducing Charles Kuralt, I talked about the significance of his *On the Road* stories to the *Evening News*.

"Not least of all," I said, "because they give us all reassurance that an America of small towns and large ideals has not disappeared."

When Charles walked out on the stage a wave of genuine warmth came from the rows of seated affiliates. It was time to introduce Bill Moyers.

"In the months I've been at CBS News," I told them, "one of the rewards has been the opportunity to work with Bill Moyers. I've come to admire him not just for the quality of his work but for the integrity which is the wellspring of his journalism."

I figured I might as well hit it head-on and let this group know that the management of CBS News believed in Moyers. Bill came onstage to polite applause.

He began to speak quietly about the burden of the commentator, the responsibility to explore and ask questions, the questions that average Americans would ask if they had the opportunity. And he talked about the need to be fair, adding that even with the best of intentions he knew there might be times when he would fail. The simple honesty of that statement struck a chord among the affiliates gathered in the auditorium that day. Like the Baptist preacher he'd once been, Moyers was both honest and inspirational. He promised to struggle to be fair. The affiliates were getting a firsthand glimpse of the best side of Moyers, a man who understands the power television gives to a handful of people and feels the burden of that responsibility.

When Moyers left the stage that morning, the applause of the affiliates represented an overwhelming endorsement of his presence at CBS News.

Dan Rather was the final speaker that morning. Given the manner in which his day had started, he did a commendable job of getting through his remarks. Under the best of circumstances he would have been challenged by the odd speech he'd written. It was designed to bring the morning to an upbeat close, and it required his periodically chanting the phrase "CBS News is the Dream" in the way Martin Luther King once told us, "I've seen the promised land." The affiliates reacted to him like churchgoers whose favorite pastor has come up with an oddball sermon. If they weren't moved to an exalted state, they were least affectionate in their applause. Following Rather we all came back onstage, where CBS News was given a standing ovation.

That night at the Fairmont Hotel CBS wrapped up the meeting with the annual affiliates banquet and the usual "Parade of Stars." Few events demonstrate as clearly as this one how news and entertainment at CBS live under a common roof. Fifty or more famous faces parade before a ballroom of affiliates who have been stroked and fed and for whom this is the event of the year. After each star walks across the stage accompanied by a musical fanfare to take a bow, he or she is led down a runway and brought to an affiliate's table to have dinner and pass the evening with a general manager and his wife from Buffalo or Wichita. The breaks between courses are extended to allow the affiliates to take their cameras and move from table to table in order to pose with different celebrities for pictures one assumes will adorn a "wall of stars" in their home or office. It's amazing how the same television journalists who are so quick to denounce the encroachment of entertainment values in journalism willingly, sometimes eagerly, accept an invitation to join the "Parade of Stars." On the grand stage there is no reluctance to "blur the line between entertainment and news." After the round of applause has died down for Mary Tyler Moore, Mike Wallace may be introduced, followed by a young heartthrob from one of the daytime soaps. Diane Sawyer might precede Angela Lansbury or Charles Kuralt follow Pernell Roberts. In the old days Walter Cronkite was always the last to be introduced. I argued with the network people that the same distinction should be given to Rather. I lost the argument and they put Larry Hagman in the windup spot. What the hell, the guy once got a 53 rating.

That night in San Francisco I was seated at the Diane Sawyer table, where Mal Kasinoff, a very nice affiliate from Harlingen, Texas was falling in love. Their eye contact was broken by the arrival of Kevin Dobson from another table. Kevin Dobson is the guy who jumped to answer when Telly Savalas snapped "Crocker" on the television show *Kojak*. He'd spotted Diane and, in the style of Ma Maison, Spago, and other Hollywood meeting places, moved in to introduce himself. A few minutes later he returned to his table. While watching this exercise in unrewarded ambition, I could see Andy Rooney being escorted down the runway of stars to a nearby table. I got up and went over to greet him. Andy glared at me.

"I am never doing this again," he snapped.

CBS News correspondents have been parading down these runways for years. This was my first affiliates conference and now I was responsible for Andy's humiliation. Oh, the joys of management.

"Andy," I said, "now that we know your profession, we need only negotiate price."

It was an old joke but Andy laughed.

Bill Moyers was the other correspondent who thought this kind of evening was not quite the same as sitting on the dais for the Peabody awards. That morning after our news presentation I had gone over to thank Bill and to tell him how exceptional I thought he'd been. As we started to leave, I casually mentioned, "I'll see you tonight at the banquet."

"Ed, I can't be there," he said. "I have to catch a plane for something I've had scheduled for months and can't cancel."

He could see me grinning.

"Do you mean to say you're passing up a chance to stand on a stage with Boss Hogg from *The Dukes of Hazzard*."

Bill began to laugh. "I appreciate your understanding. I'm no good at those things. I can do you more good with the sort of thing I did this morning."

While the stars were gathering backstage that night in the grand ballroom of the Fairmont, Bill Moyers was at the airport boarding a plane for New York.

Shortly after my return British victories in the Falklands brought an end to that war, leaving Argentine generals groping for ways to explain their earlier boasts of imminent victory in the Malvinas. As that war was winding down, another war was heating up.

On June 6, 1982, Israel began its incursion into southern Lebanon. By land, sea, and air the Israelis moved to destroy the PLO.

CBS News not only had correspondents and camera crews at the scene of the conflict; it had them on both sides of the battle lines. The Israelis made their move early on that June morning. That same evening American television viewers watched scenes of the battle on the *Evening News.* Another threshold of the satellite era had been crossed.

The Israeli Defense Force shelled buildings in Beirut which they believed housed elements of the PLO. CBS News camera crews based in Beirut stood atop other buildings in the vicinity and recorded the incoming fire. Perhaps you can recall those incredible scenes of Beirut engulfed in savage fighting or the bizarre departure of the defeated PLO days later, shouting and firing their weapons in the air as they left Beirut. If so, imagine what life was like for the men and women who recorded those scenes for you. Ike Pappas was one of the brave CBS News correspondents flown quickly to Beirut. First he made the long flight from Washington, where he was based, to Damascus, Syria. There was no time to sleep and recover from jet lag. As soon as his plane landed he set out by car down the seventy-five-mile long road to Beirut. Normally the trip takes three and one-half hours, but not during war. And when Pappas finally got there, he didn't report to an American military presence which offered sanctuary; instead, he dropped whatever he'd brought at the St. George Hotel and moved out into streets which were the scenes of shelling, strafing, and bombing. This was the chaos Americans watched each evening in the comfort of their homes, thanks to Ike Pappas and others like him. As Ike later told me, "You can't go to your friendly neighborhood travel agent and get tickets to cover a war." There was so much to admire about the men and women of CBS News . . . producers, correspondents, editors who believed totally that they were involved in something important. Because of this they often sacrificed themselves, spending long and difficult hours frequently under conditions of considerable personal risk. It is the peculiar property of television news that viewers may retain the images and even the substance of a story they have seen. But more than likely it will be associated in their minds not with the reporter who went to such extraordinary lengths to bring it to them but with the anchorman who introduced it. Once again Rather had done an excellent job in the anchor chair.

It's tempting to dismiss the skills of the anchorman, the ability to read words from a rolling sheet of paper and communicate their meaning while at the same time using voice, face, and body to create some personal link with the viewer. They are largely nonjournalistic skills, yet only a few win them in the genetic lottery. Still fewer couple this ability with the training and instincts of the journalist which are essential to anchoring live coverage of a breaking news story; interviewing, interaction with reporters, the ability to receive new information through an earpiece and translate it for viewers in some coherent fashion. No one was better at this than Walter Cronkite. But during the Falklands war and then during the conflict in Lebanon, Dan Rather demonstrated these skills to an impressive degree. As the war in Lebanon progressed, I again found myself on duty, particularly over the weekends. Soon after I'd arrive in the newsroom on a Saturday morning, I'd see Rather getting briefed on the overnight developments, preparing himself for the special reports which he would do throughout the day. It was easy to be alternately amused and dismayed by Rather's constant posturing in a kind of stud-duck role. But I had to admit that his work ethic was admirable, and I did everything I could to match it by making certain sufficient resources were committed to our coverage. There was a sense of purpose within CBS News. If it took additional crews or producers or correspondents, I made sure they were sent. In looking back on both the Falklands and the Lebanon conflicts, I have to admit that I allowed, and at times encouraged, sending more correspondents, producers, and crews than, as it turned out, were actually needed. This was particularly true in Buenos Aires, where, at one point, CBS News had a force of over sixty people. Coupled with mounting satellite costs, this coverage was exhausting our budget and we were only halfway through the year. I discussed this with Van and told him we'd have to squeeze dollars for the next six months but we couldn't allow CBS News to be beaten on these major stories. We had a growing momentum and this was no time to be cautious.

An important beneficiary of both of these world crises was *The CBS Morning News*. During the Falklands war, midday news from the British Ministry of Defence was announced just in time for the morning television in the United States. In Lebanon whatever military action would take place that day would have begun by the time the morning newscasts were on the air. The producer George Merlis supplemented the news reports from CBS News correspondents with interviews done with participants and observers in Washington, Jerusalem, Beirut, and other locations around the world. Just as Rather had seized these two stories in his senior anchor role, Diane Sawyer did the same in the morning. With her State Department experience she was very much at ease interviewing diplomats, world leaders, and high-ranking military officers.

In addition, she was a devourer of research. Merlis couldn't get over it.

"No matter how much we give her," he said, "she complains it's not enough."

"That's the kind of problem you want to have," I told him. He'd actually come to see me that morning to discuss Bill Kurtis.

"We can't get Bill to take his research seriously," he said. "He seems to think he can go into these interviews and just wing it."

Unfortunately it showed. If there was a news-breaking interview in the morning or just an interview which turned out to be memorable, almost inevitably it had been conducted by Diane. Morning television is different from the rest of the television schedule because of the lifestyle of its viewers, who tend to hear more than they actually see of their favorite broadcasts. For that reason interviews are the staple ingredients of this kind of programming. An anchor who doesn't prepare for interviews and, as a result, doesn't handle them well has a real problem.

"Bill is coming to see me later this morning," I told Merlis. "Let me see what I can do to get him on track."

When Bill arrived in my office he looked ill at ease. The confident lion of Chicago television seemed lost. After a few minutes of small talk about adjustment to life in New York, I brought up the subject of his interviews.

"Bill, we're not seeing your best work. Your interviews are formless. They lack a beginning, middle, and end. You've got to block them out in your mind before you do them, and then you've got to listen carefully so you can pick up on anything new or provocative."

"I need more research help," he complained. "Diane is getting it all."

"Have you mentioned this to Merlis?"

Bill looked a little sheepish.

"No, I really haven't," he said. "I've been talking to George about getting a producer and a crew so I can go out and do some stories the way I did in Chicago."

"I can understand your getting cabin fever, particularly with these awful hours, but you're on for two hours a morning and going out to cover some story you're interested in won't fill that hole."

"I know that," he said, "but I can bring some special touches with those stories, the way I did in Chicago."

"Look," I said, "I'll talk with Merlis and tell him to help you get out in the field for the kinds of stories you can do without being away from the broadcast for days at a time."

"That's great," he said. "I really think it will help the broadcast."

"But, Bill, you've got to watch those interviews. There's an old expression: if you join the circus, learn to love the elephants. If you join the *Morning News,* learn to love doing interviews."

"You're right," he said, "they are important. But what's really missing is a sense of one person being in charge. Diane is still learning some of the anchor skills and it shows. If I could be the one to open and close the broadcasts, do the throws to special segments like weather, maybe also do the lead-ins and lead-outs for the commercial breaks the way I did in Chicago, we'd be a stronger broadcast."

This appeal didn't come as a complete surprise. Bill's contract with WBBM-TV had been filled with language guaranteeing him predominance, a legal phrase whose meaning Bill had just summarized in his requested changes for the *Morning News.* When Bill was hired for his new role at CBS News, his agent, a Chicago attorney, had asked for this kind of language in his new contract. We'd turned him down and the matter had been dropped. Judging by Bill's reaction to Diane Sawyer as his co-anchor at our meeting in Lake Forest, Illinois, he must have come to New York thinking he would be working with an attractive young woman who would be content to play the same second-banana role with him that she had played with Kuralt. Instead, he found himself paired with someone who was rapidly becoming the talk of the New York media.

"Bill, there is no doubt you are experienced in the anchor role and Diane is not," I said. "But she is the first woman on one of these morning shows to have achieved full parity with a male co-anchor. If that was changed now, you'd be seen as a terrible villain and you don't want that."

"You're right," he said sadly. "It's too late. Well, maybe she'll improve."

When Bill left the office I called Merlis.

"George, work with Bill to get him out on some story assignments. He does good work and it will give viewers another impression of him."

"I'll talk to him in the morning about it," he said. "Did you mention his interviews to him?"

"You're damn right I did, and he says you're not giving him the research he needs, that Diane's getting all the help. That's not right,
George. He shouldn't be going into those interviews without support."

The phone in my hand began to heat up.

"That's bullshit," George fumed. "We give it to him, he just doesn't
read it."

"Look, at this point I don't care if it's bullshit or not. I care about Kurtis
looking better on the air, and it's your job to make that happen."

The next morning Merlis came to see me for our usual post-broadcast
discussion.

"Kurtis is all set with a producer so he can go out and do some stories."

"That's great, George," I said. "It'll be good for the broadcast and it'll
be great for his head."

"I asked him if he needed more research," George said, "and he told
me no . . . the level of research he's getting was about right."

"Maybe somebody should try preparing specific questions for him and
see if that makes a difference."

"We'll try it. By the way, when he left your office he went to see Diane
and suggested that maybe he should open and close the segments of the
broadcast so she'd have more time to concentrate on her interviews."

"Are you kidding? No, I guess you're not. What did she say?"

"She politely but firmly declined. Until four years ago that lady was
working for Richard Nixon. He didn't even come close."

"How do you know this?"

"Diane told me about it. I think she wanted to make sure Bill wasn't
operating with your sanction. I assured her that wasn't the case."

"What's her reaction to Kurtis?"

"I think she's beginning to see him as a local anchor bimbo."

After Merlis left I sat alone shaking my head. It's an indication of how a
tumescent ego must deprive the brain of needed oxygen that Kurtis
thought for a moment Diane Sawyer would accept a diminished role.
From America's Junior Miss in 1963 to anchorwoman of *The CBS Morning
News* in 1982 with a stop-off at the Nixon White House is not a trip one
makes without drive and ambition. It was Diane, not Bill, who was attracting the attention for this new broadcast.

Newsweek called her "the Princess Di of CBS" and pointed out that until
her emergence "the woman's role on the networks' dawn patrols was
generally confined to riding shotgun to the male authority figures."

Everything possible was being done to point the spotlight at both of these new anchors. Each was used to fill in on the weekend broadcasts when Bob Schieffer or Charles Osgood was away. Later, each would have an opportunity to replace Rather when he was absent from the *Evening News.* There were plans in the works for both of them to anchor the morning broadcast from remote locations. Coverage of the launching of the third space shuttle from Cape Canaveral, Florida, was slotted for Diane. For Bill, a trip to London to be there when President Reagan paid an official visit. The London trip offered a secondary benefit as well.

Bill had been unable to overcome the "outsider" problem. The resentment by many at CBS News toward the local anchorman who'd been given a coveted network anchor role still existed and I saw London as an opportunity to dispel some of that feeling.

The producer who would be supervising the *Morning News* coverage from London was Margery Baker, an experienced, well-liked person at CBS News, who seemed to be pulling for both Bill and Diane to be successful in the new morning broadcast. Before she left for London I asked her to come see me. I talked to her frankly about my concern that Bill continued to occupy an unpopular outsider's role and how much I'd like to see that end.

"Margery," I said, "there'll be a lot of our people in London for this trip. All the White House people will be in and out of the bureau. See what you can do to bring Kurtis into the fold."

"I think I can help," she said. "Because of the time difference, we'll be doing the broadcast at noon, London time, so Bill won't have to get up at two A.M. to go to work. I'll try to organize some things where he can spend time with some of them."

"That's great," I said. "Maybe you might be able to put together a dinner where Bill could develop a relationship with some of those people. Bring the expense report, I'll see you don't have an approval problem."

The *Morning News* had been in London for two days when I called Margery.

"How's it going with Kurtis?"

"Not well."

"Is he getting to know some of our Washington people?"

"I'm afraid not. He comes in for the broadcast and then he disappears."

"I thought you were going to organize some dinners or something?"

"He's not interested. He brought his girlfriend from Chicago and they've planned a lot of sightseeing."

"Margery, you were good to even try. I'll see you when you get back."

I put down the phone that day with a kind of resignation.

Kurtis had been shaped forever by the experience of having been a major star in local television. Chekhov was right: "the most intolerable people are provincial celebrities."

By June 1982 our major preoccupation was neither the *Morning News* nor the *Evening News*. **It was the imminent delivery of the Benjamin Report.**

The announcement in San Francisco that Bud Benjamin would be conducting the in-house investigation of "The Uncounted Enemy" temporarily halted the crisis. But not a day went by without at least one reporter asking our Press Department about the delivery date for the report. Neither Van nor I could talk to the press without encountering the same question. True to his word, Bud remained silent as he went about his work.

To those associated with that broadcast it had become clear that Bud was doing his investigation "without fear or favor" and, in the process, was asking some tough questions.

Stringer, who'd been critical of Crile in conversations with me, had shared his misgivings with others and word of this reached Crile. During the discovery process of the trial which ultimately followed, CBS had to produce all memos and documents connected with the broadcast. One of those memos was written by Crile shortly before the delivery of the Benjamin Report and sent to Mike Wallace. In it he made reference to "the spectre of the hangman's knot" and began to construct a scaffold for Stringer.

"As far as I'm concerned," he wrote, "everyone did their job except Howard," adding, "The man who was supposed to protect all of us and watch out for the reputation of the News Division was Howard Stringer. And he is bad-mouthing the show."

To be precise, Stringer was not bad-mouthing the show; he was bad-mouthing its producer.

"You can't trust George," Howard told me on more than one occasion. "Once he begins to believe something he can be amoral in making the pieces fit."

Crile was a thin-boned man in his late thirties with a thick head of brown hair he combed straight back. In corduroy trousers, shirt sleeves rolled to his elbows, and with the knot of his tie loosened to allow an open collar, he looked as though he might be a graduate student from an Ivy League college visiting CBS News on a research mission for his professor. Crile was the son of a prominent Midwestern surgeon. His stepmother was the granddaughter of Carl Sandburg. His first wife was the daughter of Washington journalist Joseph Alsop.

Before coming to CBS News, Crile had been an editor of *Harper's* magazine. In 1975 he edited an article titled "Viet Nam Cover Up: Playing War with Numbers." The author of that article was Sam Adams, a former CIA intelligence analyst in Vietnam, who charged that the military faked estimates to indicate a smaller enemy force. Crile had heard Adams and persuaded him to write of his unsuccessful efforts to make his superiors aware of this deception. The article described the rivalry between the CIA and the military.

Crile had been with CBS News for several years and had co-produced several documentaries when he proposed a documentary based on what he said was new evidence uncovered by Sam Adams indicating a "full scale perversion of the intelligence gathering process." Adams's information served as the basis for "The Uncounted Enemy: A Viet Nam Deception" and Adams became a paid consultant for CBS News.

Stringer obviously had enough regard for Crile at the time to lend his support to the proposal and to serve as its executive producer. The vehemence of his denunciations of Crile was disturbing and not least of all because there was no indication these concerns had ever been raised in advance of the broadcast. I was disturbed by what Benjamin's investigation might show about Howard's own stewardship of that broadcast. True, he'd been moved to the *Evening News* a month before its completion. But for the months of planning and execution, Crile had been reporting to him as his executive producer. In an article on the controversy surrounding the broadcast, *Variety* said that "Stringer's future . . . may be riding on the outcome of the Benjamin Report." I had become enormously fond of Howard in the past half year. I had urged his move to the *Evening News,* and his energy and enthusiasm had played a key role in its turnabout. With a deft touch he was often able to dispel the black moods of the anchorman. But I didn't doubt for a minute that if Bud's report contained evidence of serious wrongdoing, Howard could not then remain at the helm of the broadcast which was the symbolic center of mass for CBS news. For that matter, what would we do if the Benjamin Report showed misconduct on the part of Mike Wallace?

An interesting phenomenon occurred a few weeks before the Benjamin Report was delivered. The intramural quarreling among those responsible for the Westmoreland broadcast stopped and was replaced by a chorus of doubts about Bud Benjamin. The chorus would swell after the report had been released. But even in advance, Stringer, Wallace, and Crile began to discuss their worries that Bud was too literal-minded, out of step with the modern community. Stringer came to see me and talked about Bud being a "bit of a purist," judging by the kinds of questions he was asking.

"Old Bud is wonderful," he said, "but he's never produced this sort of broadcast."

"Howard, Bud was producing documentaries when you were a public school brat in England."

He smiled. "There is that, I suppose. But they were those historical things. *The 20th Century* and suchlike. He's never specialized in the hard-hitting investigative documentary."

"Those *TV Guide* charges were either true or they weren't. I have no doubt that Bud will be able to tell us the answer," I said. "Would you rather have a panel of lawyers investigating this?"

Howard sighed. "No, I suppose not," he said, and he left my office.

In early July, Bud Benjamin delivered his report. Sauter and I each took a copy home to read. I locked up a number of other copies in a safe place in my office. The report was fifty-nine pages long and it was devastating. Bud had meticulously investigated the charges and subcharges and in the summary of his report he listed the principal flaws in the broadcast, supporting many of *TV Guide*'s charges: lack of balance, "conspiracy" not proved, and various violations of the CBS News Standards, a written codification of our ethics, traditions, and procedures.

The standards had first been written and distributed in April 1976 and provided the operating guidelines not only for CBS News but for the News Departments of all CBS-owned radio and television stations. Crile had done things in preparing his broadcast which sent a shudder of revulsion through every serious journalist at CBS. One key witness for the case Crile wanted to make against Westmoreland was George Allen, a former CIA officer. Crile thought that in the first interview Allen "looked like hell, looked guilty, on those questions about the CIA." So Crile took Allen into a screening room and showed him film of three other interviewees who all shared his point of view. Then Crile set up a second interview with Allen in which he asked him virtually the same questions he'd asked in the first interview. The CBS News Standards have always demanded that interviews be "spontaneous and unrehearsed." When Benjamin pointed out the impossibility of meeting this requirement if "you interviewed him twice," Crile responded, "I honestly was not aware of it being a violation of the guidelines."

Later Benjamin asked, "Why did Allen see the other interviews?"

"For the same reason as the second interview," Crile told him. "I know it's against the sensibilities of everyone here. . . . I don't think what I did there was right."

Ira Klein was the young film editor who had been present when Crile brought Allen into the cutting room and had been so appalled he provided the *TV Guide* authors with most of their damaging information.

On June 3, 1982, Klein told Benjamin, "I looked at him as if he was out of his mind. 'You're compromising me and jeopardizing the project.' Crile said, 'Don't worry. Everything will be O.K.' The next day Allen was in the cutting room again and everyone but me was told to leave. Crile said, 'Don't worry. George Allen is an old CIA man. This won't go any further.' I was stunned. They ran interviews for him."

When Mike Wallace interviewed Westmoreland, the general also looked ill at ease and was ill prepared. Crile felt neither urge nor obligation to show the general other interviews and then gave him a second chance with the same questions he'd been asked the first time.

Another *TV Guide* charge which Bud's report supported involved a failure on Crile's part to interview Phillip Davidson. General Davidson had been the top military intelligence officer in Vietnam. As Davidson said in a later letter to Sauter, "Mr. Crile totally ignored the one official, myself, who had to have been pivotal within the conspiracy he alleges."

Crile claimed he believed Davidson was too ill to be interviewed. Indeed, Wallace mentioned this to Westmoreland during the course of their interview and Westmoreland did not contradict him.

Crile told Benjamin he turned over the job of contacting General Davidson to his secretary. She said she tried to reach him many times during the workday without success. She never tried him at night. The *TV Guide* authors were able to reach him, as was Bud Benjamin, who was told by the general that he'd had no recurring signs of cancer since his surgery in

1974. He gave permission to Bud to talk to his physician. His doctor confirmed that the general was in "fine health."

A picture began to emerge from the Benjamin Report of a correspondent who had been, at best, an infrequent participant in the preparation of a controversial broadcast which would bear his famous name, and of a producer who, instead of building a broadcast as a journalist, set out to present an airtight case in the manner of a prosecutor.

Benjamin did not support the charge that "Crile's supervisors at CBS News failed to oversee his work effectively." He acknowledged the transitions which moved Stringer to the *Evening News* a month before "The Uncounted Enemy" went on the air. And he believed that Roger Colloff went far beyond what a Vice President normally does on a broadcast—reading some transcripts and meeting with the producer. To underscore this point, he quoted Bob Chandler: "Dealing with producers as an executive is an act of faith. Ninety-eight percent of it is faith. Do you trust them? The documentary area will not be a driving forceful operation unless you let them do their thing. It is a matter of their integrity, ethics, and professionalism."

What do you do, then, if you believe a producer has failed on all three counts?

There are those at CBS News who assert that a written compilation of news standards was a mistake. They claim that the reduction of a profession to a literal code is too confining. The fact is that as early as 1971 CBS had revised and issued a number of operating standards in printed form as Policy Notes from the President. The full set of standards issued in 1976 was an extension of those Policy Notes. In fact, the section which specified that all interviews must be spontaneous and unrehearsed was drafted after an embarrassing problem with the 1971 CBS News documentary "The Selling of the Pentagon," which took a critical look at the Defense Department's public relations activities. The Pentagon charged CBS News with deliberate distortion in its editing techniques. Indeed, an internal inquiry revealed that one interview had been edited in a way which gave a misleading impression, and so written guidelines for editing were distributed to the journalists of CBS News.

In the mid-seventies Linda Ellerbee, at that time a reporter for WCBS-TV in New York, was working on a documentary for the *Eye on New York* unit, the local counterpart of *CBS Reports.* She was bothered by something which had happened in the field that day and came to see me. I was then the station's news director. She brought with her cameraman Murray Wald and together they described arriving at the office of a New Jersey psychologist to shoot a group-therapy session which their producer told them took place each week at that time. As the session progressed, Linda and Murray began to worry that the participants were performing for them. They had the feeling this was something which had been arranged just for their cameras. I called the psychologist, who said, "Yes . . . of course the producer knew this wasn't a real therapy session, but it was very similar to a real session."

This was precisely the kind of staging of stories which the news guidelines prohibited. The end result was that the producer was fired and the documentary scrapped. That's how seriously we regarded those guidelines.

It was unconvincing for a producer who had been with CBS News for a number of years to plead ignorance of the guidelines. Although some of my colleagues at CBS News argued against a written codification of standards, I never met anyone who thought that what George Crile had done was right.

When Van and I took our copies of the report home, we agreed to talk by phone later that night. It was almost eleven o'clock when my phone rang.

"Are you as depressed as I am?"

"Van, it's awful. How could this have happened at CBS News?"

There was silence at the other end.

"Van, are you there?"

"Yeah, I'm here. I just don't have an answer to your question."

"You know what else I can't figure out? The film editor, Ira Klein. If he was that concerned, why didn't he go to Stringer, or Colloff, or Leonard? And we were both here a month before the broadcast went on the air. If he knew Crile had done some of those things, how could he let us sit in a screening room watching that broadcast and not say a word?"

"I don't know," Van groaned. "Oh, fuck me. What a mess. Over the next few days you and I will have to figure out how to handle this. We'll have to cover this with Jankowski, then brief Wyman, and then figure out how we make the findings public."

"What about starting with a public shooting of Crile?"

"We may have to settle for firing him," he said, "but let's hit this again tomorrow morning. I'm on overload."

That weekend we held secret meetings at Jankowski's home in Weston, Connecticut. When I arrived, everyone was gathered outside at a table near Jankowski's pool. The group included Sauter, Benjamin, Jankowski, and his Senior Vice President for Policy, Gene Mater.

I asked Mater, "Are we waiting for the lawyers?"

A mumbled "No" followed by a quick lighting of his pipe. Shortly thereafter, Mater took me aside to explain the absence of lawyers.

"Gene doesn't trust Wyman's new Law Department," he said. "They want to be more than lawyers. They want to set policy."

If Gene was involved in corporate infighting, this struck me as an odd time to exclude the lawyers.

"They'll have to be involved in this eventually," I said.

"After this weekend," he answered, "when we have a better idea of how we want to handle this."

By now everyone had read Benjamin's report, and we spent the first part of the meeting having Bud walk us through each page.

Mater was aghast.

"This is much more serious than 'The Selling of the Pentagon,' " he said.

Benjamin answered questions and was completely forthcoming in his evaluation of the broadcast and its preparation, but he scrupulously stood apart from any discussions of how we should now handle the problem.

Sauter, Mater, and Joyce dealt with that. By the end of the morning we'd agreed that, first, we'd have to go public with our unfavorable findings. Second, we would begin planning a follow-up broadcast. Something which would allow Westmoreland to respond in an unedited segment of fifteen to thirty minutes and then be followed by a discussion with advocates from both sides. Third, we would make sure that never again on a controversial broadcast would a correspondent function merely as a reader-interviewer as Wallace had done on this one. Fourth, we would appoint a Vice President for News Practices who would hold regular meetings with CBS News people throughout the world to review and discuss the CBS News Standards. Such meetings had regularly taken place in the CBS-owned television stations, but not at CBS News. Fifth, some form of disciplinary action would be needed to show our own organization that this sort of conduct was unacceptable.

However, we all agreed that nothing had emerged from either the *TV Guide* article or Bud's investigation which challenged the basic thesis of the broadcast: that prior to the Tet offensive enemy troop strength figures in Vietnam were deliberately undercounted by high-ranking American military and intelligence officials. According to Crile, when Bill Leonard first saw the "Blue Sheet," a sixteen-page proposal spelling out the proposed documentary, he said, "These things either happened or they didn't; if they happened it is a very important story and we should run it."

Bill was right, and it was Crile's credit that he convinced eight former military and intelligence officers to come forward and admit misconduct. The tragedy was that Crile could have done an "important story" without violating any of these standards of fairness.

We then discussed specific disciplinary action. All of us agreed that George Crile could never again produce a broadcast for CBS News. What about Mike Wallace? What about the other CBS News executives and executive producers who had presided over the biggest embarrassment in the history of CBS News? Should they receive some form of reprimand, indicating that while they weren't held primarily accountable, they still had to accept some degree of responsibility for allowing a producer to run amok? All of these questions involving the ethics of an institution became academic in the days that followed.

The weekend meeting in Connecticut was followed by other meetings held at Black Rock. With the exception of Benjamin, the same group which had gathered at Jankowski's home would assemble in the thirty-fourth-floor conference room adjoining Jankowski's office. In addition, there was a delegation from the Law Department headed by the deputy general counsel, George Vradenburg. Vradenburg was the de facto head of the Law Department. His boss, Jim Parker, devoted most of his time to his other job as Senior Vice President for Planning and Development. This partially explained Mater's description of a new Law Department which wanted to "set policy." Vradenburg had joined CBS two years earlier from the law firm of Cravath, Swaine, and Moore. A tall, cheerful man with glasses, Vradenburg looked more like a successful small-town lawyer than the product of a prestigious Manhattan law firm. His rumpled suits invariably hung open at the waist even when buttoned, revealing the point of his tie and a Gucci belt buckle. His affable manner didn't prevent Vradenburg from being immediately assertive. He and his staff seemed to have little doubt that Westmoreland was an odds-on favorite for a lawsuit against CBS. They understood that CBS News was planning to offer the general reply time to be followed by a discussion of the issues. If that happened, the chances of a suit would be significantly diminished. If it didn't, which turned out to be the case, and we were sued for libel, George Crile would be the key to mounting a defense with any hope of success. Crile, then, couldn't be fired. Crile had made no secret of his belief that he'd had executive supervision throughout the process of preparation and that Stringer and the others couldn't expect to walk away and leave him as a willing scapegoat. If Crile was fired he was certain to go very public with that complaint. In addition, he was the only one connected with the preparation of the broadcast, with the exception of Sam

Adams, the paid consultant, who had a working knowledge of the statistical minutiae which would permeate any trial dealing with intelligence gathering and the counting of enemy troop strength in Vietnam. Sauter summed it up with an old quote from Lyndon Johnson: "I'd rather have him inside the tent pissing out than outside the tent pissing in."

This also meant no reprimand for Wallace and the others, nothing that could damage their credibility before some future jury. What about the Benjamin Report itself? Should it be released as a public document? There was a problem here. Benjamin had set out to investigate the *TV Guide* charges and write a report to his superiors as an in-house self-examination. He had worked with two researchers who often took notes while he interviewed all of the participants, and his report included portions of interviews which he would not have included in a document for public release.

On page 26 of his report he quoted himself asking Crile, "Do you think Westmoreland was somewhat inept?"

Crile answered, "Yes, he seemed stupid."

If Westmoreland was undecided about a libel suit, the release of a fifty-nine-page document containing this sort of thing could well tip him over the edge. Many of those interviewed had spoken freely to Bud, believing he was conducting an investigation within the confines of CBS News. If he told them their words were going to be released in a public document they might well have expressed themselves more cautiously. Finally, we agreed that Benjamin and I would join Van in drafting a memo which honestly and accurately summarized the findings of the Benjamin Report. We knew that we might someday be forced to release the full report and we made every effort to represent his findings accurately.

When we had something in draft form we would let the Law Department review it. Jankowski could show it to Wyman, and then we would ask each of the key people who had been involved in the preparation of the documentary to read the full Benjamin Report, and after that the memo would be released to our own organization and made available to the public. The three of us spent hours working on this memo. When we listed the principal flaws in the broadcast, we added, "We now feel it would have been a better broadcast if:

- it had not used the word 'conspiracy';
- it had sought out and interviewed more persons who disagreed with the broadcast premise; and
- there had been strict compliance with the CBS News Standards."

We went on to list the violations of those standards and then a number of other charges which we perceived as "judgment calls" or as "unwarranted." We announced the creation of a new position, that of Vice President for News Practices. We mentioned the planning of a future broadcast on the issues treated in the original broadcast. Finally, we included the mea culpa for Wallace: "On projects of a complex and controversial nature, the full involvement and collaboration of the principal correspondent is vital. Future assignments will take this essential need into consideration."

In conclusion, having listed the flaws with what we believed to be total candor, we added, "We support the substance of the broadcast."

For weeks both Van and I had been hearing from Rather and others that all of CBS News was waiting to see the kind of stuff we both were made of. Of course, the organization had no idea how damning Benjamin's report would turn out to be. Nevertheless, there was a tradition at CBS News of stonewalling this sort of attack. Far from stonewalling, we were about to unveil a list of journalistic transgressions of stunning proportion. At least we could say that the basic premise of the broadcast was valid. That Bud Benjamin, after six weeks of investigation, joined us in that statement was essential to its being made.

The three of us hadn't agreed on everything, and the memo acknowledged those areas of difference by saying, "There are allegations that so-called sympathetic witnesses were given more gentle treatment in their interviews than those who had a contrary position. There is honest disagreement among the three of us as to whether this is correct."

I was the dissenter on this issue. I had seen and read the same interviews that Bud had. We had different reactions to the same material. For several years in the sixties a good part of my job at WCBS Radio had been that of an interviewer. I have always believed that the purpose of an interview is to produce information. Sometimes that's best done by aggressive prodding, other times by gentle tugs.

The finished memo was sent back to the Law Department to see if we had constructed any time bombs which might explode later if there should be a libel trial. The Law Department gave its approval. Both Wyman and Paley had asked for and had received the Benjamin Report itself. Now it was time to brief Wyman on the steps which were being taken in its aftermath. Jankowski, Sauter, and Vradenburg trooped to Wyman's office on the thirty-fifth floor of Black Rock. I was waiting in Jankowski's office when they returned. All three men looked grim.

"Well," I asked, "do we proceed as planned, George?"

As I think back, it's interesting that my question was addressed to Vradenburg. For all of the talk of CBS News cleaning its own house, control of this episode was already passing to the lawyers.

"We do," he said. "Tom can't understand why Crile isn't being fired, but we do."

"At least he asked the right question," I said. "Did he have any other comments?"

"Let's just say he was not pleased. He kept saying this was like a bad movie."

Van, whose beard seemed grayer to me than it had a few hours earlier, turned to Gene.

"Ed and I better head back to the Broadcast Center and get on with the rest of this wretched day."

Gene seemed pleased by the prospect of our departure.

"Good luck," he said, and he added, "Remember, this too shall pass."

Early that evening in Van's office we began to bring in the principal players.

First, Bob Chandler, whose participation had been early and minimal. His tenure as Vice President for Public Affairs had ended shortly after the broadcast was proposed and commissioned and he'd been replaced in that job by Roger Colloff. He was given, as the others would be, the full Benjamin Report and allowed to read it alone in my office. Afterward, in Van's office, he was shown the memo from Sauter, Joyce, and Benjamin which would be made public the next day. Bob didn't seem surprised by what he read. He seemed almost determined to be as noncommittal as possible.

"Very interesting" was about all he said. Shortly afterward, he left the building and went home.

Stringer was next. After reading the report and seeing that Benjamin had not shared Crile's belief that he should shoulder ultimate responsibility, he was visibly relieved. When he read through the follow-up memo, some of that relief seemed to dissipate.

"A bit hard on the rest of us, isn't it?"

"Not exactly one of journalism's shining moments, Howard," I said.

"There is that," he acknowledged.

After Stringer came Mike Wallace. Not the confident, contentious Mike Wallace we've all known for years. He was obviously agitated, so nervous he chain-smoked throughout the evening. After he'd read the report and then the summary memo he turned to the two of us.

"Jesus, guys," he said, "you're throwing us to the wolves."

Van tried to assure Mike that this was not true, but Mike wasn't buying it. He argued that we should do nothing—just say we'd received the Benjamin Report and "That concludes our investigation."

"We can't do that, Mike," I said. "We fucked up. The *TV Guide* article had us cold. I'm proud we'd tackle such an important subject, but I'm ashamed of the way we did it."

A smoldering Wallace left the office, and the last of the group to read the Benjamin Report came in, George Crile. I left him alone behind a closed door.

When enough time had gone by to make both Van and me wonder at the slowness with which he was reading the report, I opened the door a crack to check on his progress. The office was empty and the Benjamin Report was lying on my desk. Crile had left without bothering to be shown the summary memo.

Van and I sat alone in his office.

"Welcome to CBS News," I said.

"It's not what I expected." We both sat in silence and then he added, "I dread tomorrow."

"You're right to feel that way," I said. "The press will have a field day."

"There'll be no walking wounded. One group will go after CBS News for having screwed the general. The other will hit us for having caved."

As it turned out, our evening wasn't over. Van's secretary buzzed him to say that Mike Wallace would like to come back to talk some more and he'd like to bring Crile, Colloff, and Stringer.

"Tell him we're here anytime they want to come in," Van said.

A few minutes later they arrived as a group.

It was obvious they'd met, compared notes, and were here to push for a different sort of response to the Benjamin Report.

This time Crile read the summary memo and his response was that he'd delivered an important broadcast and that we were hung up on procedural violations which were ultimately trivial.

Never once that night or in the years that followed did I have a sense that George Crile felt contrite about the manner in which he'd produced that documentary or cared that he'd played fast and loose with the reputation of CBS News.

Colloff seemed to focus on a defense of the use of the word "conspiracy" in the broadcast. The word had actually appeared only once in the broadcast itself, although Van had inserted it in the advertising. Benjamin felt it was unproved. Colloff had discussed its use at an early screening

159

with Bill Leonard and said they'd both concluded that the use of the word "conspiracy" was justified. The other three echoed his defense.

Stringer argued that Bud had been too much of a literalist in reviewing all of the material. That Bud's body of work in the documentary area involved the historical *20th Century* type of broadcast, not the controversial broadcast which was the hallmark of *CBS Reports*. It was basically the same complaint I'd heard from him before he'd read the report.

Each of them spoke briefly and then they deferred to Mike Wallace. It seemed obvious they were depending on Wallace's famous techniques of confrontation and debate to turn the tide. Mike had regained some of his composure. He was still chain-smoking, still nervously pacing the office.

The Wallace face, subject of thousands of television close-ups, is so familiar and so imposing it's surprising when you realize it belongs to a man in his mid-sixties who is physically so slight he seems at times almost frail. It's as though a lifetime of compulsive energies have stripped his body of every ounce of excess flesh. Mike Wallace was already in his forties when he came to CBS News. He'd had an active and lucrative career as a commercial announcer, game show host, Broadway actor, and television interviewer. With that background, to have begun a second professional life in his middle age at a news organization which mentions the name of Edward R. Murrow the way Indian politicians invoke the name of Mahatma Gandhi was not an easy accomplishment. It required a shrewd tenacity to match his considerable broadcasting skills. He walked to the edge of the carpet with a cigarette in his hand, facing the wall, and then he turned around to us.

"Look," he said, "when you show us a finished memo like the one we saw, I know it's been cleared by the Law Department, which means it's been read by Jankowski and Wyman and maybe even Paley. I know it's not easy to go back to Black Rock and say you want to change it . . . but we need you to represent us, too."

He stopped and started to walk back to the chairs where the others were seated. Midway he halted and turned once more to Van and me.

"Remember, you two guys are our tribunes in that building."

There was an awkward moment while he sat down.

"Mike," Van asked, "knowing what's in Bud's report, what is it you would have us change?"

Mike focused on two points. The first was easy because he was right.

"You make a statement of support for the substance, the thrust of the broadcast, but it's at the very end of the memo. What precedes it is so damning it will get lost there. Nobody will remember it. Make that statement emphatically right at the start of the memo so everyone will know that regardless of the other problems at least we were right about that."

We agreed. Either we supported the main thesis of the documentary or we didn't. If we did, then we should say so and not mumble it at the end of a long list of mortal sins.

The other change was not one either of us was willing to make. For at least thirty minutes we listened to arguments against the memo's conclusion that the word "conspiracy" was inappropriate, that it would have been a better broadcast if we had not used that word. But neither Van nor I would budge.

"It's one of those red-herring words that obscure the facts which were raised," I argued. "Of course it would have been a better broadcast without it."

Van felt even stronger. "We just didn't make the case," he said, but he had a suggestion. Add a line in the memo saying, "Our colleagues involved in the production of this broadcast are convinced that the interviews and events related to this question justify the use of the word 'conspiracy.' "

The four of them left the office that night somewhat mollified by the changes which had been made.

Since the memo stated that it reflected the views of Sauter, Joyce, and Benjamin, we would have to show the revised memo to Bud. He found the changes acceptable.

The finished document was an odd hybrid of interests. It contained a litany of our sins. It referred to disagreement among the three of us who were signing our names to it. It conceded the right to those who'd prepared the broadcast to disagree with our criticism of the use of the word "conspiracy." The contradictions were so peculiar that a paragraph was inserted which read: "In reviewing this statement, it may be bewildering to some outside CBS News that within our organization there can be debate regarding editorial decisions. But ours is a collaborative business and such debates are natural, and of great value. Where we agree is in our commitment to accuracy and fairness."

Bewildering? To those outside CBS News? We'd constructed an ironic metaphor for the Vietnam War. Instead of decisive action, a series of compromising negotiations had produced a limited response which sent confusing signals through our own ranks and presented a face of moral ambiguity to an outside world. We would learn for ourselves that an "honorable withdrawal" is easy to talk about and hard to accomplish.

Two months later, on September 13, 1982, the general returned fire. At a press conference held at the Army-Navy Club in Washington, D.C., he announced that in his home state of South Carolina he was bringing suit against CBS for libel.

He named as defendants not only CBS but Van Gordon Sauter, George Crile, Michael Wallace, and Samuel A. Adams, the paid consultant for the broadcast. By then this libel action did not come as a surprise. The general and a number of his supporters had refused to participate in a follow-up broadcast and word reached us on repeated occasions that he was seeking counsel on the viability of a lawsuit. Such distinguished Washington attorneys as Clark Clifford and Edward Bennett Williams had advised him that his status as a public figure made the possibility of a successful lawsuit unlikely. But Westmoreland said he'd been approached by the President of the Capitol Legal Foundation, who offered him legal representation with the assurance he would be completely free from any burden of cost. The Capitol Legal Foundation was one of a number of conservative public-interest firms which took a Ralph Nader approach to right-wing goals. The President of the foundation was Dan Burt, a thirty-nine-year-old, five-foot-two-inch attorney whose diminutive body housed at least half of the nation's known supply of rhetorical excess. Almost immediately he proclaimed in an interview in *USA Today*, "We are about to see the dismantling of a major news network."

The offer from Burt apparently removed the last obstacle in the mind of a retired military officer who had returned from an unpopular war and discovered that America is generous only to its winners. Now CBS had revisited the war and he was accused of conduct some of his friends and supporters were telling him amounted to a charge of treason.

The press conference in Washington was covered by a CBS News crew which microwaved it back from an antenna on the roof of the building to our bureau there at 2020 M Street. From there it was fed up an open line to the Broadcast Center in New York, where Van and I watched it in his office. On the monitor we saw the general walk up to the podium and address the reporters who gathered there.

"I am an old soldier," he told them, "who loves his country and have had enough of war. It was my fate to serve for over four years as the senior American commander in the most unpopular war this country has ever fought. I have been reviled, burned in effigy, spat upon."

Westmoreland went on to portray himself as an underdog pitted against an organization of wealth and power.

He concluded by saying, "The only question is whether CBS had an obligation to be accurate in its facts before it attempted to destroy a man's character, the work of his lifetime. I trust the American judicial system and an American jury will fairly evaluate what I and those in positions of responsibility said and did, and I am pleased to put my reputation and honor in their custody."

This was not the confused, lip-licking man we'd seen in the documentary as he was interviewed by Mike Wallace. This was an old fighter who had moved from anger to determination and was obviously prepared for another long war.

"He's pretty impressive," I said.

Van shook his head. "Imagine what South Carolina jurors will think of him."

Dan Burt followed Westmoreland to the lectern. It had been set up to hold the statement which was read by the general and was so high Burt had to stretch and peer over the top to speak to the reporters, cameras, and microphones. At any other time the sight would have produced laughter, but Burt began immediately to give some of the details of the suit, including the names of the defendants.

I looked at Van as his name was called off. His face was expressionless until the last defendant, Sam Adams, was cited. Then he turned to me.

"Funny, I didn't hear Bill Leonard's name," he said.

Burt read off the first of five counts of libel and we understood why Van had been named. The first count dealt not with the broadcast itself but with the advertising for the broadcast and specifically with the word "conspiracy" which had been used in that advertising. Until now Van had been able to stand aside from the broadcast as something that had been commissioned and produced before his arrival. But he was the one who had introduced the word "conspiracy" into the advertising. Now he would have to explain under oath why he had done that and then joined Benjamin and Joyce in July 1982 in a joint memo which said, "We now believe a judgmental conclusion of conspiracy was inappropriate."

The second count dealt with Diane Sawyer's *CBS Morning News* interview of Wallace and Crile done in advance of the broadcast. The interview contained many of the charges later made in the documentary itself. The third focused on specific parts of the documentary. The fourth with the July 15 memo which summarized the Benjamin Report. The fifth claimed the previous four counts had placed the plaintiff in a "False Light."

When the press conference concluded and the monitor on which we'd watched it began showing color bars, Van turned to me.

"Well . . . what do you think?"

"Say a prayer," I said. "Pray that we get a change of venue and move this trial somewhere else. If it takes place in South Carolina, we're dead."

Eventually CBS would obtain a change of venue moving the trial to the jurisdiction of the Southern District of New York. This would be one of the many legal maneuvers our new outside counsel, David Boies, a partner in the firm of Cravath, Swaine, and Moore, would perform. George Vradenburg, who had worked at Cravath as an associate before joining the CBS Law Department, was a great admirer of the forty-two-year-old Boies, who had been with the Cravath firm for eleven years. In that time he'd carved out a reputation as a master litigator. There was just one problem. He'd never tried a libel case before. His work had been in the areas of antitrust and securities. We'd been expecting Vradenburg to bring in one of the lawyers with a history of First Amendment cases, such as Floyd Abrams of Cahill, Gordon, and Reindel or Tim Dyck of Wilmer, Cutler, Pickering. It was a bit like learning the surgeon who was about to perform your open-heart surgery was a distinguished orthopedist. At that point a change of venue was still something for which we could only hope. Vradenburg pointed out that if the case was tried in South Carolina, Boies would be comfortable in dealing with a Southern judge and jury. Indeed, he seemed to fit that bill. With his blue Sears, Roebuck suits and low-key manner he didn't look at all like a high-powered partner in a New York law firm whose annual salary exceeded a million dollars a year. He looked more like someone whose practice consisted of wills and house closings than the gunslinger who'd forced the Justice Department to abandon its attempt to break up IBM through a series of antitrust suits. Boies not only didn't fit the wingtips and pinstripes image we were accustomed to expect from our law firms; it was obvious he was no First Amendment "ideologue." He was there to win a case. If not in the courtroom, then on appeal. By October he was ready to assess our chances.

At 4:30 P.M. on October 19, Van and I sat with Vradenburg as Boies laid out his case.

"If we are going to win," he said, "I have to convince a jury not only of an absence of malice but of the truth of that broadcast. Unless they are convinced of its truth, it's unlikely they'll believe that Crile acted without malice."

Vradenburg turned to Van and me.

"The biggest obstacle David faces is the Benjamin Report," he said.

Boies nodded. "That's right. I have to proceed on the assumption that eventually we'll be forced to turn over the report and possibly Benjamin's notes to the judge. He can then decide whether or not to make them available to the jury and I'm assuming he will. My case has to be built on the premise that Benjamin approached his report from an old-line standard that doesn't distinguish between investigative reporting and standard reporting of news events."

"I don't believe that's true," I said. "George could have done that story and still played by the rules."

"George Crile is the key to winning this case," he said. "If the jury doesn't believe George, we won't win. Right now, he's capable of going off in a number of directions in an effort to justify his broadcast. I have to keep him under control, and in order to do that, I have to keep his confidence."

"Does he appreciate the fact that we are paying for his legal costs?" Van asked.

"I think he does," Boies said. "He may want his own outside counsel. If he does, I think CBS should pay for that, too. George must continue to feel that his interests and the interests of CBS are the same."

Boies paused and Vradenburg spoke up.

"David thinks George should be given an assignment to demonstrate that he's not damaged goods."

"You've got to be kidding," I said.

"If we go to trial," Boies said, "and the jury learns that he has been paid but virtually unemployed since the Westmoreland broadcast, it will be very damaging."

"Why can't you just point out that he has been working full-time on preparing for the trial?" I asked.

"I can," he said, "and I will if I have to, but the attorney for the plaintiff will use this to convince the jury that it shows CBS News does not trust George Crile to do another broadcast."

"How perceptive," I said, "since it happens . . ."

Van interrupted me.

"Ed and I should discuss this issue later," he said, "but, David, I understand your point."

After the lawyers had gone I walked over to Van's desk.

"I can see where you're headed," I said. "I have to tell you giving Crile another broadcast would be a mistake. It's a terrible message for everyone else at CBS News who has lived by the rules."

"I hear you," he said, "but I don't think there's any choice."

"Van, imagine this scenario: The broadcast goes on the air . . . and we learn that George has done it again . . . bent some of those rules that didn't seem so important at the time. This time it's on our watch."

Van stared at me.

"Nothing is more important to CBS than winning this case," he said coldly. Then he paused and his voice warmed. "And take that from a defendant."

In the days which followed, Crile was assigned to "The Battle for Nicaragua," a documentary which was scheduled to be aired in August 1983. Crile retained Victor Kovner, a distinguished First Amendment lawyer, as his own separate counsel. CBS paid the legal fees. David Boies continued to construct a defense of truth with Crile the center pole. For Boies there was a single goal, to win the case. For CBS News it would not be that simple. No one wanted to see this case lost. Still, the Benjamin Report had laid bare a broadcast which represented a low point for CBS News, which prided itself on a tradition of being both hard-hitting and fair in its journalism. We were about to begin a legal defense for a broadcast we had acknowledged as flawed. But the attorney representing us would not only be trying to ignore those flaws; he was prepared to argue against their importance. The ethical conflicts this set in motion within CBS News remain unresolved.

In the fall of 1982, few days went by without a discussion or meeting dealing with the Westmoreland libel suit.

But this was just one strand in the fabric of activity in a busy news organization. Election night was almost upon us. It might be an off-year election but it would be Rather's first time in the election anchor chair. It would also be the first real test for Joan Richman in her special-events role. Our new financial structure was now in place and had begun to function as intended. And like a "distant early warning system" it was sounding disaster alerts for the CBS News budget. The Falklands and Lebanon stories had been enormously expensive to cover. Having been right in the middle of them, I felt responsibility for our cost problem.

In the past, it would have taken months to assess the cost impact of all this coverage. With the new systems we'd implemented, we had a general idea at the end of each week, and quite a specific understanding at the end of each month, of money spent. Of course, it's not enough simply to recognize a problem. The challenge comes from dealing with that knowledge. Anyone who has ever run a business or managed a budget knows that in the face of a cost overrun the next step is to look for a cost offset. That didn't seem like a particularly radical concept to either Van or me. To CBS News it was apparently not only radical but virtually a near violation of the First Amendment. When a job freeze for the remainder of the year was instituted by Van and me, the same people who'd watched with approval as resources were poured into the coverage of major stories now began to mutter that the place was being taken over by bean counters. Because of his peculiar dress code Van was labeled an "L. L. Bean counter."

I'd always regarded controlling a budget as part of the ethical compact you made when you became a manager. It was hard for me to understand the furor created by what seemed to me rudimentary and not very painful cost-control measures. It was clear that the era of 20 and even 30 percent budget increases had gone forever. Jankowski never missed an opportunity to stress that point, and neither Van nor I was disturbed by what we saw as a fact of life.

What did disturb us was a sense that Jankowski's perception of CBS News increasingly seemed to be shaped by the Finance Department of the television network, which did all of the number crunching and analyses for his Vice President for Finance, Tim Reynolds. The documentary area was a particular target for criticism. Time and again he referred to the issue of "deadwood." Undoubtedly there were some parts of that area which, if judged solely by an MBA's work-efficiency study, might seem to qualify as deadwood. For example, Jay McMullen worked at his own pace and in his own way. Jay was a veteran producer of documentaries. His "Biography of a Bookie Joint" in the 1960s with its hidden cameras inside a Boston bookmaking parlor, was a trailblazing documentary. Now in his sixties, Jay continued to produce excellent broadcasts. In 1982 he did "The Parole Gang," a searching look at the grimy parole system. A year later he gave viewers "After All Those Years," a touching and, as many of us would come to realize, prescient look at senior white-collar workers who were forced to retire when they were no longer needed. One broadcast a year doesn't look like much when an MBA from Wharton reduces it to a work-flow chart. Jay earned approximately $96,000 a year and in return CBS News received broadcasts which earned awards, critical acclaim, prestige, and low ratings.

Jankowski was persistent about the deadwood issue and it was difficult to argue a productivity case for documentaries. Even the black humorists of the CBS News Division had dubbed this production area "Brigadoon," after the mythical town which materializes every hundred years. So I took another approach. I had our Finance Department prepare a breakdown of what could be saved if we really cut back on all but the most productive areas of public affairs. The total savings came to less than $400,000 a year. The next time Gene mentioned the deadwood issue I produced the report and told him that a $400,000 saving in a budget of over $200 million didn't make sense when you considered the symbolism of dropping the bomb on Brigadoon. Jankowski dropped the issue instead. But as I would later learn, the question of deadwood was merely being postponed and would surface again in the future.

As election night drew closer, everyone involved was beginning to feel some tension. This would be the first time in decades that Walter Cronkite would not be presiding over CBS News election coverage. Rather's nightly broadcast was now number one in the ratings. His coverage of special events had shown his capability with a breaking story. But elections and conventions are particular rites of passage for anchorpeople. Rather described the challenge in an interview at the time with the Associated Press.

"This is tougher than the space shots," he said. "There's a lot more to know. If you don't understand the intricacies of a space shot, the public is going to forgive you. They expect you to know politics."

He was right about that and he wasn't the only one feeling the challenge. The competition among the three networks to project winners on the basis of polling data is keen. In 1980 NBC had begun making calls on races based on exit poll interviews. Voters were questioned as they left the polling place. As a result, NBC had been far ahead of CBS News with their calls. At the time it was another symbolic loss for CBS News. After that election the head of the CBS News election and survey unit, Warren Mitofsky, set out to make CBS News a competitor in the exit poll business. He experimented in 1981 and, despite a bad call in the New Jersey gubernatorial race, he assured us all that on "Election Night 82" CBS News would not fall behind either of its two competitors when it came to early calls on key races.

Computer graphics was another area where CBS News had lagged behind in election coverage. ABC had pioneered in their use. Roone Arledge, the ABC President of News and Sports, had made a development deal with the Dubner company to design new ways of displaying election information. On an election night with vote data constantly changing, visual display of all of the evolving statistics was an enormous challenge.

Joan Richman had come to me months earlier with the news that the Dubner-ABC contract had elapsed and they were free to work with us. She wanted to assign Artie Bloom, a gifted director, to work with them in developing a computer graphics system which could be harnessed to a constantly changing data base and at any time show viewers the winners and losers or display those states held by each party. I asked her to have Bloom put together a presentation for Van and me showing what we might expect. Bloom came to us with crude outlines of graphs, cubes, and other animated displays which would help explain election results. Van was even more enthusiastic than I was and so we approached election night with a battery of new electronic tools.

Another challenge for "Election Night 82" involved what to do with the most trusted man in America. One thing for certain couldn't be done: put Walter Cronkite in the election set with Dan Rather. Dan made it clear that this was his election night. He'd been "a loyal foot soldier" for Cronkite on many election nights, he told us. Now he'd painfully made the post-Cronkite transition on the *Evening News*. "I can't lose that ground," he said.

There was no doubt that sitting on the same set with Cronkite on election night involved the risk of his somehow being perceived as the junior partner. On the other hand, Joan reported frequent phone calls from Cronkite asking for the details of his election night role. Dealing with Cronkite was part of the turf Van, as President, understandably held for himself. Handling someone who had been so dominant and then had been urged into semi-retirement would have been delicate under any circumstances. Paley had made this infinitely more complex by making Cronkite a member of the CBS Board of Directors.

Van asked me to review Walter's contract to see what obligations might exist. Everyone knew that over the next seven years Cronkite would receive one million dollars a year for unspecified services which could not require his time for more than a third of each year. Obviously, that was the inducement with which Leonard and Jankowski had made retirement from the *Evening News* an attractive prospect. When I read the contract I saw that the package included the prime-time *Universe* series and two unspecified prime-time *Walter Cronkite at Large* broadcasts each year. But elections were listed in the contract along with conventions, interviews, and other coverage as the sort of thing for which, if mutually agreed upon, Cronkite would make himself available. I asked Jankowski if there were verbal agreements we needed to know about. His response was that this hadn't been the case; money had been the big factor in the negotiation.

When Walter was the prime anchorman of CBS News, superstar salaries had not yet become financial novas, so his million dollars a year was in part a recognition of illustrious years when he didn't receive the kind of money now being paid to his replacement. It was also insurance which would keep Cronkite from suddenly materializing as Rather's competition on another network. Regardless of what was, or in this case was not, written into his contract, Walter had left the *Evening News* fully expecting to play a continuing role in the future of CBS News, a future which included a significant role during elections and conventions.

Perhaps if the early stage of the Cronkite-Rather transition had not been clouded by a general perception that Rather was not measuring up, a satisfactory role for Cronkite might have been found. But Dan was already on edge about his first election night. Van came away from one meeting with him worried that "the prospect of a side-by-side comparison was unsettling the anchorman."

Joan Richman came up with the solution. "Let's set up an election studio in our Washington Bureau," she said. "We'll invite some Clark Clifford types, and as the off-year voting trends become apparent we'll switch down there and Walter can interview them."

"How do you think Rather would react to that?" I asked.

"Let me propose it to him," she said.

Dan found the idea acceptable. Walter found it acceptable. Van spent the next afternoon in Rather's office.

"How'd it go?" I asked.

"I'm trying to get him to relax," he said. "He's going to be surrounded by Bob Schieffer, Morton Dean, Lesley Stahl, Bill Moyers, and Mike Wallace. Cronkite would never share the evening with them. I told Rather he ought to lean on them. It will only make him look better."

In previous years Cronkite had developed something of a reputation among his colleagues as an "air hog." He believed the anchorman's role was to keep new information moving to the viewer and was often reluctant to interrupt that flow for a contribution from one of the other CBS News correspondents. Elections nights at CBS traditionally concluded with some of the most distinguished correspondents muttering among themselves.

When the '82 election night arrived, Rather's nervous tensions seemed ideally harnessed to the task. Van and I were watching in conference room 2-E-6 on the second floor of the Broadcast Center. A bar was set up at one end of the room for the visiting executives from Black Rock, for whom election night was a traditional night of festivity. After dinner in a Manhattan restaurant they would arrive to drink, chat, watch a bit of the coverage, and tour the election set. It was an odd social ritual which resulted in the CBS News management being constantly distracted on election nights by the necessity of playing host to the visiting moguls. As much as possible, I planned to spend my time in the studio or the control room, but a total boycott of 2-E-6 would have been ill advised.

The Black Rock contingent must have been dawdling over their coffee when our coverage started, because, except for the idle bartender, we were alone in the large conference room when Rather came on the air. He began with such velocity both of us were rocked back in our chairs for a moment, but as he went on the pace decreased and was balanced by the more relaxed tone he used while talking with the other correspondents. Joan Richman's election unit was providing him with a flawless flow of election material with which to work. The calls were quick and accurate. Mitofsky had fulfilled his promise. The animated graphics were even more effective than we'd hoped. Working with these editorial and production tools, Rather and the CBS News correspondents began to report, interpret, and analyze the election returns.

Soon after the arrival of the CBS brass I left 2-E-6 for the election set, and Van followed a few minutes later. A feeling of confidence seemed to ripple through the enormous studio. I could see Rather becoming more confident every hour he was on the air. At one point during a commercial break he leaned over to Mike Wallace, who was slipping into his chair for the next segment.

"Mike," he said, "you look nice. Momma must have dressed you up tonight."

A large number of newspaper, wire service, and magazine reporters were there to write their mandatory "How Television Covered the Election" stories. Lest anyone miss the point that unlike his predecessor Rather was allowing the other correspondents to actually get on the air, Van began to describe Rather to them as "a sharing anchor." Seeing one wire service reporter hovering around Dan during a long commercial break, he walked over to the anchor desk and in a loud voice told Dan, "Your pace is perfect. You're embracing the people around you."

Not only did this mark the beginning of a not very subtle "Rather is better than Cronkite" campaign, but it ignored the fact that the one correspondent not being "embraced" by Dan was Walter Cronkite, who was sitting in a Washington studio surrounded by distinguished guests and, in a turn of wicked irony, was not able to get on the air. Each time the control room got ready to switch to Washington for one of the Cronkite interviews, Rather turned instead to one of his colleagues on the election set. It was as though he was being asked to switch to the ghost of Christmas past. On the few occasions when Cronkite did manage to get on the air his interviews were truncated because of the flow of election results. Bud Benjamin kept reporting to Joan Richman that Cronkite was becoming furious.

Rather left the Broadcast Center that night elated and victorious.

Cronkite left the Washington Bureau bitter and humiliated.

In hindsight it could be argued that an old anchor hand such as Cronkite should have understood, even anticipated, the realities of election night. But nothing in his thirty-two proud years at CBS had prepared him to participate in election night coverage as an expendable contributor.

After this election night Van's salutation to Rather, "Hello, champion," was not off the mark in capturing the way a lot of people at CBS News were beginning to feel, not only about Rather but about themselves. A "winner" psychology had developed. A year ago Roone Arledge's ABC News had seemed unstoppable, a competitive blend of journalism and technology. Now the story and the leadership had shifted back to CBS News. Even its President had become a media story. There was growing speculation about "the next job for Sauter." CBS News itself was fascinated by the story.

Stringer visited my office to quote Rather to me. "Dan is convinced Van will soon be running everything, you know."

"Do you have a hidden staff I don't know about, Stringer?" I asked. "It's the only explanation I can come up with for how all of you manage to get a broadcast on the air each night and still spend so much time discussing the careers of your management."

"Then I don't suppose you'd care to hear the rumor about yourself?"

"Only if it's a good one."

"It's the one everyone at CBS News believes will happen. Paley relinquishes the Chairman's office to Wyman. Wyman names Jankowski as his own replacement as President. Van moves to Jankowski's job as Broadcast Group President, and, sir, you become the President of CBS News."

"The ability of this organization," I said, "to shape a story out of the shreds and tatters of conjecture terrifies me. I worry that these are the same skills being used to cover the news."

Howard grinned. "We're not nearly as good as that," he said.

When Howard left I had to admit I had been somewhat disingenuous in my response. All of CBS was waiting for Paley to take the final step and relinquish the title and office of Chairman. Van and I frequently discussed what this could mean for the two of us.

"It's positioning," he would say. "Positioning and timing. Who knows, Eduardo. All you can do is ride it as far as you can, and hope it's been worthwhile. All I know for certain is that the quality of my life deteriorated markedly the day after I left California."

The last comment was one he frequently made to me. Both of us felt we'd paid a personal price for career advancement in leaving a life we enjoyed in Southern California. Van and Kathleen both talked openly and frequently about their intention to someday return to that state. That kind of move certainly didn't seem imminent. Both our fortunes for the foreseeable future were firmly rooted in New York City.

My feelings at the time were that if Van was promoted there was little doubt that I would become the next President of CBS News. We'd both be rewarded for the hard work and accomplishment. Van would get the job he wanted, and so would I.

Remaining "positioned" required continued success at CBS News. And to Van it meant remaining in the media spotlight. He often commented that "most of what Black Rock knows about us comes from what they read." That was a cynical but a shrewd appraisal of most of the senior executives of CBS. For these key executives three publications are on their desks when they arrive in the morning: the New York *Times,* the Washington *Post,* and *The Wall Street Journal.* Relevant clips from other newspapers and news magazines are collected and distributed each day. But a story in one of the three big papers can quickly change a Black Rock agenda because of the impact it can have on the rest of the press or on the financial community.

Being in the media spotlight is a fact of life for the President of a network news division, whether he likes it or not. The job requires numerous statements to the press and responses to the inquiries of that uneven group of men and women who fill the television sections of the nation's newspapers and magazines. But Van was now seeking not just the continuing flow of press coverage but the kinds of stories which would place him in the category of celebrity executive along with Roone Arledge and Fred Silverman.

Tom Leahy, our boss during our time in the stations division, joined me for lunch one day during this period and expressed puzzlement at the way Van was courting the press.

"He doesn't need it," he said. "He's already got the job. They'll love him for a while, but they'll kill him later. I saw it happen to Freddie Silverman."

Silverman was the programming wunderkind of CBS who moved first to ABC and then to NBC in that network's counterpart of Gene Jankowski's job at CBS. The press initially lionized him for his programming instincts, calling him "the man with the golden gut." Then, as his fortunes turned sour at NBC, the same reporters savaged him with equal enthusiasm.

Leahy, who had avoided the press with as much skill as Van had shown in pursuing it, was convinced he was making a mistake. Before the lunch was over I had promised to share his feelings with Van.

That afternoon I told Van about Tom.

"Leahy thinks you're doing a Silverman," I said. "He's worried about you. He thinks you're setting yourself up as an eventual target."

"Leahy doesn't understand what high-profile jobs these are," he said. "Speaking of the press"—he laughed—"when are you arranging the Kitman lunch?"

Marvin Kitman wrote a television column for *Newsday*. I'd known him from my days at Channel 2 in New York, and I'd promised to introduce him to Van. Kitman may be the only writer dealing with television who could legitimately claim to be a humorist. Out of five columns one would be genuinely funny, three readable, and the fifth demented. He had once co-written a television series, *Ball Four*, with Jim Bouton and emerged from the wreckage with both an understanding and a loathing of television. I've always enjoyed him. He has savaged me at times in his column, but the column would make me laugh and I'd forgive him, even if he was right.

I arranged the lunch, and arriving at the Oak Room of the Plaza, I was curious to see how Van would handle Marvin. He showed up wearing a tweed jacket, a bow tie, and wrinkled chinos. A good first impression. The salad hadn't come before Marvin launched into a contemptuous dismissal of the entire prime-time lineup of CBS television. Van offered a cogent explanation. The people responsible were unspeakable morons. Kitman began to fall in love. Here was a guy who hated television more than he did. By the time coffee was being served, Van had dished everyone responsible for commercial television and had agreed to allow himself to be profiled for an article Kitman wanted to offer the *Washington Journalism Review*. Kitman spent several days at CBS News "researching" his article. When it appeared in November 1982, the flames of Kitman's ardor had not died down. Sauter, he wrote, "has a print guy mentality. Any minute you expect him to drop the phone, grab his hat and his whiskey bottle and dash into the newsroom to see what's happening. Instead he has a Tab and talks to me about the past." The article also contained such hard-hitting investigative revelations as a description of the battered manual typewriter this former newspaperman used to write his own memos in an unflagging effort to upgrade television news. What a guy.

The magazine profile was exactly the kind of media breakthrough Van had been looking for. And it was to be followed by another profile in *Esquire* magazine. We all awaited the arrival of that issue of *Esquire* with a fair amount of anxiety. As certain as we had been about the tone of the Kitman article, we were equally uncertain about what to expect from *Esquire*. A few months earlier, while I'd been off for a week at my house on Martha's Vineyard, a writer from *Esquire*, Ron Rosenbaum, had come in to do a profile of Van. Rosenbaum is a stylist with a deft sense of the absurd. His previous piece in *Esquire* had been a profile of the singer Wayne Newton. Before leaving I'd urged Van to watch himself.

"It's not a problem," he said. "He's just another dipshit reporter."

When I got back I asked Van how it had gone with *Esquire*.

"Uneventful," he said.

He must have realized the answer struck me as odd.

"I talked with him for a while," he said. "Then I let him wander back with Stringer and the guys in the Fishbowl."

I walked back to the *Evening News* area and searched for Stringer.

"How was the guy from *Esquire*?" I asked.

Stringer looked sheepish and asked me to come into his office, where he closed the door.

"I don't know, mate," he said. "I think we may have a problem."

"Tell me what happened."

"What happened is that Van gave him the bloody family jewels."

"Howard, what does that mean?"

"Well, he told us to give Rosenbaum access . . . to let him sit around and observe what we did."

"You didn't let him sit in on editorial meetings, did you?"

"Ed, we flaming well let him sit in on everything. Editorial discussions, graphics discussions, broadcast postmortems. After a while we got used to him, and you know the kinds of things people say to one another here. If he drops a bit of that in his article, we look like bloody fools."

It had been a longtime policy at CBS News not to let outsiders sit in on discussions and meetings about assignments or the editorial content of its broadcasts. Not just reporters . . . anyone. For years, CBS News had shielded the editorial process—including the minute-by-minute decisions, film and tape outtakes, and reporters' notebooks—from an army of prying lawyers, judges, and congressmen. What we smugly and defiantly had refused to give the United States Congress we had now provided to "a dipshit reporter."

The day *Esquire* hit the stands we rushed for our issues to see what Rosenbaum had written. We found it on page 53 of their November issue.

"THE MAN WHO MARRIED DAN RATHER
MOMENT TO MOMENT
WITH VAN GORDON SAUTER
PRESIDENT OF CBS NEWS"

I looked at the title and I couldn't believe it. What had started out as a private joke was now splashed across the pages of a national magazine. First, Dan Rather talking about "the look of the broadcast" and how he and Sauter "fought traditional CBS News stuffiness to change that look."

Then Rather described the fight in a lineup meeting for the broadcast over which of three stories should be the lead, the Falklands, the Middle East, or Princess Di's baby. The writer had a good ear for the quotable phrase.

"I decided we had to go with the royal baby," Rather said, "on the back-fence principle."

"We might take some heat on it, but I'd defend it," Van chimed in his support.

Not once in the past year could I remember Van taking part in an *Evening News* lineup meeting.

But the trophy Rosenbaum had taken with him from his trip to CBS News came in another paragraph, where he described what he called Sauter's "theory of momentism."

"The kind of thing we're looking for is something that evokes an emotional response. When I go back there to the Fishbowl, I tell them God-damnit, we've got to touch people. They've got to feel a relationship with us. A lot of stories have inherent drama, but others have to be done in a way that will bring out an emotional response."

I could just hear Van saying this. It was exactly the kind of jazz riff he would improvise in one of his states of free association . . . the kind of articulate drivel we had often listened to, admired, and then ignored.

It was absurd to think that *The CBS Evening News* would tailor its stories to fit what *Esquire* described as a philosophy of "that's the way it feels." But there was no way we could argue that Van didn't say it. We had now escalated from "full Rothenberg" to "full Rosenbaum." He and we had been hoisted by Van's own canard.

The changes were not revolutionary, they were simply overdue. Now an obsession with packaging the story of those changes for the print press had reduced it to the Californianization of the most respected news organization in broadcasting.

I told Van I thought the article was a disaster, that it undercut everything we'd done. He wouldn't accept that. He was on a high.

"The important thing," he said, "is that they are no longer writing stories about ABC. CBS is now the story."

But the men and women of CBS News were an enormously proud collection of people. Correspondents, producers, writers, editors. They saw themselves as the people who set and maintained the standards for broadcast journalism. As a result of the *Esquire* article, they began to watch the *Evening News* with a questioning eye, on the lookout for those "moments."

For example, during this period, there were far too many stories offering amusing slices of English life. This was nothing more than a result of Howard Stringer's fondness for quirky little stories from the land of his birth. In addition to a succession of Princess Di stories the *Evening News* regularly took its viewers to the English countryside for stories about growing giant cabbages on the isle of Jersey or a village contest for quartets of singing sheep. Imagine you are correspondent Phil Jones and you got a turndown from the *Evening News* on your story about a congressional hearing on the import tariff. That night you watch the *Evening News*. You see a story from Tom Fenton in London, another from Bob Faw in Tel Aviv, and an interesting commentary from Bill Moyers. But after that, a minute and forty seconds of the broadcast is devoted to a quartet of British sheep bleating their little hearts out. It doesn't matter that the broadcast also included some significant stories from Washington. The first words out of Phil's mouth when he joins the gang for a beer that night would have to be "Did you see those goddamn sheep? It must have been one of those moments."

In the unlikely event that anyone missed the significance of the *Esquire* article, George Will summed it all up for them a few days later in his syndicated column. "If journalism becomes a quest for 'moments,' " he wrote, "then journalism becomes avowedly manipulative."

The debate had begun and, as we were to learn later, one person carefully perusing that article describing the new CBS *Evening News* and its quest for "moments" was the anchorman emeritus, Walter Cronkite.

"Jankowski has a hole in the prime-time schedule and he wants to know if CBS News can fill it."

It was December 1982 and Van couldn't suppress his excitement as he described the phone call he'd just received from Gene.

"That's great," I said.

"It's the eight P.M. hour on Tuesday nights and the Entertainment Division doesn't have a show ready to put in there."

"That's not so great," I said. "CBS hasn't had a successful show on Tuesdays at eight since *The White Shadow*."

"It's the only shot we're likely to get. A summer run on Tuesday nights is better than nothing."

"Then the ratings will come in and everybody in the television network will say, 'What do you expect, it's a CBS News hour.'"

"I'm not convinced," Van said, "that we can't produce a respectable rating."

"We'll be opposite *The A-Team* on NBC, for Christ's sake."

"They'll be in reruns and we'll have the only fresh product," Van said.

"What are you going to tell Gene?"

"I've already told him. We can do a dynamite hour teaming Moyers and Kuralt. He loves it. You and I should talk to Moyers about this and then why don't you sound out Kuralt."

So began what would become our annual and unsuccessful venture into the world of prime-time programming. Jankowski was hoping that CBS News would deliver another *60 Minutes*. With its high ratings and its modest production costs, which were less than half the cost of an entertainment show, *60 Minutes* was a major contributor to the profit picture for the television network.

Ironically, as we were planning our new prime-time venture, *CBS Reports* was working on a documentary whose subject was prime-time television, "Don't Touch That Dial," which was scheduled for broadcast near the end of 1983. Morley Safer was the correspondent and he was also writing the script. I've always enjoyed Safer's writing and I was looking forward to screening the first rough cut. Most good television writing is made up of simple declarative sentences. Safer manages to go a step beyond that with the occasional grace note of wit or irony. Most of his *60 Minutes* work these days falls into the category of "Style." If there is a story scheduled on the new fall fashion line in Paris, it's quickly earmarked by the *60 Minutes* production staff as a Safer story.

When *60 Minutes* profiled the hit show of syndicated television, *Wheel of Fortune,* Safer was assigned to do the story and he introduced its host, Pat Sajak, as "a walking, talking loaf of Wonder Bread." It's hard at times to remember that this middle-aged dandy with his polka-dot ties and English candy-stripe shirts was one of television's world-class war correspondents.

Safer came to CBS News in 1964 from the Canadian Broadcasting System, for whom he'd covered the Algerian Revolution. Initially he was based in London, but in 1965 he was sent to cover the war in Vietnam. His story of American marines burning the hutches of the village of Cam Ne shocked American television viewers. The sight of young marines using cigarette lighters to ignite thatched roofs, sending old people and children running from their homes in terror, is one of those powerful images a generation of Americans will never be able to erase. In 1970 Safer was brought back from London to replace Harry Reasoner on *60 Minutes* when Reasoner left CBS News for his ill-fated stint as anchorman for ABC's nightly news broadcast.

When the time came to see "Don't Touch That Dial," Morley joined me in the screening room. He was obviously pleased with the way the hour turned out. He had reason to be. The broadcast presented a parade of the network moguls and the producers with their own descriptions of their work and their value system. A sardonic script from Safer made it clear the state of prime-time television was not likely to improve. The most important glimmer of truth about television came during Safer's interview with Bud Grant, the President of the CBS Entertainment Division. Grant is one of those people with no flat surfaces. Everything about him is round. As he talked to Safer, he didn't seem to sit at his desk so much as float alongside it, as if he'd been brought in and inflated just for the interview. The camera moved from a wide shot to a close-up and then pulled back to a medium close-up. Grant seemed to expand and diminish as though controlled by some pneumatic process. Even his answers to questions had that elasticity.

"In the entertainment area, what is the program you feel most proud of?" Morley asked.

Grant's eyes didn't blink.

"Dallas," he said.

Morley's face took on the expression peculiar to television interviewers who think they've caused some poor dolt to commit indecent exposure of his intellect.

"Why?" he asked.

"It's the highest-rated television series in the history of television," Grant said, and swiveled an arm toward an expensively mounted set of numbers on his desk.

"That little plaque over there on the desk says 53.3. That was the rating it got for the 'Who Shot J.R.?' episode. I'm very proud that we gave so many people so much pleasure."

In the darkened screening room I could hear Morley chuckling to himself. It was obvious he thought he'd revealed for the world the philistine tastes which governed prime-time television. I laughed right along with him. We both missed the point. Grant would have no difficulty elasticizing that same answer around a Luciano Pavarotti concert or a telecast of the annual Fort Worth, Texas, Fat Stock Show if it delivered a 53.3 rating. It wasn't that he represented bad taste. He represented no taste at all. It was just numbers, and in that he was the ideal representative for his CBS bosses in New York. Success was not to be measured by any of that "Golden Age of Television" stuff. There was only one measure that counted. A plaque with the numbers 53.3.

Later that day I discussed the broadcast with Van.

"They're in trouble out there," I said, referring to the Entertainment Division. "They've got a handful of producer-suppliers who keep recycling the same old crap. No wonder people are watching less and less network television."

"They don't think they're in trouble," Van said.

"They don't produce a damn thing," I answered. "They buy it all from outside production companies."

"They don't see themselves as producers. They see themselves as programmers."

"That's why they're in trouble," I said. "We're really the only big production center CBS has. They should be begging us to produce more hours for them."

"They don't buy that," Van said. "They think *60 Minutes* was a fluke, and besides, they think we're arrogant and don't play the game."

"Arrogant I can understand, but what is this game they think we should play?"

"If they accept a pilot from Lorimar they can bring in some focus groups to look at it. Then they go back to Lorimar and say the part of the cop's girlfriend should be played by some other actress, someone with more vulnerability, or the opening scene lacks tension and needs more 'heat.' They know that if they said that to CBS News the response would be to fuck off."

"So why are we about to bust our ass on a summer run opposite *The A-Team* in a time period which has become a lime pit for decomposing sitcoms?"

Van began to laugh.

"It's madness, isn't it? Sheer fucking madness. But if we can deliver a share of audience that shows some potential for growth, Jankowski will see it as a way to program prime time more economically and Bud Grant and Harvey Shepherd will have to accept it."

"Why is it," I asked, "that I don't think permanent residence in Harvey Shepherd's House of Hits involves 'Harvest of Shame' as a reference point?"

"It's because you're a man of keen insights. Well, Eduardo, what do you think?"

"I think I'm too fine a person for this line of work, but let's get at it."

I was actually eager to get at it. By now I was beginning to share some of Van's appetite for an opportunity in prime time.

The next day we both met with Bill Moyers. It was a brief meeting because Bill was working on a commentary for that night's *Evening News* broadcast. Bill seemed enthusiastic about attempting a prime-time venture. He'd come to CBS News, he said, hoping for the opportunity to do *Bill Moyer's Journal,* a broadcast he'd done for PBS. But if he was being asked to share an hour with Kuralt, he'd be willing.

In the afternoon I met alone with Charles Kuralt in my office. I talked about the opportunity we were being given to stake a claim for CBS News on another hour of prime time. And I told him that Bill Moyers was very enthusiastic about working with him.

"I think Bill Moyers is a truly fine fellow," he said. "I think I'd probably watch just about anything he did on television. So I have no doubt this will be a splendid hour."

I began to relax. His reaction to Moyers was encouraging, but only for the moment.

"So I wouldn't want you to think that I have anything other than great respect for Bill," he continued. "But I don't see myself doing an hour broadcast with anybody. It's just not something I'd feel comfortable doing."

Kuralt looked down at the floor. He didn't pause. He just stopped talking. There was an awkward silence. Then I asked what seemed like a logical question.

"What sort of broadcast would you feel comfortable doing?"

"Well," he said, "I'd really like to do *On the Road,* the kind of stories I'm doing on the *Evening News.* I've done some *On the Road* specials and they've been well received. I think it would be just fine to do some of those."

For several days I tried to convince Kuralt that his *On the Road* stories could be incorporated in an hour broadcast shared with Moyers and that our best chance for success would come from their pairing. To my disappointment, he wouldn't budge. Jankowski believed we had the two of them lined up as a team. If we couldn't put this in place quickly, we'd have to tell him CBS News would be unable to accept the hour. In the tradition of King Solomon, we cut the hour in two. The first half hour at 8 P.M. would be *On the Road* with Charles Kuralt; the second half hour at 8:30 would be a Bill Moyers broadcast. Van and I together fashioned that compromise and I headed off to see Moyers. This time it was Bill who balked.

"Part of what's wrong with television," he said, "is that everything is squeezed into the shortest possible form. Give me a history of the world in two minutes. I've had enough experience doing hour-long broadcasts to know how hard it is to fit everything into an hour. I just don't believe my kind of television can be done in a half-hour broadcast."

In desperation I turned to Andrew Lack, who was scheduled to be the executive producer for the Moyers broadcast. Lack is in his middle thirties, with dark wavy hair combed straight back from his forehead and a chiseled nose so pronounced it's hard to remember him except in profile. Always attired in trendy clothes, he looks like the producer of television commercials he once was. He had done many award-winning documentaries with Bill Moyers, who was an announced admirer of his skills. I explained Bill's reservations to Andy.

1 8 3

"He's absolutely convinced he can't do worthwhile television in a half-hour broadcast. I know you don't feel that way. Can you meet with Bill and share some of your thoughts with him?"

"Absolutely, I can. Let me talk to him. I've been through this sort of thing with Bill before. He's always in a state of agonized uncertainty before he begins something. But it all disappears once he starts working."

A few days later Moyers called me.

"Andy and I have spent a lot of time together over the past few days discussing what we could do in a half-hour broadcast. He's convinced me that we can do good television. I have some worries, but if you and Van still want me to do this, I'm willing to give it a try."

After assuring Bill that we did indeed want him to do this, I hung up and called Van with the good news.

"That's marvelous," he said, "absolutely marvelous news. I should call Jankowski and tell him CBS News is all set to produce the Tuesday night hour."

Then almost as an afterthought, he added, "Why don't you set up a meeting in a few days for the two of us with Bill and Andy. We should hear more specifically what they'd like to do in the way of stories. Let's make sure we're not producing a half hour for pointy-heads."

I must have been tired from my rounds of shuttle diplomacy. Van's parting line didn't register and I was unprepared for the meeting which took place several days later.

I ushered Bill and Andy into Van's office and our meeting began innocuously enough. Van had recently hired a decorator to "dress the place up." In one corner there was a painted wooden parrot on a stand. Against a wall, a very old barber chair. Van worked at an old oak farm table but had a large rolltop desk against the wall behind him. There were also ornaments he'd moved from office to office. The framed text of the deranged anchorman Howard Beale's denunciation of television from Paddy Chayefsky's movie *Network:* "Television is not the truth. If you want the truth, go to God, go to your guru, go to yourself." High on another wall catching the light and dominating the room was a large work of stained glass showing a two-dollar bill which read: "In Nielsen We Trust." After we'd all helped ourselves to cold Tabs from his refrigerator, Van turned to Andy.

"Well, big guy," he said. "It's all in your hands. What have you got for us?"

"You know we want to call the broadcast *Our Times with Bill Moyers?*"

"Great title. I like it."

"How about the opening? Have you seen the cassette of the new opening I produced with the music? I gave a copy to Ed."

"He showed it to me," Van said. "The title is good. The opening is dynamite. The music is exceptional. But now you've got twenty-seven minutes to go."

"Don't worry," Moyers said. "Andy and I have some good stories working."

Together he and Andy outlined their ideas. A visit to Los Alamos, New Mexico, and a look at the moral problems troubling people who built atomic weapons there. Whistle blowers in the Pentagon, the permanently unemployed in Gadsden, Alabama, an examination of growing problems in the Philippines. I could see Van's spirits sinking. He'd been given a chance to program an hour of prime time and he obviously didn't think what he was hearing had a chance at earning a permanent place in the evening schedule. Then Lack mentioned another story they were working on which dealt with the changing meaning of marital commitment in America. It would focus on Silicon Valley, where divorce ranked just behind computers as the second-largest industry.

"That story should go in the first broadcast," Van said.

Moyers looked quickly at Lack.

"Andy and I both think Los Alamos should be our first story. Let viewers see that we're willing to deal with a significant issue in a half-hour broadcast."

"Remember," Andy said, "they will have just seen a very pleasant half hour of *On the Road* stories."

"Let me play the whore," Van responded, "and urge you two to think in terms of stories which will strike some spark of general interest."

Moyers looked away and Van continued to press for stories with a broad-based appeal. His argument continued to be interspersed with that strange request to "let me play the whore." Moyers began to stare at the floor. I watched him glance at Van, look at the stained-glass piece with its slogan, "In Nielsen We Trust," and then begin to study the floor again.

Fortunately, the lawyers had arrived for a meeting on the Westmoreland suit and we broke off the meeting. In the few minutes Van and I were alone waiting for the lawyers to come in, I stood up and walked about his office. Then I placed both hands on the edge of his desk and leaned toward him.

"You and I made a pact not to argue in front of other people here. You need to know that I was adhering to that this morning. When you buy into Bill Moyers for a prime-time hour you're not Bud Grant who can test story lines in front of focus groups. All you can do is say to Bill, 'Here's a half hour,' and trust him to do something of merit."

Van slumped back in his chair and opened another Tab.

"I hear you," he said.

Later that day Bill Moyers asked to see me. When he arrived he was obviously shaken by the meeting and uncertain about its implications for his new broadcast.

"Ed," he said, "I never thought the day would come when I would hear a President of CBS News say, 'Let me play the whore.'"

I thought for a moment before I answered. I knew the meeting that morning was disastrous. But I had become enthusiastic about these two half-hour broadcasts. If Bill became disenchanted and decided not to go ahead, then all the rest of us would be losing an important opportunity.

"Bill," I said, "Van very much wants a success for CBS News in prime time. He wants the best of two worlds. Good journalism and popular television. He knows the television network will never keep us in their schedule if we don't deliver at least a respectable rating. I happen to think we will. He was just agonizing out loud. Why don't you write off some of what he said as rhetorical overkill. You and Andy should simply go to work and deliver the best broadcasts you can possibly produce. I don't know any other way to go about it."

Whatever I said that afternoon worked. Bill left my office and he and Andy began to work on *Our Times*. I was becoming increasingly excited about these new broadcasts. And if they turned out to be successful it couldn't be coming at a better time for CBS News. They would represent not only a source of pride but a financial bright spot in a year which was appearing to have dismal prospects.

The year 1983 was starting off on a sour economic note.

T om Wyman had assured "the financial community" that 1983 would be the "turnaround" year for CBS. He'd asserted that the stock would earn $7 a share.

In order to accomplish that, the CBS Broadcast Group constructed a budget for 1983 which reflected optimistic sales projections and across-the-board cost reductions. CBS News was given a budget increase in 1983 of under 10 percent. The projected 1983 inflation rate was 9 percent. It made for an interesting challenge, because in that same year the number of broadcast hours was expanded by 70 percent. This increase in hours came primarily from the expansion of the *Morning News, Nightwatch,* and the ten prime-time hours with Kuralt and Moyers, which created an additional 1,440 program hours for the year.

By now we believed we had an accurate fix on what was required to run an efficient CBS News. When coverage of the crises in the Falklands and Lebanon sent news costs soaring, we controlled costs elsewhere to pay for that coverage. We held down bureau costs, instituted a job freeze to reduce the staff from 1,568 in September 1982 to 1,503 by March 1983. This generated a savings of several million dollars and we ended the year without running over our budget. It would be more difficult in 1983 but we believed we'd be able to stay within budget.

Van was away one day in early February 1983, and I replaced him at Jankowski's Wednesday staff meeting. Besides Van it was normally attended by Jankowski's two Executive Vice Presidents, Tom Leahy and Jim

Rosenfield, and by his Vice President for Finance, Tim Reynolds. Later in the day Van called and asked how the meeting had gone.

"I think I'm getting paranoid," I said. "Jankowski kept talking about runaway costs and looking at me."

"What did you tell him?"

"I reminded him that you and I have installed a new financial system and that, for the first time in its history, CBS News has weekly cost reports for each broadcast, for each bureau, and for all satellite and line costs, and that we're managing to stay within a very tight budget."

"Good for you."

"I'm not sure I got through. Gene's beginning to act like CBS News is his personal Moby Dick on a sea of red ink."

"I think Reynolds is feeding him that line," Van said, "and he's getting it from the numbers crunchers at the television network."

"It's really great," I said. "Your boss acts like you're pissing money away and the people here are acting like Christmas just got canceled."

"I wouldn't worry about it," Van said. "We're in good shape. Gene just wants to be sure he can keep sending golden reports to Wyman. I'll take his temperature when I get back tomorrow. I'll see you in the morning."

I was still fuming when I hung up the phone. I honestly felt that all of the elements of a news budget which can so quickly run out of control were being carefully monitored and kept in check. My description of the reaction within CBS News to this financial scrutiny hadn't been over-stated. And not just among the rank and file. Some of our own executives, Lane and Chandler among them, didn't seem to realize how big CBS News had become in the past few years. How many more hours of broadcast time we filled, how many more crews we now had in the field, how expensive the new era of videotape and satellite feeds had become. More significantly, there seemed to be no understanding anywhere at CBS of the impact of escalating salaries now being paid in network television news. Not just the CBS News millionaire's club of Rather, Hewitt, Cronkite, Wallace, and Moyers, but the huge increases which were routinely asked for by and given to a variety of correspondents, producers, and directors. The escalation began during the time of the ABC and NBC raids on CBS News in the late seventies. Bill Leonard had learned what I would discover for myself. When the morning paper runs a story about someone from CBS News joining the competition, don't expect a phone call from Black Rock saying, "I know it's tough, but hang in there."

In that climate the agents went into a feeding frenzy. They closed contract after contract containing concessions and salaries which were granted in order to head off yet another public announcement of a raid on CBS News. Each time this happened it created a ripple effect. No contract remained a secret, since almost all of them were negotiated by a small handful of agents. Richard Leibner alone represented one hundred and forty people at CBS News, including producers, directors, and such star correspondents as Dan Rather, Mike Wallace, Ed Bradley, Morley Safer, and Diane Sawyer. Each salary escalation became the floor for the next negotiation for other clients in similar jobs.

If I was impatient with Jankowski it was because I thought he of all people should recognize the difficulty of what had been accomplished at CBS News. We had put in place a new financial order. After all, at one time he'd been the controller for all of CBS. I assumed that Van was right, that Gene was feeling pressure to impress Wyman with the strength and solidity of the broadcast group under his leadership. If Wyman had told Wall Street that 1983 was turnaround time, then Gene would be determined to present him with figures which reflected that optimism.

Not very many weeks into the new year whispers began describing "a market misjudgment." Network sales executives use that phrase the same way the FAA terms an airline crash killing three hundred passengers a "pilot error."

When Wyman had pressured Jankowski for greater profits from the Broadcast Group, he in turn began to pressure CBS News to reduce its costs. At the same time he turned to Jim Rosenfield, his Executive Vice President in charge of the television network, and asked him to increase his forecast for sales revenues. Dutifully Rosenfield hiked the prices charged for commercial time. And Rosenfield made another key decision. CBS refused to give advertisers the demographic guarantees which all three networks routinely provided. In late 1982 and into 1983 the advertising marketplace softened and CBS found itself with more unsold time than either NBC or ABC. Frantically CBS began to slash prices, but it was too late.

In the first quarter of the year, the Broadcast Group took a 45 percent plunge in operating profits. Jankowski's financial staff urged him to make across-the-board cuts to compensate for the lost revenue. The more cuts he could make, the smaller the problem he would have to take to Wyman. He asked CBS News to trim $7 million in costs from the remaining months of our 1983 budget. It was obvious Gene was facing extraordinary problems and we set out to make the cuts.

There are times when it's possible to comb a large budget line by line and make reductions no one really sees. This was not such a time. Whatever we did would be visible. In a phone call Van and I explained this to Gene, who was staggering under his load of problems. His response to us was: "Everyone has to help solve this problem, including CBS News."

In the next few weeks CBS News closed or diminished bureaus in Bonn, Hong Kong, and Cairo. A dozen people were laid off.

The number of prime-time documentaries for 1983 was reduced to seven from fifteen the previous year. We produced the $7 million for Jankowski, and compared to what was to come a few years later, it was minor surgery. But for CBS News this was the first encounter with the financial scalpel and it was a demoralizing one. John Lane was particularly dispirited. Ed Fouhy had left to join ABC News as Washington Bureau chief and John was now the Vice President for News Coverage. The burden of notifying the people in bureaus being closed or reduced fell on John and he was in agony. He was concerned, for example, about Mr. Ping in the Hong Kong Bureau.

"This guy has given his life to CBS News," he said, "and we're about to throw him to the wolves."

"Do we have any free-lance work?"

"He's a driver who goes back and forth to the airport to make pickups and deliveries. All during the Vietnam War we shipped film into Hong Kong and we never missed a deadline, thanks to Ping."

"Maybe we can throw him some per diem work," I repeated.

"We shouldn't be doing this in the first place."

I bristled at that. "Do you think I'm enjoying this?" I said. Then remembering a television commercial which was running that year, I added, "Your problem is, you'll sell no whine before its time."

John just shook his head.

"Maybe my problem is I know all these people."

I was unfair to John that day. He was not alone in having difficulties adjusting to the realities of this new era.

I muttered something about "getting our ongoing costs under control so we could avoid this kind of calamity in the future." I really did believe that CBS News couldn't expect to be totally exempt from the problems which affected the parent company. If our own financial house was in order, I thought we'd have the kind of credibility we were obviously going to need in the Wyman era. If Jankowski was reacting nervously to pressures from Wyman, I felt he was still a man of decent instincts who believed in the importance of CBS News.

Within weeks of these painful cutbacks Jankowski began to learn the full extent of the "market misjudgment." The problem extended far beyond the first quarter of 1983. It was now obvious that the second and third quarters of the year would be equally disastrous. Jim Rosenfield still held out hope for the fourth quarter. Would it improve? "Dynamite" was the word he used to describe it to the trade press, particularly, he said, in automotive and packaged-goods sales. No one believed him. To make matters worse the Television Stations Division, the traditional "cash cow" for the Broadcast Group, was having its own problems because of softness in the national spot advertising market. Our house presented a dismal picture.

Vince Loncto was the Vice President for Finance for CBS News. He asked to see both Van and me because he was worried about what he was hearing from his counterparts at Black Rock.

"Gene is relying completely on the financial staff of the television network and I'm worried that they're setting us up," he said. "They're nervous about their shortfall in sales and worried that they might have to cut the Entertainment Division's budget for new pilots."

"I'm sure they are," Van said, "but that's not a setup for CBS News."

"They've started requesting a lot of financial information from my people," Vince said. "They're talking about a profitability study for all CBS News programs."

"What are they up to?" I asked.

"This mess has got a lot of people frightened," he said. "I think they're going to try and build a case that this could all be solved if CBS News trimmed fat."

I began to steam. "For the first time we've got the costs here under control and these yahoos are trying to hang a mismanagement rap on us."

Vince began to join my fulminating but Van jumped in.

"Guys . . . Jankowski is no fool. He knows what a bad situation he had at CBS News. He's not going to let it go down the drain because some wretched MBA asks for a profitability study."

A week later he wasn't so sure. Tim Reynolds, Jankowski's financial officer, informed CBS News it would be expected to make whatever cuts and reductions were required to achieve a net savings of $25 million in the nine months which remained in the 1983 budget year.

Even then, our first reaction was that this was just a probe, an attempt to see what other reductions we might be able to come up with. We were still convinced that Gene would not risk the success CBS News was now enjoying. *The CBS Evening News* not only was leading ABC and NBC by a substantial margin in the ratings but was the only one of the three network news broadcasts to actually show an increase in ratings over 1982. The *Morning News* was up 27 percent from the previous year. *60 Minutes* remained in the top ten. We were about to embark on a new venture with Moyers and Kuralt. Surely no one would jeopardize this new prosperity. But as the days passed, the question from Black Rock was not "Can it be done?" but "How soon can it be done?" Even more worrisome, a great deal of press attention had been focused on our most recent cutbacks and bureau closings and word filtered back to us from Black Rock that Wyman thought the press coverage of the cutbacks was "great." As a result of these stories, the word on Wall Street was that "Wyman must be serious about cost control if he's touching CBS News."

Once a week Van attended a Jankowski staff meeting along with Leahy and Rosenfield.

He'd just come back from one of these meetings when he opened the door of my office. He sank into a large chair with a can of cold Tab in his hand.

"Gene's really serious about these cuts," he said.

"Does he know what he's asking us to do?"

"He thinks we've got a huge budget in a year when inflation has dropped to 9 percent."

"Loncto just brought me some stuff on that," I said. "We have large bureaus in countries with high inflation. London is 16.4. Peking is 18.8. How about Tel Aviv? They have an inflation rate of 59.1 percent. We're in the business of moving correspondents and crews around the world. I don't see the airlines and hotels dropping their prices."

"Eduardo, he doesn't want to hear any of that. Did Loncto complete the contingency plan for a $25 million cut?"

"He sure did and it's gruesome."

The list included the closing of three more bureaus, taking more than $1.5 million out of the special-events budget, and the cancellation of *Nightwatch, Sunday Morning,* and the second hour of the *Morning News.* Two hundred thirty-eight people would be laid off.

Van looked at the list.

"I forgot to give you one more headline. We've got to come up with the $25 million without eliminating any regularly scheduled broadcast."

"Brilliant," I said. "We can close more bureaus, shut down special-events coverage, and eliminate all documentaries. Maybe we can subscribe to CNN to pick up all those stories we won't be covering."

Van looked weary. "I'm on overload," he said. "Let's get out of here. Tomorrow we'll see where we go from here."

The next morning Ralph Goldberg came into my office. Van had recently hired Goldberg as a Vice President and special assistant. He'd been the number three man in the CBS Law Department. He'd counseled Frank Stanton through difficult days, including the controversial era of "The Selling of the Pentagon."

"Good morning, counselor," I said.

Goldberg furrowed the forehead of a very bald head and adjusted his glasses as he scrutinized me.

"You don't look as though you've been getting enough sleep."

"A condition you would share if you were aware of the idiotic forces now unleashed in our company."

Goldberg turned and addressed the wall.

"What my client is trying to say, your honor, is that he is involved in a budget dispute with his management."

"I wish it was as simple as that."

"Why don't you tell me about it."

I laid out the full problem for him.

"I really have the sense," I said, after describing what we were faced with, "that we're going to wake up and find we've made cuts and Gene will have avoided a problem with Wyman. But by then we will have done so much damage to CBS News we won't be able to fix it."

"How does Van feel?"

"Van is really torn by this but he doesn't see any alternative."

Ralph asked a crucial question.

"Is this why you guys came to CBS News? Was it to be a part of something like this?"

The next afternoon Ralph and I took Van to the Empire Diner on Twenty-second Street and Tenth Avenue in Chelsea. In the afternoon lull we sat in a corner booth and ordered three Tabs. I asked Ralph to tell his Lloyd Cutler story. Cutler is a distinguished attorney in Washington who, according to Ralph, had once prepared for Paley an analysis of CBS. In that report, as Ralph described it, Cutler described CBS News as the "Crown Jewel" of CBS. It was what set CBS apart and made it different from just another American corporation.

"They're losing sight of that," I said. "They're so enmeshed in that business school stuff about protecting the profit they don't realize what they're doing."

Van groaned and leaned back in the booth, staring toward the Empire's Art Deco counter.

"What do we do?" he asked.

I thought for a moment and then plunged ahead.

"We have to find a way to get through to Gene. Maybe he's buying bad advice. As respectfully as possible we tell him we can't do this . . . and we'll tell him why. We tell him we aren't saying we can't cut costs. With the system we have in place we can make adjustments over some sensible time frame. But cutting $25 million out of what's left of this year's budget would mean doing things to CBS News that are just not acceptable. And we give him the Lloyd Cutler line."

Two memos were delivered to Jankowski. The first, on March 30, 1983, was from Van and it outlined the steps CBS News would have to take to save $25 million in costs in 1983. The steps included eliminating some existing broadcasts.

The second memo was delivered the next day. It was a joint memo from Van Gordon Sauter and Edward M. Joyce. It was three pages long and included in blunt language the charge that "in the face of a crisis unrelated to the performance of the News Division, there seems a sudden conviction that CBS News is somehow a culprit, a profligate, and that radical immediate action is required to correct a larger problem.

"Long before either you or we had our present jobs, we all recognized that CBS News was a very special part of the Corporation. That has been the view expressed by Mr. Paley, Dr. Stanton, Mr. Wyman, and you.

"Corporations . . . like other institutions in our society . . . live by symbols. Throughout its distinguished history, CBS News has always been associated with excellence. Over the past decades, the News Division has provided a unique service to this company. Indeed to the country. It is the best broadcast news organization in the world. In large part the positive public image of CBS is attributable, in our view, to CBS News's contribution over the years. We cannot take credit for it. We inherited it.

"But that excellence reflects the efforts of countless men and women who went about their journalistic business literally without fear or favor. In large part that independence was made possible by the willingness of the Corporation to support that independence. On the financial side, it manifested itself by a long willingness to support programming deserved to be seen by the public even though unprofitable. More symbolically (but also with significant financial ramifications) it involved resisting inappropriate external pressures from advertisers, affiliates, senators, congress-men, and even Presidents.

"If there are crucial, long-term problems, they should be worked out over a reasonable, reflective period of time, and not subjected to the narrow passions of a short-term solution.

"This organization is too vital to CBS and to the public for that form of problem-solving.

"The reductions in front of us would severely damage our journalism and the loyalty of our employees. It would repudiate our past and jeopar-dize our future. The discussions over the past few weeks strike us as critical for CBS News.

"We don't believe, Gene, that all elements within this Corporation are 'equal.' Some are more than 'equal.' Let us agree that CBS News must be considered special and must be protected."

We sent Jankowski the two separate memos on successive days to make sure he fully understood the draconian implications of his cutback request before learning that the two senior officers of his News Division were saying no. We waited for his reaction. He could fire us, he could acknowl-edge we might have pointed out some factors he hadn't considered, but he would have to do something. Which is precisely what he didn't do. At least not on the surface. About a week later Loncto got a phone call from Gene's financial guy, Tim Reynolds, asking for our timetable on the cutbacks. Jankowski was doing to us what Kennedy had done to Khru-shchev during the Bay of Pigs crisis. Khrushchev had sent him two com-muniqués. The second was demanding and belligerent. The White House ignored the second and responded to the first, which became the basis for a settlement. Reynolds came back a few days later with a revised cutback figure of $12 million. In early April we responded by advising Reynolds we had identified $7 million in possible cuts, which included over $1.5 million from the ill-fated *Nightwatch,* reducing future coverage of the space shuttle, and the delay of three prime-time public-affairs hours until 1984, when they could be absorbed by the 1984 budget.

We were told by Reynolds that Jankowski would not accept this. By now Reynolds was our only channel of communication. We took no steps to make any cuts and weeks went by. Reynolds reminded us that the longer we delayed, the larger our cuts would have to be to reach the $12 million figure. This conflict became the talk of CBS News. Whatever becomes known within the institution quickly becomes public. As press inquiries flowed in, Van began to hold off-the-record backgrounder conversations with reporters. It was the kind of story they love to run with, and it began to acquire a life of its own as "the rebellion of CBS News." As the story grew, it first had Van, then both of us, threatening to resign. I asked Van about the stories.

"Are you telling reporters we're threatening to resign?"

He looked a little abashed.

"When you send a memo to your boss telling him you won't do what he's ordered you to do, it's the same thing."

"Maybe you're right," I said, "but I'm still hoping Gene will come to his senses."

It took a papal intervention to make that happen.

The cuts we'd made earlier in the year had taken $7 million out of our budget. We said no to $25 million more and were saying the same to a demand of $12 million, but even if Jankowski relented, there was no doubt CBS News would be making do with less before 1983 was over. I was constantly being asked to find money for some special project— sending Kurtis or Sawyer on a special assignment, agreeing to purchase videotape shot by a free-lance crew which had gone into Afghanistan. Each time I'd sit down with Loncto and we would move money from one budget line to another. I began to worry I was going to become eligible for the kind of eulogy given a Texas legislator: "His books did not balance, but his heart always beat warmly for his native land."

Then Pope John Paul II scheduled a second return to Poland. This promised to be a story of significance. Coming on the heels of martial law, he would arrive at a time of renewed tension between the Church and the Communist state. The very future of the outlawed Solidarity party and its leader, Lech Walesa, would be influenced by this trip. Joan Richman reported that NBC was making a very large commitment to the story. By some accounts they ended up spending $1.5 million to put between seventy-five and eighty people in the field. They used Tom Brokaw to anchor their *Nightly News* live from Poland. ABC put about sixty people in the field and used Peter Jennings to anchor their *World News Tonight* from Poland. Joan was burning with competitive zeal. She'd just returned from a survey trip to the various cities and towns the Pope would visit. She had inspired ideas for coverage and a budget proposal of $1 million. Van looked at me and sighed, then turned to Joan.

"Come back with a smaller budget," he said.

Joan looked as though Van must have misunderstood.

"There's no way Rather can anchor his broadcast from Poland if I cut this," she said. "With this plan I cannot only have Rather in Warsaw, where Brokaw and Jennings will anchor, but also move him to Gdansk and Czestochowa, where the Pope will visit the Shrine of the Black Madonna."

"Joan," I said, "we'd need our own miracle to make that happen. Come back with a smaller budget."

A couple of days later she returned with a budget for just under $700,000, accompanied by a memo which said her new budget would create "an unacceptable risk."

By then we'd reached the $12 million impasse with Jankowski and we asked her to reduce the scope of her coverage. A dispirited Joan Richman finally came back with the plan we accepted. It would cost just under $600,000. We would put thirty persons in the field and Dan Rather alone of the three network anchors would stay home. We would be unable to do specials unless there was an assassination and if that tragedy occurred we would not be competitively staffed.

After the *Evening News* I sat alone with Van in his office.

"Life does strange twists," I said. "I'm here at least in part because I was successful in Chicago. And much of that success came because I made a decision to invest in the arrival of this Pope. I know it sounds funny but I've always thought of him as 'my lucky Pope.' Maybe we should cover this story the way we think we should and deal with the problem later."

"Look, Jankowski is staring at a $100 million shortfall," Van said. "We've told him no on his new cuts. If we add to that by blowing our budget there'll really be a shit storm."

Van sent Gene a memo telling him that because of the cuts we'd made earlier in the year the only alternative to exceeding our budget was to scale down CBS News coverage of the papal trip to Poland. The memo spelled out the disparity which would exist between ourselves and the two other networks. For the first time since arriving at CBS News we were consciously not competitive on a major story. Part of me hoped no one would notice . . . that we'd be able to skate by. The other part wanted it to be so obvious that Jankowski and Wyman would realize there were considerations which sometimes transcended the bottom line.

On the morning of Thursday, June 16, 1983, the wheels of the big jet carrying Pope John Paul II touched the ground of the Warsaw airport. I sat in my office watching all three monitors. NBC interrupted for live coverage. So did ABC. On CBS, Bob Barker of *The Price Is Right* told contestants to "come on down." The atmosphere in the newsroom was tense. It's one thing to be beaten on a story, but when the planning of a major event commits you to third place, it really hurts.

Before the day was over, affiliates, particularly from cities with large

Catholic populations, were burning the phone lines to New York wanting to know what the hell had happened to CBS News. My executive phone rang. It was Jim Rosenfield, who'd taken a number of those calls.

"Why weren't we on the air, too?"

"Because our handful of people in Poland are spread out covering this story for the *Evening News* and the *Morning News*," I said.

"I don't understand," Rosenfield said.

"Jim, I suggest you ask Mr. Jankowski."

I phoned Van to tell him about Rosenfield's call.

"They must really be taking a lot of flak from affiliates," he said. "I'm glad I sent Jankowski that memo. They can't claim they didn't know about this."

"Have you talked to Rather?" I asked. "How is he feeling about all this?"

"He's O.K.," Van said. "He knows this is a high-stakes fight. There's no doubt he wants us to win, but he's obviously going to stay out of it."

A few days later, the headline story on the front page of *Variety* read: "Budget Cuts Crunch CBS News—Wall St. Priority vs. Pope's Trip."

It spelled out the details of the "market misjudgment" which had plagued CBS, the Wyman promises to Wall Street, and the cuts in the CBS News budget. In the article Jankowski denied that he ordered any specific cuts in the Poland coverage.

"It never happened," he said. "I would never get involved in the budget for a news story."

The same morning the *Variety* article appeared both Van and I were summoned to Jankowski's office. It's a corner office on the thirty-fourth floor of Black Rock with windows which look west to the Hudson River and north to the executive offices of ABC. We arrived and were greeted by both of his secretaries. Normally you can count on a hearty greeting from Gene. He even answers his executive line with a wagonmaster's "Yo!!!" There was no such greeting this time.

"Come in, guys. Close the door."

Before we could even take seats he got to the point.

"We've got to declare a truce and stop this public war."

Then he spelled out the terms of the armistice. He was willing to rescind the $12 million cut, but he added, "You've got to come up with something."

"That's never been the issue," I said. "We can't destroy the place in the process."

"What do we do to stop this negative press?" he asked.

"I don't know where that's coming from," Van said.

Gene was skeptical. "It has to be coming from you guys."

"Gene, this has been going on for months," Van said. "Everyone in the News Division is aware of it. It was inevitable that it would become a public debate."

Gene asked for a strongly worded statement from Van that the news-gathering capabilities of CBS News had not been compromised. Van agreed. One of us suggested that Gene come to CBS News, meet with a group of senior people, and express his commitment to the welfare and continued excellence of CBS News.

"If you think that will stop the naysayers and we can get this story out of the press, I'll do it. There's one thing I want to say to you both, though. I don't agree with something in the memo you both sent me . . . the part where you say that CBS News must be considered special, that some elements are more than equal. CBS News can't expect to be treated differently from the other divisions, from Sports or Stations."

"Gene," I said, "let me tell you what Lloyd Cutler told Paley in an analysis he prepared for Paley on this company. He told Paley it was CBS News which made it more than just another corporation. He told him CBS News was the Crown Jewel."

The next morning, Gene joined a number of us in conference room 2-E-6 on the second floor of the Broadcast Center. We had brought together about twenty key people from CBS News, including executives, producers, and correspondents. Gene was terribly tense as the meeting began. I sat next to him and I could see him gripping his hands around both armrests of his chair as he began to speak. He told the group that there would be no further cuts in the CBS News budget. Then he told them that CBS News was the "jewel in the crown of CBS."

Dan Rather, who had been a silent bystander during the months of confrontation, closed the meeting with his own benediction for Gene.

"That's very good news you've brought us today," he said. "Gene, know this . . . CBS News was with Gene Jankowski yesterday. CBS News is with Gene Jankowski today. And CBS News will be with Gene Jankowski tomorrow."

In the aftermath of what had become months of obsessive confrontation, it was difficult to sort out the pieces and see what remained. My old boss Tom Leahy remarked at lunch one day, "If you guys went after me in public like you did Gene, I'd get you. I don't know when or how I'd do it, but I'd get you."

I knew Tom well enough to know he'd find a way. I also knew we would have talked it through long before it reached a point of public confrontation.

"Gene wouldn't listen," I said. "We couldn't even get to him with our arguments."

If either of us had expected thanks from within CBS News for averting a bloodletting, we would have been greatly disappointed. With a few exceptions most people were still angry about the financial restraints they were now living with or still upset about the cutbacks which had taken place earlier in the year.

I thought I'd seen something in Van which I'd never noticed before. A resolve which was impressive. It was easy to have doubts about him, to become impatient with his compulsion to swan for the press. But in a situation which risked his own ambitions, he'd been willing to fight.

I asked him one day, "Did you notice that the 'keepers of the flame' stayed firmly on the sidelines while you and I put our jobs on the line over the cutbacks?"

He shrugged. "I'm afraid they think we're two sharks from the television stations who've been putting the financial screws to them. If we got a taste of our own medicine, then tough shit."

Van's
description of the reaction by some of the people at CBS News was undoubtedly close to the mark.

I hated hearing it, but I had to admit he was probably right. As successful as CBS News had now become, we were both still outsiders to those who'd spent their professional lives there. Even worse, we'd each worked at CBS News and then left, to become successes at CBS television stations. The cost controls we'd instituted were proof of just how different we'd become. The fact that we could believe in the need for financial controls and still draw the line when we thought the welfare of CBS News was threatened didn't satisfy the skeptics. Even our own executive staff, including people such as John Lane and Bob Chandler, acted at times as if we were mutants who'd returned from some gamma-ray zone of commercial television. In the beginning I was amused by what had seemed to me an intrinsically tribal reaction. A wandering Navajo who returned to his reservation after years away and found himself forever known by the name "Lived with the Utes" might recognize the experience. I knew that Van's extravagances of conduct, particularly his statements to the press, fostered a portion of this reaction. But we'd both risked a great deal to protect CBS News and I was growing weary of an attitude I felt was not only smug but misplaced.

I was proud of the years I'd spent running successful television stations. And I was just as proud of the seven years I had been news director for WCBS-TV in New York. Surely that was a tenure record in one of the more difficult jobs in news management. As happened to me so often, becoming that station's news director was not something I sought or expected. In late 1970 I was an executive producer for special radio coverage at CBS News. I had just returned from Paris, where I had produced the CBS Radio coverage of the funeral of President Charles de Gaulle. Morley Safer, then based in London, anchored the reports. It was a job I enjoyed. I traveled a great deal but not so much that I shared the guilt feelings experienced by some of my colleagues who were never home. My personal and professional lives seemed nicely balanced. When I came back to the office from the Paris trip I started going through the mail, phone calls, and notes which had piled up during my absence. One call was from Bob Hosking, the new general manager of WCBS-TV, asking me to call when I got back. Hosking had been appointed a few weeks earlier and I'd sent him a note of congratulations. We'd known each other since 1959, when we both joined CBS Radio. During my time as that station's news director he had been its sales director.

I'd been happy when I learned of Bob's promotion and told him so in the note. After I answered a few letters I called him back. He immediately asked if I'd come to his office. I was curious enough to drop whatever else I was doing. His office was in the same part of the Broadcast Center in which I was located, so I was there in less than three minutes.

"Fast enough?" I asked.

"I'm so new here," he said, "I have no idea who else is in this building. I didn't realize you were this close, but I'm glad you are."

"How do you like your new job?" I asked.

"It'll be either great or a nightmare and right now I'm not so sure which. That's why I'd like to bounce some things off you."

I assumed that Bob had asked me there for my thoughts on how Channel 2 News was doing in their coverage of New York.

"Bounce away," I said.

"I have to replace the news director," he said, "and I offered the job to Bill Small, who accepted it."

My first reaction was: why is he telling me this? Bill Small was the Washington Bureau chief for CBS News.

"You've made a good choice," I said. "Small is a damned good newsman. But he's got a terrific job. Why does he want to make this move?"

"You're asking the right question. He felt he had no place to go from his current job. Then two days ago he changed his mind. Dick Salant convinced him his future was bright at CBS News, and he doesn't want to be news director after all."

"What are you going to do?" I asked.

"I'm desperate," he said. "This place is a zoo and I'm expected to fix it. What do I know about news? I've spent my life in sales. I want you to take the job, but I felt I had to tell you that you weren't the first choice. I wouldn't want you to learn that later from someone else."

"Bob, the last television station I worked for was WRGB-TV in Schenectady. I was a kid doing everything from writing news copy to emceeing children's shows. That was sixteen years ago."

Bob must have been desperate. He was determined to close this sale.

"I know what you can do," he said. "I knew you when you were a reporter and I watched you become a radio news director. You know how the city should be covered and you're a good manager . . . and there's one other thing."

My mind was whirling. I'd come prepared to offer a little free advice and now I was presented with an incredible career choice.

"This newsroom is out of control," he added. "A lot of people have gotten used to being their own boss and they're not going to welcome a firm hand. You won't be afraid to knock a few heads."

"Phrases like 'out of control' don't tell me much," I said. "Why hasn't your news director kept it under control?"

"I can't figure him out," Hosking said. "We're number three in the eleven o'clock ratings . . . number two and sinking fast at six o'clock. He just smiles and says not to worry."

Mike Keating had been the station's editorial director. Before moving to television he'd been an excellent reporter covering the state legislature for the New York *Herald Tribune*.

"What kind of people does he have around him?"

"He's brought in an odd bunch," he said. "They all talk about 'advocacy journalism.' It's like a guerrilla newsroom. Maybe they're great. I don't know and that's the problem. I do know the lawyers tell me a series they just produced contained scenes which appear to be staged and that scares the hell out of me."

"What does Keating say when you mention this?"

"I can't talk to the guy. There were terrible technical problems on last night's eleven o'clock news. I called Keating to ask him what happened and he told me not to call him at home . . . that he considered this private time."

Hosking looked at the expression on my face and began to giggle.

"See what I mean? It's a zoo."

Keating provided an explanation for this a few years later in his book *White Man/Black Man:*

There were television sets in my bedroom at home—one for CBS, one for NBC, and one for ABC. When the 11 o'clock news came on, I would watch the three sets simultaneously, making notes on the comparative performances for next day's analysis and smoking a joint. Within five minutes of the end of the broadcast the General Manager would call me to deliver his critique of the show and ask questions. Occasionally I would travel within on the weekend, discovering the marvels of myself and other dimensions of the world, a new perspective opened to me by LSD. I wanted to learn more, but there was little time. Isolation was needed for a good trip, and I had little of that.

Hosking gave Keating his opportunity for isolation. In December 1970, he removed him and named me as the station's news director. The description of the newsroom he had given me was not overblown. Keating had held his job for approximately eight months. In that time he'd brought in a coterie of people who had worked together in public television. My impression was that he had turned over the running of his newsroom to this group, who struck me as long on talk of revolutionizing television and short on everything else.

A few days after my arrival I discovered a plan to cancel that night's eleven o'clock news and in its place present a tribute to a civil rights leader. I canceled the cancellation and told them I thought presenting a coherent news broadcast was the prevailing obligation of our newsroom. I have no doubt this prompted numerous meetings of the revolutionary council, but by then I was beginning to identify members of the old guard in the newsroom. These were executives and producers who had been there before Keating's arrival as news director. It seemed to me they were the ones actually putting broadcasts on the air despite their resentment of their new supervisors. I chose to cast my lot with them. One by one I removed the members of the new cadre and reinstated the people I believed could build a strong newsroom.

Marty Haag, who is now dean of Southwestern news directors at WFFA-TV in Dallas, became my assistant news director. Tony Hatch, who is now an executive with the Times Mirror Corporation in Los Angeles, would soon begin assembling a team of producers for the *Eye on New York* unit, which over the next few years would produce a series of award-winning documentaries. The smartest move I made was to recognize the abilities of a young producer who was also the pugnacious shop steward for the Writers Guild, the union which represented writers, editors, assistant producers, and producers in our newsroom. Eric Ober had come to the station not long after graduating from Yale. He'd started in the Publicity

Department but had talked his way into a tryout as a writer. Within a few years he'd worked his way up to a producer's position. In his late twenties, he would arrive for work each day in blue jeans and loud shirts. With his shaggy blond mustache and twenty-five pounds of excess weight, you would never pick him for the ace handball player his friends in Brooklyn knew him to be. He had barely welcomed me to the station before he began presenting me with a barrage of writers' grievances. He was relentless, fearless, and arrogant in his demands. My first impulse was to throttle him, but it was obvious he held the loyalty and respect of my newsroom. Within a few weeks, I could see why. He was a natural leader. I made two resolutions regarding this young man. I would see him in suits and in management.

It took a while but I did. First as an executive producer and later as my assistant news director. In the years that followed we would work together in many combinations—at WBBM-TV in Chicago and at CBS News. Today he's President of the CBS Television Stations Division.

With new executives in place, I began to build a newsroom.

The real revolution happening in New York television was taking place at the ABC station and it represented the challenge I would be facing for the next several years. ABC had become number one in the New York ratings by successfully pioneering the "happy talk" formula on their *Eyewitness News* which was about to change the face of local television throughout the country. ABC's anchorpeople became as popular for their jokes as for their news stories.

The reporters specialized in what came to be known as "reporter participation" in the stories they covered. The more the reporter became the center of the story, the better their viewers seemed to like it. During my first few weeks on the job, I watched the ABC evening news, trying to understand its popularity. ABC had recently hired as a reporter a young Hispanic who had no journalism experience but had been a lawyer representing street gangs such as the Young Lords of East Harlem. I thought he had an impressive on-camera presence. One night his story dealt with the resurgence of the puppet Howdy Doody and his partner Buffalo Bob Smith. The reporter closed his story sitting on Buffalo Bob's knee with freckles painted on his face. I couldn't believe what I was seeing. I was stunned at the direction local television was taking. The young reporter was Geraldo Rivera. What would his career have been like if his early days in television had been spent in a different sort of environment?

In 1970 the impact from this sort of news operation left a lot of people in television questioning whether the days of more serious, traditional news broadcasts were numbered. The WCBS-TV broadcasts were disorganized and ponderous. If we were going to successfully compete with a popular happy talk station, I felt we had to retain a sense of being CBS and at the same time make our broadcasts more interesting than our competition, which was winning viewers by being entertaining. I was fortunate that WCBS already had a few good reporters and one outstanding anchorman. That list included Chris Borgen, the best police reporter in the country, Earl Ubell, who had covered science for the New York *Herald Tribune*, Rolland Smith, who had a sensitive touch for the New York variation of the *On the Road* story, and Jim Jensen, the most natural anchor talent I've ever seen. Blessed by luck and Danish parents, Jensen is one of those tall, strikingly handsome people who can create a wave of turning heads whenever he enters a room. I've seen that happen in cities where no one is aware that he's an anchorman on New York television. They are drawn to his remarkable presence. He is also completely at ease in front of a camera.

Having a base to build from, I began to look for reporters who, in their writing and approach to stories, would be distinct. In the sixties I had admired the New York *Herald Tribune*. No other paper contained as many memorable bylines. I wanted to achieve this for WCBS-TV. Over a period of time, I was able to find reporters who could write and report their stories with flair and style without degenerating into the silliness that plagues some of local television.

A few of them, for example Carol Martin, who is now an anchorwoman for WCBS-TV, and Ellen Fleysher of WNBC-TV, remained fixtures of New York television. Others went on to careers at the three network news organizations. By far the largest contingent can be found at ABC, among them Linda Ellerbee, John Stossel, Joel Siegel, and Lynn Scherr. Joe Witte, our weatherman, who was so lovable we nicknamed him "Bambi," is now at NBC. Ray Brady is at CBS. Some of them branched away from hard news. John Tesch left for CBS Sports and now anchors the syndicated program *Entertainment Tonight*. Rolland Smith was a co-host of the short-lived morning entertainment program on CBS.

All of these reporters worked together in the seventies in the WCBS newsroom. They were a gifted, egotistical, talented, and cantankerous group. None was more distinctive, nor more unruly, than the man who became the new anchorman of our troubled eleven o'clock news.

The reorganization, the new reporters, and a lot of hard work had begun to pay off for our six o'clock news. We were covering the hell out of the city. Our reporting was sharp and lively. Jensen was the anchorman and he responded to all our efforts like a major-league pitcher who suddenly realizes he is pitching for a great team. As a result, we were number one in the ratings. For years our six o'clock news would be either number one or tied for number one. No such luck with our eleven o'clock broadcast, which remained mired in third place. For over a year I struggled in vain to turn that broadcast around. As so often happens in television, the success of the six o'clock news not only was taken for granted; it seemed to magnify the failure at eleven. It was a terrible period. Hosking and I were summoned to the office of D. Thomas Miller, who was then the President of the Television Stations Division. Miller was a nattily attired little man who seemed to twitch with nervousness. He acted as if he couldn't believe he held the job he did and was terrified he might lose it at any moment.

"Jack keeps asking me when the eleven o'clock news is going to be fixed," he said. "I think he expects me to do something about it."

The Jack he was referring to was Jack Schneider, President of the CBS Broadcast Group and Miller's patron. I don't think I ever heard Miller talk without invoking Jack's name. They had been boyhood friends in Chicago and Miller had been the best man at Schneider's wedding. After we left his office, I muttered irritably to Hosking, "That was probably the last time he was called the best man at anything."

I was furious because Miller had made us both sit in his office and watch *Eyewitness News* on the ABC station.

At one point they came to a story which seemed to have become a regular ingredient in their news. A middle-aged male reporter did a leering story showing female models in swimsuits. Miller suddenly looked like Edison witnessing his first incandescent illumination.

"I don't suppose," he said, "it would ever occur to a journalist that people like to look at pretty girls?"

One of the historic moments in television. The President of the CBS television stations discovers tits and ass.

I wish I could claim I said that to him. I didn't. I bit my tongue and prayed for the hour to end.

Later I told Hosking that there was no way I would put on that kind of a broadcast.

"We better do something," he said. "If they don't see some numbers growth soon, they'll throw us both out."

Hosking was being kind. They would give him another shot with a different news director and I knew that. Actually, an idea for the eleven o'clock broadcast was germinating in my mind. I just hadn't put all of the pieces together. The CBS station in Philadelphia had begun originating their news broadcasts in their newsroom instead of their studio. I liked the way it looked and I thought it might be a nice touch at eleven o'clock. Some of Miller's lieutenants were enthusiasts for this approach. But we would have to do more than move the broadcast into our newsroom or we'd be hanging our hats on a gimmick. The key in my mind was our sportscaster, Dave Marash.

Marash had been a news reporter and a sports reporter for WCBS Radio. He'd come to that station after I had left for CBS News. I enjoyed listening to him. He was a bright, facile writer who brought a rare touch of literacy to sports coverage. Marash had called me saying he'd like to work for me doing sports on television. I invited him to drop by my office for a chat. I was not prepared for what walked in. He arrived wearing a broad-brimmed leather hat and an open leather vest. His hair was shoulder length and uncombed. His beard was so long it took me a few minutes to see that his shirt was open at the neck. He looked like a roadie for the Grateful Dead. That impression was not too far off the mark. Marash had been a folksinger for a period in the sixties and was then married to the ex-wife of folksinger Pete Seeger.

I talked long enough to confirm that beneath the hair was a bright man with eclectic interests. When he left I began to mull it over. To the best of my knowledge, there was not at that time a single beard in all of television news. But when you walked down the street it seemed as if a quarter of all young males in their twenties and thirties sported beards or flowing mustaches. Television sometimes lags behind the curve of changing attitudes and I thought this was such a time. I called Marash and told him I was inclined to hire him.

"Some people are going to think I'm crazy to have hired a bearded sportscaster," I said. "But I think it will be O.K. if you will go to a barber and get your hair and beard trimmed and neatened."

There was a pause.

"I don't see that as a problem," Marash said. "You've got yourself a new sportscaster."

It worked out very well. Far from being a problem, the beard was an asset. Marash was a natural for television. He was the antithesis of his colleagues. His jackets didn't fit. He wore patterned ties with bold checked shirts. In his copy he might make reference to the Court of the Sun King to describe a change in the batting lineup for the New York Mets. New York viewers loved him.

In every neighborhood bar there seems to be a guy who can quote poetry and recite batting averages. He's different, better educated than the rest of the regulars, but he's still one of the guys. He's "the poet." Marash seemed to fill that kind of role for us, and one of the viewers who liked what he saw was Founder-Chairman Paley. He shared his opinion with Tom Miller, who immediately became a Marash fan. I gave this news the widest possible distribution. I had other plans for my new addition and they weren't limited to the sports segment. Each time I repeated the story of the Chairman's enthusiasm, I added a fillip of my own.

"Of course," I said, "Paley is very much aware that Marash's background is hard news."

By the time I was ready to propose our new eleven o'clock lineup I was being told repeatedly that "the Chairman thinks Marash would be an excellent anchorman."

I don't know if Paley felt that way or not. In view of his later attitude toward Marash, I would tend to doubt it. But at the time that commonly held belief enabled me to make the changes I wanted at eleven o'clock.

I wanted Marash as the centerpiece of a fast-paced half hour which would be packed with news and packaged with a breezy informality. I saw Marash in shirt sleeves working in our newsroom as opposed to the conventional news set and paired with a more formal co-anchor. I had his partner picked, too. When I first arrived at WCBS, Rolland Smith was a weekend anchorman. I removed him from that role and assigned him full-time to feature reporting. I was honest about my reason. He was so young and boyish I thought he lacked credibility.

"Concentrate on your reporting and Mother Nature will take care of your boyish looks," I told him.

About the time I was grappling with the problems of designing a new eleven o'clock broadcast, Rolland Smith asked to see me. He had just returned from a vacation, and when he walked into my office, I took one look at him and began to laugh.

"Couldn't wait for Mother Nature?" I said.

Rolland smiled, turning his head from side to side, showing off his new mustache.

"Does it work?" he asked.

"I have to admit it does," I said. "You could probably buy a drink without showing your ID now."

"That's all I wanted to hear," he said, and he left.

There's an innocence about Rolland Smith that's surprising to find in someone with the perfect features and spotless grooming of a Paul Stuart mannequin. I began to think about Rolland Smith paired with Dave

Marash. A white bread and rye combination. In addition, I would assign some of our best reporters to work with them in the newsroom on a nightly basis. Linda Ellerbee for breaking stories. John Stossel with consumer reports. Joel Siegel with New York feature stories and stories about the music business. In the beginning Marash could also do the sports, but eventually we'd have to find a new sportscaster. When that happened, incidentally, the sportscaster was Jim Bouton, the former Yankee pitcher. I made the proposal to Hosking, who gave me the go-ahead, and within a matter of weeks the new broadcast was ready.

When it went on the air, it was everything I'd hoped it would be. Almost everything. Marash tended to overwrite. In trying to carry the style he'd developed for sports writing into news stories, he could become convoluted to the point of incoherence. But the producer and editor regularly battled him into copy which was still colorful but intelligible, and it was worth the effort. Smith wrote short simple sentences which were perfect for his fast, clipped style of delivery. The reporters were outstanding. Siegel was amusing and could turn a nice phrase in his coverage of New York's nightlife. Stossel's consumer reports were scathing and, in the early seventies, unique in television for their bite. Ellerbee was charmingly impudent covering fires and shoot-outs. Everyone on that broadcast had a style of his own. It might not have been the complete fulfillment of my hope to emulate the old *Herald Tribune,* but it was pretty damned good —a fact that seemed lost on the viewers.

As the months went by, the ratings showed scarcely a ripple. I thought the broadcast was terrific and each morning I'd look at the overnight ratings and sink deeper into despair. This was my prevailing mood during the fall of 1973. By now, I'd been a television news director for almost two years and I thought I'd put together a good newsroom. Our early evening broadcast was a success but nothing seemed to work at eleven o'clock. I had to assume that my time was running out. In addition, Joel Siegel had just completed a multi-part series on corruption in the music industry which I had approved and closely supervised. It was a solid enough series even if it contained no great revelations. Clive Davis had recently been removed as President of CBS Records after it was learned that a federal grand jury investigation in Newark had discovered documents showing he'd used CBS funds for personal expenses. I knew when we started the series that we'd have to include that incident as part of our reports. Nothing in my years at CBS prepared me for the outburst this provoked from Jack Schneider.

Hosking came to see me, ashen-faced.

"Schneider is crazed about this," he said.

"Does he think we shouldn't have reported the story in the first place?" I asked.

"No, he understands that. He just can't believe we're raking it all up in a series."

"Tell him it's a legitimate story and we can't very well do it without mentioning the Davis business."

"Edward," he said, "that man is mad enough to fire me if I tell him that. Tom Miller wants to take you to meet Goddard Lieberson."

Lieberson was one of the distinguished citizens of the music business. He'd been a Senior Vice President at CBS on the corporate level and had been returned to his old job as President of CBS Records in the wake of the Davis scandal. With Miller, who kept rambling about "the difference between facts and the truth," I met with Lieberson in his office.

He was joined by Robert Altschuler, the public relations chief for CBS Records. Lieberson was a tall, elegant man in his sixties who seemed as ill at ease as I felt and recited the circumstances of the Davis discharge. This was information already known. He assured me CBS Records had no indication of any other wrongdoing.

Afterward when I returned to the newsroom I described the meeting to Marty Haag, the assistant news director.

"They are all so nervous," I said, "it makes you wonder what they're afraid we might find. Tell Siegel and the producer they ought to make sure they're not missing something that hasn't been reported yet."

They found no new information; nor did any surface in subsequent reports by other news organizations. Jack Schneider continued to hector us. He demanded that Hosking send him the scripts of the series in advance of its broadcast, invoking the right of the publisher to know what was going to be published. With one exception no changes were made. Schneider, in I suspect a fit of frustration, demanded that we not identify Davis as "one of the most influential men in the music business until he was fired by CBS." It was an absurd request but not one which distorted the report. So we deleted the line and the series went on the air.

In a mood of considerable dejection, I decided to take a few days off and retreat to Martha's Vineyard. Both Maureen and I have always found that the island possesses recuperative powers. Part of that, I think, comes from a chance to be alone with one another.

That we met at all is a miracle of my life. For the Joyce family, the 1940s were complex years that had not been abundant in employment opportunities and my father responded by leaving Arizona. But in doing so, he seemed to lose some essential part of himself. By then he'd begun to drink and it was a problem that worsened each year. He held a variety of jobs and did well in each of them until his restlessness prevailed and the family tried to find its luck in some new place.

My brother Charles and I once counted twenty schools in sixteen towns and cities which we'd attended in less than a decade. The constant in our life then was the automobile, which made it possible to load everything and move on to take your chances elsewhere.

In 1949 "elsewhere" was the Lower East Side of Manhattan. It was my mother's idea. New York was the one place we'd never lived.

My brother and I both attended Seward Park High School. The Lower East Side was at the end of an era. The first migration from Puerto Rico was just arriving, but it was still a predominantly Jewish world. Yiddish theater was still playing on Second Avenue and Molly Picon was one of its stars. For months I roamed those streets, oblivious to a world uptown. Anything above Fourteenth Street was Westchester to me.

Fortunately, that changed. A friend of my mother's introduced me to the Blackfriars Guild on West Fifty-seventh Street, a prestigious off-Broadway theater run by the Paulist fathers. They owned their own theater and produced several original plays each year. Just then they were casting a play called *Lead Kindly Light.* They'd just signed a young actress named Geraldine Page for one role, but they were having trouble filling a small part, a teenaged beggar who was cured by a miracle. Not only did I get the part; I even received a small accolade from one of the critics. Nineteen fifty turned out to be truly a year of good fortune for me.

An exquisite redhead from New Bedford, Massachusetts, happened to be working with the Blackfriars. Maureen Jarry was small, wonderfully argumentative, and, amazingly, she liked me . . . a lot. She kept asking what I did during the day. I muttered something about "making the rounds," which was how professional actors spent their time (at least so they told me). I did not tell her I was only seventeen years old and attended high school classes by day. I had no idea she was only a few months older than I.

A serious romance between teenagers is a mixture of passion, tenderness, and naïveté. Shakespeare may have turned it into a play; Maureen and I turned it into a lifetime. We were married on July 8, 1950, and in the innocent belief that the world will somehow provide everything you need, we moved to Wyoming, where I had been accepted by the university in Laramie. Maureen worked in the office of the Dean of Men and I picked up odd jobs to help pay the bills. That summer, in another stroke of good fortune, I heard that KODI, the small radio station in Cody, needed a temporary announcer to replace the one whose week-long bender had just cost him his job. I auditioned and was hired for the summer as an announcer–floor sweeper, and learned for the first time how exciting a radio station can be.

That fall in Laramie we lived in a Quonset hut in a section of the campus set aside for married students. Life settled down to a routine of classes and basketball games and the Wyoming winter, when thirty-below temperatures were normal.

Then we learned we were going to have a child. It was a simpler time, a time with fewer choices, and it never occurred to us that we'd do anything other than have the baby and that I would leave school and find a full-time job. The previous summer at KODI in Cody had even provided me with the rudiments of a trade.

As an announcer, I'd discovered I could sit at a typewriter and string together the local events I'd collected on the phone into news stories and then sit in front of a microphone and read those stories with reasonable clarity. All I needed was someplace to pay me for doing this. Maureen's parents invited us to move in with them in their New York apartment while I looked for work. We accepted and were still there in September 1951 when our daughter Brenda was born. Her father was then earning fifty-four dollars a week showing patrons to their tables in a newly opened Howard Johnson's on upper Broadway at Seventy-fourth Street. Not too long after that, I was hired by WKTV and we moved to Utica, New York.

A few months later, I went to WRGB-TV in Schenectady, where I remained for two and a half years. It was a wonderful time for both Maureen and me. We had our second child in April 1954, Randall. WRGB was a great educational experience. It was owned by General Electric, which also manufactured cameras and other equipment for television stations. In the 1950s they operated their Schenectady station as a production showcase to demonstrate the full range of their latest equipment. As a result, there could have been few better places for a young man learning a craft. I not only wrote the copy for the eleven o'clock news but filled in for the regular announcer when he was away. We were all routinely expected to handle a variety of such assignments. In an average day I could find myself writing promotion copy, emceeing a children's show, producing a live music program, then working on the late news broadcast.

In 1954, I was offered a job at WBBM, the CBS-owned radio station in Chicago. Once again, Maureen and I moved, this time with two children.

Slowly I was acquiring whatever skills I would bring to WCBS Radio in 1959.

By 1973 the two of us had been married a long time but still enjoyed one another's company. The few days we had together at the Vineyard were marvelous. A nor'easter had swept out to sea leaving an island cleansed by salt and swept by wind. We took long walks on the beach and carried back for the fireplace pieces of timber which had washed ashore. New York and WCBS Television seemed far away.

On the third day I mentioned to Maureen that I liked her new haircut.

"I'm glad you're feeling better," she said.

"What do you mean?"

"I got this haircut a month ago."

"God, I'm sorry," I said. "I guess I've been pretty punchy. Let's go for a walk on Stonewall Beach and then pick up a swordfish steak at Poole's. It's a little chilly but we can grill it outside."

About an hour and a half later we were back. Maureen was unwrapping the swordfish and I was uncorking a bottle of Portuguese Vinho Verde when the phone rang. It was Bob Hosking and what he was about to tell me would change my life.

"Edward," he said, "I've just learned I'm being sent to Philadelphia to manage WCAU-TV."

WCBS is the flagship station for CBS. Moving from their flagship to Philadelphia was unheard of. My first reaction was that he was being demoted.

"Is it because of the Clive Davis stuff?" I asked.

"No," he assured me. "The station is facing a serious license challenge from a community group and I'm there to head that off."

Bob's replacement was going to be Tom Leahy, the Vice President for Sales of the Stations Division. I'd met Leahy once or twice but I didn't really know him. Bob and I talked about my prospects. We both agreed they didn't seem terribly bright, because of the Davis story and an unsuccessful eleven o'clock news. By the time I hung up I was thankful I'd had three days of rest. Without them I would have been in bad shape.

I finished uncorking the Vinho Verde and we sat down to discuss the future. By the time we'd finished its twin and eaten the swordfish, our plans were made. I was going to get out of the business. Enough was enough. The next morning we drove to Menemsha, the little up-island fishing port. Our destination was Seward's Seagoing Grocery, the only general store on that part of the island. David Seward confirmed that what we'd heard was true. The store he'd inherited from his mother and father was for sale. We began to negotiate for its purchase. That weekend we drove home to our house in Connecticut.

Monday morning I left for CBS and Maureen put our house on the market. We needed the money from its sale to purchase Seward's. When the house was sold, we'd buy the store and begin our new life as island merchants.

As it turned out, the Connecticut real estate market was soft. We got few visits from prospective buyers and no offers. If the market had been hot I would have become another islander grumbling about the damned summer people and I wouldn't have gotten to know Tom Leahy.

The morning I returned to CBS I brought with me a resolve that I would take no horseshit. Knowing Leahy as I do today, that was a good thing. He can be a very tough man. We had lunch that day at the Slate restaurant on Tenth Avenue and Fifty-sixth Street. He asked questions, listened to the answers, and volunteered little.

"Why is the early news so successful and the late news is not?" he asked.

"The early news has a good lead-in from the Mike Douglas show," I said. "It's also developed a tune-in habit on the part of people who are just getting home from work at that time, and it's a fine broadcast."

"And the late?"

"Different problem," I said. "You're dependent on the audience for the network show which precedes you and that varies from night to night. Your biggest fight is to keep them from switching or going to bed. It takes something very special to do that. I happen to think we're producing it with our new broadcast. But I can't argue that the ratings aren't showing."

By now Leahy was on his third cup of black coffee. I had something I wanted to say and I blurted it out.

"A newsroom is more than ratings," I said. "Every time it goes on the air the reputation of your station is on the line. You can never take that for granted. If you get sloppy you end up losing lawsuits and facing congressional hearings where you don't have the right answers. Ask Hosking what this place was like when I got here. We may not have the ratings yet at eleven o'clock, but the reputation of this place has never been better. I think I can make it all happen but I need something from you."

Leahy didn't say a word. He just stared at me. I felt I was looking into graveyard eyes, but I plunged ahead.

"Some of the people we both work for are idiots," I said. "You deal with them. Keep them off my neck and out of my newsroom. I work for you. One boss is enough."

Leahy took another sip of coffee and put his cup down.

"Do you think you could ever learn to be more forthcoming?" he asked.

My laughter broke the tension and we headed back to the station. In the days that followed, Leahy began to immerse himself in television production. He was fascinated by how it all worked.

"What's a chromo key?" he asked. "I keep hearing about the key."

"It's no big deal," I said. "Its just a light that allows you to electronically place those visuals you see over the anchorman's shoulder."

It went on like that for weeks, and he never asked the same question twice. Only later did I learn from him that he had a degree in electrical engineering. His entry into television came when he was an NBC page working on the Jack Paar *Tonight Show*. One night he saw someone arrive with a well-dressed group which was immediately escorted to the best seats in the studio.

"What does that fellow do?" he asked an older page.

"He's a network salesman," he was told.

"That's what I'm going to be," Leahy said.

That's what he became and that was the road that led him to the general manager's office at WCBS-TV.

One morning a few weeks after his arrival the executive line in my office rang. This was a hot line from the general manager's office.

"Have you seen the overnights?" Leahy asked.

"They just came in," I said. "Let me look at them."

The eleven o'clock news had held a good share of its lead in the rating services.

"Have you ever seen that before?" he asked.

"No," I answered truthfully, "I really haven't."

"It's certainly headed in the right direction," he said. "Let's hope it continues."

This didn't happen again for a few days. Then we saw it repeated. First in the ARB, then in the Nielsen service. Ratings change for television news broadcasts the way glaciers move, slowly, imperceptibly at first.

Another few weeks went by before my phone rang again.

"Congratulations," Leahy said. "The eleven o'clock news was number one for the week. It looks like you may have a hit on your hands."

When I hung up I called Maureen to tell her the news.

"Take the house off the market," I said. "When I get home tonight I'll call David Seward and tell him it doesn't look like we'll be buying the store."

Leahy was right. We did have a "hit" on our hands. All of the parts of our new broadcast seemed to have combined in a way viewers found intriguing. Our newsroom was small, crowded, and noisy. Throughout each broadcast a low hum of typewriters and teletypes filled the background. But there was something refreshing and totally noncosmetic about the environment. It was perfect for the group of people I'd assembled. Stossel, Ellerbee, and Siegel were young, aggressive, and slightly irreverent. Smith and Marash were a perfect combination. Smith actually did 60 to 70 percent of the broadcast each night. Yet it seemed evenly divided. Marash was not one who simply allowed the camera to come on him. He reached out and grabbed it by the throat. The moment the broadcast opened with its wide shot of the newsroom, viewers knew they were watching a different kind of anchorman. With his beard, balding head, overflowing waistline, and lighted cigar spiraling smoke toward the klieg lights in the newsroom ceiling, Marash was saying to viewers, "Pay attention. It's obvious I didn't get here because of my pretty face." Marash might have been an oddity for television, but for New Yorkers he was Everyman, and WCBS-TV now had successful broadcasts in both the early and the late evening. It also had a documentary unit which was busy probing slumlords, Nazis living in America, and a host of other issues which were relevant to New York viewers.

Leahy was a marvelous boss. He remained fascinated by the visuals of television and was forever complaining about graphics or bad camera angles. By now he had mastered a technical understanding of the medium. As a result, I paid closer attention to these elements than I might have otherwise and, as a result, our broadcasts were better. He was also very astute about advertising and promotion and I learned a great deal from him. To my delight he seemed to have little interest in the editorial side of my newsroom and gave me a free hand. I can't remember him ever questioning a lead or asking why we'd covered a particular story. His most frequent complaint for many months concerned Marash's cigar.

"I hear from people that they hate seeing Marash with that fat cigar in his hand," he said.

"The ratings don't show that people feel that way, Tom," I said. "It's important to David. It's his way of saying, 'This is me in this newsroom, not some anchor clone.' "

For months variations of that conversation took place until one day when Leahy called me on our exec line and asked me to come see him.

I found him in his office drinking black coffee and eating a slice of pound cake. Leahy is a trim man who constantly watches his weight. Consumption of sweets was an inevitable sign of nervousness.

"The Marash cigar has got to go," he said.

This was not his usual style.

"Tom, we've had this conversation a dozen times."

"Let me give it to you straight," he said. "The old man hates the newsroom and he hates the cigar. The newsroom is important, the cigar isn't."

At CBS a reference to the "old man" meant one person, William S. Paley.

"How could he hate the cigar?" I asked. "He started out his business career working for his father in the cigar business . . . La Palinas."

"You know what he said to me?"

Leahy didn't wait for a response. He began to quote Paley.

" 'As you might imagine, I know something about cigars. The public doesn't believe a gentleman smokes them.' "

"What did you say then?"

"I said, 'Mr. Paley, we will tell Dave Marash not to smoke cigars while he is on camera.' "

"What's the complaint about the newsroom?" I asked.

"He finds it distracting when he sees the people working in the newsroom behind the anchormen and he's bothered by the ambient noise."

"Those are the qualities which make us different. Our anchors come across as working news people."

"Relax," Leahy said. "I told him I thought it could be dangerous to move out of the newsroom into a news set. That our success was new and we shouldn't tamper with the magic."

"What was his reaction to that?"

"He's a businessman," Leahy said. "He understood."

"Well," I said, "I suppose I should be grateful for that. I guess I'll go find Marash and give him the news that cigars are bad for his health."

"Don't mention Paley," he said.

"Don't worry," I said. "I'll tell him I'm the schmuck who feels this way."

Predictably, Marash sputtered at "my decision," but he doused his cigar and spent the next few weeks defiantly presenting the eleven o'clock editors with grossly overwritten stories.

The loss was more symbolic than real. The people working both on the air and behind the scenes on the eleven o'clock news had come to see themselves as representatives of a new wave. They were disdainful of the more traditional six o'clock broadcast anchored by Jim Jensen. No group of Nouvelle Cuisine chefs ever talked of Brillat-Savarin with more condescension than the crew at eleven when they were disparaging their colleagues on the six. As a news director I rather liked this competition between the two broadcasts. It kept each broadcast on its toes.

Almost a year passed before the subject of the newsroom was revisited. This time it seemed to come out of the blue. Leahy had been gone from the office all morning when he called me from Black Rock.

"I'm headed back to my office," he said. "Please don't go to lunch until I get back."

"Sure," I said. "What's up?"

"I'll be back in a few minutes. I'll fill you in."

I was waiting in his office when he returned and it was obvious he wasn't bringing good news. His face looked like the breaking up of a bad winter on the Hudson River.

"I've spent the morning with the old man," he said.

I knew what was coming.

"It was supposed to be a general review of the station," he continued, "but he started in on the newsroom at eleven o'clock and he wouldn't let up. His friends have stopped watching; everywhere he goes people complain about the noise and the confusion while they are trying to listen to the news."

"Did you tell him that's not reflected in our ratings?"

Leahy looked at me like a combat veteran who was not receiving the proper understanding that war is hell.

"Of course I did," he said. "He was ready for that. He told me he thought the eleven o'clock news would be just as successful in a setting which was more appropriate to the image of CBS."

"Who was there with you?"

"Jack Schneider and Tom Miller. They didn't open their mouths. They sat there looking at me like I was crazy to argue with the Chairman."

"So what did you do?"

"I must be crazy. I kept arguing. Then Paley began to speak very softly. Could we move the broadcast into the set used by our six o'clock news for a few weeks and see if it creates a problem? Couldn't we just try it? I knew the discussion was over and I said, 'Yes, Mr. Paley, we can certainly do that.'"

I didn't argue with Tom. I'd worked for one general manager who'd argued with Paley and been shipped off to Venezuela. I didn't want that to happen to him.

We made the change and there was no immediate drop in our viewership. That took months to happen and the broadcast still remained a respectable competitor to its rivals on NBC and ABC. But, to use Leahy's phrase, "the magic was gone." Marash in a jacket sitting in a traditional television news set was a competent anchorman. But he was no longer the intellectual poet from the neighborhood bar and New Yorkers sensed that. In later years Roone Arledge hired Marash for his *20/20* program on the ABC television network. Then Marash returned briefly in 1981 for an unsuccessful anchor role on WCBS. He's now with WRC-TV in Washington, D.C., and enjoying success in that city. But nothing he's done since has approached the excitement he brought to television in the seventies sitting in his shirt sleeves in a small, noisy, smoky newsroom.

Tom Leahy would go on to become President of the Television Stations Division in 1977 and then Executive Vice President of the Broadcast Group. I would go with him first as the Vice President for News for the five stations, then as Vice President and general manager of three of these stations in Chicago, Los Angeles, and New York. More than ten years later I would return to CBS News as its Executive Vice President.

I felt I came back with some battle ribbons.

I n early 1983 it looked as if another victory might be shaping up. Another glacier beginning to move.

For the first time in thirty years *The CBS Morning News* had come within striking distance of *The Today Show,* with a 3.5 rating and an 18 share of the homes using television to *Today'*s 3.9 rating and 19 share. The fact that both were dwarfed by *Good Morning America,* with its massive 5.1 rating and 25 share, was, for the moment, unimportant. We were making real, measurable progress. Ironically, it happened in the midst of the protracted budget struggle with Jankowski. As a matter of fact, a great deal occurred in the midst of that lengthy argument.

In April, Dan Burt, the attorney for Westmoreland, won a victory when Judge Pierre Leval ordered CBS to turn over the Benjamin Report. He ruled that by releasing the Sauter memorandum which had summarized the report, CBS had rendered the Benjamin Report clearly discoverable. Fortunately, the memorandum containing the conclusions of Sauter, Joyce, and Benjamin accurately reflected the report itself. Burt would find no smoking gun in the report, but it meant still more exposure of the embarrassing details of an internal investigation. Also in April, Paley stepped down as Chairman of CBS and turned the office over to Wyman, who announced that, for the immediate future at least, he would also retain the office of President. Jankowski was not enjoying a championship season. His network was showing a shortfall of millions of dollars. He was involved in a public dispute with his own News Division. Now the day he'd planned for had arrived and Wyman was showing no indication that

Jankowski, or anyone else for that matter, would share in the running of CBS. And in that same general period, George Merlis was removed as the executive producer of *The CBS Morning News*.

The problem had been building for several months. Diane Sawyer had asked to see me and arrived with Bill Kurtis in tow. They presented a litany of complaints: not enough research help; no effort being made to develop new segments; a lack of organization.

"Diane, have you discussed this with George?" I asked.

"I can't reach him during the day," she said. "He doesn't return my calls and he's always behind a closed door with one of his researchers."

"Diane is right," Bill echoed. "George seems overwhelmed."

From all indications the *Morning News* was becoming a success. Eliminating the executive producer would preclude any possibility of his being credited with that accomplishment and diverting attention away from its two stars. Perhaps the visit of these two anchors was nothing more than an irresistible drive to commingle their energies in the destruction of the hapless Merlis. Just an average day in the television news business. Still, I couldn't ignore the possibility that they might be right.

Several times I asked Merlis how things were going between his two anchors.

"No problems there," he said. "I spend more time with Bill. Diane's hard to reach once the broadcast goes off the air."

"That's no good," I said. "You've got to spend time with her, too."

"Maybe I should try her at Paley's," he said.

I let the reference slide. The octogenarian Paley had now been widowed for several years and his dates with the anchorwoman of *The CBS Morning News* were frequently mentioned in gossip columns.

It was hard to chastise Merlis, though, for his reluctance to demand that Diane be more accessible in the hours after the *Morning News* went off the air.

Once a week I held a *Morning News* review in my office. The meeting was usually attended by the two anchors, Merlis, Margery Baker, and Jon Katz, his new planning editor for the *Morning News*. Katz was a former managing editor of the Dallas *Times Herald*. He'd written a letter to Van describing himself as an out-of-work newspaperman who would like to try his hand at television. Van had never met him and handed me the letter. I brought him in for meetings with Van and me. He impressed us both as one of those bright, facile people who find it easy to generate ideas. But he knew nothing about television. After he'd left it was Van who thought of the *Morning News*.

"Let's give him to Merlis," he said.

"As what?"

"I don't know. Let's try an experiment. O.K., newspaper guy, we'll pay you to sit and generate ideas for the *Morning News*. If it works, you get to learn television and we benefit from your ideas. If it doesn't, we cut you loose with nothing lost."

Merlis took one look at our gift to the *Morning News* and was repulsed. Katz arrived wearing what I would come to know as his standard wardrobe. Baggy khakis from an Army-Navy store . . . the tail of a checkered shirt billowing over a waistline which was a testimony to years of self-indulgence . . . a loosened tie hanging below an open collar. As a pained Merlis escorted him out of my office, Katz paused at the door.

"Joyce," he said, "remember this day. I've done a lot of dumb things in my time . . . but I've never hired me."

Merlis led him to a vacant desk, assigned him the menial task of logging the program highlights of the competitive broadcasts, and tried to ignore him. Weeks went by without a word exchanged between the two of them. But Katz was not a man to be ignored. He began to size up the situation on the *Morning News* and set out to impress the two anchors. The *Morning News* was a gaping maw which had to be fed each morning with enough material to fill two hours. In addition, we had instituted an early morning news broadcast which preceded it from 6 to 7 A.M. Stations carried it as a half-hour broadcast either at 6 or at 6:30 A.M. Merlis was confronted each morning with the need to fill a total of three hours. At the same time our Financial Department was now alerting me each time his budget soared because of satellite and line costs or excessive travel time for crews and producers. I was now receiving reports showing the number of crew days for each story covered by any CBS News broadcast. If a story took one, two, or even three days, that was acceptable. If I saw a story which had taken five shooting days, I would circle it and send it to Merlis with a demand for an explanation.

As a result, he was receptive when the two anchors began to lobby for Jon Katz's ideas for segments on new products and other back-of-the-book features from food to fashion and architecture. They could be done live in the studio by the anchors without the days of travel and shooting needed to do a traditional story. Newspaper editors have spent years developing low-cost easy-read features to fill their pages. Katz arrived with a grab bag of these and Merlis began to rely on him, even formalizing his role as planning editor. The broadcast continued to present more hard news than its two competitors, but these features became an important part of the personality of our broadcast and our growing number of viewers seemed to underscore their importance.

Just as we appeared poised for a move past *The Today Show* (we had actually tied them for one week) the executive producer who'd been so vital in making that happen went into a daze. He suddenly seemed intimidated by his anchorwoman. At the weekly meetings Diane Sawyer would present her ideas, perhaps a segment on photography or finding and developing a new technology expert who could regularly do features on home computers and other common tools of the modern world. Merlis invariably agreed with her and the meeting would end with the expectation of some action. Just as invariably, nothing would happen. Weeks later Diane would raise the same subject and Merlis again would be receptive and act as though it was the first time he was hearing the suggestion.

One morning I exploded.

"We are measurably improved, George, but in case you haven't noticed we are still number three. If we don't continue to improve that broadcast we will fall back on our ass. It's perfectly acceptable for you to sit at these meetings and say, 'As executive producer I don't think that's a good idea,' when someone has just presented their brainstorm. What's not acceptable is for you to sit here and say you like it and plan to do it, and then a month later at another meeting for me to learn you haven't done a goddamn thing."

The room was silent. Merlis just looked at the table. It was obvious he wasn't going to respond. Katz, who would normally parry my acerbities by telling the group "what the Ambassador meant to say," was uncharacteristically speechless. I got up and walked out of my own office.

After closing the door, I could hear Merlis saying, "Well, I guess I've just been fired."

That was precisely what I didn't want to do. Merlis had brought an understanding of morning television to a largely unwelcoming organization which even now seemed to begrudge him his success. But suddenly he seemed paralyzed, unable to act. Later that day I called on Jon Katz.

"Katz, what's happened to George?"

"No greeting, no small talk?" he said. "The man is obviously still pissed, so I won't clown around. What do you mean by what's happened?"

"He's changed," I said. "He seems like he's barely functioning."

"Part of that is personal," Katz said, "a mid-life crisis. You won't be interested in a gossipy account, so I'll get to the other part. He's traumatized by Diane. She is incredible. Nothing in my life as a newspaper editor prepared me for her."

"What do you mean?"

"I suspect you know well what I mean. Diane Sawyer is the most ambitious person I've ever met. I am convinced that she will either become the anchorwoman of a network evening news broadcast or she'll go home to Kentucky and run for the Senate. Her success on this broadcast is part of that plan. She has decided that Merlis is not measuring up. George senses that and he's terrified."

"If that's true, doesn't it strike you as a considerable overreaction?"

"Remember, George lost his job at *Good Morning America* because of a conflict with David Hartman. Now he sees it all over again with Diane Sawyer and he can't believe it could be happening twice."

"Diane says she can never reach George. Is that true?"

"No," he said, "that's not true."

"Why did you pause?"

"Because she doesn't try to reach him. She deals through Margery or me and simply doesn't talk to him."

"Where is Kurtis on all this?"

Jon laughed.

"Next time you hear Kurtis on the subject of Merlis look quickly and see if Diane's lips are moving."

For several hours after my conversation with Katz, I continued to brood over the problems of the *Morning News*. I even began to wonder if Katz hadn't been a bit dramatic about Diane's campaign against Merlis. Was he jockeying for the job himself? He had to know he was too new to television to be a candidate for such a job.

That afternoon I got a phone call from Richard Leibner, the talent agent. Ostensibly he wanted to see if I had any interest in a client who worked for another network. A few minutes later he moved to his reason for calling.

"I had lunch with a very happy client today," he said.

"Who was that?"

"Diane Sawyer, and she was singing your praises."

I knew the answer but I asked anyway: "What prompted that?"

"That must have been some meeting in your office this morning. But the strength you showed made her feel better about the future of her broadcast than she's felt in months."

Katz had not been dramatizing the situation. Diane was waging a campaign. What would be the next move? Would we start hearing that Paley was not a Merlis fan?

That evening after the conclusion of the Rather broadcast I gave Van a fill-in.

"We'll have to replace him," he said. "It sounds like he's just gone limp."

"We can't throw the guy to the wolves," I said. "He's done a lot for us."

"I have no grief with your finding him another spot," Van said. "I'd like to hit Jankowski with some ideas for prime time. Why don't we turn Merlis loose and see what ideas he can develop for new shows."

"Yeah, maybe we could do that," I said, and I let out a long sigh while I massaged the back of my neck.

"What's troubling you?" Van asked.

"Diane Sawyer. She is going to believe she mounted a victorious campaign and that neither you nor I understand how skillfully it was conducted."

"Eduardo, it's better if she thinks we don't know."

I thought about that for a moment.

"That's unfortunately a perceptive observation," I said, and returned to the kneading of my neck muscles. "I'm too fine a person for this line of work."

A few days later George Merlis was replaced as executive producer of *The CBS Morning News* by Bob Ferrante, who had been in charge of *Nightwatch,* our overnight news broadcast. Merlis was offered the development role at the same salary he'd been earning. Instead, his agent, Jim Griffin of the William Morris Agency, asked for and received his release so that he might accept the job of executive producer for the syndicated television show *Entertainment Tonight,* based in Hollywood.

At any other time this changing of the guard on the *Morning News* would have been a matter of paramount importance. Because it came at the time of the Jankowski conflict, it seemed almost peripheral. For all we knew, another management team would be sitting in our offices next week.

On the morning of June 13, 1983, I was meeting with Van in his office when we were interrupted by a phone call from George Vradenburg in the Law Department. I could only hear Van's side of the conversation.

"I don't believe what I'm hearing. . . . I fucking do not believe this. . . . Yes, we should definitely meet. . . . Whenever you can get Boies here we'll drop everything else."

He put the phone softly in its cradle and turned back to me.

"You will not believe this either. George Crile, a familiar name in our life, surreptitiously tape-recorded phone calls with individuals in conversations he'd assured them were off the record. Those individuals are Robert McNamara, George Ball, Matthew Ridgway, and Arthur Goldberg."

Unable to help myself, I began to laugh, shaking my head at the same time.

"Van, if you told me now that Crile had been arrested with his pants down outside Westmoreland's house and charged with mooning, I would not be surprised."

"Keep laughing. You haven't heard it all," Van said. "Last Friday, Dan Burt called Boies and said that Ira Klein, our former film editor, told him about a tape of a conversation with McNamara that had been kept in Crile's desk in the lower left-hand drawer. Boies called Crile and asked him if he'd made such a tape."

"And Crile said, 'Oh, I meant to tell you about that,' " I added.

"No, it gets better. Crile said he remembered making the tape but it was either lost or reused. So Boies calls Burt, who is pissed off and who then tells the New York *Times* that what CBS is doing amounts to destruction of critical evidence. Boies then tells the *Times* it's a Dan Burt smoke screen and the tape had been destroyed or erased in the usual course of business."

"Rosemary Woods lives."

"Not so fast. This morning Boies gets a phone call from Crile, who says he did a sweep of his home over the weekend and he found a cassette with part of a conversation. And guess what it also contains? Off-the-record conversations with Ball, Ridgway, and Goldberg."

"So once again CBS News comes out looking smarmy. That's just great. Van, we've got to do something about Crile this time."

"Ed, we can't fire him. Our entire defense in this case is built around him."

"I remind you, he's working on another documentary. He's been down in Nicaragua shooting it. We can't let that get on the air."

"He's already shot thousands of feet of film."

"Van, fuck the film. Shelve it—burn it. This guy has not played straight."

"What do we do with Crile?"

"Suspend him from all editorial work. Give him to Boies full-time to work on the preparation of the trial. If we don't at least do that we are telling everyone who works for CBS News that the standards we're so quick to trumpet are just bullshit."

Both of us were on edge anyway because of our financial woes.

"I can't believe this," Van said. "Hit to hit . . . back to back . . . wall to wall. It just doesn't seem real."

"Maybe Gene will fire our asses out of here and we can open a 7-Eleven store somewhere in northern California."

Van smiled. "Not the worst of all possible scenarios. I'll let you know when Vradenburg and Boies arrive."

That was about two hours later. They arrived together and the usually unflappable Boies looked crestfallen. He began by repeating the sequence of events Vradenburg had given Van earlier on the phone.

"This is terribly embarrassing to me," he said, and added, "I've about had it with Crile."

"David," I said, "just out of curiosity, has George offered any comment about the morality of telling someone it's an off-the-record conversation and then tape-recording them?"

"He sees no difference between making a recording and taking notes."

"And the fact that it's a practice specifically prohibited in the CBS News Standards?"

Boies looked sheepish.

"He says he was unaware that it violated the guidelines."

Vradenburg had been watching my face during this exchange and he began a lecture on Crile's importance to the winning of our libel trial, but Van interrupted him.

"Gentlemen, I have been a supporter of George Crile. Ed and I have disagreed on this . . . but everyone has a tip-over factor and I've reached my tip-over factor on Crile. Ed and I both agree that Crile cannot continue to work on anything of an editorial nature for the foreseeable future. We are going to suspend him and make the organization aware of that suspension. David, he'll be available full-time to work with you."

Vradenburg and Boies looked worried but not surprised.

"It's important," Boies said, "that in being suspended George not walk away believing there is any lessening in our belief that we will win this trial. Who is going to tell George?"

"I think Ed should tell him," Van said. "He can do it tomorrow, so you have time to prepare for the inevitable questions from the press."

The next morning Bob Chandler was in my office when Crile arrived. I'd asked him to be there. Roger Colloff had been shipped to a position on Gene Jankowski's Broadcast Group staff and Chandler was now the CBS News Vice President for Public Affairs.

It was a short meeting. Crile arrived looking like someone who was there to keep an unpleasant appointment with his dentist to have his gums scraped. I had the impression he'd been briefed by Boies on what to expect. His only comment when I told him he was being suspended was "It seems terribly harsh."

"The irony," I said, "is that over the past year we have come to believe that we will ultimately win this case on a truth defense . . . but your credibility has diminished to the point where it is virtually nonexistent. With this last incident, we don't feel we can have you working on any more editorial product."

The suspension of George Crile was just one more episode in the frenetic spring of 1983. It was a period of time made even more tense by the ugly dispute over the financial destiny of CBS News. I emerged from those months with an enormous fondness for Van Sauter. That he could be a rascal, I had no doubt. I cringed at times at the sheer extravagance of his conduct. But these had been some of the most complex and trying months of our lives, filled, it seemed, with a constant barrage of incoming fire from unfriendly sources. I was proud of the stand I had taken in the face of what seemed like irrational demands to eviscerate CBS News, and I was proud of Van, too, because I had watched him struggle with the pulls of his own ambition and ultimately take the position he thought was morally right. I found myself feeling oddly protective of this bearded chameleon who could be Falstaff one moment and Iago the next. More than most, I thought I'd gotten a glimpse of the man behind the guises and I liked that person—enough to worry at the fatigue I saw on his face in the days following our budget compromise with Jankowski.

"Sauter, you look terrible," I said. "You need to take a day off."

"I do?" he said. "Maybe it's time to make a speech."

That was an inside joke we both shared because I was fully aware that he was involved in a licit love affair.

Van may have taken up fly fishing as a mechanism for spending leisure hours with Rather, but his infatuation with the sport was real. As a result, he began to search for excuses to travel to areas with good fishing. He was forever making speeches in such locations to broadcasting associations, Rotary Clubs, or whatever civic group might be of importance to a local CBS affiliate. I stopped asking why he was going to Sioux Falls, South Dakota, for yet another speech to some local group. Joe Floyd's people at KELO-TV were there to whisk him out to the countryside for a day of fishing. I'd get the inevitable phone call from a fishing site, give him a briefing on whatever had happened that day, and then have my secretary switch him over to Jankowski's office so he, in turn, could brief Gene authoritatively on CBS News issues ranging from the Westmoreland trial to a vacation replacement for Dan Rather. There would be something delightful about a senior executive of CBS inventing reasons to fly himself to the great fishing streams of North America and then conducting his business with the Group President from a pay phone outside a Texaco station on the edge of some town with a name like Chickamauga Falls. It was a small exercise in roguery which reflected a mixture of self-confidence and contempt for authority.

As it turned out, I was the one who took the day off, to attend the funeral in Washington, D.C., of Gene King, my oldest friend. Gene had been the program director of WCBS Radio when I joined them in 1959. Gene had helped me make the transition from just another announcer to producer and reporter. When Jim Brooks, a young newswriter, and I went to him with an idea for a documentary on the newest wave in bohemia, a group called the Beats, his enthusiasm for the idea made it possible. Brooks went on to become an Oscar-winning writer-producer-director in Hollywood. I remained at CBS. We both have a debt to Gene King for one of those "leg-ups" everyone needs in his career. The day I flew back from Gene's funeral I was consumed by guilt. I knew I hadn't been a very good friend in the past couple of years of his life. It was always Gene who called or who dropped in unexpectedly when he was in New York. I had become so involved in my life at CBS News I had closed the other part of my life which should have been spent with old friends. He was the last of a trio of close friends who'd died in the past few years. George Barnes, the finest jazz guitarist I've ever heard, was gone and with him the nights of staying up late, drinking too much, and listening to scratchy 78 rpm records while George showed me how he learned more from Bix Beiderbecke playing his cornet than he did from any other guitar player. Sam Schraage was dead, too. I'd met the outspoken rabbi from Brooklyn's Lubavitcher sect when I was a radio reporter and he was forming a neighborhood self-defense group call the Maccabees. Our families became friends as well. We'd visit them in Crown Heights and they would visit us in Connecticut, bringing with them a kosher meal for the paper plates we'd have waiting.

"You're great friends," Maureen would tell them. "I never have to cook."

When you are in your fifties and good friends die, part of the pain you feel comes from knowing your future will be less rich than you'd believed it would be. The sense of being deprived of time you'd taken for granted is a part of that sorrow. At Gene's service in Washington the rabbi asked me to speak. For my short eulogy I recalled something Henry Adams had once said: "One friend in a lifetime is much; two are many; three are hardly possible. Friendship needs a certain parallelism of life, a community of thought, a rivalry of aim."

After the service for Gene that quote kept turning over in my head all the way back to New York.

I came back to my office a little before five o'clock. Van stuck his head in my door a few minutes later. I'd often talked to him about Gene and we closed the door while I described the service. I told him I'd suddenly remembered that quote from Henry Adams and I repeated it, saying I thought it was a perceptive observation on the rarity of real friendship.

Van mused over that for a moment before responding.

"It's funny, I was talking to Kathleen about the same thing last night. This wretched business is so devouring. I realized I didn't have any close male friends. I meant friends in the sense of your Henry Adams quote. Then I realized something else. The person I spend the most time with and most enjoy spending time with is you."

Van seemed almost embarrassed by what he said. Neither of us said anything for an awkward moment and then my phone buzzed. Van's secretary was relaying a message to call Gene Jankowski as soon as he could.

He returned to his office to make the call and I sat alone, reflecting on what he'd said. We were an unlikely pair of friends. I was by nature as private and reserved as he was outgoing and gregarious. Our differences were reflected even in the way we dressed and looked. Wearing a suit to the office was for me as normal as the suspenders I'd worn all my adult life. I was someone who would shave a second time in one day if I was going out for the evening. Van had solved the problem years ago with a full beard, and casual clothes hung on a frame which also carried seventy pounds of extra weight. I ran five miles a day to fend off the expanding evidence of having reached the age of fifty-one. The only exercise Van enjoyed involved walking along the side of a trout stream. Even our personal lives and our politics were different. Van was now in his second marriage. I'd been married to the same woman for more than thirty years. In my middle age I was a liberal who'd moved to the center and was surprised at how often he found himself slightly to the right of that line. Van had been more consistent. He was what he'd always been, a die-hard conservative. But in our years at CBS we'd experienced "a certain parallelism of life." Working closely together had required "a community of thought." And without a doubt there was often "a rivalry of aim."

To Adam's list I would add a fourth requirement. At least for me. A bond of common laughter. We'd often seen humor in the midst of some tense and difficult occasion. That instant recognition of the absurdity of it all was like sharing a secret in a world of somber faces. If we hadn't come to CBS together, we would have remained content with occasionally running into each other during the flow of our lives. But in working together we had become friends, and friends we would remain.

"Take a look at this," Van said, and handed me a sheet of yellow typing paper, the kind used in radio for news copy.

It was a memo to Gene Jankowski which Van had typed himself on his old manual typewriter a few days after Gene King's funeral.

"Take it into your office for a minute," he said, "then come back when you've read it and tell me what you think."

Four minutes later I was back. The memo contained a proposal to Jankowski for the reorganization of the CBS Broadcast Group executive lineup. It began by telling Gene that his being surprised by a shortfall of millions of dollars was an indication of the pressing need to reorganize his executive staff. The memo was very hard on Jim Rosenfield, the Broadcast Group executive who had presided over the pricing fiasco which had precipitated the problem. In his proposal Van suggested that the television network be taken away from Rosenfield and divided into two parts. The Entertainment Division would report to Tom Leahy. The other part of Rosenfield's job, network sales along with the Operations and Engineering Departments, would go to Van in a newly created Executive Vice President post which would also include responsibility for news and sports. Roone Arledge at ABC was in charge of both news and sports. Rosenfield would be given executive responsibility for the five company-owned television stations and anything that might fit under the heading of new business. I would become President of CBS News with responsibility for the day-to-day operation of the News Division but would report to Van in his newly created job.

"Well, what do you think?" Van asked.

"It's audacious, I'll say that for it. Why do you think Jankowski would be receptive to a proposal from a guy who a few weeks ago was telling him to screw off."

"He's desperate," Van said. "He knows he's got a mess on his hands and he doesn't know what to do about it. Wyman didn't give him the President's job and Gene is worried he'll either decide to remain Chairman and President or bring somebody in from the outside."

"How do you know that?" I asked.

"I've been discussing this proposal with him and he asked me to put something in writing. I'm going to send it over like this. I don't want my secretary to see it."

"Are you really creating a job you want?"

"Look," he said, "with you running CBS News I'd have no worries. Neal Pilson is doing a good job as Sports President. You two would be the biggest users of Operations and Engineering services anyway. They're a thorn in the side of both News and Sports. I'd really like to fix that. As for Sales, we both had Sales Departments when we ran stations. There's nothing approaching brain surgery there. I think I could make it work."

"Yeah . . . but think of what the reaction in the News Division would be to their President reporting to someone who also has a sales responsibility."

"That's the way it works now," Van said. "I report to Jankowski, who is ultimately responsible for sales and profits."

"But this way there'd be another layer between News and top management," I said.

"The big advantage is that I would be at Black Rock in a position to run interference with Jankowski when some bean counter sends him a memo on CBS News and the erosion of the profit picture."

I stopped pressing the point. It was just a proposal and, besides, President Joyce had a nice ring to it. But I repeated an earlier question.

"Do you really want the job?"

Van took a moment to light his pipe while he mused over the question. By the time he answered, the room was filled with the sweet smoke of an aromatic tobacco.

"I guess I don't have a lot of faith in the way the place is being run. I figure I might as well go for it and ride this thing as far as I can."

"Maybe," I said, "you could develop a little support for our Kuralt-Moyers hour. Jankowski's obviously distancing himself where that broadcast is concerned."

"It's not showing the numbers he's after," Van said. "Gene won't get behind it unless he can wave ratings at Bud and Harvey."

"Wait a minute," I said. "It's done better in the eight P.M. Tuesday time slot than anything since *The White Shadow.*"

"But Shepherd will argue he's building a house of hits and we're pulling down the nine to ten P.M. period by providing him with a lousy lead-in."

"You and I have had this conversation so many times," I said, "I can now play both parts, but there are days when I feel like we've all been created by Joseph Heller, only he did it better."

Van tapped the contents of his pipe into a large ashtray and picked up the yellow paper containing his memo to Gene.

"I'm heading across town," he said. "I'll lay this on the Jank and we'll see what happens. We'll marry up later this afternoon when I get back."

The premiere of the Kuralt-Moyers hour took place on Sunday, June 26, immediately following *60 Minutes.* It was scheduled there on a one-time-only basis in an effort to acquaint a large audience with these new broadcasts.

Kuralt's *On the Road* half hour included a wonderful piece of Americana on the building of San Francisco's Golden Gate Bridge. His story combined grainy black-and-white film of its construction with glorious photography of the bridge today. Throughout he wove in interviews with surviving members of the original construction crew who recalled in vivid detail those dangerous days of their youth. At 8:30 P.M. Bill Moyers devoted his half hour to the nuclear scientists of Los Alamos. If Bill had harbored any remaining doubts about his ability to do quality journalism in a half-hour broadcast, they had to have been removed by this experience.

When the first ratings came in Kuralt was in the top twenty broadcasts that week. The Moyers broadcast was not far behind. On June 28 both broadcasts were moved to their regularly scheduled spot from eight to nine on Tuesday evenings, and immediately fell out of the top twenty listing. Both Kuralt and Moyers worked tirelessly on their broadcasts. For his July 5 *Our Times* broadcast Moyers had gone to China with the playwright Arthur Miller, who was staging a Chinese-language version of *Death of a Salesman.* Van thought it was dreadful. I thought it was brilliant. The producer Harry Moses had come up with what I considered an inspired technique for making the Chinese-language scenes understandable. He obtained the rights to clips from the original film of *Death of a*

Salesman with Lee J. Cobb. He showed a scene from the film and then cut to the same one done by the Mandarin-speaking Chinese actors, providing a sense of the universality of the character Willy Loman. Watching it in a screening room, I felt a lump in my throat when the camera showed a close-up of a Chinese woman in a theater seat hearing in her own language the plea that "attention must be paid" and breaking into quiet sobs. It was exactly how I had felt the first time I heard those words in English. I was taken aback when Van muttered to me, "This is something that belongs on *Sunday Morning,* not in prime time."

"I really like it," I whispered.

When the scene was over, I congratulated Harry Moses, the producer who had gone with Moyers to China. He was there with Andy Lack, the executive producer. Moyers was out in the field working on another story for the series. Harry thanked me and looked enormously pleased.

Then Van turned to Lack.

"I'm not sure that an Arthur Miller play has much hope of appealing to a wide audience," he said.

Harry no longer looked quite so pleased, and Lack seemed downright glum.

"It was a brilliant use of television," I said stubbornly.

"What's scheduled for next week?" Van asked.

"A story set in Gadsden, Alabama," Lack said, "about a generation of people who have now become permanently unemployed."

Van's features seemed to recede into his beard.

"And the week after that?"

"It'll either be a story about whistle blowers in the Pentagon or another one we've been working on about the illegal dumping of hazardous waste by organized crime."

By now Van's chin was down on his chest and he looked like one of those birds on the Great Plains that can fluff their feathers into a huge muff to protect themselves against the cold winds sweeping down from the Arctic.

"Hazardous waste is so serious a problem it may rival the issues of nuclear arms control," I said, "and yet it doesn't seem to register on the consciousness of the public."

Lack looked hopeful.

"I think we'll be helping people understand this with our story," he said.

Van gave me one of those "now see what you've caused" stares, the kind Hardy reserved for Laurel when he'd done something particularly stupid.

"I think it's time you and I headed back to our offices," he said, clearly anxious to get me the hell out of there.

We left together and neither of us mentioned the broadcast. Our mixed signals must have left the two producers confused. I didn't give it that much thought until later in the day when I met with Howard Stringer to discuss his request to borrow Jane Bryant Quinn from the *Morning News* to do some economic reporting. We'd worked out the details for that and I was showing Howard a tape of Sandy Gilmore, an NBC correspondent who had expressed an interest in coming to CBS News.

"Andy Lack says he'd much rather work for you than Van."

The statement was such a non sequitur it took me by surprise.

"Where's he coming from on that?"

"You know that Andy and I are old friends and we talk a lot. He told me about the screening. He's more than a bit intimidated by old Van."

"Tell Andy if he's got something on his chest he ought to have the balls to say it in front of Van," I said.

"It's just that every time he meets with Van he walks away feeling like an idiot who lacks a commercial touch."

"In case Andy failed to notice," I said, "both Van and I spoke our minds and then we walked away to let him produce his own broadcast."

"He quite appreciates that," Howard persisted, "but you're so used to Van you sometimes forget the impact he can have on people."

"Those people you refer to would do well to remember not just what Van has said but what he's done—which was to defend this institution at a time when it was about to be raped."

"I'm not attacking Van," Howard said. "I quite like him and I know what you both went through."

My irritation was clearly showing and Howard let the matter drop. My short temper was prompted not so much by what he'd said as by the fact that this sort of conversation was becoming a frequent occurrence with others as well and I found it distasteful. At the slightest indication of a difference of opinion between the two of us, I would find myself hearing not very subtle criticisms of Van. There was the obvious expectation that I would join the chorus. When I didn't, there would be an immediate retreat. I couldn't help remembering the silence of these voices when Van and I had been engaged in our struggle with Jankowski.

The morning Van had showed me the reorganization memo he was taking to Jankowski he'd seemed confident, even ebullient. When he returned from Black Rock he appeared less so. He'd come into my office and helped himself to one of the cold Tabs I kept in a small refrigerator.

"How did Jankowski react to your opus?" I asked.

"He just took it and put it in his desk drawer." Van sighed and added, "He wanted to talk about Cronkite."

"What's that about?" I asked.

"Apparently for some time now Walter has been criticizing CBS News at the board meetings," he said.

"Lovely," I said. "What's he saying?"

"His theme, according to Gene, is that *The CBS Evening News* is getting soft."

"That's a bit transparent, isn't it? Not like it was in the good old days when he was at the helm?"

"Gene says that Wyman has been very supportive and that Paley told Cronkite he thought the broadcast had never looked better."

"There's been a lot of stuff in the press recently," I said, "about Rather now having a bigger rating than Cronkite did. Do you think that's a factor in all of this?"

"Who knows. It's just a contribution to the grief factor that none of us needs."

"When he says soft what does he mean?"

"Less of a headline service and more features."

"Well, he's right about the first, but I think he'd have a hard time proving the second. Unless he considers an enterprise or a sidebar story a feature."

"He mentioned the singing sheep."

"Poor Howard," I said. "His obit will include a reference to those fucking sheep. But that's a cheap shot anyway. When Cronkite did the broadcast, more often than not they closed the broadcast with a light story."

"You know what I think our attitude should be?" Van asked. "Fuck him. You and I have busted our ass for this place for a year and a half. I think we deserve a few thank-yous, which we're only going to get if we give them to ourselves. We ought to get the hell out of this wretched city for a couple of weeks and go visit some of the foreign bureaus."

"Can we both afford to be away from here for that long?" I asked.

"We are involved in running a worldwide enterprise, and except for a four-day visit last year to London and Paris, neither of us has done a troop inspection. Have you ever been to the Warsaw Bureau?"

"Never."

"You've helped spend a small fortune in that bureau. Don't you think it would be a good idea to see it for yourself?"

"You've convinced me," I said. "You know another bureau we should definitely visit? Tel Aviv. It's consistently one of our most active spots."

By the end of that afternoon we'd worked out our itinerary. London first, since it's the biggest overseas bureau, then Paris and Rome. After that Warsaw, then Tel Aviv and home. I began to prepare for the trip, setting up meetings with the foreign desks and the broadcasts to get their ideas and opinions on how these bureaus were performing. I peppered them with questions. There were five good correspondents in London, Tom Fenton, John Blackstone, Mark Phillips, Martha Teichner, and Doug Tunnell. Of the five only Fenton got on the air with regularity. Why? When I asked that question of Stringer and his senior producer, Lane Venardos, they had slightly different responses.

"Tom is clearly our senior man," Stringer said. "It's only natural that we would want to use him first if he's available."

"Then why do we need four other correspondents in that bureau?" I asked.

"I think there is a good answer for that," Venardos said.

Lane Venardos is one of those people who respond in short declarative sentences. A man of great girth, heavyset in the manner of the last century or the farm belt of today, his terse sentences are often interspersed with bits of sardonic humor.

"And I give you my word as a senior producer that it's true," he continued, watching me closely for a reaction.

"Even with your name written on the back of that I don't think I would take it to the bank," I said.

"In that case, why don't I tell you what I think. Blackstone and Phillips have been rotated in and out of Beirut and Warsaw. Those are not necessarily assignments which will get them on the air every night. But when something happens you certainly want to have a good correspondent on the scene."

"You won't hear an argument from me on that," I said, "but what about Tunnell?"

"The argument holds there, too, but only up to a point."

"What would happen if we moved Doug to Bonn? He could still be swung into the Middle East, but when he's home he could cover stories in West Germany."

Venardos looked at Stringer before answering.

"Pardon me for bringing this up," he said, "but I seem to recall that we closed a bureau in Bonn less than a year ago."

"Lane, this could be our little secret," I said. "No fanfare. No announcement to unnerve the bean counters. We kept a crew and a small presence in Bonn. So we quietly shift Tunnell out of London, where he's not doing much, and see if we get more from him in Bonn."

"I like that a lot," he said, and turned to Howard. "You might want to discuss it with Dan so he could pretend that it was his idea. And maybe also discuss Martha Teichner with Mr. Joyce before he asks again why she doesn't get on the air more often."

Howard looked uncomfortable.

"I'm afraid we have another Rita Flynn situation," he said.

Rita Flynn had been the number two reporter at the State Department. During the tense dark days of the *Evening News* in early 1981, she had been less than diplomatic in her complaints when a story she'd worked hard on was taken away and incorporated in a report from the White House correspondent. Neither the occurrence nor the reaction was uncommon in a business filled with hardworking, compulsive people. Rather might have remembered some of his own struggles with New York during his years as a young reporter in Washington. Instead he chose to ostracize Rita Flynn. She and I discussed it, and in an effort to ease an ugly situation, I had Rita assigned full-time on Washington stories for the *Morning News*. I told her that "in six months this will all blow over." Six months later a crestfallen Rita Flynn came to see me. She had just come from a meeting she'd requested with Rather.

I knew the answer just from looking at her, but I asked anyway.

"How did it go?"

"Terrible," she said. "He's still angry. He told me I was arrogant. He'll never forget. This was humiliating and I can't go through it again. Will you let me out of my contract?"

"Rita," I said, "you've been doing a good job on the *Morning News*. They're very happy with you."

"I really think it's best if I go somewhere else," she said.

I released her from her contract with CBS News. A few weeks later she joined ABC News as a correspondent based in Washington. Now a year later Stringer and Venardos were telling me the problem had replicated itself, this time with Martha Teichner.

"Martha is a fine writer and a good reporter," I said. "What's Dan's problem with her?"

Stringer looked at the ceiling.

"Where does one begin?" he said. "In the old days before our arrival Dan began holding meetings with different reporters. Teichner was one of them and apparently the session did not go well."

"According to Dan," Venardos said, "Martha was blunt about her preference for *Sunday Morning.*"

"No returning from that, is there?" sighed Stringer.

"Why is it," I asked, "I don't believe Martha would have said that?"

"Ed, it doesn't matter, does it?" Stringer said. "The point is, that's the way Dan believes she felt. Old Dan has a problem with our young women journalists. He'll meet with one of our young men and end up in a Dutch uncle role. With one of our women he's likely to end the meeting feeling angry."

"It's like that Rex Harrison song from *My Fair Lady,*" I said.

Stringer thought for a moment.

"Why can't a woman be more like a man? Yes, there is that, I'm afraid, but with an extra twist. He doesn't think they've earned it the way he had to."

"Guys, what do we do?" I asked. "We can't let this happen."

"Well, it's hard, isn't it?" Stringer said. "No matter what story she does he can nitpick it so relentlessly the path of least resistance is for the producer to try to avoid using her."

"What if we moved her to another bureau? Maybe Dallas," I said. "Someplace where she'll be the only correspondent available. I'm convinced her work would stand on its own. Let me tell Rather what's on my mind. I'd prefer to get this out in the open."

Forty-five minutes later I was offering Dan a cup of black coffee and describing a plan to move Martha Teichner to Dallas.

"The woman is rapidly becoming untouchable," I said, "because so many people around here are convinced they'll offend you if they say a good word about her. I think we got off easy with Rita Flynn." I paused a moment to let that sink in. "I think she could have chosen to make it ugly and she didn't. I don't think any of us need or want the grief that would go with a 'Rather is unfair to women' story."

There were several other names I could have added to those of Flynn and Teichner, but I thought I'd made my point and I stopped while he sipped his coffee.

"Ed," he said, "first of all, thank you for the bluntness. It cuts through a lot and saves us time. Yes, I was angry. No, I do not think I've been unfair. Those were dark days for me before you and Van arrived. When Martha Teichner sat in my office and told me she preferred working on *Sunday Morning* I was furious. Having said that, I take your point. There ought to be a statute of limitations on everything, including Dan Rather's anger. Move her to Dallas. I'll do whatever I can to make it work."

"Dan, I can't ask for anything more than that," I said. "Do you have any thoughts about the London Bureau you want to share with me before I go?"

"As a matter of fact there is," he said. "I've mentioned this to Van but I'd like to share my feelings with you. It troubles me when I hear that Cronkite has said something unflattering about the *Evening News.* I worked hard for that man when he was in my chair, but I figure Walter's just having trouble handling his retirement. What really burns me is when people come back from London and tell me Sandy Socolow is talking the same way."

"I haven't heard that, Dan," I said. "Not from anybody."

"Well, you can take it as gospel that he is," Rather said. "In fact, Howard Stringer is picking up the same thing from his British friends in that bureau. I figure this outfit's been good to Sandy and I think somebody ought to set him straight."

"I'll talk to him when I get there, you can count on it," I said. "And, Dan, thank you again for your openness about Martha Teichner."

Three days later I was sitting with Martha Teichner in the CBS London Bureau. I told her of our plan to move her to Dallas. I did not mention Rather. Martha was terribly shaken by the news. I had tried to couch the transfer in terms of an opportunity to be on the air more often. She had fallen in love with London and wanted to stay. I could understand that. A petite woman with a touch of style in her dress, she looked very much at home walking up Sloane or Kensington streets.

"Martha," I said, "we all have to face the fact that you've been here for well over a year and it hasn't worked out. There may be a hundred reasons for that, none of which are your fault. The fact is that I didn't create them and I can't alter what happened. What I can do is put you in an environment with better chances for success."

She'd been staring at the floor and now she looked up, brightening as she did so.

"I'll go to Dallas and I'll try to do my best work. Now can I ask you two questions?"

"Fire away."

"Have you heard that I told Dan Rather I preferred working on *Sunday Morning?*"

"I have. Why do you ask?"

"Because I keep hearing that this is what he says and it never happened. I had one meeting with him and it lasted all of five minutes. He kept bombarding me with questions and one of them was 'What kind of stories do you believe you do best?' I told him I thought I was best at the longer enterprise stories where I have more time. Ever since then, I've kept hearing how I told him I preferred working for *Sunday Morning.* It's all been terribly puzzling."

"Martha," I said, "don't worry about it. Just go to Dallas and do good work. What's your second question?"

"Why can't I go to Beirut?"

"Why would you want to go?"

"Because John and Mark are always complaining about the frequency with which they're sent there. I think they feel I'm not carrying my share in this bureau. If I'm being kept out because I'm a woman, I think that's wrong. But I can never get an answer when I ask."

"Well, I can get an answer," I said. "If it's because you're a woman, I promise you a tour of Beirut before you go to Dallas."

After Martha left I looked at Van, who had come into the office for the last few minutes of our conversation.

"She's a gutsy woman," I said. "I really like her. I wonder if there's some unspoken policy not to send women to places like Beirut?"

"It's almost noon here," Van said, looking at his watch. "John Lane will be having breakfast right now. Why don't you call him at home and ask him?"

Because I could direct-dial John's home number, I had him on the line in less than a minute. When he heard my question he paused a moment before answering.

"I don't have to tell you, my friend, that Beirut is a very dangerous place," he said.

"John, that's not fair," I said. "Reputations in our business are earned in dangerous places."

"I guess I have to plead guilty," John said. "Maybe it's just that I'm of a certain generation, but there's no doubt about it, Martha has not gone to Beirut because I didn't think we should send a woman there."

You could always count on John Lane for an honest response. Even if he knew you believed he was wrong.

"John, work her into the rotation for Beirut," I said, "and when she gets back she knows we're going to move her to Dallas."

"I hope Mr. Rather will let up on her now," he said.

"Dan has assured me he'll do everything he can to make it work," I said.

"I pray that happens, my brother. He's not a very forgiving man."

After my call to Lane I looked at Van.

"We have to make this one work," I said. "Too many people are terrified of crossing Dan and it's unhealthy."

"That's a problem for two weeks from now when we get back to that wretched city," Van said. "It's one-thirty and it's a beautiful August day in London. Let's go walk around for a couple of hours."

Shortly after our visit to London, Martha Teichner left for Beirut, where her reports from its embattled streets earned her the praise of her colleagues at CBS News. Later when she began her assignment in Dallas, Rather remained a critic but no longer blocked her appearance on the *Evening News.* For years, though, producers who might be involved in an admiring discussion with me of her work would quickly fall silent if Rather entered the room.

Van and I left London for Paris with the beginning of a plan for reorganizing the European bureaus and with new wardrobes. Trilbies from Herbert Johnson's on Old Burlington Street, shirts from Turnbull and Asser on Jermyn Street, and ties from New and Lingwood in the Burlington Arcade. London is a Disneyland for men and future trips together invariably involved these self-indulgent shopping expeditions. For Van it was the beginning of a sartorial transformation from his celebrated L. L. Bean look to a more donnish appearance. The flannel and tweed look of an Ivy League professor not solely dependent on the university for income. It was great fun going on a trip like this. We had both purchased tickets for our wives for the London-Paris-Rome leg of our trip. The two of them liked one another and would go off sightseeing while Van and I spent our days in the bureaus, then join us for dinner with a bureau chief or a correspondent. It was the most painless travel imaginable. Someone from the bureau met you at the airport, made sure your hotel rooms were satisfactory, arranged for dinner reservations, and then got you back to the airport, undoubtedly breathing a great sigh of relief at your departure. British generals in the last century traveling to the limits of the Empire could scarcely have received more attention at each point of their journey.

In Paris we told Don Kladstrup, a correspondent in the bureau there, that it was our plan to move him to Chicago. Van, who'd once been the

Paris Bureau chief, felt that Kladstrup was not the kind of stylist who could capture the flavor of stories which were peculiarly French. Rather had fueled this by complaining that Kladstrup wouldn't allow the bureau to place a television set in his apartment. But Kladstrup had covered Beirut during some of the worst fighting and had always been a willing volunteer for such assignments.

The meeting with him did not go well. He'd just come back from an assignment in Chad and still had vestiges of the fever he'd acquired there. He and the Paris Bureau chief, David Miller, had been at odds for months and he obviously blamed Miller for his problem. As it turned out, besides moving Kladstrup we ended up replacing the bureau chiefs in both Paris and Rome. Neither of them spoke the language of their host countries and, as a result, seemed isolated from events around them, totally dependent on translators. They were unable to even read the local papers or understand the news they watched on television.

We left both Paris and Rome somewhat dispirited and considerably fatigued from plane flights and quick turnarounds on the ground.

In Warsaw, nothing about the sight of that gray city lifted our spirits. Warsaw was bombed to rubble during the Second World War. Except for an old-town section which was lovingly rebuilt, the city is made up of block after block of depressing socialist gray buildings.

At the time of our arrival in Warsaw, martial law had recently been lifted. The mood of the city was still tense. Long lines formed at every opportunity to purchase consumer goods from toilet tissue to poultry. The only stores whose shelves were stocked with goods for sale were the government PEVEX stores, which accepted only Western hard currency. There was something obscene about the sight of Poles walking by store windows crammed with items all of which were unavailable in their daily lives.

We checked into the InterContinental Victoria Hotel and had dinner that night with Les Pawlowicz, the Polish-born American bureau chief. He'd been a unit manager in the public-affairs area in New York until the declaration of martial law in Poland. The ability to speak Polish and understand the contortionist nature of Polish society earned him a quick promotion to bureau chief. We had dinner at a so-called free-market restaurant in the suburbs of Warsaw, and over glasses of *sok,* a wonderful black-current juice the Poles should export by the barrel, he depressed us further with how hard it had been for our crews. Technically, they worked for the government-run Interpress Agency, which billed us for their services. But in covering government crackdowns and Solidarity rallies they had all run great risks to get the story of their nation's trauma on the television screens of America. Some, including one young woman in the bureau, had been beaten up. Others were arrested and held in detention. Still they eagerly went out on assignments with all the spirit of a nation which for centuries had depended on miracles for its continued existence.

The price they paid for this was getting their names on the lists kept by Polish Security of known troublemakers. A cameraman or an editor whose name appeared on such a list was unlikely to ever find work again for one of the state-run organizations such as Interpress or Polish TV.

"What would happen," I asked Les, "if the Polish government should at some point decide to close down our bureau?"

"Our people would have a very hard time," he said. "They wouldn't be able to work as cameramen or editors, and in this society you are obligated to work or else you are declared a parasite and they can put you in jail."

"What would they do?" Van asked. "What kind of work would they find?"

"I don't know," Les said. "Maybe something in a factory."

What I found myself thinking but didn't say was that as a result of the declaration of martial law CBS News had expanded its presence in Warsaw. We had gone from two or three people to sixteen in a short space of time. Inevitably, there would be less and less demand for stories each night or even each week from Poland. If this happened anywhere else, we would simply reduce or eliminate the bureau and move the people elsewhere. These crews couldn't be moved and if we dropped them they would pay a price for the coverage we had presented to the United States.

That night in our hotel I mentioned this to Van.

"It's so easy to sit in New York and make the wrong decision," I said.

"It's all part of the learning curve," he answered. "It's one reason why these trips are so valuable for us both."

I don't quite know what I expected when I arrived at the bureau the next morning. Perhaps to meet a somber group of people worn down by their environment and unnerved by their bleak prospects. The people I met that day—the crews, editors, production managers, and drivers— were vital, alert, and even ebullient. They seemed delighted that the brass in New York had included Warsaw in their swing through the European bureaus. We had been warned before leaving New York and again at dinner with Les that we should assume that our hotel rooms were bugged and even our cars and the bureau itself. If we had anything of significance to discuss, it was advised that we take a walk in the park for that purpose.

For that reason I wasn't prepared for the spirited wide-ranging conversations which took place in our bureau. Anti-Russian jokes: "If the Germans attacked Poland on one front and the Russians on another, who would you fight first?" Answer: "The Germans of course. Duty before pleasure." One young cameraman regaled us with the story of how he convinced the government to give him permission to travel to Rome at a time when travel to the West was almost completely shut off. It was just before the Pope's trip to Poland earlier in the year.

"I told them," he said, "the Italian crews understand how to cover the Pope. They know the . . . what do you call it? . . . protocol. I have to learn this, too, so Poland is not embarrassed in the eyes of the West. So I spent a few days in the CBS bureau in Rome and I came back with wonderful food and clothing for my family and friends."

"Did you have enough Italian lire to do this?" I said. "We could have helped you."

He smiled and pulled the lower lid of his left eye and with his other hand pointed a finger at the ceiling to remind me that there were limits to our conversation.

"It wasn't a problem," he said.

Van and I left for Tel Aviv the next day. There are no easy connections from Warsaw to Tel Aviv, so we overnighted in Vienna and had dinner at the Schweitzerhaus, an enormous beer garden in Prater Park, home of the giant Ferris wheel where Orson Welles met Joseph Cotton in the film *The Third Man.* The Schweitzerhaus is famous for its roast haunches of pork and large steins of Budweiser, a Czechoslovakian beer. We were both helping ourselves to generous portions of each.

"Did Carol Reed give us the symbol of that wheel with his camera in the movie or did Graham Greene do it in his script?" I asked.

"That's a good question. I just know I associate it with *The Third Man* and with a world of secret-agentry."

"Did it cross your mind while we were spending time with all of those remarkable people in our Warsaw Bureau that at least one of them works for Polish security and reported back everything that went on?"

"The other people may even know who it is," Van said.

"I don't know," I said. "Les told me that before martial law we had a cameraman who was the most outspoken pro-Solidarity person. Always making passionate speeches. The day martial law was imposed, he showed up in a new job at State Television and they knew for sure he'd been the agent assigned to CBS News."

"Did you ask Les how he feels living with this every day?"

"He says the Polish government has a law against everything. It's against the law to film a government building. And since all buildings are state-owned you are violating the law every time you roll a camera in a Polish city. He thinks that, for now at least, the Poles see the Western media as a balancing factor in holding off the Russians and so we are tolerated."

"They could find us guilty, then, of law violations anytime they chose," Van said.

"That's Les's theory anyway."

Van motioned to the waiter for a refill on the beer. It was a warm August night in Vienna and we were both sitting in open-necked shirts.

"God, these could be great jobs," he said.

"Why do you say 'could'?"

"It's all changing," he said. "I think Dick Salant may have topped off the good years. Cronkite was number one and there were no real money worries. He could enjoy being editor and publisher because being publisher meant dealing with First Amendment issues. For me—and for you —being publisher means working with less and less money."

"Sauter," I said, "I plan to follow Scarlett's advice and worry about that tomorrow. It's a beautiful night, I'm in Vienna sitting outdoors under the shadow of the King Kong of Ferris wheels, and I plan to enjoy another beer and maybe go hunting for a wine bar in one of those multitudinous houses the Viennese claim Beethoven lived in."

"Sounds good to me," Van said, reaching for the stein of Czech beer being handed to him by a waiter. He took its handle and held it over the table.

"Prosit," he said.

"That's a good phrase," I said. "To the Germans it means 'Good health.' But in the original Latin it literally means 'May it benefit you.' "

"Let's drink to both."

I raised my glass.

"Prosit," I said.

The next day, more than mildly hung over, we both arrived in Tel Aviv on the last leg of our bureau tour. There were about twenty-one people working in the Tel Aviv Bureau at that time. Given the volume of stories consistently generated from Israel, it was a reminder of how large our Warsaw Bureau with its sixteen people had become. Van and I had dinner with Warren Lewis, the bureau chief, in a small café reminiscent of numerous restaurants along New York's Columbus Avenue.

"I'd like to spend some time tomorrow with Bob Faw," I said.

Faw was our correspondent in Israel and he'd done an excellent job, particularly in reporting and interpreting the activities of the Knesset. I'd been told that Faw wanted to come home and everyone in New York from Stringer to Lane was hopeful he could be persuaded to stay for a longer period.

"Bob is planning on taking both of you to Jerusalem tomorrow."

"I've never been there. I'm excited about seeing it," I said. "I'm also interested in getting a sense of what you deal with in operating out of two cities which are a good hour apart."

"Warren, I'm going to take a pass," Van said. "If you can get me a driver I'd like to see some of the Crusader castles."

"You've been to Jerusalem before?" I asked.

"No, but I really want to see these castles."

In Jerusalem, Faw and Moshe Weitz, a young Sabra who works as a news assistant and is also a tank commander in the Israeli Defense Force, indulged my appetite for playing the role of tourist with great patience.

Jerusalem was a city I'd always wanted to visit and I didn't want to waste a minute of that afternoon. It was also an opportunity to talk with Faw and try to encourage him to extend his tour in Israel. One of his reasons for wanting to return was to take part in the 1984 political campaign coverage. In my mind I began to formulate a plan for bringing him back for a few months beginning with the conventions and ending with election night. After that he could return for another year in Israel. I wanted to work that through in my own mind and then spring it on him at dinner that night. Van and I agreed that Faw had now developed a body of expertise in the Middle East which was important to CBS News.

Dinner took place at a seaside restaurant in Tel Aviv. The conversation wandered from Faw's description of how people in foreign bureaus hunger for communication from New York to shared reminiscences of Chicago, a city in which all three of us had worked. As the evening went on, I remembered that I had come with a mission and the time was at hand to make my pitch for Faw to settle for a four-month election coverage return to the States and an extended period in Israel.

"Bob and I have been talking about his desire to come home right now," I said.

Van looked at Faw.

"I think you're smart to want to do that," he said. "You could really carve out a niche on the *Evening News*. And besides, right now you're in a one-story town."

I was so startled by this I began to laugh.

Van, who must have just remembered that I'd gone off with Faw in the morning with the express purpose of exploring reasons for his staying in Israel, grinned.

I shrugged.

"What the hell," I said. "I got to see Jerusalem."

On the
return trip from Tel Aviv to New York, Van and I went over our impressions of the bureaus we'd visited.

We were agreed on the need for bilingual bureau chiefs in Paris and Rome. This was an interesting conclusion for Van to reach. He'd been the Paris Bureau chief for almost two years and spoke no French.

"I wouldn't hire me today for that job," he said.

What became obvious as we looked at other changes was that the moment we moved or replaced two or three overseas correspondents we would immediately need to set in motion a series of other changes. For example, when Faw left Tel Aviv, who would replace him? Don McNeil, the Moscow correspondent for CBS News, was anxiously waiting for the end of his Russian tour. He and his wife would undoubtedly welcome an assignment in Tel Aviv. Who then for Moscow? A good candidate would be Mark Phillips, a young correspondent in the London Bureau who had been hired during the early days of martial law in Poland. He was among the first Western newsmen to make his way out of Poland with an account of conditions there. I'd seen some of his reports for the Canadian Broadcasting Corporation coming in on a satellite feed and was so impressed I set the wheels in motion for his hire. Who would replace Kladstrup in Paris when we moved him to Chicago? Van was convinced that John Blackstone, also in the London Bureau, was the stylist he'd been looking for to go to Paris. Currently there were five correspondents in the London Bureau and not enough assignments to keep them all busy. Dropping to three would allow us to put Doug Tunnell in Bonn and assign a full-time correspondent to Warsaw. For the past year we'd rotated correspondents from other bureaus in two- to four-week tours in Poland. Bert Quint in Rome had drawn a major share of this work. For as long as the story would demand a sixteen-person bureau, it should have its own correspondent. Someone working full-time to understand the story. By the time the plane was skimming over Jamaica Bay to touch down at JFK, we had the rough draft of a plan which we believed improved our situation in Europe.

The next day I had the CBS News Graphics Department construct a large board with the names of all the bureaus in a column on its left side. The names of correspondents were put on small cards which could be magnetically attached to the board next to each bureau. Van and I brought Rather and Stringer into my office and I walked through the proposed changes, moving correspondents to different bureaus on the board.

Rather looked at Stringer.

"Well, Howard," he said, "we can see those rumors of these two fellows having lived it up in the cafés of Europe were unfounded. This is impressive."

"Not necessarily unfounded," I said. "Just incomplete. Besides being impressive, will this make us any better?"

"Howard can speak for himself," Rather said, "but I think any news organization that would have a Tom Fenton in London, Mark Phillips in Moscow, John Blackstone in Paris, and Don McNeill in Tel Aviv could claim to have an absolute Murderer's Row."

"Howard, what do you think?" Van asked.

"I think we'd be unbeatable," he said, "but only if we also improve our bureau chiefs in some of those places."

"Ed and I both think we need to make changes in Paris and Rome," Van said, "and that we need people who are fluent in the language of the country."

"I wouldn't disagree with that," Stringer said, "but they shouldn't be replaced with administrators. We need producers in there who can work with these correspondents to turn out stories which are up to the production standards of the *Evening News.*"

"Speaking of our bureaus," Rather said, "did you have a chance to tell Sandy Socolow that I'm tired of hearing from people who've come back from the London Bureau that he had become the London voice for Cronkite's 'the *Evening News* is getting soft' campaign?"

"We both spoke to him," Van said. "Sandy says he hasn't done that."

"I'd just like to see Sandy spending a little more time initiating good

European stories for the *Evening News* and a little less time politicking," Rather said.

"He's really not very smart about it," Stringer said. "I have tons of old friends in that bureau. Everything he says comes right back to me."

"Look, guys," I said. "I told Sandy we didn't send him to London to be the *Evening News* executive producer in exile. Both Van and I told him he had to start showing us something as the London Bureau chief. If he's smart, he'll do that. If he doesn't, he has a problem. Let's hope it works out. We're about to make extensive changes in our bureaus and when it's done it would be nice if we didn't have to make a lot of changes for a while."

When Rather and Stringer left I looked at Van.

"Maybe it's the jet lag," I said, "but I have the impression Rather expected one of us to return with Socolow's head on a pike."

"Only if he could tell anyone who asked that he had nothing to do with it," Van said.

"I can hear him now," I said. " 'Sauter and Joyce were awfully hard on Sandy, weren't they?' "

"You've got it," he said. "Are you going to start the ball rolling on these changes?"

"I am. It'll take a few weeks to get this going and a month or two to get everyone in place."

As it turned out, I was hopelessly optimistic. The bureau chief moves were accomplished first. Two producers from the staff of the *Evening News* were selected. Peter Schweitzer, who spoke fluent Italian, was sent to Rome. Jennifer Siebens, who spoke French and Spanish, was given the Paris Bureau and became the first woman foreign bureau chief in the history of CBS News. Lucy Spiegel, a producer in the London Bureau, became the second a few months later when she was sent to Beirut. Making the correspondent changes was more complex.

Before this whole process was finished, we would end up shifting people in or to Moscow, Tel Aviv, Paris, London, Warsaw, Bonn, Washington, Atlanta, Chicago, and Dallas. A total of ten correspondents would be part of this global realignment. Was it worth it?

All of these changes involved the use of existing resources. We weren't asking CBS for additional funding for our efforts at improvement. For me, and I believe for Van, it was part of an effort to respond to a challenge we both saw increasing in future years. The challenge of managing CBS News in an era of declining resources.

A few weeks later I got a call from Art Sekarek, the CBS News Vice President for Business Affairs.

"Are you moving a number of people in the European bureaus?" he asked.

"We are," I said, "but they're all people who are already under contract, so your department won't be involved."

"I don't know," he said. "I just got a phone call from Richard Leibner saying he wanted to come in and discuss some of his clients who are being transferred."

I ran through the list. Eight of the correspondents turned out to be represented by N. S. Bienstock, Leibner's talent agency.

"Do any of them have contracts which are coming up for renegotiation?" I asked.

"No," he said. "They're all in mid-contract."

"Call Richard back," I said, "and tell him that. These are all management decisions involving relocations for its employees. Any of those correspondents is free to talk with Lane, Stringer, Van, or me. And when their contracts come up we'll sit down and negotiate with him for their services. We can't start dealing with agents every time we make a decision involving one of their clients."

"I'll call him," Art said, "but remember, you and Van are meeting with him tomorrow about Diane Sawyer. If I know Richard, when you finish with that he'll whip a list of these other things out of his pocket."

There was such a meeting scheduled to discuss Diane Sawyer. In November 1982, the *Morning News* had been expanded to include a half hour from 6 to 6:30 A.M. It was called *The CBS Early Morning News* but was anchored by Kurtis and Sawyer in the same set with the same people who worked on the rest of the broadcast. Leibner had attempted to present a case that we were in breach of contract because the agreement "was subject to renegotiation if she gets a new anchor assignment or receives a major change in assignment." The CBS Law Department assured us that claim was rubbish and he quickly backed off. We did give him a willing promise that if the *Morning News* was successful, next year we would renegotiate Sawyer's salary rather than waiting until the January 1985 expiration date of her contract. That was only fair. She earned less than Kurtis, and while he may have come to the broadcast with more anchor experience, she was the one who had become the central figure of a broadcast which was attracting media attention far in excess of its respectable growth in ratings.

"Come back in a year," Leibner was told, "and we'll do a new money deal."

Nine months, an agent's year, had elapsed and Leibner began reminding me of that promise. I set up a meeting in Van's office to work out the details of a new contract. Van and I knew where we wanted to end up, financial parity with Kurtis, who was currently earning $600,000 a year. We also knew we wanted Leibner to believe we didn't want to pay her that much. He knew he had a hot property on his hands, and if he got one whiff of indecision on our part, he would have visions of another million-dollar deal.

Leibner arrived at Van's office after the *Evening News* had concluded. He brought along Stu Witt, one of his associates. Witt had once worked in the CBS Business Affairs Department. I'd known him for years. We were both runners and would frequently encounter one another in Central Park, where we'd each pick up our pace to impress the other. He was a trim man, bald head balanced by a closely trimmed sandy beard. I liked him and noted with some sadness that he frequently seemed embarrassed by his boss.

Leibner, on the other hand, was one of those people who seemed incapable of embarrassment. He always appeared certain you were glad to see him. Richard Leibner's meetings began with a slightly manic performance. A wide grin, his hands gesturing wildly to make some point, and his accountant's eyes seemingly unconnected to the general tumult. Some years ago Richard Leibner the accountant had become Richard Leibner the agent, and most of him made the transition. All but the eyes.

He settled himself into a chair in the corner of Van's office and grinned at both of us.

"What does a Jewish American Princess say when she's knocked over a Ming vase at the Metropolitan?"

I saw Van's chin begin to rescind into his beard in his ruffed-grouse imitation.

"I know you'll tell us," I said.

"I'm not hurt," he answered, and began to laugh hysterically.

Stu Witt smiled and nodded his head a few times.

"By the end of our meeting," Van said, "your client will be able to buy a fucking Ming vase."

Leibner raised his right wrist in mock limpness and rolled his eyes.

"Will you stop that. You guys are getting me hot."

"Maybe not buy it outright," I said, "but she'll at least be able to make the down payment."

The hand immediately dropped to his lap. The round face of the agent went slack for a moment. Only the eyes remained alert.

"Believe me, she'll be able to buy the whole fucking jar," he said.

"Look," I said. "We're here to talk about paying Diane more money. We don't have to do anything for another year and a half when her contract ends. We're doing this because we think it's fair, but there's an old Wall Street adage we should all remember. 'There's room for the bears and room for the bulls. There's no room for the pigs.' "

Leibner began to drum his fingers on his knees nervously and small beads of perspiration formed on his bald head.

"What figure do you have in mind?" he asked.

"Right now she's earning what? A little under $200,000 a year? That was O.K. for somebody coming off the State Department beat trying to prove she could handle an anchor role. Now she deserves more. She's earned it. Maybe a fifty percent increase."

The drumming stopped and Leibner made a quick rotation in his small notebook. He looked at Witt for a moment.

"I'm not going back to my client," he said, "and recommend a deal unless I can tell her she's earning as much as that rube from Chicago."

Leibner routinely denigrated any of our people who were not clients of N. S. Bienstock. It was an ugly practice and under other circumstances I would have challenged him, but in this case we'd gotten the answer we needed to know. The dollar amount he was hoping to get for his client.

"That's a lot of money," I said. "Maybe we might be able to hit that number in the fourth year of her new contract."

"What new contract?" he said. "I just want to amend the one she's got now."

"You know we're not going to do that, Richard," I said. "If we're talking a new deal, we're talking about another four years."

"Diane would be better off waiting for her contract to end," he said. "Can you imagine what Roone would pay to have the hottest woman in television sitting next to Jennings on *The World News Tonight?* And I could take her to NBC in a minute."

Van had been sitting quietly through all this exchange, with his head down and a pipe in his mouth. He suddenly straightened up and pointed the stem of his pipe at Leibner.

"Yes, you can do that," he said. "And we'll have to assume that in a year and a half Diane Sawyer will be working for the competition. We'll have no choice but to take steps to protect ourselves."

"What can you do?" Leibner said. "You've got a star on your hands. Diane knows how valuable she is now."

"She'll be less valuable in a year and a half," Van continued, "if we stop promoting her and arranging press interviews. And we'll have no choice but to replace her on the *Morning News.*"

I picked up the argument. "You know what her contract contains. CBS has the right of general assignability just as we do with Blackstone and Phillips in London. Diane could spend the next year and a half covering floods and hurricanes out of the Atlanta Bureau."

Witt spoke for the first time.

"You wouldn't do that," he said. "She's too valuable."

Van answered slowly, spacing his words.

"Don't . . . count . . . on it."

By now Leibner was looking like someone who hadn't figured on picking up the check at dinner.

"We all know where Diane's heart is," he said. "She wants to stay at CBS. Stu and I want her to stay at CBS. But Diane doesn't want to stay on the *Morning News.*"

"Then why the hell are we all sitting here?" I said.

"I'm not saying she wants off now," Leibner said. "She feels she's been on the broadcast for two years, including the Kuralt period, and she's tired. And Don Hewitt has been telling Diane how much he'd like to have her join *60 Minutes.*"

Leibner looked at Van. "Diane says you've told her she'd be marvelous on *60 Minutes.*"

This was news to me.

"Yes," Van said. "But I meant sometime down the road."

"What Diane is looking for," Leibner continued, "is some indication that if she signs a new four-year contract, it doesn't mean four more years of getting up in the middle of the night to go to work."

"What if I gave you my assurance," Van said, "that if we do this deal, then in a year and a half Diane will go to either *60 Minutes* or some comparable assignment which might involve some new prime-time show?"

"Let me talk to Diane and see how she responds to that approach," Leibner said.

"If we do this," I said, "we need some assurance that for the next year and a half Diane will continue to put the same effort into the morning broadcast that we've been seeing."

Leibner sat up very straight in his chair.

"I want you to know that if we do this deal," he said, "you have my word of honor that Diane Sawyer will be here every morning breaking her tush to make the *Morning News* a success."

"We'll hold you to that," Van said, "because 1984 will be a hectic year. We have to get through the conventions without having to worry about this. After all, we'll need those remaining months to work out her replacement."

"When that time comes, remember I can help you with some of my other clients," Leibner said.

Van looked at me and laughed.

"Will you get these guys out of here," he said. "I've still got a couple of hundred dollars in my wallet and I'd like to keep it there."

Leibner's wrist shot up and dangled in the air.

"C'mon, Stu," he said. "Let's go before I get hot again."

The negotiation would continue for several months and eventually be concluded on the terms discussed at this first meeting.

When the door closed and the two of them had gone, Van and I looked at one another.

"That's a heavy commitment we've just made for *60 Minutes*," I said.

"We didn't have a choice," Van said. "He's right. She is the hottest woman in television right now. We can't afford to lose her. Hewitt really does want her for *60 Minutes*. He's told me this, and we get another year and a half from her on the *Morning News*."

"All Diane will be thinking about is *60 Minutes*," I said. "It will be very hard to keep her up for the morning broadcast."

"Then we should go back to Leibner," Van said, "and remind him that he gave his word of honor that this wouldn't happen."

I'd worn small half-moon reading glasses during the meeting. I tilted my head and peered at Van over their rims.

"There's a wonderful quote from Emerson that sums up guys like Leibner," I said. " 'The louder he talked of his honor, the faster we counted our spoons.' "

The next morning Leibner called to talk about the relocations.

"What's to talk about?" I asked.

"Teichner's worried about selling her house in London."

"It's not a problem, we deal with that all the time. Tell her to talk to John Lane and Art Sekarek. That's what she should be doing anyway."

"I have to tell you," he said, "that Blackstone and Phillips are talking about quitting and going back to the CBC."

"They can't do that," I said. "They both have contracts. We intend to honor those contracts and we expect them to do the same."

"You don't want unhappy people," he said. "I can work it out for them if I can tell them that in recognizing the nature of the sacrifice they're making, CBS News is going to rewrite their contracts and give them some more money."

"I know Paris is hell," I said. "A man could suffer a *crise de foie* at any time. That was French I was speaking, Richard, but you'll have to tell John to be manly about it."

Leibner just ignored this.

"Well, what about Phillips?" he asked. "Moscow is no picnic. What are you going to do for him?"

"I'm going to pay for his Russian-language lessons before we send him there," I said, "in the hopes that he will distinguish himself in the building of his journalistic portfolio. If he is as good as I think he is, I'll expect a tough renegotiation from you at the end of his contract."

"You're moving a lot of my people around right now," he said.

"Your people? Will there be a new sign-off on their pieces for the *Evening News?* 'Mark Phillips, N. S. Bienstock, Moscow'?"

When I'd finished talking with an unappeased Richard Leibner, I placed a call to Sandy Socolow in London.

"Are you hearing any rumblings," I asked him, "from either Blackstone or Phillips about being so unhappy with their transfers they're thinking of going back to CBC?"

Socolow seemed shocked.

"I'd be very embarrassed as the London Bureau chief if I was that out of touch. Neither of these two gentlemen have been shy about expressing their feelings on leaving London. But you know that. As far as I know, they both see it as a step up and they both appear to be making their plans for the move. I talked to Phillips yesterday, in fact, and he seems enthused about the stories he'll be covering."

"I'm glad to hear that," I said. "If you begin to have any different impressions, let me know. Feel free to put either one of these guys on a plane for New York to come in and talk with us if it seems necessary."

"I may do that with Phillips," Socolow said. "He would like to hit you with a request for CBS News to pay for sending his wife to Russian-language school, too."

"I'm inclined to do that," I said. "In a small bureau in a place like Moscow, a wife plays an important role. Send him in. Not next week, though. I'll be on vacation."

By now I'd devoted a good part of the morning to a matter which was growing increasingly irksome. I'd known Leibner for years. There was no doubt that since his negotiation of Rather's famous million-dollar contract he had come to think of himself as more than just another agent. Because of Rather and his extensive list of clients at CBS News, he had an awareness of our internal activities not possessed by the other agents. Now it seemed as though he was pushing for a kind of favored-nation status, a relationship which would allow him to broker, even arbitrate many of the decisions being made at CBS News. The entertainment industry is filled with super agents who dominate film projects through the power of their client list. Television news, in its competitive frenzies, had long ago granted concessions and extravagant salaries to its performers, but had stopped short of allowing agents to occupy a quasi-management power broker role.

I advanced that theory to Van, who agreed.

"We've got to keep him at arm's length," he said. "Do you know, I've even stopped having lunch at Alfredo's because Leibner is always there. It doesn't matter who you're with, if he sees you he'll come over and sit at your table for a few minutes."

"I just wanted to fill you in," I said. "I'm going to be gone next week and I wanted to make sure we were in lockstep in case he buttonholes you while I'm gone."

"Well, hopefully, it will be an uneventful week," Van said. "You ought to get a head start. What's on your schedule for the rest of the day?"

I thought about that as I got up to leave.

"I'm about to make my most important phone call of the day, to confirm my ferry reservation from Wood's Hole to Vineyard Haven."

A week with Maureen, alone on Martha's Vineyard. Rejuvenation. The island had never failed me. It's amazing, too, how many significant events in my life have occurred while I was on Martha's Vineyard. In 1979 my son was married at our house in Menemsha. In 1971 I was on the island when Bob Hosking called to tell me I had a new boss at WCBS-TV. And in 1969 my being on Martha's Vineyard resulted in my covering a news story which would earn me awards for my reporting from Sigma Delta Chi, the Silurians, and the New York Associated Press.

Midafternoon on Saturday, July 19, 1969, I was about to drive down-island to pick up supplies for a "moon party" we were giving to watch the television coverage of the first manned spacecraft to land on the moon. My mission was aborted because of a phone call from the news desk of WCBS Radio in New York. Senator Edward Kennedy had been involved in some sort of automobile accident on the Vineyard's small satellite island of Chappaquiddick. A girl in the car was killed and would I mind checking the story out? I drove to the police station in Edgartown and found a handful of regional and local reporters gathered there. The national press had not yet descended on the island. All I could learn at the police station was that the accident had taken place at the bridge on Dyke Road . . . that the senator had reported it in midmorning even though the accident and the death of Mary Jo Kopechne had occurred at least eight hours earlier. Kennedy had then left the island. There were few available details about the circumstances surrounding this tragedy other than that the senator had been attending a party at an undisclosed location. I left the other reporters and took the small two-car ferry from Edgartown to Chappaquiddick, where I drove to the bridge and parked my car. On foot I began knocking on the doors of the two houses on Dyke Road, which leads to the bridge. From these neighbors I began to learn more, that Kennedy had driven to the bridge from a party he was attending in a house rented for the weekend by his cousin Joe Gargan. They gave me the location of the house. A few hours later I drove back to Edgartown. Outside the police station I could see a growing number of reporters and curious islanders.

I walked past them and into the station to find the local police chief, Dominick "Jim" Arena, who had been telling reporters all day that he was convinced that "the accident was strictly accidental" and that "there doesn't appear from the principal evidence to be any excessive speed here."

Arena was a big man who looked like a small-town police chief.

I walked up to him and said quietly, "I've just come back from talking to the neighbors about the party in the house Joe Gargan rented. I've been to the house."

Arena quickly took me into his office and closed the door. I'd just begun to tell him there were a lot of questions that needed answering based on what I'd learned in the past few hours when the door opened and a slight blond-haired man with glasses opened the door. It was Walter Steele, the Dukes County prosecutor.

"Walter," Arena said, "this is Ed Joyce. He's a summer person up-island but he's down here for a New York radio station covering this story. You better hear what he's saying."

Half an hour later I came out of the police station looking for a pay phone. In the group gathered outside I saw Mark Monsky, a young news-writer for WCBS Radio, who was also vacationing on the island. He'd heard about the accident and had come down to find out what was happening. He'd seen me leave Arena's office and came over to ask me what I knew. I held my fingers to my lips and walked a block away to a pay phone.

"Just listen," I said. It was 5:25 P.M., four hours after I had received the phone call asking me to cover the story. Reading from notes I still have, I fed the station a story which they taped and put on the air a few minutes later. In that story I gave a description of the accident, including the skid and splinter marks on the bridge. I also described the rented house where the party took place. I quoted Arena as having told me he was "not satisfied with Kennedy's explanation of the nearly eight-hour time lag between the accident and the time it was reported to police."

"He would also like to know," I said, "more about the party that the senator and Miss Kopechne attended just before the accident."

Then I listed a number of questions which remained to be answered. "How was the senator able to mistake a dirt road for the continuing pavement of the main road on the way to the ferry he says they were trying to reach?"

In his statement Kennedy had claimed he and the young Kopechne woman were on their way to catch the last ferry at midnight and had taken a wrong turn. The senator said he had no recollection of how he came to the surface but claimed he made repeated dives into the water after the accident to see if Mary Jo Kopechne was still in the car. He described himself as exhausted and in a state of shock and recalled walking back to where his friends were eating. I'd measured that distance on my car odometer and pointed out in my story that this was a distance of a mile and two-tenths and took Kennedy past several houses, one of whose occupants told me her lights were on at the time of the accident.

I went on to ask: "Who were the friends still there at the party and then able to assist Kennedy when he returned? Were they aware of what had happened to Mary Jo Kopechne? And how was Senator Kennedy able to recross the eighth of a mile of water from Chappaquiddick to Edgartown in the late hours of the night when the ferry was not running and return to his hotel room? Chief Arena says he doesn't know the answer to that either," I said. "He indicates that only the dozen people who attended the party that night on Chappaquiddick would know. The eleven who can provide the answer apparently have not yet been asked."

When I put the phone down and came out of the booth, Monsky gave a long, low whistle.

"This is some kind of story," he said.

"Let's wait a couple of hours," I said. "Arena gave me his home phone number. You call and tell him I asked you to let him know the details of the story which is now running on WCBS Radio in New York. He may already know about it, but let's see what he says."

Because of the location of the WCBS Radio transmitter on Columbia Island in Long Island Sound, the station could be listened to on Martha's Vineyard with clearer reception than some Boston radio stations. In fact, when I visited the local service station where Kennedy's car had been towed after being pulled from Pocha Pond, I could see that the radio dial had been set on WCBS Radio.

About ten o'clock that night Monsky made the call and motioned me to the phone.

"Chief Arena would like to speak with you," he said.

"You were right," Arena told me. "There are a lot of gaps in the story. In the morning, I'm going to file a citation against the senator for leaving the scene of the accident. Look," he continued, "when you're a small-town cop and a United States senator walks into your office you snap to attention, right? But I realize he didn't give me a satisfactory explanation of the eight-hour time lag between the time of the accident and the time he walked into my office to report it."

"Richard Hewitt, the ferry pilot, told me," I said, "that he took Kennedy and two men he didn't remember back to Chappaquiddick at eight o'clock this morning. They left the ferry without a car and returned around nine, which is about the time they came to your office. Have you figured out how he got back to Edgartown in the middle of the night with no ferry running?"

There was a pause at the other end of the phone.

"I just don't know," Arena said.

At 10:30 P.M. WCBS Radio ran my bulletin reporting Arena's decision.

The next morning when I walked into his office he greeted me with a sour look.

"Thanks for keeping me up all night. Every reporter in the country called me at home to check out your story on my filing the citation against Senator Kennedy."

Walter Steele, the prosecutor, was in the office with him.

"Look, you guys," I said, "I don't think you've got a clue as to the number of reporters that are going to swoop down and park themselves on our peaceful little island."

As I said that I tried my damnedest to copy Maureen's Cape Cod pronunciation of the word "park." It came out sounding like "paak." I was carefully dressed in chinos, a madras jacket, a button-down shirt, and an old knit tie. I also had a tan. I knew the reporters who would be arriving with their pale faces and dark suits would look like they were all wearing uniforms. To Arena and Steele, I was not an island native, I was just "summer people," but at least I was *their* "summer people," and they felt comfortable with me.

"You know, Jim," I said, "you're not going to get any work done if you have to spend all your time answering questions from these people. You either, Walter. What you ought to do is arrange with the church to use their hall and hold a news conference late in the afternoon each day. Just don't talk with them the rest of the time."

Since I was now firmly established as a Vineyarder, I knew I'd continue to have access, and that was the way it worked. Over the next five days I provided a total of seventeen stories to WCBS Radio.

When I left Arena's office that morning, Monsky came up to me with the Boston and New York newspapers. This story was competing for space on their front pages with the historic moon landing. The New York *Daily News* had made it their banner headline. The New York *Times* was more restrained but placed it page one, column two. The *Times* along with the other papers relied almost completely on the statement Kennedy had given to the police in the early morning, calling it "another of a series of violent events that have hounded the Kennedy family ever since it came to prominence in American political life." The *Times* also said the Kennedy statement released by the police "does not make clear where the senator and his party has been on Chappaquiddick Island."

I read the papers quickly.

"As far as I can tell, I'm the only one who's located the house or suggested there are holes in Kennedy's story. Let's go back to Chappaquiddick and see what else turns up."

When I pulled up to the small gray shingled cottage with yellow shutters where the party had taken place, I had my car radio on. It was an incredible moment in history. Human footprints were being placed for the first time on the surface of the moon and I could hear the voice of the man who was doing it while he was doing it. It was hard to leave the car, but I did, to do something I should have done the day before. I looked in the garbage cans for any indications of the nature of the party which had taken place there on Friday night. The cans were as spotlessly clean as the interior of the cottage, which I could see through cracks in the lowered blinds. A great deal of care had gone into leaving the house in pristine condition.

I'd talked briefly the day before with Foster Silva, the caretaker for the rented cottage, who lived next door. I'd wanted to confirm, which I did, that I'd identified the right house. Now I paid him a return visit and sat in his living room with Silva and his wife and son, who told me that, while they hadn't seen any of the partygoers, they had heard them.

"So had our dogs," Silva said. They'd barked all evening because of the singing and laughter which came from the house next door.

"The party wasn't wild with any riotous goings-on," Silva said. "But they were very loud, and if they had kept it up, I would have called the police. At one o'clock," he added, "I was pretty fed up with the whole thing, but sometime between one-thirty and two the noise suddenly died down."

Kennedy's statement to the police said that he and Mary Jo Kopechne left the party at approximately 11:15 P.M. to get back to Edgartown. The eleven living people who attended the party have never publicly discussed that night in all of the subsequent years. The account of the Foster Silvas describing their barking dogs and the suddenness of that transition to the normal stillness of an island night is as much of an insight as anyone else had gotten as to what it must have been like when that evening came to a sudden end. Over two hours after the senator says he left for the ferry the party ended abruptly, switching off songs and laughter and returning the night to the softer sounds of the island cicadas and gently clanging channel buoys.

On Friday, July 25, in the District Court in Edgartown, Senator Kennedy returned to Martha's Vineyard to face the charge of leaving the scene of an accident. He was given a two-month suspended sentence and put on a year's probation.

That evening the senator appeared on radio and television in a speech which was intended for the voters of Massachusetts but which was carried nationwide. The speech, which his strategists apparently intended as a kind of "Checkers" address, raised as many questions as it provided answers. One statement made by Kennedy in that speech remains the most definitive comment on the tragic affair now known to the world simply as "Chappaquiddick."

"I regard as indefensible," Kennedy said, "the fact that I did not report the accident to the police immediately."

In September 1983 the bridge on Dyke Road was still enough of a local curiosity to maintain a steady trickle of visits from newcomers to the island. For the islanders themselves, "Chappaquiddick" ranks in the same category as such other occasions of momentary celebrity for their island as the Frank Sinatra–Mia Farrow honeymoon and the filming of the movie *Jaws*.

As the week drew to a close, I was well rested, well fed, and well ready to get back to work.

It was about ten-thirty the morning of Friday, September 16, 1983, when the phone in our island house rang. It was Van.

"I'm in a room full of people and I can't talk," he said in a hushed voice. "Make sure you are around your phone today. I've got to go. Goodbye."

There are a lot of things I like to do on a vacation and hanging around a telephone is not one of them. But I was sure Van was calling from Black Rock. I couldn't think of another environment which would have produced a call as terse as the one I'd just received. My best guess was that Jankowski was about to announce some changes in the Broadcast Group. There hadn't been any new indication of this before I left. I wondered what had been going on all week while I'd been enjoying the island in the post-Labor Day glow when most of the summer people had packed up and gone home. I described the phone call to Maureen, who asked me what I made of it.

"I could be wrong," I said, "but I think Van is about to be elevated and that I'll become President of CBS News."

She looked at me carefully.

"You don't seem excited."

"It's strange, isn't it? It's what I've wanted for years. But you're right—I don't feel excited."

"You're probably just worried it won't really happen and you're trying to protect yourself."

"Maybe," I said. "To keep myself from pacing around I'm going to go out on the porch and read. Are you finished with the Dick Francis book?"

"You can have it," she said. "I don't think it was one of his best. But you like anything with a horse in it."

It was sometime after two o'clock when Gene Jankowski's secretary phoned. She put Gene on the line. His first words were: "I'm speaking to the new President of CBS News."

"Gene, that's just great," I said. "Tell me about Van."

"I'm bringing Van over here," he said, "as an Executive Vice President. He'll have the Presidents of the News and Stations Divisions reporting to him."

"Did you say Stations?" I asked.

"That's right. The most important product of our television stations is their news, so there's an affinity. I want to see us developing some synergies."

Rather than respond to a statement I thought fell somewhere between simplistic and absurd, I asked another question.

"Are there any other changes?"

"Yes, let me walk you through them. I'm putting together the management team for the eighties."

That was a line I was sure I would be reading in the trade papers and I was right. The changes Jankowski outlined essentially gave the heart of Jim Rosenfield's job to Tom Leahy, who had been Executive Vice President in charge of the television stations, as well as radio and the other Broadcast Group enterprises such as cable. Leahy would now be placed in charge of the Entertainment Division along with network sales and affiliate relations. Neal Pilson, the President of Sports, was upped to Executive Vice President in charge of the Sports and Radio Divisions. As for Rosenfield, he was given a grab bag of responsibilities which included finance, network operations and engineering, and the cable and other new enterprises which had been Leahy's responsibility. But at the same time, he was awarded a new title, Senior Executive Vice President.

It was a sweeping organization all right. Jankowski appeared to have taken Van's proposal and expanded it into a ledge of bureaucratic basalt which was now squarely placed between himself and all of his divisions. Instead of two Executive Vice Presidents, he had a quartet, a group that would come to be derisively referred to by the other CBS managers as "the Admiral's Club."

When I hung up the phone, I didn't say anything for a moment, and Maureen grew impatient.

"Well?"

"Confusion now hath made his masterpiece."

"What is that?"

"It's a line from *Macbeth.* I saw it somewhere the other day and it is painfully apt."

"Never mind that, were you named President?"

"I am, I mean I was," I said. "I'm sorry, I thought you could tell from the conversation."

Maureen let out a yell.

"That's wonderful! We've got to call the children."

Just then the phone rang. This time it was Van.

"Did Jankowski reach you?"

"He sure did. This is a fine mess you've gotten us into, Ollie."

I heard laughter at the other end of the phone.

"I know," he said. "Isn't it ridiculous?"

"Just what you wanted, the Stations Division."

"I know," he said again. "I'm going to have to roll up my sleeves and go to work. You wouldn't believe what this place has been like for the past week."

"I can believe it."

"Jankowski has gone through fifteen versions of his reorganization plan. It changed each time someone left his office."

"I wish you'd called me."

"I almost called you several times. Then I thought: why ruin your vacation? You're going to need whatever rest you've gotten. When are you coming back?"

"I was coming on Sunday but now I think I'll return tomorrow if I can get a ferry space on a Saturday."

"Kathleen and I will be in our Connecticut house. Why don't you and

Maureen stop off on your way home. We can have a late lunch or an early dinner."

I did get a ferry reservation and the next day we arrived at the Sauter house in Connecticut sometime in midafternoon. Kathleen had a chilled soup and a pasta salad waiting. Van opened a bottle of California white wine. The afternoon was warm, more like a July than a September afternoon, and we ate out on their deck. We had our eight-month-old Jack Russell terrier with us and we were all laughing at his acrobatic leaps off the deck and his feverish runabouts in the woods around the house in pursuit of squirrels.

"You should take him to Black Rock with you," I said.

"An inspired idea," Van said. "There are enough squirrels, too." Van paused. "Is your dog getting through our fence?"

We walked into the woods and I retrieved "Bo the Wonder Dog," who was indeed trying to make the best of a small hole in the wire mesh.

"How did Rosenfield end up with an upgrade in title to Senior Executive Vice President?"

"He laid a guilt trip on Gene you wouldn't believe," Van said. "He reminded them that a year ago he'd been offered a big job at ABC and Gene and Wyman had talked him into staying at CBS. Then he told them the change would be perceived as a complete demotion for him unless he was named Senior Executive Vice President."

"We'll have to remember that," I said. "Gene takes guilt."

"It doesn't matter," Van said. "Gene's sending us all signals that the title doesn't mean anything. Jankowski cut him off at the knees."

"Jimmy is resilient," I said. "He won't even know that."

"Wait till he tries to dance," Van said.

"I guess I should feel up about this," I said. "But I honestly have to tell you I have some real concerns about how all of this will work. Gene now has a layer between himself and CBS News. It might have been different if you'd had some control at the network level, but you've got stations instead. I don't think it's healthy."

Van seemed just as gloomy. "Eduardo," he said, "just remember you're the one who's ended up with the good job. I have to go over there and live with those wretched people."

We laughed and continued to shuffle our way through layers of fallen oak leaves. On that day we were both willing if not cheerful participants in a historic change in the relationship between CBS News and the Corporation. But we had shared a great deal during the past eighteen months and both of us seemed determined to approach the future in that same spirit.

As we drove home that evening along the winding Merritt Parkway, Maureen was uncharacteristically silent for much of the trip. As I turned onto the Cross Country Parkway, she broke her silence.

"I'm worried about how you and Van are going to work together in these new jobs," she said. "All he talked about at dinner was how awful it was that he was going to have to go out now and buy suits."

"That's mostly joking," I said. "We've gone through so much and shared so much, we'll be able to sort it out."

"I know you'll try," she said. "And I believe Van will try, too. I've just been thinking about that dinner at Mr. Chow's."

I had to think a minute before I got the point. Not long after we'd arrived at CBS News we were in Los Angeles with our wives, having dinner at a Chinese restaurant in Beverly Hills. When the menu arrived, I began the usual discussion of "if I order their mystery appetizer, which we all know is seaweed, and Kathleen orders the spiced dumplings, then Maureen could order the spiced shrimp and Van could . . ."

Kathleen interrupted. "You don't understand," she said with a resigned smile.

"Don't understand what?"

"Van doesn't share. Even with his wife."

While the three of us exchanged portions of our orders, Van ordered three dishes for himself and ate varying portions of each.

By now I was speeding down the Henry Hudson to Manhattan and our apartment on Central Park West.

"I know what you're saying about Van," I said. "And it won't always be easy. I know that. One part of Van is desperate to be in that Black Rock hierarchy. If Jankowski moves up or out Van could become the Group President and he knows that. The other Van will hate every minute he's there."

"That's my point," she said. "There are two Vans and one of them will get very restless if this new job takes him out of the limelight."

Some idiot driver swerved in front of me from the right lane and sped into the exit for the Mosholu Parkway.

"Honey, I love you very much," I said. "But please knock it off. All I know is that Monday morning I'm going to walk into the Broadcast Center as the new President of CBS News and I certainly don't plan to be anything else."

270

"On Friday I received a brief phone call from Gene Jankowski while I was on vacation," I said.

"It was one of those 'you're now the President of CBS News . . . details to follow' calls. I was back in the office on Monday and then left on Tuesday to come here. As you can see, my first order of business as President of CBS News is to see if the place can run without me."

The audience at Caesars Palace in Las Vegas gave me an understanding laugh and the tone was set for the rest of the speech I was making. David Brinkley of ABC News had been the scheduled keynote speaker for the thirty-eighth annual conference of the Radio and Television News Directors Association. He'd canceled just a few days before the event and I'd agreed to take his place. About 1,500 radio and television executives from around the country attended the conference and it provided me a chance not only to make my first talk as President of CBS News but to say something to the assembled news directors I'd long wanted to say.

For years I'd attended these annual meetings and listened to speakers from the networks, usually anchormen or high-level executives, as they hectored the local news directors on their shortcomings. Most often this was accompanied by a gratuitous reference to the local anchors with their "blown-dry hairstyles." They spoke with the smugness of archbishops lecturing young novitiates on the virtue of celibacy. After almost two years of exposure to the vanities of network anchors, many of whom would flunk a truth-in-hair-coloring test themselves, I wanted to say something different. I didn't believe the networks had cornered the market when it came to journalistic competence. In the late sixties and early seventies there were stations around the country with news broadcasts which seemed descended from the comedy show *Laugh-In*. By 1983 their number had dwindled and there were as many television stations producing news broadcasts with as much care for journalistic standards as *The CBS Evening News*. So I chose to speak to the news directors about the unifying effect local stations exert on their communities during difficult times, from economic crises to weather emergencies such as floods or hurricanes. I mentioned the many stories broken by their news organizations which ranged from political developments to prison conditions. Then on a personal note I told them it was a complex and demanding and often thankless job they performed. I knew there were a lot of news directors sitting in that audience who were going through their own version of what I'd experienced. Trying to win in the ratings and at the same time run a news organization in which they could take pride. I wanted them to know that what they were doing wasn't going unnoticed. From the warmth of the applause at the end of my remarks I knew they had recognized and appreciated an attempt to break with the past by acknowledging the accomplishments of local television stations.

After the speech I walked outside in the dry Nevada air. The lighting in Las Vegas casino hotels is permanently subdued and there are no clocks on display to distract the gamblers. Midnight and noon are indistinguishable. It took a moment for my eyes to adjust to the bright sunlight, and when they did I saw Van walking toward me. He seemed to be coming from the direction of the MGM Grand, which was across the street from Caesars.

"You look like a contented man out for a noonday stroll," I said.

"It's a keen disguise," he said. "I've been meeting with some of the stations people."

"How are you finding it?"

"Chicago and St. Louis are O.K.," he said. "New York, Los Angeles, and Philadelphia are in the toilet."

"Other than that, Mrs. Lincoln, how was the play?"

"You've got it," Van said. "How did your speech go?"

"Well, there were no flying objects when I finished, so I think it went fine."

I described briefly what I'd told the news directors.

"Of course, I also included a 'libel suits are hazardous to your health' segment," I said.

"Get used to that," Van said. "I've given the speech so many times I ought to record it."

"I'll hold out for a music video."

"Speaking of our favorite lawsuit," Van said, "Boies feels that Burt is winning the public relations war."

"I know. He's told me that, too. He says Burt is constantly leaking damaging material he finds during the discovery process to friendly reporters. Boies is worried it'll be a year before the trial starts and impossible by then to get jurors who haven't been influenced."

"Another year of this. It's sheer madness," Van said. "Vradenburg would like for the Law Department to hire a public relations firm which would stay with the case right through the trial."

"That's a bit of a departure, isn't it? A Law Department with its own PR firm."

"Just for this trial," Van said. "There's a need for someone who can learn the details of this case the same way Boies has. Someone who can be as aggressive as Burt but hopefully with some class."

"Just as long as we don't lose control of this," I said. "The Law Department has a short-term goal . . . winning the trial. Let's make sure they understand it's CBS News which sets policy, not the Law Department."

"You've got it," Van said. "By the way, Jankowski is very anxious to see some announcement made on *American Parade.*"

American Parade was the name of our next entry in the prime-time sweepstakes. The network had not renewed the two half-hour broadcasts with Kuralt and Moyers. It was Jankowski's ultimate decision. His explanation to us was that there had not been enough evidence of ratings growth in the ten weeks the broadcast had been on the air. Reminders that these broadcasts had actually done better than anything the Entertainment Division had placed in that Tuesday night time slot since *White Shadow* days fell on deaf ears. Jankowski's response to Van and me was: "Try again next spring with something else." We consoled ourselves that CBS News at least had another commitment for a spring-summer run. This time we wanted to do an hour broadcast rather than two half hours. On-air promotion is important to the introduction of any new broadcast. We'd had to divide our limited allotment of promotional airtime between *On the Road* and *Our Times.* If we could use the time for the promotion of only one new broadcast, we could do a better job of attracting new viewers. We'd asked Shad Northshield to be the executive producer of the new broadcast and told him our first choice for the anchors would be a team of Kuralt and Moyers. I asked Kuralt if he would now be willing to join Moyers in an anchor partnership. His immediate response was "Yes." He'd been impressed with the *Our Times* broadcasts and hoped that he and Bill together might be able to acquire and hold on to a piece of the prime-time schedule. By then Van was being pressured by Jankowski for a commitment from the News Division that it would be able to program one of the prime-time hours in the spring schedule. We were both convinced that he wanted to demonstrate for Wyman his ability to reduce the staggering costs for programming time and we were more than happy to make that happen, if it meant a new hour for CBS News. I went to Moyers with the news that we had another opportunity, and that not only would we have Shad Northshield as the executive producer but this time Kuralt had no reservations about a co-anchor role with Bill Moyers.

Bill was less than enthusiastic.

"I don't know what I could do that would be better than what we did on *Our Times,*" he said. "I know I was difficult to persuade that my kind of journalism could be done in a half-hour broadcast. I was wrong. It can be done. My colleagues and I have just done with *Our Times* some of the best journalism on television."

"Bill," I said, "I agree with you about *Our Times.* Those were marvelous broadcasts. I'm one of the people who convinced you to try the half-hour format. I'm as frustrated as you are that the network didn't renew the broadcast. But we've got to keep trying. If we don't tell Jankowski in the next day or so that CBS News is ready to undertake this, Bud Grant and Harvey Shepherd will bombard him with proposals for new sitcoms and action adventure shows. CBS News will lose a great opportunity. We can't let that happen."

"If this is what you want me to do, I'll do it," Bill said. "I know you want to preserve whatever toehold we have in prime time. But I've never worked with Shad, except for an occasional contribution to *Sunday Morning.* How does he feel about me? Maybe I'm not his ideal choice for a new broadcast."

"Shad has told me how enthusiastic he is about working with you," I said. "I'll call him and let him know that you've agreed to do this. Then I think you guys should spend a lot of time together for the next few weeks just bouncing around ideas."

Standing outside Caesars Palace that day with Van, I was optimistic about this new broadcast. Northshield was an experienced producer and I was hopeful that Moyers and Kuralt together under the umbrella of a single broadcast would provide compelling viewing. When Van mentioned Jankowski's eagerness for a public announcement of the new broadcast, I was all for it.

"On October 13," I said, "the CBS Press Department is flying in reporters from the television pages of newspapers around the country for the fall press meeting to hype all the new shows. I'm supposed to speak to them in the morning. I can handle *American Parade* there."

"Jankowski may want to announce it himself before that," Van said.

"The more Gene becomes identified with this effort, the better. If he does it, fine. If not, I'll do it on the thirteenth. That's something of a departure for Gene, isn't it? He hasn't exactly sought a public role."

"I think we'll see Gene doing a lot more of this. He wants to become an industry statesman. His staff is busy searching for the right kinds of speaking opportunities for him. What they call 'pedestal' speeches."

"You have to admire him," I said. "He's not a graceful speaker but he'll stand there at the podium . . . start at the beginning and stop when he comes to the end."

"He's going to do everything he can," Van said, "to convince Tom Wyman to name him President."

"Well, bless him in his quest," I said. I looked at my watch. "I'd better get back to my room and pack up. This is not a town I want to stay in any longer than I have to."

"I'm heading back, too," Van said. "By the way, there is no available office space for me right now at Black Rock. They are going to knock down some smaller office on the twenty-fourth floor and construct something for me but that will take several months. I don't want to move into anything smaller over there, even in the interim. It will send the wrong signals."

"Van," I said, "I am going to miss you when you leave our building. Miss our popping in and out of one another's offices. But if you stay there for several months it will really send the wrong signals."

"I hear you," he said. "Maybe there's some space in one of the other CBS buildings in midtown."

As it turned out, there wasn't, so I wouldn't physically occupy the CBS News President's office until early in the new year.

I flew back to New York to find that my suggestion that Moyers and Northshield "spend a lot of time together just bouncing ideas around" would not qualify for inclusion on a list of great ideas. My first indication of this came from Bob Chandler, who'd replaced Roger Colloff as Vice President for Public Affairs when Colloff was shipped out of the News

Division to a staff job at the Broadcast Group. Chandler was a man in his mid-fifties who'd been a reporter for *Variety* before joining CBS News. For years he'd been a deputy to Bill Leonard, working primarily in the planning and coordinating of convention and political coverage. In 1977 he was appointed Vice President for Public Affairs, a job he held until the early eighties, when Leonard moved him to a news administration position. This enabled Leonard to make room for Colloff in public affairs at a time when he was trying to provide some journalistic experience for his young protégé from Washington. Now Chandler was back for a second tour. Bob took pride, even delight, in being blunt and outspoken. This sometimes grated on some of the creative personalities in the documentary unit. Mostly I found his candor refreshing and had come to respect Chandler for being someone who would rather roll up his sleeves and get a job done than spend days discussing how difficult it would be. A heavy man who never seemed to be without a cigarette, Chandler labored to make himself heard with a thin voice which ranged from husky to wispy.

"It's not going well with those two guys," he said.

"What do you mean?"

Chandler inhaled a lungful of cigarette smoke and brushed some ash from his vest before answering.

"Well, Shad says Bill wants to spend hours discussing the direction they're going to take. Not just the kinds of stories Bill would do but the entire broadcast."

"What's wrong with that?"

"Shad's used to working with Charlie on *Sunday Morning*. As long as Charlie can do his own writing he's happy to let Shad worry about what goes in the broadcast in the way of stories."

"It won't work that way with Bill," I said. "Until he's actually out in the field shooting his stories, he's going to need a lot of time with Shad discussing everything. Shad must recognize what an asset Moyers is."

"He has great respect for Bill," Chandler said. "But you know Shad. He's used to running his own empire."

"Shad Northshield has spent a lifetime at NBC and CBS working with some very difficult and talented people," I said. "He's had an easy few years with Kuralt. I know Bill can drive you crazy with his indecision and his constant agonizing over seemingly little things. But Benjamin calls him 'the remote from Elsinore.' But in the end he's worth all that effort because what he puts on the air is so remarkable. Can you remind Shad of that and run some interference here?"

"I'll do my best," Chandler said, "but I'm worried about it."

A few days later Chandler was still worried, so I met with Shad. During the previous two years Shad had come to me on a number of occasions asking for help for *Sunday Morning,* most often the use of some correspondent for one of his special features such as "Cover Story." Usually I was able to provide the help and in the process gain an insight into the skillful manner in which Shad, with limited resources, produced a weekly broadcast outside the mainstream of day-to-day activities in the News Division. The morning Shad came to see me I felt comfortable getting right to the point.

"I hear you and Bill aren't really hitting it off," I said.

Shad didn't seem surprised.

"You hear right," he said. "At least I guess that's right. Maybe it's me. Maybe I'm just not the right person to produce a show with Bill Moyers. I admire the guy tremendously but I always walk away from him feeling frustrated."

"Shad, I don't follow you."

"Look, I know how to produce a show and get it on the air," he said. "I'm really excited about this show. I've got an idea for a set which would be a huge wall of television monitors, each with a separate feed receiving different images. It would be designed by the Korean artist Nam June Pak. I've found some wonderful music for the open by Charles Ives. I want to organize all this and present it to you. I don't have time for a lot of meetings on the state of American journalism."

"Is that what you think Bill wants to do?"

"I don't know what he wants. I just know that every time I meet with him I walk away feeling like I'm letting down the First Amendment. I tell him when the time comes to work on story assignments we'll know how to do that. We do it every week on *Sunday Morning* and most people think that's pretty good."

"Shad, it's better than pretty good," I said. "I know that and you know that and I have no doubt that Bill knows that, too. The reality here is that until Bill actually starts working and can see for himself how this broadcast is shaping up, he's going to need constant reassurance that he's involved with something of high quality. You may feel it's a pain in the ass having to do that because your reputation ought to speak for itself. But it's worth it. You'll get stories with a vision and insights you wouldn't get from anyone else."

"I guess you think I should try harder with Bill," Shad asked.

"I guess I do. In the end what will matter is what we put on the air. Bill will make it better."

After my meeting I called Chandler and gave him a fill-in on the conversation. I asked him to keep an eye on how things were going.

"I will," he said, "but I'm not optimistic that those two will ever hit it off."

A few days later Chandler called to alert me to a problem.

"You may be hearing from Moyers," he said. "He and Shad had a meeting yesterday that, at least according to Shad, went poorly."

"As a matter of fact," I said, "I've got a message here that Bill is trying to set up an appointment with me. I'll let you know what he says."

I had my secretary call Bill and tell him I was available immediately if he was free to come to my office. When he arrived Bill looked tired, as though he might not have had a full night's sleep. His friendly smile didn't prevent me from noting the circles under his eyes. I wasn't feeling all that well myself. I'd awakened with an aching head and my usual remedy of Tylenol and Tiger Balm, a Chinese analgesic, had failed to remove the pain.

"I'm afraid I'm here to increase the burden of your office," Bill said.

"I'm throwing myself on your mercy, Bill. Judging from the pain in my head this morning, I am being punished not only for all past sins but for all future sins. So go easy."

Bill looked concerned.

"We can do this next week if you want."

"From the look on your face when you came in, I think we ought not to postpone this."

"You're right," Bill said. "Ed, I don't think I should be a part of this new broadcast."

"Why do you feel that way?"

"For me to do my best work I need to work with someone I can be open and honest with about my feelings, including any misgivings I have. Sometimes I'm wrong about those and I need someone to tell me that, too. I've been fortunate to have that here, first with Howard and then with Andy."

"Do you feel you wouldn't have that with Shad?"

"Shad towers over the landscape like a Hercules," Bill said, "and his producers on *Sunday Morning* swear by him. But he is one of those people who seem to work best by creating an atmosphere of tension. That is not an atmosphere in which I work well."

"Bill, has there been some incident which has convinced you of this?"

"Shad has been very open about the problem. He told me yesterday that my role inhibited him not only on my pieces but across the board for the whole program. So I believe it's better if I just step aside."

"Bill, I'm going to ask you for a favor," I said. "This is so important it deserves clarity of thought on my part, something my throbbing head makes impossible at the moment. May I take you up on the offer you made at the beginning? Can we think on this over the weekend and talk again on Monday?"

"Of course we can," Bill said, and he left.

I opened a small jar of Tiger Balm and rubbed a layer of its gentle fire in a soothing band just above my eyebrows. A few minutes later it began to work its minor miracle and I moved on to other matters. Toward the end of the day my secretary brought me a typewritten note from Bill: "Dear Ed, I am stricken with guilt as I leave for the weekend that I gave you that headache, and I regret it."

The note went on to suggest ways that this new broadcast could "get off to the best possible start toward quality, class and popularity."

Bill's first suggestion was that I detach Howard Stringer for "at least four months." I felt we'd made a commitment to Shad which ruled that out. I could also imagine Rather's reaction if he was told the executive producer of the *Evening News* was going to absent himself for a quarter of the year to work on another broadcast. Bill's second suggestion, however, seemed more achievable.

"If that is impossible, I can take Harry Moses" (Moses had worked with Bill on *Our Times*) "and do the best possible job of contributing to the broadcast those significant pieces it will need irrespective of who is senior executive producer. And on that score, I have to say that I really don't know who is more likely to make the other part of the broadcast work as efficiently as Shad, provided he is calm at the core."

As unorthodox as that might be, I thought, it was at least worth a try. Bill closed his note by saying, "In the meantime, I am ordering you a year's supply of Tylenol; would you like it sent to the office or your home?"

Over the next few days I argued a reluctant Chandler and a clearly irritated Northshield into acceptance of the Harry Moses role.

"In the end," I said, "you will have first-rate stories for your broadcast."

That done, I went to see Van to keep him abreast of this latest change and the reasons for making it.

"Is Moyers really worth all this?" he asked.

"I believe he is," I said. "He'll give the broadcast an intellectual edge we wouldn't otherwise have."

"It's a Nielsen edge that Jankowski is asking us for."

"Well, he could help that by giving us the kind of promotional support the Entertainment Division gives to its new shows."

"I'll bring that up to him," Van said, "but I'm not all that optimistic that he'll come through."

"It's a great system," I said. "The Entertainment Division allots the airtime for all the promos and we're not exactly high on their priority list. Maybe you can improve this when you're over in Black Rock. Any progress on your new office?"

"Oh, it's still weeks away from being finished. They're rebuilding the southwest corner of the twenty-fourth floor into an enclosed suite. Anyway, Jankowski wants me to be involved with *American Parade* while I'm still over here. You can get very busy in your new job."

Since Van was reluctant to initiate conversations with either Moyers or Kuralt, I didn't give much thought to that. As it turned out, the events of the next few weeks would keep me very busy.

On Friday, October 21, 1983, Don Hewitt called. He was excited.

"I've got my hands on some stuff that's dynamite," he said, "and there's no way I can get it on this Sunday's *60 Minutes*.".

Usually when Hewitt talked like that I held on to more than my wallet. He hadn't kept *60 Minutes* where it was for all those years by giving away hot stories.

"What have you got?"

"I've got a copy of the FBI tapes showing John DeLorean accepting a suitcase full of cocaine from their undercover agents."

"Where did you get them?"

"I'm not sure I can tell you."

"Don, they can't go on the air unless I know the answer to that. The guy's on trial in federal court. We're not going to automatically put this on the air."

"O.K. Hold on to your seat," he said. "I got the tapes from Larry Flynt."

"Larry Flynt as in *Hustler* magazine? You've got some interesting friends."

"I've been talking to him because he claims he's got some tapes of a Hollywood bimbo having sex parties with high-level members of the current administration. You've got to admit that would be a helluva story."

"One of my favorite categories," I said. "Interesting if true. How did the DeLorean tapes become a part of your conversation?"

"He just brought them up out of the blue," Hewitt said. "When I saw them there was no doubt they are the real thing. I have no idea where he got them."

"Given the character of your source, if we use them I think we'd have to disclose where we got them."

Don was silent for a moment.

"I think I'd better call him and tell him that."

"O.K. Make sure he knows we're not paying him a nickel, and that no strings are attached."

Half an hour later, Don called back. He'd reached Flynt.

"He doesn't care if we say the tapes came from him."

"Does he realize the FBI will be on his ass in a flash trying to find out how he got them?"

"I told him that. The guy just doesn't care."

"I didn't ask before," I said. "Where are you?"

"I'm in Los Angeles. I figured I could take the tapes into the bureau."

"I'd feel better if you came back to New York with them on a plane tonight," I said.

Hewitt headed for the airport and I called Rather. If these tapes were what Don claimed they were, part of any rationale for running them would be their basic "newsworthiness." This meant we'd have to run them on Saturday and not hold them for the *Evening News* with Rather on Monday. I wanted him to hear about the tapes from me instead of learning about them for the first time watching Bob Schieffer on Saturday. Rather took the news with unusual calm.

"Hewitt's remarkable that way," he said. "You never know exactly what he's going to come up with. You'll catch some flak for running them, though."

"I figure it this way," I said. "As Don describes them, there's nothing in the tapes which the FBI hasn't already described in detail to the press, and a jury is going to see them anyway. But the opportunity to actually view the tapes for the first time makes this intrinsically newsworthy. Besides, enough cases like ABSCAM produced tapes which were publicly viewed and the courts have held that this didn't violate the defendant's rights. There's lots of precedent for showing them. The question is: are they real? I'll know more tomorrow when Don gets here."

I expected to have an active weekend. I didn't know how active.

I was still in a deep sleep when the phone rang in the early hours of Sunday, October 23, 1983. It was John Lane telling me a terrorist bomb had devastated the Marine barracks near the airport in Beirut. He didn't have a figure on the death toll but there was every indication it would be high. I threw on some clothing and rushed out of my apartment. I was able to get a cab almost immediately and was in the newsroom within twenty minutes of John's phone call. The news from Beirut got worse with every passing minute. We waited for a satellite feed to see the videotape which would give us our first look at scenes of destruction. Rather arrived two hours later. By then it was almost seven-thirty. We began a grim watch which saw the death toll gradually mount throughout the day until it finally reached 241. At midmorning, when the first videotape came in by satellite, I was sitting in the control room with Joan Richman. News people are used to watching scenes of tragedy and devastation. The hush in the control room that morning was chilling. Throughout the day and into the evening, CBS News presented numerous special reports as more of the terrible details became available.

Because of the Beirut story, Dan anchored the Sunday evening news. Two production units worked side by side—one producing the special reports, the other producing the broadcast. In the midst of this we were looking at Hewitt's DeLorean tapes. There was no doubt about their authenticity. The pictures were in grainy black and white and the audio was muffled, but I could see and hear the automaker discussing his ties to the Irish Republican Army and his need to obtain financing for his faltering car company in the North of Ireland. Then, in a memorable scene, FBI undercover agents gave him a suitcase filled with cocaine. DeLorean looked at its contents and exclaimed, "It's better than gold." A moment later the tape showed an FBI agent entering the room and arresting a stunned DeLorean, who put his hands behind his back to be handcuffed.

There was no doubt that these were indeed the actual arrest tapes. They were everything Hewitt had described and a bit more. Watching the tapes gave you something none of the printed reports had been able to capture. A sense of how far the government had gone in an elaborate masquerade which culminated in DeLorean's arrest. When a jury finally acquitted DeLorean, the ethics of this kind of ABSCAM deception had become an issue in their deliberation.

CBS News had planned to run the tapes on Saturday and advised DeLorean's attorney of this fact. As a result, U.S. District Judge Robert Takasugi issued a temporary restraining order barring their broadcast. CBS lawyers appealed and the three-judge panel of the 9th Circuit Court of Appeals heard arguments in an unusual hour-long hearing Saturday afternoon before ruling that the tapes could be aired. Lawyers for the defense then sought a U.S. Supreme Court stay, but two justices, William Rehnquist and Chief Justice Warren Burger, refused to intercede.

By that time it was too late to show the tapes on our Saturday broadcast. The Sunday broadcasts presented not only the DeLorean tapes but the first questions being raised about the wisdom of the President's decision to send a "peacekeeping force" to Lebanon. Was the Marine contingent stationed in a low-lying area of maximum vulnerability? Given the history of terrorist bombings, had adequate security precautions been taken? CBS News correspondents reported these and other questions which were being raised in Washington and elsewhere. In the weeks ahead this would become a thorny issue with some of the CBS affiliates who seemed to feel that CBS News was somehow being too hard on Ronald Reagan. Any reporting which appeared to challenge the official statements of this popular President could produce mutterings from some of the affiliates.

Another rumble of discontent was produced by our having broadcast the DeLorean tapes. Bill Moll, the President of Harte Hanks Broadcasting, a communications group which owned our affiliate in San Antonio, Texas, wrote me a letter saying, "America will not soon forget nor forgive CBS and its affiliated partners for meddling in the judicial order of things." He sent copies of his letter to both the outgoing and the incoming chairman of the CBS Affiliates Board. I knew and liked Moll and thought he was capable of better judgment.

I responded in a three-page letter detailing the reasons I believed he was wrong. Looking back now, I am amazed that I found the time to write such a letter.

Two days after the bombing of the Marine barracks in Beirut, another story involving U.S. military forces dominated the news. On Tuesday, October 25, the United States along with six Caribbean nations invaded the island of Grenada and removed its Marxist government. Once again I learned about this from John Lane in a phone call which awakened me from a deep sleep.

"Sorry to wake you, my brother."

"No problem," I mumbled. "What's up?"

"Do you know where Grenada is?"

"It's down in the Caribbean somewhere."

"No wonder you're the new President of CBS News. Well, after today a lot of people will know where it is. The United States has just invaded it."

"No shit? Who's got the pool?"

"That's one of the reasons I'm calling you. There is no pool. No reporters will be allowed to cover this, on the grounds that it's not safe."

"What bullshit," I said. "Is Beirut safe? These guys just don't want us watching if they screw up."

"Hey, I'm on your side," John said.

"Have Jack Smith rattle all the cages," I said. "If they still say no, I'll send a letter of protest to Weinberger. If there's enough of a storm maybe we might be able to at least get a pool reporter and crew on the island."

Jack Smith and the Washington Bureau hit a stone wall at the Department of Defense. By midafternoon my letter was hand-delivered to Secretary of Defense Caspar Weinberger. It was a protest not only of the restriction of news access to the island of Grenada but of the attitude which had been expressed by the DOD Public Affairs Office. The letter quoted the "statements of Colonel Robert O'Brien and Lt. Colonel Leon DeLorme to our correspondent Bill Lynch saying that 'we learned a lesson from the British in the Falklands.' " Weinberger never responded but in interviews said that the decision to bar the press was made by the military commander of the American task force in Grenada and that he wouldn't overrule him on this issue. So the American public, which had received firsthand information from the press in Vietnam, in Korea, and in the Second World War, was denied firsthand reporting from Grenada. On the third day of the invasion, the Pentagon began to release its own videotape, which clearly represented what the government wanted the public to see and believe. It may have been an accurate portrayal. Without verification from an independent press, there was no way of knowing. This official tape certainly raised no questions about the competence of a large military force which had great difficulty routing 400 Cuban technical advisers from the island. Since this was the only tape available, we showed it on our broadcasts but followed the policy used in dealing with other governments which imposed their restrictions on what we could show. As the government-approved scenes of the Grenada invasion were broadcast on CBS, a super appeared in the lower third of the picture which said, "Censored by the Department of Defense."

When the press was finally admitted to Grenada, it was compelled to operate in a restricted fashion for the first several days. We saw what our government wanted us to see, when our government wanted us to see it, for as long as our government deemed appropriate.

It wasn't until the sixth day of the invasion that the press was allowed to cover Grenada in a more meaningful fashion and move about on its own. Paradoxically, some of the CBS News coverage was so "positive" from the U.S. point of view that the stories would not have had the same credibility had they been issued with the imprimatur of the Pentagon. For example, we sent the CBS News survey unit to Grenada to conduct a poll of Grenadians. The results showed that the islanders overwhelmingly supported the invasion.

The issue was never one of military censorship. I believed then and believe now we were dealing with political censorship. Whatever need for silence for security's sake existed before the invasion, it disappeared when the first American soldier set foot on Grenada. The enemy knew he was there. I asked Jack Smith during this period if he thought the Pentagon was having any second thoughts.

"Just the opposite," he said. "They think it's worked out great. All those guys who were second lieutenants in Vietnam and are now bird colonels at the Pentagon are congratulating one another for not letting the press lose this war, too."

Toward the end of the week I received an invitation to testify on the impact of this situation before the House Subcommittee on Courts, Civil Liberties, and the Administration of Justice. It was an opportunity I eagerly accepted. There was a developing perception in Washington, one which persists to this day, that the public supported the exclusion of the press from Grenada at the time of the invasion. I didn't believe it, and two months after the invasion Lou Harris conducted a nationwide poll which showed that 65 percent versus 32 percent of those questioned thought that "a small group of reporters should have been allowed to accompany the troops to Grenada." And 63 percent versus 34 percent worried that "by not allowing at least a small pool of reporters to report an invasion, a President or the military might be tempted to cover up mistakes or lives lost."

I felt there was nothing more important at the time than making sure this remained a public issue which would not soon die down. If the issue quickly disappeared it might convince the military and those in government that similar action could be taken whenever they wished to keep the public in the dark.

CBS News was not the only news organization alarmed by what seemed like an attempt to conduct an off-the-record war. A number of us watched with discomfort a satellite feed shared by a number of foreign broadcasters reporting the Grenada invasion for their home countries. In one story which was beamed to the Pacific rim, an Australian journalist told his countrymen, "We have just seen the end of two hundred years of press freedom in the United States."

In this climate of concern I was surprised that Van seemed largely indifferent. He also didn't appear to be all that involved with the affairs of the Stations Division, which was his new area of responsibility. His attention was focused instead on the upcoming *American Parade*. What with the events in Beirut and Grenada and my upcoming testimony before the House subcommittee I had my hands full. Nevertheless, I found myself breaking away from those matters with irritating frequency because of phone calls from Van's secretary asking to set up meetings with Chandler, Northshield, and me. I postponed them as often as I could, not only because of the pressure of the news but because I thought Northshield was in danger of being "coached" into total confusion. I had pressured him relentlessly on the continued role for Moyers. Van was applying the same kind of pressure on the matter of story assignments. The plan for the broadcast was that Moyers and Kuralt would be the anchors and that each would contribute one story a week. Other stories for each broadcast would be contributed by Kurtis, Sawyer, and Andy Lack. Lack, who'd been a producer, had a long-standing promise which predated both Van's and my arrival that he would be given a chance as a correspondent. When we met with Shad, he would enthusiastically go through his list of stories which were currently being researched.

"Charlie's got some great *On the Road* stories working," he said, "and Bill's got good stuff, too. He wants to do a piece on the banking crisis in Brazil, which he thinks is a threat to the hometown bank in this country. Kurtis wants to profile Muhammad Ali and bring out the issue of whether too many fights have caused brain damage."

"We need more stories like Ali," Van said. "We need the kinds of names *People* magazine would put on their cover. Are we trying for the Woody Allens and Michael Jacksons?"

Shad looked at Chandler for help.

"We can find some stories like that," Chandler said. "But celebrity stories are not the kind of stories most people would instinctively want to do."

Before Van could answer, I jumped in.

"That's understandable," I said. "And that's not what the entire broadcast should contain anyway. Van is talking about promotability. When you promote a broadcast that asks if Muhammad Ali is brain-damaged from too many fights and also asks if your hometown bank could go bust because of loans to Brazil, you attract different kinds of viewers and, hopefully, the total number will have increased."

"All of that sounds good," Chandler said, "but it's not going to be that easy finding stories to do about famous people that don't turn out to be pure fluff."

Van had been staring out the window while I'd been talking to Chandler. When he heard Bob's last remark his head snapped back and he looked as though he'd been suddenly awakened from a sleep and didn't know whether to bark or bite. Before he could say anything, I jumped in again.

"Nobody wants fluff," I said. "The Ali story doesn't sound like fluff. *60 Minutes* can tackle important subjects and still find a way to profile a Lena Horne or a Yul Brynner."

I looked at Shad, who appeared thoroughly demoralized.

"Shad, I think the best thing we could do right now is let you get the hell out of here and go back to work. And I've got to talk to the lawyers about what I'm going to say in my statement to a congressional committee."

Shad smiled at me.

"That's the best idea I've heard since I came in here."

After they'd left Van paused at my door.

"That fucking Chandler," he began.

"He's just trying to be a buffer for his producer," I said. "Let me talk to him this afternoon."

Later in the day Chandler came to see me.

"You guys are going to give Shad a breakdown," he said. "He's doing his best to come up with a good show and these sessions with Van and you aren't helping."

"Maybe there's an answer here," I said, holding up a piece of paper. "Shad is sending us his assignment sheets. At this stage all those stories are only research anyway. Can you make sure these sheets include some stories being researched that at least reflect some of these discussions?"

"Shad would be happy to get a Woody Allen or a Michael Jackson," he said. "They won't give interviews, and if they did it wouldn't be on a new show nobody has ever heard of, but we're trying. Sure they can go on that list, but just because it says 'approved' and has a budget number next to it doesn't mean anything."

"Robert, it means we can stop going round and round in these meetings," I said.

"My next list will reflect this," he said, and he left.

I stayed at my desk and began poring through a stack of material the Research Department had prepared for me on the history of military press censorship. It was fascinating reading. During the Second World War, for example, the military set forth the governing principle for the employment of field press censorship that "the minimum amount of information will be withheld from the public consistent with security." What happened in Grenada was closer to the impulse Thomas Jefferson described in an 1813 letter. "The first misfortune of the Revolutionary War induced a motion to suppress or garble the account of it. It was rejected with indignation."

And in Vietnam, despite the tensions between the press and the military, the press had voluntarily observed military security rules. According to Barry Zorthian, who was then director of the Joint U.S. Public Affairs office in Vietnam, "In over four and a half years, and in dealing with approximately 2,000 news media persons, only six security violations were considered by the military to be serious enough to involve Department of Defense accreditation."

I packed it all in a briefcase to take home for weekend study. As it turned out, there were no middle-of-the-night phone calls, so I spent the next two days going over material for my testimony. By the time I arrived in the office on Monday morning, I was beginning to feel well prepared and comfortable with the prospect of appearing before a congressional committee. As a matter of fact, I was feeling good about the past week. CBS News had handled itself well in the coverage of the tragedy in Beirut. All our effort of the past two years was reflected in that coverage. I knew the decision to air the DeLorean tapes was controversial, but I was confident I'd made the right decision. Grenada was disturbing, but I felt good that CBS News had been one of the first news organizations to protest the news blackout. Today, six long days after the invasion, we along with other news organizations would be allowed for the first time to move freely about the island. I was pleased at the opportunity to tell Congress this kind of press restriction was not what a free society was all about. I'd even had a good reason to deflect my phone calls from Richard Leibner for the past week to Art Sekarek, reminding the agent that this was the purpose in having a Vice President for Business Affairs. Being constantly busy had its rewards after all. I brought my suitcase into the office and planned to spend a couple of hours signing the stacks of personnel and purchase forms for which the Corporation demanded the signature of a division President. Normally, this was an irksome chore, but I was in such a good mood I found myself humming as I scratched out innumerable EJ's in the small boxes at the bottom of the forms.

As so often happened at CBS News, any mild euphoria was not only short-lived but often a precursor to some new problem.

In this case it came, while I was happily initialing corporate papers, in the form of a message from my secretary that Bill Moyers would like to see me before I left for Washington. It was 10:20 A.M.

"Tell Bill I'll see him right now," I said, "but I must leave for the airport by eleven."

At ten-thirty Bill walked into my office carrying a piece of paper.

From the look on his face I knew that paper didn't contain suggestions for my testimony in Washington. I offered Bill a seat on the sofa at the far end of my office and sat in the chair next to it.

"I know you have a plane to catch," he said, "so I'll move right to my reason for being here. I wrote this over the weekend, and because I want to be very clear, I'd like to read it to you."

In a quiet voice and with the same cadence with which he delivered his frequent commentaries on the *Evening News,* Bill sat in my office and read the three-page letter he had brought me. While it would not be the last, it was the first time this had happened, and it was a strange experience watching this man I so much admired who was obviously distraught as he sat on my sofa reading a letter out loud.

"Dear Ed," he began. "The time has come for me to leave CBS."

I became terribly depressed as I listened to Bill ask to resign and leave as quietly as possible.

"*American Parade* is not my kind of journalism. I don't believe in it and I can't do it. It's that simple."

He recalled his initial reluctance to do the broadcast and his frustration over the cancellation of *Our Times*.

"We had demonstrated that it isn't necessary to take shortcuts to make journalism work in a dramatic form in this medium."

He said he'd feared that this was a thinly disguised effort to create yet another magazine infusing journalism with the entertainment ethos that now pervades broadcast news.

"My fears are confirmed now," he said. "There is circulating the first list of *American Parade* projects approved by management and assigned a budget number for production. As I suspected, what is developing is a hybrid imitation of *60 Minutes* and *20/20,* precisely the kind of broadcast I have said over and over again I do not wish to do."

The list he read to me was the one containing Woody Allen and Michael Jackson. It also included, to my surprise, a profile of someone whose name I'd never heard of, Annie Liebovitz, with the explanation that "she shoots the stars."

Ms. Liebovitz appeared to have been the clincher for Bill in concluding that he "would be out of step on *American Parade.*"

He took a pause in his reading and his voice got even quieter as he continued.

"The audience would see the hypocrisy on my face as I pretended that a report on the tragedy in Lebanon or the banking crisis in Brazil belonged in the same broadcast with a portrait of little Annie Liebovitz who shoots the stars."

As he came to the end of the third page he looked up at me for the first time and read the last two lines.

"CBS has been very generous to me, and I have a lot more friends here now, including you, than when I came back. Sincerely, Bill Moyers."

Then he handed me the letter.

I tried to prioritize what seemed like a hundred separate thoughts careening through my brain. The list which had tripped the scale for Bill existed because of my attempt to keep Van relaxed while Shad worked on his broadcast. I couldn't very well tell Bill that the list was largely fiction. There was no going back for Bill as far as *American Parade* was concerned. I had to face that reality, but I wanted to persuade Bill that walking away from that broadcast didn't have to be accompanied by a complete departure from CBS News.

While I sorted this out in my mind I made a pretense of studying the letter Bill had given me. Then I began my response.

"Bill, I think you're right about not doing *American Parade,*" I said. "But I don't think you should leave CBS News. Let's work on other ideas for prime time. Given the failure rate of the network's alleged entertainment programs, there'll be other opportunities."

Bill was determined to leave.

"It's obvious to me," he said, "that my journalism is not going to stand alone in prime time by the network's standards of commercial success. I think you need to be free of my chronic disconsolation over the direction this business is taking, and to save all that money you are now paying a misfit."

"Bill, I wish I had more misfits like you. And I'm not going to defend the network. Those guys are what they've always been. If televised hangings could produce a rating, they'd make speeches in favor of the death penalty. But they're failing too often and too expensively. They're going to need us."

"Ed, I know you believe that," he said. "There are a number of us who have said to one another Ed Joyce would put quality journalism on the air if he had a free hand, but he doesn't have it. The system won't permit it and the man you work for is Van Sauter, who doesn't for a moment support quality journalism. He's the same man who said to me in your presence, 'Let me play the whore.'"

Half an hour had gone by and I couldn't miss my plane.

"If this trip to Washington wasn't so important," I said, "I'd cancel everything on my schedule and not let you out of here until I'd convinced you how wrong you are. But I can't do that. Bill, promise me we can continue this discussion when I get back."

"Of course we can," Bill said, "but I'm convinced the honorable thing for me to do is leave, for us to shake hands and go our separate ways. I need to find some way to regain the momentum I had twice here and lost: first on the *Evening News* and then with *Our Times.*"

After Bill left I called Howard Stringer and described what had happened. He'd worked closely with Bill and knew him better than anyone else at CBS News. I asked for his help.

"Unfortunately," I said, "I have to walk out of this door for the airport within two minutes. Will you talk to Bill and try to convince him that the *Evening News* needs him? And don't forget, in two months we start an election year. Bill will have a big role in the primaries, conventions, and election night."

"It may be just as well that you're out of town for a few days," Howard said. "Let me work on Bill. It would be terrible to lose him."

"We can't let that happen," I said.

"I've lived through a few of these with Bill," Howard said. "If I can get to him before he beings sharing his decision with friends I may be able to turn him around. Otherwise, he can become quite bloody-minded."

"Why are we still talking?" I asked. "Hang up and call Bill."

I grabbed my suitcase and rushed for the airport. As President of CBS News, I had a car and driver, which assured me a few minutes of peace and quiet on the way to the airport . . . as long as the car phone didn't ring. It didn't and I spent the time considering the Moyers dilemma.

To Van there was not a shred of doubt that the single most important person on the air for CBS News was Dan Rather. It would have been hard to argue against the importance of the person who anchored the broadcast which was the equivalent of our front page. Moyers, unlike a Rather or a Cronkite, was not someone from the traditional anchor mold with the skill to convincingly and authoritatively read news copy prepared by someone else. But neither was Edward R. Murrow. Despite the evolution of his broadcast beyond the role of headline service, Rather was much more a descendant of Cronkite than of Murrow in his attitude toward television journalism. What excited him was covering breaking stories and the challenge of developing an informational edge over the competition. Moyers alone of the senior CBS News correspondents shared the Murrow vision which enabled him to delineate those forces and issues which were shaping and creating the headlines. As a result of this ability to anticipate what would become important, he devoted three prime-time half hours of his *Our Times* series in 1983 to stories about subjects which were reshaping the world. His trip to Peking with playwright Arthur Miller was an early indication that the new Chinese regime was unlocking the door with which they had barred Western culture for decades. A few weeks later he devoted a half hour to the tensions in the Philippines. The crisis he described led to the eventual overthrow of President Ferdinand Marcos. And in August 1983 Moyers devoted a half hour of prime-time television to the AIDS disease. It was a chilling prediction of an epidemic.

The loss of those insights for CBS News would be far greater than many people, certainly Van, realized. I believed it when I'd told Bill that the failure rate at the network, coupled with the growing need to control costs in the Entertainment Division, would create a future demand for other efforts from the News Division. This would provide the opportunity for other Moyers broadcasts. If Bill felt so strongly about not being part of this kind of a magazine broadcast, we'd eventually come up with something else. The concern for the moment was keeping him at CBS News, although my more immediate problem was preparing for my congressional testimony, which was now two days away.

When I arrived in Washington, I checked into the Four Seasons Hotel and spent the remainder of that day and all of the next in a suite on the fifth floor with Gene Mater, Ralph Goldberg, and an assortment of CBS lawyers. For two days they took the parts of the congressional committee members and bombarded me with questions about the role the press should play during sensitive military engagements. This was a first-time experience for me. Mater and Goldberg, who'd spent years accompanying CBS executives to Washington hearing rooms, were particularly skilled at playing the part of both sympathetic and hostile questioners. Every few hours I would break off and go to a phone in the bedroom of the suite we were using to get a progress report from Stringer on Moyers. By Tuesday afternoon he was assuring me I could relax.

"Bill is enthused about returning to more commentaries on the *Evening News*," he said. "We're already talking about some things we'll do during the election year."

"Stringer, I think you've missed your calling," I said. "You should have been a druid. I think you invoked some magic spell over Bill."

"He quite likes you," Howard said. "Remember, he had no relationship with Salant . . . he and Bill Leonard were never on the same wavelength . . . and he thinks Van is the devil incarnate. You're actually the first News President, sir, with whom Bill feels he can sit down and talk."

"With all that," I said, "I've come terribly close to running him off the reservation."

"You're also succeeding in keeping him at CBS News. Why don't you call Bill and tell him I've told you about his enthusiasm for doing more for the *Evening News*."

"I'll do that right now," I said. "Howard, I'm terribly glad you have a green card. While I'm down here in Washington, I'll put in a word for you at Immigration."

"Oh, thank you, governor," he said, breaking into a cockney accent. "The name is Stringer . . . S-t-r-i-n-g-e-r."

Mater and Goldberg could hear my laughter from the next room. With relief I dialed Moyers's number. He was in his office.

"How are you going down there?" he asked. "When do you testify?"

"Not till tomorrow."

"Well, good luck. I know a bit about that experience. It's never something you can prepare for with too much care."

"I'm certainly in a better frame of mind," I said, "than I was when I left New York. Howard has told me about the conversations you two have been having about the *Evening News* and I couldn't be happier."

"Howard's wonderful that way," Bill said. "We've been able to sit together and spark ideas. If you and Howard both feel I can make a contribution to the *Evening News,* then I'm ready to devote my energies to earning that confidence."

"Bill," I said, "1984 will be an exciting year for all of us because of the political story. We should also kick around ideas for documentaries."

"I'd like that," he said, "but you shouldn't be wasting your time talking with me right now. You should go back to your study hall."

When I went back to the living room of the suite, Gene Mater immediately returned to the role he'd been playing when we'd halted, that of a hectoring congressman.

"Mr. Joyce," he asked in his deepest baritone voice, "how could we trust you journalists to keep secret an impending military action after what you did to our boys in Vietnam?"

I was in such an ebullient mood I couldn't resist a chance to shock this very sober inquisitor.

"Congressman," I said, "if you'll forgive me . . . that's a dumb-ass question."

Mater gave me the look homeroom teachers reserve for spitball throwers.

"That's not a response I think you should give to a United States congressman," he said.

As it turned out, he was quite right to prepare me for that question. Vietnam did come up as a justification for the military's reluctance to believe that even a small pool of reporters for the wire services, newspapers, and broadcasting could be counted on not to breach security. I reminded the committee of the Zorthian quote that after four and a half years, and in dealing with approximately 2,000 media persons, only six security violations were considered by the military to be serious enough to involve Department of Defense accreditation. And that in Vietnam the press was voluntarily observing military security rules.

Generally the hearing turned out to be far less adversarial than I'd anticipated. The subcommittee was chaired with evenhandedness by Robert Kastenmeier, a Democrat from Wisconsin. My panel consisted of John Chancellor of NBC News, David Brinkley of ABC News, and me. Both of them made it clear at the outset that they were speaking as individuals, which left me as the only panel member responsible for the policies of his news organization. Early on in my testimony, I made the statement that CBS News was not seeking to report military secrets or to jeopardize lives. There was, I pointed out, a history of working relationships between the press and the military which spanned three wars and had been sadly violated in Grenada. Testimony lasted for about an hour and a half. I had a sense of the committee becoming increasingly receptive when I agreed that there were circumstances which could require temporary military censorship for security reasons. Even the die-hard supporters of the administration struck me as uncomfortable with how far the military had gone with their press blackout of the invasion. When the hearing was over I walked outside with Gene Mater into the fall air of Washington. It seemed particularly cool after the hot television lights in the hearing room.

"Thank you for the preparation," I said.

"You handled yourself well," Mater said.

"I was lucky my debut was not in front of a hostile committee," I said. "That could have been tough."

"Would you like to share a cab to the airport?" he asked.

"I have to stop by the Washington Bureau first," I said. "I want to say hello to Jack Smith and I'm supposed to spend a few minutes with Charley Rose."

Rose was the new host of the ill-fated *Nightwatch.* Successive cuts in its budget had reduced it from a four-hour news broadcast to a two-hour interview program with four-minute news inserts in each half hour. The live two-hour program was broadcast from 2 to 4 A.M., after which it was rebroadcast on tape from 4 to 6 A.M. The program had also been moved from New York to Washington to achieve further cost savings. In the complex bookkeeping system of the Broadcast Group we discovered we would be charged a lesser amount for the use of a studio and technicians if we did the broadcast in Washington as opposed to New York. It achieved no net savings for CBS and was an absurd reason for relocating a broadcast. But it removed approximately a million dollars in annual cost from our budget and helped keep *Nightwatch* on the air.

When I arrived in Jack Smith's office I found a stack of telephone messages waiting for me. One of them was from Art Sekarek asking me to call him as soon as possible. I asked Jack to close his office door while I dialed Sekarek. When I reached him a torrent of words poured into my ear.

"I'm sorry to bother you . . . honest to God . . . I know what your last few weeks have been like . . . but Leibner and Witt are on a tear. I've tried not to burden you because I could see everything going on and I knew you were up to your ass and . . ."

"Art," I interrupted him. "What's Leibner's problem?"

"Well, for one thing, he can't stand it that he's not cutting deals directly with you, and that you keep referring him to me."

"Does the guy ever watch a news broadcast?" I asked. "There have been a few things going on in the world. Besides, he's dealt with you in the past."

"Richard has changed ever since he made the Rather deal. This morning he said to me, 'What does Joyce think I am, just another agent?' "

"As far as I know, he's still collecting commissions," I said. "Did I miss an announcement about N. S. Bienstock becoming a nonprofit institute?"

"No, you didn't miss it," Art said. "Let me go down the list. Leibner and Witt are still trying to negotiate the Blackstone and Phillips moves. Witt is now saying he can move them to the CBC even though they have contracts with us."

"That's nonsense," I said. "A series of worldwide moves are being held up for months because Leibner doesn't want to be just another agent. We are not going to renegotiate for people who are merely fulfilling the terms of their contracts. Phillips knows there's going to be a salary increase. How about Blackstone?"

"No, he doesn't know that yet."

"When you're discussing the arrangements for his move, make sure he understands we'll be bringing him up to $110,000, which will put him on a level with the people in the other foreign bureaus. I assume there is nothing in his contract which prohibits us from paying more?"

"No, we can always pay more," Art said. "That's a very generous increase of almost twenty grand."

"Yeah, but it's fair," I said. "These are bigger assignments. After you've told Blackstone, call Witt or Leibner and as a courtesy let them know, but stress the point that this is based on our own review and is not part of a negotiation. And another thing. Tell them I've talked to Phillips and I'm talking again next week with Blackstone. Let them know that I believe they have taken a very small problem and turned it into something larger. They've tried the same thing with Teichner, Tunnell, and Sheahan. They are way out of line when they begin interfering like this in the operation of CBS News."

"I'll tell them," Art said, "but I'm afraid I'm not through with my list. Did you give Leibner permission to shop Kladstrup?"

"Weeks ago he told me that Don Kladstrup would like to stay in Paris and not be moved to Chicago. He asked me if he could find him another job in Paris, would I release him from his contract, and I said yes."

"O.K., I just wanted to make sure," Art said. "I think they've placed him at ABC. Have you also given him permission to shop Gary Shepherd?"

Shepherd was a correspondent in the CBS News Los Angeles Bureau. His contract was coming to an end and we had been renegotiating for several weeks. Our last salary offer had been $120,000, which represented more than a 20 percent increase.

"No, as far as I know we're in the midst of a good-faith negotiation."

"He says ABC has approached him about Shepherd and he can get another twenty grand from them."

"Shepherd's a good guy," I said, "but that's too much money for a general assignment correspondent. Art, what the hell's going on?"

"I think Leibner would like to move a couple of people to ABC so he can establish another atmosphere of 'raiding.' It worked with Leonard and he thinks it'll put the same pressure on you to avoid that kind of publicity."

"And if I cave on Shepherd, that'll become the floor for future negotiations. How many of our people does Leibner represent?"

"I don't have the exact number but it's over a hundred."

"Get me a complete list," I said. "I'd like to see it. If we fall for this, the additional twenty thousand for Shepherd gets multiplied by the next twenty negotiations for other general assignment correspondents. And what about somebody who's already earning $140,000 a year? What's his expectation? . . . 180? . . . 200? I don't know of any business that routinely grants forty, fifty, sixty, and a hundred percent increases. It's crazy."

"Ed," Art said, "that's the way Leibner's had it for the past few years."

"Yeah, and it adds up to millions of dollars. It's one of the reasons we closed some bureaus earlier this year. Then Jankowski demands a cut, or holds next year's budget down, but we're locked into all of these escalating contracts and we end up closing bureaus so the gravy train can roll on. Art, what else is on your list?"

"Witt says Bob Simon wants to move to New York."

Simon was a correspondent in the Washington Bureau who'd recently moved there after several years in the Tel Aviv Bureau.

"Tell Witt," I said, "the appropriate thing for Bob to do is come up to

298

New York and discuss that with his management. I don't appreciate hearing about this first from his agent."

"Wait a minute," Art said. "There's more. Witt has been negotiating a new contract for Harry Radliffe with Bob McCarthy."

Radliffe was a producer in the London Bureau and McCarthy was Art's deputy and the director of business affairs for CBS News.

"I've got a copy of McCarthy's deal notes in front of me," Art continued. "According to those notes, Witt says when you and Sauter were in London you were kissing Radliffe's ass and telling him what a great producer he was."

"He's a fine producer," I said. "We both told him so."

"Well, Witt says he expects to see that reflected in a lot of dough for the new contract. He claims he's already checked ABC, and if the dough's not there, he'll give ABC a combination of Simon and Radliffe in London."

"I've known Witt for year," I said. "So have you. In fact, he used to have your job here. This doesn't sound like him."

"I think it's all part of Richard's big power play," Art said. "You've just moved into this job and a lot's happened in the past few weeks to keep you jumping. If he can establish some new ground rules for himself now while you're occupied with everything else, he'll have it made."

"Art, we're not going to change a thing," I said. "Leibner's a power broker only if I allow him to be one and I won't do that. We'll talk some more when I get back."

The next message I'd received was from John Lane, also asking me to call before I left Washington. When I reached Lane he wanted to discuss our ongoing coverage of Grenada in the aftermath of the invasion. When he'd covered that he moved on to another topic.

"Your close personal friend, Mr. Leibner, makes my head hurt."

"Welcome to the club," I said. "What's he done now?"

"Yesterday I called Gary Shepherd just to tell him I knew we were renegotiating his contract and wanted him to know how much we liked him and how I was sure it would all work out fine. You know what he told me? 'My agent says you guys in New York don't give a shit whether I live or die.'"

"The era of the super agent," I said. "How do you like it so far?"

"Not a hell of a lot," Lane said. "Can we offer Shepherd more money?"

"God, it would be easy to say yes to that," I said. "He's a good reporter and it's only another twenty thousand. But I seem to remember how sick at heart you were when we closed bureaus and laid people off. John, I put my ass on the line to stop another wave of layoffs. If I don't get a handle on these salaries, Black Rock is going to be back for more. I don't want that to happen."

"Amen to that," Lane said. "When are you coming back?"

"I'll leave the bureau in a couple of hours. That should get me back to the office about four-thirty. I want to see the tape I'm taking to Acapulco."

Acapulco was the location of the 1983 meeting of the CBS Affiliates Board.

Once there I knew I would hear complaints from them about Moyers and Lesley Stahl, the CBS News White House correspondent, complaints about my opposition to the press blackout in Grenada, and because of the Bill Moll letter, a few gripes about the use of the DeLorean tapes. Most of the grumbling, I was warned, would reflect a growing resentment of stories criticizing President Reagan for his decision to send a Marine "peacekeeping force" to Beirut and the controversy over whether there had been adequate security safeguards. According to Tony Malara, President of the Network with responsibility for sales and affiliates, a number of the Affiliates Board members were convinced that CBS News coverage had been excessive and unfair.

In the past two years I'd had enough experience with this group to know that the loudest criticisms would come from people who hadn't actually seen the coverage themselves. Usually such grievances were reflections of the chatter at Rotary meetings or the country club. I knew what our coverage had been like and I was not about to offer any apologies. I also remembered what it had been like sitting in a control room that Saturday morning looking at the first satellite feeds of the mangled bodies of those young men in Beirut.

I got off the plane in Acapulco with a videotape which condensed our coverage of both Beirut and Grenada. If the affiliates wanted to complain, I'd answer them, but first I was going to make damn sure they'd actually seen what it was they were complaining about. The temperature had been brisk in New York, even for mid-November. Leaving an air-conditioned plane for an airport which wasn't was a body blow. The temperature reached the nineties and the humidity was just as high. How lovely, I thought, the affiliates will find it too hot to play golf or tennis. They'll all huddle in the shade with adult beverages until they've margaritaed themselves into a state of posse comitatus and then go on the hunt for the new President of CBS News. It was Saturday and the CBS News presentation to the board wasn't scheduled until Wednesday morning. I got a taste of what the next four days would be like at the cocktail reception at our hotel before dinner that night. I spotted Red Martin, a silver-haired man in his late sixties who owned and operated WCAX-TV in Burlington, Vermont. Red was a former chairman of the Affiliates Board and had been a source of constant difficulty for Dick Salant and Bill Leonard when they'd held my job. He was a naturally disputatious man who seemed to love contention for its own sake and reserved real anger only for those who tried to ignore him. I liked him, thought he ran a good station, and when I saw him that night in Acapulco, walked over to say hello. Red wasted no time in bringing up Grenada.

"You're just dead wrong on this Grenada business, you know. The military has to be able to keep a secret on a thing like that."

"I thought we sent all of you affiliates a copy of my statement to the subcommittee," I said. "I didn't say there aren't times when you have to live with the military censorship to protect the lives of soldiers. But first of all, there could have been a small pool of reporters attached to the invasion force and secrecy arrangements could have been worked out. Second, we didn't get to move around that damn island for six days after the invasion."

"Have you ever been shot at?" Red asked.

I thought back to the summer of 1967.

"Sure, on the streets of Newark, New Jersey."

"Just what I thought," he said. "Too young for the big war, too old for Vietnam. If you'd ever had some character trying to shoot you, then you'd know what I mean."

"Red, I'll never get you to change your mind," I said. "We're just going to have to disagree on this one. I hear that some of your fellow board members are ready to take some shots at me on Wednesday."

"I've been trying to settle those fellows down," he said. "They've got short memories. Things are pretty good at CBS News these days and they ought to consider that."

We were interrupted by the arrival of several other affiliates and in a few minutes I walked over to Van, who'd just arrived from California.

"How was your flight?" I asked.

"Uneventful," he said. "But nothing prepared me for this heat. I was soaked by the time I got to the hotel. I'm not sure Mexico produces enough beer to replenish my fluid loss, but I'm about to find out."

"I'll join you," I said, "but after dinner I'm taking a pass on the hospitality suite. Affiliates with access to unlimited firewater could be hazardous to my health."

"Yeah, we gotta figure a way to lie low," he said, "until the News presentation on Wednesday."

"Peculiarly enough," I said, "Wednesday I don't mind. I'm going to lay it all out."

"You know what we should do? Jankowski has the company plane waiting to take him back. We should borrow it and fly to Mexico City and spend some time with our stringer there, George Natanson."

"Great idea," I said. "We know Manuel Alonso, the press secretary to President De la Madrid. We could have Natanson arrange for us to have lunch with him."

"That's what I'll tell Jankowski. A high-level meeting requires our absence for a day."

"Of course, Gene, nothing less could tear us away, because our hearts are really here in Acapulco," I said. "But as long as we're in Mexico City we should take a few minutes to see the Diego Rivera murals."

"Gene, the affiliates would want it that way," Van said.

"What if he says no?"

"Maybe we can arrange to be kidnapped."

The day in Mexico City went exactly as planned, including a side trip for the Rivera murals. It was also a brief respite from the high humidity of Acapulco in November. I got a sense of what I'd missed Tuesday evening at dinner, when I kept getting a succession of storm signals from affiliate relations people who would leave their tables and come over to me to whisper the latest complaint about CBS News coverage. We were "tough on our President. How could the country pull together if CBS News was pulling it apart?" By eleven o'clock Wednesday morning, the time for the News presentation, which was held in a large meeting room at the hotel, I was thoroughly pissed off.

Malara functioned as the host for these events and in introducing me he used the phrase "Van Sauter's replacement."

I began by saying I thought of myself as having "succeeded Van . . . replacing him is something else again."

Then I added, "You may have noticed that I've been a bit busy since I took the job, but not so busy that I haven't corresponded with some of you." I described the letter I'd gotten on the use of the DeLorean tapes and gave them several paragraphs of my response. "Now, I'd like to address those who felt we pushed too hard on the issue of press exclusion from Grenada," I said, and used as an example a letter of complaint from an affiliate in Mississippi which my secretary had read to me on the phone that morning. One part of that letter had particularly stirred me and I'd asked my secretary to read it back at least three times while I wrote it down.

"We elected Presidents to make these heavy decisions concerning the protection of our national freedoms," the writer said, "and sometimes to protect freedoms, some must sadly be relinquished temporarily, so please let us not jeopardize all of our freedoms for the sake of holding on to a temporarily lost Freedom of the Press."

I quoted that paragraph and paused for a moment to let it sink in. Then I offered another quote from quite a different source.

"Why should freedom of speech and freedom of the press be allowed? Why should a government which is doing what it believes to be right allow itself to be criticized? It should not allow opposition by lethal weapons. Ideas are much more fatal things than guns. Why should any man be allowed to buy a printing press and disseminate pernicious opinions calculated to embarrass the government?"

Again, I paused and looked up at the hundred or so Affiliates Board members and CBS executives.

"Those words were spoken in 1920 by Nikolai Lenin," I said, "and that's what's at issue here, making sure the information flow is not controlled by the state. I keep hearing that some of you were also disturbed by our coverage of the bombing of the Marine barracks in Beirut and some of the questions which were later raised. I'd like you to see some of that coverage."

The lights were lowered, and on television monitors around the room as well as on a big screen behind the podium from which I was speaking, the tape I'd brought with me began to roll. It was twelve minutes long and it was a skillfully edited chronological account of the Beirut bombing with its terrible scenes of the deadly wreckage of the Marine barracks and of the overlapping invasion of Grenada. It contained portions of our Washington coverage and a Moyers commentary. The tape concluded with the wrenching sight of President and Mrs. Reagan walking among and consoling bereaved families in an enormous military hangar which contained a sea of flag-draped coffins . . . bodies of dead marines which had been flown home from Beirut. The camera closed on one of those flags while a Marine bugler played taps. I'd seen the live coverage and now was viewing this tape for a second time and I still had a lump in my throat.

When the tape ended, the lights stayed down for a short time and then were raised. I looked at the affiliates for a moment before I spoke.

"Any questions?" I asked.

There was silence, and I just let it hang there.

Finally, Charley Brakefield, the head of WREG-TV in Memphis, Tennessee, broke the silence. I liked Charley Brakefield and as the lights had come up I'd seen him holding a handkerchief to his eyes.

"Ed, it's kind of hard to ask a question after what we've just seen," he said.

"That's because you've just shared what our viewers and what the men and women of CBS News experienced over the past few weeks. Thank you for being here. I'll see you all at lunch."

At lunch I circulated among as many Affiliates Board members as possible. Not one of them voiced a complaint about CBS News coverage. It was as though a spell had been broken and we were once again a happy affiliate-network family. In the years which would follow this meeting in Acapulco, I would have my share of conflict with this group and indeed be at times the object of their ire. Eventually I would conclude that an adversarial relationship was inevitable for any News President who tried to be protective of his organization. Despite this I came to like many of the individual affiliates, men like Ken Hatch of KIRO-TV in Seattle, Washington, one of the stations of the Bonneville group; Jim Babb of Jefferson Pilot Broadcasting in Charlotte, North Carolina; and Ward Huey of Belo Broadcasting in Dallas. They were able broadcasters and good businessmen and there were others like them. But gathered in a large group, the moderate affiliates often deferred to their more strident colleagues. The result was a collective voice of considerable hostility which acquired many decibels of amplification from a large CBS Affiliate Relations Department whose purpose seemed defined by the principles of Chicken Little.

Two days later I returned to New York. I was in my office early the morning of Friday, November 18, 1983, to get a head start on the mail and memoranda which always stacked up when I was out of town. It was shortly after 8 A.M. when my phone rang. My secretary hadn't come in yet, so I picked it up and was greeted by a familiar voice.

"Hiya, babe. I had a hunch you'd be in early today."

Start off each day with a smile, I thought, resolving to let the phone ring the next time. It was Richard Leibner.

"I've got good news and I've got bad news," he continued. "The good news is I got a job for Don Kladstrup in the Paris Bureau of ABC News. He really appreciates your letting him out of a contract. You will do that, right?"

"Richard, of course I will. I told you I'd do that weeks ago. I hope it works out well for Don."

"I'll need a letter from you," he said, "for the ABC Law Department. Now for the bad news. Gary Shepherd is going to take the offer from ABC."

I made a decision to seem as indifferent as possible to this news.

"I wish him well, too. Anything else? I'm kind of busy this morning."

"If there's not more flexibility in the offers you make you're going to lose people. ABC was happy to pay a hundred and forty."

"What can I tell you? They've got a couple of good guys."

"I might have been able to keep Shepherd for you if I hadn't had to deal with Art," Leibner said.

"I can't negotiate every one of these contracts and still run this place," I said. "Obviously if it's a big contract, that's different."

"I've got a lot of clients at CBS," he said.

"I appreciate that, Richard," I said. "You and I have been negotiating contracts with one another for more than ten years. I know going in that you're going to try for whatever the market will bear. What I'm saying is that the market will no longer bear the kind of increases you've been getting for the past few years. It's been a rich period for you, but it was an aberration and it couldn't last forever."

"That kind of attitude is only going to hurt CBS News," he said.

"What's going to hurt CBS News is if I have to gut our news-gathering capability to pay for a lot of fat-cat contracts. The people I work for are putting the financial brakes on this company. It's a fact of life for both of us."

"We were only twenty thousand apart," he said.

"You're not listening to me," I said. "Twenty thousand is not the issue. You've got a dozen other clients here at the Shepherd level. If I coughed up another twenty for him you've got a new floor to work with for all the rest and then we're pushing a quarter of a million dollars and that's only one group."

"I never link one deal to another," he said.

"Spare me that bullshit, will you? Save it for your public statements. You're in the business of forcing up market value. We both understand that."

I could hear a giggle on the other end of the phone.

"Listen, babe . . . it's called the free enterprise system."

"The system also allows me to say no," I said, "and with the pressure I'm getting to reduce costs I'm going to have to say no more often."

"I can't believe CBS didn't learn a lesson the last time," he said.

"It was that last time that created the problem. You not only got your million-dollar deals but you jacked up salaries for producers, directors, and a lot of journeymen correspondents."

"Hey . . . I don't carry a gun. It was management that said yes."

"I don't disagree with you there," I said, "but now management is saying no."

"You'll learn, sweets," Leibner said. "You can't treat people that way."

After talking with Leibner I dialed CBS Operator 51 and asked her to connect me with Art Sekarek at home.

"I wanted to catch you before you left for work," I said, "just in case I get tied up this morning."

I described the conversation I'd had with Leibner.

"I didn't want to bother you in Mexico," Sekarek said, "but Stu Witt is now refusing to speak to me. He's doing his deals with McCarthy."

"What's that all about?"

"When I called him to tell him that we were giving Blackstone some more money and this was a courtesy call, not a negotiation, because the guy's in mid-contract, he went bananas. Now he's demanding an apology from me and an assurance it won't happen again."

"Let me see if I've got this straight," I said. "He's angry because we decided to give more money to someone who works for us and because we told our employee what we were doing instead of asking his agent to tell him?"

"Sure," Sekarek said. "Witt wanted to be able to call Blackstone and say, 'Look what I got out of those pricks in New York.' Now Blackstone knows his agents have done nothing for him. By the way, according to McCarthy's deal notes for November 9, Witt was still so mad he began to scream, 'I've declared war on CBS News.' "

"Those two guys belong in the Polo Lounge," I said, "negotiating the square footage for dressing rooms. They'd better be careful who they declare war on."

"Leibner said to me, 'If Joyce has money to reopen Bonn, add Teichner to Dallas, and plan on opening a small bureau in Denver, then he can find the money for my deals.' I told you before I thought he was making his move."

"Maybe I should give him an office next to mine. That way I could check with him before I make any decisions."

"I think he'd like that," Art said. "When the date for Leonard's retirement was approaching, I remember him saying he wished he could afford to take the job."

"In Hollywood," I said, "agents frequently end up running the studios. Maybe that's in store for us, too. How much money do you figure Leibner takes out of CBS News?"

"I sent you that information along with the full Bienstock client list. It should be there on your desk. I added up the salaries of all of his clients at CBS News. You'll see all the names, more than a hundred. It comes close to $16 million."

"We're dealing with fucking K Mart here," I said. "Of the ten top agents we do business with, does anybody else have a list like that?"

"Ralph Mann at ICM and Jim Griffin at the Morris office might each have ten people," Art said. "The others less."

"And they're very professional to deal with," I said. "What do you think Leibner nets from us alone?"

"Well, his commission varies," Art said. "It's five percent for just negotiation but more if he handles taxes and other business things, which he does for a lot of his clients. So I figure he nets anywhere from eight hundred thousand to a million from us."

"He's got the same number of people at ABC News," I said, "slightly less at NBC. His wife represents people at local television stations across the country. Besides Witt and his hired help, do they have much overhead?"

"I've been in his office. They've got some accountants and office help, that's it. It's a family business owned by Leibner and his wife and they probably clear at least three million a year after overhead, and we don't know what kind of shelters he's got set up, so maybe it's more."

"Now I understand why the guy turns green when I talk about holding down contract increases," I said.

"Are you kidding? Look at what he's been getting for his big stars like Rather or Wallace or Sawyer. And even for his small-fry correspondents or producers he's come to think of a thirty percent increase as normal business. You better believe he shits a brick when you talk about holding increases close to the inflation rate. If you stick to a seven percent increase except for the bigger stars, that will affect at least eighty-five of those hundred-plus people he represents here. And if CBS News does it, it will eventually affect what NBC and even ABC are paying. You could cost Mr. and Mrs. Leibner a million or more bucks a year without trying too hard. If I were you, I wouldn't cross any streets without looking both ways."

After talking with Art I leafed through the folder of papers my secretary had left on my desk and found the Bienstock client list he'd sent me. It was like looking through the membership sheets of a trade union. In this case, a profit-making union. No wonder Leibner had come to see himself as the head of a kind of shadow government. His reach into CBS News was extraordinary. He had most of the major stars. Rather, Wallace, Safer, Bradley, Rooney, Sawyer, and a host of well-known correspondents such as Bruce Morton, Ray Brady, and even David Martin, our Pentagon correspondent, whom I'd hired when I spotted him on a public television panel program while he was working for *Newsweek* magazine. All of those were names of people whose contract negotiations would have required my involvement. But the list showed another and much larger group whose contracts were routinely handled by the Business Affairs Department— the bureau correspondents, directors, and producers. Art was right. By imposing ceilings on their increases I was depriving Leibner of a significant portion of his future income.

My phone sounded again and I was tempted to let it ring. It was not yet nine o'clock and my secretary wouldn't be in for another few minutes. But each ring of a telephone always seems louder than the one before and by the fourth ring it was deafening, so I picked it up and found myself saying good morning to Jack Smith.

"How was Mexico?" he asked.

"Ninety degree humidity and crawling with Affiliates Board members. On the other hand, I wasn't in New York and my morning so far is filling me with nostalgia for faraway places."

"Well, I won't try to add to it," Jack said. "I just wanted you to know what I'm hearing out of Defense in the aftermath of your Grenada testimony."

"Did we make a dent?"

"We may have," he said. "I'm told that the Chairman of the Joint Chiefs, General Vessey, is going to ask Winant Sidle, a retired major general, to chair a committee which is supposed to come up with recommendations for ways to handle media coverage of future military operations, including joint exercises. In another few weeks you should be getting a letter from General Sidle, so you should be considering your response."

"Jack, you have no idea what a pleasure it is to be talking about the news business. That's very good news. Our response will be affirmative . . . of course we'll take part. Hopefully, we can work toward some pool arrangement for future military exercises."

I did receive a letter from General Sidle a few weeks later. Jack Smith represented CBS News on the committee and the end result was a working arrangement for a pool which would service both print and broadcast. Responsibility for the television pool rotated among the major broadcasters. The output of the pool would be shared and disseminated by them throughout the country. The pool was activated on several occasions for military exercises, and at those times when CBS News had responsibility, Jack selected a correspondent and crew for the assignment, then notified the Vice President for News Coverage and me. Awareness of the exercise was confined to our small group in an attempt to protect security. While the system works well for military exercises, it has yet to be tested in a situation as serious as the invasion of Grenada.

The next few days which followed my return from Mexico were the first since I'd become President of CBS News which might be described as routine. They were filled with meetings. A meeting with Jonathan Rodgers, the new executive producer of the *Weekend News.* Another on *Nightwatch.* A long meeting on Central America. Did we have too many people there with close to thirty in El Salvador and Nicaragua? No, but we'd watch it, was our conclusion. Should we open a one-correspondent bureau in Mexico City the way we had in Boston and San Francisco and were about to do in Denver? I was for it. John Lane and Peter Larkin, the foreign editor, argued that because of air travel and communications, it made more sense to continue basing our Latin American activities in Miami. My days were busy, productive, and after the whirlwind of the past two months, they seemed by comparison uneventful. That wouldn't last long.

Shortly before noon on Wednesday, November 23, 1983, I'd just finished meeting with Charles Kuralt. He had concerns about balancing *Sunday Morning* and traveling around the country for his *On the Road* stories for his new broadcast. He also now had to be present in the studio each Tuesday evening at eight o'clock. He'd been counting on being part of a team with Moyers. This would have allowed him to miss a few Tuesdays while his partner anchored the broadcast. To my surprise he talked about leaving *Sunday Morning* if *American Parade* should be continued in the prime-time schedule.

My response was that it would be nice to have the need to wrestle with that kind of problem. Charles laughed good-naturedly and agreed it was a decision for the future.

Following Kuralt, I met with Van and Gene Mater. The Law Department had retained John Scanlon, an experienced public relations representative, to work with David Boies in countering the guerrilla warfare Dan Burt was conducting in the media. Scanlon was a man of considerable charm whose white beard and rotundity masked an aggressive streak when selling a story to the media which rivaled that of Boies in a courtroom. Mater wanted to discuss his concern that a Law Department with its own public relations arm had the potential for improvising policy on an ad hoc basis. It was much the same concern I'd raised with Van in Las Vegas and one he obviously didn't share. We had just begun a discussion when my secretary interrupted with a phone call from Ted Savaglio, the West Coast Bureau chief, who'd told her it was important.

"There is something in this morning's *Daily Variety* I think you would want to know about," he said.

Daily Variety is published each weekday in Los Angeles, and while it primarily targets the Hollywood community, it's a miniature version of the larger weekly *Variety*, which is published in New York and which aims for a national readership in the entertainment and communications industries.

"It starts on page one," Savaglio continued, "and moves to five columns on page twenty-four. It's got a headline that says: 'CBS' Gary Shepherd and Don Kladstrup Jump Ship for ABC News.' "

"Is Richard Leibner quoted?" I asked.

"Yeah," Savaglio said. " 'The moves do not represent any pattern. Each and every situation is approached individually and stands on its own.' "

"What about ABC?"

"They quote David Burke, one of their Vice Presidents," Savaglio said. "Let me read it to you. 'Elaborating on ABC's clearly established pattern of recruiting proven talent from CBS, Burke said the company is constantly upgrading and enriching our ranks.' "

"Teddy, thank you very much for the call," I said. I hung up the phone and described the article to Van.

"Well, Leibner's making his move, isn't he?" Van said. "Every negotiation is going to include the threat of more stories about another talent drain at CBS News."

"What will Jankowski's reaction be?"

"Oh, I think he'll be O.K. on this," Van said. "How he'll react if there's a series of these is something else."

"Yeah, he didn't exactly stand tall for Leonard, did he?" I said.

Mater spoke up for the first time.

"Guys, you ought to be thinking about the weekly *Variety,*" he said. "It comes out next Wednesday and they would normally just rerun a story like this from the daily. When they do, every television columnist in the country will pick it up."

"Look, this 'jump ship' stuff is bullshit," Van said. "Shepherd was a throwaway to influence future negotiations . . . and you released Kladstrup from his contract so he could go. You can now read Leibner's thank-you for your having been a gentleman in *Daily Variety.* Leonard bled to death because of this kind of warfare. You've got to show Leibner that this won't work with you because you'll fight back. Mater here should call Jack Loftus at *Variety* and tell him we're all upset about the story in *Daily Variety* and that you'd like to meet with him to set the record straight."

"Any doubt where this is coming from?" Mater asked.

"A 'jump ship' angle did not suddenly materialize in the mind of a *Daily Variety* reporter," Van said. "It may have been Leibner or a surrogate, but it's a shot across our bow to let us know what's in store if we take a hard line on contracts."

"I'm afraid Van's right," I said. "Tell Loftus I know he has a Monday deadline, so I'll meet with him anytime except Thanksgiving Day."

Later that day I visited Dan Rather's office in the *Evening News* area.

"May I close your door?" I asked.

Rather was all attention at that request.

"Here, let me do it," he said, and quickly moved to the door. With the noise of the newsroom sealed off, the room was very quiet. The loudest sound came from the air bubbling in his large tropical fish tank.

"I've never talked with you about Richard Leibner," I said.

There was a freezing of the smile on Rather's face . . . the same expression television viewers see when he says, "We'll have more news in a moment," and waits for the camera to go off him and the commercial to begin.

"As an agent he's done very well by you and I'm aware of the relationship that's grown out of that. But I feel his actions in the past few months have been inappropriate. As you know, it's taking forever to complete our European bureau reorganization. Richard should not have been involved in that the way he was. Now with this fiction of an ABC raid it's pretty clear he's trying to dance on my head the way he did on Leonard's. I don't plan to sit still for that and I just wanted you to know that."

Another moment of quiet before Rather answered. Brightly colored fish chased one another around long strands of undulating greenery.

"You're right, we've never discussed Richard," he said. "That's probably been the correct way for us to handle it. I figure Richard is a big boy, and if he's in for some shots, that's what he gets paid for."

On Friday, November 25, 1983, the executive offices of CBS were closed for the holiday, so I was alone without a secretary when Loftus arrived. Loftus was the editor of the television section of *Variety*. He'd obviously been briefed by Kevin Goldman, the reporter who usually covered CBS News.

"You're unhappy with the *Daily Variety* story and angry at Leibner, right?" he said.

"What else do you know?" I asked.

"You released Kladstrup because he had some problems anyway and you were not going to stand in the way of his getting another job in Paris."

"What else?"

"That you're upset about Shepherd, but I can't understand that. He was free to go."

"Of course he was," I said. "That's not an issue. But in the midst of a negotiation if his agent tells him he's not appreciated at CBS, which Leibner did, that's clearly an attempt to move his client somewhere else."

"Why would Leibner want to do that?"

"How many clients do you think Leibner has at CBS News?"

"Quite a few, I would think . . . twenty-five . . . thirty."

"What if I told you it was well over a hundred and that their salaries total over $15 million a year?"

"Those are nice commissions."

"Yes, they are, and we're just one source. That's why the trading of players and the pressure in the press take place. The *Daily Variety* article was part of this effort. It's 1981 all over again. We see a pattern to exert pressure and force the market up."

"What's wrong with that?" Loftus asked.

"CBS News didn't cover the arrival of the Pope in Poland earlier this year because of cost problems. You wrote about that for your paper. The issue is whether we're going to control our own business or be dominated by the demands of agents like organized sports or the motion-picture industry. We can either make the agents and all their clients rich or cover the news. For a while we could do both but that era is ending."

Our conversation lasted for almost an hour. As Loftus was getting up to leave, he turned to me with a last question.

"If you had to sum up your feeling about this in one line, what would it be?"

I thought briefly.

"I am determined not to let the flesh peddlers affect the caliber of our broadcasts," I said.

The following Wednesday Loftus's story appeared in *Variety*. It included the quotes from me and a response from Leibner calling the CBS accusations "farfetched." The Thanksgiving weekend must have been slow for *Variety;* they placed the story on their front page with a banner headline: "CBS News Declares War on Agent . . . Too Much Jack in the Bienstock."

"Jankowski thinks the *Variety* article is very helpful," Van said.

We were on our way to a lunch with Jankowski in the executive dining room on the thirty-fourth floor of Black Rock on the day the article appeared.

"In what way?"

"It shows Wyman how serious the Broadcast Group is about holding its costs in check."

"Well, I hope he remembers that," I said. "We're going into 1984 with a skinny budget for a year with primaries and conventions, not to mention an election. God help us if other news breaks out."

"Is there a lot of buzz in the newsroom?"

"It's all people are talking about," I said.

"Maybe some of his clients will stop and think about how rich their agent has gotten."

"Wishful thinking," I said. "To most of them he's the guy trying to get them more money and I'm the guy who doesn't want to pay it."

"You may be right," Van said, "and Leibner will be on the phone with every one of them. He's already done a quick change from aggressor to victim."

"How do you know that?" I asked.

"He sent me a hand-delivered letter this morning. It made me think of your Emerson quote about counting your spoons. He wants a meeting with Jankowski and me."

"That's predictable," I said.

"I'll draft a response telling him to fuck off and show it to you," Van said.

"After the holidays there should be a meeting," I said. "Maybe you should be there so he can see there's no division of thought. We can establish a framework for future dealings. Part of the mystique he's peddled is instant access to top management. That's clearly shut off and it ought to stay that way. I should get involved with negotiations for the big contracts and Business Affairs should handle the rest."

"He should be dealt with in the same way CBS News deals with other agents," Van said. "This is the perfect time to stop any favored-nation idea."

"I wonder how Rather is going to handle all this?" I said.

"It'll be complex for him. He's shrewd enough to know Leibner got out of hand. But at the same time Leibner is very involved in the lives of the Rathers. He handles all of their business affairs and I don't think we can begin to guess at everything that involves, like that large ranch in New Mexico he owns with Donald Rumsfeld."

"How do you know that?" I asked.

"Kathleen has developed a relationship with Jean Rather, and she says that Jean is always running into the Bienstock office to go over business matters."

"I'd better touch base with him when I get back this afternoon," I said. "On Thursday I'm going on jury duty for two weeks. I hope lunch doesn't run too late. Can you tell me why we're having lunch with Trent Lott?"

Trent Lott was a conservative Republican congressman from the 5th District of Mississippi. He'd become the Republican Whip through a combination of hard work and shrewdness and was a devoted supporter of administration policies in the House.

Van looked uneasy.

"Oh, it's part of Gene's campaign to show the people on the Hill that CBS is run by good and decent Americans."

"Come on," I said, "it's certainly more than that."

"Bill Lilley has been sniping at CBS News," he said. "He's been the point man for Wyman in the struggle in Washington over financial interest in syndication programming."

William Lilley III was a Senior Vice President for Corporate Affairs. All three networks had been lobbying Congress for a change in the law which prohibited networks from having a financial interest in programs which could be syndicated for sale to local stations. The Hollywood production companies which owned and produced these programs saw this for the threat it was and hired Jack Valenti, a former official in the Johnson administration, as their lobbyist. Valenti was as skillful as the networks were clumsy in pressing their case. President Reagan even came out publicly for his old friends, the Hollywood producers, and the battle was lost and with it an opportunity for millions of dollars in additional revenues for the networks.

"What is Lilley saying about CBS News?" I asked.

"He claims that every time he went in to lobby some congressman, it quickly turned into a litany of complaints about CBS News," Van said.

"And Gene's solution is that we all have lunch with Trent Lott?"

"It's simply Gene trying to show Wyman he's a statesman," Van said. "We'll just smile a lot, eat our chicken, and go back to our offices."

On the surface, the lunch was innocuous enough. It was also attended by the other Executive Vice Presidents and Jankowski's staff. Lott was a tall dark-haired man with glasses in his early forties who treated Jankowski and his staff with an ill-concealed condescension. Just another lobby group. He was a bit more cautious with Van and me but seemed quite pleased at being so obviously courted in the home base of what conservative mythology portrayed as a bastion of the Eastern liberal establishment. Watching him throughout lunch, I kept thinking of a chipmunk at a picnic who has just stolen your Fritos.

Later Van called and asked me for my reaction.

"It's a bad mixture of agenda," I said. "A company like CBS inevitably will have to lobby Washington. It's a fact of life. But CBS News is in the business of pissing those people off. That's also a fact of life. I think we send conflicting signals at a lunch like that. Politicians respect power and are quick to sense weakness. Lobbying is essentially an admission of weakness. I don't think it's in the best interest of CBS News to be thrown into that kind of gathering."

"I'll discuss this with Gene," Van said. "He's really into this Washington thing."

"I'll be glad to call him and tell him my feelings."

"No," Van said, "let me do it. That's what I'm here for."

"O.K.," I said. "I'm running out of time. My jury duty starts tomorrow and I want to see Rather before I get out of here."

Rather arrived about twenty minutes later.

"I'm sorry to be so long getting here," he said. "I had to record my radio commentary."

Rather does a daily commentary written for him by a radio newswriter.

"No problem," I said. "I'm going to be on jury duty for the next couple of weeks, so I probably won't be showing up here until about six o'clock each evening. I wanted to make sure I told you I understand how difficult this conflict with Leibner must be for you. But I also wanted you to know I thought it had to be done for the best interest of CBS News."

I poured him a cup of black coffee while he answered.

"Well, you're right," he said. "It is difficult for me. Richard is and will remain a friend, as I consider you a friend."

"Look, Richard and I will have to deal with one another. He has to deal with CBS News and he has important clients."

"I'm glad to hear you say that," Rather said. "Right now Richard is obsessed by this. It's all he's talking about. And frankly he's worried about the impact on his business."

"When I'm finished with jury duty," I said, "I'll meet with him and we'll clear some air. But he'll have to understand he's an agent and not someone with a voice in the management of CBS News."

"Oh, I think he understands that now," Rather said. "Richard may be a lot of things but he's not stupid. He's gotten that message. But I think the sooner you meet with him, the better. You should know he was particularly stung by that 'flesh peddler' quote."

"Frankly, I think it was harsh, too," I said. "I wish I hadn't said it, but I was trying to make the point that the news business has no place for that Hollywood power agent stuff."

"I tell you this under the heading of 'news you can use,'" Rather said. "Richard feels there were overtones of anti-Semitism in that remark."

A knot formed in the pit of my stomach.

"Richard knows me better than that," I said. "No matter how great our quarrel he can't really believe that. My God, Swifty Lazar made a speech last year boasting that modern agents have come a long way from the street hustlers who used to be known as flesh peddlers."

"Ed, I am only telling you this," Rather said, "because if Richard says this to me, he is saying it to other people, and he talks, as we both know, to a lot of people. If you have any regrets about that remark, then when you meet with him you ought to say so and put this to rest."

"I'll do that, I assure you," I said, "and I thank you for sharing that with me."

When Rather left I sat alone, thinking not of Hollywood but of William Shakespeare and *The Merchant of Venice.* How on earth could I have been such an insensitive dolt that I didn't make that connection? Regardless of what I thought of Leibner, I would tell him I regretted using that term. I owed him that. It would make the rest of the conversation more difficult because I couldn't allow him to turn the clock back again. For everyone's good, I thought, including his clients, there had to be some limit to appetite. Almost half of our entire news budget was used to pay salaries. If they kept progressing at the rate they'd been going, the inevitable result would be major surgery on the News Division, complete with the elimination of numerous employees. The reluctance to accept this was not limited to Leibner. Most people inside CBS News didn't believe it. It was ironic. As a news organization, we had begun covering the story of disinflation and its impact on the American economy. But our own people seemed to assume that CBS was somehow exempt, that the competitive wars among the three network news organizations would continue to inflate salaries and budgets as they had in the past.

The next morning I left for Foley Square in lower Manhattan and jury selection. In my briefcase I carried several rolls of dimes for the pay phones scattered throughout the building which houses the New York State Supreme Court. For almost two weeks I conducted the business of CBS News from those phones each time the jury was given a recess. I recalled stories of "Dimes" Korshak, an attorney in the entertainment industry in Los Angeles with ties to Chicago and the group of businessmen there who comprise what is euphemistically known as "the Outfit." Because of the curiosity of certain federal agents as to the exact nature of the business arrangements between Dimes and his Midwestern friends, he conducted all of his business in phone booths, where the likelihood of electronic eavesdropping was reduced. As I fed in dime after dime to satisfy the insistent demands of the phone company, my respect for Korshak's business acumen, if not his choice of friends, increased immeasurably. I was selected as a juror on a murder trial involving a drug war in Harlem. After the past few years at CBS, the managerial style of the accused seemed enchantingly simple. I had particular cause for reflection on Tuesday, December 6, when I learned that Walter Cronkite, who up to now had confined his observations of the *Evening News* to a few close friends and the entire CBS Board of Directors, had gone public. In an interview with the New York *Times,* our Public Relations Department informed me, he said, *"The CBS Evening News* has become more concerned with entertaining audiences and less committed to covering all the major news stories of the day." Dan Rather had no comment. Did I wish to make a statement? Several dimes later I hurriedly dictated something to the effect of "I hold no one in greater respect than Walter Cronkite, but in this case he's dead wrong." Having delivered that limp retort, I rushed back to the jury room just as the judge called us back into the courtroom, where the defense attorney seemed to be trying to reduce an offense of second-degree murder to a lesser charge of restraint of trade.

When the accused took the stand and began a denigration of the business practices of his former and now dead rival, I resolved to hold out for a charge of Murder Two even if it meant being locked overnight in a hotel room with my fellow jurors. I also resolved that in 1984 I would find a way to spend some time with Cronkite. For two years Van had wanted to be the one to "handle" Cronkite because of his role on the board. Now I wanted to give it a try and see if there wasn't some way to bring an end to this warfare.

The pace of each day varied from hours of testimony which required concentration to hours of inactivity waiting for the trial to resume. Along with my rolls of dimes, my briefcase was stuffed with papers my secretary had delivered to me each day at the courthouse. Papers to sign, material to read. During one long recess I read a profile of myself in *Electronic Media,* a weekly publication for broadcasters. Much of the article consisted of a long interview I had done with Diane Mermigas, one of their reporters. At one point in the interview she had asked me for a comment on Ted Turner and his Cable News Network. Turner was for some reason a name whose very mention could cause Jankowski to vituperate. The suggestion that *Nightwatch* had been created to fend off Turner's encroachment on our affiliate body always prompted angry denials. Puzzling, since it was quite true. Executives of the Broadcast Group were frequently exhorted to remind the world that one overnight broadcast of *Nightwatch* reached a larger audience than Turner's CNN achieved over a week-long twenty-four-hours-a-day schedule. When the interviewer asked me for my comment, the pomposity of my response was matched only by my total lack of prescience.

Dripping with condescension, I told the readers of *Electronic Media* that "I regard Ted Turner just about the way General Motors regards Harley Davidson. It's an interesting small business."

Sitting in a courtroom in lower Manhattan was an odd way to close 1983. In the roughly three months I'd been President of CBS News, I had been faced with events in Beirut and Grenada, the issue of the DeLorean tapes, the temporary resignation of Bill Moyers, testimony before Congress, a public fight with an agent, a temporary rebellion of affiliates, not to mention the ongoing process of the Westmoreland trial as well as the difficulties of starting up *American Parade* under the added burden of having succeeded a good friend who had moved up but not out. No wonder the jury box seemed like a refuge. The hours of waiting provided the only moments of reflection I'd enjoyed in months. I emerged from this convinced of the need to hire someone to replace me in my previous job. This was not something I had planned on doing.

But the whirlstream of those three months caused me to worry about what the future might hold. Since 1981, when I first arrived, CBS News had almost doubled the percentage of the network schedule for which it was responsible. In 1978, it produced 14.1 percent of the CBS television network schedule. In 1981, 17.4 percent. In 1983, it made the largest contribution in its history, contributing 33.3 percent of all network airtime. It was a lot to manage even in tranquil times, and as I had just been reminded, there were no assurances of future tranquillity. It made sense to appoint a new Executive Vice President based on the needs of the *Morning News* alone.

A lunch I'd had with Diane Sawyer at the end of November confirmed my worries. She was bitterly at odds with Bob Ferrante, the executive producer who had replaced Merlis. After lunch I asked Bill Kurtis for his reactions and he lip-synched Diane's complaints. Ferrante was rigid, unimaginative, lacked the spark of George Merlis, who was now being canonized in absentia by them both. Whoever I hired would have to quickly assume the role of godfather for that broadcast. By the time the trial was over and I returned full-time to CBS News, I'd pretty well resolved to discuss the job with Howard Stringer. Howard was a known quantity within CBS News. His appointment wouldn't produce an outcry from the xenophobes. He'd been an imaginative executive producer of the *Evening News* who had reshaped the broadcast and developed a corps of producers who were the best in the business.

Not the least of his skills had been demonstrated in his handling of the black moods of an anchorman. I had a few reservations. For one thing, Howard was not an American citizen. Although he'd worked in the United States for more than twenty years and, in addition, had served in the American Army in Vietnam, he remained a citizen of Great Britain. I'd had some concern about that while he was an executive producer. In fact, I was surprised that not once had anyone questioned the appropriateness of America's most watched network news broadcast being in the charge of a foreign national. If Howard became the Executive Vice President of CBS News, he would be the number two executive at one of America's most important news organizations and an obvious candidate to become its President if I should ever leave. American citizenship would, in my judgment, become an essential qualification. When I discussed the job with Howard, I would have to make that abundantly clear. Howard lacked experience in certain business fundamentals, particularly the development and control of a large budget. But I'd never believed that process required much more than common sense and I was sure he could grow into that part of the job. By far my biggest reservation was the absolute delight Howard took in the sharing and soliciting of each day's bumper crop of CBS factoids. If CBS News had long ago developed rumoring to assembly-line perfection, Howard had become the model worker. In his years at *CBS Reports,* Howard had craftily concluded that while Nielsen seldom awards a winning rating to a documentary, another rating system takes place in the television columns of major newspapers. Over the years he'd become a friendly source of information for writers such as Tom Shales of the Washington *Post.* A relationship such as this gave Howard access to the ear of an influential writer and helped shape his perceptions of television. There were times when this was beneficial, but it could be worrisome to read a Shales article, see some bit of what had been confidential information, and wonder if Howard had provided it in an attempt at ingratiation. He and Van shared an instinct for indiscretion, the need to make, in Shakespeare's words, "the babbling gossip of the air cry out." With all that, Howard was still my candidate for the job. We'd simply have to talk candidly about what I felt was a shortcoming. If he was given this new job he would have access to a level of information about CBS News he'd never had before. In moving from producer to manager he would relinquish the ability to regularly use the word "they" as in "they say" or "you won't believe what they are doing now." By accepting the job he would be accepting membership in the third person plural pronoun club, the "they" who are in charge. Discussing all this with Howard went onto my list of things to be done early in 1984.

The trial moved toward its conclusion. The prosecution and defense presented their closing arguments, and the jury began its deliberations. For the first time I learned what the others in the jury box thought. My fellow jurors had also concluded that the accused was more than an aggrieved businessman. We returned a verdict of second-degree murder and were released to our regular lives with a thank-you from the judge for having been an attentive and thoughtful jury. I left the courtroom and headed back uptown for CBS News and a new year.

Van's secretary came into his office and closed the door.

"Mr. and Mrs. Leibner are here," she said.

Van looked surprised.

"Did you know he was bringing Carole?" he asked.

"No, but it's a good idea," I said. "She's a good balance for him when he begins to get manic."

It was an evening early in 1984, shortly after 7 P.M. The news had just finished its first feed and we'd been waiting for Leibner's arrival. In the weeks which had followed my public clash with Leibner, the Bienstock agency had negotiated a number of contracts for clients at CBS News. Leibner and Witt had dealt with our Business Affairs Department and the negotiations had been conducted in a professional, albeit subdued, manner. Earlier that day I'd asked Sekarek for an assessment of the negotiations.

"The deals are getting done without the bullshit" was his pithy description.

Rather's description of Leibner's being "obsessed" wasn't overblown. Hardly a day passed without my hearing from someone who'd just encountered Leibner. Sometimes it was one of his clients telling me that Leibner was worried about his business and wouldn't I please ease up. The truth was, I was fully prepared to do that. The point had been made and as long as Leibner behaved like an agent instead of a power broker I saw no reason why Bienstock and CBS News couldn't arrive at some modus vivendi.

Besides, I'd embarrassed myself with my stupid and unfeeling use of the term "flesh peddler" and I was anxious to put it behind me.

When Van's secretary brought the Leibners into his office, they both looked understandably tense. Carole Cooper is a thin dark-haired woman who mostly represented on-air people at local television stations across the country.

The two of them walked immediately to a couch at the far end of the office and sat down next to one another. Leibner was as subdued as I'd ever seen him. There were no ethnic jokes, no spasms of wild gesticulation. He sat with his hands on his lap.

Rather than let an awkward silence continue, I decided to address a sore point.

"Before we discuss anything else," I said, "I want you to know I regret the 'flesh peddler' quote in *Variety*. You didn't deserve that and I'm sorry I said it."

"Why didn't you call me Shylock?" he said.

"I didn't intend that for a minute," I replied, "but even the Hollywood reference I did intend was too harsh, so I'll tell you again I wish I hadn't said it. But that's all I regret. You have been way out of line lately and when I saw that *Daily Variety* piece I was not about to let you do to me what you did to Bill Leonard."

Leibner looked as though he was about to burst from a paroxysm of rage.

"I didn't give that stuff to *Daily Variety*," he said. "I didn't even talk to the reporter."

"Richard, you were quoted in that article," I said.

"I mean, I didn't give him any of that business about 'jumping ship,'" he said.

Van, who'd been silent until now, took a pipe out of his mouth and began loudly banging the ashes into a large ceramic ashtray.

"I think we'll waste an evening which is already getting late," he said, "if we bog down in a line-by-line examination of what appeared in those articles."

Leibner persisted.

"Why did you have to talk to *Variety*?" he asked.

"For two reasons," I said. "One, because you planted or at least influenced the tone of the *Daily Variety* article. Two, Kevin Goldman, who covers CBS for the weekly *Variety*, made no secret of the fact that you had allowed him to spend time in your office that week watching you conduct business. I can imagine the story which would have appeared if I hadn't talked to Loftus."

"Richard, you shouldn't be quoted anywhere," Van said, "on your dealings with CBS News."

"I did a favor for Kevin," Leibner said. "He told me he wanted to learn something about how an agency works just to broaden his professional knowledge. His being there was just a coincidence."

I didn't believe that for a moment, but this discussion was now spinning its wheels and I wanted to get moving.

"Maybe it was a coincidence," I said, "but now you can see how your fingerprints seemed to be all over that article."

Leibner seized at that.

"Yes, I can see that, babe."

Suddenly I was babe again.

"But I would never do that," he added.

I let it drop and moved to the next subject.

"Regardless of any argument or any fight, we're going to end up dealing with one another. You have important clients and we need them. You need CBS News. It's best for everyone if that's done in a calm, professional manner."

"I've got to be able to deal directly with you," Leibner said quickly.

"That's not always going to be possible," I said, "not if I'm going to get the rest of my job done. On the big contracts I'll be there. For the rest, Sekarek can handle them."

"What do we do to clear the public air?" Leibner asked.

"We do business in a normal fashion," I said. "Word will get around."

"That's true here in New York," he said, "but not around the rest of the country. That's where I'm getting hurt. Carole is already encountering that from some television stations who are following the example of the CBS News lead."

Carole Cooper nodded glumly at that.

"Look," I said, "I'll put the word out here that you and I have had an amicable meeting. It'll spread. And if any reporter should ask me I'll say the same thing."

"Do you think you could get Loftus to write that in *Variety?*" he asked.

"Loftus will write what he wants," I said, "but I can tell him what I've just said to you."

The rest of the conversation drifted into upcoming contracts for various Bienstock clients and the evening ended with a round of assurances from Leibner that his primary goal was the welfare of CBS News.

After they'd left, Van and I sat alone comparing notes.

"Eduardo, no one will ever thank you for it," he said, "but you've turned an important corner for CBS News. Leibner's golden era is over."

"He's not going to give up that easily. He'll be busy trying to regain ground."

"But not as an aggressor. He's afraid of you now. He knows you took his measure."

"You can never really measure a snake till it's dead," I said, "and that one's far from dead."

The next morning at my regular staff meeting I waited for the normal routine to finish as each executive briefed his colleagues on what was happening in his area of CBS News.

"You might be interested to know that I met last evening with Richard Leibner. N. S. Bienstock and CBS News are once again doing business on an amicable basis. I also want you to know I told Leibner I regretted my 'flesh peddler' quote in *Variety.*"

Joan Richman gave me a wide and supportive smile.

"Way to go, boss," she said. "Good for you."

After the staff meeting I asked my secretary to locate Howard Stringer and have him come to my office. He'd just finished his morning conference call with the domestic bureau chiefs and a few minutes later appeared in my doorway.

"Good morning, chief."

"Stringer, come in and close the door while we discuss drastically altering your life."

"Oh, good . . . I'm being fired off the *Evening News.* I hope I'm being treated as well as Socolow was. Remember, if you make me the London Bureau chief I'm simply going home."

"The story of your life, Howard . . . semi-prescient. But that's not quite what I have in mind," I said. "I'm thinking of filling my old job."

Howard became serious.

"We've all been wondering if you were going to do that."

"The demands of the past few months have convinced me," I said, "and I'd love to see you in that job if we can extract you from the *Evening News* without unbalancing the anchorman."

"He wouldn't block me," Howard said. "Not after all I've done for him." He stopped, seeing the smile on my face. "That was silly of me," he said. "Of course he would. I'll have to work on him."

"The first thing you have to do is decide if you want the job," I said. "The hours are longer . . . it's seven days a week, twenty-four hours a day, and you won't earn any more money than you're making right now.

In fact, you'd probably earn more over the next year or so if you remained with the *Evening News*. On the plus side, there's the exhilaration of running a great news organization . . . and if I should be hit by a speeding car you'd stand a good chance of being the next President of CBS News."

"It would be a long time before I'd be ready for that," Howard said. "Both you and Van came to these jobs with years of management experience. If you think I can do the job I'd love to try it and, hopefully, while I'm learning the job still make a contribution with those things I do know."

"Howard, the most important thing you could do is replace me as shepherd for the *Morning News,*" I said. "That broadcast has had precious little management attention for the past several months."

"I'd quite like that."

"There are a couple of problem areas I'd like to put on the table," I said. "One is your tendency to enjoy the role of the artful dodger with your colleagues and more importantly with people like Shales at the Washington *Post.* In this job you would know everything that was being planned or discussed at CBS News. Along with a new office we'll be issuing a size-twelve zipper for your mouth."

Howard looked hurt for the briefest moment before he began to laugh.

"Ah . . . hard but fair," he said. "Never one to mince words, old Joyce. You have my assurance that won't be a problem."

"I don't know how you'll feel about the other matter I'm going to bring up," I said, "but the only reason to leave the kind of job you now have and become the Executive Vice President is the hope that one day you'll be President of CBS News. Howard, they could never give that job to someone who is not an American citizen. You've been here since the sixties . . . you were in the American Army in Vietnam, but you're still one of Her Majesty's subjects. Unless becoming a citizen is something you'd planned on doing, I would in good conscience have to tell you this is not a job you should take."

"I should have done that years ago. I've been on the verge of it so many times. After all these years my life is here, isn't it? But it's been a difficult break for me to actually make."

"I can understand that," I said. "I've spent enough time in England to appreciate your feelings. It's a tough decision and maybe you want to think about it for a few days."

"No," he said. "It's something I've intended to do. You may operate with the assumption that I will begin the process of citizenship."

"You won't mind, then, if I start calling you Yank?"

Howard looked so pained I walked over to where he was sitting and put my hand on his shoulder.

"Welcome aboard, Howard. Now go to work on Warden Rather. If he grants your parole, I'll meet you at the gate."

A few days later Howard was back in my office.

"Dan is being bloody awful about my leaving the broadcast," he said.

"In what way?"

"I told him I'd heard you were considering appointing an Executive Vice President. I didn't tell him you'd offered me the job. Instead, I asked for his support in trying to convince you to give it to me."

"Why on earth would you do that?"

"That way he could feel he'd helped orchestrate it. His man in the front office . . . that sort of thing."

"Howard, consider this part of your learning curve," I said. "That's exactly what you don't want him to believe. It's difficult enough as it is without expanding his territory."

"I may not be moving anywhere," Howard said. "Old Dan is being frightfully cunning. He said if I want the job he will of course support me. Then he quickly adds that he thinks David Buksbaum would be ideal as my replacement."

"Checkmate," I said.

"Exactly," he said. "The producers would resign en masse if that happened. They're used to expressing opinions. David would think his first goal was to dominate them."

"When your only tool is a hammer," I said, "everyone begins to look like a nail. It seems to me there are three senior producers on the *Evening News* who are the leading candidates to replace you."

"Lane Venardos, Mark Harrington, and Tom Bettag," Howard quickly responded.

"Of course," I answered. "They're the obvious choices. Dan can't be serious about Buksbaum."

"I don't think you can overestimate the degree to which Dan counts on total loyalty and obedience from David."

"There's no doubt that David is someone who will get things done," I said. "He's been good working with the crews. They'll tell you the equipment situation in the bureaus has never been better."

"It's more than that," Howard said. "If Dan woke up in a room with two dead bodies, an open suitcase stuffed with hundred-dollar bills, and no idea of how he got there, the first phone call he would make would be to David Buksbaum."

"Fascinating, isn't it?" I said. "David's instrumentality would become more important to Dan in that job."

"And it would destroy the broadcast. Dan has come to believe his own publicity. He's forgotten how helpless he was without us."

"Hey, when *U.S. News & World Report* lists Dan with David Rockefeller, Katherine Graham, and Punch Sulzberger as one of six people who received top ratings in their survey identifying influential Americans in the private sector, that's pretty heady stuff. And in their follow-up last May they placed him with Lee Iacocca and Senator Robert Dole as one of six Americans whose influence is on the rise. I can assure you that Dan does not say to himself, 'I'm just the symbol for all those dedicated men and women of CBS News,' or 'I owe it all to Stringer and his skilled producers.' He won't say that even to himself, for the same reasons I won't hear my name mentioned either. We're all uncomfortable reminders that while people on the outside may think he's in charge, we know what he knows, that it's not the case."

"And the only one here who acts like Dan's in charge is Buksbaum," Howard said.

"You've got it. With the rest of us he has to settle for being terribly important. That was all right when things were bumpy, but now he's number one. The people who write for newspapers and magazines know less about the inner workings of television than they do of the Central Committee in Moscow, so Dan gets lumped in there with media barons and captains of industry. That leaves our anchorman trying to figure out why he's not calling all the shots like Sulzberger, Graham, and Iacocca."

"There are times," Howard said, "when I'd just like to walk away . . . say, 'Sod it all . . . here, Dan, it's all yours, see if you can make it work.' "

"Don't be discouraged, Howard," I said. "This will just slow us down a bit."

"We can't very well just name someone and let Dan read the release along with everyone else," Howard said. "He'd bugger the poor devil in a matter of weeks."

"It's more than that," I said. "Dan's contract is quite specific. He's 'entitled to participate substantially in management decision making with respect to the *Evening News.*' Jankowski gave him that . . . it's part of what you will come to know as the challenge of management."

"I haven't made a very good start, I'm afraid," Howard said, "but I won't give up. I'll have another go at him after tonight's broadcast."

"This time," I said, "I suggest you appeal to his self-interest . . . not his gratitude."

While Howard went off to have "another go" at the anchorman, I left to meet with Van on the subject of exit polls. The political primary season was beginning. The Iowa caucuses and the New Hampshire primary were just weeks away. The House Subcommittee on Elections was planning to hold hearings on the practice by the three networks of projecting winners on election night on the basis of information obtained through exit polls. For years all three networks had interviewed voters as they left the voting place, asking them who they voted for, the reasons for their vote, and other questions which identified the race, religion, sex, and socioeconomic background of each voter. The purpose of this had been to provide material for post-election analysis. But in 1980 NBC took it a step further and used the exit-poll data to project winners in that election. That year CBS was still using its slower Vote Profile Analysis, which was based not on asking people how they voted but on votes actually cast and tabulated in sample precincts. Throughout the evening NBC was first to project the winners in numerous states while CBS executives ground enamel off their molars and began to formulate catch-up plans. The catch-up occurred in 1982, when CBS News made successful calls using exit-poll data during its coverage of the off-year election. The congressional committee members correctly anticipated that the three networks would be competing furiously on election night 1984 to make the first calls in key races, including the presidential contest. They acknowledged that the exit-poll results were accurate enough to withstand challenge on that basis. Their complaints centered instead on the charge that this new method for projecting winners in elections was so fast and so early it created a situation in which voters in the Western time zones would know the winner of a presidential election before many of them had even gone to the polls, hardly an incentive to believe they would be casting an important vote. As a result, they argued, many voters would simply decide to stay at home. Indeed, NBC in 1980, on the basis of exit-poll information, declared Ronald Reagan President-elect at 8:15 P.M. EDT, two and three-quarter hours before polls closed on the West Coast. But the argument had less merit when you considered that in 1980, 42 percent of the actual vote had been tabulated nationwide before the polls had closed in California. At that time Ronald Reagan was leading in states that accounted for 396 electoral votes and had amassed a margin of 2.7 million in the popular vote. It takes 270 electoral votes to get elected. So even without projections, the message to viewers would have been the same . . . a Reagan landslide. In fact, President Jimmy Carter had conceded his defeat before the West Coast polls were closed. But this didn't deter the three most vocal members of the subcommittee, Al Swift, a Democrat from Washington, Tim Wirth, a Democrat from Colorado, and William Thomas, a Republican from California, the chairman and ranking minority member of the House Subcommittee on Elections. Their message to the three networks was clear.

"You're harming the democratic process because you are discouraging West Coast voters from going to the polls by telling them the race is over. Show some restraint or we'll seek legislation which imposes restrictions."

The networks' response was that exit polling was an accurate way of correctly informing voters of the outcome in their particular states once their polls had closed. For years CBS had been arguing that the problem was one of staggered poll closings in a country with multiple time zones. The solution was to adopt a uniform poll-closing time throughout the nation. That would be a far better solution than asking television news organizations to withhold from the public the outcome of elections known to us at a time when the vast majority of polls in the nation were closed. The networks, too, had at least the basis of an argument. But the argument had less merit when you considered that the information had been developed in the first place by the networks' own survey and polling units and that the motivating impulse behind using exit-poll data to project winners had less to do with the public's right to know and more with the competitive worry that the public would choose to watch on election night whichever network provided the earliest returns.

When I arrived in Van's office I had pretty much anticipated what I would hear.

"Jankowski says Wyman would really like us to get out of the exit-poll business . . . at least stop using them as the basis for projections."

"It's not that easy," I said.

"According to Gene, Bill Lilley is citing this as one more way CBS News manages to piss off Congress."

"That may be true," I said, "but it doesn't mean we should let Congress tell us how to practice journalism."

"Remember, I testified before this subcommittee a couple of years ago on exit polls," Van said. "They're not going to drop this issue."

"Frankly, I wish CBS News hadn't started making calls with the damned things," I said. "It was only because NBC cleaned their clock. But I don't see any face-saving way we could discontinue the practice without looking like we were caving to pressure from the Hill. If they go for restrictions, they'll walk into a mine field of First Amendment issues."

"Oh, I don't think it's a legal issue we worry about," Van said. "It's a

331

public relations problem. We're going to start hearing all that shit about the arrogant networks. Lilley will be whispering into Wyman's ear and Gene will be a man in agony."

"It's so tempting to say yes," I said. "What the hell, we withhold other information . . . we wouldn't hesitate to embargo demands from kidnappers if reporting them endangered the victim . . . but when you start letting Congress tell you how to cover the news you're standing on a slippery slope."

"What do I tell Gene?" Van asked.

"Tell him I know it's not uncommon to resort to expedience when honor gets a little risky," I said, "but I can't do it."

Van looked at me for a long time before he responded.

"I'll tell him it would cause a shit storm in the News Division if you did this," he said. "You'd be perceived as a sellout."

"That, too," and I laughed as I said it because there was no doubt that half the decisions made by a President of CBS News were reviewed in the corridors of CBS News and measured against a past whose legend was approaching Arthurian proportions.

"Before I get out of here," I added, "I should fill you in on the latest in the Stringer-Rather saga."

"I have a pretty good idea," Van said. "Rather called me this morning to ask me to get behind Buksbaum for the executive producer role."

"What did you say?"

"I told him I'd never thought of David in that sort of role."

"And?"

"He said he thought David had a lot to offer."

"No," I said. "I mean what else did you say about Buksbaum? Did you tell him David would be all wrong for that job?"

"No. I thought what I said was sending a signal."

"It'll take more than that. If he keeps pushing for Buksbaum I'll have to leave Stringer where he is."

"Why don't you and I take both Rather and Stringer somewhere out of the building to discuss this . . . someplace where there won't be any interruptions and we'll wear him down."

The next morning the four of us gathered in a suite at the Dorset Hotel. The suite was stocked with hot black coffee for Rather, tea for Stringer, and iced Tabs for Sauter and me. When everyone had helped himself, I opened the discussion.

"Hopefully, we'll leave here this morning agreeing on a replacement for Howard."

I looked at Howard. "If we don't, you'll experience what in corporate jargon is known as the mid-career stall."

Rather stared at the black recesses of his cup.

"Let's begin by listing the names of the candidates for the job," I continued. "As I see it, they are Venardos, Harrington, and Bettag, three of the senior producers. They've all been a part of the rebuilding of the broadcast. Of those three Venardos is the most senior. The fourth name is David Buksbaum. Dan, would you agree that's the list?"

"I would," he said. "We might add a dark horse with the name of Andy Lack. He doesn't have the hard-news experience but neither did Howard."

"Andy is a close friend," Howard said, "but I think it would be wrong to pass over people who've worked on the broadcast for the past two years."

"Dan, I take it your candidate remains Buksbaum?" I asked.

"Those are all excellent candidates," Rather said, "and I take your point that if we don't agree on one of them, Howard would experience a career stall. That wouldn't be fair to him, which means we need to pick his replacement this morning. Perhaps I'm just uncomfortable with change. My relationship with Howard has been very close and very good these past two years. I feel the two of us have achieved a real bonding. So in considering his replacement that sort of relationship is important to me, and I feel that of this group, good as they all are, David Buksbaum is the person I would feel best about. But mark this," he added, "it's not just because of friendship that I say this. Yes, Dan Rather and David Buksbaum have been friends, are friends, and will continue to be friends, but I also think he is the best person for the job."

He paused briefly, then concluded by saying, "But they're all excellent people."

I saw an opening here. The last thing Rather would want would be for any of the other candidates to learn that he had not been their supporter.

"They're excellent, but you don't think you could develop the bonding you talked about?"

"No, I'm sure that could develop," he said. "It's just that it already exists with David."

"Howard, what do you think about Buks for that job?" I asked.

"I'm frightfully uncomfortable with the idea," he said. "We have a group of people who like one another and are terribly open with one another. Old David, bless him, can be a bit of a bully. I know he gets things done, but the litter of bodies can be costly in the long run."

"Howard, I know you think that," Rather said. "I also know David has that reputation, but I've known him longer than any of you."

"David has done an excellent job in the operations area, Howard," I said.

Stringer paled as I said that.

"If I was a Marine general who wanted to see the flag planted on the next mountain crest," I said, "Buksbaum is the kind of guy I'd turn to and know the flag would be flying there the next day. He's a hard charger, but the role of executive producer for the *Evening News* requires more than aggression. It requires editorial and production skills and it certainly requires motivating a large number of talented people. David has a bright future, but I just don't see him in this job."

I looked at Van.

"Van, you've been very quiet this morning. What are your thoughts on this?"

Van walked over to the large serving cart in the corner of the suite. He took a bottle of Tab from the bucket which was filled with iced bottles. He looked different this morning and for a moment I couldn't put a finger on it. Then I realized he was wearing a suit, a gray one with a faint chalk stripe. He opened the bottle and walked back to his chair before responding.

"Like Ed, I have a high regard for David," he said, looking at Rather. "My perception of David's interests and of his skills would never have led me to think of him for this job. That's just one man's perception, of course."

Rather turned back to me.

"Ed, a moment ago you said you believed David has a bright future. What do you think that future would hold?"

What did I think? The asking of that question could well be the tidal change in this discussion, so my answer would have to be persuasive.

"It seems to me," I said, "that David's talent should be discussed in terms of our need to constantly improve our news-gathering capability. I could see him in the Joan Richman spot, or if John Lane should change jobs, I could imagine David in that kind of position. You have to believe that anyone who was beaten on a story would hear about it fast."

Stringer picked up the theme.

"That would be meshing the man with the job," he said. "David would be admirably suited for that, and we would benefit from his experience."

Rather nodded his head.

"There's no doubt that David is hard news with capital letters," he said.

"While he is still my leading choice, not my only choice, but my leading choice for the *Evening News* . . . I can see why you might think of him for other roles."

"Gentlemen, the issue is becoming very clear," Van said. "There are three excellent candidates currently working on the *Evening News.* I think Ed is quite right: we should look for the best way to use David's talents. But right now our goal should be to choose one of the three senior producers as Howard's successor."

I began to feel better. Rather had backed off the Buksbaum candidacy in exchange for a vague commitment to future opportunities. For the next seven hours, right through a lunch which two waiters in white jackets brought to the suite, we deliberated over the choice of the new executive producer for *The CBS Evening News.* Sauter, Stringer, and I were agreed that the job should go to Lane Venardos. Venardos was the person on the broadcast the others turned to in Stringer's absence. He was a well-organized producer with sound news judgment. In both the asset and the debit column one would have to list his comedic abilities. More than one moment of tension in the Fishbowl had been dispelled by a Venardos comedy routine.

Dejected faces brightened, for example, at Lane's imitation of a small-station disc jockey. A deep voice would roll out of Lane's three-hundred-pound body announcing "tall tower, full power, we break in when the news breaks out."

But in this new job he would have to exercise an authority in situations which couldn't be resolved with a stand-up routine. Before our meeting I had discussed Venardos with both Van and Howard, and we had agreed that he was our choice. Not the least of the reasons I felt that way was the number of times Lane had argued when Van or I had criticized an *Evening News* story he felt was sound. He'd been firm and persuasive with his arguments, something I respected and believed would be important qualities for dealing with the anchorman.

By the time lunch was finished, we were unanimous in our selection. Rather had returned again and again throughout the morning to the concept of bonding, but the three of us assured him that Venardos and he would be bonded within weeks.

When we left the Dorset, Howard and Dan grabbed a cab to return to the West Side and the Broadcast Center. I walked the few blocks with Van to Black Rock.

"A productive morning," he said.

"I think it was. But the amount of time we spent discussing bonding was fucking unbelievable."

"That's an issue that's incredibly important to the anchorman."

"You know those job description forms the Personnel Department creates for every position at CBS?" I asked. "They're going to have to do a new one or at least expand the one they've got for an executive producer . . . something like 'a degree in journalism is desirable, willingness to submit to bonding essential.' "

The changes were announced in mid-January 1984. On his first day in his new job Howard arrived in my office shortly before 9 A.M.

"Good morning, Your Grace," he said. "Now what do I do?"

"You could start today off by spending a little time with the *Morning News,* " I said. "They need attention."

"I'll have to be careful there in terms of my relationship with Dan. He's already advised me it wouldn't be good for my career to become too involved with the *Morning News.* "

"Did he really? Howard, he'll have to realize that you now have other responsibilities in addition to the *Evening News.* "

"Bit like a jealous lover, our Dan, isn't he?"

"More than a bit, I'd say. How will he feel about your getting involved with *American Parade?*" I asked.

"Less jealous than the *Morning News,* I should think," he said. "It's a public-affairs broadcast, not another hard-news broadcast which uses the bureaus and their correspondents and crews."

"Well, poke around there for me. You spent years with all those people in public affairs. I don't have a sense of *American Parade* building a bank of good stories the way *60 Minutes* has always done."

"Actually, I've already done that," Howard said, "and you're right to be worried. You've got the Balkans on your hands there, mate. Most of my old crew from *CBS Reports* are now working on *American Parade* and they've all been calling me at home telling me how bad things are."

"Be specific."

"They say that Shad is trying to replicate *Sunday Morning* in prime time. Remember, a lot of these people have produced some distinguished documentaries and they resent being lectured on how good *Sunday Morning* is."

"Where is Chandler in all of this?" I asked.

"These people all recall Bob from his first tour as Vice President for Public Affairs. They're calling it 'the return of Nixon.' "

"I don't believe this place. No wonder stories aren't being stockpiled. Everyone is too involved arranging the next dirking."

"Shall I continue with me report?" Howard asked.

"Yes, I suppose so."

"According to my little group, Shad is spending his time working with the designer of the new set with the hundred television screens and Chandler sees his main function as fending off Van."

"A dangerous pursuit on his part," I said. "Van is beginning to mutter about getting rid of Chandler."

"I'm for that this morning," Howard said. "Chandler hasn't exactly greeted my appointment with jubilation. Nor, for that matter, has John Lane."

"What did they say to you?" I asked.

"Chandler wished me good luck and then added, 'And you'll need all of it,' and Lane won't even look at me."

"Don't worry about it," I said. "It's just the standard CBS News greeting for a new executive. It's about the way I was greeted when I arrived."

"You came from the flaming Stations Division," Howard said. "I've worked at CBS News my whole bloody life."

"You're admirably trained to deal with it. You were a scholarship boy at a public school in Britain. Either charm them or ignore them."

"The only way I could charm Bob Chandler would be to douse myself in something suitably flammable and hand him a cigarette lighter."

"They were both established executives when you were just a young researcher and then a young producer," I said. "It's the young-pup syndrome. Not only have you grown up but you've become a lead dog. They're still in place pulling the sled and now they have to stare at your fat ass."

Howard smiled. "There is that, I suppose."

I was actually more concerned about the reaction from both of them than I indicated to Howard. Chandler was almost condescending in his dealings with Howard. Lane seemed traumatized by the appearance of Howard Stringer in his new executive role. Shortly after the job change I held a meeting of the domestic bureau chiefs in New Orleans at the Pontchartrain Hotel. Both Howard and John were there to join in on two days of discussions with the seven bureau chiefs and the domestic editor. Meetings such as this are only effective if they can be turned into free-wheeling discussions with the formal agenda serving mostly as a point of departure. The bureau chiefs were prepared for this kind of meeting and so was I. It was distressing to watch John Lane, who was by nature gregarious, sitting silently throughout these meetings. At dinner one night I tried to break the ice with a toast to Howard which actually would have been more appropriate for a roast. I reminded the group that Howard was Welsh and recalled the circumstances in which Sir Thomas More, the Lord Chancellor of England, was executed in 1535. He was convicted by his protégé Richard Richards, who gave perjured testimony against More and then became attorney general for Wales. More looked at him and said, "I know it might profit you to gain a whole nation for the price of a soul—but for Wales?" I concluded by suggesting a toast "to a man who would never settle for so little but whom I shall watch with particular care whenever the stakes are low."

Both wine and water glasses were raised to the sound of laughter around the large table in the private dining room of LeRuth's. Across the table I witnessed the listlessness of an obviously depressed John Lane.

A few days later back in New York I found myself discussing this with Van.

"I'm really worried," I said. "John is a well-liked figure. If his attitude toward Howard begins to create some echo within the institution, it will be terrible."

"You'd have to remove him before that happened," Van said.

"And that would be terrible, too. I really like John."

"So do I," Van said, "but it would solve one problem. We're going to have to deliver on Buksbaum for Rather."

"I don't feel any particular pressure on that. There was no time frame in our discussion of David."

"Rather mentions him every time we talk," Van said. "It's going to become a manhood issue for him if he can't produce for his boy. You're the one who described Buksbaum as the kind of hard charger who would make a great replacement for Lane."

"I certainly did, didn't I? And when Lane retires we should certainly consider it."

"Are you really willing to jeopardize your relationship with Rather?" Van asked, his concern obvious. "You don't want to get off to that kind of start with him in the first few months of your new job. Look, I'm having lunch with Lane tomorrow. We've had this scheduled for weeks. Let me take his temperature. Maybe because of Howard he'd prefer to be in some other job."

The next afternoon at about two-thirty Van burst enthusiastically into my office.

"Well," he said, giving the word the same excited reading Jack Benny used on radio. "I have some news for you. John Lane would like to be the London Bureau chief."

"You're kidding."

"I am not kidding. He told me at lunch."

"I wouldn't mind transferring Socolow," I said. "The last time you and I were in London we told him he had to show us more and it really hasn't happened. Besides, he's been there three years. John Lane would be great in that job, and it would be a face-saving way to remove him from working directly with Howard."

"And it would mean Buksbaum could move into the job," Van said.

"Look," I said, "I got myself into this with my own bullshit, and now I'm stuck with it. David will work his ass off in that job. What I don't know is if he can rise above his servile relationship with the anchorman and stop grinning every time Dan tells him about the rabbits."

"Now, now, Eduardo, allow for growth, as our old boss Tom Leahy used to tell us."

"You're right, and I will," I said. "I'd better go talk to John Lane."

"My advice is to leave it alone for now," Van said. "John has told me of his desire to go to London. . . . Get the other pieces in place. Get ready to make the announcement and then tell John about the change."

Those other pieces involved transferring Socolow to Tel Aviv as bureau chief, and returning Chandler to his previous job as Senior Vice President for Administration. Gene Mater, who'd been handling those responsibilities, had accepted a job with CBS International, making it possible to remove Chandler from his involvement with *American Parade* without, I hoped, causing him undeserved embarrassment. I could pluck him from what I was certain was a collision course with Van. It also provided an opportunity for me to bring in Eric Ober, then Vice President and general manager of WBBM Television in Chicago. He had first worked for me in the seventies at WCBS-TV as producer, executive producer, and assistant news director. He'd left there for his first news director's job at WCAU-TV in Philadelphia. In 1979 I brought him to WBBM-TV in Chicago as my news director, a job he held until 1981, when he became Vice President for News for the five CBS-owned television stations. Now he was back in Chicago, this time as its general manager. The young man who'd been the aggressive shop steward of the Writers Guild unit was now a middle-aged television news executive of considerable experience and, in my judgment, great competence. We'd talked frequently about Eric's desire to come to CBS News so we could once again work together. Eric was both smart and tough, a product of a Brooklyn boyhood and an education at Yale, where he'd acquired a master's degree in African history. He'd need both of those qualities if he was going to survive the usual welcome at CBS News for a new executive, particularly one from the outside.

I first met with Chandler and thought it best to be direct in my explanation of why he was being returned to his previous job.

"Robert, I want to get you out of the hot seat with *American Parade* before it blows up on you."

Bob took the news calmly. He inhaled his usual lungful of cigarette smoke before responding.

"I'm not entirely unhappy with this," he said. "You and I have been able to work together, but Sauter drives me crazy."

My next conversation took place on the phone with Socolow, who seemed at first resigned though unhappy with the prospect of leaving London for Tel Aviv. In coming days he would flirt with the idea of leaving CBS but instead he accepted a New York-based job as a *60 Minutes* producer.

Then I called in David Buksbaum and offered him the new job, which combined responsibility for both news coverage and operations. Buksbaum didn't even pretend to be surprised, but he did seem ill at ease and, to his credit, concerned for Lane.

"I feel funny replacing John," he said. "He's first-rate."

"Don't worry. John has told Van he wants to go to London."

When I'd finished talking with Buksbaum, I asked my secretary to locate John Lane and ask him to come see me. London was by far the largest of the overseas bureaus of CBS News. It was more than just a bureau; it was a clearinghouse for material from the rest of Europe as well as the Middle East and Africa. There were approximately ninety people in the CBS News offices in Bowater House in the Knightsbridge section of London, including correspondents, technicians, producers, accountants, and thirteen *60 Minutes* staffers. I sometimes indulged myself in fantasies of being the London Bureau chief. It struck me as a great job, a chance to live in a gracious city and manage an important bureau. I could understand why Lane would see that as a desirable alternative to what he was currently doing. When he arrived in my office I enthusiastically laid out his new job for him.

"You know, this may be the best job at CBS News," I said.

John seemed dumbstruck. It was a moment before he could respond.

"Hey, I don't want to go to London," he said.

"Didn't you have lunch with Sauter a few days ago and tell him you'd like this job?"

"Yeah, but I didn't mean now. I meant some day down the road."

"Didn't you tell him you'd never been happier than when you were the Chicago Bureau chief and that you'd like a chance to run London and live in Europe for a few years with your wife?"

"I did say that. I absolutely said it," he repeated for emphasis. "But we were talking about things we'd both like to do at some future point in our lives."

John Lane was one of the most honest men I'd ever dealt with. If he claimed that was all he said, there was no doubt in my mind that he spoke the truth. Besides, I'd taken part in countless conversations like that with Van. With the two of us it usually centered on early retirement and the things we could do with free time. He'd fish every river in North America and I'd raise horses. I also knew that neither of us had any immediate plans to do so. But there was no turning back from these changes and I told John this was the case. The announcements were made on February 7 and John flew off for a few days in London to meet with the bureau and to look for a flat to let, something not that easy to find in the high-priced Knightsbridge, Belgravia, and Chelsea neighborhoods with proximity to the bureau. A few days after his return John came to see me.

"I have a chance to go to NBC News," he said. "Larry Grossman, the new President, is looking for a number two guy to run their hard-news activities. He comes out of public television and advertising, not news, so I think he'd rely on me a lot. I know I'm under contract to CBS News. I'm hoping you'll release me from that contract."

"John, you don't want to leave CBS News," I answered.

"I never dreamed that day would ever come," he said, "but I really don't want to go to London. I've got a daughter just starting college here and I don't want her mother and father to be on the other side of the Atlantic from her."

"What if I found you some other job in this country? Would you go back to Chicago and be bureau chief?"

"I should leave CBS News," John said. "Mr. Rather's opinion means more than ever before around here. I have to face the fact that I'm never going to get on his right side. I sure have tried . . . but it's not going to happen . . . so I really need you to release me from my contract."

I agreed to do so and it completed what was a terrible mistake on my part. I ended up losing for CBS News someone who was not only a sound news executive but a good and decent man. In his job I placed an uneven, divisive individual who defined his job in terms of praise from the anchorman. Providing Rather with his personal Vice President gave him, for the first time, an obedient representative in the executive councils of CBS News.

Great blunders, Victor Hugo wrote, are often made, like large ropes, of a multitude of fibers.

"Shirley, call Bill Moyers at that number you have for him in Bermuda," I said. "Buzz me when he's on the line."

While my secretary left to place the call I waited in my office with Howard Stringer, who had urged me to speak with Bill. John Lane had gone to NBC News a month ago and I had been urging Howard to quickly establish his presence at CBS News and fill the gap, something I feared would be impossible for Buksbaum. One of the impressive things Howard had already done was to pull together a group from Special Events and the *Evening News* to prepare Dan Rather for the task of moderating the first debate of presidential candidates on network television since 1960. A few months earlier the FCC had changed its rules regarding equal time, an action which was upheld in court. CBS News invited Walter Mondale, Gary Hart, and Jesse Jackson to take part in a debate in prime time on the night of March 28, 1984. I was concerned that Rather would approach his moderator's role in a state of fevered machismo.

We all remembered his performance at the 1974 presidential news conference which was held in front of a live audience in Houston, Texas. When Rather rose to ask his question of then President Richard Nixon, he followed the format of the news conference and identified himself and his network. The audience responded with a mixture of applause and boos, prompting the President to ask, "Are you running for something?"

Perhaps it was being in his own hometown or the tension of being in front of a live audience, but Rather's response had a combative edge.

"No, sir, are you?" he said, and to many viewers across the country he seemed like a smart-ass who wasn't showing the proper respect for the office of the President of the United States. It was not the kind of episode we were anxious to see repeated when we brought together the three Democratic candidates before a live audience at Columbia University's Low Library. Prior to the actual broadcast Stringer staged a mock debate in front of a small group, using members of his impromptu task force to portray the three candidates, and then critiqued the way Rather performed as moderator. As a result, he was relaxed on the night of the debate and the evening produced an opportunity for each of the three candidates to comfortably express himself without having to contend with a moderator more concerned with how he was being perceived than with exploring the ideas set forth by candidates for the nation's highest office. Joan Richman and her director Artie Bloom shot the debate with cameras placed on all four sides of the debate table in a television equivalent of theater in the round, with an audience completely surrounding the three participants.

I was enormously pleased, much more so than I'd been the night when *American Parade* had premiered. This was why I was now sitting with Stringer in my office waiting to talk to Bill Moyers in Bermuda.

American Parade was a disaster, a confusing mishmash of a broadcast which reflected no distinctive vision. Shad Northshield had been so buffeted by the time the first broadcast went on the air that the evidence of his creativity could be seen only in his extraordinary set with its enormous wall of television monitors, each with separate inputs allowing it to electronically coalesce into a huge American flag. This special effect concluded a wonderful opening, designed by Shad, which was cut to accompany the music of Charles Ives and which was a minor tour de force in modern television techniques.

Kuralt was a charming host, but he contributed only one of the five stories it took to fill an average broadcast. The rest of the hour was filled each week with a ragtag assortment of undistinguished stories by Bill Moyers, Diane Sawyer, Morton Dean, Andy Lack, and other CBS News contributors. The stories included an "ideal" nursing home, paraplegics in Galveston, and a Diane Sawyer profile of a community activist in the Roxbury section of Boston who was so uninteresting even Diane seemed bored. But a low point occurred in the fourth broadcast: unable to deliver Van's celebrity interviews with Woody Allen or Michael Jackson, as Bob Chandler had predicted, *American Parade* offered instead a painful profile of the marriage of comedian Robert Klein and opera singer Brenda

Boozer, a segment which could hardly have advanced either of their careers and certainly ensured the demise of *American Parade.*

After the broadcast, I received a phone call from Van, now ensconced in his new office in Black Rock. Van had finally moved out of the Broadcast Center, allowing me to physically occupy the President's office nearly six months after assuming the job.

"Gene asked me if CBS News could come up with a quick replacement for *American Parade,*" he said.

"We might be able to do that if I can convince Moyers to take the part."

There was silence for a moment on the other end of the line.

"See what you can do," he said.

The result was an idea for a broadcast called *Crossroads.* Andy Lack would produce and Moyers and Kuralt would jointly participate. The key would be convincing a reluctant Moyers to agree to the idea. I had described the problem for Stringer and asked him to get Lack to help him enlist Bill for this new effort.

"Listen, mate, I'll give it my best," he had said, "but when the discussion turns to Van, Bill is going to tell me to piss off."

"Howard, that won't be a problem on *Crossroads,*" I said. "Believe me, Van won't come within twenty city blocks of *Crossroads.* He's been talking up *American Parade* for months, and he's now sitting over in Black Rock picking shrapnel out of his ass from the bomb we've put on the air. I think you may comfortably tell Bill you don't think Van will be involved in *Crossroads.*"

"Well, that will help. Even with Bill it will be hard to get momentum going on this broadcast. There were such great expectations for *American Parade.* I don't think we can count on another rave from Shales."

Tom Shales, the media reviewer for the Washington *Post,* had given *American Parade* a glowing and, as far as we were concerned, undeserved review, going so far as to write that "if *American Parade* doesn't succeed, we may as well abandon prime time as if it were a ravaged slum, one so terminal that urban renewal is out of the question."

"He'll be afraid to go out on a limb again," Howard said.

I didn't know it at the time but Howard had even hired a young man who was a friend of Shales to be a producer in Washington for the *Morning News.* I'd asked Howard about the wisdom of hiring a producer with no television experience but had accepted his explanation that the young man's background as a staff assistant to a U.S. senator would help in setting up the Washington interviews the broadcast felt it needed for Diane Sawyer.

"Look, reviews are nice," I said, "but what really counts is getting decent broadcasts on the air."

Howard sighed. "There is that, isn't there? I shall give it my best."

A few days later he was back in my office with a telephone number in Bermuda where I could reach Moyers.

"Andy and I are not having much luck with Bill. He feels he's just hitting his stride again with his commentaries on the *Evening News.* He doesn't think the network will show any more support for this new broadcast than it did for *Our Times.*"

"Did you tell him Jankowski would love to show Wyman how an inexpensive public-affairs broadcast can lower the soaring costs of producing the prime-time schedule?"

"Ed, I did all of that," he said. "I all but threatened to throw my body across the tracks of the A train if he didn't do the broadcast. If he's going to change his mind it will take you to do it."

By the time Shirley buzzed to tell me Moyers was on the line from Bermuda, I'd jotted a few notes for myself on a pad. One of them said, "Simply tell Bill the truth." Moyers patiently listened to my request that he take part in the new broadcast and then he listed his reasons for declining, most of which I'd already heard from Howard. He also mentioned his concern that since Kuralt and he produced such different forms of television, they might prove incompatible to viewers. Then he added another reason.

"I honestly don't believe the people you work for want to see public affairs succeed in their prime-time schedule. I know you believe differently, but the only reason I can see for their consistent lack of support is that they really don't want us there."

I looked down at the note I'd written for myself on the pad on my desk.

"Bill, I'm not sure that you're completely wrong," I said. "It's pretty obvious they feel that way about documentaries. Even when we have the money in our budget to do them they schedule them on Christmas night or opposite the Academy Awards on NBC. But I guess in a peculiar way I think that's why it's so important to keep trying to come up with some regular broadcast which provides a place to deal with the kinds of issues that have been done in the past only in documentaries. If we can get a head of steam going with *Crossroads* we can begin to hope for a regular slot where we can slowly build an audience."

"Ed, I wish I had your optimism," Bill said.

"There's one other thing. *American Parade* is an embarrassment to CBS News. Regardless of what the network thinks of *Crossroads,* or whether they renew us for the fall, I want to see us produce something that restores our self-respect."

I took a deep breath after I'd said that and waited for Bill's response.

"Ed, I'm still pessimistic," he said, "but if you want me to do this broadcast, I'll do it."

After I'd thanked Bill and put down the phone I realized I'd been gripping the receiver so hard my right hand was trembling.

Howard, who'd been sitting quietly in my office during my conversation, walked over and patted my shoulder.

"Well, chief," he said, "Bill Moyers can never say you weren't straight with him. Your description of the network attitude toward documentaries was appallingly true. Do you think they'll be any more supportive of *Crossroads?*"

"It all depends on Jankowski. With Bill on board we'll do good broadcasts . . . we both know that. So it depends on what kind of balls Jankowski will have when Bud Grant calls him and says, 'Those *Crossroad* shows are nice but Harvey Shepherd doesn't think the series has legs.' "

I called Van later that day to tell him we were now set with a replacement for *American Parade.* I was feeling a bit guilty that my exasperation had been so obvious to Stringer a few days earlier when I'd assured him Van would not take part in the production of *Crossroads.* I'd have to watch this. Van and I had been through too much for me to snipe at him, even obliquely. Besides, I was concerned for Van in his new role. He seemed at a loss, almost dispirited, and now he was increasingly bitter toward Chandler and Northshield because of the failure of *American Parade.* He'd obviously been counting on another success. Perhaps it was his weight loss, the sixty pounds he'd shed on a liquid fast diet. The energy and drive which was so much a part of him seemed diminished. A phrase once used to describe Disraeli in decline, "a burned-out volcano," kept crossing my mind. I didn't have a sense of his immersing himself in the affairs of the five CBS-owned television stations. Eric Ober, who'd just come from the Chicago station, said Van was "uninvolved." But Jankowski continued to describe his new tier of Executive Vice Presidents in glowing terms. He told *Broadcasting* magazine it was a demonstration that "the whole is greater than the parts . . . that two divisions if they work well together wind up being more successful than the individual components would be."

In practice none of this happened. Each Wednesday morning Jankowski met with his four executives: Van, Tom Leahy, Neal Pilson, and Jim Rosenfield. The description Van gave to me of the weekly meeting of this group was demoralizing. He painted a picture of rudderless, pointless mornings with no sense of anyone in charge. Most of my glimpses of life at Black Rock came from our discussions. With his reorganization Jankowski had so isolated himself that I seldom saw him more than once a month and that was at a large monthly meeting attended by the four Executive Vice Presidents and the five Presidents of the News, Entertainment, Sports, Radio, and Television Stations Divisions. Jankowski's staff also attended the meetings, so there were approximately twenty-five people seated around a large table in Jankowski's conference room. These sessions were a dismal counterpart of the smaller weekly meetings Van had described to me. Each executive present was expected to speak for a few minutes about his area of responsibility. When I first started attending these meetings I described what I believed were the problems facing CBS News and how we were attempting to deal with them. The escalating talent salaries, for example. I quickly came to realize that this was neither expected nor particularly welcome. The required skill was to be able to speak for your allotted time without discussing anything of importance. So I would arrive at meetings with a list gathered for me by my secretary. "The President is going to Santa Barbara next week. . . . Rather is going on vacation and Charles Kuralt will fill in. . . . The *Evening News* had a four share point lead over NBC this week and five over ABC." Heads would nod around the table. Then I would in turn listen to the other executives intone their own lists of the meaningless incrementa of their divisions. If there is some special hell to which television executives are consigned for eternity in punishment for their abuse of the public airwaves, I am certain it takes the form of a never-ending Jankowski staff meeting. I, at least, could leave the meeting, walk out of Black Rock, and return to CBS News. Van couldn't, and it appeared to be taking a toll.

Among my reasons for calling Van that afternoon, along with wanting him to know that Moyers had agreed to do *Crossroads,* was the issue of who was going the handle the negotiation of Dan Rather's contract. In 1979, when Rather signed his contract to anchor *The CBS Evening News,* it was widely reported as a ten-year agreement. And, in fact, CBS News had a ten-year contractual obligation to Rather. What only a handful of people knew, however, was that the anchorman had an absolute right to walk away from CBS at the end of year five by giving three months' notice either on, or in advance of, December 22, 1984.

Richard Leibner had asked to see me in connection with Rather's contract a few days earlier. He arrived in my office and seemed nervous as he began the discussion.

"This is going to be a busy year for Dan and for you," he said, "with the campaign, the conventions, and the election, December is going to be here faster than you think. We should start dealing with Dan's window now."

"Makes sense to me," I said. "I assume Dan has no desire to leave."

"Dan has no intention of leaving CBS News. He has told me he doesn't even want me to test the waters at ABC or NBC and you can imagine what they'd offer to get the number one anchorman in America."

"There are a lot reasons why he's number one, Richard," I said. "They wouldn't necessarily be there at the other places."

"Dan is very happy."

"He should be, he's anchorman of the most watched news broadcast in the country. And he's earning two million dollars a year."

"That was a lot of money for an anchorman with no record of success," Leibner said, "but look at what he's done since we cut that deal. I'm telling you I could walk into Roone's office with a check for any figure I picked and he'd sign it on the spot."

"I thought Dan told you not to talk to Roone."

Leibner lifted both hands in the air, palms forward.

"I haven't said a word to Roone, I swear to God. I'm just making a point that if Dan Rather untried was worth that much to CBS five years ago, he's got to be worth more today."

"Hey, I think you're right," I said. "When do you want to start the negotiation?"

Leibner averted his eyes from mine while he reached into his briefcase.

"You and I have a relationship that's important to me," he said. "We can talk and we understand one another. I don't want there to be any misunderstanding about what I'm going to say, so I want to show you a letter from my client."

He gave me a brief handwritten note he'd received from Rather asking that the negotiation begin as soon as possible. It also expressed his desire that Gene Jankowski, rather than Van Sauter or Ed Joyce, negotiate with Leibner because Gene had conducted the previous negotiation.

"There was a discussion when we got the five-year window," Leibner said, "and Gene Jankowski knows there was an implicit understanding that the next deal would be improved if things worked out well. But I swear to you that's the only reason."

"Richard, relax," I said. "I don't know if Gene will want to handle this

. . . that's up to him. But it won't break my heart if I'm not the one who does it."

I could see the tension begin to drain from his face, which softened with a knowing smile.

"I'll bet it wouldn't," he said. "Let someone else handle this hot potato, because I'm talking major dollars."

I had asked Van to pass this request on to Jankowski and the afternoon I called him about Moyers and *Crossroads* I asked him if he'd gotten a reaction from Gene.

"He wants you to do the negotiating," Van said. "He doesn't want to be a part of it unless it looks like we might lose Rather."

"We're not going to lose him. What does Gene say about implicit promises of more money after five years?"

"He says the only reason he gave a five-year window was to assure Dan he had an option if he missed the life of a reporter."

"That strikes me as pure bullshit," I said. "I need some guidance here. What's my ceiling?"

"Whatever it takes. We can't lose this guy. Look at it this way: if Gene handles it you can be sure that Leibner wouldn't leave the table with less than five million a year. Anything less than that is money saved for CBS News."

"I want to try something," I said. "You know how Leibner likes to complain that he's dealing with a difficult client in a negotiation? I want to use Jankowski that way. Act as if I think he's being totally unreasonable but I'll try to talk some sense into him. But I need to know that Gene will go along with being cast in that role."

"I'll tell him what you want to do."

"One other thing," I added. "Gene has to promise he'll refuse to take any phone calls from Leibner during this negotiation."

The next day Van called me.

"Gene loves it. Make him the heavy."

"Will he duck Leibner while this is going on?"

"Don't worry." Van laughed. "When Wyman learns we're going to pay Rather more money, Gene will be a happy man if none of his fingerprints are on the deal."

Leibner and I fenced with one another for months while I constantly and deliberately complained about Jankowski's obstinacy. Finally I offered a set of increases which I was quite sure would be accepted: an additional $750,000 the first year followed by future increases which would take Rather to $3 million in the second year and up to $4 million in

1990, the seventh year of his ten-year contract. I asked Van to run those figures past Jankowski before I put them on the table. He called me back in a state of ebullience.

"Eduardo, the Jank thinks you're a magician. If you can close at those dollars, he'll be delighted."

"It takes a big wheel to talk in circles," I said. "Isn't he the same guy who wants us to hold salary increases to seven percent?"

"He knows what ABC would pay Rather," Van said. "He knows what he would end up paying if he was negotiating. You're saving CBS between one and two million dollars a year."

"Well, it's not done yet," I said, "but I think this will do it."

That night following the *Evening News*, I met with Leibner in my office. He arrived wearing a leather coat and a frown.

"You look troubled," I said.

"I'm bothered by the way this Rather thing is going."

"In what way?"

"The signals that seem to come from Jankowski that maybe these numbers might be getting too big . . . that maybe Dan isn't worth all that money. I'm beginning to think maybe I should just shelve this negotiation until it's deadline time. Then I could watch Jankowski kiss my ass to match the kind of offer I'll have from ABC."

"Richard, what can I tell you? Wyman is breaking Gene's balls on costs. But Gene is still being receptive when I give him some suggested numbers and tell him this is what it will take to keep Dan at CBS."

"That's important for me to hear," he said, "that there's some respect for what my guy has accomplished . . . some respect for the kind of professional he is."

"I can tell you Gene has that kind of respect. But if we don't close a deal soon I can't guarantee that Wyman won't step in and call a halt."

"You think Wyman might get a look at these dollar figures and say, 'No way, José'?"

"He's not a broadcaster, he's a businessman."

"Maybe I ought to hear what you've got for me," Leibner said.

"I spent the morning with Gene convincing him that this offer made sense for CBS," I said. "He's worried about it but he'll go along with it."

Then I laid out for Leibner the offer which would take Rather up to $4 million in the seventh year of his contract. The frown lines disappeared from his face. He nodded his head and took notes as I laid the yearly figures out. Over a ten-year period his client would earn $36 million.

"I think we're close," he said. "You may have to sweeten it a little but I'm very encouraged."

I leaned close to Leibner and looked him in the eye.

"Let me tell you something. I've had a tough time leading Jankowski this far. Before I left his office, he told me 'not another nickel.' You know what else he said? 'When you start throwing around three or four million dollars a year, you're entering Larry Hagman territory.' "

I didn't know what Larry Hagman was earning, and I hadn't discussed this with Jankowski, but I knew there was truth to the point I was making and so did Leibner. This was an unheard-of salary for a journalist, even a television journalist. This negotiation could have been taking place in the Polo Lounge of the Beverly Hills Hotel, and Leibner loved it.

He called Rather and we closed that night.

I called Van at his apartment late in the evening to give him the news.

"Congratulations," he said, "you've done a great job."

I laughed. "Only in television could someone get kudos for shoveling up $36 million. You don't think there's a chance that Gene will feel I spent too little?"

"I don't think that will be a consideration."

"I don't know. He's the great trailblazer. I'm not sure I measured up. After all, he not only introduced the million-dollar salaries, he gave Rather a two-and-a-half-mil signing bonus with another three million in deferred funds with fat interest rates."

"Joyce, you really are a cheap bastard, now that I think about it."

"Well, tomorrow," I said, "I'm back to the humdrum of business . . . trying to keep the Warsaw and Johannesburg Bureaus in next year's budget, all the little things I also do in addition to being banker to the stars."

"And you'll get at least one phone call from Leibner," Van said, "telling you how much your relationship means to him."

"I'm too fine a person . . ."

"For this line of work," Van finished. "Go home and pour yourself a glass of wine, Eduardo. You deserve it."

"I think I'll take a shower first. I feel like I've done the butterfly stroke through five miles of floating sewage."

"Hey, big guy," Van said, "it's just another day in American broadcasting."

The Place des Vosges in the Marais section of Paris had an exquisite elegance in the moonlight of an April night.

With its pink-and-white matching Renaissance houses, covered arcades, and steeply pitched slate roofs, you almost expected the wraith of Victor Hugo, who lived there in the 1830s, to materialize for his evening stroll. Van and I ended up there because we were enjoying one of the compensatory benefits that occasionally alternated with cutting deals and cutting budgets for CBS News—foreign travel. We had called a meeting of foreign bureau chiefs and correspondents at the Hotel Bristol in Vienna. It was the first such meeting in the recent history of CBS News and it had been a success, bringing together producers and executives from New York with their colleagues overseas. Jankowski had even flown to Vienna to address the group at lunch and had attended a dinner for them at the Palais Schwarzenberg. After Vienna, Van, Howard, and I had taken Jankowski and his wife to Warsaw. I was eager for Gene to see that a bureau such as this which was only sporadically productive was an important part of the connective tissue of a worldwide news-gathering organization, something his financial staff was unlikely to include in their analysis of the CBS News budget. For Gene it was an opportunity to visit the country of his origins. After Warsaw we'd all flown to France, where the Jankowskis accompanied us on an inspection of the broadcast sites we were selecting for our upcoming coverage of the anniversary of D Day. The trip had been an opportunity, I hoped, for Gene to learn that foreign bureaus were a lot like firehouses. Those seemingly idle people sitting at their desks on a slow day were the same ones who, twenty-four hours later, might be dropped into the anarchy of Beirut, be reporting from a desert in Ethiopia, or be asked to provide a sophisticated explanation of the latest military maneuvers of the Warsaw Pact countries.

On our last night in Paris, the Jankowskis made plans of their own, so Van and I headed for Bofingers, an Alsatian restaurant near the Place de la Bastille. After dinner we walked up the Rue St. Antoine in another of the postprandial jaunts we'd by now enjoyed together in cities around the world.

"God, this has been a great trip," Van said.

"Yes, it has. We've got some fine people in these bureaus."

"They're a hardworking bunch, aren't they?"

"They're a reminder of what's so special about CBS News," I said. "I'm so tired of hearing Ed Murrow's name invoked by someone who's on his way to dinner at Le Cirque. It's redemptive to be around people like this."

"I think it's been good for Gene, too," Van said.

"I hope so," I answered. "He's been more like the man I used to know before he began running for President of CBS."

"I know what you mean. And you don't live with it every day."

"It's strange," I said, "the one quality he had which was so great was an optimistic certainty about everything. The day Wyman didn't name him President a blanket of indecision swept over him like snow in October."

"He needs to get out of his tower more often. He's such an innocent."

"No shit. I knew that when I watched him get off the airplane in Warsaw."

"Wasn't that hysterical?" Van said.

We'd flown from Vienna to Warsaw in a chartered jet, and as Gene stepped onto the tarmac of the Warsaw airport with a camera hanging from his neck, he began to raise the camera to photograph the airport control tower and the numerous military aircraft which were taxiing in front of it. This movement was not lost on what seemed like a battalion of military policemen who started running toward Gene, brandishing their weapons.

"If you or I had done that we'd be dead," I said.

"Which is what I thought Gene would be at any moment," Van said.

We reached the Place des Vosges, then walked up the Rue de Birague and turned right onto the Place. Victor Hugo's apartment, which is now a museum, overlooks the lovely square. We stopped for a moment to look at it.

"He wrote one of the wisest things I've ever read," I said. "Every parent should be required to commit it to heart. 'The supreme happiness of life is the conviction that we are loved.' "

"I've never heard that quote," Van said. "It's really a marvelous thought. When you were a child, did you feel loved?"

"Astoundingly so, given the sort of childhood I had," I answered. Perhaps it was the wine from Bofingers or simply the headiness that comes from knowing you're alive on a spring night in the loveliest city in the world, but for whatever reason, the two of us spent the next hour strolling the streets of Paris and describing our childhood.

I talked about my mother and father and the nomadic life my brother Charles and I had led, what it was like to go to six different schools in a single year. I reminisced about my father and the pain his recurrent bouts with alcoholism inflicted on our family.

"I have a theory," I said, "that the children of an alcoholic acquire an acute sensitivity to embarrassment which stays with them throughout their lives."

Van thought about that for a moment.

"That would be understandable," he said, and he paused for a moment. "I never knew my father. My parents were separated. He was a fireman who worked out of a firehouse less than two miles from where we lived in the same small town in Ohio, and I've never talked with him . . . not once."

"Jesus, that beats my two pair, Van," I said. "I never once doubted that my poor troubled father loved my brother and me and would be there in our corner no matter what we did."

We ended up crossing the Seine and standing at the foot of Notre Dame staring up at the gargoyles illuminated by spotlights scattered around its base. It was almost midnight.

"It's been a good evening, Eduardo," Van said. "I've enjoyed it. Why don't we fall into a cab and head back to the hotel. In the morning we can marry up with Jankowski, head for the airport, and fly back to madness."

I'm an enormously private person. That wasn't the kind of conversation I'd often had with anyone outside my immediate family. Neither, I suspect, had Van. When two friends unlock a gate, it's unlikely that either will ever find it easy to close it again.

The weeks which immediately followed the bureau meetings in Vienna were mostly occupied with *Crossroads*, the *Morning News*, and *Nightwatch*. Kuralt was busy stockpiling *On the Road* stories for his new broadcasts along with other stories which would provide a different display of his interests and abilities. They would include a profile of New York's governor, Mario Cuomo, who was scheduled to be the keynote speaker at the Democratic National Convention later in the year, and a look at an experimental drug—minoxidil—which it was believed might offer new hope for curing baldness. Moyers had plunged into this new broadcast without another moment's hesitation and was hard at work. The menu of stories he was producing was a reflection of his range of interests: the conflict between a couple and the Christian Science Church over the responsibility for the death of the couple's child . . . a look at the security problems at the Marine compound in Beirut prior to the 1983 bombing . . . the battle over "Star Wars," the Reagan administration's controversial space defense system . . . a look at the United States' covert war in Nicaragua . . . an interview with the Pulitzer Prize-winning playwright David Mamet. I'd asked Bill to help us produce something that would restore our self-respect, and he was going at it with a vengeance.

In the years at CBS News in which we worked together, Bill alternated between fallow periods and times of intense activity. How I regret those fallow periods for what was lost on the television screen. He could be one of the most difficult, frustrating people to work with, but I can't think of anyone for whom an extra effort was more rewarded by excellence than Bill Moyers.

That sort of gratification was not nearly so likely to arise from efforts to shape up the *Morning News*, as Stringer was discovering, a situation complicated by the fact that Diane was losing interest in the broadcast. The promise of joining *60 Minutes* at the beginning of the next year must have made awakening at two each morning even more of a chore than it had been. She remained the most written about newswoman in television, but the ratings on the broadcast, which had moved so dramatically, had, for the time being at least, reached a plateau. *The Today Show,* which had looked so vulnerable with the introduction of sportscaster Bryant Gumbel in the anchor role and Jane Pauley absent on maternity leave, was now regaining its balance and Gumbel was displaying a formidable skill at interviewing.

There is nothing unlawful or immoral about ambition and Diane's zeal to join *60 Minutes* was understandable. I'd urged Howard to do everything he could to keep her buoyed up and involved in the broadcast until we were past the political conventions and the election so that we could devote our attention to her replacement and her graceful departure.

Bill Kurtis was another matter. Diane's success left him in a permanent state of petulance. We hoped that when she left the broadcast he might develop a different outlook. My biggest worry was that he was simply miscast on a program which depended so heavily on interviews.

In late February and early March, Stringer had urged that we remove Bob Ferrante as executive producer and replace him with Jon Katz, an idea which enjoyed the support of both anchors. Howard felt that a combination of his television skills and Jon's editorial innovations could provide the broadcast with the boost it needed. Although relatively new to television, Katz undoubtedly was a man of both ideas and enthusiasm. I remembered how Merlis and I had worked together in 1981 and 1982 and hoped that Howard and Jon could strike some of the same sparks together.

And I was concerned about Howard. The Westmoreland trial was hanging over his head like a darkening day. He arrived for work one morning looking tired and haggard.

"Late night?" I asked.

"Couldn't sleep. I was up half the night."

"Anything wrong?"

"It's this bloody trial."

"I know," I said. "Mike Wallace came to see me the other day. He's working on his depositions during the discovery period . . . something we'll both do eventually. He's as nervous as I've seen him. He kept repeating, 'That fucking George, he didn't have to do it that way, the story was there.' "

"I know how he feels," Howard said, "and I was the executive producer. Now I see my career going down in flames."

"It could be a year before this case goes to trial," I said. "You can't let it get to you."

"Ed, friends of mine called me at home last night. They'd been to a party with Dan Burt, who was telling them this trial will destroy Stringer's career."

"And they did exactly what he wanted them to do, which is call and tell you what he said."

"I suppose you're right."

"I know I'm right," I said. "You're going to have to summon up your British resolve or he'll have you talking to yourself before the trial begins. I'd rather have you talking to Katz about ways to lift the *Morning News*. If that doesn't happen I'll return you to the anchorman."

"Not likely he'd take me." Howard's face thawed into the makings of a mischievous smile. "Two mornings in a row, he's dropped by my office and my secretary has told him I was in a meeting with Katz and the *Morning News* staff."

"There'll be no going back now," I said. "Great news for Venardos."

"Any sense of how it's going between them?"

"Funny you should mention that. I asked Dan that very question this morning. He says things are fine, they just haven't bonded yet."

"Old Dan does have that thing about bonding, doesn't he?" Howard said.

"I'm sure it'll happen," I said. "When it does, perhaps you should give Lane a shower."

After Howard left my office, I placed a call to Jack Smith in our Washington Bureau. I was considerably more optimistic about the future of *Nightwatch* than I was about the fate of the *Morning News* and for reasons which had absolutely nothing to do with the size of its audience. Right from the beginning it seemed *Nightwatch* had existed on the edge of extinction. Each year would begin with a budget for the broadcast which extended only until May. Its continuation beyond that date was dependent on Jankowski's confidence in the financial picture for the remaining months of the year. If the picture dimmed, *Nightwatch* would go to black, permanently. It was one of the odd ways the Broadcast Group held its financial cards beyond the vision of Wyman and his corporate staff. Each month I would provide the Broadcast Group a flash report showing our financial situation for the month, for the year to date, and for the projected total year. Time and again when that report showed us exceeding our budget, CBS News would be ordered by the Group to lower the flash prediction so the Group would not have to reveal a problem to the Corporation, in the hope that before the year was over prosperity would have returned. By May we would invariably be flashing red ink for *Nightwatch* because its allotted funds for the year had come to their scheduled end. *Nightwatch* was by now reduced to an interview program hosted by Charley Rose and it had been moved from New York to our Washington Bureau, where we were charged a lesser rate by the television network for production facilities.

I was calling Jack Smith that morning to enlist him in a campaign I hoped would be the salvation of the beleaguered *Nightwatch.* Now that the show was located in Washington, many of its interviews involved politicians—members of the administration, representatives from the Hill—mostly the lesser lights of Washington who seldom made the cut for an *Evening News* story or an appearance on *Face the Nation*, often the same people who complained to CBS lobbyists that they were ignored by CBS

News. *Nightwatch* might be on at an ungodly hour, but it was still network television, and an under secretary or a congressman from East Dismal was delighted with an opportunity for a national forum. I told Jack that I wanted to paint *Nightwatch* as Washington's newest idea mart for aspiring movers and shakers.

"I'd like you to send me a weekly list," I said, "naming all the pols who appeared on *Nightwatch*. I'll give that list some circulation in Black Rock."

"I'll get the executive producer to do one for both of us," Jack said. "Anything else?"

"If you're talking to Jankowski or any of his execs, tell them how these guys love coming in to appear on *Nightwatch*."

"That's easy. They really do love it."

I began circulating the *Nightwatch* guest lists to Black Rock with attached notes about the interest the broadcast was generating in Washington. I knew that Jankowski was searching for ways to demonstrate to Wyman that he was fulfilling his mandate to build bridges between Black Rock and Washington.

If he believed *Nightwatch* had become an important broadcast in the minds of the nation's lawmakers, Jankowski would never cancel it. A few weeks later I could tell the idea was taking hold. During a phone call with me, Tony Malara, who had responsibility for television network sales, suddenly blurted out, "Will you stop it with those *Nightwatch* guest lists?"

"What do you mean, Tony?"

"You know what I mean. I know what you're doing. I know why you're doing it. But you're breaking my balls with those lists. Jankowski keeps coming into my office, waving it in my face, wanting to know what we're doing to sell more spots on *Nightwatch*."

Again I called Jack Smith in Washington.

"Keep those lists coming," I said. "And tell the people on *Nightwatch* who've been worrying about cancellation that they can relax . . . at least for now."

Washington was very much on my mind a few days later, the morning of May 13, when I boarded the CBS jet to fly to Los Angeles for the 1984 affiliates convention.

I was the first from the CBS group to arrive. I smiled at the sight of an empty plane, headed toward one of the two seats in the rear which I always tried to occupy, and settled back to watch one of my favorite corporate rituals.

The small Gulfstream jet had four seats in the front where passengers sat facing one another in twos. Another four seats in the middle were similarly placed but with a table between them, and two more were located at the back of the cabin. Unwritten corporate protocol dictated that front seats be held for Wyman or Jankowski. I opened that morning's Washington *Post* and pretended to read as the other executives began to arrive and mill about the aisle, making casual small talk to avoid taking a seat. Over the top of my paper I saw Wyman and Jankowski take their seats and the CBS corps de ballet begin its performance. The implicit requirement of the dance was that it be done without pushing or shoving and that the final descent into the seat seem almost casual. Not once did the senior executives of the Broadcast Group take their eyes off one another as they moved about in the aisle next to Wyman. Leahy and Rosenfield, in particular, seemed to be engaged in some complicated pas de deux in which each of them had to remove a jacket and carefully fold it. Suddenly Leahy was a blur of motion which clarified itself in the seat opposite the CBS Chairman. Rosenfield stared at the one seat which was left but continued to turn his jacket inward, placing one shoulder neatly inside the other and shifting his considerable bulk to block the aisle, making it impossible for his competitors to do anything other than acknowledge his occupancy. But in doing so, Rosenfield had failed to notice the late arrival of William Lilley III, Wyman's aide and Washington point man.

Lilley was a short man with dark wavy hair and glasses. An ample waistline, testimonial to the chefs at numerous Washington restaurants where he regularly entertained congressional staff members, caused him to walk with a slight waddle. But on this day, he moved with astonishing fluidity. Without stopping to hang up his overcoat or stow his small suitcase, he poured himself down the aisle, dodged underneath Rosenfield's chin, and spun himself into the last seat with a balanced grace which made a Baryshnikov entrechat seem like a drunken stagger.

"Good morning, guys," he said.

When Rosenfield had taken a seat in another section of the plane, Lilley got up for a moment to hang his overcoat in the cabin closet and to place his bag on its floor. As he returned, I could hear him address Wyman.

"Great article in the Washington *Post* this morning, Tom."

I'd been holding the *Post* in front of me for the past five minutes but I hadn't read a word. I hastily began leafing through its pages until I came to the business section, whose first page contained a photograph of Wyman and a long, laudatory article about his management of CBS since being elevated to Chairman.

"Under Wyman's leadership," it declared, "CBS has recovered much of the luster it lost in the late 1970s, erased a set of bad ventures, restored management stability and shown a new concern for bottom line planning." The article quoted a financial analyst at the First Boston Corporation who said that Wyman had "substantially reinforced the company's credibility with the investment community."

Not all of the article was as commending. It quoted "a source close to the company" as saying, "He is still viewed in the Broadcast Group as someone managing something like a packaged goods company who doesn't have an excitement about the business." And, indeed, Jankowski and his staff consistently muttered about the people around Wyman, which by implication at least suggested a sense of unease with the new Chairman. On page four of the business section my eye was caught by a separate story with the headline "Wyman Seeking Better Reception for CBS on Hill." In the story Wyman attributed the failure of the networks to win repeal of the financial interest and syndication rules to the strength of what he called "a suspicious and negative" attitude about the networks in

Washington, particularly on Capitol Hill. The article pointed out that in 1982 Wyman considered relaxation of the rules the number one subject on the CBS agenda but that today Wyman is focusing on building bridges between Black Rock and Washington instead. The article bristled with quotes from Wyman that were disturbing, even though the obliqueness with which he spoke made it necessary to read them several times. Referring to the antipathy he'd encountered on the Hill, he said, "The really scary thing is when somebody says to you, 'Look, Tom, I don't have any feeling about financial interest and syndication, but I do have a feeling about the fact that you guys are just too muscular and you exercise your power in ways that are not attractive to me.' " Lest there be any doubt that he was giving an example of criticism of CBS News, he added, "The work of CBS News is not something that is enormously helpful because, from time to time, if you're doing your job well you're going to irritate people who have a different point of view. If you do it badly you will irritate an even larger number of those people." Then he redeemed himself with "None of that we can change very much. This is the business we're in and we must be in it vigorously."

I looked up and saw Wyman walking toward me. He'd seen me reading the *Post* and was undoubtedly about to ask for my reaction. He was smiling broadly, obviously pleased by the article.

"Ed, what do you think the reaction will be at your place?"

"Frankly, they're going to be unnerved by it," I said.

Wyman looked puzzled and his smile vanished.

"Simply because I want to reach out and make a few friends in the Washington community?" he asked.

"It's what those friends might ask for," I said.

"I thought I was pretty emphatic about that, when I talked about not being able to change the business we're in."

"I know you said that to the reporter," I told him, "but it's kind of buried in a long article which makes quite another point."

"I certainly have no intention of telling you people how to cover the news," Wyman said testily.

"I believe you," I said, "and that's certainly what I'm going to tell our people."

"And if you need me to tell anyone that, in a form which is more direct, I stand ready to do it," Wyman said.

He returned to the front of the plane, where I was sure Bill Lilley would tell him what stuffy asses the news people at CBS were and to ignore our carping.

I sat there for the remainder of the flight to Los Angeles studying Wyman. He intrigued me. The occasions on which I'd found myself in his company were for the most part budget presentations or the quasi-social functions of a corporation. They weren't all that frequent, but they had tempered my initial and unfavorable impression of the man I had first met in Chicago in 1980. Since then, I had invariably found him to be sophisticated and courteous, with a droll sense of humor. At one particularly tedious affiliates lunch I had walked past his table heading for a phone in response to a message to call my office. Tony Malara was at the podium introducing the chairman of the Affiliates Board. A steely grip on my right wrist brought me to a quick halt next to Wyman's chair.

"This isn't fair," he whispered. "You're not allowed to escape unless you take me with you."

"We rendezvous at the plane," I whispered back. "The bomb goes off in here in five minutes."

In the background the Affiliates Board chairman had just told the first of a succession of not very funny jokes. The laughter in the room was dutiful but strained.

"Too late," Wyman said, "it just went off."

Late in the day in my room at the Century Plaza Hotel in Los Angeles, I got a phone call from Jack Smith, our Washington Bureau chief.

"Has the *Post* article on Wyman caught up with you out there?"

"I read it on the plane coming out," I said. "What's the reaction in the bureau?"

"You can probably imagine it's not going down too well with our folks," he said. "There's a lot of talk about the end of an era and the beginning of a new CBS."

"Jack, Wyman was on the plane with me. He thinks he was supportive of CBS News in that article."

"Well, no one here thinks that," Jack said.

"He went so far as to tell me he had no intention of telling us how to cover the news."

"I wish there was some way of getting that across to our people."

"There may be. Tomorrow at lunch I'm going to introduce a panel of our correspondents who will talk to the affiliates about the election. Rather will be there. So will Lesley Stahl, Bob Schieffer, and Bruce Morton. Maybe I can set the record straight in my remarks."

"Stahl and Morton are two of the people who're buzzing the most about this," Jack said. "What you say might go a long way to reassure them that the new Chairman is not about to put a muzzle on his News Division."

By the time lunch arrived on May 14, I knew what I wanted to say to the affiliates. My remarks weren't really directed at them, although it couldn't hurt for them to hear them, too. They weren't even aimed at the CBS News correspondents on the panel. I decided to use the occasion to speak to the management of CBS and to publicly interpret Wyman's interview. I also wanted to set the record straight on what I believed should be the proper relationship between CBS News and those in power in Washington. If Wyman or Jankowski felt I was wrong they'd have to tell me so directly.

The large ballroom was filled with hundreds of affiliates and CBS executives. For the occasion CBS had decorated the large room in the style of a political convention with a sign containing the name of one of the fifty states placed at various tables.

I began by telling the audience that the reporters they were about to meet were an important part of a system by which our leaders are held accountable to the public. I talked for a moment about the sophisticated, costly public relations efforts used by governments to get the citizenry to buy their explanation of the facts, and I added, "That's O.K. . . . that's also the way our system works . . . and these reporters come along and they report those facts . . . but they also report other explanations of those facts . . . they even go out and seek out disputatious voices."

Then I moved to the point I wanted to make.

"One of the facts of life as we at CBS News go about our daily chores is that we bring some amount of grief into the lives of our colleagues in other parts of CBS. I know that when some of my friends go down to Washington on business that's totally unrelated to CBS News, there are times when they're made to feel about as welcome as a polecat at a picnic.

"That's just a fact of life," I said, "when a large corporation chooses to house a great news organization."

Then I urged the group to read the Washington *Post* article which had appeared the day before. I described Wyman's reference to unhappiness in Washington when CBS News "reports a story in a way they might disagree with," and I repeated his quote that "none of that we can change very much. This is the business we're in and we must be in it vigorously."

"And we, in turn," I said, "have an obligation to be fair, to be balanced, and to be accurate."

I introduced the panel of CBS News correspondents and returned to my luncheon table to hear them analyze the campaign for the CBS affiliates. I sat down next to Van and leaned toward him.

"Maybe Gene will stop inviting me to his Washington dinners," I said. Van looked at me for a moment.

"I don't think that will be an issue," he said.

Neither Jankowski nor Wyman ever mentioned my remarks to the affiliates that day.

After the lunch my attention was quickly diverted by the sudden need to begin damage control on an episode involving Howard Stringer.

Two years earlier, in 1982, when the affiliates were meeting in San Francisco, *TV Guide* published its scathing attack of the Westmoreland documentary. In preparing that article, one of the two *TV Guide* reporters, Don Kowet, had conducted a telephone interview with Stringer, a large portion of which they had both agreed was "off the record." Kowet, angered by CBS criticism of a book he'd subsequently written on the making of the documentary, turned over thirty-seven tape recordings he'd made with people at CBS to attorneys for General Westmoreland.

Dan Burt made the tapes public and the *Evening News* reported the story on May 14. I watched from my hotel room as Rather presented excerpts of the Kowet-Stringer conversation. Kowet's interview with Howard was devastating because it revealed him speaking to Kowet in a low, almost hushed voice and thoroughly trashing George Crile. I was stunned by what I heard. Howard was saying many of the things he later said privately to me. But he was saying them to a magazine reporter who at that time was obviously preparing a slashing critique of a broadcast for which Howard had been the executive producer. I placed my head in my hands when I heard Stringer tell the *TV Guide* reporter, "As you may have gathered, we have our own suspicions about George Crile anyway."

After hearing Kowet describe what he claimed *TV Guide* had learned about Crile's conduct in preparing the broadcast, Howard responded by saying that if Kowet's charges were correct, "then it does devolve on me because I should have known I wouldn't get fair journalism off him."

I was in a rage when I reached Howard on the phone.

"How could you have said those things?" I asked. "You didn't share your thoughts with me until *TV Guide* had published their story and blown the whistle. You sounded like a schemer who was trying to save his own skin at any price."

"That wasn't it, mate," he said. "I was unnerved and angry at George when Kowet began to tell me what he'd learned. . . . It was so obvious he had the goods on him . . . that I was just stupid enough to say those things."

"Why the hell didn't you come to me and tell me what *TV Guide* was on to? We could have salvaged some honor by conducting our own investigation before the article came out."

"Oh, Ed," Howard said, "I was so sick about it all I kept hoping it wouldn't be as bad as I feared."

Van was more philosophical. His anger was directed at Kowet for violating an off-the-record agreement.

"You suspended Crile for doing the same thing," he said. "Remember that."

"I remember. It's reprehensible. But my new Executive Vice President is not exactly off to an auspicious beginning."

"What are you going to do?" Van asked.

"I'm going to do what we've all been doing since we first had to pick up this tar baby," I said. "I'm going to get up on the stage of the Plitt Theater on Wednesday and tell those affiliates I stand by the substance of this broadcast. Then I'm going to attack Kowet for turning over those tapes and say that Howard, like the rest of us, is convinced that the broadcast was accurate."

The affiliates who were gathered in the auditorium on Wednesday seemed satisfied by what I told them and I shifted my remarks to the subject of the replacement of *American Parade* and the addition of Bill Moyers to our new prime-time hour. Then I introduced Bill.

I'd asked him to come to Los Angeles and join me in speaking to the affiliates because he'd been so effective two years ago before this same group. "Give them a sense of what we hope to do with *Crossroads,*" I said. "I think the time has come when we need to start developing affiliate support for our efforts in prime time."

Bill spoke first about his hopes for *Crossroads*. Then in remarks obviously aimed more at CBS management than the affiliates, the man who'd once been the publisher of a major newspaper spoke of twin goals.

"CBS News," he said, "can deliver to the network a broadcast which will bring both profits and pride. The profit will come from the lower cost of reality programming in relation to the revenue it generates should it catch on. The pride will come from realizing that we in the CBS family have found yet another way to pay our civic rent while also paying our stockholders as well."

For us all it was a pragmatic reminder that the dual responsibilities of paying civic rent and paying shareholder dividends are not automatically in conflict. From the edge of the stage I looked at the rows of affiliates in the darkened theater and began to feel some optimism. From the looks on their faces they were not being unreceptive to what Bill was saying. Then I saw my old boss Tom Leahy sitting in the third row and watched while he leaned over to Bud Grant in the seat next to him. He whispered something in his ear and they both smiled.

After the News presentation, Bill again used the pressure of his many assignments as a reason for missing that night's "Parade of Stars," and headed for the airport. The evening produced the usual mobilization of CBS television luminaries from soap operas, sitcoms, and journalism.

Late that evening I headed for Portland, Oregon, where *The CBS Evening News* would originate its Thursday and Friday night broadcasts. KOIN-TV, our affiliate there, had just constructed a handsome new building filled with state-of-the-art production facilities. Mick Schafbuch, its general manager, had asked for help in making the inauguration of his new station a memorable event. The bulk of the broadcast, including the packaged stories and the graphics, continued to originate from New York. The introductions and other short news stories which were written for Rather were read by him in his Portland studio in front of a traveling flat which replicated the one in our New York studio. KOIN-TV made the most out of these two days. Rather was booked as the featured speaker at breakfast, lunch, and dinner. He moderated a panel discussion with a number of CBS News correspondents before a packed auditorium and the television cameras of the local public television station, which later broadcast the entire event.

It was a chance for me to watch Dan handle himself in the public spotlight. Not only on the speaker's stand but at the cocktail parties which preceded lunches and dinners and with the local press. Buksbaum had brought the usual two bodyguards to Portland to help shepherd Rather. He took on the role of chief of security for the anchorman, entering every room first, head up, making no eye contact with anyone while he swept the room before indicating to the two bodyguards that Rather could enter. Switchboards at hotels where Rather stayed were instructed not to put calls through to his room unless the caller asked for a code name. All this created an air of tension around Rather's travels.

"I worry about the toll this sort of thing exacts," I said to Van.

"It goes with being the anchorman," Van replied. "Cronkite had to do it and so does Dan."

"Cronkite could do these things and just be himself," I said. "Dan can't do that. It's as though he's constantly inventing who he is or what he is."

"That's the nature of the guy," Van said. "He's like a political candidate at these things, trying to impress everybody he meets."

"That's why I said he's constantly inventing himself. Did you hear him refer to Venardos at the luncheon speech when that young woman in the audience asked him about the *Evening News* staff?"

Dan had pointed out Venardos and said, "I believe in hiring people who are smarter than myself."

"I was watching Lane's face," Van said. "He was probably wondering why he couldn't remember being hired by Dan."

"Van, the anchorman is redefining his role. The full Rothenberg stuff was something we could laugh at, because we felt confident that Dan didn't really believe he wrote, edited, and produced the whole broadcast. But this is the first chance I've had to watch him in public over an extended period. He's beginning to believe his own bullshit and that's something we ought to worry about."

"All we can do is keep an eye on it," Van said, "and if it becomes a problem, deal with it then. This is a pressure year for Rather with the conventions and the election. I worry that all the colds he's had are related to the pressure he's feeling."

"If we get him through both conventions and election night without one of his attacks of laryngitis, it'll be a miracle," I said.

"If he goes belly-up, who do we turn to?" Van asked.

"There's always the most trusted man in America."

Van looked stricken at the thought of Walter Cronkite regaining the anchor chair.

"Have you nailed down Cronkite's role at the convention yet?" he asked.

"I have a date to go sailing with Walter next month when we're both going to be on Martha's Vineyard. I hope to work it out then."

"Just remember," Van said, "it's got to be Dan's show."

368

"And after we go sailing," Cronkite said, "Betsy and I would like you and Maureen to be our guests for dinner at the Edgartown Yacht Club."

"Sounds great," I said. "What's the dress code at the Yacht Club?"

We were each at our island homes, talking with one another by phone.

"They're a little stuffy. You might get away with a jacket and an open shirt, but you probably should wear a tie."

I began to laugh.

"In the years I've had this house I've never kept a jacket here, much less a tie. I brought one with me the year my son got married in our meadow but I made sure I took it back. I'm in Chilmark, you know. I'm not one of you fancy Edgartown folks."

"Don't worry. I'll loan you something," he said.

I'd spent weeks trying to find a convention role for Cronkite. Each time I broached the subject to Rather, he was adamant that he couldn't imagine a role for Walter, "other than the anchor chair, of course." If Rather was adamant, I knew Van would also be opposed. Joan Richman, on the other hand, was if anything even more anxious than I to find some way for Walter to participate, and ultimately she provided the solution for clearing the impasse. She had come to me because Cronkite had sent Bud Benjamin to discuss the conventions with her. She was smart enough to see an ugly confrontation in the making.

"You know, boss," she said, "the press will be on this before too long. The 'where is Cronkite?' question will begin to drive us all crazy. It'll be a shame to have Dan's first convention as anchorman marred by something like this."

Sitting in Rather's office half an hour later, I felt like a parrot.

"You know, Dan, the press is bound to pick this up, and you and I are going to be spending our time explaining why Walter is not with us in San Francisco and Dallas. It's not exactly how I'd like to see you positioned for your first convention."

Before I'd left his office Dan was telling me that there might be "a whole lot of value in viewers being able to see this veteran anchorman joining me for a few minutes at the convention."

I thought to myself that it might be more than just a few minutes but kept my counsel and headed off to call Cronkite. When I reached him we agreed to get together on the Vineyard. To emphasize the importance of our talking, I sent him a handwritten note dated May 7, 1984: "As I said on the phone, we should really spend some time one-on-one and see if our common interests and common sense can't transcend past disagreements. Dealing through emissaries creates nothing but misunderstandings and the perception of rudeness. Let's see if we can't move beyond this."

The screened porch of Cronkite's gray shingled house which faces Chappaquiddick across a narrow strait of water turned out to be a perfect location to work out the problem. Betsy, Walter, Maureen, and I had gone for a sail aboard Walter's boat, the *Wyntje,* named after a Dutch ancestor, and then on to dinner at the Yacht Club. Wearing his blazer, his shirt, and his tie, I turned to Walter during dinner and said, "I feel comfortable in these clothes. Let me see if I've got the rest of it right," and lowering my voice, added, "And that's the way it is."

The subject of conventions wasn't raised until later in the evening. We'd gone back to their house for a nightcap. Walter and I were alone on the porch while Betsy was showing Maureen the rest of their home.

"We need to work out your convention role," I said.

"I hope we can do that," he answered.

"Tell me what's on your mind."

"I don't want to find myself again in the situation I was placed in on the last election night," he said, "off at some remote location where you can't get on the air. I worked hard for a lot of years to develop whatever reputation I have. Today, even though I'm no longer in the anchor chair, I'm asked to do a lot of things, go a lot of places because of that reputation. I can't take a role which will diminish or squander that reputation."

"That's language I can really understand," I said. "Let me be as direct with you now. These are Dan's first conventions. He has to be clearly seen as the anchorman. We've also got Bill Moyers in what used to be the Eric Sevareid role. With both of those as givens, what kind of part do you think you could play?"

Cronkite didn't miss a beat in answering.

"Here's what I think I could do and make some contribution to the coverage. I've covered a lot of conventions over the years. I know something about how they work. I'd like to follow the events during the early part of each evening. But later in the night when some patter is developing Dan could turn to me and say something like 'Walter, you've seen a lot of conventions. What do you make of this?' "

I could hear our wives returning.

"I don't see why that shouldn't happen," I said. "When I get back to New York I'll ask Joan Richman to work out the details."

I stood up when Betsy and Maureen walked onto the porch.

"What a great day this has been," I said. "A few hours on the water, then a great dinner with the two of you, and no wear and tear on my own clothes . . . but I think we'd better be headed back up-island. Betsy, I'll be seeing you in San Francisco."

Betsy Cronkite is a charming and very bright woman who, like her husband, has invested a lot of years at CBS News. Her face brightened, I thought, when I said that, but she turned to her husband for confirmation.

"Betsy hasn't missed a convention yet," he said. "You can count on her being there."

For the network news organizations the two political conventions have traditionally generated a sense of combat which is quite different from their daily rivalry. Correspondents and camera crews routinely see their counterparts at the rival networks when covering the same story. Not so with broadcast producers, executives, and others for whom the competition, while intense, is less personal. Under one roof at a convention site that changes. The three news organizations encamp in common space allotted to them by the political party. Several years of preparation precede their arrival and images of military engagement come easily to mind.

The general in command of this campaign in 1984 for CBS News was Joan Richman. Every mile of cable, every plate of glass for a movable anchor booth, every gross of typewriters, every rented trailer was the result of her planning. This was the first time she'd been in charge of convention coverage and she'd done it all with an added burden: she'd been given a budget several million dollars less than CBS had spent for the 1980 conventions. For two years each budget she'd proposed had been rejected—first by Sauter, then by me—as inflated. In December 1983 Joan took a contingent from her staff to Tampa, Florida, to watch CBS Sports cover the Super Bowl, and the lessons learned resulted in the leanest approach to convention coverage anyone at CBS News could remember. In the past, elaborate control rooms were constructed at each convention site, only to be torn down when the convention was over. In 1984 CBS News would have, instead, a control room in a large trailer which would be moved from the Democratic convention in San Francisco to the Republican convention in Dallas. Instead of building two expensive anchor booths, Joan came up with a prefabricated booth which would be used at both locations. In past years VIP rooms with carpeted floors were constructed for Paley, Stanton, and other top executives. Not so in 1984. I felt confident that we had not cut back in ways which would affect our coverage, but had eliminated the cosmetic trappings of an era when financial accountability played less of a role in the life of a CBS News President. Joan preceded me to the Moscone Center in San Francisco along with Rather. She called me the first day and sounded worried.

"You may have to come out here sooner than you thought," she said.

"What's wrong?"

"Dan has gotten a look at the setups for NBC and ABC. They're doing it like they've always done it and we look pretty shabby by comparison. We've got no carpeted areas, no fancy control room, and no big signs."

"I'm sure they look like Bloomingdale's and we look like the Pottery Barn," I said, "but will the viewer at home see the difference?"

"Boss, I don't think so, but rehearsal doesn't start until tomorrow."

"If there is a problem tomorrow I'll get on a plane," I said.

I turned to Stringer, who'd been sitting in my office when Joan called.

"One of us should have gone out there with Rather to hold his hand."

"I thought Joan was doing that," he said.

"She's one busy woman right now, and if Dan gets into one of his 'how do you expect me to pull a wagon with square wheels?' episodes, it's a full-time job trying to put him straight."

"We're spending a flaming fortune out there as it is," Howard said.

"By year's end we will have spent thirty-six million for political coverage and over twenty of that will be for the two conventions," I said. "I guess you're right . . . that's a flaming fortune . . . less than this place has historically spent but still a bundle."

The next morning I breathed a sigh of relief when Joan called after the first rehearsal.

"Dan's fine," she said. "We look great."

I arrived at the Moscone Center in San Francisco a day later feeling elated. We weren't going to do gavel-to-gavel coverage, but we planned to take to the air early each evening as the main events of the convention began and continue until everything of importance had concluded for the night. There's an atmosphere of excitement and hoopla to a convention which is peculiarly American. Part civics lesson, part carnival. Even now, when the primaries have changed in nature and there is no longer the fevered brokering in smoky rooms where a compromise candidate could suddenly emerge. Where else can one speech create a future candidate? Once every four years, through television, millions of Americans are brought into the process of nominating the person who will govern the life of their nation. A political convention is a coveted assignment for those in network news. Working out of a series of gray trailer offices, the kind you see at construction sites, our people had come from New York and Washington, from bureaus across the country, and even from overseas, contributing a sense of reunion to the high spirits.

Josephine Franc, my secretary from New York, was in the executive trailer when I arrived. Van, Howard, and I would work out of here for the duration of the convention and then it would be moved to Dallas. She handed me a list of calls and notes, and I was going through them when Van arrived.

"I am so bored with this fucking convention," he said. "I'm on overload and it hasn't even started. I can hardly wait to go home."

I knew immediately what was wrong, and I knew that by the end of the day Van would repeat it to everyone he saw. The destructiveness of Jankowski's executive overlay was never more obvious than at the conventions. Van had no clear role at the conventions and yet, as the Executive Vice President of the Broadcast Group to whom the News Division reported, he was burdened with accountability. In his previous job he would have been ebullient, charged by the electricity of the convention. Instead, he was embarrassed by his lack of purpose and was hiding that embarrassment behind a façade of disinterest. For two weeks we were going to share an office trailer in San Francisco and Dallas, sit together in control rooms, and pretend that two people had to be there. Van was in the more senior role, yet I felt I had come to San Francisco as the President of CBS News and I was not about to temporarily relinquish that position. We were two stallions turned loose in the same field and only friendship prevented us from destroying one another. In the days before the convention began, Joan and others would come to me with advisories and questions, the normal routine between us. I would discuss these issues with them in

373

front of Van. Occasionally he would make a comment. To break the tension of being cooped up like this for hours in our small trailer, he or I would suggest lunch at Fisherman's Wharf or a visit to the local Orvis store to examine their fishing gear.

By Monday, the first night of the convention, I was on overload, too, and could also hardly wait to go home. The coverage went smoothly, however, and to conclude our broadcast Joan used a taped package which was a nicely produced look at San Francisco and how it was reacting to the Democrats. I congratulated Joan and Artie Bloom, the director, for a good opening night and with Van walked back from the control room outside the Moscone Center to our office, which was inside on a lower level. By the time we got there our phones were ringing with messages of an affiliate revolt.

Our coverage of the Democratic convention had run past the starting time of their late evening news broadcasts and, as a result, many of our affiliates had gotten on the air with their local broadcasts at a later time than their ABC or NBC competitors. ABC and NBC had allowed local stations to cut away from their coverage, something I had chosen not to do.

After we'd each taken a few calls, Van and I compared notes.

"I've just talked to Tony Malara," he said. "This is a real shit storm. You're going to get a telegram from Joe Carriere, the chairman of the Affiliates Board, protesting tonight's runover into local news time."

"You could make an argument that a prepackaged piece on San Francisco at the end of the convention was not exactly hard convention coverage," I admitted. "But glancing at the schedule for the rest of the week, it looks to me like we'll be running over every night and I don't plan to go off the air if something is happening here."

"You'll have to watch Joan," Van said. "When the convention wraps up she's going to want to stay on the air and let the correspondents bullshit with one another."

"We may just have an obligation to explain to our viewers some aspect of what they've been watching," I said. "That's part of covering a convention."

Ironically, after having operated three television stations, I understood the sensitivity of a station manager to network overruns. Many times I fumed when my weekend news broadcasts were delayed following an NFL football game. The sportscasters continued to chat away in post-game analyses while my news people sat idly in a hot studio waiting to get on the air. But I would never have been outraged if we were delayed or pre-

374

empted because of network coverage of a national political convention. This was a fundamental change in the attitude of the affiliates and their relationship with CBS News. In the past they would simply have taken it for granted that one of the services a network provided for their viewers was coverage of the political conventions, and that it was important to the country and essential to the reputation of CBS News. In 1984, however, the thirteen-member Affiliates Board voted unanimously to protest and request shorter-form broadcasts. They then released their protest to the press. When called by the Associated Press for a reaction, I said that I anticipated giving the Republicans roughly the same amount of time and that I thought the disagreement was "a collision of interests." Because I was trying to be diplomatic I didn't say that I thought this reaction had less to do with concern for lost local news than it did with local advertising. I didn't have to say it. The Associated Press called Cullie Tarleton, the general manager of WBTV, the CBS affiliate in Charlotte, North Carolina, and he spelled it out. He told the AP that the time slot was particularly important in July, which is one of four sweep months that measure ratings and set advertising rates. "Late-night news is a very marketable product," Tarleton said, adding that if they went on late, "we have to offer make-goods to our advertisers. This really impacts on revenues." I wasn't so naïve that I could be surprised by this response from some of the station managers. I was surprised to encounter it from so many of them and surprised, too, that no rebuttal of that position was forthcoming from affiliate managers I believed to be responsible broadcasters. The Yeats lament that "the best lack all conviction, while the worst are full of passionate intensity" never seemed as apt as it did for me that week in San Francisco.

The next morning I sat down with Joan Richman and described the affiliate revolt we were facing.

"I feel comfortable defending our staying on the air as long as anything of significance is taking place on the convention floor or if there is some form of developing news," I told her. "I find it hard to defend running feature pieces of long correspondent round-table discussion once the convention has wrapped up and we've moved into local station news time."

We were all beginning to feel the pressure of the week. Joan took a furious drag on a cigarette.

"Why have we all been working for the past two years if not to come to San Francisco and put on the best convention coverage anyone has seen?" she asked. "Part of accomplishing that is having the right tape package to drop in or having the best correspondents in television sit together at the end of the evening and explain to viewers what it all meant. I can't believe CBS News is going to allow a bunch of affiliates to tell us we can't do that."

"In case you haven't noticed," I said, "CBS News is the only one of the three networks not providing a cutaway cue for its affiliates at eleven o'clock."

That same night, in fact, many NBC stations would cut away at eleven and miss anchorman Tom Brokaw's interview with the Reverend Jesse Jackson.

"Joan," I continued, "you produce the broadcast, but when the events on the floor are concluded and I feel we've discharged our obligation, I'm going to walk over to you and say, 'Get off the air.' When I say that . . . get off the air."

By now Joan's face was white with anger.

"Yes, sir," she snapped.

For the remainder of the week, at the end of each convention session a tense scene was enacted in the control room in the CBS trailer outside the Moscone Center. As we moved into local news time, Van—who by now was sitting behind me instead of at my side—would begin to groan and sometimes storm out of the control room. I would pretend to ignore him and watch the monitor. When the convention had concluded and our analysis of the events of that evening was taking place, I would listen intently, and when the correspondents reached that point where they seemed to be filling rather than analyzing, I would walk over to Joan and say, "Let's get off the air."

Returning to my seat, I would hear her speaking into the mouthpiece of the headset she wore throughout our coverage.

"Let's wrap it up."

Sitting in the control room that Tuesday night, I had been amazed to look up and see that ABC had left the convention floor and returned to *Hart to Hart,* the action adventure series which was their regular Tuesday night programming. After only twenty-five minutes they were forced to abandon *Hart to Hart* and return to the convention floor, where Jesse Jackson, the first black candidate for President to stand before a convention, was about to speak. The ABC decision was difficult to comprehend and seemed even more so the next morning when executives at ABC were quoted in the press defending their *Hart to Hart* decision in a way which was clearly writing off future coverage of conventions. One ABC executive referred to the conventions as dinosaurs. ABC Vice President David

376

Burke said, "These gatherings have become political endorsements with little news value to the public," and added, "Four years from now everyone will be doing what we did Tuesday night."

Even Larry Grossman, the new President of NBC News, was quoted as saying, "The whole thing could have been tape-delayed."

I couldn't believe what I was reading. CBS research estimated that when Jackson addressed the convention, over thirteen million Americans were watching him on CBS alone, and that was 85 percent of the number of viewers who had watched a movie on CBS on the same night one week earlier. In fact, it was estimated that some fifty-six million Americans watched CBS News convention coverage at some point during that convention week. How could anyone argue that leaving the convention for a rerun of a so-called action adventure series was in the public interest? While ABC was running *Hart to Hart,* there was no shortage of provocative and important information on the convention floor. During this twenty-five-minute period, Diane Sawyer interviewed one of the many black delegates who were enraged that Georgia delegate and fellow black Andrew Young was not supporting Jesse Jackson. Later Young was actually booed by a contingent of black delegates. Ed Bradley interviewed a Mondale campaign manager on the senator's relations with Jackson and the possibility of a Mondale-Jackson ticket, and Bob Schieffer talked with Senator Fritz Hollings about reports that Jackson might make a run for the Senate in South Carolina.

When Jackson spoke at 9:25 P.M., who was better prepared—CBS viewers or ABC viewers abruptly ripped away from the *Hart to Hart* rerun? To me the answers were very clear. And so was the reason for the remarks by the news executives at the other two networks: the commercials in *Hart to Hart* commanded a higher price than commercial time in convention coverage. The groundwork was being laid for 1988 and a further reduction in convention coverage. It was one thing to move away from gavel-to-gavel coverage, but the heart of the convention process took place in the evening hours in prime time, where the cancellation of network programming cost each network millions of dollars in reduced ad revenues. Deriding the conventions as "pep rallies" or "dinosaurs" so a public obligation which took place for two weeks every four years could be further eroded struck me as being unspeakably cynical. Most disheartening to me was the certainty that if this idea gained ground at ABC and NBC, the pressure at CBS to follow suit would be unstoppable. I made a decision to do whatever I could to disparage the "dinosaur" idea before it gained respectability. I publicly called such remarks "cynical, bad journalism, and perhaps bad citizenship." To the New York *Times* I said, "Conventions may be ceremonial, but CBS News is in the business of broadcasting the ceremonies of the nation. That's part of our obligation of service."

Responding to an ABC suggestion that in 1988 they might choose to provide highlights of the convention each night at 11:30, I said, "Showing highlights of the Jesse Jackson speech is not comparable to seeing the Jackson speech live. A description of Mario Cuomo's speech is not the equivalent of sharing the keynote with the nation. These are events that occur every four years in the life of the United States and they deserve to be treated seriously and with respect."

And I said variations of the same thing to a dozen newspapers and the two wire services. I did my best to make reducing future convention coverage fit somewhere between canceling Mother's Day and bombing the Lincoln Memorial. By the following week *Variety* was reporting that "Joyce's remarks apparently hit home, for Larry Grossman, President of NBC News, was sounding more thoughtful, saying it's foolhardy to sit here now and say what you're going to do four years down the road."

Van and I never discussed this issue. After the first night of the convention, communication between us about runovers into affiliate time was limited to the groans I heard each night behind me in the control room. Jankowski was consistent. I had no conversations with him at all during the conventions. The only indication I had of what the senior management of the Broadcast Group was thinking came in a phone call from my old boss Tom Leahy, who told me he thought Burke of ABC was staking out "the smart business position."

Then he added, "I can't believe you're continuing to run over into affiliate time each night."

"Tom," I said, "you've known me a long time. I don't think it's even close on this one. I don't know what the hell they think we've come to San Francisco to do. They may think it's possible to have a network news organization available only when it's convenient for them . . . but it doesn't work that way."

"These guys are never going to forget this," he said. "They'll find a way to get you."

I hung up thinking that with Leahy you knew where things stood and that was preferable to the opacity which increasingly marked the Jankowski style.

In the midst of this, Howard came to me in my office trailer with Jon Katz, saying it was urgent we spend a few minutes discussing the *Morning News*.

"Katz, this will have to be very important to trigger my Give a Shit meter," I said.

"I've had an offer to be the night city editor for the Albany *Times-Union*," Katz said. "Show me some respect."

I looked at Stringer.

"Do you think there's a chance he might take it? It would brighten my day."

Katz pulled both hands out of the pockets of clean but wrinkled chinos and clapped them.

"He's tired," he said. "He's single-handedly trying to salvage television coverage of conventions but he's still got the time to lash out at me."

"Very good. A taunt and a compliment rolled into one. I knew you were a natural for television. Now get to the point."

"The Press Department has been receiving a steady stream of calls from newspapers all over the country," Stringer said, "wanting to know if it's true that Diane Sawyer is leaving the *Morning News* for *60 Minutes*."

"That will be wonderful for the *Morning News*, won't it?" I said. "Five months of trying to build an audience with an anchorwoman who's leaving."

"That's why we're here," Stringer said. "Jon and I think it's best just to let her go now . . . let Hewitt have her."

"And what do we do about a replacement?" I asked.

"The fact is, she's hardly been on the broadcast for the past six weeks," Katz said. "We've been using Meredith Viera and Jane Wallace as fill-ins and they're both pretty good. Meredith is doing the show this week, in fact, while Diane covers the convention."

"And I'll begin an immediate search for other replacement candidates while we continue using the two of them," Stringer added.

"Guys, this sudden barrage of press inquiries about Diane's leaving didn't start by some stroke of coincidence. What's going on?"

Howard and Jon looked at one another and Katz responded.

"I've come to know Diane pretty well since I came to CBS. I admire her a lot, but I wouldn't want to be standing in the way of something she coveted. Think of how far she's come and how fast . . . Junior Miss . . . weather girl . . . and just a few years ago she was sitting out in San Clemente doing research for Nixon on his memoirs. Now she's got a commitment to join *60 Minutes* next year. But that's almost six months away. She's terrified that something will develop . . . a ratings collapse on the *Morning News*, something that will burst the balloon. Does that answer your question?"

"No, it doesn't. Howard, do you believe she's behind this? Because five more months of this could become very unpleasant."

"It's obvious to me, mate," Howard said.

"One other thing I should say," Katz added. "Diane is tired . . . and that's real. She leads an active life. She'll have lunch with Henry Kissinger, then go home and take a nap . . . and that same night she'll be at a dinner party. And when she goes home she'll read the research for the next morning before she sets her alarm for two A.M. and goes to bed. She's a relentless person but you forgive her because she works her ass off."

My secretary interrupted to tell me Joan Richman had just gotten the convention lineup for the night from the Democratic officials and wanted to discuss it with me.

"Guys, give Diane a message from me," I said, and I shot both hands straight up in the air. "Tell her I surrender. When this convention is over she can start at *60 Minutes.* Hewitt will be delighted. It will give him extra months to stockpile her stories for next season."

"I'd better tell the Press Department they can confirm those inquiries from the press," Howard said.

"By all means, and then start looking for a replacement. You're going to find it's not that easy."

Many months later I had a frank discussion about this with Diane, who was emphatic, almost emotional, in denying that she had tried to steamroll her departure from the *Morning News.* By then she was an established member of the *60 Minutes* team and the subsequent history of the morning broadcast had confirmed her good judgment in wishing to depart.

By the last night of the convention I felt drained. When I first arrived in San Francisco, I started each day with a five-mile run through Golden Gate Park. By midweek the extra two hours of sleep was too precious to trade for the exercise. I thought the job we'd done had been excellent. So, apparently, did American viewers. CBS News convention coverage was top-rated in the Nielsens. Rather had handled himself well and the presence of Moyers and Cronkite in the anchor booth gave our broadcasts a sense of perspective and history.

More importantly, the convention itself had been a fascinating event. Any convention which produces the first black presidential candidate for the nomination and then goes on to actually nominate the first woman ever to run for the office of Vice President can rightfully claim a special place in the history books.

Bill Moyers sensed this. He turned to Rather in the anchor booth and said, "Something enormously powerful is happening in this country. They'll be making movies about this long after we've retired to Texas."

But would networks still be covering conventions? I wondered. Was the dinosaur theory a more accurate reflection of the new reality for network television than I liked to believe? When I left the control room after the last night of the convention and headed back to the trailer inside the center, I was tired and dispirited. Jankowski had been silent on both the conflict with affiliates and the "dinosaur" issue, which had been widely reported in the press as a conflict in news philosophies among the three networks. I had to assume I could count on no sympathy for the positions I'd staked out for myself. Equally silent was the anchorman of *The CBS Evening News.*

Rather, who immediately sensed a tension he'd never felt between Sauter and Joyce, avoided mentioning either issue during the entire week. By the time I reached the executive trailer that last night Maureen was there with Kathleen Sauter. They'd both flown out for the convention and, as they so often did when traveling together, had made plans for a celebration.

"You go with them," I said. "I just want to go back to the room and crash."

In a millisecond she registered and categorized the degree of my unhappiness.

"We'll go there together. Let me tell Kathleen."

Van, who'd spent most of the night in the executive trailer instead of the control room, walked over.

"I understand we're having a late supper."

"I think I'm going to head back to the hotel room," I said.

"We should crack a bottle of wine and try to relax."

"I'm not up for that," I said. "It's been a long week and not the week I expected. I think I've been on the right side of some important issues, but the affiliates would like to field-kick my nuts from here to Dallas, Joan Richman thinks I caved in to pressure by not letting her stay on the air until the obvious had been stated at least a dozen times . . . and you . . . I don't know where you are . . . but I know where you weren't, and that was in my corner."

I turned away and walked toward the door, where Maureen was standing. I took her arm and we left for the hotel.

On Thursday morning, July 26, 1984, the week after the Democratic convention, David Burke of ABC News and I both appeared live on *The CBS Morning News* to debate the future of network coverage of conventions.

I chided the way his network dropped out of the convention in order to play a *Hart to Hart* rerun. And he scored a few telling points with the argument that the primaries are now the decision makers. But I thought he'd gone too far by saying that "partisan political events that are sculptured for the very fact that we have our cameras there may not be truly a service to the public."

That struck me as a bit much coming from the network which had seen *Hart to Hart* as a greater service.

"David, what I don't understand," I said, "is how a great network such as ABC, which will put two weeks of Olympic coverage in prime time and which puts twenty nights of football into prime time on Mondays, can balk at covering once every four years the conventions of the two great parties of the United States."

"Ed," he responded, "in 1988 you'll be doing it like we did this year."

I liked David Burke, perhaps more than one should like a competitor. He had served on the staffs of prominent politicians, among them Senator Edward Kennedy of Massachusetts, before making a mid-career change and taking a staff job at ABC News, where he handled business and policy issues for its President, Roone Arledge. As I removed my makeup after the broadcast, I thought to myself that perhaps not having a background in journalism was an asset in this new era. Of the three network News Presidents I was the only one who'd ever covered a news story or run a newsroom. Arledge of ABC News had come from that network's Sports Division and Larry Grossman of NBC News had arrived at his job from a career in advertising and public television. I went back to my office and began to work through the usual mountains of papers which awaited. At about 8:30 A.M. my exec phone rang. It was Tom Wyman.

"CBS three . . . ABC zero," he said. "We were certainly on the right side of that issue."

With the exception of the phone call from Tom Leahy in San Francisco, this was the first time in almost two weeks I'd heard from anyone at Black Rock. I took a deep breath and launched into a description of the blood-lines of certain key affiliates with particular emphasis on the uncertain caliber of the kennels.

I hung up the phone that morning puzzled once again by Tom Wyman. Every conversation with the people on Jankowski's staff produced a description of the pressure Gene was under from Wyman, and most often there was an accompanying lament that Wyman lacked respect for the traditions and values of CBS News. I knew my own initial resentment of Wyman's decision to drop gavel-to-gavel coverage of the conventions. Yet in my subsequent dealings with him he never revealed an attitude toward his News Division that was in any way hostile. That he could be obtuse was evident in his Washington *Post* interview, but I could only wonder again about the kind of counsel he was receiving from those around him, including Jankowski.

I called Maureen at home that morning to let her know about his call, partly to reassure her but also as penance for her long flight home from San Francisco sitting next to a silent husband in a black funk.

"You'd do well to let a few people at CBS know about that call," she said.

It was good advice and the first person I called was Van.

"That's wonderful news," he said. "I'll circulate that word over here." He paused and then he added, "I want you to know I spoke to Rather yesterday and I told him he and everyone else had to get behind you in Dallas to fend off the affiliate pressure."

I asked Joan Richman to come see me. She brightened at my description of Wyman's attitude toward future convention coverage. Then I added something else.

"Joan, I took a ton of shit in San Francisco from all sides. I have no intention of going through a replay in Dallas. I'm going to be under the same pressure from the affiliates about runovers and I'm going to tell them the same thing again, that CBS News will make the decision about when its broadcast should end. But when the story ends for the night down on that floor, I'm going to be there again telling you to get off the air and I don't want to be treated like I've just spray-painted graffiti on Ed Murrow's tombstone."

In midafternoon I walked back to my office from a visit to the Fishbowl and my secretary told me Gene Jankowski had called on my executive line. I rang him back, and he answered with his standard wagonmaster's call.

"Yo!!!!! Jankowski."

"Ed Joyce, Gene."

"I understand from Van you got a nice phone call from Tom."

"I did. He thinks ABC has gone too far in talking about cutting back convention coverage."

"Well, I just wanted you to know I think our affiliates are being unreasonable."

"It might be helpful at the next affiliates meeting, even one of the regionals, if you told them so."

"I'll do that."

Somehow I suspected that he wouldn't and I was right. But I slept better that night than I had in weeks.

The next day I had occasion to wonder again about Wyman and his relationship to CBS News. On July 27 a memo from Wyman was delivered to Jankowski, Sauter, and me. Attached was a copy of an article from the New York *Times* headlined "The Networks Debate Convention Coverage." The arguments in the piece were similar to those raised in the debate between Burke and me over the future of conventions. But toward the end it contained a paragraph which obviously had attracted Wyman's attention.

"At CBS," the *Times* said, "the tradition of strong coverage of major events was formed under the chairmanship of William S. Paley; under the chairmanship of Thomas Wyman, some in the news organization no longer feel the complete security and support they remember."

In his note to the three of us Wyman said he "was very pleased that we are portrayed accurately on the right side of an important issue," again emphasizing his support for future coverage of conventions. But he was less than pleased by the rest of the article.

"My reason for sending you this note is to make it clear that I am more than weary of reading the thoughts expressed in the final section of the article.

"If any of you feel that there is substance to this thesis, I hope you will share your thoughts with me. To date, you have not, which has led me to conclude that you might share my view that the charge is inaccurate and, hence, unfair. It seems clear that a number of people in the News Division must feel that they have less support from this office than they used to. If you believe that this relates to communication failures on my part, I hope you will tell me so. As you might gather from the foregoing, this subject is important to me, and I will appreciate your thoughts and advice on it."

I canceled all the appointments I could for the rest of the day and began working on a response. This was an opportunity I'd been hoping for, a chance to tell Wyman as candidly as possible how he was perceived at CBS News and some of the reasons why. By day's end I had drafted a three-page memorandum which I thought might open his eyes to the problems he was creating for himself and for me as the individual now charged with running the News Division. I was particularly struck by the "to date, you have not" line in his memo, where he asked for thoughts from anyone who believed there was truth to the charge expressed in the *Times*. Clearly, Jankowski had not been frank in his dealing with Wyman on this subject. If nothing else, my memo would be candid.

Shortly before the *Evening News* went on the air that night, Van called to tell me Jankowski wanted to respond to Wyman for all three of us and that if I had any thoughts on the subject to send them to Gene.

I pondered this for several days and on July 30 sent Gene a three-page memorandum containing much of what I'd written for Wyman:

"Since you are going to respond to Tom Wyman for all three of us I offer a couple of thoughts for your consideration," it began. "I know it's a painful and at times demoralizing experience when you see yourself described in a manner you believe to be totally at odds with the splendid individual you know yourself to be. But let's put that aside for a moment in the interest of candor.

"The News Division, rightly or wrongly, believed itself to be a particular source of pride for William S. Paley. I suspect a Warren Mitofsky poll of the News Division's employees would reveal the following . . . a belief that the new Corporate management of CBS perceives CBS News as: 1) a cost problem and 2) a Washington problem for a corporation which often needs the goodwill of the legislature and the Executive Office, not to mention the various regulatory agencies.

"Future events will offer ample opportunity to provide Tom with a moment where he may express more public support of the News Division at a crucial time. When there is an opportunity to express pride, either internally or publicly, in some accomplishment of the News Division (if indeed pride is justified) I think it's essential that this be done.

"Washington, D.C., is a small village, and when representatives of CBS are quoted as saying that the defeat of the financial interest rules came about because of the antagonism on the Hill towards CBS News, it is inevitable that a shudder will run through the News Division.

"With this as background, it is perhaps understandable that Tom's interview in the Washington *Post* was interpreted by some at CBS News as an articulation of ambivalence towards CBS News as a journalistic entity within the larger Corporation. I don't think this problem is going to go away immediately. I think it very likely that Tom will find this criticism running through stories in print about CBS like a leitmotif.

"One of the many things that make CBS News different from other divisions at CBS is that its employees constantly deal . . . both professionally and socially . . . with those who write articles in the newspapers and magazines of the nation about television and, in particular, about CBS. This means that what would start and end with hallway chatter in another division inevitably works its way into the private and public consciousness of the industry.

"Perhaps it would be constructive for Tom to consider using some industry or journalistic forum to deliver a speech which would outline his and CBS's commitment to a strong and vigorous news organization. While, given the human consideration, such a speech will not put to rest all of the problems he identifies in his memorandum, it might be a very helpful development."

I had my driver hand-carry this to Jankowski's office and then deliver a copy to Van. As an analysis of the perceptions which continued to hover over Wyman like a spectral aura in the minds of the News Division, it stands the test of time rather well. Jankowski never commented on it or even acknowledged its receipt and I have no idea if he ever shared its contents with Wyman.

The days between the two conventions passed quickly. I traveled to Washington for three days at the beginning of August to prepare for and then testify before a Senate committee on network use of exit polls for projecting the outcome of elections. Meredith Viera and Jane Wallace alternated in replacing the now departed Diane Sawyer on the *Morning News*. Howard began his search for other candidates. He was dismayed to read in the press that Kathleen Sullivan has been re-signed by ABC. He'd hoped, he said, to surprise me by proposing her as Diane's successor and had had a number of lunches and dinners with her discussing this possibility.

Just before leaving for Dallas I told Bill Moyers I was putting eight prime-time documentary hours in the 1985 budget. I said I wasn't optimistic about the network's renewing *Crossroads* and I wanted him to help me in rebuilding the documentary unit. His first reaction was that the time had come for him to leave CBS News. He'd returned to CBS in 1981 with the hopes of doing a regular prime-time broadcast of his own. Moyers had a window in his contract which would allow him to leave if he wished. I urged him to stay and even went so far as to tell him that his departure in the midst of the Westmoreland trial would be a symbolic loss to CBS News which would be particularly hurtful to our already endangered reputation. He seemed adamant when he left my office. But the following morning he came back, saying he'd grown excited by the prospect of rebuilding *CBS Reports,* that he not only would remain at CBS News but also would like to start work right after the Republican convention on a documentary dealing with the rise of fundamental Islam in Arab nations such as Egypt and Saudi Arabia, whose leaders were frightened by this phenomenon, and that he would put a researcher to work on this immediately.

I went to Dallas feeling confident that Moyers would produce broadcasts for the coming year which would bring pride to CBS News.

When the Republican convention began on Monday, August 20, I was less ebullient and more realistic about the week that lay ahead than I'd been on my arrival in San Francisco a month earlier. The atmosphere was actually more relaxed. Van seemed more at ease, no longer describing himself to anyone who would listen as being on "overload."

At a party for about one hundred CBS News people prior to the start of the convention, I presented Joan Richman and Dan Rather with enormous stuffed dinosaurs. Joan had asked our Graphics Department to design large political-type pins with a whimsical dinosaur and a large heart in the style of I Love New York pins. They quickly became a coveted convention trophy. Each night as we entered "magic hour," as the local news time for affiliates had come to be known, Joan would look to me for an indication of whether or not we would be staying on the air. The affiliates remained relentless in their demands that we relinquish the airtime. The night George Bush was nominated as the Republican vice presidential candidate the nominating process ran late and entered "magic time." The calls of protest from angry affiliates began to pour in when we stayed on the air.

In its own way the Republican convention was as interesting as the Democratic convention had been. The nominations of Reagan and Bush were unsurprising. But this was the beginning of the 1988 race and all the hopefuls were there: Jeane Kirkpatrick, Bob Dole, Jack Kemp, and an array of dark horses such as Pierre du Pont, the Republican governor of Delaware. The Convention Center swirled with the conflicting tides of conservatism. This was the group which would spend the next four years struggling to define the nature and role of their party for the decades to come.

The convention might have lacked suspense, but not conflict. A tug-of-war emerged between the managers of the convention and the networks over what came to be known as "the film." The Republicans had produced an eighteen-minute documentary about the President which they planned to screen in the convention hall and they wanted the networks to run it in its entirety. This was nothing new. Past convention managers for both parties had even gone so far as to extinguish all the lights to force the networks to turn to the film being played. Technology now allowed the networks to do with less light, and of course interviews could be conducted from other locations, including the anchor booth. In San Francisco the Democrats had exhibited films about Harry Truman, Eleanor Roosevelt, and Walter Mondale. None of the three networks chose to show them. The argument against it usually boiled down to "we're here to cover a news event, not a contrived film."

In Dallas the Republicans had taken it a step further. Instead of the usual nominating speech, they planned to have Vice President Bush speak first and then conclude by introducing the eighteen-minute film, which was partially narrated by the President himself, who would then appear in person at the speaker's stand. Their argument, contained in a letter to me from Frank Fahrenkopf, the chairman of the Republican National Committee, was that since we had carried the live introduction of Walter Mondale in San Francisco by Senator Edward Kennedy, which lasted twenty-two minutes, the airing of an eighteen-minute film which the Republicans were using for the introduction of their candidate would be "the only logical course."

News columns and editorial pages had a field day with this issue. The Washington *Post* ran an editorial declaring that it "gets you to the point of saying that the whole convention could be taped and would still have to be televised." Most editorial opinion took the opposite stand, and many of us had a sense that the Republicans were stoking this fire in order to buttress Fahrenkopf's point in his letter to me—and I'm sure my counterparts at ABC and NBC—that the film was "a genuinely newsworthy document."

Charles Manatt, the chairman of the Democratic National Committee, of course saw it differently. In his letter to me he argued that "it would hardly be reasonable, much less in good faith, to allow the Republican National Committee and the Reagan Presidential campaign to make a filmed prime-time presentation on behalf of their party and candidate, while denying this opportunity to the Democratic Party."

I simply replied to Chairman Manatt that "the selection by CBS News of the stories, events, and materials to include in our coverage of the political conventions has reflected—and will continue to reflect—the professional news judgments of CBS News personnel."

My response to Fahrenkopf had to wait until the Republicans made available to us a copy of their film. I pressed Joan Richman to keep hounding them and finally, on Wednesday, August 23, she phoned to say it had arrived. A few minutes later Van and I were sitting in a makeshift editing room where a CBS technician played for us the tape cassette copy of the film. It was stirring and beautifully produced—and it was a commercial with all of the effects and expensive production values which are used in modern political advertising. By claiming it was their introduction to the candidate, they were hoping to get eighteen minutes of free airtime for a commercial which would be viewed by millions of Americans. It could be argued that the conventions increasingly had been structured for our cameras as a televised event. Still, until now conventions had remained events for delegates and the candidates which the networks were allowing the country to witness through their coverage. The networks were now being asked to cross another threshold and turn over a significant portion of airtime to a free political commercial. When the tape finished and the lights went on in the trailer which housed the edit booths, I could see a number of our reporters and crew members straining to catch some indication of our reaction.

"That's a powerful film," Van said.

"Why don't we take Joan and discuss this in private in our trailer," I said.

"She should ask the anchorman to join us," Van said. "He'll have to deal with the decision on the air."

I turned to Joan, who was not far away.

"Meet us in our trailer in about five minutes. Bring Rather and ask Stringer to join us, too."

Our trailer, as it turned out, was not the best place to hold an important meeting. Too many phones ringing. Too many people constantly coming in and out with the questions and problems which at another time would have been routine. I told my secretary to find us another location.

"Shirley," I said, "you know the spare trailer we use for press interviews, the one we put Wyman and Jankowski in to make their phone calls. I'm confiscating that for the next hour. Unless it's an emergency, don't tell anyone where we are."

The five of us entered the small trailer and closed the door. We pulled a small couch and several chairs into a circle at sat down to confer.

"We have to make a decision on whether or not to run that film," I said. Everyone nodded in assent.

"Our decision is going to attract a lot of attention. The Press Department tells me two-thirds of the calls they're receiving are to ask if we've made up our minds yet. It's wonderful when we become the story."

"The White House is doing everything it can to fuel that," Rather said. "They hope to make this such a public issue that we'll feel the film had become newsworthy."

Good, I thought. If the anchorman gets his macho rolling, it will support what I'm about to say.

"It may turn out," I said, "that the film has become a news story, but it doesn't follow that we have to run all eighteen minutes of it."

"But it just seems to me," Van said, "that a lot of people are going to want to see that film. It's fine stuff, beautifully produced. We are, after all, in the television business. Why should we deny someone the right to use the medium in a sophisticated manner?"

"No doubt about it," I said, "it's a well-produced, effective eighteen-minute commercial. They can easily use portions of it in their commercials during the campaign. But in San Francisco we didn't show the Democrats' films about Harry Truman, Eleanor Roosevelt, and Walter Mondale."

"Wait a minute," Van argued, "we did carry Ted Kennedy's twenty-two minute speech introducing Walter Mondale."

"Sure we did, because it was a live news event, the kind we've always covered at conventions. It wasn't a political commercial."

Van got up from his chair and began to pace the room.

"A lot of people in this country want to see this film," he said. "They're going to be very angry if we don't carry it and I think we'll pay the price in the ratings if we don't."

He quickly added, "I'm not saying we should carry it just because we might lose in the ratings. I think it's a fine film which stands on its own."

Rather, Stringer, and Richman had been following these volleys like spectators at the U.S. Open. But Rather seemed surprised by the possibility of an impact on the ratings if we didn't run the film, and suddenly his head stopped turning.

"Ratings are not something Dan Rather knows a lot about," he said. "That's why you two fellows are paid those handsome salaries. But if you think enough people know about and want to see this film, maybe there is an argument that it's a newsworthy event."

I was sure I could count on Joan.

"If we carry this film," I said, "then we'll have turned the conventions into dinosaurs after all, because the next logical step will be for the parties to prepackage more and more of the elements of a convention. Why take a chance on a speaker who may not have the power to energize and illuminate? Then we'll start asking why cover the convention at all, why not just do a wrap-up every night when it's all over? Joan . . . you've been very quiet, what do you think?"

"I think it would be a terrible mistake to run this film."

"Dan?" I felt sure that he would not run the risk of anyone ever hearing that he'd been less than the staunchest defender of journalistic independence.

"If you are asking me what I think we should do," Rather said, "the answer is no. I do not think we should run this film. Yes . . . I think we should recognize that we very likely—we don't know for certain—but very likely will pay a price in the ratings. But again, no, I don't think we should run this film."

"Howard?"

"One could certainly make an argument for running the film," he said, looking at Van, "but I agree with Dan that we shouldn't run it."

"Van?"

"You all know how I feel," he said. "But if it's the sense of this group that we shouldn't run it, then so be it. I think we should walk out of here and announce the decision of CBS News and not refer to any disagreement among us on this issue."

A few hours later the following letter from me was delivered to the Republican national chairman, Frank Fahrenkopf:

"After reviewing the film and giving the matter the most serious consideration, CBS News has decided not to show the film. We do intend, however, to take note of the issue surrounding the broadcast of the film and to use brief excerpts from the film in our convention coverage.

"In covering both the Democratic and Republican conventions we believe we are all best served if the two parties produce the conventions as they choose and we produce our news coverage based on our best judgments.

"We do not take issue if you choose to present an eighteen-minute campaign commercial partially narrated by the candidate immediately before the candidate presents a live address to the nation.

"In the same spirit we believe we have the right and the obligation to use our professional news judgment in determining what to broadcast during that time."

What CBS News ended up doing while the eighteen-minute film was being played in the Convention Center was to share with its viewers the nature of the controversy and to illustrate it with brief excerpts from the film itself. Bill Moyers and White House correspondent Bill Plante joined Rather in the anchor booth to discuss the affair and its implications. ABC News did much the same thing in its coverage. NBC News broadcast the film in its entirety.

The next morning when the alarm went off in my hotel room, I called for the overnight ratings. They showed that the largest number of viewers had tuned in the NBC News coverage. I opened the door to the corridor outside, where a stack of morning newspapers had been left in a neatly tied bundle. Leafing through them, I noted that *USA Today* accused CBS News of having treated the Reagan film as if it were "pornography."

I groaned and began to throw clothes into a suitcase. In a few minutes Van and I would be leaving together on a four-day fishing trip in northern New Mexico. It was something we'd planned and arranged months earlier. Van had suggested it and Maureen had encouraged me to go.

"It'll be good for you," she said. "I see how Van looks before he goes fishing and then how he looks when he comes back. You love the outdoors, but the only time you see it is from an airplane window."

Howard Stringer was less enthusiastic when I told him about the trip.

"Oh, Ed, you can't do that. This whole place thinks Van took up fishing merely because of Dan. You're just beginning to separate yourself from Van in the minds of a lot of people and that's been good for the place."

"Howard, Van and I are friends. If the two of us can't go fishing for a few days without the resident Kremlinologists having to rework their latest analyses, I'm sorry, but I'm not going to lose sleep over it."

Packing for that trip in my Dallas hotel room that morning, I wasn't so certain the trip was a good idea after all. The tension between Van and me in San Francisco had been palpable, and though both of us had tried our best to avoid confrontations in Dallas, the issue of the Republican film had brought us into conflict again. In our old relationship, when Van had been the News President, I would have simply raised my objections and then deferred to his right to make the final decision. In this new structure I felt I couldn't do that, any more than I would automatically defer to Jankowski or Wyman. Van was still my boss, but now I was the President of CBS News, a role that increasingly seemed to have me playing Becket to his King Henry. This was an analogy which came to mind too often these days, particularly the admonition of one of T. S. Eliot's Tempters that Thomas didn't used to be "so hard upon sinners when they were your friends. Be easy man. The easy man lives to eat the best dinners."

At the Dallas airport Van was accompanied by his youngest son, Jeremy, a college student who had spent part of his summer working as a convention page for us in San Francisco and Dallas. I was fond of Jeremy. I thought him to be a fine young man. As a result of his presence, however, neither Van nor I mentioned the convention or the NBC ratings win. There were long periods of silence on the flight to Albuquerque, where we rented a four-wheel-drive vehicle and began the several hours' drive north to the Vermejo Park ranch, an enormous working cattle ranch of almost 400,000 acres nestled in the alpine meadows of the Sangre de Cristo mountain range. A limited number of guest fishermen have access at any one time to the ranch's twenty-five miles of rivers and streams, seven major lakes, and a reservoir. By the time we pulled into ranch headquarters we'd seen deer, wild turkey, and enough pine and aspen forests to tell us we were in for something special. Growing up in the West, I'd thought of this as the natural world. Now the vast mountain ranges seemed as alien to me as the reaches of China when I'd walked along the ramparts of the Great Wall. But that sense of estrangement quickly disappeared. Over the next few days I felt at home and began to relax. Even with the help of Bob Pelzl, a gifted guide and fly-fishing instructor, my fishing skills didn't match Van's. But I could sit a horse or drop instinctively on the backs of my heels and balance for a long talk with one of the hands on the ranch. "Hunkering down" was what my dad used to call it.

In one of those talks, which turned to the subject of dogs and the trouble they could get into, I found myself reaching for a childhood memory and saying, "One of those porkypines can tear a dog up pretty good." I think if I'd had some Bull Durham I would have rolled one of my own. I glanced up at Van, who was smiling, trying not to laugh, wondering, I'm sure, what had happened to the fellow who introduced him to Turnbull and Asser shirts, trilbies, and silk foulards.

For four days we rose early, fished until dark, and had dinner with Jeremy and more than a few beers at the ranch headquarters. By the last night at dinner we were so tired we sat for long periods of time without talking. But this time it was silence without tension, the quiet that can be enjoyed by two friends so comfortable with one another that neither feels a compulsion to fill the void. Then one of us would be inspired to recall for Jeremy some episode from shared experience, such as a dinner in Hong Kong aboard the big ship *Jumbo* in Aberdeen Harbor, where I'd introduced Van to the durian fruit, a delicacy esteemed above all others in Asia. A peculiarity of the durian is that while it has a sweet delicate taste, the fruit produces a malodorous aroma, something Anthony Burgess described in one of his novels as like "eating a sweet raspberry blancmange in the lavatory." I promised to produce for Jeremy a photograph I had of Van sitting next to Mr. Ping from our Hong Kong Bureau taken shortly after sampling his first durian.

"I should have suspected something," Van said, "when you asked the waitress to serve the durian. The poor woman looked like you'd just asked her to perform an indecent act."

Another period of silence followed that story while the three of us devoured enormous slices of lemon meringue pie from the ranch kitchen.

"Every religion has its own ideas on an afterlife," I said, breaking into the silence. "It wouldn't be bad waking up and discovering paradise was exactly like this."

Van was filling his pipe from a large soft pouch.

"Eduardo, I just hope that the day will come when the two of us can walk away from CBS in a position to live a life with some degree of grace where we can do the things we both enjoy."

"I don't know, Van, the way the business is going. I have this vision of a car pulling up to the filling station where I'm pumping gas in some small Western town and a voice saying, 'Didn't you used to be Ed Joyce? What ever happened to Van Sauter?' And I tell him, 'You can find him two miles down the highway managing the 7-Eleven store.'"

Van smiled and a circle of aromatic pipe smoke floated above the table and its empty pie plates.

"Not the degree of grace I had in mind," he said, "but also not the worst of all possible worlds. At least we'd be able to go fishing together."

"Home is the fisherman. Welcome back, sport."

The nettlesome greeting came from Howard Stringer, who was waiting in my office the morning of my return from New Mexico.

"Did Van come back, too?" he asked. "Or will his body be found in the mountains this winter by fur trappers?"

"He's back," I said. "We both had a good time."

"I'm glad to hear it. Did you thrash out his behavior at the conventions?"

"Believe it or not, neither of us mentioned the conventions once."

"Oh, I can believe that, because it's so frightfully British," Howard said.

"I think we were saddened by the tensions between us and made an unspoken pact to move past them. A few days of immersion in pursuit of the elusive trout does restore perspective. You should try it sometime, Howard."

"I think it preferable that people here see that one of us doesn't fish," he said, "if you don't mind."

"Speaking of perspective," I said, "the two of us should be working on next year's budget. This time of year it gets locked in."

"What sort of mood would Group Captain Jankowski be in?"

"A good one, I should hope," I said. "The *Evening News* dominates the network competition. The *Morning News* is chugging along. *60 Minutes* remains in the top ten. And Gene thinks *Nightwatch* is winning all those Washington hearts. Why shouldn't he be happy?"

"Well, I hope he retains that mood when he reads the fine print and sees that you're opening a small bureau in Seattle, expanding in Hong Kong, and adding eight hours of *CBS Reports* documentaries next year."

"Seattle and Hong Kong are small potatoes," I said. "It's been stupid to operate in Hong Kong with an office but no bureau chief or correspondent."

"What about the documentaries?"

"For two years," I said, "we've been raping *CBS Reports* to pay for shows like *Our Times, American Parade,* and *Crossroads,* telling ourselves it was justified by an opportunity to establish a new magazine in prime time. But even as we speak, I feel the rug moving underneath our feet on *Crossroads.*"

Howard looked surprised.

"Think about it," I said. "*Crossroads* was on for three weeks, then preempted by the Democratic convention. It came back on the Fourth of July, had a couple of outings up against the Olympics—I couldn't even get Maureen to watch—and then it was bumped for the Republican convention. Now it will appear on the Labor Day weekend—marvelous timing."

"I thought Jankowski wanted a low-cost public service hour in the prime-time schedule," Howard said.

"Howard, let me tell you how it will work," I said. "They'll have a program meeting over in the Tower of Jell-O. We won't be there, of course. Bud Grant and Harvey Shepherd will stand in front of a big board and lay out their proposed schedule for the new season. Jankowski will look at it and say, 'I don't see *Crossroads.*' That will be Harvey's cue to say, 'Based on the ratings performance of *Crossroads* over a ten-week period, I believe it would destroy any possibility for the network to enjoy a successful Tuesday night.' Tom Leahy will then deliver his part of the script and say, 'Harvey's right. *Crossroads* has no legs.' After that meeting Gene will tell us what a shame it was that *Crossroads* couldn't find an audience. Actually, he'll say it to Van, who will deliver the message to me. I'll point out that there was really no audience to find, but without the ratings Gene will never overrule the Entertainment Division."

"Moyers compares it to having a picnic in a graveyard at midnight," Howard said.

"He's not wrong," I said. "Do you think for a minute they'd treat one of their entertainment shows this way? Bullshit they would. That's why I want those documentaries in the budget for next year. We will have done a total of four documentary hours this year. I'm not exactly proud of that. Which is pretty much what I told Moyers just before I left for Dallas."

"Bit risky, wasn't it?"

"I had to. He had a window coming up in his contract which would allow him to leave. I couldn't very well let that window close and then say, 'Oh, by the way, Bill, I think *Crossroads* is about to become history.' "

"I take it Bill is staying," Howard said.

I described for Howard the two conversations with Moyers. How he had been about to leave but had then reversed himself.

"He seems quite enthusiastic about some documentary ideas," I added.

"Congratulations on keeping Bill aboard," Howard said.

"I continue to keep him, and I continue to fail to provide a regular broadcast which uses his talents. In the beginning I had hopes for *Crossroads.*"

"Old Van didn't give you much help there, did he?" Howard said. "I thought he was supposed to be the News Division voice in Black Rock."

"Not his kind of broadcast," I said. "I don't think I fully understood how far out Van had gone in his optimistic descriptions of *American Parade.* If *Crossroads* had sparked in the Nielsens, I'm sure Van would have gotten behind it for us."

"But as you noted a moment ago," Howard said, "the network managed to keep *Crossroads* a well-guarded secret. What would Gene's response be if Bill Moyers went to him and said, 'I don't believe it's possible to get serious journalism on the air in your prime-time schedule'?"

"I know exactly what he would say, because I've heard him say it," I said. "Gene would look at Bill with a hurt expression and ask, 'How can you say that, Bill? The record shows CBS News has more airtime, more employees, a larger budget, and more resources at its disposal than ever before in its history.' "

"Of course," Howard said, "but that's because of the expansion in the morning, or the addition of *Nightwatch,* or because they want to be bloody number one in the evening news. Is Gene aware that he's mouthing sheer sophistry?"

"Howard, if I knew the answer to that, it might make it easier to know what to do."

I looked at my watch.

"Jesus," I said, "I've been back half an hour. I arrived feeling rested and I'm already depressed. Thanks a lot. What's happening with your search for a Sawyer replacement for the morning?"

"No one's developing as a good candidate from the outside. Jon and I are quite high on Jane Wallace these days. We'd like to discuss her with you."

"Fine, let me plow through whatever else is waiting for me here and then we'll talk."

The news about Jane Wallace was encouraging, because I was impressed with her, too. As a reporter in our Miami Bureau, Jane had drawn quite a few Central American assignments. She had waded through jungles and battled bugs with the best of them to report the confusing stories of Nicaragua and El Salvador. As an anchorwoman she was obviously inexperienced, and it showed in as fundamental an area as reading a TelePrompTer. That's a skill which has less to do with intelligence than it does with coordinating one's speaking and motor skills. Reading words from yards of paper which roll relentlessly for two hours each morning takes some practice. I was convinced that Jane would improve. And she'd already developed a far more important skill, the ability to conduct a series of interviews each morning with guests who might vary in a single hour from Henry Kissinger to Calvin Trillin. She was intelligent, charming, and engagingly audacious, and I was certain that viewers would warm to her. To my surprise, Van didn't share my enthusiasm. Each time I pressed her case or praised something she had done that day, he would invoke Jankowski's name.

"Gene will never buy into Wallace," he said one morning.

"I know she's a little green," I said, "but so was Sawyer in the beginning. Remember that ice queen stuff?"

"Gene wants somebody presold."

"What does that mean?"

"Someone already known to viewers," Van said. "Someone viewers would automatically want to watch. Gene doesn't feel it has to be somebody with a news background. It could be a Sarah Purcell or a Mariette Hartley."

"We can't put some actress on *The CBS Morning News*."

"That's another thing," Van answered. "Gene thinks maybe it's time to change the name of the broadcast to give it more flexibility."

We continued to alternate Meredith Viera and Jane Wallace on the *Morning News*.

Howard came to me during this period and asked if he should expand his search list.

"Should I be calling the agents and finding out if the Sarah Purcells and Mariette Hartleys are available?"

"Absolutely not," I said. "We'll wait Gene out. We'll keep using Meredith and Jane and in a couple of months we'll tell him we can't go on like this any longer and CBS News feels strongly that Jane Wallace should do the broadcast. Gene will find it difficult to say no."

Jon Katz bearded me regularly with his worry list about both of his temporary anchorwomen.

"Meredith tires easily. I worry about how she'd handle these brutal hours. And Jane has a tough time dealing with all the stress that goes with a show like this. She blew her top at a couple of my producers this morning over some last-minute changes."

Happily, Katz was trying to take hold of this broadcast now that he was the executive producer. Howard had been devoting more and more time to getting ready for his inevitable testimony in the Westmoreland trial. He'd spent weeks first preparing and then giving his deposition in the discovery portion of the pretrial proceedings. This had kept him away from CBS News and had diminished his participation in the morning broadcast. So Katz had been very much on his own.

David Boies had come to me saying he felt it was essential that Stringer be present in the courthouse on a full-time basis once the actual trial started. Boies shared with me his concern about Howard's anxiety over Dan Burt's cross-examination. He felt it was important that Howard be present for all of the other testimony which would precede his own. Since the trial was now scheduled to start in mid-October, this meant I could look forward to months without a deputy with whom to share the running of CBS News.

But Howard was on hand the Monday morning in mid-September when Bill Moyers asked to see us both. I assumed Bill wanted to fill us in on the progress he was making with his documentary on the rise of fundamental Islam. The instant Bill walked in the door I knew something was amiss. The man who took the seat I offered looked less like the teacher of civics and history I'd always imagined him to be and more like someone whose pursuits were nocturnal and dubious.

His face was sallow and puffy. His gray suit was wrinkled. And in his hand he held several typewritten pages.

"I spent a very difficult weekend deciding something which is important for all of us," Bill said, "and because I write more clearly than I can talk I want to read this to you."

And he did.

He began by reminding me that he had come to CBS in 1981 stubbornly believing his chief purpose was to try to create a public-affairs series, but when *Our Times* received no more support than it did, he returned to the *Evening News* and after a struggle of a couple of months was back in stride. He then recounted how after what he called the "bitter *American Parade* experience" and the plan to transform it into *Crossroads*, he had responded to our entreaties to do this new broadcast, despite his reservations about its chances for success and his reluctance to again appear less frequently on the *Evening News*.

He pointed out that in August he had been prepared to exercise an escape clause in his contract which was there to provide him with a way out if he was not regularly involved in a public-affairs series. This was when I asked him instead to stay and work with me in restoring *CBS Reports* by producing documentaries.

Now Bill raised his head for a moment and looked at me before continuing.

"I know I came back to you and told you I would stay," he said, "and that I said I was enthused by the prospect of doing these *CBS Reports* broadcasts. Ed, I was not being truthful. For the first time in a career which has contained many changes, I made a decision for the wrong reasons. The night before I told you I would stay, I went home and discussed this with Judith. She said what my wife has always told me—that the important thing was to make the decision I felt in my heart was the right one. We went over our finances and talked about the ways we would adjust to the loss of income, because we both know that million-dollar salaries are a rarity, even in television. I hardly slept that night but I came in the next morning and told you I wanted to stay. Ed, I did that because I didn't want to give up everything CBS provides me and so I came to you and told you I was enthusiastic when in my heart I believe that occasionally scheduled documentaries have too little impact for the time and trouble involved. I know you don't feel that way and I admire you for it, but I think it's almost impossible for a documentary with little promotion and usually an obscure spot to do well in the ratings. I know you've argued that a documentary doesn't have to produce big ratings but the ratings competition is so fierce it fights against getting serious journalism of depth and relevance on the network. I've been tormented by this since then. I left your office having agreed to do something I felt was wrong and now that I've made a decision to leave I feel liberated and so should you. You can use my salary for other purposes. CBS will be relieved of my frustrations, and I can find a place where I can once again be productive."

With that Bill folded the papers and placed them in his jacket pocket. What seemed like an eternity of silence ensued until I finally spoke.

"I don't know what to say . . . I'm so unprepared for this. In my mind you were happily at work doing the homework for your next documentary. I guess I just don't understand how it is that you seemed so up and so challenged by the idea of breathing life back into *CBS Reports* and now you're leaving."

For the first time in the years we'd dealt with one another, Bill showed anger.

"I thought I just explained that. I lied. I came here and I lied to you."

I let out a long sigh. Even if it was true, I didn't want to hear it. Right now, I just wanted to bring an end to this meeting.

"Bill, I'll need to be able to explain to the people I work for why I think you should be released from your contract. May I have a copy of what you just read?"

"These are only my notes," he said. "I'll put them in a letter for you."

Bill stood up and turned toward Howard, who had been a silent observer.

"Howard, I asked that you be here because I didn't want a situation where you would come to me afterward to try and talk me into staying."

Now it was my turn to be angry.

"I can promise you one thing, Bill," I said. "I will not ask Howard to try and persuade you to stay."

Bill left, and Howard and I sat alone in my office.

"In a lifetime filled with bizarre meetings, that may lead the list," I said.

"Are you really going to let him go?" Howard asked.

"Yes. All along I've believed that we would ultimately find the role, the outlet for Bill. But when he sits here and says, 'Ed, I lied to you,' I just don't know how to handle it."

"Maybe I should go to Bill," Howard began to say.

"NO . . . absolutely not," I said. "No one wants Bill Moyers to stay more than I do. But as we've just seen, it's dangerous to approach him with plans unless he's convinced he wants to be a part of them."

I never received the letter from Bill asking to be released from his contract. Howard and I discussed this often and one day he came to me with what he thought was the reason.

"Bill and Andy Lack have been talking to NBC," he said. "They've been chatting with Larry Grossman about going there to do a weekly prime-time broadcast."

"How do you know this?"

"Andy Lack and I are old friends," he said. "Andy has told me all about it."

"Lack's contract is up," I said. "He'd be free to go and so will Bill when I give him his release."

"Andy doesn't really want to go," Howard said, "but right now we've got nothing for him to do."

"What does he want to do?"

"He'd like to work on a new prime-time show idea for us," Howard said.

"With Bill?"

"No. That's one of the reasons he doesn't really want to go to NBC. He says he'd like to produce a show without having to design it around established on-air people, and that includes both Bill and Kuralt. He'd prefer to use some of our younger correspondents instead. He thinks they would be more flexible."

Andy Lack was one of the more innovative producers in television news. I was interested in seeing just about any program he proposed.

"Tell Andy to go to work," I said.

"What about Bill?"

"Bill has told us he wants to leave, but I still haven't received his letter. Maybe he's been holding off until he has the NBC deal lined up. In the meantime he's continuing to do his commentaries for the *Evening News* and election night is only a few weeks away. Unless I get a formal request from him in writing, I'm going to operate with the assumption that Bill is with us for the foreseeable future."

By late October, Bill's letter still hadn't arrived, and I was content for the time being to wait until after the election to resolve the issue.

And in October I was prepared to make the push to name Jane Wallace as the replacement for Diane Sawyer. Jane and Meredith Viera had been alternating in the anchor seat long enough to give rise to considerable speculation, not only within CBS but in the press, over which of the two would be chosen. As a result, both Meredith and Jane were growing increasingly snappish. They felt, not without some justification, that an embarrassing Miss America aspect had attached to their contest for this role.

Van continued to remind me of Jankowski's determination to find presold talent and he now added that Gene was eager to satisfy affiliates who were demanding larger ratings in the morning. Just as persistently, I reminded him that Sawyer had not become a name until after she joined the *Morning News.*

"I'd like a chance to tell Gene this," I said.

Van agreed to arrange a meeting with Jankowski in his office. I was invited to bring both Stringer and Katz. In advance of our trip across town

I met several times with the two of them to discuss the importance of pushing for Wallace.

"We have to nail this down—now," I emphasized.

"To believe Van, Gene is still quite adamant," Howard said.

"I'm sure he will be," I said, "but, guys, we're all agreed we don't want to go down the Sarah Purcell, Mariette Hartley road. We need a journalist and Gene has to be made to see how strongly we feel about this. Jane's the best candidate on our horizon. She may not be perfect but she'll grow. Besides, we can't go on any longer without naming a permanent replacement. We're all going to look like fools if we don't act soon."

The day we rode up in the elevator at Black Rock to the thirty-fourth floor I looked at my two companions. Howard was wearing a blue suit and an English shirt with strawberry candy stripes and a white collar. Even Katz had eschewed his usual baggy chinos and had managed to find a pair of gray flannel trousers and a blue blazer.

"For you, this isn't bad, Katzo," I said. "Anyone else would have managed to wear a suit."

To my surprise he let the gibe go unreturned.

"I don't own a suit," he said quietly. "Is this O.K.?"

I realized how nervous he was. I looked at Stringer, who also seemed tense. I tried another icebreaker.

"Howard . . . cheer up. It's only your career that hangs in the balance here."

He smiled.

That's more like it, I thought as the elevator doors opened on thirty-four.

Jankowski's office was large, with a western view which extended across the Hudson River to New Jersey. At the eastern tip of the office was a door leading to a private bathroom.

Easy chairs and a sofa had been gathered around a coffee table and as soon as we sat down a waitress from the private executive dining room served coffee and tea in white china cups.

"The *Morning News* has come a long way in the past couple of years," Gene said.

"It really has," I agreed. "Despite those critics who were so vocal when we first made the changes."

"You can't pay attention to the naysayers," Gene said. "They'll always be there. I take credit for the ratings growth. When I made the decision to take *Captain Kangaroo* off the air and expand the *Morning News* I heard from lots of naysayers then, too. But that's when the ratings started to climb."

So much for Merlis, so much for Joyce, so much for Sawyer, I thought. Gene actually believed that deep-sixing the poor Captain had caused the turnaround.

"Now with Diane going to *60 Minutes* we have another opportunity," he said. "Who has the News Division come up with to replace her?"

"The delegation from CBS News wishes to announce that its candidate is Jane Wallace," I said.

Van didn't say a word. He smoked his pipe and stared out the window toward Jersey City.

"I don't think the affiliates would like that," Gene said. "When the show was less successful it wouldn't have made that much difference. But now we've built it into something bigger and the level of expectation is that much greater."

Gene looked at Howard.

"Is that really the best the News Division has been able to come up with?"

Howard's face turned the color of his strawberry candy stripes.

"No one believes that Jane is the ideal candidate," he said.

"She's a fine reporter but a neophyte at anchoring. Her troubles with the prompter have been obvious. And she doesn't handle stress that well," Katz added.

I began to steam.

"Jane Wallace may not be ideal, but she has great promise, and in addition to everything else, she's smart. Smart counts for a lot. Howard here has been conducting our search on the outside for other candidates. You might tell Gene about the lack of success you've experienced."

"Well, I thought for a while I had a good shot at Kathleen Sullivan at ABC," he said, his face now a glowing cerise.

"I'm not sure she would have been right either," Gene said.

"Perhaps I should cast my net wider," Howard said. "Have another go at the agents."

"You might call Harvey Shepherd on the Coast," Gene suggested. "He looks at a lot of pilots. Maybe he's seen one of those information-based shows with someone who might be right."

"Good idea," Howard said. "I'll do that."

I made another attempt to salvage Wallace.

"We've gone too long now without a replacement for Diane," I said. "We could bring Jane along quickly."

"We shouldn't allow ourselves to be rushed into such an important decision," Gene declared. "I don't see how CBS News can go to the affiliates and say the best person we've been able to find to replace Diane Sawyer is a young woman who's never anchored before."

I started to remind him that neither had Diane but I didn't. The meeting was over and I knew it.

"We'll continue to search," I said.

When the three of us left Gene's office, Van, who hadn't said a word during the meeting, remained behind.

During the elevator ride down to street level I was silent. I said nothing until we were in the back seat of my car being driven to the Broadcast Center.

"Well, you two assholes really blew Jane Wallace out of the fucking water."

"We always said that Jane wasn't the ideal candidate," Howard said.

Katz quickly added, "I told you right along I didn't think she could handle the stress of this show."

"Bullshit," I said. "You both lost your guts and you caved. Now we're going to go on for God knows how long without naming a new anchor, and we're going to look like we're running the Monty Python School of Journalism."

"I'll begin immediately to talk to the agents and scour the bloody country," Howard said.

"You'd better be quick," I said. "In another few days you'll be spending your time in lower Manhattan sitting in a courtroom and leaving the search to your partner there who's been in television for at least twenty minutes."

Weeks went by and neither Stringer nor Katz had additional candidates to put forward. Our best chance had been eliminated and we were about to begin a long, cold winter.

Stringer, indeed, was tied up in court during the Westmoreland trial, which began on October 11, 1984.

I made a point of occasionally attending as well, and took comfort from watching David Boies in action. He was an incredibly gifted lawyer. Surprisingly, this was not my impression of Dan Burt, who'd come across as such a formidable street fighter. While George Crile was testifying, for example, Burt appeared almost inept. Crile had spent the last two years doing virtually nothing except prepare for this day. As a result, he could summon up in obsessive detail the most arcane elements from the volumes of intelligence-gathering minutiae compiled during the Vietnam War.

Nearly all of Burt's witnesses up to this point in the trial had given testimony on the issue of truth. With Crile, however, Burt was trying to build a prima facie case of malice. Since Crile was being called as a hostile witness, Burt was in effect conducting a cross-examination, his first. He did so with the same histrionics he had displayed in his press conferences. He was sarcastic, sneering, actually putting his hands on his hips and rolling his eyes toward the ceiling when Crile spoke. He was so denunciatory that the judge gave Crile great leeway in his response. As a result, Crile delivered long self-serving statements demonstrating his undeniably impressive knowledge on the subject. It was obvious that Burt's strategy was backfiring. He was getting nowhere with Crile and he'd been going after Crile for days as though his pride wouldn't permit him to stop.

During a recess I mentioned this to Boies.

"If I had a witness like that," Boies said, "I'd get him off the stand as quickly as I could because I'd be afraid he was scoring points for the opposite side with the jury."

Then he confided to me that Burt had come to him complaining that even the other lawyers on the Westmoreland side were urging him to get Crile off the stand.

"What did you say?" I asked.

Boies smiled.

"I told him I've had the same problem myself, and that sometimes even your own people don't understand what it is you're trying to accomplish. That when this happens I just ignore them. I also told him, 'I think you're doing great, Dan.' "

A small group from CBS News sat together in the courtroom each day: George Crile, Mike Wallace, Howard Stringer, and Sam Adams, who'd been the paid consultant. This group would expand to accommodate the arrival of the occasional visitor such as Van or me. By contrast, General Westmoreland was usually accompanied only by his wife, Katherine, known to friends as Kitsy, who brought wool and knitting needles. Her hands were constantly in motion throughout the long weeks of the trial. The general was tall and dignified, a lonely figure who, before the trial ended, would have to sit through unflattering testimony from men who'd been his subordinates in Vietnam.

One morning Stringer nudged me with his elbow.

"Look at Wallace."

Mike Wallace had walked over to the general and his wife, and the three of them were engaged in an animated, seemingly cheerful conversation.

"He's been working on them for days," Stringer said. "Now they greet him each morning like an old friend."

"Mike has probably convinced the general they were both the victims of their junior officers," I said.

With a trial of such significance taking place a few miles from the newsroom, it was difficult at times to concentrate on the daily routine of business. Correspondent Eric Engberg and producer Suzanne Allen were assigned to cover the trial for CBS News. I made it a point not to screen or ask to see scripts of their stories before they went on the air. I even tried to avoid talking with either of them in the halls of the Broadcast Center or during visits to the courtroom. I knew this perturbed our general counsel, George Vradenburg, who told me repeatedly that David Boies believed CBS News coverage came down harder on CBS than either of the other two networks.

In this atmosphere of tension, election night seemed like a welcome diversion. Rather had given us a scare when the sore throat virus which seemed to plague him at times of major coverage reduced his voice to a rasp a few days before the night of the election. But he bounced back, thanks, he said, "to Mother Rather's famous recipe for red-hot Texas chili," and his energy level on that night was never higher, so high in fact that one television critic described him as "wired as a fox terrier."

He was joined that evening by Diane Sawyer, Bill Moyers, Bob Schieffer, Bill Plante, Lesley Stahl, and Bruce Morton. One face familiar to CBS viewers was not present. The kind of negotiation I'd conducted to find a role for Cronkite at the conventions was less successful in this case. I'd again gone to Rather in an attempt to persuade him that it might be a good idea to bring Walter in late in the evening on election night.

"Walter could do a smaller version of what he did at the conventions," I said. "There was something good about the sight of two generations working together."

The new anchorman wasn't buying it.

"I think I gave a lot to Walter at the conventions," he said. "I brought him right into the anchor booth with me under the heading of 'it's all right to test my good nature, just don't start abusing it.' Walter will have to understand that he's had a lot of election nights. This one is Dan Rather's."

By midafternoon on election day our exit-poll data were showing quite conclusively that Reagan would win a second term and by a wide margin. But at 6:30 P.M., when Rather came on the air for the first time, CBS News took pains not to project a winner when it was still midafternoon in California and the other Western states. Rather cautiously told viewers that "there were indications that a substantial win for Ronald Reagan may be borne out if voting trends don't change by the time all the polls have closed." This careful language failed to satisfy the congressional critics. Later that evening Representative Tim Wirth of Colorado issued a statement that network coverage fell short of the restraint he'd hoped for and Congress had asked for. Before the night was over he was calling it a "real disregard for the integrity of the electoral process." Evidently we could expect more congressional hearings and quite possibly an attempt at restrictive legislation.

Shortly after election night I got a phone call from Van on the West Coast.

"I just had lunch with the Hook," he said.

The Hook was Ed Hookstratten, a Los Angeles agent who represented among others Tom Brokaw of NBC and Tom Snyder, the newsman turned talk-show host. Both Van and I had dealt with Hookstratten during our days in Los Angeles. The Hook was a balding fellow in his fifties and built along the lines of William Conrad, the actor who played the private eye Cannon on television. Frequent diets had modified, but only slightly, the clear evidence that for Hookstratten breakfast, lunch, and dinner were business expenses. During my days at KNXT in Los Angeles he'd represented several of our on-air people, including sportscaster Jim Hill. I'd found him relentless during negotiations and honorable once an agreement had been reached. A profile of him in the New York *Times* quoted me as saying, "He's the kind of guy you like to play cards with." I wasn't surprised to hear from Van that the two of them had lunched together. In fact, I was mildly envious, knowing what a trencherman Hookstratten was.

"Who picked up the check?" I asked.

"Have you ever known an agent to pick up a check when there's a CBS Amex card in the room?"

"Not in my lifetime."

"Listen," Van said, turning serious. "Ed has a client he says is dying to do *The CBS Morning News.*"

"Who's that?"

A brief pause.

"Phyllis George."

To me Phyllis George was the very pretty woman who sat next to Brent Musburger on Sundays during *The NFL Today.* I knew she was a former Miss America who had become a sportscaster, one of the first women to break the sex barrier in television sports. I'm a runner. And I fish, swim, and ride horses. But team sports have always bored me stiff. My pulse does not quicken during the World Series, and Super Bowl Sunday has always represented a marvelous opportunity to avoid the lines at a movie I've been eager to see. Except for the Olympics, the Iron Man Triathlon, and the rare rodeo, I do not watch televised sports.

"Phyllis George. Well, you know I never watch sports," I said. "Is she any good? Is she smart? She worked for you when you ran Sports, didn't she?"

"Correct. I think she's a hardworking, bright woman. She's done a lot of interviews. I know your concern about finding someone with a news background. But Phyllis has the sort of name Jankowski is looking for and she's not from some Hollywood sitcom."

"Is she traveled?" I asked. "Is she a sophisticated person?"

"Well, she was First Lady of the state of Kentucky," Van said.

"That's right. I forgot she's married to John Y. Brown. Hey, if she lives in Kentucky and flies in on weekends for *The NFL Today,* that's one thing. But would she want to move to New York and get up in the middle of the night to do a morning show?"

"I only know what Hookstratten tells me. He says more than anything else, Phyllis wants to do this morning program. We could revamp the format. Let Kurtis do all of the news material and let her handle feature interviews, hand-overs to the weatherman, that sort of thing."

"I don't know, Van. I still think we'd be better off going with Jane Wallace."

"Ed, I've told you for months that Jankowski is never going to buy into Wallace. You can't go on much longer with no replacement for Sawyer and not have Jankowski begin to ask questions about the way CBS News is being run if it can't come up with someone better than Wallace. I've mentioned Phyllis to Gene and he thinks it's a dynamite idea. Why don't you talk to the Hook and see if he could get Phyllis to come in for a few weeks on the broadcast as a replacement. Then make up your mind. I'm afraid if Gene doesn't see some movement he's going to start thinking seriously about turning the time period over to the Entertainment Division."

The first call I made after talking to Van was not to Ed Hookstratten but to Bob Morse, the general manager of WHAS-TV in Louisville. I'd known Bob since the early seventies when we both were television news directors. The previous May, Maureen and I had been his guests at the Kentucky Derby. I felt at ease explaining to Bob the reason for my call.

"What can you tell me about her?" I asked.

"First of all, I can tell you without a doubt that John Y. would not have been elected governor without her."

"What kind of First Lady was she? Did she handle herself well?"

"She was an excellent First Lady," Bob said. "She initiated some fine programs and handled herself well in public. She's very popular here in Kentucky."

My next call was to Ed Hookstratten, who proceeded to tell me quickly he'd never seen anything like it.

"All America loves Phyllis George."

If I'd had the slightest gift of clairvoyance I would have said, "CBS News will fix that."

Instead, I made the arrangement for Phyllis to do a two-week replacement with the proviso that we not refer to it publicly as a "tryout."

Then I called Katz and Stringer and told them what we were doing.

Stringer was immediately enthusiastic.

"She's certainly presold, I'll say that."

Katz was skeptical.

"Do you really think this is a good idea?"

"Unfortunately, it's the only idea," I said. "We pissed away months grooming Jane Wallace, who's dead in the water. None of us—and I include myself—has come up with an acceptable candidate who fits the presold definition. Under the theory that any strategy is better than no strategy at all, I think we'd better watch Phyllis George with an open mind."

The press did not for one moment accept the simple replacement explanation for the arrival of Phyllis George. Shrewdly, they saw it for the on-air audition it was. The day that Phyllis arrived for her first rehearsal, I looked up from my desk and saw a very pretty woman standing in the doorway. It took me an instant to recognize who it was. She walked in and immediately gave me a big hug and then began to laugh. We'd never met before.

"Ed told me to do that," she said. "I told him I was nervous about meeting you. I said he's going to be some hard-boiled newsman who's used to dealing with Dan Rather and all those correspondents. Ed said you're really a nice man and I should just come in and give you a big hug."

From that day on I liked Phyllis George. She is a lovely woman who was tragically miscast by a number of us in a role where she would inevitably fail.

Most of those who worked with her during her two-week tryout on the *Morning News* were impressed by her willingness to work and to learn, and by her extra effort to make it clear that she was not pretending to be a newswoman. Even Katz, who'd been initially suspicious, was now enthusiastic.

"Maybe it's just that I've never been around a star before," he said. "But they are different."

Katz was referring not only to the deluge of requests for interviews with Phyllis from newspapers and magazines but to the entourage which accompanied her arrival: her own makeup man and a full-time public-relations woman, unfamiliar trappings even in television news.

"I think if we redo the format we can make it work," Katz said. "Let Kurtis do the news blocks. We're going to have to add a heavy in Washington to conduct political interviews because now neither one of our anchors can handle this. Phyllis because she shouldn't, Kurtis because he's just not good at it. There are plenty of topics suitable for a morning program, from health to parenting, which Phyllis can do."

The initial reaction to Phyllis George within CBS News was remarkably temperate considering the history of that stormy institution. Even veterans such as Joan Richman were surprisingly supportive of her arrival. Joan went so far as to come to me and tell me she knew Phyllis from Sports and thought "she just might be terrific."

Over the next few days I negotiated a contract on the phone with Hookstratten. It was a straightforward agreement with no special arrangements for dressing rooms or limousines, and was typical of many other CBS News contracts. The first year's salary was $700,000.

On December 3, 1984, CBS News announced that Phyllis George would join *The CBS Morning News* on a permanent basis. The next morning the New York *Times,* in reporting this, quoted Richard Salant, a former CBS News President, someone I admired very much and still do. Salant told the *Times* that appointing an anchor without journalistic experience "demeans news and places that division in the realm of entertainment."

I still felt uneasy about the hire of Phyllis George but relieved that, for now at least, the threat of losing that time period to the Entertainment Division had been headed off. The selection of someone from outside television news was not without precedence for CBS. In the sixties, Harry Reasoner for two years had shared the role of host on a midmorning program called *Calendar* with a Broadway actress named Mary Fickett, who'd been selected by Dick Salant. In the seventies, Salant chose Sally Quinn, a writer for the "Style" section of the Washington *Post,* to join Hughes Rudd as co-anchor of *The CBS Morning News.* Quinn was known at the time for her breezy portrayals of life on the cocktail-party circuit in Washington and had never worked in television. Then, in the seventies, Dan Rather hosted a prime-time magazine broadcast titled *Who's Who.* His partner was Barbara Howar, a lively young woman whose tour of television talk shows while promoting a book on the social foibles of Washington had brought her to Salant's notice.

So hiring Phyllis George was not quite the heretical departure some were claiming. On the other hand, this past history did not suggest that hiring Phyllis George was a wise idea. I justified it to myself by reflecting on the number of people who would be unemployed at CBS News if Jankowski should ever follow through on the threat to turn the morning time period over to the Entertainment Division. I crossed my fingers and determined to do everything I could to assure Phyllis's success.

In November, I received a note from Bill Moyers which seemed to indicate his intention to remain at CBS News. He had never sent me the letter asking for a release. The note I finally received some two months later began by saying, "All this time we thought the ball was in one another's court." Moyers described having stayed late composing his letter. The room with the copy machine, he said, had been locked, so he had placed his letter in a gray CBS envelope marked "personal and confidential" and pushed it under the door of my office and left for home. I smiled as I read the note; I knew I had never received such an envelope. Bill concluded with "on the other hand we've both been busy." I took that as an indication that he was no longer intending to leave CBS News and I was delighted. What's more, I had an idea for a documentary subject. I knew that Bill had been hurt when Andy Lack agreed to stay, but I was sure that losing Lack as a partner had probably made him less anxious to move to NBC. I met with Bill and encouraged him once again to undertake some documentaries for *CBS Reports.* I suggested that he examine on his first broadcast the complex issue of immigration. He seemed interested. Then I broached another matter I found troubling.

"Bill, I normally try to ignore rumors and you know what a rumor factory this is . . . but I'm hearing with increasing frequency that you've been telling some of the senior correspondents that you're trying to set up a meeting with Wyman."

The truth of the matter was that he'd had such a conversation with Bill

Kurtis, who'd then told Katz, who immediately picked up the phone to alert me to what he called in barely suppressed amusement "the Decembrist plot."

Bill couldn't mask his surprise that I'd found out about this.

"I wasn't going to tell you, Ed," he said. "I tend to work ideas through my own mind by testing them on people to see how they react. That I am then quoted shouldn't surprise me, I suppose. But yes, I am going to ask to see Wyman. I plan to tell him about the frustration many of us feel with the executive structure under which you work. I have nothing against Van. He is a charming and bright individual. He just doesn't stand for quality in journalism. That's not where his interests are to be found. A number of us believe that you're quite different. That if left alone, Ed Joyce would help us get serious journalism into prime time. If left alone, Ed Joyce would not hire a Phyllis George. But you can't do it when the man you work for is Van Sauter. You are not in the role where you can speak as the executive voice of CBS News to Jankowski or Wyman. That's why they have Van there. His is the voice who interprets CBS News for them and that's why we have these problems. I'm going to urge Wyman to find some other role for Van . . . something he'd be more comfortable with anyway, I'm sure . . . and to allow you to do your job with a free hand."

"Bill, I won't tell you not to see Tom Wyman," I said. "But before you seek such a meeting I think you should consider it in the context of what's taking place right now on Foley Square. CBS is defending itself in one of the most significant libel suits in history. It's made more complex because many of us are ashamed of the way that broadcast was prepared. If you say to Tom Wyman what you've just said to me, he's not going to know if you're totally right or completely wrong. He won't know how to react; so he'll go to Gene Jankowski, who created the structure in the first place. Gene will probably discuss it with Van and he'll certainly ask Rather's opinion. I will hear about it through Van, not directly from Gene. You've already discussed it with a number of people here, so we'll have all the makings of a civil war. The reputation of CBS News is already on trial in one courthouse and being raked over each day in the press. This is all they'd need. CBS News might never recover."

Bill left my office and called me later that day to say he would not meet with Wyman. Instead, he would start researching the topic of immigration for a future *CBS Reports* broadcast, and he added, "I hope I've made the right decision."

The Westmoreland trial was very much on my mind. A few days earlier Mike Wallace had been admitted to Lenox Hill Hospital suffering from "exhaustion." The past twelve months had not been kind to Mike. After years of marriage, his third wife, Lorraine, had left him and moved to Fiji to be near a son by a previous marriage and her grandson. Mike seemed devastated by this and I concocted a research assignment in the South Pacific to allow him to visit her. He'd returned with the news that they'd mutually decided to seek a divorce. On top of that he faced the inevitable day when he would have to take the stand and answer questions about his involvement or lack of it in the preparation of the Westmoreland documentary. Mike's hospitalization was the result of this pressure. While Mike was still in the hospital, Jankowski's office began to get phone calls from an unidentified male voice claiming to have proof that Mike Wallace was hospitalized because of a drug overdose. David Fuchs, the Senior Vice President on Jankowski's staff, arranged a meeting with the caller at the Hilton Hotel. Fuchs came away from the meeting convinced of two things. One, that we were dealing with a disturbed person who in exchange for silence wanted a job in broadcasting. Two, that he did indeed have a copy of the Lenox Hill admittance records for Mike and that they contained some reference to drugs. It fell to Don Hewitt and me to call Mike in his hospital room and tell him about this bizarre extortion attempt and also advise him that someone was threatening to send copies of the hospital records to the local papers. I waited for Mike to say there was nothing to it. When he didn't I became more direct.

"Mike, this is not an area I'm comfortable in as an intruder," I said. "But if this guy does have something and is going to send it to the papers we have to know how to handle it."

"Ed's right, Mike," Hewitt said. "If this nut sends something like that to 'Page 6' at the New York *Post,* imagine what they'll do with it."

Mike authorized us to talk with his doctor, who gave us an account of what had actually happened. Mike had been so agitated and so despondent his doctor placed him on medication to help him sleep and to decrease the level of his anxiety. As a result of the use of these prescription drugs, Mike had suffered a reaction at home one afternoon and with a friend had walked on his own to the emergency room of Lenox Hill Hospital. The records at the time of his admittance substantiated the doctor's account. Consequently, Fuchs told the would-be extortionist to disappear and not to expect enhanced career opportunities at CBS. A few days later our Press Department got a call from "Page 6" asking questions about the cause of Mike's hospitalization.

The matter was never pursued and quietly died. Mike came home a few days later and began attending the trial once more on a regular basis. It seemed at the time to be just one more bizarre development growing out of a broadcast which would plague us all for years to come. Dan Burt's boast that he would dismantle CBS News was one he failed to fulfill in the courtroom. But there is no doubt in my mind that what he failed to do before a judge and jury he accomplished in other ways.

For almost three years CBS News was placed on the defensive by an old warrior and his feisty lawyer, who had said from the outset that Westmoreland sought neither money nor vengeance, that the issue was whether a television network can rob an honorable man of his reputation. The more frequently our public statements repeated our support for what we called "the substance of the broadcast," the more we were viewed by some Americans as an arrogant media giant. We carefully watched the Nielsen ratings for signs of disaffection for either the *Evening News* or *60 Minutes* and saw none. The *Evening News* sailed along several share points ahead of its two competitors in the Nielsen ratings and *60 Minutes* stayed on the list of television's top ten programs. We continued to be successful, but to a group of men belonging to the National Congressional Club in Raleigh, North Carolina, we also remained powerful, much too powerful. And they were determined to change that.

The membership of the club consisted of a group of political activists who were longtime political and fund-raising associates of Jesse Helms, the conservative Republican senator from North Carolina. Together they created a group called Fairness in Media, whose purpose was to challenge what they considered to be the pervasive liberal bias in American journalism.

In early January, Jack Smith, our Washington Bureau chief, called and the first thing he said was "Have you heard anything about an article in the Raleigh *News & Observer?*"

"Not a thing."

"They're reporting that Jesse Helms has sent a five-page letter to conservatives around the country urging them to buy CBS stock."

I chuckled. "Is Helms a stockbroker on the side? What's that all about?"

"You got me, but according to the newspaper, his letter urges conservatives to buy up stock in CBS so they can take control of the network and—are you ready for this?—become Dan Rather's boss."

This time I laughed out loud. "I ought to invite him up here for a week to see how he likes it. His next letter would begin 'On second thought.' Jack, I'll call the Law Department and see if they know anything. I hope Vradenburg doesn't laugh me off the phone."

Vradenburg, as it turned out, wasn't laughing.

"Yes, it's true," he said. "They're filing the required documents today with the SEC. We're meeting now on a lawsuit we'll file against them in federal court. We think this group, FIM, is in violation of federal securities laws."

"A lawsuit? Isn't that overreacting a bit? Does anyone really think that Jesse Helms and a bunch of people nobody ever heard of down in Raleigh are going to take over CBS?"

"We're worried about what this might trigger, that some corporate raider might start thinking about a move on CBS," Vradenburg said. "Look, you guys can't report any of this. The SEC has very strict rules relating to proxy solicitations of shareholders."

"George, I can assure you that when you watch *The CBS Evening News* tonight you're going to see this story in some form."

"I don't know how the SEC would regard . . ."

I interrupted him. "Then I would say the SEC would be in direct collision with the First Amendment."

"You may be right, but make sure that no one at CBS News issues a response to Helms until we've sorted ourselves out with the SEC."

"How long will it take?"

"A few weeks," he said. "Perhaps longer."

"Tomorrow morning I'm flying to Richmond to speak at the Virginia Association of Broadcasters lunch," I said. "Whatever I say there will be reported by the wire services and picked up by papers around the country. The President of CBS News can't very well speak about journalism but say 'no comment' when Jesse Helms is telling people they should take over CBS and become Dan Rather's boss."

"Ed, the SEC is very strict on this business of proxy solicitations. You're an officer of the company. They would consider this a case of your using a public forum to speak to CBS shareholders."

"George, I appreciate that, but I'm going to have to say something. I'll write it on the plane. If CBS as a company has prepared a response by then, I'll be glad to use that. But I've got to say something."

By the time my plane touched down the next morning in Richmond, my response to Fairness in Media was written.

"Now we are hearing from groups with names that begin 'Truth in,' 'Accuracy in,' 'Fairness in.' Inevitably these are groups that want their narrow ideological biases to dominate the media and ultimately the country. They just don't want their voices to be heard, they want theirs to be the loudest voices.

"When you hear from one of these deceptively named organizations, recognize clearly that you are hearing from those who would like to bring upon us all the Dark Night of the Yahoos."

For over three years I'd watched CBS News at work and I believed the charge of liberal bias was unfounded. Excesses and/or misjudgments committed by television news are likelier to arise from competitive frenzy, the adolescent exaltation in being first in the Nielsen ratings, than from ideological bent.

FIM claimed it had targeted CBS and Rather for its campaign because it believed CBS was the most anti-Reagan of all the networks. Similar complaints had been raised in the past by supporters of Lyndon Johnson, Richard Nixon, and Jimmy Carter. I believed CBS News had been selected as the focal point of the FIM campaign because the Westmoreland trial had placed us in an adversarial relationship with a military figure respected by the right wing and because CBS was number one. If CBS News could be punished, the other networks would become more cautious and fall in line. I had no idea what Rather's own politics were. I never had that sort of discussion with him. For the same reason that I was registered as an Independent voter I took care to avoid acquiring any sort of political label. I would have been particularly sensitive to any attempt to inject a partisan tone into the news product of CBS. When in 1984 David Gergen left the Reagan White House, where he'd been assistant to the President for communications, he said in an interview in *Broadcasting* magazine that he thought it was true that "CBS is the hardest-nosed and the hardest-edged in its coverage," but he added, "If we were a wildly liberal administration, I think they would have the same hard edge." I thought Gergen was right on the money. Even George Crile's ethical lapses in preparing the Westmoreland documentary never struck me as the result of a political philosophy. If Stringer was right, Crile was a die-hard conservative. Pride, ambition, and greed might lead to our downfall, but not ideology.

At the Richmond Hyatt, with minutes to go before my speech, I called New York and was given the CBS statement in response to the Helms-FIM offensive. It was mild but firm in tone and I was glad to see that much at least.

"To seek control of a corporation for the sole purpose of subjecting its news operations to political influence is to contradict the traditions of a free and uninhibited press. CBS intends to take all appropriate steps to maintain the independence and integrity of its news organization."

I incorporated that into my speech along with what I'd written on the plane. It was the first of many talks I would give defending CBS News from Helms and others interested in becoming "Dan Rather's boss," and in this role I was strangely alone. The senior executives of the corporation were muted in their initial public response.

Rather came to see me after the Richmond speech, expressing his concern over the lack of public statements from Wyman, Jankowski, and Sauter defending CBS News against the charge of liberal bias and over the increasing number of speeches by Helms, who'd begun to refer to me as "the august Mr. Joyce."

"Ed, I want you to tell Tom and Gene," he said, "that if it's felt I've become a liability to CBS, I want them and you to know they only have to tell me that and I'll step aside."

I've encountered more sincerity in a call congratulating me for being eligible to buy $50,000 worth of group term life insurance if I would just supply a few simple details. The anchorman made his short speech and then stopped, his face assuming the same half smile he uses at the end of his broadcast right after he's laid four extra vowels into "good niiiiight."

For the briefest second I was tempted to say, "Tom and Gene have been discussing this possibility with me, but, Dan, it hasn't come to this yet." However, the image of myself pouring cold Perrier on the unconscious face of the world's most expensive anchorman helped me control that impulse. Instead, I described the mood at Black Rock.

"No one over there thinks Helms and his crew have a prayer of controlling CBS. What they're worried about is who else might be out there deciding that CBS is an attractive target. Have you been watching our stock shoot up? This company is in play and that's what shakes them up."

None of that seemed to register on Rather.

"But I'm the one being targeted," he said.

"Dan, you're just a symbol in this fight because you are the nightly face of CBS News. No one in Black Rock holds you responsible for this."

Momentarily mollified, he left.

CBS stock, which had been priced at $73.88 a share when Helms and FIM announced their campaign, approached $90 a share by mid-March and the nation's financial press was paying close attention. *Business Week* magazine ran an article in March with the headline "Even the Networks May Be Fair Game. Talk of a CBS Takeover Has Everyone Thinking the Unthinkable." It quoted the merger chief of a major Wall Street investment bank as saying, "If you were going to bust up a network, the values would be fantastic." The same article went on to say, "In fact, stock market interest in the networks was stimulated by a conservative group, led by Senator Jesse Helms, which was formed to raise money to buy CBS stock in protest of what group members consider biased news coverage."

In the midst of the Helms attack and the Westmoreland trial, Phyllis George made her debut on *The CBS Morning News*. She arrived at the studio accompanied by Vincent, her hairdresser, and Dee Emerson, her public-relations representative. Phyllis paid for the services of Dee and CBS paid Vincent. I'd balked at this at first, but Katz had convinced me it was something we should do.

"The guy's not just a hairdresser, he's an important part of her life. They get into screaming matches about her hair or the clothes she should be wearing, but she loves him. When she's tense, he gives her neck massages to relax her."

Katz saw the look on my face.

"It's not like that," he quickly added. "Vincent is a very smart, very nice guy. I was talking to him about commuting each day to New Jersey and he mentioned that he lives there, too, with his wife and kids. I guess he could see me staring at his leather suit and he said, 'Oh, this? It's just a look.' Hey, if he can help keep Phyllis relaxed and focused on the job, it's in our best interest to have him around."

Wherever Phyllis went, somewhere in her vicinity was a reassuring figure dressed in pants and a tunic made of black leather.

Katz was less kindly disposed toward another member of the Phyllis George family, the Hook.

Hookstratten flew in from California for the first broadcast and showed up in the control room. For the CBS News production staff the sight of an agent in a control room was something of a shock. Katz reassured them that being surrounded by old friends and familiar faces helped reduce the tension Phyllis was understandably feeling. A few days later he wasn't so certain. Shortly after 9 A.M. he came to see me. The broadcast had just gone off the air, and he arrived in my office looking more disheveled than usual, his shirttail out, a cloud of cotton plaid dropping from the folds of a black wool sweater.

"I'm going to kill that fucking Hookstratten," he said.

"And good morning to you. What's wrong?"

"You know he showed up the first morning in the control room?"

"Yeah, I know. You thought that was fine."

"Well, he's been there *every* morning."

"I didn't know that."

"Phyllis'll arrive in a great mood and we've got interviews set up for her . . . a nice range of things she can handle . . . William DeVries, the heart surgeon, or Billy Crystal, the comedian. She'll be so happy that Vincent doesn't even have to rub her neck. Then the Hook descends on her and she's like a little girl who's been scolded by the teacher. Suddenly she's nervous, pouty, and it affects her on the air."

"What is he telling her?"

"I know exactly what he tells her because Phyllis tells me," Katz said. "The woman is absolutely guileless. He's telling her she'll never make it unless she starts doing hard-news interviews like Kurtis."

"That wasn't what she was hired for. She knows that and so does Hookstratten."

"This morning at the end of the broadcast, she stopped and said, 'Jon, I want to do some interviews that make news. I want to interview that Gandhi woman.' "

"Jon," I said, "I think that request should remain our little secret. Did you point out that Mrs. Gandhi was assassinated some time ago?"

"I did. I said, 'Phyllis . . . she's dead.' And her answer was 'Oh . . . well, somebody like her.' "

"Stay where you are," I said. "I'm going to see if Hookstratten has gone back to his hotel room."

My secretary buzzed a few minutes later to tell me he was on the line.

"Ed, I've known you for a long time," I said when I picked up the phone, "so I won't beat around the bush. Stay the fuck out of this building."

I described the openness Phyllis was receiving from people at CBS News.

"But that won't last long if she attempts to be something she's not and starts trying to do interviews she can't handle. And I can tell you for sure it won't last if a perception develops that she's some lightweight who has to have her agent there every morning holding her hand."

I described her request to interview Mrs. Gandhi and told him that if that sort of story began to circulate, the results could be devastating.

"Ed," I said, "I like you . . . you're a nice guy . . . but stay away."

Hookstratten laughed. "O.K., you big prick, I'll stay away. But I gotta tell you . . . you newsies suck."

Phyllis had difficulty remembering who was alive and who was dead. In the interview with Billy Crystal, who was a wonderful mimic, she asked him if Fernando Lamas, Crystal's favorite impersonation, ever wrote or called Crystal after one of his appearances on television. The straight-faced response from Crystal was "Well, I think he died a few years ago."

From that day on, lists were kept.

Katz and his hardworking staff came up with an idea for a group of interviews which they felt would show Phyllis at her best. They called it the "Women of Influence" series, and it gave Phyllis an opportunity to talk with Sally Ride, Gloria Steinem, Jane Fonda, and Dianne Feinstein. The interviews were taped outside the Broadcast Center rather than done live, and even though they benefited from editing, they boosted the staff's morale. Phyllis seemed comfortable chatting with these bright achievers.

When I complimented Jon on the series, he replied, "Well, we managed to get it done in spite of every obstacle David Buksbaum could mount. He treats the requests we make for camera crews like an assault on the *Evening News.*"

"Have you mentioned this to Howard?"

"Howard's in and out these days because of the trial, but yes, I've mentioned it. Howard doesn't want to get on Rather's wrong side."

That afternoon when Howard returned from Foley Square I collared him.

"You've got to run some interference for Katz. Buksbaum will walk all over that broadcast unless you step in and say the *Morning News* helps pay for correspondents, crews, and bureaus. They have a right to use them, too."

Howard looked uncomfortable. "Dan's got it in his mind that the *Morning News* is draining resources from his broadcast and David is busy showing him that he's putting a stop to that."

"I'll remind David that he's a CBS News Vice President, not an *Evening News* executive," I said, "but you've got to stay on top of it, and by the way, it's absurd. The *Evening News* has never had as many resources as it does now."

Howard sighed. "I know that, mate, but try telling it to Dan."

"You know," I said, "in 1981 it was a great challenge to make this organization more responsive to the *Evening News,* to give Rather the support he needed from the bureaus. But Jesus, he's become like that ornamental vine from Japan, the kudzu, that was introduced in Georgia a few years ago. Now it's spread its tendrils all over the whole damned South. Buildings actually collapse from the weight of the kudzu weed and that's what's going to happen here unless we find a way to prune Dan back."

"It won't be that easy, I'm afraid," Howard said, "and he now has a Vice President in charge of the preservation of kudzu."

One bit of good news occurred in early January. Two of the most relentless critics of the networks on the issue of early election projections and characterizations based on exit-poll information came up with a way to break the impasse. Congressman Al Swift of Washington and William

Thomas of California proposed seeking legislation to introduce a uniform poll-closing time throughout the country on election day if the three networks would agree not to use exit-poll data to project winners or characterize races before the closing of the polls. They were particularly concerned about characterization, the description of the likely outcome of a race using phrases such as "shaping up as a possible win" or "it looks like an upset is in the making." All three networks jumped on this opportunity to gracefully get out of this aspect of the exit-poll business. At the time, achieving a uniform poll closing seemed as likely as reintroducing prohibition, but it was a face-saving way for the networks to discontinue their practice without the appearance of withholding information from the public because of congressional pressure.

A few days after the announcement I was the guest at an editorial lunch at the New York *Times.* It was hosted by Arthur Gelb from the "Arts and Leisure" section of that newspaper and their two reporters who covered television at that time, Sally Bedell Smith and Peter Kaplan. I'd been looking forward to the lunch. It was not just a social occasion but a two-hour question-and-answer session with the understanding that everything said was on the record and would quite possibly result in an article in the paper. Before lunch I jotted a few notes for myself on issues I thought might be raised, including the recent announcement on exit polls. As it turned out, exit polls weren't mentioned. The *Times* wanted an answer to the question I would be asked for months wherever I traveled in the country: "Why did you hire Phyllis George?" I responded as I would again and again, that Phyllis was a seasoned broadcaster with a personality and presence we believed would be valuable on the *Morning News.* Then I threw in what would become a standard caveat—that Bill Kurtis would handle the news blocks and the interviews and reports on such subjects as politics and government policy. I didn't mention that I was in the process of hiring a New York *Times* reporter, Terence Smith, to become the Washington interviewer for the broadcast because Kurtis was as inept in handling such interviews as Phyllis George. Following the lunch, Sally Bedell Smith, who had been assigned to write the story, spent several days talking to a cross section of people at CBS News. The article which appeared in the Sunday "Arts and Leisure" section on February 3, 1985, was headlined "CBS News Is Changing, Cautiously." It described me as "reserved" as my predecessor, Van Sauter, was "garrulous," and went on to say, "So far Mr. Joyce, who is fifty-two, appears to have successfully straddled the force of change and traditions at CBS News. He has continued to modernize and transform the structure of the organization; yet he has begun to talk about rejuvenating the documentary form, a CBS tradition that for several years has seemed in jeopardy. Simultaneously, he has kept operations running smoothly for the nearly four months that CBS News has been in a New York courtroom."

Consistent with my long-standing practice of always providing one quote for each interviewer which when reduced to print would make me wince, I endeavored to explain the ingrained resistance to change at CBS News by saying, "Whatever we do, there is always a Greek chorus in the background humming 'this time we've gone too far.' " As usual, I was amused when saying it and embarrassed when reading it. The truth was, my attempt to reinstitute the documentary at CBS News was very much influenced by a desire to effect change and still preserve tradition in a way that would earn the approval of the Greek chorus. In general, though, it was a positive appraisal in an important publication at a time when most newspaper articles about CBS dealt with Jesse Helms vs. CBS or the ongoing Westmoreland trial. Van's shrewd analysis of how perceptions were formed at Black Rock— "all they know about us is what they read in the press"—was brought home to me in the days immediately following the *Times* piece. Jankowski's monthly staff meeting took place that week. During the morning almost every executive in the conference room found a way to mention the article with comments which ranged from "Good ink" to "Who's your press agent?" Van was the only one of the group who didn't comment. This was so unusual I spent the rest of the day thinking about what might be bothering him. The *Times* had asked about our relationship to one another given the fact that Van's job required him to "put a final stamp on decisions" and I'd answered as truthfully as I could without getting into specifics. "Obviously there are times when we do disagree. Sometimes he prevails and sometimes I do."

That night I picked up dinner for Maureen and me at one of the Chinese restaurants on Columbus Avenue, and our kitchen counter was lined with cardboard cartons filled with steamed dumplings and General Ching's chicken. I was uncorking an inexpensive Muscadet and the cork was crumbling and falling back into the bottle.

"Damn," I said, "we'll be drinking pieces of cork all night."

"I'll give you some cheesecloth," Maureen said. "You can use it as a strainer."

"By that time the dumplings will be cold."

"Then chew cork," Maureen advised. "You're in a grumpy mood."

"I guess I am. I'm irritated with Van." I described his silence. "It particularly hit me at Jankowski's staff meeting," I said. "Each time someone would make a comment about the article, even give me a little needle, Van would grow more morose."

"It's the geranium principle," Maureen said.

"The what?"

"The geranium principle. See my flowers on the windowsill here? They're lined up side by side because when I had them in double rows the plant in the back couldn't get enough light. The geranium in front blocked the light. That's what you're doing to Van."

"Hardly," I said. "I think he spends half his days talking to reporters."

"That's my point. That's his sunlight. He needs it. You'd be just as happy if you never talked to a reporter. The kids and I can't even get you to keep a scrapbook."

"Oh, don't start on me with that again."

"We've given up," she said, "but I don't know why you're so surprised at Van's reaction. Do you think he's happy in that job?"

"I think he's torn. He wants to be there but he doesn't want to be there. He's finally beginning to spend more time with the Stations Division. They're trying to get some syndicated show going to run in the afternoon as a lead-in for their news broadcasts."

"Good," Maureen said. "Do you realize this is the first time you've admitted to me you don't think Van is happy in his job?"

"Must be the cork in this wine."

"Pour yourself another glass," Maureen said, "and maybe you'll tell me whose idea it was to hire Phyllis."

I folded tinfoil over the top of the wine bottle in place of the ruined cork and put the bottle in the refrigerator.

"It wasn't my idea," I said, "but I sure as hell didn't throw my body in front of the tracks to stop it. Now I've got to make it work. May we please knock this off? Why don't we eat our dumplings and talk about our grandchildren."

The next morning I'd barely settled in at my desk when my secretary told me Dan Rather had called asking if he could drop by for a cup of coffee. Waiting for him to arrive, I found myself smiling. I'd peeled that tinfoil off the bottle of white wine the night before and Maureen and I found ourselves talking, of all things, about *The Best Little Whorehouse in Texas*. Neither of us had seen the play or the movie until some friends had invited us to join them at a local dinner theater in Connecticut. The show had been performed by a cast which could most charitably be referred to as semi-professional. Maureen had remembered how entranced I'd been by one character in the musical, a Texas politician with resonances of LBJ who sings and dances a number called "the sidestep." One line from the song particularly amused me. "I'm a poor boy come to greatness, so it follows that I cannot tell a lie . . . ooo . . . I love to dance the little sidestep—now they see me, now they don't."

"You laughed so hard I was embarrassed," Maureen had said.

"I couldn't help it," I answered. "You've asked me what it's like to work with Dan. That's him."

Now he was about to come into my office and I found myself almost eager for the performance. It didn't take long for it to begin. After a few sips of black coffee and several assurances that "my troops sure admire the way you've spoken back to Helms," I could almost hear the melody begin.

"You know I respect Tom Wyman as a leader of this company."

"I know you do, Dan. You've said that many times."

"But a lot of my folks were expecting more from that speech he made this week at Duke University."

On Tuesday, February 5, 1985, Wyman had been the guest speaker of the Sloan Colloquium in Communications at Duke. His subject was "The First Amendment and Professional Broadcast Journalism." He'd addressed the Helms challenge in spite of advice I knew he was receiving from the CBS Law Department not to mention it lest the SEC view his remarks as proxy solicitation. He said the issue before us was "who is to monitor the objectivity."

"People," he continued, "tend to have very mistaken views about the relationship of CBS corporate management to the CBS News Division. While corporate management is clearly accountable for all that takes place in the company, our standards dictate a 'separation of powers' when it comes to reporting the news . . . and they should. We believe it is essential to maintain the independence and integrity of our news organization."

And he added, "It is this professional independence and integrity which the senator and his supporters would have you overlook."

I thought it was a low-key but nevertheless supportive speech and I told Rather so.

"I suppose we were all expecting a speech that would raise hell from here to hoorah," he said.

"And what you got was a measured statement."

"That's right."

"Dan, I think you have to appreciate that by its nature the soul of a corporation is timid. There are certainly voices around Wyman urging

4 2 6

him to lie back and let people like Joyce take the public heat. I think we need to support and encourage the guy to do more of this. It doesn't much matter how well it was done."

"I take your point," he said. "At least something got said."

"It's like the walrus at the circus who does a few tricks and then applauds with its huge flippers," I said. "It would be rude to point out that the beast is clumsy. It's amazing enough that he's doing it, so we applaud, too."

"I like that description," Dan said. "I may use it to fire up some of my people. Maybe I'm just edgy because the Helms people have used my name."

"Dan, you make a lot of speeches."

"This SEC concern holds me back, though."

"Not really," I said. "Hell, I'm an officer of the company and I've spoken out. Vradenburg might not appreciate my saying this, but from an SEC point of view you're just another contract employee." I caught myself quickly and added, "Our most important contract employee, of course."

"Well, that comes under the heading of news I can use," Rather said.

A few minutes later he left, and I sat alone in my office feeling certain of two things: that he would continue to complain to others that Wyman's address at Duke had been inadequate, and that there would be no speech from Dan Rather lambasting Senator Jesse Helms.

That same week was a big one for Howard Stringer. David Boies told him that because Burt had so botched his cross-examination of George Crile and had dragged it through so many additional days, it was unlikely he would have time to call Stringer to the stand. Howard was ebullient. It was also the week he was sworn in as an American citizen. In a courtroom on Foley Square in lower Manhattan, Howard raised his right hand and agreed to relinquish all loyalties to foreign monarchs. Van and I had accompanied Howard and his wife, Jennifer, to the courtroom, and I felt a tug of sympathy for the conflicting emotions an Englishman must feel when he becomes an American and must abandon his Queen. As one who had scolded Howard constantly about the need for him to acquire citizenship, I was touched by this and told him so. The new American still retained his British humor.

"Ah, mate, I'm surprised at you," he said. "You're usually a more observant fellow. I had my fingers crossed."

If Howard had seemed ebullient about evading the witness stand, Van was ecstatic after a phone call from George Vradenburg on Wednesday, February 13.

Actually it was a conference call which connected Vradenburg with both Van and me in our offices. Dan Burt had asked to meet with him to discuss a settlement in the Westmoreland trial. This was a surprising bulletin; shortly before Crile had taken the stand, Burt had offered to settle if CBS would pay $5 million in legal fees and issue a statement saying CBS now believed General Westmoreland had not misled his superiors about enemy troop strength. Vradenburg had come to Van and me at the time and we had told him CBS News would not agree to such a settlement. Then, as recently as January, Burt had returned, dropping the demand for money and offering to settle for just the statement. We still felt such a statement would have been completely at odds with every public utterance about the broadcast made by all of us over the past four years. It, too, was rejected and we took it for granted that the Westmoreland trial not only would go the jury but would be with us for years to come as both sides dealt with the appeal process.

"I don't see what we could give Burt at this late stage," I said. "We've already turned him down twice."

"I agreed to meet with him," Vradenburg said. "But just to make it clear I wasn't jumping at the opportunity, I told him my calendar was full tomorrow and I couldn't see him until Friday."

"What does Boies say about this?" Van asked.

"I haven't told him," Vradenburg said. "David has his hands full in the courtroom. I don't want to distract him unless I think we have something to talk about."

"Well, you've made my day," Van said. "Let's marry up on Friday after you've met with Burt."

Vradenburg laughed. "Van, I didn't think you'd object to this trial ending without your being called to the stand. But, fellows, if I'm going to tell Burt no money, no retraction, no apologies, that boils down to the same kind of statement we would make even if the jury returned a verdict in our favor. That's not a lot to take back to his client."

"Why don't you tell him we have never questioned the general's patriotism or his loyalty," I said, "and we'd be willing to put that in a statement."

"I think," Van added, "you should tell Burt CBS never believed this should have gone to court and we'd be very amenable to a statement which allowed both sides to retire under circumstances of grace and dignity."

On Friday morning, February 15, Vradenburg had breakfast with Burt at the Westbury Hotel, Burt's home during the trial. Afterward he met with Van and me to describe the breakfast.

"Well, big guy, how'd it go?" Van asked.

"Better than I could have expected."

"Wellll!" Van said, his Jack Benny imitation an expression of relief at the news. "This calls for a cigar while I listen to you."

He removed a Davidoff from a humidor and began to clip one end while Vradenburg reported on his meeting.

"Burt started off by telling me that this would be our last chance for a settlement before the case went to the jury. I told him I'd already discussed this with my client and that all we'd be willing to do is issue a statement which talked about the general's patriotism and the general's loyalty . . . no money, no retraction, no apology."

"And Burt said?" The words came bursting out of Van's lungs in a wreath of gray cigar smoke.

"Burt said he understood that," Vradenburg said, "and that he'd like to work on a draft of a joint statement and send it to me later today."

"You should take pride," Van said. "It's over."

George was still cautious. "Let's wait and see how the statement from Burt reads. I'm going to be tied up for a good part of the day with the Corporation on papers we're filing with the SEC. I would suggest that a number of us meet tomorrow to discuss this. I would also suggest that we do it at the Cravath offices in lower Manhattan. The chances of some sharp eye spotting us all arriving for a summit conference are diminished if we meet down there.''

The next morning I arrived at One Chase Manhattan Plaza. The offices of Cravath, Swaine, and Moore occupy several floors of this skyscraper in the heart of New York's financial district. Vradenburg had been right. On a Saturday morning in February, the streets were deserted and the arrival of a large contingent of CBS executives went unnoticed. In addition to myself, the group that gathered in the Cravath conference room included Van Sauter, Gene Jankowski, David Fuchs, a Senior Vice President on Jankowski's staff, George Vradenburg, Catherine Flickinger, an assistant general counsel for CBS, and David Boies. The sense of excitement was palpable. The case that *Newsweek* had called ''the libel trial of the century'' might be on the verge of being settled out of court. Vradenburg began with a recap of his call from Burt and their meeting at the Westbury.

Then he said, ''Before I present Burt's draft of a joint statement, I think you should all hear from David Boies and get his best thinking on what he sees as the likely outcome of this trial if we don't reach a settlement.''

Boies seemed subdued, almost depressed, I thought. A thoroughbred who'd been reined in before he could gallop the final furlong. He presented a brief and expectedly cogent summary of the case so far, saying that he believed CBS would win a favorable verdict on the matter of malice but the issue of truth could go against us. This was a stunning revelation for most of us in that room. In all of his previous estimates Boies had been optimistic about our winning on both charges. Even more so on the appeal level. Then he sobered us up even more with a precise estimate of our chances.

''In fact,'' he said, ''on the truth issue I think we have less than a forty percent chance that the jury will come back with a verdict favorable to CBS.''

''What about the appeal process?'' someone asked.

''The judge has worked very hard, and I think very successfully, to make this an appeal-proof case,'' he answered.

''I don't know about the rest of the people here,'' I said, ''but I'm staggered by what you're saying. I understand you never know what a verdict will be until a jury returns it, but I've been under the impression from all our conversations that we were in better shape than this. First, Burt was so inept with Crile, then Gains Hawkins sat on the stand and testified that Westmoreland had imposed 'a dishonest ceiling' because higher figures were 'politically unacceptable.' ''

Hawkins had been chief of the order-of-battle section of MACV Intelligence.

"Let me answer that in two parts," Boies said with what I thought was a sad smile. "Burt blew his best chance at malice when his cross-examination of Crile fell apart and I just said I think we're all right on the matter of malice. Gains Hawkins was good for us on the truth issue but his cross-examination is not over." In Hawkins's deposition, in fact, he had said he received no such order from Westmoreland about cutting or imposing such a ceiling. "But all of that aside," Boies continued, "the judge has said from the beginning that 'clear and convincing' would in all likelihood be the standard of truth.

"This jury has gotten to know the general very well during this trial. For five months he's been here each day. So has his wife. I've watched the way the jurors look at the Westmorelands. They like them. I know the press made a lot of the general stumbling at times in his testimony. I think he handled himself well and I think the jury does, too. I don't think this jury will come back with a verdict that says General Westmoreland was dishonest or lied to his superiors."

I let out a low whistle while the rest of the group around the long conference table stared into space.

"George, maybe you'd better show everyone the statement Dan Burt gave you," Van said, and I had the impression he might have had an advance look.

Most of the statement seemed straightforward enough, but one part of it I found disturbing. Dan Burt was asking CBS to say that during the course of the discovery process and the trial CBS learned new facts, and if it had known them prior to the broadcast, they not only would have been included but would have significantly altered the content of the broadcast.

"I'm troubled by that," I said. "I don't see how we could possibly agree to say that."

"I'm more than comfortable saying that," Van declared. "It's just one of those lines that will slide right by."

Vradenburg looked worried.

"In view of what we're getting, it doesn't seem like much to give back," he said.

I persisted. "Can you give me an example of what we came across during the trial that we didn't know before?" I asked.

Vradenburg turned to Boies.

"You've lived with the details," he said. "Give Ed a specific."

"Well," he said, "during the course of the trial we uncovered a memo from Army archives describing a briefing attended by Westmoreland's military superior, Admiral Sharp."

"And you feel certain that Crile, if he'd had the memo, would have included it and significantly altered the thrust, or the nature, or the conclusion of his broadcast?"

"I can't be sure, of course," Boies said, "but he might have."

Vradenburg looked across the table at Van, then at me.

"You've heard David say he thinks we have less than a forty percent chance of winning this case. When you consider that, does this statement still bother you?"

"It does, I'm afraid," I said. "If our chances are that slim, David, why do you think Burt wants to settle?"

"First, no one ever knows with certainty what verdict a jury will return. And I think Burt knows he hasn't handled this case well in the courtroom. He'd like to get it behind him."

"Burt also told me," Vradenburg said, "that it's been very hard on his client sitting there in the courtroom hearing critical testimony from his junior officers."

"Gentlemen, gentlemen . . . and lady." Van stood up next to the table. He began to walk around the room. "This is a subparagraph in a big story. It will get lost in all the coverage of the settlement of this fucking lawsuit. The headlines will say, 'It's Over!' "

"Van," I said, "everything about this case will be written about for years."

Van continued his striding.

"Don't worry," he said. "As soon as we make the announcement of a settlement we'll put our own interpretation on it. We'll turn loose the spin doctors."

This produced a chorus of laughter around the table.

"But the problem," I persisted, "is I don't think anyone here really believes this statement is true. There are four books that are going to be published on this case and those are just the four we happen to know about. It's going to be pretty obvious on reflection that this was bullshit."

"Who cares," Van said. "It'll be history by then. We'll get the spin doctors to encourage more books. If enough of them are written, each with its own interpretation, people will be so turned off and so confused they won't know what the fuck happened."

Another round of laughter. Jankowski and Fuchs, who hadn't said a word, looked like two theater patrons who'd arrived for the last twenty minutes of *Nicholas Nickleby*, were enjoying it immensely, but hadn't yet figured out the plot.

Vradenburg moved to close the matter down. He looked directly at Jankowski as he spoke.

"I could go back to Burt and say, 'My client can't live with this statement.' Maybe he'd still agree to settle. I just don't know. But we have an opportunity to save the Corporation millions of dollars in continued legal costs and in possible damages if we lose the case and I think we should take it."

I tried again. I knew I was being an obstinate pain in the ass. Vradenburg believed what he was saying and he also saw a chance to emerge as the individual who'd cut the deal with Burt and saved CBS from continuing a trial it might lose.

Van claimed he was totally comfortable with the statement. But a settlement of the case would mean he could avoid what was sure to be a tough cross-examination on his insertion of the word "conspiracy" in the advertising for the documentary. I worried that this was such an attractive prospect it might be clouding his judgment.

"You know," I said, "the Benjamin Report showed a very clear pattern in which dissenting voices and information were winnowed out of that broadcast. For CBS to issue a public statement saying this trial revealed new information which Crile or even Wallace would have included when it's obvious they chose to ignore other information is very risky. For months some of the smartest reporters in the country have been sitting in the courtroom covering this trial. They've heard what Crile and Wallace have said over and over again. They'll know that statement's not true. We're constructing our own Watergate here."

I saw Boies's head nod ever so slightly in what I hoped was agreement.

"David," I said, "the smart reporters, the ones who've followed this carefully, will they know that statement's a lie?"

A pause and then: "Yes . . . I think they might."

This time Jankowski spoke up. "Well, we don't want to be part of a lie," he said. The issue was settled.

The group then proceeded to work out a statement which a pessimistic Vradenburg took that afternoon to Burt, who agreed to study it and give it consideration. The next day the same group met again in the Cravath conference room. Vradenburg told us that Burt had called him at home during the evening to ask for minor word changes. "Issues fully explored at trial" was changed at Burt's request to "matters explored over two and a half years of discovery and trial." He had not shown it to Westmoreland

433

as yet. It was a cold February morning and the Cravath people apparently didn't get word to the building supervisor at One Chase Manhattan Plaza that there would be a need for heat that Sunday morning. As a result, the room had a chill to it which was more than matched by Van's attitude toward me. It was reminiscent of the conventions. While Vradenburg moved to a private office to call Burt, Van and I sat there not saying a word to one another.

A few minutes later Vradenburg opened the door of the conference room and from the expression on his face we knew the answer.

"We've got a settlement," he said. "The general said yes."

I got out of my chair and walked over to Van.

"You would have been great on the stand," I said. "Now you're just a former indicted co-conspirator."

Van sat there for a moment taking in a deep draft of air.

"Eduardo," he said. "It's just another day in American broadcasting. What could go wrong?"

Mike Wallace and George Crile had both been asked by Boies to come to the Cravath offices that morning. They had no idea that a settlement was in the works. Boies had simply said he needed them to go over material for the courtroom on Monday. They had been taken to an office on a separate floor and were unaware that all of us were in the building a floor below them. Boies went up to give them the news. A few minutes later he returned with them in tow.

Wallace by now had the same pleased Cheshire cat expression Van was wearing. Crile, however, looked perplexed. A settlement was obviously a good thing, but from his point of view a favorable verdict on the issue of truth would have been more desirable. Vradenburg was about to leave to take the joint statement to Burt for his signature. We all read it one last time. It was only two pages long:

"General William C. Westmoreland and CBS today jointly announced the discontinuance of the *Westmoreland* suit against CBS, Mike Wallace, George Crile and Sam Adams. The suit pertained to a CBS News broadcast, 'The Uncounted Enemy: A Viet Nam Deception,' broadcast on January 23, 1982.

"The matters treated in that broadcast—and the broadcast itself—have been extensively examined over the past two and a half years both in discovery and then through documents and witnesses presented by both sides in Federal court.

"Historians will long consider this and other matters related to the war in Viet Nam. Both parties trust their actions have broadened the public record on this matter.

"Now both General Westmoreland and CBS believe that their respective positions have been effectively placed before the public for its consideration and that continuing the legal process at this stage would serve no further purpose.

"CBS respects General Westmoreland's long and faithful service to his country and never intended to assert, and does not believe, that General Westmoreland was unpatriotic or disloyal in performing his duties as he saw them.

"General Westmoreland respects the long and distinguished journalistic tradition of CBS and the rights of journalists to examine complex issues of Viet Nam and to present perspectives contrary to his own."

That was it, that short statement. After three years of fierce combat, the general abruptly withdrew from the field. We would never know, nor would he, if the jury believed CBS News acted without malice or produced that broadcast from the outset with malicious intent; never know if the jury thought the documentary whose basic thrust we had so publicly supported was truthful. In the opinion of our own lawyer, a man whose skills were universally respected, we would have had a less than 40 percent chance of being found truthful. In every likelihood CBS News had escaped a final judgment which would have imposed not only a considerable financial penalty but a reputational penalty of devastating proportions. In exchange CBS gave the general a public statement saying it did not believe he had been "unpatriotic or disloyal in performing his duties *as he saw them.*" As retired Admiral Thomas Moorer, a former Chairman of the Joint Chiefs of Staff, would later say, "You could have said that about Hitler." Why this elderly general, who by now had devoted four years of his life to the retrieval of his honor, would have settled for so little remains a mystery. The only clue we received as to what had actually gone on in the Westmoreland camp came when Vradenburg returned from the Westbury with copies of the statement signed not by Burt, as we'd expected, but by Westmoreland. The story that Vradenburg told the group waiting for him in the Cravath conference room would seem to support later charges that Burt had not even consulted the other members of his legal team and it was he alone who convinced the general to withdraw.

"Did you talk with the general?" I asked Vradenburg when I saw the signature.

"No," he said. "I would have accepted Burt's signature since he's Westmoreland's attorney."

"What happened?"

"It was actually embarrassing," he said. "You know, attorneys play a game with one another about how impossible their own clients are to deal with. I've said to Burt at times, 'You may think the military is tough to deal with but they're easy compared to these arrogant CBS News people.' That sort of thing. When I handed him the statement to read we were in the lobby of the hotel. Burt looked at it and said, 'Wait here. I'm going upstairs to get Westmoreland to sign it. I don't trust the son of a bitch not to change his mind.' "

The laughter in the conference room at a statement that Vradenburg, to his credit, found offensive worried me.

"The tone we take from now on is very important," I said. "We really have to take the high road . . . nothing celebratory . . . nothing that would appear like gloating."

Mike Wallace nodded his head immediately. "I couldn't agree more."

As we all gathered our belongings to leave, I stopped Van in the Cravath hallway.

"I heard Vradenburg talking to Boies about a party," I said. "I hope they'll cool it, too."

"It's just a lawyers' thing," he said. "Boies and his team have worked their ass off for us. You should put in an appearance."

"They did and I will," I said. And I left.

The announcement of the settlement was made the next morning. It was a stunning surprise for many, including the contingent of reporters who'd spent the last five months in the federal courthouse writing about what they believed was a landmark libel trial. They bombarded both sides for interviews. The plaintiff and defendants were much-sought-after guests on television interview programs ranging from *The Today Show* to *Nightline*. The general tried to strike a conciliatory note in the early hours. He characterized himself and Mike Wallace to reporters as "victims of circumstances."

This, of course, was a perception Mike had artfully cultivated in countless courtroom chats with the general and his wife, Kitsy.

But by midday Mike was swashbuckling through his interviews in the style familiar to television viewers. Gone was the man who'd crumpled from his dread of the witness stand. Gone, too, was any sign of the agreement with me on the importance of not seeming to gloat. A smiling Mike Wallace dressed in a trench coat talking to reporters on the courthouse steps began to savor the taste of victory. He told the New York *Times*, "I don't feel a liaison with him as a victim of circumstances. I am

4 3 6

proud of the documentary. We received in the court a vindication of the accuracy of our documentary."

Don Hewitt and Dan Rather took Mike to a celebratory lunch at the "21" Club. A reporter from the *Times* was given access to a scene in a taxicab after lunch and it was reported in the next day's issue.

"Mr. Rather, grinning, turned and made a mock-gallant toast to Mr. Wallace. 'To Mike,' he said, 'congratulations. Your hide has never been thicker and your spine never straighter!' "

According to the *Times*, "Mr. Hewitt laughed, and Mr. Wallace smiled without mirth."

The note was struck, and by Tuesday evening the melody was being sung by a huge crowd at a glitzy New York discotheque. The party which had been described to me as "just a lawyers' thing" was held at Régine's and it was far from a party for lawyers. John Scanlon, the public-relations man hired by the Law Department, had been instructed to invite all of the reporters who'd covered the trial. Régine's was packed and the atmosphere was charged with the kind of jubilant electricity found after a winning game or a landslide election.

I walked in and looked for David Boies. I saw him standing at the edge of the dance floor talking with several of the young attorneys who'd worked with him on the trial. I walked over and shook his hand.

"David, congratulations," I said. "We were damned lucky to have you handling this case."

I talked with Boies for a few minutes more. Then I took a final look at the carnival that had been staged and I left.

The next morning in my office I sat at my typewriter and began writing a long note to Bud Benjamin. It started out as a simple thank-you note to Bud for having undertaken the unpleasant task of conducting our in-house investigation of a controversial documentary. But as I thought about Bud and the integrity he'd brought to his assignment, I realized that he epitomized the virtues of CBS News and that he wasn't alone. There were many others like him and their ethos needed to be voiced before a revisionist history of the entire episode of the Westmoreland broadcast was created.

The memo I wrote to Bud Benjamin that day was distributed to the nearly 1,500 men and women who were employed at CBS News:

"It is a bitter historical irony that I cannot reach you to tell you of the withdrawal of the Westmoreland suit, because you are on assignment in Cambodia and Vietnam. I cannot, however, allow my own relief at the conclusion of the unfortunate episode to distract me from expressing my gratitude to you for having undertaken our own internal inquiry into the charges then being made about the manner in which the broadcast was produced.

"Bud, you didn't volunteer for this assignment, but I recall your telling me that you took on this burden because 'nothing was more important than CBS News.' How fortunate we all are that an individual of such unblemished integrity was willing to accept this kind of responsibility.

"Your findings were both painful to us and encouraging to us. They pointed to embarrassing transgressions of our own CBS News guidelines. They also pointed us toward a statement which you, Van and I were able to make in July of 1982 that 'we stand by this broadcast.'

"Floyd Abrams was quoted yesterday in the New York *Times* as saying, 'CBS ought to have gotten a lot more praise than it did for the Benjamin Report. The internal investigation is precisely what I think more people would want a news organization to do.' I know for certain that you have not gotten the credit you deserve.

"In the years that followed the delivery to us of your report, one could look in vain through the volumes of clippings about this matter for any direct or blind quote from Bud Benjamin. While others with far less knowledge than you succumbed to the temptation to opine, you remained a repository of silent wisdom. As painful as it was to acknowledge the flaws in our broadcast, I believed then and I believe now it was right to do so. Our own news guidelines are a codification of the value system that is inherent to CBS News. They represent the fibre of our journalism.

"Because of you, I believe everyone at CBS News feels more protective of those principles. I am proud of what you've done and we are all enhanced by your presence at CBS News."

In writing and giving such wide distribution to this note to Bud Benjamin, I knew full well I was making a public statement.

So I was not surprised when a New York *Times* reporter called to ask why I had written such a memo.

"This is a time for us to feel relief but not jubilation," I told him. "And I think it's time for us to reflect, and then go about the business of good journalism."

The *Times* story appeared the next morning and prompted a phone call at my apartment from an agitated Mike Wallace.

"What do I say to people," he asked, "when they tell me the President of CBS News was obviously saying the broadcast was not good journalism?"

"Mike," I said, "it's easy. Tell the truth. Tell them the President of CBS

News was just saying the same thing you've heard him say for almost three years."

Another of the former defendants who'd hit the interview circuit was Van. He'd started out with a restrained tone but by the third or fourth interview had joined the ranks of Wallace and Crile in treating the general's withdrawal as a vindication of the journalistic soundness of the documentary. I knew my memo to Bud and my subsequent quotes in the *Times* placed me squarely at odds with what he had been saying for two days. I finished dressing and hurried for the office.

It was a different story there. Throughout the day I received an outpouring of thank-yous in the form of phone calls, visits, and notes from people at CBS News. A handwritten note from Shad Northshield said he believed I represented the "correct embodiment of the spirit of CBS News." And added that he was "extraordinarily proud to be a part of it right now."

Another handwritten note . . . this one from Bill Moyers.

"This member of your crew was very impressed by your efforts to restrain a jubilation that might have turned a narrow escape into an orgy of celebration in behalf of professional malpractice, and by your quiet call back to the basics."

The reaction within the News Division seemed magnified by its contrast with the muteness of Black Rock. After the Democratic convention I'd experienced a similar isolation and I had no difficulty this time interpreting the total silence of my executive phone line. It was as though it had been disconnected for failure to pay a bill. I wasn't surprised, either, that the anchorman was making no requests to share "a cup of coffee." This time, though, I felt none of the turmoil I'd experienced after San Francisco. I felt no tug from Becket's Tempter—no indecision over doing the "right thing for the wrong reason," no twinge of doubt about the rightness of what I'd done and why I'd done it.

That afternoon a note from Tom Wyman was delivered to my office. Wyman began by saying, "Job satisfaction takes various forms." He'd read the *Times* article and said he "particularly liked the lines 'I think it is a time for us to reflect, and then go about the business of good journalism.' It could not have been said better and I thank you most sincerely for saying it."

It wasn't a smile of appreciation that crossed my face as I read Wyman's note, although I had to acknowledge that the timing of his gestures of support, whether by design or coincidence, had been remarkable. I smiled because at the bottom of his note his secretary had typed "cc: G. Jankowski, V. Sauter." I knew that service on my executive phone was about to be restored.

"That was a good story Moyers did for the *Morning News,"* I said to Lane Venardos.

It was a relief to be talking about something other than the Westmoreland trial, which had ended several days earlier. Any resentment of my depriving CBS of a public-relations victory with the Benjamin memo was silenced by Wyman's support. The anchorman still had not called for his coffee but had begun sending emissaries instead, which was why Venardos was in my office.

"You liked the Moyers story?" he asked.

"I did." Bill had dealt with the controversy surrounding a New York radio station which had presented some pro-Arab voices as part of a dialogue on the tensions in the Middle East, and the station had consequently been bombarded with criticism.

"Bill is angry because we didn't run it on the *Evening News,"* Lane said.

"I wondered how he ended up on the morning broadcast," I said, "but you've rejected other stories before."

"I don't think this was handled quite as well as it should have been. We didn't exactly reject it. It just sat there on our shelf for days. Finally Bill took it away and gave it to the *Morning News."*

"I'm surprised he didn't say something to Dan."

"I'm afraid he did," Lane said.

"And?"

"The anchorman told Bill he didn't know anything about it."

"Did he?"

Venardos looked at my office ceiling.

"Must have slipped his mind," he said. "You know how busy he is."

"Is that why you came here this morning? To tell me about this?"

"As a matter of fact, no," Lane said. "Although I'm glad you brought it up, because I'll try to repair the damage with Bill. I came to see you because the anchorman and managing editor of *The CBS Evening News,* the same person we've been discussing, has an idea, and he's very anxious to see this done."

"I'm all ears," I said. "Go ahead."

"He would like to conclude the broadcast each night by showing pictures of missing children."

"You may not believe this," I said, "but Harvey Shepherd made the same suggestion. I told him no. Would you like to know why?"

"I think I'd better take notes," Lane said, "since I will be relaying this to the anchorman."

"The network is on the air twenty-four hours a day," I said. "Twenty-two minutes of that time is allocated to the *Evening News.* You may use it to cover stories about earthquakes, blood shortages, or missing children. If you start carving up your news hole for appeals for earthquake relief, blood donors, or the return of those children, you'll end up with requests from hundreds of other equally worthwhile causes. That's why the network allots time for public service messages and allocates you your twenty-two minutes to cover the news."

Lane had been massaging his jaw while I talked. He began to pull at his chin.

"Hmmmmm . . . what do I tell the anchorman?" he mused.

"I'm not through yet," I said. "I have another reason why I'm saying no. There's a legitimate debate about whether the number of missing children has actually increased. Some people argue that most of these are cases where a child has been taken by one parent in a custody case."

"Maybe we should do a story about that," Lane said.

"That's the business you're in, Lane, and it's your decision to make."

He began to lift his considerable bulk off my couch in preparation to leave.

"I will relay all this," he said, raising himself up.

"Talk to him about the Moyers business," I said. "If he didn't like Bill's story, then Bill should know that."

Lane stopped before opening my office door.

"I will. One other thing I should mention before I leave. Bernie Goldberg. The anchorman really, and I mean really, does not want to lose Bernie Goldberg."

That was at least the fifth message I had gotten from Rather on the subject of Bernie Goldberg in the last two weeks. Each time it was delivered through an emissary. With David Buksbaum it had been "Mr. Rather is very worried about the possibility of losing Bernie." Goldberg was a correspondent and quite a good one. Something of a stylist in his writing, he was one of a growing number of correspondents who worked exclusively for the *Evening News,* often coming up with his own ideas for story assignments. Every two or three weeks Goldberg would appear on the *Evening News* with a story which might emanate from anywhere in the country, sometimes anywhere in the world. It would reflect his interests and be written and delivered with style: for example, a wry look at the deteriorating quality of life in New York. Detractors called this group the "auteur correspondents." But I felt they added a touch of class to our broadcast which set it apart from its competition. They were, I thought, a throwback to the "byline" reporters in print, men and women whose flair with words attracted the interest of readers.

In February 1985 Bernie Goldberg was earning the more than respectable salary of $130,000 a year. As his contract began to approach its expiration, he was someone I felt we would wish to renew and would go to some extra lengths to make happy. I didn't anticipate quite how happy Bernie expected to be. With the Westmoreland trial over I was urging Howard Stringer to become more active with the *Morning News* and to assume some of the other responsibilities I'd handled when I'd held his job. Among those were contract negotiations for key people. I told him I would call Richard Leibner, Goldberg's agent, and tell him Howard would be the one he and Bernie should talk to about a new contract.

"It's going to take $300,000 a year to keep Bernie happy," Leibner said when I reached him.

"That's too happy, Richard," I said. "That kind of money is not in the cards."

"Dan would not want to lose Bernie Goldberg," he said.

There was that message again. This was the most blatant example I could recall of Leibner's invoking the name of his richest client.

"Then I hope Dan is prepared to pay part of Bernie's salary," I said.

Leibner laughed. "He may not be that anxious to keep him. We can get to money later. There are some other little things on Bernie's mind that he can mention to Howard . . . mostly housekeeping items."

A few days later I learned that the house Bernie wanted to keep was in Florida. Stringer called me after a lunch with him to tell me Bernie was sick of living in New York and wanted to work out of the Miami Bureau.

"Would he really want to give up the great spot he's got with the *Evening News* to be a bureau correspondent? Most of the assignments in that bureau are in Central America."

That wasn't quite what Bernie had in mind. He didn't want to be sent off to places like El Salvador and Nicaragua with the other reporters in that bureau. He wanted to be based in Miami but continue to do the same stories he'd been doing for the *Evening News*. And there was a complication. His girlfriend was a producer on the *Evening News*. If we moved him to Miami, then he wanted us to find a job for her in that bureau, too.

"You just wanted to see my face when you told me this," I said. "This has to be a joke."

"Actually," he said, "I've gone over it with Venardos and he could work with Bernie based in Miami since he travels so much anyway. We'd bring him into New York to edit the pieces."

"And the girlfriend?"

"She's quite a good producer, as it turns out," Howard said. "We could move her there."

"And what do we say when someone else's contract comes up and they want to live in San Francisco or New Orleans?"

"We'd have to say this was a special case, I suppose. Keep an open mind on this. Dan is absolutely rabid on the subject of not losing Goldberg."

"What else did you and Bernie talk about?"

"We began to run out of time," Howard said. "He's going to put it all in a note for me."

"I can hardly wait."

"Do stay open on this, though," Howard said. "Dan is feeling bruised because of your turndown of his missing children idea. You also rejected the new music for the commercial bumpers. It might be a good idea to let him win one of these."

I reached for a piece of paper in the out box on my desk.

"I'm about to send this over to Jankowski," I said, holding it in front of me. "Let me read you the first paragraph. 'During the four weeks from January 28 thru February 24, 1985, the *CBS Evening News* audience was up slightly (2%) over one year ago, averaging a 14.7 rating/24 share or 2.5 rating points better than NBC's *Nightly News* (12.2 rating/20 share) and 3.2 rating points better than ABC's *World News Tonight* (11.5 rating/19 share).'"

I dropped the paper back in the box.

"We have a four share point lead over our nearest competitor. This should be a time for Dan to enjoy life and feel secure with what's been built around him the way Cronkite did. Instead, he's increasingly restless."

"In many ways it was easier when Dan was so frightened," Howard said. "Now if the ratings dip for a week all he thinks he has to do is wear his silly sweater. Nevertheless, chief, keep an open mind on this one."

The next morning an agitated Howard called, asking if he could see me right away.

"Bernie Goldberg said he'd put his contract demands on a piece of paper," Howard said. "I've got it. I think you should see it, too."

Howard was slightly less flustered when he arrived in my office.

"I don't know what goes through the minds of these flaming correspondents," he said. "Is it the agents telling them what stars they are? Let me read this list to you."

I'd spent a good part of a lifetime by then dealing with the outsize egos of television performers. But the list Goldberg presented to Stringer couldn't have included more if he'd been asked to give it to the genie he'd just uncorked from a magic bottle.

In addition to a relocation in Florida for Goldberg and female friend, he wanted a "title," some way, he said, of "institutionalizing my role on the *Evening News.*" He wanted to do in-field essays/commentaries "in addition to the bread and butter." A commitment for one documentary a year and five *Evening News* series "in order to maximize the time I spend on the bigger, more significant stories." Foreign assignments, "two per year, as per Dan's request." He preferred to report to Fishbowl producers. And he also wanted "a major say, within reason of course, in picking the producers with whom I work."

He was just as concerned about the way his work would be promoted. "When the *Evening News* chooses to promo a piece I've done I want my name mentioned in the promo—as a way to showcase some of my stories."

There were other odds and ends he wanted attended to: right of first refusal on any new CBS News magazine-type program; a CBS Sports assignment; and then, as his final point, a discussion on what his girlfriend's role would be in Miami.

By the time Howard had finished reading this list of contract terms from one of Murrow's heirs, he looked like he could use a stiff drink. If it hadn't been nine-thirty in the morning I might have offered him one.

"He can't be serious," I said. "That's just fantasy stuff in case we're nuts enough to say yes."

Howard put his hand on his chest.

"Ed, it's not. He bloody well means it. I watched the man's ego growing right before my eyes. It was like one of those sci-fi movies."

"The ego that ate Miami," I said.

"Like that . . . right," Howard said. "Now what do we do? Rather and Leibner have got Bernie convinced he's going to get these things."

"I'll tell you what we don't do. We don't dignify this list with any kind of point-by-point discussion. Tell his agent that. If he ends up working someplace else, so be it."

Over the next few weeks I continued to hear how much Dan Rather did not want to lose Bernie Goldberg. I even got a phone call from Jankowski inquiring about the Goldberg negotiation.

"We're very far apart," I told him. "You know we're holding most contract increases to your seven percent lid, but we would pay more than that for Bernie."

Jankowski's response was memorable.

"I hope we never lose anyone we really want to keep over money," he said.

"The issues are not just financial," I answered, "but there has to be some limit to how much we give a Bernie Goldberg because of the impact it will have on other negotiations."

"I know Dan would be very concerned if he went to another network," Jankowski said. "He thinks it would be a symbolic loss."

There it was, the same sort of signal flashed to Bill Leonard a few years earlier. Jankowski was fond of saying that CBS News had more airtime, more people, and more budget than ever before, without ever acknowledging that the additional airtime accounted for the extra people and the larger budget. The truth was that CBS News was covering the world each year with a smaller real budget than it had the previous year. And we wouldn't be able to survive many more years of this cost squeezing and still support an enormous payroll of contract talent. Of the more than 1,500 people who worked at CBS News, about 650 of them were under contract, most of them represented by agents. This one payroll required a third of a budget which exceeded $250 million. (Another 22 percent of that budget went to pay salaries of camera crews, directors, videotape technicians, and other employees whose salaries were negotiated with various labor unions.) At an annual budget meeting I arrived with an enormous chart for Jankowski and Wyman. It showed that if they continued to hold CBS News to the same modest annual budget increases while at the same time costs for the talent payroll continued to soar, the results would be disastrous. CBS News would be forced to reduce its resources and in less than a decade would have no camera crews, no bureaus, and none of the resources needed to report and broadcast the news . . . just a large group of very rich anchors and star correspondents. Out of that demonstration came the mandate to hold increases to 7 percent. But now in the Goldberg negotiation Jankowski was invoking his old saw about not letting mere dollars stand in the way of keeping the talented. It was that philosophy which resulted in less than 20 percent of the people who were under contract at CBS News earning more than half of the huge talent payroll.

I knew all of that. Finally, however, I had to do the same thing Bill Leonard had done before me. I approved a contract with Goldberg, thus precluding a story in *Variety* or one of the other trade publications about the defection of a CBS News correspondent to another network, complete with its assortment of anonymous quotes saying what a devastating blow to morale at CBS News this loss represented. Bernie's salary was escalated from $130,000 to $200,000 a year and the two CBS News employees were moved from New York to Miami. The $70,000-a-year raise and a relocation to a warmer climate sufficed. We did not grant any of the other demands. Still, I would read newspaper and magazine stories for the next year which included references to how close I came to losing Bernie Goldberg.

Among the items on the list I did not agree to was the request for a title, or as Bernie had put it, "a way of institutionalizing my role on the *Evening News.*"

However, a few weeks after Bernie had moved to Miami, I heard Rather on one broadcast introduce him as "CBS News National Correspondent Bernard Goldberg." I called Venardos and asked him to point out the error to Dan. Four nights later Rather did it again. After the broadcast I walked back to Rather's office and closed the door. It was quiet, except for the bubbling of Dan's tropical fish tank.

"I gave Bernie a new contract which pays him a great deal of money," I said. "Then I agreed to move him and his girlfriend to Miami. I think it was a foolish thing to do, but I did it. I did it because you believe he is so important to your broadcast. That's the only reason. I turned him down on a number of other requests, including a title, and you can't unilaterally bestow one on him."

Dan smiled and agreed not to use the title again.

As months went on and I continued to read repeated accounts of how I would have lost Bernie Goldberg if Dan Rather hadn't interceded, I often remembered that smile.

I'm convinced that Bernie Goldberg's memo to Stringer should be mounted in the Museum of Broadcasting as a symbol of the changing values in network television news. For years many of us had believed that these excessive, egocentric demands were inspired by agents, were part of their strategic probing for the limits of a negotiation. But now, in the Goldberg memorandum, there was proof that the Me Generation at CBS News had come of age. The star system we had all created now had the supporting players standing in line to get theirs, too.

Any suggestion to these people that the time had come to curb their appetites must have seemed at best incongruous and at worst hypocritical when each day the financial pages of their newspapers carried the latest analysis of the spiraling price of CBS stock. At the same time, reports from Washington were indicating that Ted Turner, the cable operator, was preparing for a takeover of CBS. Supposedly he and his lawyers were in the nation's capital holding talks with the FCC regarding the mechanics of station license transfers.

In early March, Wyman felt compelled to distribute a memorandum to all "Officers, and Department Heads of CBS, Groups and Divisions."

He acknowledged that the sharp increase in the activity in CBS stock had "attracted heavy press coverage and speculation." Then he dismissed the Turner rumors: "As we have indicated we have no interest in any kind of association with Ted Turner. To the best of our knowledge there is no substance to reports that he plans a network takeover attempt. It would appear that his financial resources are already rather fully engaged."

When read in hindsight, that last line, a droll dismissal of the flamboyant entrepreneur from Georgia, makes one wonder about the kind of advice Wyman was receiving to have so badly misjudged the capacity of Turner. Most of us might have been forgiven for never having heard of junk bonds. Little in a life in broadcasting prepared an executive for the realities of this new chapter in American capitalism. But Wyman was the professional CEO and he should have known better. Still, in the eyes of many of us at that time he was beginning to display a taste for combat which was impressive.

He definitely impressed me when he called to tell me that Paley had recently been a dinner guest at the White House.

"It must have been a special evening," he said. "He was seated next to Nancy Reagan."

Wyman paused, but since all of his conversations were filled with such gaps, I wasn't certain he was expecting me to react to this update of Paley's social calendar.

"Aha," I said.

"Yes," Wyman continued, "and apparently the First Lady spent a good deal of the evening sharing with Mr. Paley the distress that she and her husband feel because of the invasion of their privacy when they're at their ranch in California."

He paused again and this time there was no doubt he was waiting for my reaction.

"The long lens?" I asked.

"Exactly. Just so I have some idea, can you explain why CBS News would think it was a good idea to position a camera on a distant mountain-top to get those shaky, poorly focused pictures of the President at his ranch?"

"Because we're denied access to the ranch," I said. "Because this not very young President is skillfully isolated from a press corps which knows only what his advisers are willing to tell them about what's going on there. The White House was very unhappy with us during the KAL crisis when the Russians shot down that plane. The White House press office, many miles away in Santa Barbara, was busy telling the press, and through them the world, that the President was huddled in conference at the ranch with his advisers. But our camera showed him happily astride Old Paint on a trail ride."

Wyman chuckled. "May I assume that if the President or the First Lady was involved in anything of a personal nature while outdoors CBS News would not find that newsworthy."

"You certainly may," I said.

"Well, we seem to have a problem here," Wyman said. "It so happens that when Nancy Reagan told Mr. Paley about this he assured her that he had no idea this was going on and he would see to it that the practice was immediately discontinued."

"Oh, that's lovely."

"Do I correctly understand CBS News feels that using its customary standards of good taste, it should continue to photograph the President with this camera?" Wyman asked.

"You have a precise understanding of our position."

"I'll tell Mr. Paley," Wyman said. The tone of his voice made it clear it was not a message he relished delivering and I could understand that.

In an earlier era that sort of fiat from William S. Paley would have been executed immediately. No one, not Frank Stanton, not Dick Salant, not

Walter Cronkite, would have challenged such a command. But this was a different time. Wyman never raised the subject with me again, although every few months Jankowski would call asking for verification of reports he'd heard that NBC was no longer photographing the President's California ranch with a long lens. The reports were untrue.

Jankowski made no bones about the fact that he was responding to inquiries from Paley, or "the Chairman," as he always called him. When Jankowski began a conversation with the words "The Chairman has heard a report . . ." I immediately understood he was referring to Paley, not Wyman. CBS News continued to photograph the President at his Santa Barbara ranch. Whatever Wyman told Paley overrode "the Chairman's" hasty assurance to the First Lady that this practice would be abolished immediately, and was an indication of the control Wyman exerted. As the corridor lore of Black Rock put it, "Wyman had the board." That was understandable, when you considered that CBS profits had risen from $183.8 million in 1980 to $212.4 million in 1984. During that time the television network had remained in the number one position in the ratings race. Wyman jettisoned such nonperforming businesses as Fender Guitar and Fawcett Books, and CBS was now embarked on a number of new ventures. The acquisition of twelve consumer magazines from Ziff-Davis publications had just been completed. In 1984 Wyman's own income from CBS totaled $1,164,808, not a pittance, although considerably less than the salaries paid to Dan Rather, Mike Wallace, and Don Hewitt.

On March 13, CBS held its annual corporate meeting with security analysts. It was a rosy affair. The broadcast advertising market was strong, the Ziff-Davis acquisition was generally hailed as a smart move, and most important of all to the assembled financial analysts, the earning outlook was promising.

A few days later another network made news and in a big way. ABC announced it had agreed to be acquired for cash and warrants valued at $3.5 billion by Capital Cities Communications, a company which owned and operated television and radio stations. This was the largest acquisition in broadcast history. The price of ABC shares rose more than $31, or 42 percent. CBS shares began to feel the impact of this announcement. In the five trading days which ensued, CBS stock rose $20.25 per share, or 23 percent. There was no longer any doubt that CBS stock was "in play." Someone was buying CBS stock but no one at CBS seemed to know with certainty who the predator was. On April 1, Ivan Boesky notified the SEC that he had acquired 8.7 percent of CBS shares "for investment purposes." Obviously Boesky knew that Ted Turner was preparing to launch his takeover attempt. Most of us at CBS News learned a new word: "arbitrageur," one who purchases large blocks of stock of companies in takeover situations in the hopes of reselling that stock at a higher price.

On April 9, CBS sued Boesky, alleging that he had financed his CBS stake by borrowing more than Federal Reserve Board margins allow. This suit, which would ultimately force Boesky off the stage, struck most of us as an arcane struggle between Wall Street druids. But one thing seemed clear to us all. Wyman was a fighter. He was tough and the lawsuit was just one example of his combative side which we would see in the days ahead.

"That Tom Wyman," Rather mused one night in the Fishbowl after the broadcast. "He's showing me something. I thought he was slow off the mark when Helms came on the scene, but I sure like what he had to say about Turner."

Wyman had publicly stated that he didn't believe Turner had the conscience to run a television network.

"Do you know Turner?" I asked.

"Not really," Rather said. "I've met him. But I know that he's someone who'll go to Jesse Helms and talk Southern: 'You're right about those network people, Jesse . . . they all ought to be hung for treason.' But he's the same Ted Turner who'll fly down to Cuba and go duck hunting with his pal Fidel Castro."

Rather's statement typified the CBS News reaction to Turner as a possible owner of CBS. Few would argue that he had not been foresighted and innovative in the creation of his Cable News Network. But Turner had developed a public persona over the years which most people at CBS News found offensive. His public drunkenness after winning the America's Cup and his demagogic speeches about the lack of patriotism at the networks served to shape his image as a ready-made bogeyman.

In late March I'd been in Moscow and I recalled for Rather the Soviet curiosity about the Turner threat to a major American broadcasting company. I had a meeting at the Soviet Foreign Ministry with Vladimir Lomeiko, the chief of its Press Department, and Valentin Kamenev, the deputy chief. Both were urbane, sophisticated men. In fact, I realize now I was encountering a preview of "Glasnost," the new Soviet openness. They were well informed about Turner. He was a frequent visitor to Moscow as well as other world capitals. I responded to their questions with the CBS equivalent of "the party line," dismissing Turner as overly ambitious without adequate resources. As I was leaving, Kamenev, who'd spent eight years in Washington as press counselor at the Soviet Embassy, stopped me at the door.

"Don't underestimate this Turner," he said, and he smiled. "Remember, the Bolsheviks were a small group and they took over an entire country."

When I repeated this story for Rather that evening in the Fishbowl, he laughed but didn't give the Soviet warning much credence.

"Just the same," he said, "I'll put my money on Tom Wyman."

"It's amazing," I reflected to myself. "Wyman's not only got the board . . . he's got Rather."

A few days later, on April 16, 1985, the New York *Times* ran a story on Turner's expected bid for CBS. The stock, the article pointed out, had now risen to $109. Just three months earlier it had been valued at $73.88. The *Times* article quoted Wyman's unflattering description of Turner, then continued with a surprising paragraph: "However, one member of the CBS Board of Directors, Walter Cronkite, the former anchorman of the CBS Evening News, said recently that 'he could not prejudge what Mr. Turner might do at CBS. It might be very much like becoming President of the United States.' Mr. Cronkite said, 'Maybe the office makes the man. He has proved flexible in the past. What he says he is going to do and what he does are not always the same.' "

I arrived at my office at eight-thirty that morning and as I was unlocking the door I could hear my executive phone ringing. I rushed in to pick it up.

"Do you know where Cronkite is?" It was Wyman.

"No, I don't, but I can try to find out."

"I wish you would, as quickly as possible. Did you read the quote in the *Times* from Walter?"

"I'm afraid I did," I said.

"We have a board meeting tomorrow in Chicago. As you might imagine, that's not one of the most constructive things a board member might say just before such a meeting."

"The reporter was Sally Bedell Smith. I've never known her to misquote anyone."

"That's what bothers me," Wyman said. "A number of other board members are very anxious to talk with Walter and have him explain himself in advance of that meeting."

"I know it's early," I said, "but did you try his office?"

"Actually, I've reached his secretary. She either doesn't know or won't tell me where Walter is."

"I'll try to track him down," I said.

Within minutes I'd learned from Bud Benjamin that Cronkite was in

Las Vegas, where he'd made a speech the night before. If he was keeping to schedule, he would be boarding a flight to Chicago in about forty-five minutes. I remembered that Eric Ober, our Vice President for Public Affairs, was also in Las Vegas attending the annual meeting of the National Association of Broadcasters. I woke up Eric in his hotel room and gave him both the background of the *Times* article and Cronkite's flight number.

"Throw some clothes on and get out to the airport," I told him. "If you can find Cronkite anywhere in the terminal, take him to a pay phone and call me."

Ober broke some sort of speed record that morning. Exactly twenty-two minutes later my secretary buzzed me to tell me Eric was on the line.

"Ed, here's Walter," he said.

"What's this all about?" a familiar voice asked.

"It's about your quote in the *Times* on Turner," I said, and described the request from Wyman to locate him.

"How did he sound?"

"Not very happy," I said.

"I guess I should call him."

"I can switch you over to his office," I said.

I could hear Walter clearing his throat.

"All right," he said, "let's do it so I can get on this plane."

I switched the call to Wyman's office and then put down my phone, no longer quite so certain that "Wyman had the board." Cronkite held an allegiance to Paley, who had placed him on the board. What discussions had gone on between the two of them? I couldn't imagine for a moment Paley endorsing a Ted Turner takeover, but was this sort of public difference with Wyman an indication that some board members would be more open to another candidate? The New York *Times* had reported that William Simon, a former Treasury Secretary, had pulled back from working with Turner but might be preparing a bid of his own. Speculation such as this was quickly becoming a way of life for us all.

Ray Brady, our financial correspondent, would pass on the latest rumor to the *Evening News* staff, sometimes directly to me. Some of these rumors were true. For example, Larry and Zachary Fisher, two brothers who had made millions in New York real estate, were described by sources as trying to gain control of CBS, and it turned out they actually acquired one million CBS shares. Until an investor crossed a legal threshold which required disclosure to the SEC, we had no way of verifying these reports, and investors such as the Fisher brothers were not about to advertise their maneuverings.

On April 18, 1985, the Turner Broadcasting System filed its bid to acquire CBS with the SEC. Working with E. F. Hutton and Company, Turner proposed an unusual no-cash leveraged buyout of CBS expected to be worth up to $5.3 billion, which would work out to $175 per share. The market price of CBS stock that day was $108. However, Turner offered no cash at all. Instead, he asked CBS shareholders to participate in the buyout by trading their stocks for a package of securities that would include junk bonds and some equity in the new company. The simplest explanation of junk bonds from the Wall Street experts boiled down to "high yield and high risk."

For the battle ahead, CBS retained the Wall Street firm Morgan Stanley and Company as its investment adviser. For legal counsel, Cravath, Swaine, and Moore. Once again David Boies would be representing CBS. On the face of it, Turner's offer to shareholders looked too thin to be taken seriously. I asked George Vradenburg, the CBS general counsel, why such an elaborate defense was being mounted.

"There's a lot of money loose in the marketplace," he answered. "If Turner can make any progress, others will ask to join him and he'll be able to improve his offer."

His answer made sense to me. And like a lot of other people, I found myself agreeing to Rather's reaction to Tom Wyman.

W yman was demonstrating leadership qualities at exactly the right time.

The atmosphere of tension at CBS which had begun with Westmoreland, and been heightened by Helms, was now crackling because of Turner. To the frequent press inquiries about the impact of all of this on CBS News, my standard response was that there was no impact, that everything was "business as usual."

Nothing could have been further from the truth. All of us were experiencing some degree of uncertainty. My executive line rang frequently with calls from an array of senior executives such as Leahy or Rosenfield anxious to know if CBS was picking up anything new "on the street." Several times a day Van called to mine the latest lode of rumors. He was, as he put it, "servicing Jankowski." Stress has become a much-written-about area of study in the field of psychiatry over the past twenty years. In fact, two psychiatrists at the University of Washington Medical School, Dr. Thomas Holmes and Dr. Richard Rahe, had even devised a scale rating stressful events. Topping the list was the death of a spouse, but ten of their other forty-three common stressful events were work-related, ranging from "fired at work" to "trouble with boss." Such a medical team would have found CBS News in 1985 a fertile field of study. Under normal conditions news organizations, with their deadlines and competitive pressures, are stressful environments, producing exotic outbursts from colleagues obviously feeling the heat. But even by the standards of CBS News there were patterns of behavior during this period which could only be described as bizarre.

Don Hewitt was a case in point. Here was a man in his sixties earning approximately $2 million a year as executive producer of the most successful magazine broadcast in the history of television. Yet dealing with Don was like contending with a hyperactive child. In a matter of hours he could shift from temper tantrum to wild enthusiasm and back again. Most of us felt an affection for this talented man who'd presided over *60 Minutes* for the past seventeen years. But even those of us familiar with Don's mood swings were astonished at the almost obsessive jealousy he developed during this period for Andy Lack.

Lack had gone on to produce a pilot of the magazine program he'd outlined for me after the end of *Crossroads*, which was not scheduled for a summer run. As he'd requested, he'd been allowed to work with a group of younger, less established reporters. He'd chosen Jane Wallace and Meredith Viera, who'd been the most frequent replacements on the *Morning News*. He also selected John Ferrugia, a first-rate reporter who'd been the backup to Lesley Stahl and Bill Plante at the White House. Then as the fourth member of his reporting team he'd picked Bob Sirott, a young entertainment reporter whom I'd first hired at WBBM-TV in 1980.

Lack was making a statement with this group. They were neither from the ranks of CBS News heavyweights, which included Kuralt and Moyers, nor from the first tier of established CBS News correspondents, the Lesley Stahls and Bruce Mortons. He'd assembled a collection of young, competent reporters whom he hoped would strike a responsive chord with a group of viewers he wanted to bring back to network television. Surveys indicated that Americans in their twenties and thirties were watching less and less network television. Lack's strategy was to offer them not only reporters who were their contemporaries but the kinds of stories they might be reading in *Rolling Stone* or *Mother Jones* magazines. A clone of *60 Minutes*, he reasoned, would suffer by comparison and be unlikely to succeed.

Where *60 Minutes* had done profiles of Yul Brynner and Lena Horne, his broadcast would do a report on the aging Bo Diddley, Brook Benton, and Big Joe Turner, who represented a whole generation of rock-n-roll singers not being paid for the music they had created.

As it turned out, there were some stories which could easily have been done on *60 Minutes*, such as an exposé of consumer frauds by anti-abortion groups. But there were segments about the dangers of so-called designer drugs, a football player struggling to maintain his standing without the super strength from the steroids he'd stopped taking, and a computer hacker showing how easily he could break into corporate files.

An average story on Lack's broadcast ran eight minutes, half the time of a *60 Minutes* piece but still more than four times the average length of a story on the *Evening News*. Even the title seemed to break with tradition: *West 57th*.

It opened with a fast-cut montage of the production staff at deadline time. Images of the four attractive young reporters swept through this opening, accompanied by a driving musical beat. Undoubtedly it was a departure from traditional CBS News ventures, and for that reason carried with it a degree of risk.

Howard urged me to allow Tom Shales, the Washington *Post* television critic, to have a private advance screening of the pilot broadcast. Howard had spent hours on the phone describing the broadcast to Shales and thought it would help ensure a favorable review. I agreed to the screening and Howard was proved right. Shales sent Lack a note of praise which concluded with "I have seen the future and it's the future."

Unfortunately, Shales's favorable reaction began to circulate throughout CBS News and Hewitt asked if he could have a look at the new pilot, too. Lack was reluctant to accommodate him, and so was Stringer. I argued that Don would eventually see the broadcast anyway, and that as the ultimate professional he would applaud Andy's attempt at innovation. I was quite wrong. Don took one look at the broadcast and immediately disliked it. His scathing attacks continued for months on the premises of CBS News and inevitably some of his caustic comments made their way into the newspapers, including the New York *Times*. Hewitt knew he'd gone too far and immediately sent notes to me acknowledging that he'd been "bush" and to Andy Lack offering to come to the *West 57th* production area and "personally apologize to everybody." It was too late; the lines were drawn.

The *60 Minutes* staff rallied behind Hewitt. Those working on *West 57th*, many of whom had worked in the *CBS Reports* unit, dubbed themselves "the video-fluent" and began calling the *60 Minutes* crew "the over-the-hill gang." At any time I expected to be told that an *Animal House* food fight had broken out in the CBS cafeteria. The first clue as to what was truly bothering Don came from Eric Ober, who had daily responsibility for *60 Minutes* as well as *West 57th*. In one of their recent sessions together Don had turned to Ober and said, "Do you know what those guys are trying to do? They're trying to make Lack into another Don Hewitt." When Eric told me this I understood why Jankowski had gotten a phone call that morning from Ron Konecky, Hewitt's agent, asking to discuss his contract. I was puzzled at first because the contract had considerably more than a year to run. It was Jankowski who'd originally made Hewitt the richest executive producer in television news, and his $2 million a year dwarfed the $300,000-a-year salary of an Andy Lack. Just as Jankowski had not wanted to be a part of the last Rather contract negotiation, he was not anxious now to deal with Hewitt's agent. Sauter and I were asked to handle it, with the instructions "no more money for Hewitt." By the time of our first meeting with his agent, Don had begun floating descriptions of conversations he claimed to have had with Grant Tinker, the head of NBC, about a future role there if he should leave CBS.

At that first meeting Konecky struck me as a bright man who knew he'd been sent on an impossible mission. Nevertheless, he argued that Don had created in *60 Minutes* such a remarkably successful prime-time show that he was entitled to an equity position in the same way Hollywood producers owned all or part of the programs which they'd created. I responded by saying this was an argument Don had raised many times in the past, usually after having dinner with Norman Lear.

"Don has to understand," I said, "that Tom Wyman would like to see CBS News producing at least five more *60 Minutes* precisely because CBS owns it all, not some Hollywood producer."

I have no doubt that Konecky gave Hewitt an accurate account of the meeting, but Hewitt was not to be deterred. Don's pursuit of a new contract would go on for months, as would his attack-first, apologize-later relationship with Andy Lack and *West 57th.*

Tensions were running high throughout CBS and were exacerbated each day by some new takeover rumor. It was easy to recognize the symptoms of Dan Rather's nervousness. His voice began to trouble him. Until now I'd associated this recurring ailment with major news events. A cold, a virus, whatever produced the Rather laryngitis, seemed to pounce each time we were nearing an occasion of special coverage. Back in 1984, as election night approached, we wondered if our anchorman would be with us. He showed up, however, and as the night wore on, his failing voice actually seemed to improve rather than deteriorate—the result, he said, of off-camera helpings of "Mother Rather's famous Texas red-hot chili."

Now the problem seemed to flare up even without the pressure of a big story. So I was pleased when Rather mentioned he was seeing Dr. Wilbur Gould, a throat expert whose specialty was the human voice. The Mercedes he drove even sported a vanity license plate which proclaimed "VOICE." When Dr. Gould asked if he could come in and watch Dan at work, I made all of the arrangements and even provided a cameraman to tape Dan during the entire half hour of his broadcast. Gould was as interested in watching Dan during the commercial breaks as he was when Dan was reading the TelePrompTer. He made a few minor suggestions at the time. Could smoking be forbidden in the area? Could the camera with the TelePrompTer be moved any closer to Dan to make it slightly easier to read?

A few weeks later Dan came to see me.

"I'm learning a lot from Dr. Gould."

"I'm glad to hear that," I said. "I believe he can be helpful."

"You know, I've always told people that Dan Rather is a natural reporter but Dan Rather is not a natural anchorman. I've never even had a speech lesson and that's why I'm here. Dr. Gould thinks there are a number of techniques I could learn which would reduce the stress he feels I impose on myself when I'm on the air, and that they might even improve what I'm doing."

"You want to be a little careful there," I said. "There's an old Zen proverb about the caterpillar who was asked how he was able to run about and coordinate his hundred little legs. When the caterpillar thought about it, he took three steps and tripped."

"I admit I'm a little concerned about that," Rather replied. "Dr. Gould is bringing in a team of experts next weekend for a two-day around-the-clock working session. I know you've got better things to do with your weekends, but I was wondering if you could come along just to keep an eye on things."

I was tempted to say, "You're damned right I'll come along. I don't want you sounding like José Ferrer." Actually I was pleased that Dan had asked.

On Saturday, April 27, I was scheduled to sit on the dais at the annual dinner of the White House Correspondents' Association in Washington.

"Where is this two-day session going to take place?" I asked Rather.

"In East Hampton."

"I'll come out there with you on Saturday," I said, "and I'll have the company plane pick me up at the local airport and fly me to Washington later in the afternoon. President Reagan will also be on the dais and I really shouldn't cancel. But to make you comfortable, I'll get Howard to join you on Sunday."

The morning of April 27 was the beginning of a glorious spring day in New York. I walked across Central Park toward Rather's East Side apartment, enjoying the bright yellow of the forsythia blossoms. As I turned onto East Seventy-fifth, I could see a large chartered bus parked in front of Rather's building. Aboard the bus were Dr. Gould and the team of experts he'd assembled for the Rather case. They were obviously excited at the opportunity to work on one of America's most familiar voices. Dr. Gould was a bespectacled avuncular man in his sixties. His team included a vocal coach who dealt with actors and opera singers, a voice coach and researcher from the recording and research center of the Denver Center for the Performing Arts, a former television newswoman familiar with their techniques who was identified by Dr. Gould as the interpreter, and a professional masseuse.

I was the last to arrive, and after being introduced I took a seat while the bus pulled out and headed toward the Hamptons.

The treatment began on the bus. The voice and speech team had analyzed the tapes I'd provided for Dr. Gould and concluded that Rather needed to work on a variety of problems which included shallow breathing, incorrect head posture, tightness of jaw and tongue, hard glottal initiation, hypernasal voice quality, and lips which their report said held "some degree of tension chronically" with the result that "the mouth appears smaller than it actually is." Bearing down on these problems, they told Dan, "will make a significant difference in your degree of vocal skill and mastery." Listening to this with the sound of midtown traffic in the background, I was convinced Rather would ask to get off the bus before we made it to the Queens-Midtown Tunnel. But, astonishingly, he seemed enraptured, so much so that I began to worry. Maybe it was a good thing I was here: I might have to break him away and take him to a deprogrammer. But as Dr. Gould and his associates began to outline the specific techniques they would be teaching for the next forty-eight hours, I felt reassured. Almost everything they proposed would be aimed at eliminating Dan Rather's excess tension. The more they talked to him about the principles of breathing and relaxing, the more I settled back in my seat and relaxed. By the time the bus pulled in front of the 1770 House in East Hampton, where everyone would spend the night, I was reflecting on how the quality of life would be improved for a lot of people at CBS News if the good doctor could pull this off. Everyone quickly dropped suitcases in their assigned rooms and returned to the bus, which took us to Dr. Gould's nearby weekend home. His basement was set up with a television camera, recorder, and monitor. Dr. Gould wasted no time putting Dan through his paces. The team began instructing him in full-bodied yawns, spine rolls, the flapping-wing stretch, and jaw massage. This was followed by specific voice and speech techniques. Dan was shown how to give his face a light massage and then asked to practice a series of sounds which began with "woo-woo-woo-woo," then moved through "woe-woe-woe-woe," "waw-waw-waw-waw," and finally "wow-wow-wow-wow." Dan intoned these with the same earnestness he might bring to bear while asking a cabinet officer, "When did the President first know about this?"

Standing in the back of the room, I turned to the masseuse, an attractive young woman in her thirties with a lingering trace of a European accent, possibly German.

"What's your role going to be in all of this?"

"I'll show you," she said, and began to massage my neck and shoulders. She was marvelous. After several minutes I could feel the tension draining from my body, and yet I wasn't the least bit drowsy.

"I haven't been this relaxed in years," I said. "You have a real gift." She held her two hands in front of her.

"Dan says these are what got him through election night."

"I didn't know that."

"Yes, I gave him a long massage before he went on the air that night."

"My dear, we're all in your debt," I said. "Those hands were good for at least four Nielsen points."

I thought to myself, "So much for Mother Rather's famous Texas red-hot chili."

Sunday night I called Stringer at home to find out what happened on Day Two in Dr. Gould's basement. The two sessions had been practically identical.

"What was Dan's reaction when it was all over?" I asked.

"He was ecstatic. Told me he felt great."

"You have to hand it to him, don't you? That can't have been an easy weekend."

"Are you kidding, mate?" Howard said. "That's anchorman heaven, isn't it? An entire weekend with a team of experts and the two senior executives of CBS News concentrating on nothing else but Dan Rather?"

"Well, I'm still kind of touched that he felt comfortable with our being there. After all, Dr. Gould is his doctor."

"There is that, I suppose," Howard said. "Perhaps I'm just tired. I think I'll pour myself a glass of mother's ruin and go to bed."

A few weeks later I was even further touched. Rather had Dr. Gould send his bill to me. It came to well in excess of $20,000. I approved it, telling myself the expense would turn out to have been a good investment if it helped stabilize our anchorman at a time when each day at CBS seemed to bring some new whisper of uncertainty.

Not all of the tensions at CBS were derived from the outside. We managed to generate a significant amount on our own. For instance, Van was now refusing to speak to Jon Katz. He'd taken Katz to lunch for what was intended as a chance for two former newspapermen to deride the insanity of television. It didn't quite work out that way. After the lunch Katz asked to see me, and when he arrived he seemed unusually quiet. Something was obviously wrong.

"What's the matter, Jon?"

"I've just had a very strange lunch with Van which I feel I must tell you about."

Their conversation had begun with the usual badinage, but shifted at some point to a discussion of Howard Stringer.

"Van was very hard on Howard," Jon said. "So much so that I couldn't figure out why he was telling me those things. After all, Howard is one of my bosses."

"What did he say?" I asked.

"That he didn't know what Howard did all day," Katz said, "except sit in his office and talk on the phone. That when you had that job he knew exactly what you were doing, but that he doesn't think Howard is working."

"Jon, I'm rocked by all this," I said. "Obviously I'm going to have to discuss it with Van."

"I realized that when I decided to see you. I can only assume Van knew I would feel I had to tell you. I even wondered if he was using me to bring you a message."

"I doubt that, Jon. I'm going to call Van and I would appreciate it if you didn't mention your lunch to anyone else, especially Howard."

When Katz left I began to steam, and I dialed Van's executive line.

"Van, are you free to talk for a minute?"

"I'm all alone."

"How was your lunch with Katz?"

"It was a great lunch. He's a wonderful guy."

"He shared with me some of your observations of Howard," I said. "If you have misgivings I'd like to hear about them first. This job is tough enough without learning that you've trashed my deputy to an executive producer."

I went on to repeat Katz's account of their luncheon conversation.

"That asshole," Van exploded. "I will never speak to that idiot again."

"That's not really the point, is it? The point is, you shouldn't have been saying those things in the first place."

"He totally misunderstood or misrepresented what I told him," Van insisted.

I never received a satisfactory explanation from Van about his lunch with Katz. There was no doubt that Stringer had been derailed for months by the Westmoreland trial, but I felt he was finally beginning to regain his footing now that the proceedings were over. I encouraged him to take more responsibility and I feared for his self-confidence if he learned that Van was not only having doubts about him but sharing them with others at CBS News. I never heard Van quoted on the subject after that, but from then on he refused to speak to Katz.

One morning Katz asked to see me to discuss what he described as "a great idea."

He arrived in my office dressed in gray flannel trousers, a blue blazer, and a plaid button-down shirt with a dark knit tie.

"What's going on, Katz?" I asked.

"I wish to be taken seriously this morning. Listen, O great one, I know your day is filled with matters that are much more important to you than the miserable piece of shit I produce each morning. I'm sure you're busy finding more crews for Rather or dealing with important First Amendment issues, but I have a proposal which can give a lift to the *Morning News* and can be a wonderful opportunity for Phyllis as well."

He immediately began to spread a series of papers across the surface of my desk. He was proposing that the *Morning News* be allowed to originate the broadcast in Europe the week of May 6 to coincide with the fortieth anniversary of VE Day.

He had an ambitious plan which involved live remotes from Covent Garden, Trafalgar Square, and the Cabinet War Room in London, as well as locations in Rheims and Paris in France. He even had permission from the East German government to originate live from the Russian War Memorial in East Berlin, encouraged no doubt by Soviet anxiety that Russian suffering in the Second World War might be ignored in the blitz of Western media coverage. Besides the remotes he proposed a round-table of past and current CBS News correspondents which included Walter Cronkite, Winston Burdett, William Shirer, and Eric Sevareid.

He planned to ask Rather to fly to London to moderate the roundtable. His hope was that if Rather was participating in this week of coverage,

Buksbaum would be less inclined to bottle up the crews which Katz would inevitably require. Because this effort would be so complex, Katz frankly admitted that he might be taking on more than he was capable of handling. He suggested that we ask Joan Richman to go to London and coordinate all of the special-events aspects of his proposal. I thought he was smart to acknowledge his shortcomings and began to look at his proposal with interest.

His ideas for Phyllis were not only interesting; they were realistic and achievable. Interviews with the Queen's fashion designer and British music stars such as Phil Collins and a tour of the stately British country homes.

"Look, we'll find some things connected with VE Day for her to do, too, but we'll produce her and protect her and at the end of the week people will see that she can make a contribution with interesting material while the others handle the weightier stuff in a traditional CBS News manner."

I gave Katz a go-ahead and the week he produced with Joan Richman's help generated more enthusiasm for the *Morning News,* at least within our own organization, than I'd seen in over three years. Even Rather, who had first turned down an invitation from Katz to moderate the correspondents' roundtable, changed his mind. Realizing he might be missing out on an opportunity to publicly invoke Ed Murrow's name, he hastily flew to London.

When Katz returned home he came to see me looking tired but enthusiastic.

"This week proved something," he said. "Now I've got to keep the momentum going."

"You're right," I agreed. "I can't remember the last time I heard people here talking about something they'd seen on the *Morning News.*"

Katz laughed. "Even admitting they'd watched the *Morning News* is a big give for some people here."

"What's your next brainstorm? And keep in mind that I can't provide you with money to originate in Europe every couple of weeks."

"We don't need that," he said. "I'm a realist. I know that I'm not going to suddenly find that I can get crews and correspondents . . . and if I did I know that Rather would simply unleash Buksbaum. I want to work with a handful of beat reporters of our own. We've already got Terry Smith for Washington stuff and Bob Krulwich for financial stories. If I can find six or eight more of those, I'm in business. Then if CBS News will just provide five-minute news blocks in each half hour, you'll never have another complaint from Rather about the *Morning News* using correspondents. We'll do it ourselves."

"And Phyllis?"

"That woman worked hard in London," Katz said. "She took direction and she handled herself well. Everyone saw that. I think we're over the hump."

Phyllis thought so, too. She came back from London brimming with confidence. If asked about her ambitions, Phyllis was guileless.

"My dream is to do this morning program and also some prime-time interview specials like Barbara Walters," she would reply.

After London she mentioned this dream more frequently.

One morning Katz called to say that he had just rejected an interview request from Phyllis.

"She wants to interview the Secretary of State," he said.

"What prompted that?"

"Barbara Walters," Katz said. "Hookstratten is telling her she'll never be Barbara Walters until we let her do some news interviews."

"Look," I said, "Phyllis is not going to interview George Shultz. But on the other hand Hookstratten may have a point. Keep her out of politics and international affairs, but there's always a flow of stories about societal issues, drug abuse, foster children, you know what I mean, serious subjects."

"But not geopolitical issues," Katz said.

"Exactly."

"And in fairness, she's done some of those," Katz said. "I still don't think that will satisfy Hookstratten."

"Don't worry about that," I said. "You've got some momentum going. Don't let it stop."

A few days later, the *Morning News* had Phyllis scheduled to do one of those "serious subjects." It involved a convicted rapist, Gary Dotson, who'd been serving time in an Illinois prison when the woman who'd accused him, Cathleen Webb, suddenly recanted her testimony. Dotson had been released from prison three days earlier and the two of them were actually making the rounds of the television talk shows together. So far they'd appeared on *The Today Show* and *Good Morning America*. Now they were scheduled for *The CBS Morning News* in the 8:30–9:00 segment, and I arrived in my office in time to watch the interview.

I turned on the three television monitors in the far corner of my office, and in the center screen, which was adjusted for CBS, I saw the familiar "Newsmaker" graphic which always preceded this segment. The camera opened on Phyllis, then pulled back to a group shot which included Cathleen Webb, Gary Dotson, and Dotson's lawyer, Warren Lupel.

"What were the first words you said to each other at your meeting last night?" Phyllis asked the couple.

"Not bad," I thought. A lot of people would wonder about that.

Webb answered indirectly. "I don't remember who spoke first," she said. "I asked for Gary's forgiveness and it was given sincerely."

Dotson said, "I was nervous, but I'm glad I met her."

"Did you have dinner together?" Phyllis asked.

While they were both saying no, I was shouting at my office ceiling, "Jesus, Phyllis, this wasn't a date!"

Phyllis got back on track.

"Why did you go on morning talk shows?"

"That's better," I said. Another question on a lot of minds.

"To show Gary's character," Webb said. "Gary doesn't have the character of a rapist."

I began to relax. The rest of the interview seemed innocuous.

Phyllis moved to wrap it up.

"How about you two shaking hands at the end of a long day?"

I cringed a little at that but told myself Phyllis could get away with it because she was just being natural and human. While they shook hands I began to take off my jacket and get ready to organize the rest of my day.

I wasn't even looking at the monitor when I heard Phyllis's voice saying, "How about a hug?"

My head snapped back in time to see the abashed Webb and Dotson not complying with her request. I turned off the sets and sat alone in my office, holding my head in my hands. It was over, and I knew it. The worst part was that Phyllis wouldn't even know how truly terrible that moment had been until someone told her. Nothing in the life of this lovable woman equipped her with the instincts, let alone the professional background, for the role in which we'd cast her.

The first press reaction to the interview came from Tom Shales the next morning in the Washington *Post* in a three-column story called "Invitation to a Hug." Shales began: "Collectors of seemingly idiotic remarks made by Phyllis George on the CBS Morning News hit a vein yesterday." Shales had even reached Phyllis, who told him, "I wanted to get the personal side. I don't think it's such a big deal."

That was just the beginning of the deluge of derision. For another four months Phyllis George was the recipient of an unrelentingly hostile press coverage steadily eroding the charm and vitality which had been her natural assets.

At CBS News the most common reaction was embarrassment, and a firm conviction that the hiring of Phyllis George had been a monumental blunder.

"We're very happy with Phyllis. We think she brings something that's needed to the broadcast."

I was standing at a microphone in the Grand Ballroom of the Arizona Biltmore Hotel on an afternoon in June 1985, responding to questions from approximately 150 reporters and critics from newspapers and magazines around the country. Twice each year the network scheduled a four-day event to provide reporters an opportunity to screen new programming and question network executives and producers. My session was to be followed by a press conference with the star and producers of the network action adventure show *The Equalizer*.

I answered a variety of queries, but most of the grilling focused on Phyllis George. Following the week of successful broadcasts from London, Van and Gene had cautiously begun to expose themselves as having been instrumental in her selection. But after the "invitation to a hug," they quickly retreated and left any public defense of her selection to me. It wasn't easy. Phyllis by now had become a kind of public joke, and increasing numbers of potential guests on the show declared they would not appear if they were to be interviewed by Phyllis. The irony of my defense of Phyllis in Phoenix that day was that I was by now regularly arguing with Van that we should replace her and Bill Kurtis to give the show a fresh start. Phyllis had been a foolish choice and was now permanently damaged. Kurtis in his own way had been equally miscast from the beginning. He was now becoming increasingly public about his unhappiness.

I knew that WBBM-TV in Chicago not only would take him back but would pay him even more money than he was earning at CBS News. I proposed this to Van since the television stations fell under his supervision and, as a result, the Chicago station began negotiating for Kurtis to return. But Van remained adamant on retaining Phyllis.

"If we replace her," he said, "there'll be a shit storm."

Bob Schieffer, who anchored the Saturday *Morning News,* agreed to take over the anchor reins after Kurtis left. Schieffer, a former newspaper and television reporter from Fort Worth, Texas, first joined CBS News in 1970. In the years since, he'd been assigned to the Pentagon, the State Department, and the White House. He was one of a number of CBS News correspondents who had anchored the *Morning News* in the past. He enjoyed doing the broadcast, particularly the interviews, but he made it clear he saw this as a temporary assignment and was not anxious to uproot his family in Washington, where he was based, to move to New York. Schieffer brought journalistic credibility to the broadcast at a time when we needed it and he was unfailingly cordial to Phyllis at a time when she was so fragile. With that anchor seat secured, at least temporarily, I could keep up the pressure to remove Phyllis. At the same time I was trying to protect her in my public statements, and that day in Phoenix I'd answered so many questions about her and offered so many endorsements I was relieved when one reporter shifted the topic and asked, "If Ted Turner were to acquire control of CBS, would you want to remain at CBS News?"

"I would think not," I replied, "and I would think he wouldn't want me to remain. I have never met Ted Turner. I only know what I read. He doesn't strike me so much an ideologue as a privateer who is willing to sail under any flag as long as he gets his share of the plunder. That's not a value system I would feel comfortable with. We've been blessed over the years at CBS News. The Corporation, going back to the beginning, under the leadership of Paley and Stanton, and today under Jankowski and Wyman, has felt that the News Division ought to be left free from interference from government, from advertisers, and from the Corporation itself. That's remarkable."

Missing from that list of threats to the freedom of the division was an institution which seemed about to interfere in the life of CBS News, an institution indifferent to its history and traditions . . . Wall Street. But Wall Street was very much a topic at CBS when I returned to New York. While nothing was ever said officially because of SEC concerns, the phrase "leveraged buyouts" was buzzing about Black Rock. The consensus seemed to be that CBS could construct what in Wall Street jargon was called a "poison pill" by buying back a large block of its own stock. CBS would borrow money for the purchase, thus saddling itself with enough debt to make Turner's bid, which itself was contingent on heavy borrowing, unworkable. But not all the money for such a repurchase plan could be borrowed. Wyman's corporate planners were bombarding the Broadcast Group with requests for answers to a number of financial questions. What would the projected profit be from the sale of KMOX-TV in St. Louis? What would the cost reduction numbers be as a result of layoffs of various percentages of the Broadcast Group work force? Those were alarming questions which indicated to me that Wyman and those around him now had reason to believe the threat from Turner or someone allied with Turner was even more serious than I'd believed. Not only was the prospect of a layoff disturbing but the thought that CBS would actually sell one of its television stations was astounding. Buyers were lined up around the country ready to make offers on any station which came on the market precisely because they were limited in number and extremely profitable businesses. Even thinking about selling one was extraordinary. In fact, one of the most compelling arguments raised by Wyman and others in the struggle with Turner was that if Turner took over CBS, he would be so saddled with debt that he would be forced to implement layoffs and sell large portions of the company.

The prospect of covering the news with fewer resources grew more likely with each day following my return to New York. It was very much on my mind on the evening of June 12 when I arrived in the Fishbowl for my usual post-broadcast visit. The moment I opened the glass door I had a sense that something was wrong. The senior producers were silent and Rather was glowering at the floor.

"Boy, this group doesn't look happy," I said.

"Well, frankly we're not," Rather replied. "Before you came in I was saying there is something wrong when the *Evening News* can't get its hands on the best correspondents at CBS News."

What Rather said disturbed me. I was unaware that the broadcast was having such a problem.

"What happened?" I asked.

"Well, tonight two of our major pieces were done by Karen Stone and Chris Kelly. Now I ask you, is that the best CBS News has to offer?"

Stone and Kelly were two solid reporters. But, undeniably, they were not on the Dan Rather "A list," which included correspondents such as Lesley Stahl, Bernie Goldberg, and Bob Simon.

"First of all," I said, "I saw the broadcast and those were two good pieces. But that's irrelevant. I can't believe the *Evening News* can't get its hands on just about anybody it wants."

Almost on cue the senior producers joined the anchorman with their cries of poverty. This was a group of people I liked a great deal. It included Linda Mason, Steve Jacobs, Tom Bettag, and Andrew Heyward. I thought they were the best in the business. Linda and Tom were CBS News veterans. I'd lured Steve away from ABC News for his gift with graphics, and Andrew had been one of my producers at WCBS-TV during my days there as news director.

"You must admit," Andrew said, "that *West 57th* has really deprived us of some important talent."

"Wait a minute," I said. "Let's look at the people on that show. Bob Sirott came from WBBM-TV, John Ferrugia was backup at the White House, which meant he worked mostly for the *Weekend News,* Jane Wallace has spent most of the past eight months working for the *Morning News.* Now I admit Meredith Viera was a regular on your broadcast but . . ."

"She was important to us," Heyward said.

"But," I continued, "when CBS News is given a chance to do a prime-time hour we have to use our good people to do it . . . and since the good people are all involved in one way or another with your broadcast, it means you can lose someone like Meredith."

"Ed," Rather persisted, "I am telling you flat out that the *Evening News* is not able to get its hands on the good people of this News Division. I don't know where they are, working on *Sunday Morning* or just hiding, but I know they are not on this broadcast."

"I'll tell you what I'm going to do," I said. "I'm going to leave here and start putting together the usage sheets we compile for all the correspondents, and if you're right, it'll get fixed."

All of that material was in my office when I got there. I received a monthly report which listed the number of times each CBS News correspondent appeared on the air and the broadcast on which the appearance was made. As I read through it, I began to shake my head at what had just taken place in the Fishbowl. The loss of Meredith Viera, a favorite of Rather's, to *West 57th* had been transmogrified into a state of correspondent famine for the *Evening News.* But studying the work output of the entire correspondent corps of CBS News, I could see that so completely did the *Evening News* now control the resources of CBS News it was a wonder that the other broadcasts, such as *Sunday Morning,* the *Weekend News,* and the *Morning News,* got on the air. The complaints of Rather and his producers were preposterous. I was someone who had played a major role in canalizing the output of the entire News Division to flow into this single *Evening News* broadcast, and I began to question the wisdom of what I'd worked so hard to create.

The next morning I had my secretary copy a list of the names of seventy-six CBS News correspondents throughout the country and around the world. Attached to it was the following note:

"Take a close-hand look at the extensive list of correspondents available, almost exclusively, to *The CBS Evening News*.

"I have not included in the list the other CBS correspondents attached to *60 Minutes, West 57th, Sunday Morning, Nightwatch*, or Radio. The people on this list work at virtually nothing other than your twenty-two minutes a night. Three years ago, not only did fewer people do this, but they were heavily involved in the *Morning News*. If you end up on as many nights as you claim without the presence of correspondents whose work you most admire, it's time for a serious review of how you are managing for us what may have become a disproportionate share of the total resources of CBS News."

This was distributed to Bettag, Heyward, Jacobs, Mason, Rather, and Venardos, with copies to Buksbaum and Stringer.

Shortly thereafter. Howard came to see me.

"Chief, I'm worried," he said. "I wish you hadn't sent that note."

"Howard, if you want to worry, worry about an order coming out of Black Rock for cutbacks. If that happens this place will be hell to operate. This kudzu stuff from the *Evening News* has got to stop. We can't have duplicate resources for each broadcast."

"Dan is back there now holding a war council with his producers, and the buzz of this is all over the place."

"Let him steam," I said. "We're all entitled to bitch about our bosses once in a while."

Later that afternoon my secretary told me Dan Rather would like to see me. "Good," I thought. "I'll let him let off a little steam before I walk him through the realities of what we're facing."

But Rather hadn't come to my office to let off steam.

"Ed," he began, "I wouldn't want the sun to set on anything that could even be perceived as a quarrel between us."

I was surprised at this, but I assumed that Dan had built a few fires during the day with his posturing and was looking for a way to tamp them down.

"I'm glad to hear you say that, Dan. These are tough days for all of us and we shouldn't let such things get blown out of proportion."

"For the life of me I don't know how these things get started," Rather said, "but people around here have the idea that you and I are involved in some big quarrel."

I should have been listening for the background music.

". . . I love to dance the little side step. Now they see me, now they don't."

Instead, I heard Dan Rather say, "You and I know we don't have a problem, Ed, but I'll have to calm my producers down."

After the broadcast that night Dan and I made a point of engaging in obviously cordial conversations in front of the news staff. I assumed the matter was dropped.

The next morning a worried Lane Venardos came to see me.

"This friction between you and the anchorman troubles me," he said. "I don't know where it's all headed."

"Don't worry about it. Dan and I have discussed it and he feels it will blow away as people see the two of us involved in business as usual."

Lane paused. "Then why isn't he saying that to the producers?"

"He probably is finding it difficult to immediately back off his initial tantrum," I said, "but I'm sure that will happen now."

Lane didn't look convinced when he left.

A few days later someone leaked a version of the story to *Variety*, which then ran an article headlined "Rather and Joyce Tiff at CBS over Staffing on *Evening News.*" The story contained a litany of complaints about understaffing at *The CBS Evening News.*

By then, however, I was concentrating on a more important story, the hijacking of TWA Flight 847.

On Friday, June 14, a plane carrying 153 passengers and crew members, mostly Americans, was on its way from Athens to Rome when two passengers with guns and hand grenades ordered the pilot to fly to Beirut.

For days the nation watched this event unfold on television. The plane shuttled from Beirut to Algiers, then back to Beirut, where one of the hostages, a young Navy diver, was killed and more heavily armed hijackers boarded the plane. It then flew to Algiers once more but returned to Beirut, where Shiite Moslem Amal leader Nabih Berri announced that his group had taken control of the remaining American hostages. But Berri said he supported the demands of the original hijack group, who were members of the more radical Hezbollah. The hostages were moved to an unknown location in Beirut.

CBS News got off to a rocky start in its coverage of this story. Western news people, particularly Americans, had become targets for kidnapping in Beirut. Along with many other Western news agencies we had withdrawn our Western employees but kept in place a staff of Lebanese camera crews and drivers plus the office manager Walid Harati.

In the first chaotic forty-eight hours of the hijacking of TWA Flight 847 we had correspondents on site in Algiers and Cyprus, but Harati alone carried the burden in Beirut. He was linked by telephone to our crews on the scene and to a contact in the airport control tower. Harati would talk with them, then relay his information to us in New York.

Because Harati was an office manager, not a trained journalist, a number of us, including Rather and me, would listen to his reports and make a determination as to what would be carried in our broadcasts. Our major concern was that nothing be broadcast which would endanger the hostages. Initially this was not much different from what the other news networks were doing in their coverage of the story. Buksbaum, who often needed restraining, seemed instead to be paralyzed by this story. He was reluctant to move people back into Beirut because of the danger of kidnapping.

As a result, when ABC newsman Charles Glass arrived in Beirut we were still relying on Harati. By the time our own reporters were on the ground in Beirut, Glass, an able reporter who'd spent years covering the Middle East, was off and running. He persuaded members of the Amal militia to drive him across the tarmac and up to the TWA plane, where he was able to obtain a brief interview with the TWA flight crew, including its cool captain, John Testrake.

All of us watched the tape of the interview as it was fed in by satellite. I was standing in the control room along with Joan Richman.

"Is that a pool feed?" I asked.

"There was some confusion over that," she said, "but the answer is no. Glass got it on his own."

"So we'll be seeing this shortly on ABC?"

"I'm afraid so. Boss, can you light a fire under Buksbaum? We need to get more people into Beirut."

I went looking for Buksbaum and found him with Rather.

"Guys, we need more people moved into Beirut fast."

"They're on their way," Buksbaum said, and listed the names of crews and reporters who were now being flown in.

"Something fishy about that Glass interview," Rather said.

"What do you mean?" I asked.

"Our policy doesn't allow us to pay money for interviews. But I don't think you get that sort of cooperation from the Amal without laying out some big dollars."

"I don't know," I said. "Glass has spent a lot of time with those people. He's no stranger and that could explain why they helped him."

"I'm hearing different," Buksbaum said. "I'm hearing it was money."

That sounded like bullshit to me and I threw him a challenge.

"If you can verify that I'll make a public issue out of it. In the meantime, let's get those people into Beirut."

This time Buksbaum didn't mention his worry about kidnapping. And he never responded to my challenge. But Rather continued to insist that Glass had a special arrangement of some kind with members of the Amal. As a result, that story began to gain some acceptance within CBS News. Inevitably this whispering campaign began to reach a wider audience. Roone Arledge, the President of ABC News, even felt compelled to publicly comment on the stories and to deny them. On June 21, I sent a letter to Arledge: "Congratulations on the interview your reporter, Charles Glass, obtained with the TWA flight crew. To the best of my knowledge, no one at CBS News believes that Glass obtained that interview through anything other than reportorial skill and enterprise. He has my admiration."

I distributed copies of that letter to a number of people at CBS News, including Rather and Buksbaum, and the rumor died down.

Every hour seemed to bring some new development in the hijacking. In those first days most of us were in the newsroom on an around-the-clock basis and the pressure to stay on top of the latest developments was intense. I believed our frequent bulletins were justified because of the extraordinary nature of this bizarre story. On one day we interrupted programming seventeen times. Joan Richman was usually in the control room and Rather was at the anchor desk to maximize our ability to take to the air quickly.

On one occasion I was sitting in the office of the foreign editor when I looked up at a monitor and saw we were interrupting network programming. I turned up the audio and was stunned to hear that we were quoting a Phalangist radio report in Beirut claiming that Israeli gunboats had invaded Beirut harbor. Phalangist radio was notoriously unreliable and it turned out that this report was false. I tore into the control room looking for Joan and found instead Ernie Leiser, who was sitting in for Joan while she took a short break.

"Ernie, ninety-nine percent of Phalangist radio reports are bullshit and we all know that. This is a tense enough situation without interrupting the network for fucking rumors."

Ernie was uncharacteristically meek in his response.

"All right, we'll see that it doesn't happen again."

I was mildly surprised by Ernie's reaction, mostly because he was a naturally disputatious personality who seldom seemed to entertain the thought that he might be wrong about any issue. It caused me to wonder if he'd simply acquiesced to a request from Rather to go on the air with that flash. The aggressive reporting from ABC had Rather in enough of a competitive frenzy to make that possible. I went looking for Rather. To avoid discussing this subject in front of others I asked if we could step into his office. Inside I closed the door, and shared my feelings on what we'd just done.

"If we were already on the air and in the course of a broadcast mentioned a report from Phalangist radio, it would be one thing. We've done that before with all of the caveats. But when we interrupt with a bulletin telling people that Phalangists are saying Israeli gunboats have just invaded Beirut harbor, we give that credibility . . . and it's irresponsible."

Dan reacted as if he'd been struck. I could see him struggling with an impulse to explode. For several seconds he stared at the floor.

"You're probably right," he finally said. "ABC's been awfully good today and I guess I was just looking for something to move our coverage along."

I left Rather's office disturbed by his reaction to editorial criticism but also believing we needed something to regain the edge from ABC News. It turned out to be Jon Katz who provided the key.

The *Morning News* had brought in a guest expert, Fouad Ajami, director of Middle East studies at Johns Hopkins University, and a Shiite himself, who explained the many factions in Beirut—particularly the Lebanese Shiites—in simple, understandable language.

A few hours after my meeting with Rather, Jon Katz called to ask me if I'd seen Ajami that morning.

"I did and he made more sense describing who's who in that crazy city than anybody I've heard."

"I'm probably cutting the throat of my own broadcast," Katz said, "but you ought to talk with him."

"I'd be glad to, but why?"

"Because he's plugged into all of those people there, like Berri, the head of the Amal. He talks to them every day."

"He does?" I said. "Do you think he could arrange for Rather to interview him?"

"I think he can. Of course, if you or Joan find him valuable you will immediately take him away from the *Morning News* as a way of saying thank you, Katz."

"Katz, we really need this," I said. "We're falling on our ass."

"We can all see that," Jon said. "That's why I called."

Fouad Ajami was a slight man who spoke an English filled with phrases of exquisite politeness. Yes, he would be "honored" if he could be of "any service in assisting an organization I so much admire." His first suggestion was that he call Colonel Akef Haidar, Berri's deputy in Beirut, and put me on the phone.

"I will first of all tell him in Arabic how important you are," Ajami said. "He will like that. Then you can talk with him and discuss an interview with Nabih Berri."

It didn't take long for the call to go through and whatever Ajami said to Colonel Haidar must have worked, because he was immediately receptive to the idea of an interview and said he would pass it along to his leader.

A short while later I found myself talking with Nabih Berri, who assured me that the hostages were safe and agreed to be interviewed by Dan Rather.

I hung up the phone and signed Fouad Ajami to a contract as a consultant to CBS News. Then I sallied into Rather's office with the news of the Berri interview. He was elated.

"Ed, I can't begin to tell you what a difference it makes to this organization to have a hands-on President. It's the major difference . . . and it makes me all the more sorrowful that we would have someone in our outfit who would call a reporter at *Variety* and feed him that nonsense about a quarrel between us."

In the telephone interview with Rather that day, Berri claimed there were forty remaining prisoners and that six of them were being held separately "under the control of the hijackers [the Hezbollah] because maybe they don't trust me so well, but I have their word." He then discussed terms for the release of the hostages which involved the release of a large number of Shiites in an Israeli prison.

Critics of that interview with Berri and others which followed charged that it represented a step over the line from journalism to diplomacy which would be better off left in the hands of official negotiators. That argument has the appearance of validity but doesn't stand up very well under realistic scrutiny. If we accept that it is journalistically sound to seek out the man who is controlling and negotiating the fate of the hostages, then it is equally sensible to ask him questions about the terms or conditions which would lead to their freedom. If he replies with conditions that the negotiators at the other end are hearing for the first time, that can't be helped. One should not fault the journalist for asking the right question.

Berri also allowed some of the hostages themselves to be interviewed by the three networks. It seems evident that this decision to make the hostages available to the media was coupled with a decision to keep them alive. In any hostage situation a fundamental goal is to keep the kidnappers talking. Nabih Berri acquired a growing stake in the safe release of the hostages through his interviews. At the same time, the opportunity for the American public to see that the remaining hostages were at least alive and in apparent good health probably lessened pressure on the administration to take some immediate action.

At the end of the eighth day there was no way of knowing if this was a situation which might go on for months. I appointed Stringer the duty officer for the next week and told him we would alternate weeks after that.

But Rather's last interview with Nabih Berri took place on Sunday morning, June 30, 1985, when Berri told him all thirty-nine Americans would be freed that day.

At 10:56 A.M. EDT, CBS News interrupted regular programming with a bulletin from Bob Simon in Beirut confirming that Red Cross cars with all hostages had left Beirut for Damascus, and freedom.

Months later an article on Dan Rather by Tony Schwartz appeared in *New York* magazine which said: "When ABC was scooping CBS at the scene of the TWA airline hijacking in Beirut last summer, Rather managed virtually single-handedly to keep CBS competitive merely by working the phones, most notably in securing a transcontinental interview with Nabih Berri."

T he hostages were free. But the news for our budget was not quite so wonderful.

Shuttling crews, correspondents, and producers around the world, along with the costs for two weeks of almost nonstop satellite time, had left the budget in ruins. And one of the biggest costs came from our own television network for keeping the Rather news set on a standby basis in order to take to the air quickly for bulletins. It was an inflated charge which my own financial people estimated as almost double what we would pay to an outside production facility. But its impact on us was real. Now we were learning there would be a Reagan-Gorbachev summit in Geneva that fall. Great for world peace, terrible for the CBS News budget. At first I tried to shrug it off as one of those unfortunate things that sometimes happen to news organizations. Jankowski was not receptive to that philosophical approach, as I learned from Van.

"Gene says CBS News has to find the offsets," Van said.

"The problem is," I replied, "not only did the hijackers blow our budget but now we have a summit coming up we didn't know about when we put the budget together and God knows what else will happen before this year is over."

"Gene is not going to tell Wyman at a time like this that CBS News is running over budget," Van said. "There'll be a shit storm."

"Well, I'll tell you one thing that we'll have to cut for sure. The *Evening News* is planning to originate from Japan in August for the fortieth anniversary of Hiroshima and the end of the Second World War. They've made elaborate and very expensive plans. I'm going to have to tell them they can't go. In the wake of my most recent collision with the anchorman, I'm sure this will be, to use your delicate phrase, another shit storm."

"Go ahead and make that cut," Van said. "Let me talk with Rather. I think I'm going to have to start spending more time with him and find out what's unsettling him so much."

"I wish you'd do that. Dan and I are never going to be friends in the way the two of you are. But Cronkite and Salant were not close personal friends either and that worked well for a lot of years."

"I'll have Kathleen call Jean Rather and set up a weekend," Van said. "I'll let you know what I hear."

I did cancel the *Evening News* trip to Japan and predictably the anchorman was unhappy. Just as predictably, the CBS News Press Department began to receive phone calls inquiring about a controversy within CBS News over this cancellation. I'd made no public response at the time of the *Variety* article about the dustup over the correspondents for the *Evening News*. This time I issued a short statement, which was released on July 3, 1985.

"Events taking place in Japan on August 5–9—for the fortieth anniversary of Hiroshima and the end of World War II—will be thoroughly and extensively covered on the *Evening News* and the many other CBS News broadcasts on both radio and television. However, our broad-ranging coverage of the TWA 847 hijacking just concluded and our anticipation of the U.S. Soviet summit this fall have given us need to reassess our plans for the remainder of the year. One of our decisions is not to originate the entire *CBS Evening News* broadcast from Japan during the anniversary week. Actual news coverage will remain undiminished."

That may be one of the franker statements made by a network official. I had flatly said that CBS News had deep but not bottomless pockets and that if the *Evening News* didn't originate from Japan as it had planned, the story would still be covered in a normal and satisfactory manner.

More significant news came out of CBS on July 3, however: CBS announced a complicated plan for buying back 21 percent of its own stock. This would be done with borrowed money. But Wyman promised to reestablish the financial health of CBS with a restructuring that would dispose of $300 million in CBS assets by mid-1986 to reduce that debt. He also promised to trim operating costs for the company by 1987. As a result, CBS was left with a debt in excess of $1 billion, a "poison pill" of sufficient toxicity to cause Turner to withdraw his offer by August.

However, CBS would end up swallowing some of its own witches' brew. The debt-to-equity ratio, a measure of corporate financial health, shot up from a conservative 24.9 percent to a questionable 69.8 percent. One expert, Elizabeth Toth, an analyst with the Provident National Bank in Philadelphia, said bluntly, "CBS has substantially weakened its financial position."

What's more, the percentage of stock owned by CBS may have jumped from 7 percent before July 3 to 28 percent after the purchase, but that still remained a minority interest. The repurchase plan may have been enough to fend off a suitor with weak financing such as Turner, but the stock remained in play. Rumors continued to circulate that the Fisher brothers were buying CBS stock. But it was another pair of brothers who moved quietly into the life of CBS: the Tisch brothers, sixty-two-year-old Laurence Tisch and his fifty-nine-year-old brother, Preston "Robert" Tisch. Working closely with his brother, Laurence had made Loews, the company he headed, one of the nation's ten largest diversified companies with $17.5 billion in assets. CBS at that time was valued at $5 billion.

On July 22, 1985, the Loews corporation informed the SEC that it had acquired 9.9 percent of outstanding CBS shares. By early August, Loews filed the necessary government form stating its intention to acquire up to 15 percent of CBS stock. Later filings in September and October revealed the intention to eventually increase those holdings to as high as 25 percent.

The word from Wyman was that Larry Tisch saw this primarily as an investment but had also been motivated to help CBS because he believed it important that CBS retain its independence from such ideologues as Senator Jesse Helms. According to Wyman, Tisch had no intention of trying to take over the company. It looked at the time as if the best kind of "White Knight" had arrived on the scene. Here was someone who was content to be an investor rather than an owner. A few skeptics did some homework and discovered that Laurence Tisch had acquired a substantial stake in the CNA Financial Corporation in 1974. CNA was a $3.7 billion insurance company headquartered in Los Angeles. Tisch, they pointed out, had told CNA's chairman he had no intention of taking over the company, but a few months later he was running CNA. Until his investment in CBS, the single largest shareholder had been Paley, who owned 8 percent of the total stock.

But Tom Wyman was our general who would lead the fight to hold off Helms, Boesky, and Turner. If he was comfortable with the assurances of Larry Tisch, then most of us were prepared to believe that CBS was now secure against any hostile takeover. For that reason no great tremor ran through CBS on July 22 when Laurence Tisch announced that Loews had raised its CBS stake to 20.98 percent. The price of CBS stock rose to $135⅝. By midsummer the price we would all pay for averting a hostile takeover was becoming known. The 1986 budget increase for CBS News would have to be held below 4 percent.

That message was delivered in a matter-of-fact manner from the Broadcast Group Vice President for Finance to his counterpart at CBS News. The message was a bombshell. Twenty-nine percent of that budget was required just for the talent payroll. It had grown at a 13.3 percent rate in 1985, thanks to the impact of the new Rather salary and a number of negotiated increases for such superstars as Morley Safer, Ed Bradley, and Charles Osgood, not to mention hefty increases for such supporting players as Bernie Goldberg. Of the 650 people in the "talent" category, 20 percent of them now earned 50 percent of that payroll.

Other CBS News employees, most of them in unions, earned the next 22 percent of the total budget. They had contracts which called for raises far in excess of 4 percent. That was half the budget, and another 27 percent was needed to pay for moving crews and correspondents around the world, cable and satellite costs, and the charges to us from our own network for the use of its studios and other facilities. All this was the very heart of the news-gathering and broadcasting process. CBS News was what economists describe as a "labor-intensive" business and the only way to meet the demand to hold increases in the year ahead to 4 percent would be to significantly reduce that labor force.

I called Van and asked him if he was aware of the new budget figure.

"Yes, and I'm afraid Gene means it," he said. "There will have to be layoffs at CBS News."

"No kidding. We could be talking about a lot of people."

"I would guess two hundred," Van said.

"Does Gene understand that?"

"Of course he does," Van said. "Look, this is not 1983. It's a different ball game. The company is going to sell the toy division and get rid of its share of Tri-Star Pictures and, confidentially, I've just come from a meeting on selling KMOX-TV. They're not fooling."

"If this has to be done, then I guess it has to be done. But CBS News can't be singled out. It shouldn't be asked to carry more than its share."

Van paused before answering. "This is the time to remove the deadwood at CBS News."

"Van, listen to me. There is deadwood here. I know it and you know it and some of it will go. But if there are layoffs at CBS News that aren't matched throughout the rest of the company, there'll be hell unleashed on us all."

"Tell that to Gene when you see him," Van said. "He'll be meeting with the Division Presidents to talk about the seriousness of this situation. By the way, the network sales forecasts for the fourth quarter suck."

"Jesus, you're filled with great news. What's the next bulletin? Some mutual friend with cancer?"

"Just a typical day . . ." Van began.

". . . in American broadcasting," I finished the line.

Unfortunately, it was fast becoming a "typical day." The new Cap Cities management which was taking over ABC was blunt about its intentions to prune costs at that network. So far NBC seemed immune, but before the year would end General Electric would take over RCA, the NBC parent company, bringing the last of the three networks into this new era.

When Jankowski held his meeting he stressed that all divisions of the Broadcast Group would be expected to carry proportionate shares of the retrenchment. The headline from the meeting, though, represented one bright note.

CBS, Gene said, would soon be offering an early-retirement incentive program for employees past the age of fifty-five. The final details were still to be worked out, but it appeared that CBS was prepared to credit an additional ten years of service and an equivalent number of years to the age of anyone in that category. This would significantly increase the dollar amount of their pension. They would have a brief period of time to accept if they wished to retire. This was a bright note, at least to me, because CBS News had a large number of employees in that age group who might be happily inclined to accept such a proposal. For each who did I would decrease our layoff list by one.

The meeting was held in Jankowski's large executive dining room. At least twenty-five senior executives of the Broadcast Group sat around a long table and listened to Gene describe the enormity of what had to be done. He closed the meeting with his familiar benediction: "The future is in our hands."

As we were filing out, I walked over to him and said, "Gene, this will be very hard for people at CBS News to understand. It would be helpful if they saw some evidence of layoffs and cutbacks elsewhere at CBS before we made our announcement."

"That may not be possible," Jankowski said. "The Entertainment Division may achieve its cutbacks by reducing its number of pilots for next

4 8 3

year. Those people affected don't work for CBS, they work for Hollywood production companies."

"Gene, I've told Van that if CBS News has any sense of being singled out, the roof will cave in."

"Every division will share in this," he said. "But each division may do it a little differently. CBS News can only achieve these reductions by eliminating people."

I left Black Rock that day hoping I'd gotten a straight answer. The dimension of the problem seemed clear and the dilemma real enough. CBS had acquired an enormous debt through borrowing money to buy back its own stock. To retire the debt service would require the sale of assets and a reduction of costs. I was now preparing to implement across-the-board layoffs of a magnitude never known before at CBS News in an effort to support this protective step. But Jankowski's response had a déjà vu quality reminiscent of 1983, when he'd said, "CBS News can't be expected to be treated differently from any other division."

I assigned Stringer to begin meeting with executive producers, department heads, and the various Vice Presidents. I asked him to look for jobs which did not directly affect our ability to cover the news. For that reason I told him to try to avoid the bureaus as much as possible. No single broadcast should be sacrosanct and that included both the *Evening News* and *60 Minutes*. I also told him not to discuss the list he compiled with anyone else for now. I didn't want a master list of those about to be laid off suddenly materializing in *Variety* or some other publication. I told Stringer to make sure that each executive he dealt with saw only the list which that particular person helped compile for his own area of responsibility.

Next I asked Bob Chandler, an honorable, fair-minded man, to work with the CBS Personnel and Law Departments as well as our own Business Affairs Department to make sure we violated neither the human nor the contractual rights of anyone who ended up being laid off.

None of us had been through anything like this before. The only body of expertise within CBS to which we could turn for advice was the corporate Personnel Department, which drew up procedures for all groups and divisions of CBS. It was a checklist of chilling thoroughness which included provision of temporary office space for those employees who were laid off because they would be expected to vacate their desks within forty-eight hours. It also included instructions to ask the employee for all CBS credit cards and identification.

The role of the Law Department during this period was to help avoid possible lawsuits because of violation of human or contractual rights.

In this gloomy atmosphere the summer premiere of *West 57th* might have gone almost unnoticed. But the controversy which Don Hewitt had first introduced continued to surround the broadcast. A viewer who hadn't seen the show but who read Tom Shales's review in the Washington *Post* would believe he'd missed an outstanding hour of creative innovation. Indeed, Shales later ranked *West 57th* third on his list of the ten best broadcasts of 1985, right after *Death of a Salesman.*

If the same viewer had been reading John Corry in the New York *Times*, he would have concluded he'd been spared the ultimate substitution of entertainment for journalistic values.

Hewitt, who seemed constantly propelled to his typewriter by either anger or remorse, dashed off a note to the *60 Minutes* staff on August 14, the morning after the premiere.

"I think it behooves all of us to salute them," he said. "It didn't even come close to the 'mess' John Corry said it would be, although neither was it the millennium that Shales thought it was. It was a quite good broadcast and every bit as entertaining as most of TV's summer fare."

Don's note stopped short of a more important point. In a television landscape dominated by *Dynasty, Dallas,* and *The A-Team, West 57th,* whose first broadcast included stories on the Oregon cult of Bhagwan Shree Rajneesh, battered wives, and the impact of the Live Aid mobilization on Ethiopian famine, was still a public-affairs broadcast struggling to survive in a hostile environment. The fact was totally lost in the debate which continued over whether *West 57th* was serious journalism or a shallow pandering to the yuppies. Andy Rooney had no doubt about the answer to that question. He sent me a long, thoughtful note telling me *West 57th* was "trash journalism," adding that "it violates the most basic rule by which CBS News has operated. It is trying to give people what they want to see, not what they ought to know." At the end of his note he said, "I don't intend to make a public announcement of my opinion on this matter but could not keep myself from saying it to you."

He was true to his word, for which I admire him.

Dan Rather had been off the air for a few days in August, away on a fishing trip in the Laurentian Mountains of Canada. After he'd been back a day we had lunch at the Maurice Restaurant in the Parker Meridien Hotel. Dan had come back from vacation with a cold. Rather's colds always worried me but he seemed in good spirits. We talked about his trip for a while and he mentioned that he and Van planned to go fishing the following weekend on Connecticut's Housatonic River. I was happy to hear that, and made a note to ask Van the following week if he'd gotten any new insights into Rather's psyche.

After the maître d' had taken our order, Dan brought up the *Variety* article again.

"Ed, I'm still puzzled by that story of a great fight between the two of us last June. For the life of me I don't know how those things get started."

"It was strange," I said. "Someone reading that would have gotten the idea that we were going after one another hot and heavy."

Then once again I heard him say, "But you and I know there's nothing to it."

I was puzzled that he would even bring up the subject after this much time had gone by, and switched topics by asking him how he liked watching Bob Schieffer on the *Morning News*.

"Well, you know I'm a big admirer of Bob's," he said. "He's good help. But can you tell me how much longer this outfit's going to stick with Phyllis George?"

"Do you feel it's time to cut bait?" I asked.

"I didn't like it when she was hired in the first place. I didn't say anything because I knew what all of you were trying to do to make something out of that poor morning program. But, yes . . . I think it's time to cut bait."

"I appreciate your saying that," I said. "I really do, and when you go fishing this weekend with Van, I'd appreciate your saying something to him. He ought to hear how you feel."

"Are you two having a disagreement about this?" he asked.

"No, not at all. We just see this one a little differently and I think it would be very helpful if you shared some of your feelings with Van."

At this point the maître d' appeared with two waiters bearing our lunch on silver serving trays.

"If somebody had told me I'd be eating lobster salad and drinking Perrier in New York when I was a kid loading boxcars in Lewiston, Idaho, for a dollar an hour, I'd've smiled for weeks," I said.

"I know what you mean," Rather said. "I always say the best part of these jobs is there's no heavy lifting."

After a few more minutes of ritual poor-boy talk I shifted the subject to the coming layoffs.

"These are going to be painful, Dan," I said. "A lot of good people are going to lose their jobs."

"It might be helpful if I had some idea of who was going," he said.

"Here's why I don't think that's a good idea. A company can't lay off that many people and not have some lawsuits. If you're involved in the selection process, or even have access to the list, sure as hell some smart lawyer is going to get you on the stand to answer questions. That would mean guaranteed press coverage. It's better if you can just say, 'I had no idea who was on that list.' "

"I never thought of that," Rather said, and dropped the matter like an empty lobster shell.

"You know," I said, "on those occasions when you talk to Jankowski or Wyman, anything you can do to dispel the idea that we're a fat organization would be helpful."

"Well, as a matter of fact I've done that. I made a note to mention to you that I saw Gene yesterday and he asked me what the reaction at our place would be to these layoffs."

"Great. What did you tell him?"

"I said, 'Gene, we are already lean and mean . . . we are already making do with less than our competitors put out in the field, but we'll just have to get by with less. Make no mistake,' I told him, 'it will hurt . . . but we can do it.' "

I dropped my own empty lobster shell on the plate and signaled the maître d' for the check. It came to $89.14. I signed for it with my CBS American Express card.

It had certainly been a business lunch.

That afternoon back in my office William Lilley III called on my executive line asking how soon I'd be able to execute the layoffs and make a public announcement.

"This is an important statement for Tom to make to the financial community," he said.

"We're not ready," I answered. "This is a complex business, reviewing the list with the Law Department and with Personnel. You don't want to see a wave of lawsuits because this was rushed and sloppily handled."

"I suppose you're right, but let's do this as fast as we can. This is an important statement."

Later in the afternoon Van called with the same request.

"They really want to see this done soon," he said.

"Why is it so important that CBS News be the first big shoe to drop?" I asked.

"They feel that if the financial analysts see that layoffs are taking place at CBS News, they'll believe that CBS really means what it says about reducing costs."

"Van, who are *they?*"

"Well, I'm quoting Jankowski, but I assume he's reflecting Wyman's feelings," he said.

I gave Van the same answer I'd given Lilley.

In fact, that week the list was complete but I was holding it back. Howard Stringer had taken on the miserable task of targeting 125 jobs which he believed could be eliminated without bringing CBS News to a standstill. We had reached that number by reducing costs in a variety of areas big and small. Our cutbacks virtually destroyed the capacity of our Los Angeles Bureau to update the *Evening News,* which was recorded in midafternoon Pacific time but broadcast to the Western states several hours later. This saved almost a million dollars.

All bureau chiefs were admonished to hold down their costs because, as David Fitzpatrick, the domestic assignment editor, put it in a memo outlining belt-tightening procedures, "if we don't save the money we have to save, we are going to be in more people trouble."

Ted Savaglio, the Los Angeles Bureau chief, sent a similar memo to his staff, telling them, "We must work hard to save money in order to have the money to cover breaking news." Then he added, "This is not a budget pinch, crunch or squeeze. . . . It is a vice [sic] that is still turning." At the time I didn't know if Savaglio was peculiarly perceptive or just a poor speller. Today I believe it was the former.

And we saved still more money by canceling documentaries planned for the remainder of the year. Rebuilding *CBS Reports* would have to wait for another year.

I had told Stringer and Chandler I wouldn't veto the names on the layoff list unless I saw some obvious injustice. And in some cases I did. As I reviewed the list, I spotted the name of a woman in an overseas bureau who had spent her life at CBS News and had once been wounded in a terrorist attack.

"She may be deadwood now," I said, "but there was a time when she wasn't. Take her off."

Also listed was a producer overseas who was now in his fifties and who had covered the pestholes of the world as a reporter for CBS News. He would never make it onto Rather's "A list" but he'd been jailed in Africa and Asia because of his willingness to go into dangerous areas. I removed his name as well.

I'd been holding back the final list because CBS had made its early-retirement offer to employees over the age of fifty-five and had set a deadline after which it would be withdrawn. I was not anxious to drop 125 people and then discover weeks after their departure that many of them could have been saved if I'd known the exact number of early retirees at CBS News.

Chandler, Stringer, and I had met with Van in my conference room to review the layoffs and I'd expressed my concern about this subject, urging that we wait.

"That could take weeks," Van said. "The company doesn't have that sort of time. This has to be done as soon as possible."

I threw out another idea.

"If ever there was a time to put *Nightwatch* out of its misery, this is it. It's a money loser. It's just an interview show in the middle of the night with a minuscule audience. It's only there because it's a launching pad for all those jet-fueled egos in Washington. If we took it off we'd save $4 million and we could lay off about forty people. The *Nightwatch* staff is a group of young people who haven't been with CBS very long. They'd have an easier time finding jobs than some of the older people on the list."

Van bristled. "You've got a list that's almost complete. Let's get on with it. Jankowski is never going to agree to take *Nightwatch* off the air."

"I outsmarted myself on that one," I said. "I regret the day I ever sold him that bill of goods about *Nightwatch* the great friend maker."

Van obviously thought I was being indiscreet to mention this in front of Chandler.

"Look, this is an unpleasant business for us all," he said. "Let's do it . . . get it over . . . and get it behind us."

Van and Howard left and I asked Chandler to stay.

"Bob, I have real misgivings about these layoffs," I said.

"I think they're absurd," he said. "The whole thing is crazy."

"There's no holding them off. The whole company is going through a retrenchment. But you and I can delay them until we know who's going to take early retirement."

"Black Rock," Chandler said, "and that includes Sauter, doesn't give a shit about our people. Their attitude is, if we lay off more of them than we have to, so what?"

"Let's not personalize this with Van," I said. "You're the one who's reviewing the names on the list with Law, Personnel, and Business Affairs. You're the only one who knows what each of them is saying. So if you and I both say all the names haven't been approved and reviewed, no one will know the difference."

"I'll be glad to do that," Chandler said, "and in the meantime I'll start trying to find out who's going to take early retirement. Speaking of that, I just received my package of information in the mail. I'm going to go over the numbers, and if they look as attractive as I think they are, I'm probably going to take it."

"Bob, do whatever is right for you and your wife. But I wouldn't want this moment to go by without telling you how much I hope you don't take it. How much I think you're needed here."

I really meant that. I'd started out sizing up Chandler as one of the stuffy mossbacks of CBS News but had come to value him for his bluntness and his willingness to roll up his sleeves and take on difficult tasks. I was also aware of how secure I felt asking him to share in delaying the layoff without worrying I might read about it in the papers or learn that word of our collusion had gotten back to Black Rock.

"I appreciate what you say," Chandler said. "You and I have gotten along rather well even though we've disagreed with one another at times. But I'm pretty sure I'm going to take this. I just don't want to work for a company run by Gene Jankowski."

"Do you feel that strongly about him?"

"I watched him when Leonard was here and I watched him with Sauter and I've watched him with you in the job," Chandler responded. "That man is determined to bury CBS News and I don't want to be here when it happens."

When Chandler left I sat alone in my office pondering what he'd said. You could certainly build a case for his charge. What would I do, I wondered, if I was over fifty-five and eligible for early retirement? I was then fifty-two. The answer I gave myself was: I would take it. Van and I had spent enough idle hours discussing the imagined joys of life after CBS. But those talks were half game, half therapy. Now I was seeing in Chandler someone only a few years older than myself presented with the opportunity to actually do what we'd so often talked about, and I was envious.

I shook off my despondence that day by attending a screening of Moyers's upcoming documentary on immigration. I was joined by Eric Ober and by Perry Wolff, the executive producer, and Elena Mannes, the producer. I'd known Elena since the early seventies when she'd worked as a producer for me at WCBS-TV. Perry was someone who rivaled Bud Benjamin for the title "Mr. Documentary." He joined CBS News in the early fifties and produced the documentary series *Air Power*, which was narrated by Walter Cronkite. Now in his sixties, he was a slight man whose dark hair had thinned but whose energy remained undiminished. Any Perry Wolff documentary was one I looked forward to viewing, but I was particularly anxious to see what he and Elena, collaborating with Moyers, had produced.

Bill was out in the field working on another broadcast but had sent me a note generously thanking me for urging him to take on the subject of immigration. He'd just screened the final material before writing me and he described the broadcast as "a drama of America wrestling with its destiny. This nation of immigrants is engaged in a hard debate over whether we can go on admitting everyone who wants to come."

What Bill didn't refer to in his note but what I saw and heard that day in the screening room was his remarkable ability to listen to Americans. Not once did he fall into the trap of polemicizing. Instead, he allowed the real people of his "drama" to tell their story. Among them:

- A Jewish woman in Miami (whose family came here from Poland) leading a campaign to "save the English language."
- The Cuban owner of a shoe store declaring that his children have the right to speak their native tongue.
- Two black women—sisters—who lost their jobs as janitors to Hispanics describing how they sued (successfully) to get them back.
- Illegal Mexican hard hats calmly and eloquently saying they came to Dallas "because their families back home are starving and this is the only way we have to feed them."
- Redneck hard hats, standing close enough to overhear the interview with the illegals who work on the same construction site, stepping into focus to say their own wages have been depressed from $16 an hour to $11 because of these very workers.

When the lights went on at its conclusion, I turned to Perry and Elena.

"I'm so proud of what you've done. I can't think of anything which has been done on this subject that even comes close."

"Wait till you see what Bill is doing with his next documentary," Elena said.

"That's right," said Perry. "He's using some of these techniques to show the disintegration of the black family structure. It's going to be very controversial."

I left the *CBS Reports* area that day feeling both refreshed by what I'd seen and depressed by the thought of hours which would be lost because of the budget cuts. Twelve hours of documentaries were included in my 1986 budget, but who was to know if they would ever get on the air?

Walking back to my office with Eric, I said, "Bill can be a terrible pain in the ass, but you forget all that when you watch the kind of broadcast we've just seen."

"No doubt about that," Eric said. "Speaking of pains in the ass, can Katz and I see you?"

"Sure . . . what's up?"

"Let him tell you. He's waiting in your office."

Katz was sitting in a chair in my office, holding a piece of paper.

"If it costs money, forget it," I said.

"That's not why I'm here," he said. "I'm not that crazy. This is a list of guests who have turned down opportunities to appear on the *Morning News* because of Phyllis. They not only won't be interviewed by her, they won't appear, period, and that attitude is not limited to people outside CBS News. Some of our own correspondents don't want to appear on the broadcast."

Eric Ober had no real responsibility for the *Morning News*. His area was the public-affairs world of *60 Minutes, West 57th,* and *CBS Reports.* But both Howard and Katz frequently turned to him for help and advice.

"Eric, is this true," I asked, "or is it Katz being cute?"

"I've been accused of a lot of things in my life," Katz said, "but cute has never been one of them."

"Cute as in cunning," I said. "Eric, what about it?"

"I'm afraid he's telling you the truth," Eric said. "There's been a controversy over *West 57th* but at least there are two camps. This whole place is now on edge because people know layoffs are coming. Phyllis has become a symbol. Is she a scapegoat? Maybe. But I think the longer she stays on that broadcast, the more she's going to be seen as proof of the bad management of CBS News."

"Can't really blame them for that," I said. "Let me get Howard to join us."

When Howard arrived I put the question to him.

"These guys feel that Phyllis is becoming an increasingly divisive symbol for the News Division. What do you think?"

"I think most people here believe we're all bloody idiots for having stayed with her this long," Howard said.

"When I tell Van that Phyllis has to go, will you still feel that way?"I asked.

"Mate, the way I feel these days," Howard said, "if he and Jankowski continue to insist that Phyllis stays, they should move the whole bleedin' mess to the Entertainment Division and let them sort it all out."

"They might be inclined to do it," I said, "but at some point it may be preferable to seeing CBS News trying to produce an entertainment show instead of a news broadcast."

"I'd be glad to express my view on the matter," Katz said. "Unfortunately, Mr. Sauter refuses to speak to me, although he mentions my name to enough people these days."

By now Van had developed a theory that Phyllis needed a new producer in the morning and was being widely quoted as saying that as soon as Katz was replaced the broadcast would begin to improve.

"Thank you, Katz, but you're not invited," I said.

"Seriously," he said, "if it would help get Phyllis out of there by telling Van you are also removing me, then do it."

"Jon, we probably will replace you at some point and bring in a new executive producer, but we need you now to provide some continuity if we put a new anchor team in place."

The team I had in mind was actually a trio. The early morning news was anchored by Forrest Sawyer and Faith Daniels. Sawyer had been an anchor in Atlanta, as Daniels had been in Pittsburgh. I'd hired them in the past year for the early bird news. Faith had arrived first and had quickly impressed her co-workers as a serious, hardworking newswoman. Forrest had come a few months later and was handling himself well, particularly in the interviews. I wanted Faith to take over the news blocks for the *Morning News* and Forrest to replace Schieffer. As the replacement for Phyllis George I hoped to bring in Maria Shriver from our Los Angeles Bureau. I'd hired Maria in 1983 to cover the entertainment industry for the *Morning News*. At the time she was a co-anchor on Westinghouse Broadcasting's syndicated magazine program, *PM Magazine.* Art Kaminsky, an agent with clients in news and sports, had sent me her tape. I agreed to look at it mostly as a courtesy to Kaminsky. I knew that Maria was the daughter of Sargent Shriver and Eunice Kennedy, but to me she was just another in the blur of names I associated with "the Kennedy clan." I was surprised at what I saw when I played the tape. An assortment of stories and interviews done with obvious intelligence by a young woman who had a real presence in front of the camera. I was impressed enough to hire her.

In the two years she'd worked in the Los Angeles Bureau she'd developed a corps of supporters led by its bureau chief, Ted Savaglio. I believed that Maria Shriver had the ability and, just as important, the instincts to conduct the interviews for the morning broadcast. I also thought that as viewers came to know this young woman who had grown up in an environment of politics and glamour they would grow to like and respect her. There was just one problem. In a few months Maria was going to marry Arnold Schwarzenegger, the body builder turned actor.

Schwarzenegger obviously had the brains to match his brawn. He successfully used his bulging pectorals as the basis for a movie career which was making him one of the richest men in Hollywood. I didn't know if Maria would be willing to move to New York for a job which involved awakening each morning at three o'clock.

I put the question to Katz.

"I have good news on that front," he said. "I mentioned this to Kaminsky and he says she would definitely move here for that job."

"Katz, I don't trust Kaminsky on this one," I said. "When he brought me Forrest Sawyer the guy was working for our affiliate in Atlanta. I told him I'd want to get permission from them to talk to Forrest. Kaminsky told me they knew he was leaving because Forrest had a better offer from a station in Washington. Like a dope, I believed him, and I really sandbagged the poor guy who runs that station. He didn't have a clue about what was happening until Kaminsky notified him his anchorman had just been signed by CBS News. Why don't you call Maria and tell her you've just had this bright idea but before you mention it to me, you want to know if she'd move here."

Late that afternoon Katz called me.

"I spoke to Maria," he said. "The answer is an unqualified yes."

T he next day Howard and I had lunch with Van. Before going I reminded Howard of his promise to remain firm when Van struggled, as I knew he would, to keep Phyllis on *The CBS Morning News.*

The restaurant I chose was about as far away from the midtown influence of Black Rock as we could go without leaving the city. We met at Frank's, an Italian steak house complete with pressed-tin ceiling and sawdust on the floor in the heart of the meat-packing district on West Fourteenth Street.

After the waiter had taken our orders, I turned to Van.

"I could discover a cure for cancer now and my obit would still read, 'Joyce, who hired Phyllis George in 1985.' I've been a good soldier. I've defended her with affiliates, praised her to the press, but I can't do it anymore."

"Phyllis is not the problem," Van said. "She just needs a good producer who understands her."

"I'm not going to shift this into an argument for Katz," I said. "He probably should be replaced sometime soon. I think he'd welcome it. But Jon Katz didn't hire Phyllis George. You and I did and it was a terrible mistake."

"Jankowski still thinks Phyllis is right for the show," Van said.

"Then let Jankowski produce the broadcast or give it to the Entertainment Division. He's been threatening us with that long enough. I've come to believe it would be better for CBS News to lose it than keep on producing something which is so alien to everything it represents."

Howard joined in with alarm in his voice.

"Ed, you don't really want that to happen," he said. "We'd lose more jobs."

"What we're losing may be more important than those jobs," I said. "We've become a joke."

"I'm not convinced," Van said, "that CBS News will ever be able to get behind the kind of program it takes to be competitive in the morning. Maybe I should set up a unit within the Stations Division which would produce the morning show and let CBS News provide the news blocks in each half hour."

Howard looked horrified. "You can't mean that," he said.

"Maybe you should," I said, "but if that fails and CBS News has dismantled its morning operation, what do you do then?"

Van didn't answer. The food arrived at the table. He took a few bites of his angel-hair pasta, then pushed the bowl aside and reached for his pipe.

"Look, it's over with Phyllis," I said. "Keeping her there is going to rip our place apart. She has to go. I want to replace her with Maria Shriver and bring Forrest Sawyer and Faith Daniels on board in a broadcast that's appropriate for CBS News."

"Remember the question Leahy used to ask us?" Van said. "Will they sell tickets? What you want to do won't sell tickets."

"Maybe . . . maybe not," I said. "Who the hell knows? But I can promise you one thing—it won't be an embarrassment."

Van leaned back in his chair. All three of us were in our shirt sleeves.

"Howard, what do you think?" he asked.

"I think Phyllis was worth a try," he answered, "but I think we have to accept her failure and move on."

Van groaned. "It's going to be a shit storm," he said. "But if that's what you want to do, go ahead. I'll tell Gene what's happening. You should call the Hook before you talk with Phyllis. When would you plan to make the announcement?"

"If I can get my ducks in a row I'd like to make it the Friday afternoon of the Labor Day weekend. It will minimize the press coverage."

In my car on the way back to the Broadcast Center, Howard gave me a pat on the arm.

"Well done, chief. Old Van will thank you for this someday."

"I know Van," I said. "Believe me, he regards what we're doing as an interlude until he can come up with his own plan for the morning."

"We'll have to make it so good he'll change his mind."

"Let's just try to do a broadcast we feel good about," I said. "You should start the negotiations going. Get Ober to help you. He's good at that. Kaminsky's got a problem representing both Sawyer and Shriver. He'll have to do matching deals to avoid one of them feeling slighted. Phyllis is earning seven and Kurtis eight. We shouldn't pay more than five each for their replacements. Remember, we're going to be paying off Phyllis's contract for the next three years."

"Mate, it's worth every penny," Howard said.

On Friday, August 30, Kaminsky finally accepted an offer of $500,000 for each of his clients. I called Hookstratten in his office in Los Angeles.

"I'm glad you phoned," he said. "I've been telling Van for months that you ought to get rid of Katz and get Phyllis a producer who recognized her value. Last week he said I ought to tell that to you and . . ."

"Ed, stop," I said. "The purpose of my call is to tell you we're going to take Phyllis off the broadcast."

"That's a terrible mistake. All America loves Phyllis George."

"Not anymore," I said. "For four months she's been savaged in the press on an almost daily basis. I don't know how the poor woman has been able to keep her head up. And that's not going to change, because we never should have put her in that spot in the first place."

"She's still got a lot to offer."

"I'm sure she does, but not to CBS News," I said. "I'll level with you, Ed. Her presence is ripping this place apart."

"Those fucking newsies," he said. "You can't program for their taste."

"Ed, we should think about how we announce this," I said.

"I'll work out a statement with Phyllis. We'll say that she asked off because of conflict with family responsibilities. But I need your word you'll continue to recognize that it was your decision to remove her and that you have a contractual obligation to pay her for the next three years."

"You've got it," I said. "I want to call Phyllis and tell her. Do you want to talk to her first and prepare her?"

"No, Phyllis likes you. I think she should hear it first from you."

Phyllis was in Kentucky with her husband and children when I reached her.

"You wouldn't believe how beautiful it is here," she said. "I am so looking forward to this weekend. Are you going to be able to get away at all?"

"I hope so," I said. "Phyllis, I'm calling you with some bad news. We're going to replace you on the *Morning News*."

There was a pause before she answered.

"I'm sure you wouldn't be calling me unless your mind was made up," she said. "Has it really gone that far?"

"I'm afraid it has. You've worked so hard and you're such a decent person, I want you to know I feel terrible about the public bashing you've received."

"It's been pretty terrible," she said. "Does Ed know about this?"

"I just finished telling him. He'll be calling you in a few minutes."

"I won't pretend I'm not very, very hurt by this," she said. "But I'm a big girl and I'll get over it."

I put down the phone with sadness, reflecting that this was probably the first big rejection in the charmed life of this lovely woman. Suddenly the door of my office was flung open and Eric Ober rushed in, looking pale.

"Have you talked to Phyllis yet?"

"I just got off the phone with her."

"Oh my God," he said. "I wanted to stop you. Kaminsky says we may not have a deal with Maria."

"My ass we don't have a deal," I said. "When her lawyer accepted it and said he'd discussed it with his client, we had a deal. He knows that."

"He does know that. He said he was talking to Maria by phone. She's up at the family compound in Hyannis Port for the weekend. She was very happy, he said, but suddenly Arnold Schwarzenegger ripped the phone away and screamed, 'Those terms are not good enough for Maria. The deal is off!' "

"I don't believe what I'm hearing," I said. "I know that fuck played the Terminator in a movie, but he can't do this."

"Kaminsky says he's tried to call Maria back and Arnold won't let her speak to him."

"In the meantime, Hookstratten is preparing a statement from Phyllis," I said, "and if I know him, he's already on the phone with the press trying to get his angle into the story."

As if on cue, my secretary buzzed me to say that Sally Bedell Smith from the New York *Times* was on the phone and wanted to discuss the Phyllis George resignation.

"Tell her I'll call her back in a few minutes," I said, then turned back to Ober. "Is there such a thing as a stomach transplant? I think I'm going to need one. Look, you call Kaminsky back. Tell him you have known and worked with me since the early seventies. Tell him in all those years you've never seen me go crazy like this. That I'm calling in the CBS Law Department because I plan to sue both Art and his client. That when I'm through, both of them will look like dog meat, and that CBS News will never deal with Kaminsky again because he's an unethical shit. I know that's all just talk but it's all we've got right now. Act like somebody who's just seen an angry Richard Nixon with his finger on the nuclear button."

Five minutes later Eric called to say Kaminsky had pleaded for one more hour to straighten things out.

"Tell him in one hour we're going public with this whole affair," I said. "I don't know if that will scare him but it scares the shit out of me."

The next hour was like a death watch in my office. I was joined by Katz, Ober and Stringer while we waited for word from Kaminsky. Having bulled through the firing of Phyllis George in spite of the wishes of both Sauter and Jankowski, I was fully aware of the position I'd be in if the announcement of her departure was not coupled with the name of her replacement. The list of reporters calling the CBS News press office was now growing. Each time my secretary buzzed, the group would freeze, hoping it was Kaminsky. Finally my secretary opened the door and said, "Art Kaminsky is on the phone."

I took a deep breath before picking up the phone.

"Yes, Art," I said in a quiet voice.

"You have a deal."

"I'm very glad to hear that," I said, in the same quiet voice, while my office erupted in a scene of pantomimed jubilation. Katz was actually hugging Eric Ober.

"I'm sorry about all this," Kaminsky said. "I do a lot of legal work for that family. I finally told them that if you took me to court I'd testify that I agreed to a deal."

"Art, what happened?"

"I don't really know. But Maria's brother Bobby is the hero. He and Sargent straightened this out."

"What did they say?"

"They told Arnold that in their family a deal was a deal, and Maria had one."

When I finished with Kaminsky, Katz and Ober rushed off to inform the *Morning News* staff of the changes.

Howard remained behind.

"Well, you cleared that hurdle, sport."

"Howard, the big one's ahead."

"Don't worry," he said. "We'll make something of that show yet."

"I'm sure it will be better now, and this had to be done. But Jankowski and Van are never going to support the new team. And the affiliates would like it better if we were announcing Wink Martindale and Annette Funicello. Pray for some movement in the ratings. We're going to need something to help us."

The headline the next morning on the television page of the New York *Times* read: "Phyllis George Quits CBS Morning News." The second paragraph of the story included her statement: "I have come to the conclusion to rearrange my priorities."

The article then continued:

"E. Gregory Hookstratten, Miss George's agent in Hollywood, said in a telephone interveiw, 'I think she is tired. I don't think she found the rigors of the early morning to be compatible with her family life, which is really in Kentucky. She wants to stay at home in Kentucky."

"In a statement yesterday, Mr. Joyce expressed gratitude for the hard work Phyllis did for CBS News. 'I can understand how difficult this year has been for her and her family,' he said. 'We will miss her.' "

Most of the press accounts of the departure of Phyllis George were equally straightforward. Van seemed relieved that her removal had not precipitated the storm of negative press he'd expected. His mood changed on Wednesday, September 4, however, when the weekly *Variety* came out with a story headlined "Sauter's Luster Fades at CBS: 'I Want Phyllis' Mistake Costly.' "

For any one of us, that sort of article would be annoying, even infuriating. For Van it seemed to be a personal calamity. He was convinced that Katz had somehow engineered the story as revenge for his expulsion from Van's luncheon tables. The mystery of "who got Van?" became a prime topic of discussion at CBS News, fueled by his obvious rage over the article. Rather told him it was clearly a "Black Rock bushwhack." I felt that Van was overreacting considerably, but Eric Ober saw it differently.

"Are you aware of how bad things are these days in the Stations Division?" he asked.

"No. I haven't paid much attention."

"You should be aware that New York, Los Angeles, and Philly have terrible news ratings. Chicago has not exactly welcomed Kurtis back like the conquering hero. To make room for him they not only paid him $1 million a year, they blew out Harry."

Harry Porterfield was a distinguished black reporter. I'd signed him to his first anchorman's contract in 1979.

"The black community is so pissed off," Eric said, "that Jesse Jackson is organizing a boycott of CBS-owned television stations. And the division invested in the development of that syndicated show, *America,* so they'd have an early news lead-in. Van was deeply involved in planning that show. It's been such a flop it's wiped out the ratings for the early news on three CBS-owned stations. Also, there's KMOX-TV in St. Louis."

"Yeah, I know they're going to sell it." I said.

"They ought to. Their local news dropped from first to third place in the last two years."

"That fits with something I heard the other day," I said. "In '84 their pre-tax profits were just under $6 million. This year they'll be lucky if they hit $4 million."

"That's my point," Eric said. "Van has to be worried that someone is going to pick up that story and begin asking what happened to the television stations in the two years he's been in charge."

"Eric, I want you to do me a favor. Don't discuss this around here. Not with Howard, not with Katz, not with anyone. Most people in the News Division are so insular they have no idea what else goes on. If you enlighten them, it'll work its way right along the vine into some column."

"I won't," he said. "But keep your eye on those stations. Van has some real problems there."

Eric provided me that day with a missing piece to something which had been puzzling and troubling me for weeks. Van seemed unusually tense and moody. I'd attributed it to the difference between us on the issue of Phyllis George. But his reaction to the negative story in *Variety* became almost obsessive. Kathleen Brown Sauter had even called Maureen to discuss the article, describing Van as "morose."

Maureen and I believe that marrying Kathleen was the single best thing that had happened to Van. The four of us had spent a great deal of time together over the past four years. We had traveled to Europe and Asia, and while Van and I occupied our days with the bureau people, the wives went off on their own adventures, a day at Oxford, the Bullet train to Kyoto, a tour of GUM, the huge department store on Moscow's Red Square. And in May 1985, Maureen and Kathleen had even conducted what could have been a difficult business negotiation. We'd sold our summer home on Martha's Vineyard—our life at CBS seemed to preclude the kind of summer vacations which had once made that house so precious to us—and we were searching for something closer to New York which would be accessible on weekends yet near enough for me to return quickly to the newsroom if a major story developed. As it happened, the Sauters were about to sell a house in upper Fairfield County, Connecticut. They wanted to move further up in that state to the area around the

Housatonic River, which offers some of the best fly fishing in the Northeast. When Maureen first mentioned buying their house, I ruled it out.

"Van and I can't very well dicker with one another over the price of a house," I said.

"You don't have to," she said. "Kathleen and I can handle it."

I was still somewhat dubious but had to laugh that night when I heard Maureen discussing the house with Kathleen on the phone.

"You and I are both big girls. We can do this without involving the men. Quote me one price—the price you think is fair and realistic. I'll say either yes or no."

As a result, we bought a weekend house in Connecticut.

So I was not surprised that Kathleen would feel comfortable telling Maureen how "morose" Van had been lately. She even speculated that it might have something to do with the approach of his fiftieth birthday, and asked us to attend a surprise party on Saturday, September 14, at their new house in Litchfield County.

It would be a small gathering, she said. The Joyces, the Rathers, the Stringers, and the Brokaws. One of Kathleen's best friends was Meredith Brokaw, wife of Tom Brokaw, the NBC News anchorman. It was a friendship which originated in California during the time Tom was a local anchorman with KNBC Television and Kathleen was married to her first husband, a West Coast attorney.

Driving along Route 7 that Saturday on my way to the party, I was curious and more than a bit concerned about how Rather, who was so accustomed to being the center of our universe, would react to the presence of another bright star, Brokaw, in the same room. The first clue came at one o'clock in the parking lot of a gas station in the town of Kent where all the guests were to rendezvous before arriving en masse at the Sauters'. The Rathers were not there when we pulled in. The Stringers were. Forty-five minutes later we had pretty well exhausted the scenic opportunities available from the gas station and there was still no sign of the Rathers. A small Japanese car cruised into the lot. Looking out of the driver's window was the familiar face of an anchorman, Tom Brokaw.

"Kathleen asked me to drive down and see if you were here," he said. "She was beginning to worry she'd given all of you the wrong day."

I turned to Howard. "Let's go. I think we've waited long enough."

Howard looked worried. "I don't like to think of Dan arriving and finding no one here."

"I didn't drive two hours to spend the day watching oil checks," I said. "You can wait if you want."

Our small caravan pulled out of the filling station and in ten minutes arrived at the Sauters' new house, a lovely country home on a hill which had been owned by the American artist Eric Sloane.

Van seemed in good spirits. He offered cold beer and a tour of the house which included his newest toy, a large satellite dish with which he could bring in the television programs his remote location made inaccessible by a regular antenna. At least another hour went by with no sight of the Rathers. I'd never met Brokaw before and was finding him pleasant and relaxed. I have no idea what he's like to work with, but in a social environment he's good company. It was a glorious September day and I was standing outside in a garden area enjoying the warm sun with Brokaw and with Kathleen and Maureen when the Rathers drove up. Jean Rather carried a present for Van into the house and Dan walked up the small hill to where the three of us were standing. He was wearing dark glasses, a safari hat, and a "why am I here?" look on his face. I could see his jaw muscles were clenched. I had seen that look before. He was now experiencing the kind of tension that blocks peripheral vision and bursts blood vessels.

As he approached us I heard him mumble "Hello, Tom," without actually looking at Brokaw. Nervously he went over to Kathleen and kissed her on the cheek, then to Maureen for another kiss. Coming toward me, he was watching Brokaw out of the corner of his eye. I stuck out my hand and said, "Hello, Dan." He shook hands and leaned toward me in a daze. I felt a wet kiss on the side of my face. I looked at Maureen, who was trying not to laugh. But I avoided eye contact with Brokaw, who'd been standing next to me.

Finally I said to Rather, "We were worried about the two of you."

Rather stared at me as if realizing for the first time who I was.

"Traffic was terrible. We got a late start." Then to Kathleen: "Sorry about that. I know you wanted all of us to arrive together."

By the time that afternoon was over I could understand why Brokaw had been successful for so many years as the host of *The Today Show*. He treated Rather like a difficult interview and drew him out with a long series of friendly questions. He learned that Dan was planning on staying overnight at a nearby house because he hoped to do some fly fishing the next morning on the Housatonic. At one point Brokaw disappeared for a while and returned with a number of trout flies from a nearby tackle shop which were right for the Housatonic hatches in September. Gradually Rather relaxed and everyone began to have a good time.

We were all in good spirits if not fine voice when we gathered around a tape machine which was playing an instrumental version of "You're a Grand Old Flag." Holding specially prepared song sheets which Kathleen had ordered from a specialty shop in California, we sang such memorable verses as "Happy birthday, Van, you're a truly great man—with a beard so fine and a pipe that's divine—you look so fab—here, have a Tab."

It was true corn and even Rather was laughing as he sang. I haven't seen Brokaw since that September day in Litchfield County. I have no idea how he reacted to the sight of the anchorman of *The CBS Evening News* greeting the CBS News President with a kiss. I've often mused over his drive home that night with Meredith Brokaw.

"Do you think they're always that affectionate with one another, Meredith? Is that what it takes to become number one?"

Whatever laughter we'd enjoyed that weekend would have to last for a long while. The months that followed offered few occasions for mirth. I returned to work knowing this would be the week of the layoffs. Thursday, September 19, was now the designated day. The atmosphere at CBS News was agonizing. But a strangely upbeat mood prevailed at Black Rock. In fact, on Wednesday, September 18, Jankowski summoned a group of his senior executives, including me, to a large screening room to watch a film he'd commissioned called "Making Television—Inside CBS," a skillfully produced look at the Broadcast Group. Jankowski said he'd had it put together in order to have something to show to schools and to "influential members of the Washington community." I had just left a meeting with Stringer and Chandler in which I had said I believed there were certain people who should learn about their layoff directly from me. The Vice Presidents, for example. The three of us were approaching the next day with a sense of dread. Now I was sitting in a darkened room watching a film about the Broadcast Group which was not intended for broadcast and which cost at least $50,000 and perhaps as much as $100,000 to produce. After the screening, I would be offered cocktails by waiters in white jackets. All of this on the eve of the largest cutbacks and layoffs in the history of CBS. It was unreal. There was a particular moment which seemed almost hallucinatory. The CBS News segment of the film came on the screen and I saw the faces of people who, I knew, would discover the next morning that they no longer had jobs. When it was over, Jankowski spoke for a few minutes about the Broadcast Group and told us that "the future is in our hands."

The next day was every bit as terrible as I'd feared. A day of incalculable sadness at CBS News. A number of people had accepted the early-retirement offer and some recent job openings had not been filled, so the total number of those laid off had been reduced to seventy-four. But this was no consolation to those who were now out of work. Everyone had old friends who would be going, and the coming departure of the early retirees was equally regretted: Bob Chandler, Ernie Leiser, Bud Benjamin, and many others who'd been part of the fabric of CBS News would be leaving, too. Bud had called me a few days earlier.

"I would't be able to sleep nights if I didn't take early retirement, knowing some poor devil might lose his job if I don't," he said.

As I walked through the halls that day I could sense the hurt and the hostility around me. At one point I walked past Marian Glick, a news editor in network radio, whom I'd known and worked with for over twenty years. She typified the professional news person who'd made CBS News an organization of such high standards. She was among those retiring early. She must have sensed something in my face, because she walked over to me and kissed me. The memo I'd sent to the organization describing the scope and the reasons behind the layoffs had just been distributed.

"I know how terrible you feel," Marian said.

I walked into my office, closed the door, and sat alone for several minutes before I could continue. Rather didn't come to work until 5 P.M., and he left shortly after the broadcast. The next day a violent earthquake erupted in Mexico which devastated Mexico City. Venardos came to me with a proposal for taking Rather to Mexico for special coverage of the tragedy. I agreed and Rather left within twenty-four hours. Now he could focus all of his pent-up vitality on covering a single terrible event and he was superb. I was glad I'd agreed to send him even though the cost of our special coverage of the earthquake sent its own aftershocks through our devastated budget.

But the Mexico City earthquake accomplished the impossible at CBS News. For the next few days people sublimated the pain of the layoffs by working around the clock on that horrifying story.

However, on October 3 something happened which caused the anguish and anger to resurface. Charles Collingwood died. Collingwood had retired from CBS News in 1982 after forty-two years. Since then he'd drawn a "special correspondent's" salary in return for occasional services. There is a famous story about the time Murrow interviewed a twenty-three-year-old Collingwood at the Savoy Hotel in London and came close to not hiring him because Collingwood arrived wearing argyle socks, a statement of dandyism which to Murrow seemed inconsistent with serious reporting. It's yet another tribute to Murrow that he could see through Collingwood's Beau Brummel façade and bring to CBS News someone who would not only slog through the mud and cold of European battlegrounds but continue to report with distinction through the Six-Day War in the Middle East and the conflict in Vietnam. In fact, at the height of that war, in 1968, he became the first American network correspondent to be allowed to visit Hanoi.

For all those years he remained very much the dandy with his bespoke suits and trilby hats which earned him the affectionate nickname "the Duke of Collingwood." Morley Safer, who'd been mentored by Collingwood during the time they shared in the London Bureau, was only one of many open in their admiration of this remarkable journalist. But there are people whose early years are so truly golden that it seems almost inevitable that fate will impose some balance of sadness in their later life. Collingwood lost his wife, the former Hollywood actress Louise Allbritton, to cancer. Also, his heavy drinking had been one of the open secrets at CBS News, and just when it seemed that his problem was under control he learned he had cancer himself. I heard of his illness from Morley Safer just before the beginning of 1985, and I sent him a note telling him how much his presence at CBS News was missed, adding, "As all of us enter 1985 we do it on the shoulders of men like Charles Collingwood, and I wanted you to know how aware we are of that debt."

A few days later he responded with a handwritten note relating some of the details of his illness, and went on to say, "What I have just told you is not at all confidential—I feel no shame or guilt over what has happened to me; it strikes the virtuous and the wicked without discrimination." A few months later, in March, Rather mentioned he'd seen Collingwood, who had come home from the hospital and was worried he might have to relinquish his office at CBS News. I sent him another note telling him I had just made sure that "your office facility was extended into the indefinite future. I didn't want you to have any worries about that at a time when all of your energies should be focused on prevailing."

A thank-you note followed a few days later on March 6, 1985: "It's a funny thing about offices, one has become so used to them it has become difficult to work anywhere else. I find that the vestiges of an office routine keep me from sitting around the house in a dressing gown all day, letting ole rockin' chair git me, which I do not want to happen."

Not long thereafter, the CBS News Business Affairs Department notified me routinely that the Collingwood special correspondent contract was about to expire. It didn't pay Collingwood a large sum, but I was certain that it was important to him, as was his continued association with the news organization to which he'd devoted his life. I wrote him asking if he would consider a renewal. If so, CBS News would be honored to continue the relationship.

"Having mulled over your suggestion that I might continue my present situation as a CBS News special correspondent," he responded, "I have come to the conclusion that that is just what I would like to do.

"I suppose I am a rather conventional person and one of the major conventions of my productive life has been my long association with CBS. It would be a real pang for me, especially now, if that association were to end.

"I suspect that you are suggesting this as much from personal consideration as from expectations of my future productivity. I welcome it, nonetheless."

Now, a little less than five months later, Charles Collingwood had died.

On Wednesday, October 9, St. Bartholomew's Church on Park Avenue was packed with those who wished to pay their respects and to hear eulogies from Morley Safer, Dan Rather, Bill Leonard, and other colleagues of "the Duke."

After the service a slightly smaller group gathered in the large downstairs room of the Century Club; many of those on hand were in their fifties and sixties. I had arranged for CBS News to pay for this gathering as my own gesture of respect for this wonderfully elegant man. Nothing so obviously right should be looked upon in hindsight with regret, but this occasion brought together in one room a very larger number of past, present, and soon-to-be-past employees of CBS News, and in the murmur of that large room I could hear questions being asked about the state of CBS. "Were the layoffs really necessary?" "How could this have happened at CBS News?" "Would it have happened if Paley was still in charge?" "Was it really caused by the takeover threat, or was it because of CBS blunders in publishing, toys, musical instruments, and theatrical films?"

What had been intended as a remembrance for Charles Collingwood—which, ironically, I was sponsoring—had become instead a wake for an era in television which was being destroyed. One of those present was Don Hewitt, who in the grip of this mood began to consider an idea I would learn about in a few days.

Milling among the guests, I began to encounter an almost palpable hostility. I would engage someone in conversation only to discover him finding a reason to walk away. I spotted Stringer and walked over to him.

"I'm not sure this was a good idea," he said. "The rage building up here is incredible."

"I'm sensing the same thing. No one has quite built up the nerve to tell me what they think yet."

"I'm beginning to get those 'how can you be a part of . . . ?' questions," Howard said.

"There's a fair amount of firewater being consumed here, Howard. Some of the elders particularly are knocking it back. We might do well to quietly depart."

In the car on the way back to the Broadcast Center, Howard and I compared notes.

"I've managed to reach my mid-forties without experiencing anything remotely like this," he said. "You could cut the anger in that room with a knife, particularly from those in their sixties. Even Bill Leonard avoided me."

"I know. It was like *Cocoon* gone sour."

"Old Van's a crafty beggar," Howard said. "He didn't even attend the funeral."

"He was out of town, Howard."

"Of course he was."

The most perceptive articulation of the rage at CBS News came from Andy Rooney. Andy had joined Eric Sevareid and other old friends of Collingwood in a eulogistic roundtable discussion on *The CBS Morning News.* He made a comment to the effect that Collingwood had not been treated all that well by CBS in his declining years. I sent him a note telling him I thought he'd been unfair. Andy wrote me back citing a time a few years earlier when Collingwood had done a first-rate job narrating and writing a Brezhnev obituary and how deeply hurt he'd been when his voice was taken off the report and the script read by Rather. Andy had to have known that this incident occurred before my arrival at CBS News because he added something else.

"Perhaps I was unfair to CBS in my comments but I was not talking about you. Many of us at CBS feel we have been loyal to something which no longer exists. Perhaps we are in love with our own loyalty. Each of us had friends who were fired in what seemed like an unnecessarily efficient manner. 'There but for the grace of . . .' was the feeling we all share. CBS got rid of some deadwood but it got rid of some wood that wasn't dead, too. And, I suspect, that like a forest, there's a purpose for a little deadwood."

That captured with exquisite painfulness the anger and the grief which was sweeping across CBS News. To make matters worse, no significant layoffs were taking place in the other divisions or groups of CBS. Jankowski seemed indifferent to the turmoil to the point of insensitivity.

The same week of the Collingwood funeral approximately two hundred executives of the Broadcast Group were asked to come to the Titus Theatre of the Museum of Modern Art for an 8:30 A.M. screening of his lobbying film, "Making Television—Inside CBS." In the question-and-answer which followed, Jankowski was asked why the numerous CBS people seen in the film were not identified by name. His answer brought a hush to the room.

"I'd like the film to have a long life and some of those people may not be here," he said.

The silence which followed was broken by scattered and self-conscious laughter. At the Titus Theatre, Gene told the group once again that "the future is in our hands." He clasped his hands and extended them when he said this.

Jankowski's Vice President for Communication and Information, George Schweitzer, who'd supervised the production of the film, had repeatedly and persistently asked to arrange a screening for the *Evening News* staff, many of whom appeared in its scenes. I went back to my office and wrote a memo which I sent to Schweitzer, with a copy to Van, telling him not to bring that film to the *Evening News:* "CBS News remains a bruised and lacerated institution. Gene's remarks this morning at the Titus Theatre that supers were not used because some of the people in the film might not be here within the film's life span represented a prophecy which had already and singularly come true for CBS News."

At this time one of the most bizarre hijackings in this modern era of the terrorist occurred. A band of Palestinians took over the Italian cruise ship *Achille Lauro,* making hostages of its five hundred passengers. Leon Klinghoffer, a sixty-nine-year-old American, was murdered and his body thrown overboard. Again CBS News went on a twenty-four-hour alert and began moving crews and correspondents around the world. Late in the day during our coverage of the story I received a phone call from William Casey, Director of the CIA.

"Mr. Joyce," he said, "I'd like to discuss a story one of your reporters uncovered and is planning to broadcast. He's learned that we are intercepting and listening to radio communication between the terrorists aboard the *Achille Lauro* and an Arab state. This is true, but if he broadcasts that information those signals will stop and that will lessen our ability to rescue those passengers. It will place the lives of the passengers in even greater danger."

I thanked the Director for the information and made no commitment, saying only I would quickly look into the issue. My first call was to Jack Smith in Washington. He confirmed that David Martin, our Pentagon correspondent, had the story. I told Smith about the phone call I'd just received from the CIA Director and I concluded, "I don't think there is any way we can justify reporting that information at this time."

"I agree with you," Jack said. "So does Martin. But you'd better talk to Dan."

I headed back toward Rather's office and asked Venardos to join us there. It was now 6:15 P.M., the first feed of the *Evening News* was at 6:30. I told them both about my phone call from Casey and began listing my reasons for not broadcasting the story. I saw the by now familiar sight of the anchorman growing rigid with fury as I continued.

"In the interest of time," he said, "let me stop this. I can see where this is going and how it's going to end up. Let me just say for the record that every time we let this administration tell us what we can and cannot broadcast we are making a mistake and that shouldn't happen."

I started to argue that there were damn few times when government interference was justified and this was one of them. Then I realized he was correct about one thing: we were close to airtime, and the issue was settled anyway.

"We'll have to discuss this when we all have more time," I said, and left. I was hoping for a quick and happy ending to the plight of the remaining hostages on the *Achille Lauro,* and not just for humanitarian reasons. The CBS News budget was being hijacked as well and it couldn't be happening at a worse moment.

I was attending frequent meetings at Black Rock to discuss the 1986 budget and at each of them I was asked about the '85 budget, which was now headed toward an overrun of millions of dollars because of our special coverage. We'd just eliminated 125 jobs but we were moving even more deeply into the red. At one of these meetings, Jankowski turned to me angrier than I'd ever seen him before.

"CBS News has proved it's very good at one thing," he said. "Running over its budget."

The financial pressure assailing all of us was unparalleled in my lifetime at CBS.

Wyman had even decreed that the fleet of CBS aircraft be sold. Aside from the revenues the sales would produce, it was an effective piece of symbolism. CBS executives loved those planes the way Bedouin chieftains love Arabian stallions. Paley was described as so angry about this decision he was making plans to buy the large Gulfstream jet for himself. It was the first clue I'd perceived that there might be renewed tension between Paley and Wyman. I was so busy dealing with layoffs, major stories, and a budget which was rapidly spiraling out of control that a great deal of what was going on in the Corporation escaped my notice. I was worried about how CBS News was going to cover the Reagan-Gorbachev summit conference in Geneva when every dollar we spent for that coverage would be over budget.

Increasingly I felt like someone trying to do the sidestroke in a whirlpool. Then, in the middle of October, Laurence Tisch finally completed his last purchase of CBS stock, bringing his holdings to 25 percent of the total shares.

The stock had been valued at $73.88 when Senator Jesse Helms and the Fairness in Media group first began urging conservatives to "become Dan Rather's boss" through ownership of CBS. Now it had risen to $117.50 and CBS offered Tisch a seat on its Board of Directors. He accepted. And I barely noticed. I was trying to dig my way out from underneath an avalanche which had been triggered a few days earlier by Don Hewitt.

Anyone who has ever enjoyed a sunny October day in New England knows the special pleasure that comes from what could be the last warm encounter with the outdoors until spring.

That was the sort of afternoon I had on Friday, October 11, 1985. I had taken the day off for a head start on the long Columbus Day weekend.

The year hadn't provided many opportunities for this kind of self-indulgence. I was tired. The past ten days had taken a toll. The past ten months, for that matter. Helms, Westmoreland, Boesky, Turner, and Tisch. Major layoffs and budget slashes at a time with an uncommon number of major news stories. The TWA hijacking, the tragedy of the *Achille Lauro,* the earthquake in Mexico City, turmoil in South Africa, and an unexpected summit meeting in Geneva. Critical, demanding events for a news organization. Costly events for a News Division facing relentless pressure to slash its budget. In an earlier era the cost of coverage would have been considered the price a corporation would be willing to pay for choosing to house a great news organization. Not this year. Perhaps not ever again.

I was determined to check this baggage in for the weekend and not reclaim it until Tuesday morning, minutes—perhaps seconds—before my arrival in my office at the Broadcast Center. I had just come back to my new house in Connecticut after a five-mile run with "Bo, the Wonder Dog," my overachieving Jack Russell terrier, on the dirt trails of a nearby state park. Bo was enjoying a bowl of fresh well water and I was about to diminish a can of Amstel Light when the phone rang.

It was Howard Stringer.

"Hello, sport. Sorry to intrude on your weekend, but I have a bizarre one for you."

"Stringer, it will take a lot to activate my 'Give a Shit' meter, but do your best."

"It's that bloody Hewitt."

"What's he done now?"

"He says they want to buy *60 Minutes* and the *Evening News.*"

"Howard, who is they?"

According to Howard, Hewitt had approached his famous co-workers on *60 Minutes* with his latest inspiration: they could use their celebrity to attract the financial backing with which to buy CBS News, or at least the key parts of it.

The stars of *60 Minutes* are bright, traveled people. Through their position in one of television's top ten broadcasts, they had reaped the kind of financial reward and security most Americans can only hope to achieve through winning a lottery. In a world where so much is amazingly accessible, why not consider owning your own broadcasts? And wasn't this just a variation of what Hewitt had been seeking anyway? In an earlier era, D. W. Griffith, Douglas Fairbanks, Mary Pickford, and Charlie Chaplin had seen just such a dream come true when they formed United Artists. Why not let Don explore it? Perhaps this was the start of "United Anchors."

"Howard," I asked, "where is the anchorman in all of this?"

"As far as I can tell, he's not part of it. He says Hewitt is just doing this to try and reopen his contract . . . but it's obvious he's discussing it with Don."

"It's so farfetched," I said, "I can't imagine Rather getting within ten feet of it. What's the situation as of now?"

Howard said that Hewitt had tried to get through to Jankowski, who was unavailable. He then called Jim Rosenfield, the most senior of the four Executive Vice Presidents, and laid the idea out for him. Rosenfield reached Jankowski, who agreed to meet with Don on Tuesday to hear his proposal. Since I had the day off and Howard was in his office, Rosenfield had described all this to him.

I listened patiently, shaking my head.

"Howard, I think Dan is probably right. This is really a cover for Don to get a meeting with Gene so he can bring up the issue of a new contract. Gene will tell him CBS News is not for sale. He'll tell him it's the center jewel in the great crown. Not once will he refer to the principle of never allowing inmates to run an asylum. He'll think it, but he won't say it. Let's just consider this another example of Don being irrepressible and try to enjoy the weekend."

That Tuesday morning I drove in from Connecticut and arrived a few minutes later than usual, shortly after nine. Waiting for me was the message that Dan Rather wanted to come by. When he arrived it was to talk about Hewitt.

"Don is trying to get me to join him today for his lunch with Jankowski."

It was interesting: Dan simply took for granted that I would know what he was talking about.

"Are you going?"

"I have a long-standing lunch date with Lesley Stahl and I don't plan to cancel it."

"That strikes me as smart," I said.

"Don has a way of dragging other people into things like this. I'm not going to be used so Don can reopen his contract."

The conversation was brief. Rather left and I started to prepare for the day ahead. Gorbachev was now planning a trip to Paris in advance of the Geneva summit. Venardos wanted to meet with me and present a request to take Rather and the *Evening News* to Paris. The fact that Rather hadn't mentioned it this morning did not surprise me. Increasingly he used surrogates for that sort of request. Ambassadors moving between two powers.

My executive phone rang and it was Tom Wyman.

"Can you believe how bush this Hewitt proposal is?" he asked.

"I really can't," I said. "Even for Don, who can come up with some off-the-wall ideas."

"If anyone has the notion that Mr. Paley might have played a part in that, I can assure you it's not the case," Wyman said. "I've talked with him about it and he thinks it's absurd."

Actually I had wondered if there was a Paley connection. Don and his wife, Marilyn, were frequent social companions of Paley. A chance to mention a weekend with Paley in the Hamptons was something Don never passed up.

"Larry Tisch feels the same way," Wyman continued.

"I'm glad to hear that."

Then Wyman moved to the obvious reason for his call.

"Where does Rather fit into all of this?"

"He just left my office a few minutes ago. He doesn't want any part of it. He thinks it's just Hewitt trying to reopen his contract."

"I'm glad to hear that," Wyman said. "It is so terribly bush."

I received no phone call from Jankowski that day. I did hear from Van in midafternoon.

"Gene had his lunch with Hewitt," he said.

"How'd it go?"

"Gene told him CBS News was not for sale. Then he says Hewitt began to tell him how bad morale is at CBS News."

"What did you say to Gene about that?"

"I told him anytime you lay off a lot of people you can expect morale to be bad."

It turned out Hewitt had said considerably more than that. He told Jankowski that morale was bad not because of the layoffs but because the President of CBS News no longer reported directly to Gene . . . that people felt CBS News no longer had that favored status which always had made it special. Jankowski replied that Don shouldn't worry, because "we'll either fix it or change it." If he'd held a press conference that statement couldn't have circulated with greater speed. By the end of the day his quote was known to everyone at CBS News.

The next day Van called from another city telling me the Broadcast Group press office was getting a lot of phone calls.

"They're asking if it's true that you're on shaky ground. What's going on?"

"Our press office is getting the same calls, only the question is being asked about both of us," I replied.

Eric Ober had just left my office a few minutes before Van called. He had heard Hewitt's replay of the Jankowski lunch to a group in *60 Minutes.* I described it to Van.

"We'll either fix it or change it," I repeated. "That's not quite a ringing endorsement for the executives who have just implemented Mr. Jankowski's layoffs."

"No, it's not," Van said.

"The story is now all over this place," I said, "and the only one who can stop it is Jankowski. He has to make one strong statement of endorsement and it'll be over. I'm going to call and tell him that."

"No," Van said, "let me call him and tell him that."

"Tell him something else. This is a tough job in good times and these are bad times. Managing news stars is like being a lion tamer. You walk into the cage with a chair, a whip, and a gun. The chair will break, the whip won't hurt them, and the gun fires blanks. All that keeps you alive is the fact that the big cats don't know that. I think Gene just gave the secret to the cats."

"Are you going to talk to Hewitt?"

"I've just tried to reach him and he's not in his office."

"Why don't you hold off," Van said, "until we get a better idea of what's coming down."

"Sure. Besides, Gene is the one who has to talk to Don."

Later that afternoon Eric Ober came to me with the report Don had just given *60 Minutes* staffers of his latest conversation with Jankowski.

"According to Don, Gene called him and said, 'Remember I told you we'd either fix it or change it? Well, we're not going to change it, we're going to fix it.' "

"Lovely," I said. "Once again Gene comes through as a tower of strength. Can you tell me what the fuck that means?"

"Ed, I don't know."

"When they make a movie of this," I said, "why is it I think I'm going to be played by Woody Allen? Would you believe that in five minutes I'm going to be serving tea and exchanging gifts with officials from Tokyo Broadcasting who are here to open their new bureau? And tomorrow I'm flying to Paris so Rosenfield, Sauter, and I can have a dinner with executives of the French phone company to celebrate our new satellite deal with them. Eric, keep your ears open while I'm gone. God only knows what you'll hear."

In Paris, Van and I had lunch at Bofingers. In the past, dining together here had always been an occasion for celebration. This time it was different. We were both depressed. Van had been in the bureau earlier in the day and had encountered Hewitt, who was there to help edit a *60 Minutes* story.

"I told Don he was a destructive asshole," Van said. "It just bounced off him."

"That's Don. In that sixty-three-year-old body there lives a fourteen-year-old adolescent."

"A ton of negative press is being generated by all of this," Van said. "Before I left New York I was interviewed by Tony Schwartz for an article in *New York* magazine. I think it's going to be rough on me, rough on you, and rough on Wyman."

"Jankowski?"

"He didn't mention him."

"It's amazing," I said, "how he goes unnoticed. You know, the irony is, we are by far the most successful of the three network news organizations, but we're the place that's on fire. You would think that Jankowski would have automatically responded to Don by saying that to him and talking about the tough year we've come through."

"Eduardo, Gene doesn't do strength," Van said. "He's not into firm position."

"At some point," I said, "you cross a pain threshold and begin to ask yourself serious questions about what you're doing with what remains of your life. I look at those guys who took early retirement with a certain amount of envy."

"Hey, I wish I was eligible," Van said. "I've got to tell you, when I'm fifty-five I'm out. There are just a few more years in school for Kathleen's children."

"I'm past that. It's just Maureen and me and we don't spend as much time together as we'd like to anyway."

Van looked at me.

"You know, if you ever decided to pack it in, I think I might come back."

I chuckled. "I don't think it's ever possible to move backward like that. It's never what you think it's going to be."

"I don't know," he said. "I think I could return . . . like the Dauphin."

Most of the rest of the day was spent in the Paris Bureau on the phone with New York. The Hewitt "Buy CBS News" story had produced a flood of negative press just as Van had predicted. "Discord in the House of Murrow." "Morale at CBS News Low." The stories were hard on me, hard on Van, and hard on Wyman. Jankowski was hardly mentioned.

Our dinner with the high-ranking officials of the French phone company was a formal affair, with numerous toasts. After the dinner Rosenfield, Sauter, and I adjourned to a nearby piano bar where a black American jazz pianist, Joe Turner, was performing. We sat drinking wine, listening to medleys of jazz standards, and talking about CBS. Rosenfield stunned us both by saying he had decided to accept the early-retirement package.

"The numbers are right, and I just don't know what my future is at CBS. I told Gene I'd stay if my duties were expanded and he didn't respond, so I'm going."

"That's a shocker," I said.

"Gene's reorganization in 1983 made it impossible for any of us to do our jobs," he said. "There are layers within layers within layers now. It's crazy. We're all tripping over one another."

He raised his wineglass.

"It's too bad, fellows, we had a good thing going."

I looked at Van, remembering the role he'd played in convincing Gene to make those changes in 1983. He raised his glass and clinked with Rosenfield's.

"Big guy," he said, "you're right . . . it was a good thing."

That night after leaving Rosenfield, Van and I called Stringer in New York and asked him if there were more stories. There were.

"They're all claiming that Hewitt tried to get both your scalps," Howard said. "Don gets quoted saying it's not true, then the rest of the article is filled with anonymous quotes about how bad things are. It's a bit like knowing there's a fire but not knowing where the smoke is coming from."

"We'll be back tomorrow," Van said. "In the meantime why don't you bring in that kid from *Variety*, Goldman, and sit him down with a few people—Joan, Eric, you. Get Rather to join you and tell him what Ed has done for CBS News."

I was touched by that since Van was as much the target of these stories as I was.

"What Van and I have both done, Howard," I said.

Before the week was over, variations of the Hewitt offer to buy CBS News and the turmoil in the News Division appeared in the New York *Times,* the Washington *Post, Newsday, Electronic Media, TV Guide,* and other publications.

The *Variety* article which grew out of Van's suggestion was not particularly helpful. In it Ober responded to a charge that I had ambitions for a high position at Black Rock by averring, "I have never heard Ed Joyce say he wants any other job than being President of CBS News."

And Stringer, to an allegation that I was "not in touch with staffers at CBS News," replied, "He's at the *Evening News* every day."

Richman was the most articulate: "With all the things facing the corporation and with all the financial pressure," she said, "to run the News Division to the level of success he's run it shows how cockeyed some of the rumors are."

The quote from Rather struck me as odd but at least it was supportive: "Joyce has been among the most vocal supporters on First Amendment issues."

Even Van was quoted: "There will be no changes in the management of CBS News."

Until then we'd both been joint targets. After that the situation gradually began to shift. The by now famous Hewitt-Jankowski lunch was being reported as a meeting at which Hewitt had asked for "Joyce's scalp."

Incredibly, all of the stories which dealt with his offer to buy CBS News reported it as though it was something which conceivably could have happened. None of the reporters even asked if the News Division could possibly survive as an independent entity. A look at our disfigured budget would have provided the answer. Certainly CBS News as it existed in 1985 could not have survived without the financial resources of the rest of a Broadcast Group which included a television network and the five profitable television stations. These same reporters also failed to take note of the fact that Hewitt's proposal involved the possibility of purchasing the *Evening News* and *60 Minutes.* The less profitable areas of the News Division, such as the *CBS Reports* documentary unit, were not part of this initial inquiry.

Van and I returned to New York on the Concorde and were in our offices by 10 A.M. I'd flown the Concorde twice before. Once on an upgrade; another when I'd paid the difference in fare out of my own pocket. It seemed justified this time because of the obvious crisis which was taking place in the News Division. Someone at CBS pointed out the Concorde flight to a reporter at *Variety,* who then ran a story citing it as an example of lavish spending at a time of budget cuts and layoffs.

I walked into my office that morning carrying my suitcase and found a copy of a memo from Don Hewitt, addressed to Jankowski, with copies to Sauter, Joyce, Rather, Wallace, Safer, Sawyer, Moyers, and Rosenfield.

"Dear Gene," it began. "What started out as an effort to let you know that six of us who helped build CBS News were interested in buying it if it ever came on the market has degenerated into what is being perceived as a 'get Ed Joyce movement.' I, for one, want to go on record as disassociating myself from that."

I found the memo interesting for more than the obvious reason. Ed Bradley and Harry Reasoner were not among those sent copies. But Moyers and Rather were. By now Dan was publicly saying he had not been a serious participant and was trying to distance himself from the proposal.

The rest of the memo was equally fascinating.

"If this continues to be perceived as a 'cabal against Ed Joyce' as Van told me it was, I no longer want any part of it and will henceforth confine myself to the job I am paid to do and will consider what happens to the rest of CBS News none of my business."

I looked up from the memo and saw Eric standing in my doorway. "Come in," I said. "Take a look at this."

I handed him Hewitt's memo to Jankowski. When he finished he nodded his head.

"That fits with what Don is telling me he said. That's why I wanted to see you, and also to tell you about the meeting we had with Goldman from *Variety*."

"Thanks for doing that."

"This thing is crazy, but I want to tell you about Rather at that meeting. Howard convinced him to do it and he showed up like he didn't want to be there. Then while the rest of us were telling Goldman how much you'd done for this place, it was like Dan was trying to bury you with faint praise. To call you a vocal supporter on First Amendment issues, while the rest of us are reminding Goldman of how successful this place is in spite of the bombs that have been going off for the past years, just seemed bizarre."

I sighed. "Well, I suppose in view of the number of times I've overruled him and the tensions between us during the past few months, I should be happy he showed up at all."

"Ed, that guy owes you a lot, but he doesn't want to admit it."

"Maybe not even to himself, Eric. What about Hewitt?"

"That's another bizarre one. Don is now telling me that Rather has seized on the turmoil that was created by the offer to buy CBS News to make it an anti-Ed Joyce campaign."

"I plan to call Don this morning anyway," I said. "Do you think he will tell me that?"

"He might. Don is very angry at Dan right now. But he's also afraid of him, like everyone else at CBS News."

"Eric, you've been a good friend. This whole thing is like fencing with shadows."

"Well, you may be learning who's casting one of them," he said.

When Eric left I called Hewitt and asked him to come see me.

A few minutes later a head peeked around the edge of my door. It was Hewitt, with a sad smile on his face.

"Is it safe to come in here?"

"Sure it is."

I walked Don over to a sofa and sat in a chair next to it.

"I am so sorry I started this whole thing," he said.

"It was crazy," I said. "They're not going to sell the News Division—it's the cement that helps hold the whole affiliate system together. Without us they wouldn't have a network."

"I know that. Now I know it. Even Paley has told me I went on a fool's errand. Look . . . lemme tell you how all this got started. That thing at the Century Club after the Collingwood funeral. It turned out to be a meeting of the CBS News old-timers' club . . . and we were all talking about the layoffs and how terrible things were . . . about how you don't report to Jankowski . . . about how the company doesn't give a shit about CBS News anymore. It was like we were all attending a funeral for CBS News. I came back to my office afterwards and I was sitting at my desk feeling depressed, staring out the window, and I had this idea. The company is selling its toy division and other stuff. Maybe they'd really like to get rid of CBS News. If they would like to, then some of us should get together and buy it. I figured with our names we could get the dough. That's the God's honest truth, Ed. I'm sorry about what it turned into."

"Don, how have I suddenly become the target?" I asked.

Don got up from the sofa and walked over and softly closed the door.

"You got a problem with the Texan, kid," he said. "And I don't mean Moyers, who happens to think you're a pretty good guy."

"Dan says he wasn't part of this."

"Boy, does that piss me off," Hewitt answered. "I may be crazy, but I'm not so crazy I'd go to Jankowski with that proposal if the anchorman of *The CBS Evening News* didn't think it was a good idea."

Don came back and sat down on the sofa.

"Let me tell you something else," he said. "When this thing first blew up as a big story in the press, Dan came back to see me. He sat right in the chair in my office and he looked at me and he said, 'Keep going, Don, you've got Ed Joyce on the run.' He wants you out and he wants Sauter back. It's as simple as that."

By now Don's motor was running in a way which is familiar to anyone who's ever dealt with him. He'd left the sofa and was pacing around my office, waving his arms as he talked.

"I told Dan the last thing I want is to see that guy back. When he was here as President he couldn't get out and over to Black Rock fast enough."

Don cocked his head at an angle. "Are you sure Sauter isn't egging Rather on?" he asked.

"Don," I said, "everyone here knows Van and I are friends. We've made no secret of it."

"I hope you're right, kid," Hewitt said, "because something's got Rather all riled up."

When Don left the office I started to call Van to put this on the table. I was interrupted by my secretary informing me that Tony Schwartz from *New York* magazine was calling. "Jo, has he called this office at any time in the past two months?" I asked.

"No, he hasn't," she said.

Not only was Schwartz calling about the article he was writing on CBS but he had only a few hours remaining before his deadline. When I mentioned my surprise that he was waiting until now to call, he said he'd gotten the impression from the CBS News press office that I wouldn't be available. I had mentioned at a staff meeting that I'd heard Schwartz was working on an article which had the strong likelihood of being unfavorable. Perhaps that had been taken as a signal by the press people that I wouldn't be interviewed. I let the matter drop. Schwartz had obviously spent a great deal of time reading everything which had been written to date on the affairs of CBS News. I hung up the phone after talking with him convinced I wouldn't enjoy reading his article. Then I dialed Sauter, deciding to mention my Hewitt conversation without using Don's name.

"Let me give you the rumor du jour," I said. "Rather is being described as waging a campaign to move me out and bring you back."

There was a pause before Van answered.

"I've heard that, too," he said. "I've spent a lot of time with Rather in the past few months and I have never heard him say anything which would lead me to believe that's what he wants to see happen. He has said he liked it better when we were all there together and Howard was his executive producer. But that's the most I've ever heard him say."

"I don't know, Van. This has a ring of accuracy."

"Look, there's enough shit flying right now that's real," he said, "without starting to chase every account we hear of how an anchorman does or doesn't feel. He's perfectly capable of saying things to people because he thinks that's what they want to hear. If he thinks they want to hear something negative about you, he'll give them what they want . . . but that's Rather. We've always known that side of him, and it's not new. Right now we should be worried about *New York* magazine and their story on CBS."

"I guess you're right," I said. "By the way, Tony Schwartz did call me . . . just now, a few hours before his deadline."

"Why did he wait so long?"

"He said our Press Department had given him the impression I didn't want to talk with him. I pointed out he'd never called my office until now."

"What tone did he take?"

"Professional. He's got a lot of detail and he's also picked up all the gossip and innuendos. But at least he floated it past me so I could knock some of it down."

"Like what?"

"He'd heard that one of the *60 Minutes* stars had been trashing me. I pointed out I'd recently gotten a note from that person telling me how much he respected me. He also claimed he had it on good authority that Rather had come to me pleading two special cases in the layoffs and that when I turned him down he went to you and you bailed one of them out. I told him it wasn't true, but I don't think he believes me."

"You know," Van said, "this article is going to be more of the same, only in greater detail, and it's just going to feed this whole monster. There'll be no walking wounded."

Worry about this article increased when our Press Department was notified that advance copies of *New York* normally available on Fridays, would not be distributed to the press. The magazine explained it was concerned that elements of its CBS story would appear in daily newspapers without appropriate credit.

On Thursday night, October 24, I attended a party for CBS Rome Bureau chief Peter Schweitzer at his brother's apartment on West End Avenue. Maureen had driven up to Connecticut to deal with builders who were constructing additions to our new weekend house. Peter's brother George worked on Jankowski's staff, so the party included a cross section of people from CBS—Jankowski, Sauter, Rather, and Stringer. The magazine article and what it might contain was the number one topic of conversation. Was there some smoking gun which none of us knew about? Why else would they impose such secrecy? Stringer sidled up to me in a corner of the living room.

"Listen, mate," he said, "I can get my hands on an advance copy in about half an hour. I have a friend who does a lot of work for the magazine."

A few minutes later both of us said a quick good night to the guest of honor and the host. I had my driver drop me off first at my place on Central Park West and then take Stringer to his friend's apartment. I paced the floor for the next hour waiting to hear from Howard. When the doorman buzzed saying Mr. Stringer was here, I opened my front door and waited for Howard to get off the elevator. He emerged smiling.

"Nothing you'll like, sport, but there's no smoking gun."

As I read the article, I could see Howard was right. It contained nothing that hadn't been reported elsewhere. But it was the lengthiest, most detailed recap of the turmoil at CBS yet, and appearing in a major magazine, it was bound to have an impact. It was hard on Wyman, quoting an unnamed television executive as saying, "He doesn't understand the psyche and the personalities of people who make an entertainment company great." The article described his performance as "spotty," pointing out that a costly video text venture had yet to be introduced commercially and the revival of a CBS theatrical-movie division had failed to turn a profit. Two joint ventures, CBS/Fox, a producer and marketer of video-cassettes, and Tri-Star Films, a feature-film company, were described as not having provided any substantial contribution to the CBS profit picture. The purchase of a group of Ziff-Davis consumer magazines was portrayed as a blunder in which CBS had overpaid by at least $40 million, something which had already been substantiated by a lawsuit filed by CBS against Ziff-Davis.

As for Wyman's acquisitions in the "other" category, mostly toys, the article pointed to a loss of $52 million in the first three quarters of 1985. The clear implication was that Wyman's mismanagement, not the threat of a takeover, had contributed to the woes at CBS News.

Sauter was depicted as someone who "hadn't come up through the News Division and now his loyalty was clearly to his corporate bosses." The anger over layoffs was described as "directed at Sauter as much as Joyce." As for Joyce, he "was less able than Sauter to disarm with collegial charm, and he was much more openly a corporate man." Among his sins, Joyce "made a series of moves that suggested he would be ruthless about holding down costs, and called Rather's agent a 'flesh peddler.' " The article included a quote from me saying, "I regretted using the term and that if it showed insensitivity, that's something I genuinely regret." The article went on to describe me as continuing to take a hard line on contract negotiations. An an example of what was wrong with this practice, it cited the near-departure of Bernie Goldberg until "CBS upped its offer at the last minute."

And, finally, the whole episode of my memo to Rather and the *Evening News* producers on correspondent staffing for the broadcast was reported in its by now familiar form, but with one new addition.

"Asked if the incident had seriously damaged his relationship with Joyce, Rather replied, 'No comment.' "

Both Sauter and I were criticized for not opposing and preventing the recent layoffs as we had successfully done in 1983. I could see a reporter wrestling with a difficult story. Most of his quotes were from unnamed sources, and they were harsh, so he felt compelled to write, "It is ironic that the turmoil should be intense in a division that is doing so well. *The CBS Evening News with Dan Rather* remains the highest-rated and by broad consensus the best of the three network newscasts. *60 Minutes* in its eighteenth year on the air remains among TV's top ten shows and generates $70 million a year in revenues for CBS. And while critics had been deeply divided over the quality of CBS's newest news show, *West 57th*, the simple fact is that no other network has ever even attempted to program two hour-long prime-time news magazines."

What fascinated me was not what was in the article but what wasn't, or more precisely, who wasn't. In a total of seven pages of the President of the CBS Broadcast Group, Gene Jankowski, the senior executive responsible for everything in radio and television at CBS, was dealt with in two short paragraphs.

"Janowski is an executive widely known for his relentless optimism and high spirits, and those closest to him say he has never complained about the management structure. However, these same executives say that Jankowski has expressed disappointment that he hasn't been able to forge a closer relationship with Wyman.

"Before Wyman came on as chairman, Jankowski was considered a leading candidate for the presidency of CBS, Inc. In Wyman's current management structure, that possibility has been precluded."

And while there were photographs of Wyman, Tisch, Joyce, Paley, Rather, and Sauter, there was none of Jankowski.

When I'd finished reading I handed the magazine back to Howard.

"Well, I guess I'm identified for all time as someone who wants to move up the corporate ladder on the backs of the poor newsies."

"There aren't enough people who know you, chief," Howard said. "You've been too busy trying to keep the bloody place glued together to get around and do any glad-handing."

"Howard, I appreciate what you say but I wouldn't have been the glad-handing type even if I hadn't been under siege for so many months. And I can't very well change who I am. I know you don't want anyone to know how you got a copy of this, but can I at least call Van and tell him the gist of it?"

"I don't want to jeopardize my source."

"I'll tell Van he's got to keep his mouth shut," I said.

Howard laughed. "Lots of luck on that, but all right."

When Van heard we had a copy of the magazine he insisted on coming over. To my surprise, Kathleen was with him. They both looked tired and worried. I ushered them in, handed Van the magazine, and fixed drinks for everyone, Glenlivet for Howard, glasses of Pouilly-Fuissé for Van and Kathleen. The room was silent as Van read each page and handed it to Kathleen. Suddenly he startled us all with a loud bellow.

"Goddamn!"

"What's wrong?" Kathleen asked.

"There's a description here of Bill Lilley as a lightning rod and a source of fear and mistrust."

"It's true," I said.

"People are going to know it came from me," he said.

"But it's not one of your quotes."

"I've used that description of Lilley to people on the thirty-fourth floor . . . at least the lightning rod part. They'll know it came from me."

"Schwartz says in this piece that you insisted on having a public-relations person present for your interview and on taping it."

Van looked a bit sheepish.

"I talked to him a few other times on the phone," he said. "It was off the record."

When he finished reading we sat around my living room and compared notes.

"There really wasn't anything new, was there?" Howard asked.

"There didn't have to be," I said. "It's the first long article pulling together all of the rumors, factoids, and truths."

"Ed's right, Howard," Van said. "And this will now start another round going in the press. Everyone who writes about television is now competing on this story."

When I was finally alone I called Maureen in Connecticut to tell her what had happened. I described the article.

"I was surprised," I added, "when Van arrived with Kathleen."

"Do you want my reaction to that?" Maureen asked.

"Sure I do."

"I don't think Van knew what might be in that article, but he was worried that it might have something which would produce a strong reaction from you. He knew if Kathleen was there your reaction would be tempered no matter what it contained."

Usually this sort of point about Van produced an argument. This time I only listened, and I went to bed that night remembering Van's description of Bill Lilley and wondering how many other off-the-record conversations he was having.

Van was certainly right about the competitive frenzy among those who would be writing about the CBS story. Virtual replicas appeared in *Time* and *Newsweek* and newspapers across the country. Liz Smith, the savvy gossip columnist for the New York *Daily News,* even posed the question of how this was happening.

"I suppose you think it was all a big coincidence?" she asked, referring to the fact that on the same day her column carried an item about the turmoil at CBS, the Washington *Post, New York, Newsweek,* and *Time* all had big takeouts as well.

"How did it happen," she wondered, "that everybody got planted with the seeds of the News Division's internal unhappiness at the same time? Is the inky press so smart? Oh, I fear not, dear reader." Her point was that the skids were being greased for Wyman, Joyce, and Sauter, and that "some if not all will have to go."

Once again Jankowski's name was absent.

"Wyman's not exactly showing grace under pressure, is he?" I put the question to Van.

It was midafternoon on Friday, November 1. We were sitting alone in my office, discussing an interview with *The Wall Street Journal* in which Wyman had promised there would be no more layoffs and then commented that the layoffs at CBS News had been handled with "clumsiness." He was referring specifically to the fact that once the layoffs had been officially announced they were implemented immediately. Seventy-four people learned on a Thursday that Friday would be their last day of employment at CBS. This had been a source of particular bitterness.

"We weren't given a lot of choice in that, were we?" Van asked.

"Are you kidding? Wyman's management committee dictated that as a procedure for the entire company. Showalter said Wyman personally reviewed the plan."

Joan Showalter was the corporate Vice President for Personnel who'd briefed Wyman on the layoff details before going to the various CBS divisions with instructions for the procedures to be followed.

"It's amazing the way this is turning," I said. "They're not Wyman's layoffs, and Jankowski has gone to ground, so they're not his layoffs, so it must be that Joyce came to work one Thursday morning and decided that seventy-four people ought to be gone by the next day."

"I think we're seeing Wyman's surprise that Larry Tisch is not going to be a passive investor."

"What makes you say that?"

"It's just what I'm picking up over there," Van said. "Jankowski's staff is running around gathering information to answer the questions Tisch is asking."

"Such as?"

"Mostly it has to do with who all the people are in that building and why are there so many of them in jobs which don't actually produce anything."

"That's the right question to ask," I said. "But you think that's why Wyman is trying to put space between himself and the layoffs over here?"

"Wyman has had Paley pretty well checked, but now he's got someone who owns twenty-five percent of this place and who is asking questions about the way he's running it. I think one of these questions is about the furor at CBS News and I don't think Wyman has good answers."

"Well, if he has half a brain he's got to be able to see that this story is not remaining hot copy without a lot of inside effort," I said. "Didn't he read Liz Smith?"

"That fucking Hewitt. He plays with matches and then he says, 'I'm sorry the house burned down.' "

"Van, let's be straight with one another. Rather is playing a big part in this. For a while he was willing to say I was a defender of the First Amendment. He'd give me that much. Now it's become 'no comment.' And in stories which are now reporting speculation that I might be asked to resign, that's corrosive."

Van looked uneasy.

"I think Dan is just waiting to see how this all shakes out and staying on the sidelines," he said.

"No, it's more than that. He's a player."

There was a very long and awkward silence. I made no effort to break it. Van looked away from me and let out a long breath of air before speaking.

"Rather thinks you've got to go. He thinks you should go and I should come back."

"If that's what's going on," I said, "if that's what this past month is all about, I don't think I want to be here anyway."

"I don't believe you can function in this job," Van said, "if you don't have Rather. What else would you like to do?"

"There's no other job at CBS I would want. I've got three and a half years left on my contract."

"Gene would probably pay that off and let you go if it would calm Rather and bring an end to all of this," Van said.

"Maybe I should do that. If I were two years older, that's about what I would have gotten in one of those early-retirement packages."

"Wouldn't you like to be out from under all this shit?" Van asked.

"You know there are a lot of people here I'd miss. But I can't argue that I haven't had a bellyful of some of our stars who talk like Ed Murrow but act like Willie Sutton. What do you think Jankowski would say?"

"I think he'd prefer you to stay," Van said. "Maybe to run the stations or take over the international business stuff for CBS."

"Van, I don't think so. I don't really like what's happening to CBS. Rather is leading this kind of charge on me. He's got the whole bitterness of the layoffs behind him and it's ripping the place apart. Every day there seems to be a new obituary for CBS News in some paper. That's so destructive."

"Hey, it's the end of a long and awful week," Van said, "another one. Why don't we both go home for the weekend. I'll fill Jankowski in on this and you and I can talk details on Monday."

Van started to leave but stopped when I began to talk again.

"You know, Van," I said, "I don't think you realize how difficult it would be coming back here a second time. If Gene would just look Rather in the eye and say, 'Dan, we all work for someone, and this is the guy you work for, and . . .' "

Van interrupted me, and I saw an expression on his face I recognized.

"That would hold Dan for a few months," he said, "maybe longer. But eventually you'd be dealing with the same problem. You don't want to live that way. Let's talk some more on Monday."

He moved toward the door and turned to me before opening it.

"You, sir, have handled all of this insanity with remarkable good grace. Go home and share a bottle of wine with Maureen." Then he left.

I told my secretary to hold my calls, and sat alone at my desk, remembering where I'd last seen that expression. It was on a fishing stream in northern New Mexico when he realized a trout had struck but had not yet taken the fly and that he had milliseconds in which to set the hook.

I picked up the phone and dialed the direct line for Jankowski.

"Yo!!! Jankowski," he answered.

"Gene, Ed Joyce. I need to see you for a private talk."

"All right, but we shouldn't meet here in my office. It will just start a bunch of rumors."

We arranged to get together at his Fifth Avenue apartment at four-thirty that afternoon. Gene's daughter let me in and told me he would be a little late because he'd "gone up to see Mr. Wyman." He arrived about five-thirty and we made small talk for a while about his new pied-à-terre. Then I came to the point.

"Gene, how bad is it?"

"I don't know," he answered. "You tell me. I'm certainly not going to remove you. You've done what Tom Wyman and I required you to do."

"You need to know that Van believes I have an insurmountable Rather problem."

Gene looked out the window, then back at me.

"How well do you know Van?" he asked, then quickly added, "No . . . don't answer that. It's not a fair question to ask you about your boss."

"Gene, this is important. I'm only here for some straight answers. What you see is what you get."

"I know that. Look, we all know what Van is. He's a politician . . . he leaks to the press, spreads rumors. But he knows the tube. I wouldn't just take his opinion on what Rather thinks. Dan has never said to me that he thinks you should go and he's had plenty of opportunities. Talk to him and ask him."

Gene looked out the window again.

"You do know," he said, "that Van and Dan have been talking for months about Van's coming back?"

Hewitt had posed that question to me a few days earlier and I'd dismissed it, saying Van and I were friends.

My mind flashed back over the past few months, recalling Rather's increasingly erratic behavior, and my encouraging Van to spend more time with him.

"No, I didn't know that," I said, "but, Gene, that's the ball game then, isn't it?"

"I don't think it's a good idea. They're too close, those two. Talk to Dan."

"All right, I will," I said, and got up to leave.

As I was walking out, Gene mentioned something else almost as an afterthought.

"If there's a problem, I'd have no choice. I'd have to make a change. There are lots of Presidents. There's only one Dan Rather."

It was early evening when I left Jankowski's apartment. I didn't return to the office but drove to my house in Connecticut. Because of the heavy weekend traffic it was well after nine when I got there. Maureen had dinner waiting, chicken with shallots, a favorite of mine. I picked at the food and described the events of the day, beginning with my conversations with Van and my talk with Jankowski.

"How do you feel?" Maureen asked.

"I'm really tired," I said. "I'm tired of CBS. It's as if a company were having a nervous breakdown."

"Do you want to leave?"

"That's what I was prepared to do when I was talking to Van this afternoon," I said. "I thought it might be the best thing to do."

"But?"

"But after hearing Gene say that Van and Rather have been talking about this for months, I'm not inclined to make it that easy."

"Does it surprise you that Van would have discussed this with Dan?"

"Yes, it really does," I said. "Given the tensions between the anchorman and me, Van must have known he was pouring kerosene on a fire."

"If you want to leave, I wouldn't be unhappy," Maureen said.

"God, CBS has been your life, too, for a lot of years."

"And I have no complaints," she said. "They've been good years for me. We've been able to do a lot of exciting things together because of the jobs you've held. I know that, but I'm angry about what CBS is becoming and I don't see a happy future."

We talked through a good part of the night about CBS, about leaving, about staying, about our finances. It was after one when we finally decided to go to sleep. I saw Maureen setting the alarm for 8 A.M.

"Why so early?" I asked.

"I thought I'd go over to the nursery and buy some bulbs for us to plant tomorrow afternoon."

"You've got to be kidding," I said.

"I certainly don't intend to mope around this house. We've almost missed the season as it is."

"After the day I described to you, you actually expect me to dance around stuffing daffodils in the earth in some stupid autumnal celebration?"

"You're wearing your Pitiful Pearl expression," she said.

"Thanks for your support."

"That's what you're getting, dummy, just like when we were going to buy Seward's," she said, and started to cry.

"My God, am I that far gone?" I put my arms around her.

"I hate what this job is doing to you," she said. "You're like a character in an episode of *Dynasty.*"

"Make it *Dallas.*" I began to laugh. "Except that everybody ends up being J.R."

"I'm serious," Maureen said. "You've got to get out of there."

"There's a big part of me that would just like to walk away."

"And?"

"And my pride just won't let me."

"Oh, it's that Cap Joyce nonsense about never running away from a fight," she said.

I laughed again. "No man is a hero to his wife."

"That's not true. You're the one who said you envied Chandler and those other people taking early retirement."

"This is different now," I said. "I'm being positioned as the one who is doing terrible things to CBS News when I think I've often been the only one who cared about that place. If Gene wants to remove me he'll know where to find me."

"And Van?"

"I don't know whether to be angry or sad about Van. We've both lost the chance to be old men together going fishing and laughing about the crazy days at CBS."

"What will Dan say to you on Monday."

"He'll look me in the eye and say there's no problem between us. Then I'll repeat that to Jankowski and Dan will continue to do whatever it is he's been doing."

"Something will have to give," Maureen said.

"Oh, it will. They can remove me and bring Van back . . . keep me but have me report directly to Jankowski . . . or remove me and bring in someone else."

"Can Van survive if he comes back?"

"I don't think he could last a year," I said. "He'd owe his survival to Rather, whose ego would bring down CBS News."

"If you're right about Rather," Maureen asked, "what are you going to do after you've talked with him?"

"I'm going to be very open," I said, "about the fact that I believe Hewitt was right when he said the President of CBS News should report directly to Jankowski."

"And?"

"And then I'll wait and try to keep CBS News running with its now nonexistent budget. You know, T. S. Eliot gave Thomas a great response when he was urged to flee. Thomas said, 'All my life they have been coming to me, those feet. Death will come only when I'm worthy.' I could do worse than to remember that when I go to work on Monday."

"A little grim for my taste," Maureen said, "but I'll tell you what I've always told you. Do what you believe is right, and whatever the consequences, we'll make it work."

"You always have," I said, "and if I end up leaving I assure you there'll be life after CBS."

"Now," Maureen said, "I suggest that tomorrow night you and I go out for a Chinese dinner. I'm wonderful company . . . and I share."

I winced and put my arms around her.

On Monday morning I called Rather and asked if he could come by my office for a moment. Seconds before he arrived Van walked in, obviously there to continue Friday's conversation. Rather saw him and stopped in the doorway.

"I can come back later," he said.

"No, please stay," I said. "Will you excuse us, Van?"

I took Rather by the arm and led him into a small anteroom opposite my office and closed the door.

"This won't take long," I said. "I just want to discuss the palace revolution that's going on here."

Dan looked worried.

"I've never seen anything like it," he said. "I wish someone could tell me what's happening."

"Several things," I said. "People are angry and hurt by the layoffs and people don't like the fact that the News President doesn't report directly to the President of the Broadcast Group. They're right about that and it has to be changed. What's being lost sight of, though, is that the good name of CBS News is being muddied day after day after day. If this bad-mouthing isn't brought to a stop soon, it may be impossible to repair. I think we can bring it to a stop. I think it can be fixed. But not if there's a perception of an insurmountable problem between the two of us. If there is, then I shouldn't stay here. Dan, if such a problem exists, now is the time for you to put it on the table."

Rather didn't even pause before answering.

"I take your point about the good name of CBS News being muddied," he said. "I also agree that the problems are fixable. That's not to minimize how serious things are. This place is hotter than a hickory fire. Have there been problems between the two of us? The answer to that is yes. I thought you were too hard on Richard Leibner and I didn't like that memo you sent to me last June."

I didn't stop him to point out the number of times he'd come to me in the past months to say precisely the opposite of what he was now telling me.

"But is there an insurmountable problem between us? Absolutely not. Ed, if you have a problem, it's not with Dan Rather."

When Rather left I walked back into my office to find Van gone. We never again discussed our Friday afternoon conversation about my leaving to make room for his return. In fact, most communication between us took place either by phone in short, curt discussions or in the form of memos. What had been happening was now out in the open. There was nothing to discuss.

I took a moment to make notes of my conversations with Rather and called Jankowski.

"That's what I thought he'd say," Jankowski replied when I read him the notes. "Go back to work."

After I put down the phone I thought to myself, "That's what I thought he'd say, too, Gene."

My next phone call was to Don Hamburg, a lawyer with the New York firm of Weitzner, Levine, Hamburg, Maley, and Walzer. The firm specialized in trusts and estates, but Hamburg represented a small number of people in television.

I'd first met him because he represented Rolland Smith, who was then an anchorman at WCBS-TV in New York. Among his other clients had been Jessica Savitch, the NBC newswoman who was killed in a tragic car accident. I had always been impressed by Hamburg as a smart, straightforward attorney who genuinely cared about his clients.

I briefly described the situation at CBS and asked if he would represent me if it was required. Later that day he came to my office and together we reviewed my contract. He confirmed what I believed. If I was removed as President of CBS News, CBS would be obligated to pay me for the three and a half years which remained before my contract expired or offer me a flat sum settlement. Minus annual bonuses, which were not part of the contract obligation, this would come to over $800,000.

"What if they offered you another job?" Hamburg asked.

"I have no contractual obligation to take it, do I?"

"No, but what would you do?"

"I have probably never been as miserable as I've been in the past few months. One part of me would really like to see it end. But if I go, and Sauter comes back totally dependent on Rather for his survival, the entire organization will be in thrall to an ego which will see anything resembling dissent as a threat. A lot of good people all around the world will be hurt. So if I'm removed and offered another job, the answer is no, I wouldn't want to remain at CBS."

"Look, I'm your attorney as of now," he said. "Promise me one thing. If they offer you another job, don't give them an answer until you've called me."

"Sure," I said. "I promise. But after I've called you I'll want to go. This isn't a CBS I remember anymore and I'm afraid I've helped bring that about."

The next day I had lunch with David Fuchs, the senior Vice President on Jankowski's staff. I asked Fuchs to tell his boss that the unrest at CBS News would not end until the reporting structure was changed and the News President reported directly to him.

"Tell him," I said, "I realize that sets in motion a musical-chairs procedure in which I may find myself without a place to sit. But for the good of CBS News this has to change."

"I think Gene feels that if he makes a change before the first of the year it will look like he's giving in to Hewitt," Fuchs said.

"Don is not the issue here," I said. "Either remove me or have me report directly to Gene. Nothing else will stop the tumult."

Even that remedy sounded like wishful thinking when Howard Stringer arrived in my office later in the day carrying the latest issue of *Broadcasting* magazine.

"This won't make your day any brighter, chief."

The magazine had interviewed a cross section of senior CBS executives about their participation in the cutbacks at CBS and plans for layoffs in their areas. With the explosions still going off at CBS News, none of them wanted to admit they were even considering layoffs. William Lilley III did his best to distance Wyman and the Corporation from any responsibility.

"At the corporate level CBS has no layoff policy," he said. "This is a large company with some 30,000-odd people. We have not been advising people how to handle situations like this."

Broadcasting also interviewed the executives in the Broadcast Group, and you could see them running for cover.

According to *Broadcasting*, "Tony Malara, President of the Television Network Division, said, 'We have a couple of jobs that will remain unfilled into the next quarter.'"

Out on the West Coast, Bud Grant, President of the Entertainment Division, told the magazine, "There will probably be staff efficiencies but if so they will be very minimal."

"We've been had, mate," Howard said.

"You noticed," I said.

"Our people are never going to believe that they haven't been screwed."

"No doubt about it," I agreed, "and wait till they read this week's issue of *TV Guide*."

I handed it to Howard.

The article quoted Edward Atorino, a media analyst for Smith Barney, who described himself as optimistic about Wyman's chances of success, particularly in connection with the News Division.

"The News Division has been living in a dream world for a long time," he said. "They're a bunch of high-priced underworked people suddenly having to toe the line and they can't understand it. I think Wyman may be pursuing a strategy that might work."

"Be a spot of fuel on the old fire, won't it?" Howard said. "What a time for you and Van to have had a falling out."

"You know about that?"

"It's all over the place," he said. "Rather's quite chatty about it."

"I'm sure he is."

"There's no sentiment in this place for Van coming back," Howard said. "Just Dan, and Gene could nip that in the bud with one lunch or even one phone call."

"Not Gene's style, I'm afraid."

"When you find out what his style is, let me know," Howard said, "although Lord knows you could spend half your life underestimating that man's ability to survive."

"Gene could well want me out, even though he says not. I've been a pain in the ass from Westmoreland to Phyllis George. And to CBS News I'm now the grim reaper who scythed down a lot of good souls."

"Yes," Howard said, "reading the press, one might conclude that Tom and Gene were a bit surprised at your hastiness in removing those people."

"Howard, you're in a tough position and I know that. If Van comes back you'll be working for him. But I think you owe me this much . . . an honest answer to one question. When did you first learn that Van and Rather were talking about Van's coming back?"

Howard looked uneasy and then sheepish.

"At Van's birthday party," he said. "My wife and I stayed overnight to have a Sunday in the country and so did the Rathers. We all had dinner and drinks together that night and at one point Jean Rather began to talk about Van returning."

"Howard, why didn't you say something to me?"

"Oh, mate, I wish I had. But you and Van were such close friends. It's always been hard to talk honestly about him to you and I suppose I hoped it might have been nothing more than the sort of loose talk that goes with wine."

Howard's description of the awareness throughout CBS News of Van and me had not been exaggerated. A steady stream of people came to my office each day, outspoken in their hope that I would stay and equally candid about their fear of Rather and what it would mean if Van returned. Bureau chiefs, correspondents, *Evening News* producers, people who even today are dependent on Rather's favor. I promised to keep their visits to myself but it meant a great deal to me at the time.

The 1986 budget had not yet been approved. It was scheduled to be presented to Wyman on November 25. In advance of that date I was asked to give a preliminary briefing to Wyman's financial team, which included Louis Rauchenberger, the CBS treasurer, and Fred Meyer, the chief financial officer of CBS.

I arrived in the corporate conference room with books and charts and began to walk them through next year's CBS News budget. I explained that the cost of the ongoing activities of CBS News for the year ahead would be 3.8 percent over last year's budget, but then began to describe some new activities which would impose other additional costs.

The television network had asked us to produce some one-minute pieces on the Constitution called "We the People" at a cost of $1.2 million. I pointed out, however, that the network would generate three times that amount in revenue by selling "We the People" as part of the year-long observance of the Constitution scheduled for 1986. Rauchenberger and Meyer were, to me, surprisingly disinterested in this information. What concerned them was bodies. Why did we have so many?

"Who are all these people?" Meyer asked.

Fred Meyer was a Swiss, a pleasant, heavyset, bespectacled man in his fifties who enjoyed talking. He'd come to CBS from Sandoz, an enormous international pharmaceutical company headquartered in Switzerland. Lou Rauchenberger was about the same age but taller and less voluble. Solid and stolid was the way I thought of the two of them and I wasn't surprised that it would be Meyer asking the questions.

"What people are you talking about, Fred?" I asked.

"All these CBS News employees. You've got more people now than you did last year."

"That's not so. We've just eliminated a hundred and twenty-six jobs. Remember those people we laid off?"

"Exactly," he said. "Yes, that's my point. You laid them off and now you've got still more."

We argued that point back and forth for several minutes. I noticed he kept referring to a page in a black notebook on the table in front of him. When I asked about it he told me he had a report on the number of per diem employees we had used during a time period which included both the TWA and *Achille Lauro* hijackings. It was the practice at all three networks to work with free-lance crews during times of crisis. It would be financially unfeasible to have enough crews on the payroll for all emergencies; hence the per diem practice. The use of free-lancers depended totally on how many stories on the scale of the Iran hostage crisis or the TWA hijacking might occur. In some years none at all. I explained this as carefully as I could and then prepared to move on to the rest of the budget, but Meyer seemed obsessed by these per diem crews.

"After the beating Tom has taken in the press," he said, "now I learn we've got still more people. He's not going to like this."

I tried again to explain, searching for metaphors I thought a Swiss would find meaningful.

"Instead of a permanent army of this size," I said, "we work with a smaller group of regulars and then in emergencies call on our volunteer force."

That produced a stare of total incomprehension.

"We only call on them when an avalanche comes crashing down the mountain," I said. "The rest of the year they return to their homes."

Another stare. I remembered a bit of sixties trivia. Sandoz Chemical held the patent on and was the only legitimate manufacturer of LSD, the hallucinogenic drug. I thought about using that as a springboard into some point about alterations of reality when Meyer began to shake his head.

"I don't know, I don't know," he said. "Tom's not going to like this, after all we've been through."

"Tell Tom that's the way these stories get covered, and while it may seem like a distortion of reality at first glance, a close look will show it's actually cost-effective to do it that way. But the price you pay is a huge tab when an extraordinary story blows up. It does not logically follow that we should be laying more people off, in case that's anyone's conclusion. I would hope what you are all reading each day would convince you that cutbacks at CBS News are a little different from getting rid of toys."

I had forgotten that for the past year the unprofitable CBS toy division had reported directly to Meyer.

A hush fell over the room. A bishop who had lectured two members of the Curia on the need for a change in the proscription of birth control would recognize that hush.

"Well, we'll have to discuss this among ourselves," Meyer said. "Thank you for coming over to this building at a time when I know how busy you are."

The next day I got a phone call from Tim Reynolds, the Finance Vice President for the Broadcast Group.

"Ed, we've had a little change in signals here. This year the budget procedure will be a tad different. No Division Presidents will be on hand for the presentation to Wyman. Just the four Executive Vice Presidents. So Van will handle both Stations and News."

A few minutes later I gave Joan Richman the go-ahead for our coverage of the Geneva summit.

"You're sure you need twelve crews?" I asked.

"Boss, according to the credentials requests I've seen, ABC and NBC are each sending eighteen. There are a lot of locations to cover and we've got to be ready from morning till night with our coverage."

"O.K.," I said, "we don't have the money for one crew, so why not send twelve?"

"I like your spirit. By the way, Mr. Rather wants to fly over in business class instead of first. He thinks it would be good for morale."

"He's nothing if not gestural," I said. "Why not."

"Of course, he'll have to come back on the Concorde," she added, "so he can be in Washington in time to anchor the President's report to Congress."

I laughed. "Joan, I have no doubt that when you need him you will beam him down."

While Gorbachev and Reagan were establishing some spirit of accord in Geneva, my own summit meeting was enjoying less success. The location, the luxurious Ritz-Carlton in Laguna Niguel, California. The occasion, the annual convening of the CBS Affiliates Board.

Howard joined me for this event, and on the morning of our report to the Affiliates Board he gave a short description of the plans for the morning broadcast. For a change he was able to cite some favorable reviews in the press. The Baltimore *Sun* had described the broadcast "as more credible, more competent, more worthy of the news part of the show's title. Sawyer comes off as intelligent and informed. He could be a star. And anyone who gives Maria Shriver a chance will instantly recognize she handles herself well, far better than George ever did."

That same week the Washington *Post* reviewed television coverage of the summit in Geneva and told its readers, "The media story of the week may have been the comeback of the CBS Morning News. Anchorman Forrest Sawyer proved a tough interviewer with U.S. and Soviet administration spokesmen, and in New York Maria Shriver held her own with Robert McNamara."

Howard concluded his remarks with a plea for support and patience for the time it would take for this new morning team to make its full impact. When he finished, Phil Jones, the new chairman of the Affiliates Board, stood up in the audience.

"I speak," he said, "for many affiliates this morning when I tell you we don't think you have found a winning combination. Many of us wonder if you shouldn't do some research and see if you can't come up with a program that will quickly appeal to a larger audience."

Howard started to answer but I placed my hand on his forearm.

"In our business," I said, "I suppose it's inevitable that we will make mistakes and I hope that's forgivable. What's unforgivable is if we don't learn anything from the experience."

I looked out in the audience and saw Jankowski and, standing in the back of the room, Van.

"Hiring Phyllis George was a mistake. It was a terrible blunder and we can't repeat it. Whatever broadcast CBS News produces in the morning has to be in harmony with its own value system."

I saw Jankowski shift in his seat and look at Van.

Phil Jones wasn't through.

"Ed," he said, "then many of us wonder if the time hasn't come for CBS to ask the Entertainment Division to produce the morning show."

How many times had I heard that threat over the past four years? Now here it was out in the open.

"Ultimately that's a decision for Gene Jankowski to make," I said. "But think about this. What if the Entertainment Division doesn't come up with a hit? By then CBS News will have dismantled its morning staff. And do you really want an entertainment show on your air when there's a hostage crisis or some other big story? You may regret what you get."

After the news presentation Howard and I spent a few minutes walking along the bluff which overlooks the Pacific Ocean. It's at least a hundred and fifty feet above the beach, and the view is dominated by blue water, sand, and the gardens and courtyards of the affluent Southern California coastline.

"That was more than a bit discouraging," Howard said.

"It's incredible, isn't it?" I said. "We try to work inside a system that's basically crazed and it's amazing that we ever make it click. Affiliates, stockholders, anchorpeople, they're all the same—they're walking, talking appetites, demanding more."

"I guess it's always been like this," Howard said, "and I was just a producer worrying about my next documentary."

"It was never like this. I first came to CBS in 1954 and I spent half the years since then in some form of news management. I was never under any illusion that I was working for the BBC. Almost every boss I've had here has been some sales guy, but part of the deal was that News was something special. Now I don't think they can afford to feel that way anymore. Everything relates back to the price of the fucking stock."

"One would think the affiliates would resent that," Howard said.

"Those guys are going through the same thing. Most of the stations are owned by groups which are listed on the exchange right along with CBS. Westinghouse, Cox, Meredith, Storer. Hell, Storer is a takeover target right now. The financial analysts are watching them the same way they watch us."

We both stared silently for a few minutes at the white sails which dotted the blue water of the California coastline, in a stunning visual tribute to the rewards of free enterprise.

"Those are undoubtedly many of our stockholders out there," I said, and looked at my watch. "If you're going to drive me to catch my flight we'd better get going."

I arrived in New York about the same time the CBS News crews were returning from Geneva. Our coverage had been excellent. The Washington *Post* said, "Certainly the CBS Evening News seemed the most vital and aggressive of the scheduled broadcasts from Geneva" and singled out Bill Moyers's commentaries for praise. "He has no real competition."

A number of people who'd been in Geneva sought me out to tell me that Rather had been open in his prediction of Van's return to CBS News. But at the post-broadcast discussions each evening Rather and I conducted ourselves as though nothing unusual was happening. On November 27, 1985, I sent the CBS News monthly report for November to Jankowski.

"During the four weeks from October 18 to November 24, 1985, *The CBS Evening News* recorded a 13.5 rating/23 share, a half rating point increase over its audience level of one year ago. The NBC *Nightly News* (12.3/21) is currently in second place, and ABC's *World News Tonight* (11.7/20) is third."

The report also said that *The CBS Morning News* was in third place with a 3.2 rating and that *60 Minutes* had shown an 8 percent gain over the previous year and had been number one among all CBS prime-time programs for the past two weeks.

The financial section of the report showed that because of the large number of unscheduled new events in 1985, including the Geneva summit, CBS News would exceed its budget by 4.1 percent which would amount to $13.2 million. Part of that overage, the report said, was also caused by requests from the network for episodes of *West 57th* and the "American Treasury" announcements as well as *Nightwatch,* which had been budgeted only through May. As I initialed the memo I smiled to myself. Not bad, I thought. I can live with that.

A few days later, on December 3, Moyers came to my office. He looked worried and I was glad to see he wasn't carrying sheets of paper. At least he wasn't going to read me another note of resignation.

"You once talked me out of going to see Tom Wyman to tell him Van should be removed," he said. "I've always regretted letting you do that."

I smiled.

"I'd be hard pressed to argue with you now," I said, "but it's a failing I'll just have to live with."

"I want you to know that I'm having lunch tomorrow with Gene Jankowski. I'm going to tell him what a terribly destructive thing it would be to bring Van Sauter back to CBS News. Ed, I have talked to many people here in recent days. Many of us feel you are a man of integrity and that we can work with you if Van is out of the picture. Don Hewitt tells me he is going to tell Jankowski the same thing. I won't speak for Don tomorrow, but I wanted you to know what I'm going to do and what I'm going to say."

"Bill," I said, "I'm certainly not going to ask you this time not to have such a conversation. What you've just said means a great deal to me. But I must honestly tell you I think your chances of success are virtually nonexistent. If Rather wants me out and Sauter back, I'm afraid his is the voice Gene will listen to."

"I've discussed this with Dan," he said. "He knows what I'm about to do. I've asked him outright, 'What's your problem with Ed Joyce?' He never answers except to say you're not supportive of the *Evening News.* I told him, 'Dan, we all need . . . I need, you need . . . someone who will tell us we're wrong, who will say no. Ed Joyce will tell us that. Van Sauter won't.' That was not something he wanted to hear."

"I'm sure it wasn't," I said. "Bill, if you're going to do this, I have to be honest with you about something. There are many things I've done here that I'm proud of. But when day after day I see stories written that I've been aloof and insensitive to the layoffs, I have to be honest with myself. There's been a willingness to believe that here, and that's a failure on my part."

"I think that's true," Bill said. "Part of that is your personality. You're a reserved man. You can be tough, you can be strong . . . and some of us know there's more to you than that. Unfortunately a lot of people here haven't seen the other side of you. Because of your friendship with Van, you've allowed . . . you've even enjoyed Van as the performer, and that's prevented a lot of people from learning who you are. So if Dan or someone else tells them that you were aloof and insensitive when it came to laying these people off, they have no frame of reference. But that can change if you want it to. The important thing is that Jankowski be made to understand that Dan does not speak for most of us. I'll call you after my meeting with him tomorrow."

The next afternoon Bill came to see me.

"Well, I had my lunch with Gene," he said. "I told him everything I had planned to say. I'm afraid I had the feeling I was talking with someone whose mind was made up. He kept saying, 'You make my job very difficult. No matter what I do someone will be unhappy.' Ed, I told him we believe you stand for something and that Van does not. I told him how destructive it would be to CBS News if he made a decision to bring that man back. But he just kept repeating, 'You make my job very difficult.'"

"Bill," I replied, "I'm not terribly surprised and I'm terribly honored by what you said. I thank you for that."

That night I returned home late in the evening after attending an award ceremony for twenty- and thirty-year employees of CBS. Maureen told me the CBS Press Department had called to advise me of Hollywood gossip columnist Rona Barrett's appearance on the television program *Entertainment Tonight.* She had reported that I would be replaced by Sauter as soon as a "face-saving position" could be found for me.

The Associated Press ran a similar story that evening, saying "CBS sources have been critical of what some believed was his insensitive handling of the recent layoffs of CBS News employees."

I called Jankowski at home and described both reports.

"Ed, there's not going to be any change," he said.

"Gene, we both know there'll have to be some change in this management structure," I said. "But there's an immediate problem tomorrow."

"What's that?"

"I'm scheduled to get on a plane in the morning and fly down to Tampa for a regional conference of CBS affiliates from the Southeast."

"Go ahead," he said.

"Gene, they will obviously want to know about these reports."

"Tell them we don't speculate on rumors."

"Look, I don't know what your plans are," I said, "but it strikes me that someone has very cleverly forced your hand. You have to either shoot me or endorse me before that meeting takes place."

There was a pause while Gene thought about that.

"Why don't you hold off on your flight down there until we can talk about this tomorrow."

"I can be in your office first thing tomorrow," I said.

"I have a breakfast scheduled with Rather. I'll call you afterwards."

Maureen, who'd been listening to my side of the conversation, waited until I'd finished and placed the receiver back in its cradle.

"What's going to happen?" she asked.

"At breakfast tomorrow Rather will say a few nice things about me to Gene. Likes children, kind to horses, that sort of thing. Then he'll take the mask off because he'll be worried that Gene has been hearing dissenting opinions from Moyers and others. He'll say that he can't work with me and he'll imply without actually saying it that if I remain he may just go fishing."

"So it's all over," Maureen said.

I kissed her.

"Only the CBS part," I said.

"What are you going to do if Gene offers you another job?"

"I promised Don Hamburg I'd call him before I responded to that sort of an offer. But I don't want to stay at CBS."

"Thank God," Maureen said.

"So I'll confer with Don and go back with him to work out the terms of my departure. I've negotiated a lot of deals for CBS. Tomorrow I'll negotiate mine."

Late the next morning I received a phone call from Jankowski asking me to come to his office in Black Rock.

Gene was direct.

"Ed, why don't you come over here and work for me. I'd like you to be the Senior Vice President for Worldwide Enterprises. Rosenfield was handling this and you'll report directly to me."

"You've obviously made up your mind?"

"I had breakfast with Dan this morning. He believes it has to be done."

"Have you heard any other viewpoints?"

"Many of them," Gene said. "Just yesterday from Bill Moyers. You are described each time as a man of integrity, and opinions on Van are mixed."

"You're that worried about this change and still you're making it?"

"After my breakfast with Dan this morning I don't feel I have a choice."

I kept my promise to Hamburg and told Gene I wanted a few hours to think it over and to discuss it with my attorney. I left Black Rock and went directly to Hamburg's offices at 230 Park Avenue.

Methodically, he laid out the options as he saw them.

I could accept the job.

I could leave and be paid for the next three and a half years.

I could ask for the contract to be paid off in a lump sum.

"They aren't obligated to give a lump-sum payment," he said. "It's over $800,000 and they will probably offer a smaller amount. It's called present market value."

"I don't think that will be a problem," I said.

"It would be helpful," Hamburg said, "if you tell me what you think will be going through Jankowski's mind when we meet with him."

"Jankowski wants to put out a fire in the News Division, but he's worried that he's just going to make it worse. He knows it's absurd that the layoffs have been dropped on my doorstep and he has to be uncomfortable with what's gone on between Rather and Sauter. He has to be worried that I'll make a public issue of all of that. What he doesn't know is that the last thing I want is for CBS News to be battered apart any more than it already has."

"Right now, it's better if he doesn't know that," Hamburg said.

"You're right. I've been out of my office for most of the day. On the heels of those press stories last night CBS News will be awash in speculation. He's got to get this announcement out by the end of the day and he's hoping he can say I've been moved to another job. So the later in the day we meet with him, the more pressure he'll feel to get me to agree to take that job. A week from now when this story dies down he won't care. Today he'll care."

Hamburg was making notes for himself on a long yellow legal pad as I talked.

"Are there any other factors that you've left out?" he asked.

I thought for a moment before answering.

"The Tisch factor, I suppose. Tisch has been asking a lot of questions about the bureaucracy. Who are all those people? What do they do? This has pinpointed the absurdity of Jankowski's 'Admirals Club.' Why can't the News President deal directly with the President of the Broadcast Group? Both Wyman and Jankowski get a chance here to show Tisch they're being responsive to his concerns."

"Is that it?"

"I think so."

Hamburg put his pencil down on top of the legal pad.

"O.K., here's what your attorney recommends. You accept the other job for a clearly defined and limited period of time, at the end of which you resign. At that time CBS will not only pay you the full value of your contract but also pay you an amount which we will negotiate as a recognition of the unusual circumstances involved in your departure."

I considered that, then answered.

"For two months. No more than that, Don."

We delayed the meeting with Jankowski until 4 P.M.

When we arrived in his office he was joined by Haskell Paul MacCowett, Wyman's Senior Vice President for Administration. Hamburg and Mac-Cowett reviewed my participation in various CBS plans, the pension plan, the investment plan, the stock options I'd been granted over a period of years. It was detailed and it was time-consuming and I could see Gene looking at his watch. I knew the pressure he was feeling to issue a press release on the changes.

"Don," I said, "could you review my vesting rights in the pension plan again? Some of those numbers didn't seem quite right."

I looked at Gene.

"I understand you have an announcement you want to make, but it's very unlikely I will choose to stay and this is important information."

"Let me make a proposal," Gene said, "in the interest of time. If you will accept this job, we will recognize your right to resign at any time in the next year and at that time we will pay you at least $1 million. That's apart from any money you have in the pension plan or in stock options, which is legally yours anyway."

Hamburg looked at me. It was exactly what we were going to propose.

"All right," I said, "until February 15. Then I want to go."

Gene excused himself to tell George Schweitzer, the Vice President for

Communications, that statements announcing the changes could now be released to the press. MacCowett left, too.

"Get it on paper, Don," I said. "I'll wait for you outside."

It was late in the day and darkness was just setting in. Lights were starting to go on in Black Rock and the other buildings along Sixth Avenue's media row. I stood on the sidewalk waiting for Don and looking up at Black Rock, thinking about the years in which that building had been a totemic presence in my life.

"What are you looking at?"

I turned and saw Don Hamburg, who was carrying my termination agreement.

"At CBS," I said. "It's a fascinating place, isn't it? Even in the twilight."

I returned that evening to my office just as the broadcast was ending, and decided to go back to the Fishbowl one last time and say goodbye to the producers. I was talking with Tom Bettag, one of the senior producers, when Rather walked in. He seemed surprised to see me but I was now unavoidable.

"Ed," he said, "I just hope that someday someone will explain to me how all this happened."

It was so wonderfully consistent. The next day I received a handwritten note from Wyman which was just as consistent.

"Many people," he wrote, "including myself have been a part of whatever problems CBS News faces today. None of us can feel comfortable that you are bearing the central burden of getting from here to someplace else."

And in Los Angeles a few days later Gene Jankowski and Van Sauter met with the television press and told them CBS News had been running very well. According to the Los Angeles *Times,* when asked why then a change had been made Jankowski said, "It's no secret that everyone within the News Division wasn't marching to the tune of the same drummer."

Van also responded.

"In a news organization," he said, "bonding is essential if we are to do our tasks well."

POSTSCRIPT

- Dan Rather decided to originate all of his broadcasts during the week of February 24, 1985, from Texas to highlight the plight of the American farmer. Unfortunately, this took place while the regime of Philippine President Ferdinand Marcos was being toppled. The news resources of ABC and NBC were poured into the Philippines story.

- Don Hewitt received a new contract.

- Bernie Goldberg was granted the title of National Correspondent.

- The proxy statement of the CBS Annual Report revealed that Gene Jankowski had been given a new contract in November 1985. His base salary was raised from $275,000 to $475,000. He was granted a $200,000 signing bonus and annual bonuses of $150,000.

- In July 1986 *The CBS Evening News* dipped briefly to third place for the first time in four years.

  In that same month, CBS News implemented another round of layoffs. Seventy people were laid off. A total of ninety jobs were eliminated. In a memo to the staff, Van Gordon Sauter said, "I regret the burden this layoff adds to our shared task, but we can and will absorb it."

  Also in July, Sauter announced that CBS News would no longer produce *The CBS Morning News.* A new unit outside the News Division, but reporting to Sauter, would produce a more entertainment-oriented program. Actress Mariette Hartley was chosen to be the hostess.

- During the week of September 1, Dan Rather introduced his new sign-off for *The CBS Evening News.* Each night that week he closed the broadcast by looking at the camera and saying, "Courage." The one exception was his Wednesday broadcast, which he signed off in Spanish with the word *"Coraje."* This new closing was abandoned at the end of the week.

  And in early September, new layoffs and the loss of *The CBS Morning News* created so much dissension within CBS News that *Newsweek* made the issue its cover story. The cover art showed the CBS Eye broken in half. It was titled "Civil War at CBS . . . The Struggle for the Soul of a Legendary Network."

  A few days after this *Newsweek* issue appeared, the CBS board met and requested the resignation of Tom Wyman. William S. Paley and Laurence Tisch had worked in tandem to force Wyman out. The next day Van Gordon Sauter was fired. He had returned to CBS News nine months earlier. Bill Moyers resigned from CBS News to return to public television.

- On October 5, 1986, Dan Rather was attacked and beaten by two men while walking on Park Avenue at 10:45 P.M. In his statement to police he said he didn't know who the two men were and that they repeatedly asked him, "What's the frequency, Kenneth?"

- On October 30, 1986, Howard Stringer was named President of CBS News. One of his first responsibilities was to negotiate a contract for a news star, Diane Sawyer. She signed a new contract with CBS News which paid her $1.2 million a year.

- In January 1987 the CBS Board of Directors selected the new leadership for CBS. Eighty-five-year-old William S. Paley was named Chairman and sixty-three-year-old Laurence Tisch President and CEO.

- On March 5, 1987, Howard Stringer announced the layoff of 215 employees of CBS News. Among those who lost their jobs were 14 on-air reporters, including Ike Pappas, who'd worked for CBS News for over twenty-two years.

  The New York *Times* headline on March 9 proclaimed, "Sadness Turns to Anger over CBS dismissals" and quoted Andy Rooney, who said, "This guy Tisch put his money into the company, but I put my life into the company and so did Ike Pappas."

A few days later, Laurence Tisch told *The Wall Street Journal* that the image of CBS had been "broken by negative reporting on the cutbacks."

- On April 7, 1987, a CBS proxy statement mailed to shareholders stated that Tom Wyman would receive $400,000 a year for life as part of his settlement. In addition, the statement said he could select either $3.8 million in ten annual installments or one lump sum of $2.8 million. Van Gordon Sauter would continue to be paid his salary, estimated at $300,000 a year, until September 30, 1990, when his contract expired.

- By June 1987 the ratings for *The CBS Evening News* dropped to a record third-place low. It was the worst audience performance since 1964, when Cronkite had been a relative unknown.

- For the week of August 10, 1987, Dan Rather altered his on-air delivery in an effort to speak slowly and quietly. The experiment was abandoned at the end of the week. The Washington *Post* called him a "Valium." Rather told the *Post*, "I tried it and it didn't work."

- On September 11, 1987, angered that a tennis match which was being carried on CBS was running late and would spill over into the *Evening News* time, Rather stormed out of the studio. The match concluded a few minutes later and the sports announcer signed off. With no anchorman in the studio, the network went black. CBS affiliates and their viewers were left with an empty screen for over six minutes until Rather finally agreed to return. The London *Times,* reporting from Los Angeles, asked, "Is Dan Rather, bishop of the nation's news business, losing his marbles?"

  Also in September, the new *CBS Morning Program* with Mariette Hartley dropped to its lowest ratings ever in the Nielsens (1.9). A few days later CBS announced its cancellation after nine months on the air. The News Division would be asked once again to fill that time period with a *CBS Morning News.*

- In the fall of 1987, the A. C. Nielsen Company introduced a new method of measuring television audiences, the so-called people meters. By early October the new rating system showed *The CBS Evening News* in first place.

  Also in October, *Variety* reported that Van Gordon Sauter was "making an ironic segue from entertainment-oriented news to reality-based entertainment. The former prez of CBS News charged by critics with blurring the line between news and entertainment is developing a first run half hour strip about doctors for syndication." According to *Variety*, "the idea occurred to him that if courtroom shows have done so well, why not a doctor's show in syndication?"

- In November 1987, *Manhattan Inc.* magazine profiled Laurence Tisch, pointing out that the $951 million he had paid for a 25 percent interest in CBS was now worth around $1.6 billion. "In the world of takeovers," it said, "his bagging of CBS is the steal of the century. An all timer."

- On November 18, 1987, CBS agreed to sell its records division, the world's largest record company, to the Sony Corporation for $2 billion in cash. In addition to the sale of CBS Records, the company had already sold its book publishing operations for $500 million, music publishing for $125 million, and magazine publishing for $650 million. As a result of the sale of these assets, CBS would be left with approximately $3 billion in cash. The New York *Times* noted that CBS appeared "generally saddened by the news." It quoted someone described as a longtime CBS employee as saying, "This is a great entertainment and communications company. Now half of its presence in the world is being lopped off."

  Two days later *The Wall Street Journal* ran an analysis of the Tisch takeover of CBS with the headline "Tisch Does What CBS Feared in Turner—Stripped-Down Concern Ends Era of Diversity." The article began: "Ted Turner must be smiling. When the Atlanta broadcaster launched a takeover bid for CBS in 1985, the company vigorously fought off his attack in part because directors feared he would dismember CBS." The story then pointed out that Tisch had done what the directors feared Turner would do, adding, "CBS has been stripped in one year of much of what it built in 60, largely at Mr. Tisch's initiative."

INDEX

ABOUT THE AUTHOR

Ed Joyce was President of CBS News from 1983 to 1986. In nearly thirty years at CBS he was Executive Vice President of CBS News; Vice President and general manager of CBS-owned television stations in New York, Los Angeles, and Chicago; Vice President of News for CBS-owned television stations; director of news and public affairs, WCBS Television, New York; news director, WCBS Radio, New York; reporter-producer, WCBS Radio. In 1969 his reporting of the Chappaquiddick story received awards from Sigma Delta Chi, the Society of Silurians, and the New York State Associated Press.

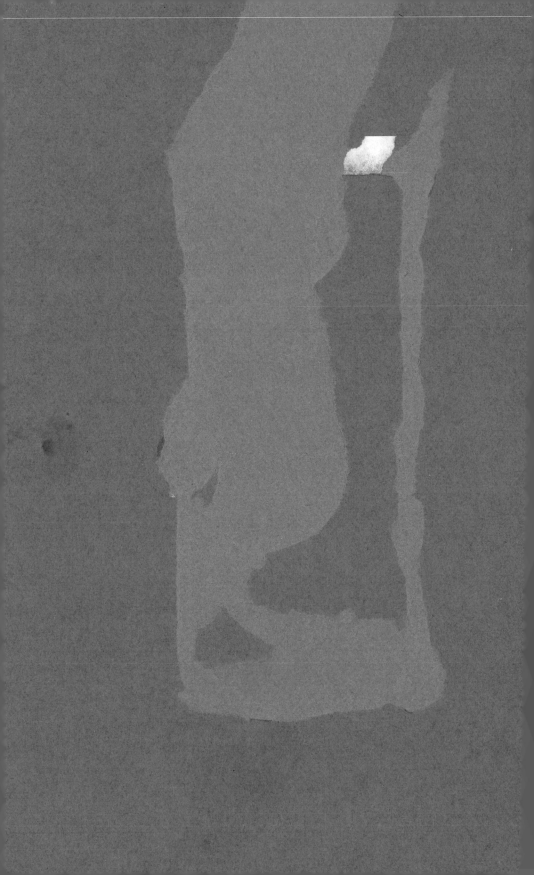